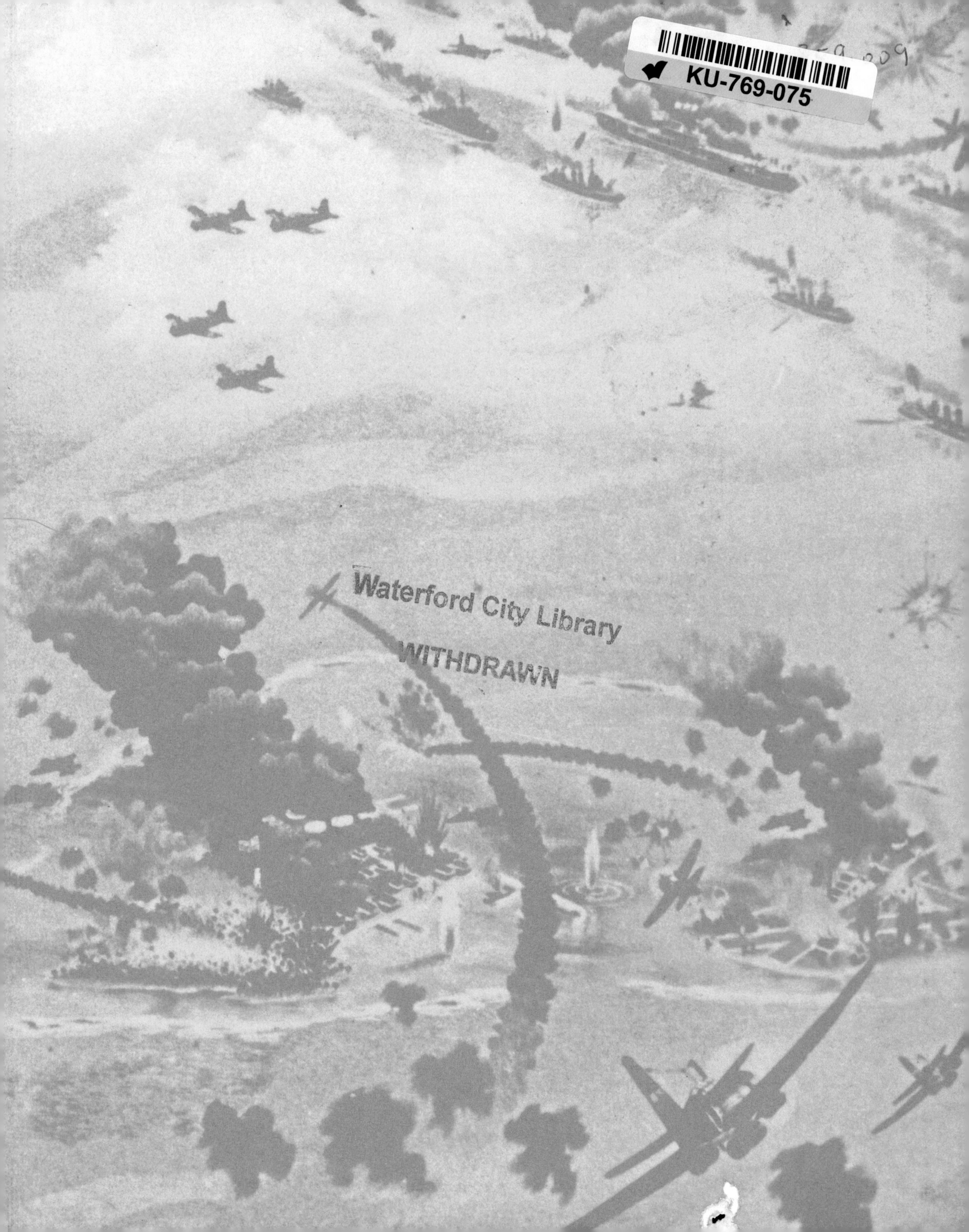

BATTLE
AT SEA

BATTLE
AT SEA

3,000 YEARS OF NAVAL WARFARE
R.G. GRANT

LONDON, NEW YORK, MELBOURNE,
MUNICH AND DELHI

SENIOR ART EDITOR Gadi Farfour
PROJECT ART EDITOR Victoria Clark
DESIGNERS Philip Fitzgerald,
Amy Orsborne

SENIOR EDITOR Alison Sturgeon
PROJECT EDITORS Ferdie McDonald,
Tom Broder, Andrew Szudek

EDITORS Kim Bryan,
Marcus Hardy, Nigel Ritchie

INDEXER Helen Peters

MANAGING ART EDITOR Karen Self
MANAGING EDITOR Debra Wolter
ART DIRECTOR Bryn Walls
PUBLISHER Jonathan Metcalf

CONSULTANT Captain Christopher Page

PICTURE RESEARCHER Sarah Smithies
DK PICTURE RESEARCHER Romaine Werblow

PHOTOGRAPHY Gary Ombler,
Chester Ong, Graham Rae

ILLUSTRATION Darrell Warner, Philip Gamble

CARTOGRAPHY Encompass Graphics

PRODUCTION EDITOR Lucy Baker

PRODUCTION CONTROLLER Linda Dare

First published in Great Britain in 2008
This edition published in 2010 by
Dorling Kindersley Limited,
80 Strand, London WC2R 0RL

Copyright © 2008, 2010 Dorling Kindersley Limited
A Penguin Company

2 4 6 8 10 9 7 5 3 1
ND111 – 05/10

Colour reproduction by MDP Ltd, UK
Printed and bound by Leo Paper Products Ltd, China

Discover more at
www.dk.com

CONTENTS

FOREWORD

Samuel Johnson said in 1759: "No man will be a sailor who has contrivance enough to get himself into a jail; for being in a ship is being in a jail, with the chance of being drowned." In fact, the great man had understated his case. He was talking of sailors in general, not of those serving in navies in time of war. The naval prayer, first recorded in the 17th century and still part of the church services of Britain's Royal Navy, asks for preservation not only "from the dangers of the sea" but also "from the violence of the enemy". It is this "violence" that is the overriding theme of this book.

Naval warfare is almost as old as conflicts between armies on land, and as in land campaigns, it is the great battles that catch the imagination, the titanic clashes that can be said to have changed the course of history. Some, such as Cape Ecnomus between Rome and Carthage, or Leyte Gulf between the US and Japan in Word War II, involved vast fleets; others, such as the battles of Chesapeake Bay or the Nile, were fought by a relatively small number of ships. In spite of this, their strategic consequences were equally momentous.

While most nations have a long history of fighting on land, the list of countries that can be termed "maritime nations" is much shorter. There are certain nations and peoples that appear again and again as participants in the battles recorded in this book: in the Classical world the Carthaginians and the Greeks, in the Middle Ages the Venetians and the Genoese, in the age of European exploration the Spanish, the English, and the Dutch. Geography plays a key role, and some countries have little or no coastline, or difficult access to the high seas. For some, history teaches that the threat to national existence and way of life comes from across a land border, and this ever-present fact naturally colours thinking about defence. For maritime countries the sea looms larger in their national consciousness.

Historically, those nations with strong navies have developed in this way as a result of experience, sometimes harshly taught. They tend to depend on trade. The sea has always been the major highway for international commerce. Transporting goods in ships is much cheaper than moving them by land, and today, by air. International systems throughout the ages have depended on the free passage of people and

things around the world. When these systems break down because the sea lines of communication are severed or threatened, naval action is required. Uninhibited movement of the vast majority of the traded goods around the globe relies, in the last resort, on the famous phrase of the 19th-century American naval officer, and historian, Alfred Mahan: "command of the sea". The world today is fortunate that trading nations are able to move materials almost anywhere without interference, something we all take for granted.

What naval history tells us, however, is that this freedom, like most others, is not cost-free, and that, periodically, a price has to be paid. The classic way of ensuring command of the sea is to find the battle fleet of the enemy, and destroy it. This has the added benefit for maritime nations of reducing or preventing any chance of invasion. The incidents resulting from the attempts to deny or maintain command of the sea are the battles recorded in this book.

These battles, usually short in duration, tell just a part of what sea power is all about. A key part of historical experience is the ability of maritime powers to project their land power over huge distances, often to a place of their choosing rather than that of their antagonist, to impose a seemingly endless blockade upon an enemy, and to deal with piracy and illegal commerce. They also have the power to do good around the world: working for the abolition of the slave trade, providing assistance to disaster-hit lands, or simply "showing the flag" to reassure friends and deter enemies.

Naval warfare is the story of the use of the most modern, high-tech, and sometimes expensive equipment that a nation can procure. A technological advantage could sometimes define the difference between victory at sea and defeat. The study of naval battles, however, confirms that they are really about people, not just the senior commanders, famous, or notorious, as they might be, but the ordinary man doing extraordinary things under the most stressful of circumstances out of loyalty to his shipmates, his ship, and his country. He is the true hero of this book.

CAPTAIN CHRISTOPHER PAGE
ROYAL NAVY

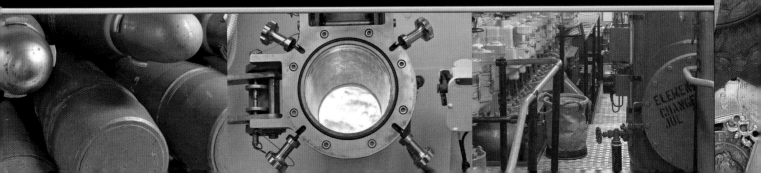

ANCIENT GALLEYS

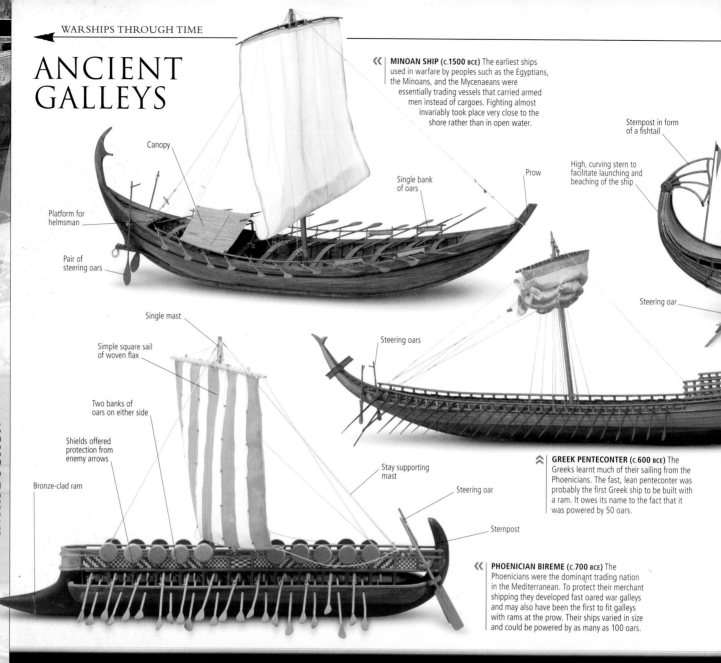

Canopy

Platform for
helmsman

Pair of
steering oars

Single bank
of oars

Prow

Sternpost in form
of a fishtail

High, curving stern to
facilitate launching and
beaching of the ship

Steering oar

Single mast

Simple square sail
of woven flax

Two banks of
oars on either side

Shields offered
protection from
enemy arrows

Bronze-clad ram

Steering oars

Stay supporting
mast

Steering oar

Sternpost

« MINOAN SHIP (c.1500 BCE) The earliest ships
used in warfare by peoples such as the Egyptians,
the Minoans, and the Mycenaeans were
essentially trading vessels that carried armed
men instead of cargoes. Fighting almost
invariably took place very close to the
shore rather than in open water.

ᴧ GREEK PENTECONTER (c.600 BCE) The
Greeks learnt much of their sailing from the
Phoenicians. The fast, lean penteconter was
probably the first Greek ship to be built with
a ram. It owes its name to the fact that it
was powered by 50 oars.

« PHOENICIAN BIREME (c.700 BCE) The
Phoenicians were the dominant trading nation
in the Mediterranean. To protect their merchant
shipping they developed fast oared war galleys
and may also have been the first to fit galleys
with rams at the prow. Their ships varied in size
and could be powered by as many as 100 oars.

WARSHIPS THROUGH TIME

THE HISTORY OF WARSHIP DEVELOPMENT is an epic one,
stretching from oared galleys and longships to modern aircraft
carriers and nuclear submarines. As well as superb fighting
machines, many warships have been masterpieces of design.

THE MEDITERRANEAN was the focus
for the early development of warships.
The first boats used in battle were
civilian vessels turned to military use, such
as those made from pitch-coated reeds that
the Egyptians utilized in the 12th century
BCE. They were used to carry soldiers and
served as platforms for archers and spearmen

During the 1st millennium BCE, maritime states
around the Mediterranean developed fighting
galleys, the first purpose-built warships.

GALLEY WARFARE
Galleys were propelled in battle by banks of
oars. The galley's sail, typically on a single mast
in the centre of the ship, was generally not used

in combat. Greek and Phoenician naval
designers created the penteconter, then the
bireme (two banks of oars) and trireme (three
banks). Fast and manoeuvrable, these galleys
were themselves weapons – a ram at the bow
was used to smash the hulls of enemy boats.
Over time more oars were added to drive much
larger galleys called polyremes, which could be
packed with soldiers and with catapults serving
as shipborne artillery. Galleys remained the key
warships of the Mediterranean throughout the
period of the Roman Empire and its successor,
the Byzantine Empire, whose dromons were
frequently armed with the formidable
incendiary weapon known as "Greek fire."

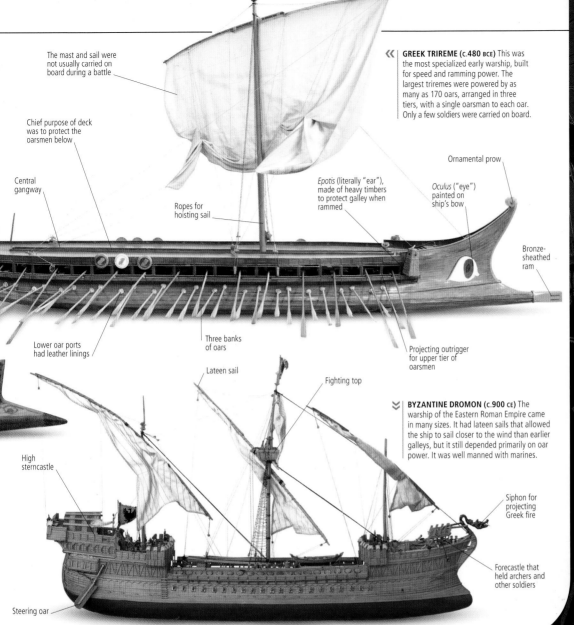

The mast and sail were not usually carried on board during a battle

Chief purpose of deck was to protect the oarsmen below

Central gangway

Ropes for hoisting sail

GREEK TRIREME (C.480 BCE) This was the most specialized early warship, built for speed and ramming power. The largest triremes were powered by as many as 170 oars, arranged in three tiers, with a single oarsman to each oar. Only a few soldiers were carried on board.

Epotis (literally "ear"), made of heavy timbers to protect galley when rammed

Ornamental prow

Oculus ("eye") painted on ship's bow

Bronze-sheathed ram

Lower oar ports had leather linings

Three banks of oars

Projecting outrigger for upper tier of oarsmen

Lateen sail

Fighting top

BYZANTINE DROMON (C.900 CE) The warship of the Eastern Roman Empire came in many sizes. It had lateen sails that allowed the ship to sail closer to the wind than earlier galleys, but it still depended primarily on oar power. It was well manned with marines.

High sterncastle

Siphon for projecting Greek fire

Forecastle that held archers and other soldiers

Steering oar

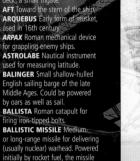

GLOSSARY

An explanation of less familiar nautical and military terms used in the book is given below.

1ST RATE British ship of the line with more than 100 guns on three decks.
2ND RATE British ship of the line with 90–98 guns on three decks.
3RD RATE British ship of the line with 64–80 guns on two decks.
4TH RATE British ship of the line with 46–60 guns on two decks.
5TH RATE British frigate with 32–44 guns on a single deck.
6TH RATE Small British warship with 20–28 guns on a single deck, a small frigate.
AFT Toward the stern of the ship.
ARQUEBUS Early form of musket, used in 16th century.
ARPAX Roman mechanical device for grappling enemy ships.
ASTROLABE Nautical instrument used for measuring latitude.
BALINGER Small shallow-hulled English sailing barge of the late Middle Ages. Could be powered by oars as well as sail.
BALLISTA Roman catapult for firing iron-tipped bolts.
BALLISTIC MISSILE Medium or long-range missile for delivering (usually nuclear) warhead. Powered initially by rocket fuel, the missile descends to its target in freefall.
BARBETTE Armoured cylinder supporting the large gun turrets of 19th- and 20th-century warships.
BAR SHOT Cannon ammunition, consisting of two half-cannonballs linked by a solid bar. Used, like chain shot, for attacking spars and rigging of sailing ships.
BATTLECRUISER Class of heavily armed ship developed in years leading up to World War I as a kind of fast battleship.
BATTLEGROUP Formation of surface ships, originally centred on battleships, but in recent times consisting of a carrier with guided missile destroyers, anti-submarine destroyers, cruisers, and frigates.
BEAM The breadth of a ship at its widest point.
BILGE Lowest part of the interior of the hull, where water collects.
BINNACLE Mount for a ship's compass, in sailing ships usually sited on the quarterdeck.

INTRODUCTION

MEDIEVAL WARSHIPS

INTRODUCTION

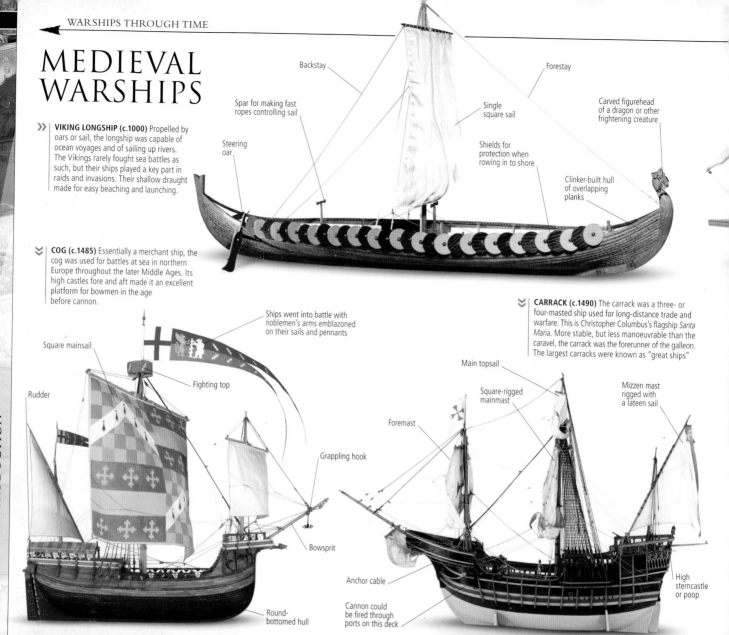

VIKING LONGSHIP (c.1000) Propelled by oars or sail, the longship was capable of ocean voyages and of sailing up rivers. The Vikings rarely fought sea battles as such, but their ships played a key part in raids and invasions. Their shallow draught made for easy beaching and launching.

Backstay

Spar for making fast ropes controlling sail

Steering oar

Forestay

Single square sail

Shields for protection when rowing in to shore

Carved figurehead of a dragon or other frightening creature

Clinker-built hull of overlapping planks

COG (c.1485) Essentially a merchant ship, the cog was used for battles at sea in northern Europe throughout the later Middle Ages. Its high castles fore and aft made it an excellent platform for bowmen in the age before cannon.

Ships went into battle with noblemen's arms emblazoned on their sails and pennants

Square mainsail

Fighting top

Rudder

Grappling hook

Bowsprit

Round-bottomed hull

CARRACK (c.1490) The carrack was a three- or four-masted ship used for long-distance trade and warfare. This is Christopher Columbus's flagship *Santa Maria*. More stable, but less manoeuvrable than the caravel, the carrack was the forerunner of the galleon. The largest carracks were known as "great ships"

Main topsail

Square-rigged mainmast

Mizzen mast rigged with a lateen sail

Foremast

Anchor cable

High sterncastle or poop

Cannon could be fired through ports on this deck

THE DESIGN of medieval warships developed along very different lines in the Mediterranean and the seas of northern Europe. Mediterranean states continued to use oared galleys for warfare. Their shipbuilders made hulls that were carvel-built (had flush-fitting planks) and, under the influence of Arab sailors from the Indian Ocean, adopted the triangular lateen sail instead of the square sail. In northern Europe the Viking longship, the prime warship of the early Middle Ages, was clinker-built – it had overlapping planks that needed less caulking than carvel-built hulls – and had a square sail. The longship had oars, like a Mediterranean war galley, but was better suited to rough seas.

North European shipbuilders also used a clinker-built hull and a square sail on the sturdy round cargo ship known as a "cog". Cogs came to be used in warfare, in the process growing "castles" at both ends of the ship, raised platforms from which soldiers and archers could rain missiles down upon enemy ships and where they could resist attempts to board. Although oared galleys continued to play a part in warfare in northern Europe, sailing ships took precedence.

Shipborne warriors
This 8th-century carved stone from the Swedish island of Gotland shows Viking warriors aboard a longship sailing to Valhalla after a life of raids and invasions.

HYBRID SHIPS

In the 15th century a fruitful cross-fertilization between the Mediterranean and northern European traditions took place. The three- or four-masted carrack combined lateen and square sails to create a larger, more manoeuvrable descendant of the cog. At the same time the smaller two- or three-masted caravel evolved, mostly with lateen sails but sometimes with a square sail as well. By 1500 the carrack was the dominant warship of northern Europe. It provided a stable platform for cannon, used in large numbers on ships from the late 15th century. With gun ports cut into its hull, the carrack grew into the "great ship" – for example, *Henry Grâce à Dieu*, launched in 1514, which carried some 180 cannon, distributed along gun decks and in prodigiously high castles.

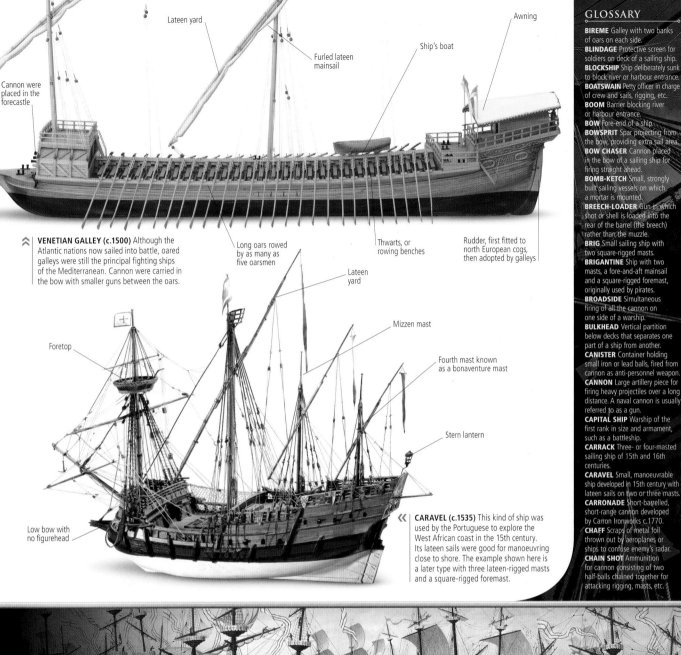

Lateen yard

Furled lateen mainsail

Ship's boat

Awning

Cannon were placed in the forecastle

VENETIAN GALLEY (c.1500) Although the Atlantic nations now sailed into battle, oared galleys were still the principal fighting ships of the Mediterranean. Cannon were carried in the bow with smaller guns between the oars.

Long oars rowed by as many as five oarsmen

Thwarts, or rowing benches

Rudder, first fitted to north European cogs, then adopted by galleys

Lateen yard

Mizzen mast

Fourth mast known as a bonaventure mast

Foretop

Stern lantern

Low bow with no figurehead

CARAVEL (c.1535) This kind of ship was used by the Portuguese to explore the West African coast in the 15th century. Its lateen sails were good for manoeuvring close to shore. The example shown here is a later type with three lateen-rigged masts and a square-rigged foremast.

GLOSSARY

BIREME Galley with two banks of oars on each side.
BLINDAGE Protective screen for soldiers on deck of a sailing ship.
BLOCKSHIP Ship deliberately sunk to block river or harbour entrance.
BOATSWAIN Petty officer in charge of crew and sails, rigging, etc.
BOOM Barrier blocking river or harbour entrance.
BOW Fore-end of a ship.
BOWSPRIT Spar projecting from the bow, providing extra sail area.
BOW CHASER Cannon placed in the bow of a sailing ship for firing straight ahead.
BOMB-KETCH Small, strongly built sailing vessels on which a mortar is mounted.
BREECH-LOADER Gun in which shot or shell is loaded into the rear of the barrel (the breech) rather than the muzzle.
BRIG Small sailing ship with two square-rigged masts.
BRIGANTINE Ship with two masts, a fore-and-aft mainsail and a square-rigged foremast, originally used by pirates.
BROADSIDE Simultaneous firing of all the cannon on one side of a warship.
BULKHEAD Vertical partition below decks that separates one part of a ship from another.
CANISTER Container holding small iron or lead balls, fired from cannon as anti-personnel weapon.
CANNON Large artillery piece for firing heavy projectiles over a long distance. A naval cannon is usually referred to as a gun.
CAPITAL SHIP Warship of the first rank in size and armament, such as a battleship.
CARRACK Three- or four-masted sailing ship of 15th and 16th centuries.
CARAVEL Small, manoeuvrable ship developed in 15th century with lateen sails on two or three masts.
CARRONADE Short-barrelled, short-range cannon developed by Carron Ironworks c.1770.
CHAFF Scraps of metal foil thrown out by aeroplanes or ships to confuse enemy's radar.
CHAIN SHOT Ammunition for cannon consisting of two half-balls chained together for attacking rigging, masts, etc.

INTRODUCTION

EARLY MODERN WARSHIPS

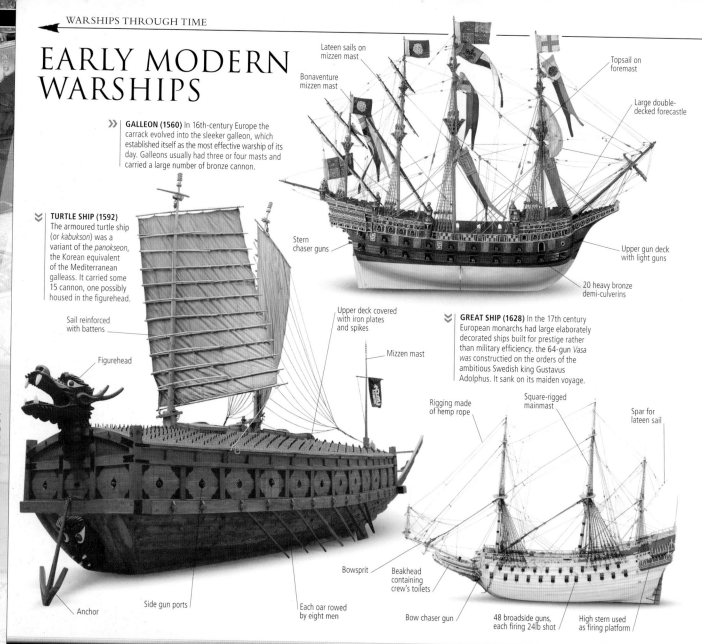

GALLEON (1560) In 16th-century Europe the carrack evolved into the sleeker galleon, which established itself as the most effective warship of its day. Galleons usually had three or four masts and carried a large number of bronze cannon.

Lateen sails on mizzen mast

Bonaventure mizzen mast

Topsail on foremast

Large double-decked forecastle

Upper gun deck with light guns

20 heavy bronze demi-culverins

Stern chaser guns

TURTLE SHIP (1592) The armoured turtle ship (or *kabukson*) was a variant of the *panokseon*, the Korean equivalent of the Mediterranean galleass. It carried some 15 cannon, one possibly housed in the figurehead.

Sail reinforced with battens

Figurehead

Upper deck covered with iron plates and spikes

Mizzen mast

GREAT SHIP (1628) In the 17th century European monarchs had large elaborately decorated ships built for prestige rather than military efficiency. the 64-gun *Vasa* was constructied on the orders of the ambitious Swedish king Gustavus Adolphus. It sank on its maiden voyage.

Rigging made of hemp rope

Square-rigged mainmast

Spar for lateen sail

Anchor

Side gun ports

Each oar rowed by eight men

Bowsprit

Beakhead containing crew's toilets

Bow chaser gun

48 broadside guns, each firing 24lb shot

High stern used as firing platform

THE DEVELOPMENT of ocean-going sailing ships in the 16th century allowed European sailors to make voyages around the world. They encountered countries with independent and highly sophisticated naval traditions. For example, in a war against Japan in the 1590s, the Korean fleet included ironclad "turtle ships", the likes of which had never been seen in Europe. China had built sailing ships larger than any that Europeans possessed. Yet the momentum of European progress in shipbuilding and arms manufacture was unstoppable.

GALLEONS AND GALLEASSES
In the second half of the 16th century the large carrack or "great ship" was surpassed as a fighting warship by the galleon. Gall...

had all the advantages of carracks – they were substantial-size ships with gun ports that could carry a heavy weight of cannon – but their designers reduced the height of the castles and lengthened and streamlined the dimensions of the ships for better handling. The sides of the ships were sloped inward from the lower gun deck to the weather deck, enhancing stability and making them more difficult to board.

While galleons dominated warfare in the Atlantic, in the Mediterranean oared galleys remained in use in battle through the 16th and 17th centuries. The Spanish and Venetians turned galleys into floating gun platforms. Venice invented the galleass, a large warship powered by sails and oars, which could mount a truly impressive quantity of cannon. But although galleasses were used outside the

Mediterranean – they formed part of the Spanish Armada in 1588 – the future lay with ships that relied entirely on sails.

SHIPS OF THE LINE
In the course of the 17th century the galleon evolved into the ship of the line. Gunnery became the primary means of engaging enemy vessels and the traditional action of boarding only secondary. Guns were arranged almost exclusively along the sides of the ship, to deliver thunderous broadsides. Ships fought in line of battle, and the ship of the line was a warship powerful enough to hold its own in such a gun duel. The forerunner to such ships was England's *Sovereign of the Seas*, commissioned by King Charles I of England in 1634. Smaller frigates and sloops played a supporting role

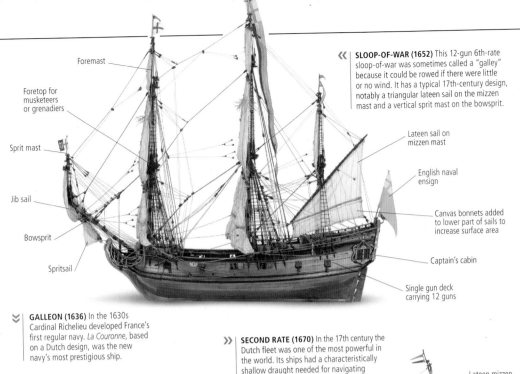

Foremast

Foretop for
musketeers
or grenadiers

Sprit mast

Jib sail

Bowsprit

Spritsail

SLOOP-OF-WAR (1652) This 12-gun 6th-rate
sloop-of-war was sometimes called a "galley"
because it could be rowed if there were little
or no wind. It has a typical 17th-century design,
notably a triangular lateen sail on the mizzen
mast and a vertical sprit mast on the bowsprit.

Lateen sail on
mizzen mast

English naval
ensign

Canvas bonnets added
to lower part of sails to
increase surface area

Captain's cabin

Single gun deck
carrying 12 guns

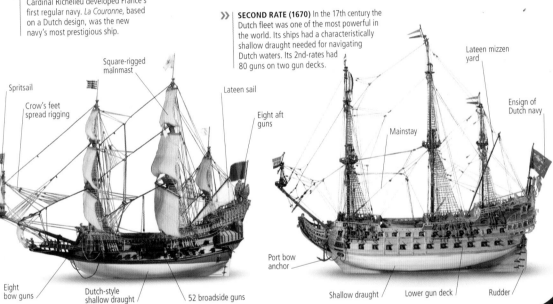

GALLEON (1636) In the 1630s
Cardinal Richelieu developed France's
first regular navy. *La Couronne*, based
on a Dutch design, was the new
navy's most prestigious ship.

Spritsail

Crow's feet
spread rigging

Square-rigged
mainmast

Eight
bow guns

Dutch-style
shallow draught

52 broadside guns

SECOND RATE (1670) In the 17th century the
Dutch fleet was one of the most powerful in
the world. Its ships had a characteristically
shallow draught needed for navigating
Dutch waters. Its 2nd-rates had
80 guns on two gun decks.

Lateen sail

Eight aft
guns

Port bow
anchor

Lateen mizzen
yard

Ensign of
Dutch navy

Mainstay

Shallow draught

Lower gun deck

Rudder

GLOSSARY

COG Round-bottomed sailing
ship developed in northern
Europe in the Middle Ages.
CONGREVE ROCKET British
self-propelled missile, developed
in the early 19th century.
CORSAIR Polite word for "pirate".
CORVETTE Small, fast, lightly-
armed, three-masted sailing ship,
like a small frigate.
CORVUS Roman device lowered
onto the deck of an enemy ship
to enable soldiers to board.
COTTONCLAD Confederate
ship in US Civil War, protected
by cladding of cotton bales.
CRUISER Term originally used
to describe ship's role – sailing
independently, raiding or attacking
merchant shipping. In late 19th
century applied to steam warships
smaller than a battleship, first the
protected cruiser, which had decks
armoured against explosive shells,
then the armoured cruiser, with
belt of armour around the hull.
In 20th century cruisers were
usually classed as light and heavy.
CULVERIN Narrow smooth-bored
cannon of 16th and 17th centuries.
CUTTER Small sailing boat with
a single mast. Also a kind of ship's
boat carried by larger sailing vessel.
DAHLGREN GUN Reinforced
muzzle-loading cannon, widely
used on gunboats in US Civil War.
DEAD-RECKONING Method of
calculating one's position at sea by
the ship's speed, the time that has
elapsed, and the direction steered.
DEPTH CHARGE Anti-submarine
weapon designed to explode near
target at depth determined by fuse.
DESTROYER Warship conceived
at the end of the 19th century as
a "torpedo-boat destroyer", then
adapted to deliver torpedoes itself.
In World Wars I and II destroyers
were widely used as escorts for
warships and merchant convoys.
Today, they are armed with guided
missiles to defend other ships from
air, submarine, and surface attack.
DOUBLE To attack a single ship
with broadsides from both sides.
DREADNOUGHT Launched in
1906, HMS *Dreadnought* gave
her name to a new generation
of battleships, faster, with more
armour and heavier guns than
any previous warships.

18TH-CENTURY WARSHIPS

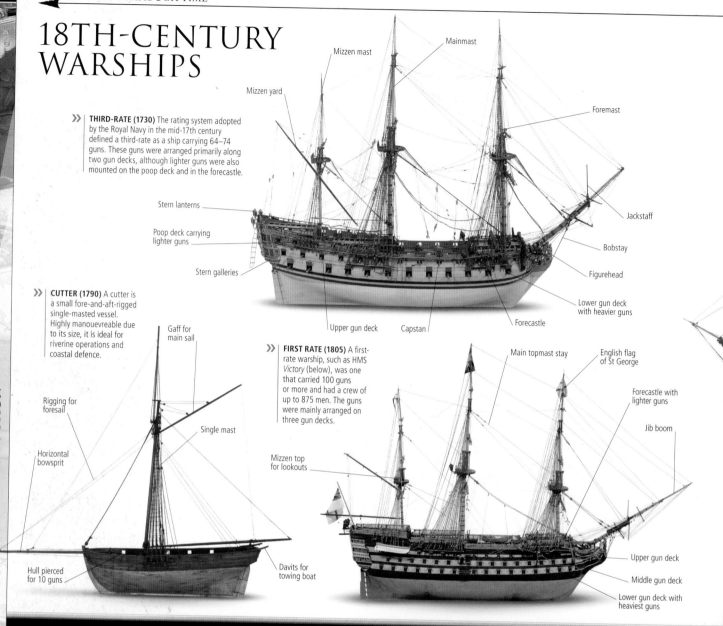

THIRD-RATE (1730) The rating system adopted by the Royal Navy in the mid-17th century defined a third-rate as a ship carrying 64–74 guns. These guns were arranged primarily along two gun decks, although lighter guns were also mounted on the poop deck and in the forecastle.

Mizzen mast

Mizzen yard

Mainmast

Foremast

Stern lanterns

Poop deck carrying lighter guns

Stern galleries

Jackstaff

Bobstay

Figurehead

Lower gun deck with heavier guns

Upper gun deck

Capstan

Forecastle

CUTTER (1790) A cutter is a small fore-and-aft-rigged single-masted vessel. Highly manoeuvreable due to its size, it is ideal for riverine operations and coastal defence.

Gaff for main sail

Rigging for foresail

Single mast

Horizontal bowsprit

Hull pierced for 10 guns

Davits for towing boat

FIRST RATE (1805) A first-rate warship, such as HMS *Victory* (below), was one that carried 100 guns or more and had a crew of up to 875 men. The guns were mainly arranged on three gun decks.

Main topmast stay

English flag of St George

Forecastle with lighter guns

Jib boom

Mizzen top for lookouts

Upper gun deck

Middle gun deck

Lower gun deck with heaviest guns

BY THE 18th century oar power as a means of propulsion in battle had finally fallen by the wayside in most European navies, although galleys still served effectively in the shallow waters of the Baltic. The three-masted, multiple-gun-deck sailing ship, fighting in line of battle, remained unchallenged as the primary warship.

THE RATING SYSTEM

The design of warships became relatively standardized. They were categorized according to a rating system developed by England's Royal Navy in the mid-17th century, which referred to the number of guns a ship carried. By the mid-18th century a first-rate was a three-deck ship with 100 or more guns, while a second-rater had 90–98

guns also on three decks. The standard ship of the line was a two-decker third-rate, typically around 52m (170ft) long and mounting from 64 to 74 guns. Fourth-rate ships, with around 50 guns, were sometimes admitted as ships of the line. The naval ships not considered fit for the line of battle included frigates, sloops-of-war, schooners, brigs, and mortar vessels (variously fifth, sixth and unrated ships), which all nevertheless performed vital support functions. Frigates became especially important in the course of the 18th century. Fast and well-armed for their size, they served to great effect as scouts and commerce raiders. The frigates of the fledgling US Navy, such as *Constitution* launched at the end of the century, could carry as many as 60 guns and were a match for any fourth-rate ship of the line.

NEW TECHNOLOGIES

The warships of the 18th century benefited from some crucial technological advances. Firstly, ships' wheels had been introduced to replace the previous tiller system of steering. The pulley mechanism allied to the wheel allowed much greater and swifter movement of the rudder, and hence improved manoeuvrability. During the late 18th century copper sheathing of hulls was introduced. By protecting the hull, the copper plate allowed warships to spend longer at sea before requiring dry-dock maintenance and repairs. The introduction of the carronade in the 1770s provided a short-range but powerful gun light enough to be mounted on the upper deck without destabilizing the ship – the heaviest guns, such as the 32lb Blomfields, had to be carried close to the waterline to maintain stability.

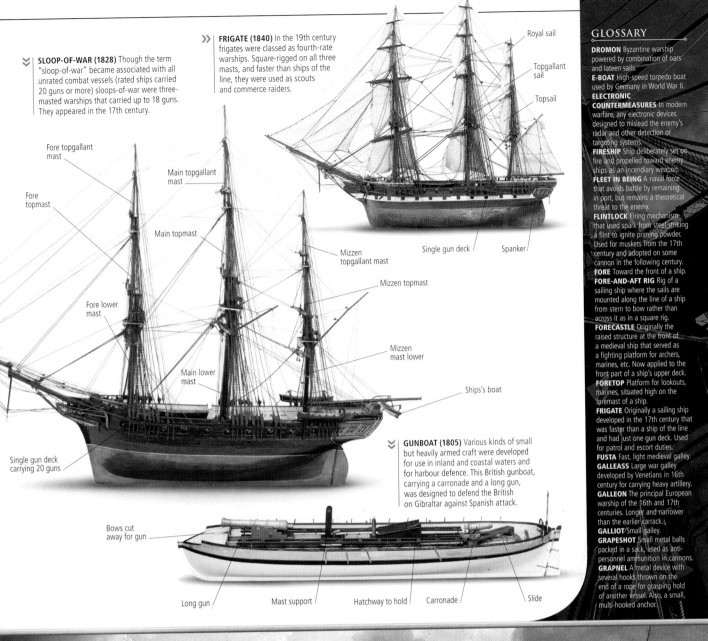

SLOOP-OF-WAR (1828) Though the term "sloop-of-war" became associated with all unrated combat vessels (rated ships carried 20 guns or more) sloops-of-war were three-masted warships that carried up to 18 guns. They appeared in the 17th century.

FRIGATE (1840) In the 19th century frigates were classed as fourth-rate warships. Square-rigged on all three masts, and faster than ships of the line, they were used as scouts and commerce raiders.

Royal sail

Topgallant sail

Topsail

Fore topgallant mast

Main topgallant mast

Fore topmast

Main topmast

Mizzen topgallant mast

Mizzen topmast

Fore lower mast

Mizzen mast lower

Main lower mast

Single gun deck

Spanker

Ship's boat

Single gun deck carrying 20 guns

GUNBOAT (1805) Various kinds of small but heavily armed craft were developed for use in inland and coastal waters and for harbour defence. This British gunboat, carrying a carronade and a long gun, was designed to defend the British on Gibraltar against Spanish attack.

Bows cut away for gun

Long gun

Mast support

Hatchway to hold

Carronade

Slide

GLOSSARY

DROMON Byzantine warship powered by combination of oars and lateen sails.

E-BOAT High-speed torpedo boat used by Germany in World War II.

ELECTRONIC COUNTERMEASURES In modern warfare, any electronic devices designed to mislead the enemy's radar and other detection or targeting systems.

FIRESHIP Ship deliberately set on fire and propelled toward enemy ships as an incendiary weapon.

FLEET IN BEING A naval force that avoids battle by remaining in port, but remains a theoretical threat to the enemy.

FLINTLOCK Firing mechanism that used spark from steel striking a flint to ignite priming powder. Used for muskets from the 17th century and adopted on some cannon in the following century.

FORE Toward the front of a ship.

FORE-AND-AFT RIG Rig of a sailing ship where the sails are mounted along the line of a ship from stern to bow rather than across it as in a square rig.

FORECASTLE Originally the raised structure at the front of a medieval ship that served as a fighting platform for archers, marines, etc. Now applied to the front part of a ship's upper deck.

FORETOP Platform for lookouts, marines, situated high on the foremast of a ship.

FRIGATE Originally a sailing ship developed in the 17th century that was faster than a ship of the line and had just one gun deck. Used for patrol and escort duties.

FUSTA Fast, light medieval galley.

GALLEASS Large war galley developed by Venetians in 16th century for carrying heavy artillery.

GALLEON The principal European warship of the 16th and 17th centuries. Longer and narrower than the earlier carrack.

GALLIOT Small galley.

GRAPESHOT Small metal balls packed in a sack, used as anti-personnel ammunition in cannons.

GRAPNEL A metal device with several hooks thrown on the end of a rope for grasping hold of another vessel. Also, a small, multi-hooked anchor.

IRON AND STEEL WARSHIPS

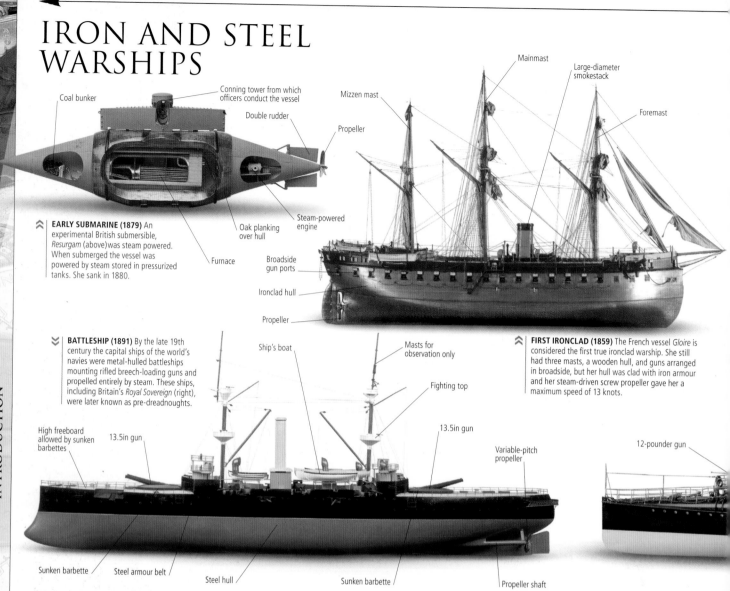

Coal bunker

Conning tower from which officers conduct the vessel

Double rudder

Propeller

Steam-powered engine

Oak planking over hull

Furnace

EARLY SUBMARINE (1879) An experimental British submersible, *Resurgam* (above) was steam powered. When submerged the vessel was powered by steam stored in pressurized tanks. She sank in 1880.

Mizzen mast

Mainmast

Large-diameter smokestack

Foremast

Broadside gun ports

Ironclad hull

Propeller

FIRST IRONCLAD (1859) The French vessel *Gloire* is considered the first true ironclad warship. She still had three masts, a wooden hull, and guns arranged in broadside, but her hull was clad with iron armour and her steam-driven screw propeller gave her a maximum speed of 13 knots.

BATTLESHIP (1891) By the late 19th century the capital ships of the world's navies were metal-hulled battleships mounting rifled breech-loading guns and propelled entirely by steam. These ships, including Britain's *Royal Sovereign* (right), were later known as pre-dreadnoughts.

Ship's boat

Masts for observation only

Fighting top

13.5in gun

13.5in gun

Variable-pitch propeller

12-pounder gun

High freeboard allowed by sunken barbettes

13.5in gun

Sunken barbette

Steel armour belt

Steel hull

Sunken barbette

Propeller shaft

INTRODUCTION

THE DESIGN OF WARSHIPS in the 19th century was revolutionized by the adoption of steam power, the replacement of wood by iron and steel in ship construction, and the development of rifled turret guns firing explosive shells. Change was at first quite slow. The first steam-powered fighting ship was the *Demologos*, an American paddle-wheel-driven harbour defence vessel of 1814, and the first iron-hulled ships emerged in the 1820s. But until the mid-19th century major navies still consisted primarily of wooden sailing ships. The advent of the screw propeller as an alternative to the paddle wheel was a crucial step forward (the first screw-driven

warship was launched in 1843) and by the 1850s almost all new-built warships had steam engines as well as sails. The universal adoption of metal construction took longer. In the 1850s ships with hulls of wood or iron were covered with thick iron plates, creating the "ironclad". In the 1870s steel began to be used both for hulls and armour, while sails finally disappeared as marine steam engines became more effective. This revolution in ship construction and propulsion was matched by changes in armament. Explosive

Explosive shell with sabot
This explosive shell from the American Civil War is attached to a wooden sabot. The shell was placed sabot-first into the muzzle to keep the shell's fuse centred; the fuse was ignited by the powder charge.

shells replaced solid shot. Firing in broadside was gradually abandoned in favour of a much smaller number of large breech-loading guns mounted in revolving turrets – the effectiveness of a turret gun having been demonstrated by the American *Monitor* of 1861. The deployment of torpedoes created new problems for naval tacticians, and gave designers a chance to create new kinds of small, fast torpedo attack craft.

UNEASY TRANSITION

Some of the large warships built during the period of transition from wood and sail to steam and steel were ungainly and even unseaworthy. The positioning of guns, funnels, and masts (still needed for observation posts) often involved unsatisfactory compromises, as did the trade-off between armour and performance

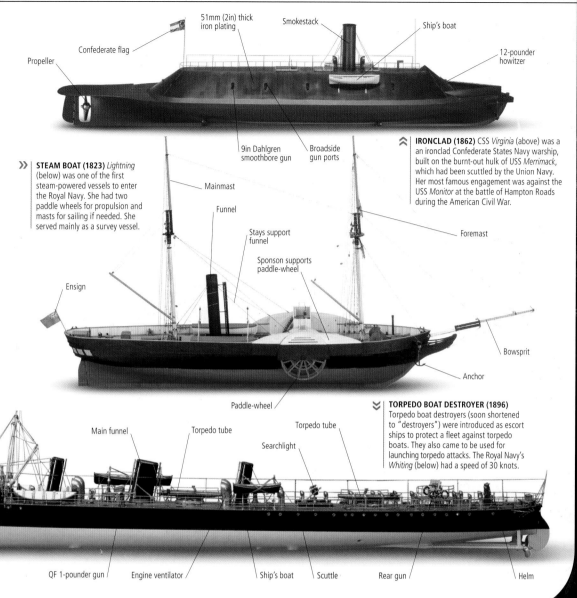

51mm (2in) thick
iron plating

Smokestack

Ship's boat

Confederate flag

Propeller

12-pounder
howitzer

9in Dahlgren
smoothbore gun

Broadside
gun ports

▲ IRONCLAD (1862) CSS *Virginia* (above) was a
an ironclad Confederate States Navy warship,
built on the burnt-out hulk of USS *Merrimack*,
which had been scuttled by the Union Navy.
Her most famous engagement was against the
USS *Monitor* at the battle of Hampton Roads
during the American Civil War.

» STEAM BOAT (1823) *Lightning*
(below) was one of the first
steam-powered vessels to enter
the Royal Navy. She had two
paddle wheels for propulsion and
masts for sailing if needed. She
served mainly as a survey vessel.

Mainmast

Funnel

Stays support
funnel

Sponson supports
paddle-wheel

Foremast

Ensign

Bowsprit

Anchor

Paddle-wheel

≫ TORPEDO BOAT DESTROYER (1896)
Torpedo boat destroyers (soon shortened
to "destroyers") were introduced as escort
ships to protect a fleet against torpedo
boats. They also came to be used for
launching torpedo attacks. The Royal Navy's
Whiting (below) had a speed of 30 knots.

Main funnel

Torpedo tube

Torpedo tube

Searchlight

QF 1-pounder gun

Engine ventilator

Ship's boat

Scuttle

Rear gun

Helm

GLOSSARY

GRAPPLING HOOK A grapnel.
GREEK FIRE Inflammable liquid
used as a kind of flamethrower in
naval warfare by the Byzantines
from the 7th century CE.
GUN PORT Opening in the hull
of a ship through which ship's
guns are run out for firing.
HAWSER Heavy rope or steel
cable used on board ship.
HEAVE TO To prevent forward
movement of a ship, usually by
bringing bow into the wind. A ship
stopped this way is "hove to".
HEMMEMA Swedish warship of
the 18th century. Powered by oars
or sail, it was used in the shallow
coastal waters of the Baltic.
HULK Old, wrecked, or abandoned
ship, often used as a barrier.
IRONCLAD Warship of the
mid-19th century, originally built
with wooden hull armoured with
iron plates.
KABUKSON Medieval Korean oar-
powered warship, fitted with
heavy cannon and an armoured
(spiked) upper deck (also known
as a turtle ship).
KAMIKAZE The suicide attacks of
Japanese pilots who intentionally
crashed their aeroplanes into
enemy ships at the end of World
War II. Usually translated "divine
wind" after the typhoon that
prevented the Mongol invasion
of Japan in 1281.
KNOT Speed of one nautical mile
per hour —1.85kph (1.15mph).
LANYARD Cord pulled to fire a
gun, e.g. to activate the flintlock
firing mechanism of a cannon.
LATEEN SAIL Triangular sail
mounted at an angle on the mast.
LEE The side (e.g. of a ship) away
from the direction of the wind.
LEE SHORE Shore on the leeward
side of a ship, i.e. with the wind
blowing toward the shore.
LEEWARD Opposite of windward,
the direction downwind of the
way the wind is blowing.
LIBURNIAN Small Roman warship.
LINE OF BATTLE Tactic developed
in 17th century, where warships
line up one behind the other to
fire broadsides at the enemy with
no risk of hitting their own ships.
LINE ABREAST Ships sailing
side by side in a line are said
to be "in line abreast".

INTRODUCTION

DREADNOUGHTS, CRUISERS, AND DESTROYERS

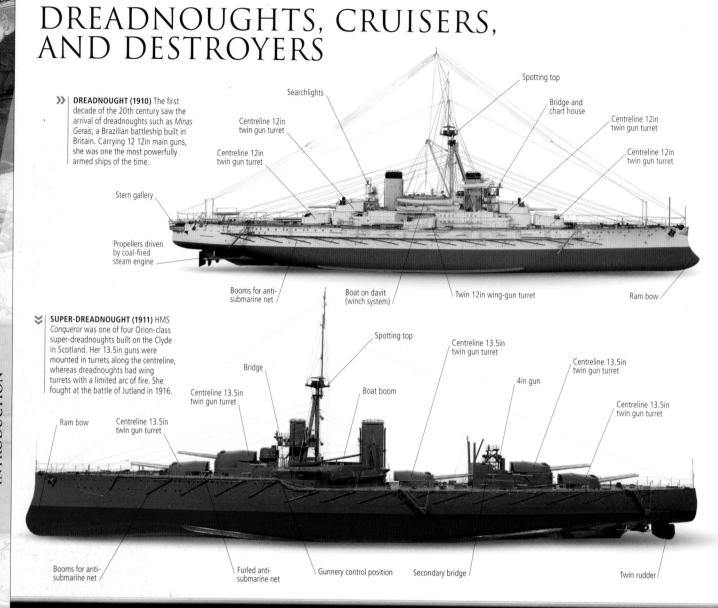

DREADNOUGHT (1910) The first decade of the 20th century saw the arrival of dreadnoughts such as *Minas Gerais*, a Brazilian battleship built in Britain. Carrying 12 12in main guns, she was one the most powerfully armed ships of the time.

Searchlights

Spotting top

Bridge and chart house

Centreline 12in twin gun turret

Centreline 12in twin gun turret

Centreline 12in twin gun turret

Centreline 12in twin gun turret

Stern gallery

Propellers driven by coal-fired steam engine

Booms for anti-submarine net

Boat on davit (winch system)

Twin 12in wing-gun turret

Ram bow

SUPER-DREADNOUGHT (1911) HMS *Conqueror* was one of four Orion-class super-dreadnoughts built on the Clyde in Scotland. Her 13.5in guns were mounted in turrets along the centreline, whereas dreadnoughts had wing turrets with a limited arc of fire. She fought at the battle of Jutland in 1916.

Spotting top

Bridge

Centreline 13.5in twin gun turret

Centreline 13.5in twin gun turret

Boat boom

Centreline 13.5in twin gun turret

4in gun

Centreline 13.5in twin gun turret

Centreline 13.5in twin gun turret

Ram bow

Centreline 13.5in twin gun turret

Booms for anti-submarine net

Furled anti-submarine net

Gunnery control position

Secondary bridge

Twin rudder

In the years between 1880 and the beginning of World War I in 1914, warship design settled into a generally recognizable format. Multiple guns were mounted along the centreline, and moving turrets provided wide arcs of fire. Armour plate, particularly around the magazine and the engine rooms, became critical, especially as guns, shells, propellants, and targeting equipment all went through dramatic improvements. By the end of World War I, battleships were sending shells of large calibre (12in or even 15in) accurately out to ranges of up to 18,000m (60,000ft).

POWER FACTORS

Propulsion also went through important changes from the last decades of the 19th century. The use of steam turbines produced better power more smoothly delivered, and during the second decade of the 20th century the major powers switched from coal-fired engines to oil-burning variants. Oil not only burned cleaner, but could be transferred easily at sea, and could power ships for longer distances.

TYPES OF WARSHIPS

Three primary types of major surface vessel equipped the world's navies from around 1900. Battleships were the capital ships, with multiple batteries of turret-mounted guns. The dreadnoughts, a generic name derived from the eponymous British battleship of 1906, almost exclusively carried very large-calibre guns for long-range ship-to-ship duels. Cruisers were faster and had longer range and lighter armament than battleships. The battlecruiser was designed to combine battleship armament with the speed of a cruiser, at the expense of much reduced armour. Finally, destroyers, developed from early torpedo boats, performed such roles as fleet defence and escort duties, as well as carrying out torpedo attacks. The bane of all surface warships was the submarine that first had a dramatic effect on naval warfare in World War I.

QF 1-pounder gun
The British QF 1-pounder was used as an anti-torpedo boat weapon during World War I.

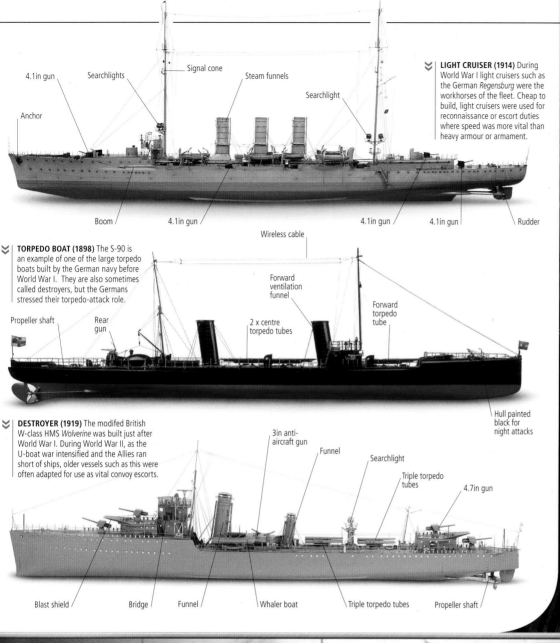

LIGHT CRUISER (1914) During World War I light cruisers such as the German *Regensburg* were the workhorses of the fleet. Cheap to build, light cruisers were used for reconnaissance or escort duties where speed was more vital than heavy armour or armament.

4.1in gun · Searchlights · Signal cone · Steam funnels · Searchlight

Anchor

Boom · 4.1in gun · 4.1in gun · 4.1in gun · Rudder

TORPEDO BOAT (1898) The S-90 is an example of one of the large torpedo boats built by the German navy before World War I. They are also sometimes called destroyers, but the Germans stressed their torpedo-attack role.

Wireless cable

Forward ventilation funnel

Forward torpedo tube

Propeller shaft · Rear gun · 2 x centre torpedo tubes

Hull painted black for night attacks

DESTROYER (1919) The modifed British W-class HMS *Wolverine* was built just after World War I. During World War II, as the U-boat war intensified and the Allies ran short of ships, older vessels such as this were often adapted for use as vital convoy escorts.

3in anti-aircraft gun

Funnel

Searchlight

Triple torpedo tubes

4.7in gun

Blast shield · Bridge · Funnel · Whaler boat · Triple torpedo tubes · Propeller shaft

GLOSSARY

LINE AHEAD Ships sailing in a line, one behind another, are said to be "in line ahead".

MAN OF WAR Large sailing ship armed with cannon on two or three decks, the standard fighting ship of European navies from the 17th to the 19th century.

MANGONEL Medieval catapult, widely used in siege warfare.

MARINE Soldier carried on board a warship.

MARQUE, LETTERS OF Licence issued by a government to a privateer to engage warships or capture merchant shipping of another nation.

MATCH, SLOW Slow-burning cord used by gunners to light the priming powder in the touch-hole of a cannon.

MIDSHIPMAN Young boy taken aboard ship as a cadet to be trained up to be an officer.

MIZZEN MAST Third mast of a three-masted sailing ship, situated behind the mainmast. Often fitted with a lateen sail.

MONITOR Class of 19th-century ironclad warship that took its name from USS *Monitor*. Often applied to shallow-draught vessels used for shore bombardment.

MORTAR Muzzle-loading gun with a short, wide barrel for firing explosive shells at a high angle.

MUZZLE-LOADER Gun loaded from the front (muzzle) end, such as cannon where the shot and powder charge have to be rammed down the length of the barrel.

NAVARCH Supreme naval commander in Sparta and other Greek city-states.

NAUTICAL MILE 1.85km (1.15 miles). 60 nautical miles = 1 degree of the earth's circumference.

OCTANT Precursor of the sextant as an instrument for measuring angle of sun, moon, and stars to the horizon.

PANOKSEON Medieval Korean war galley.

PENTECONTER Early Greek war galley, powered by 50 oars.

POLYREME Large oared galley of the Classical era with several oarsmen pulling on each oar.

POOP Highest deck of a sailing ship, situated at the stern, usually above the captain's quarters.

INTRODUCTION

WORLD WAR II WARSHIPS

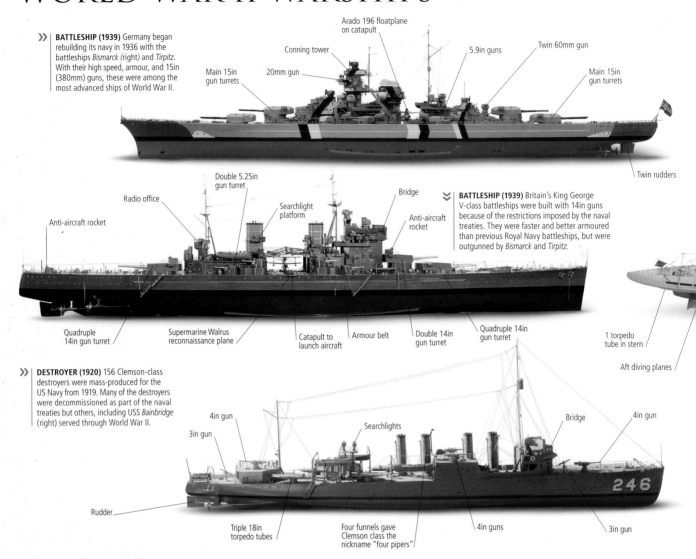

>> **BATTLESHIP (1939)** Germany began rebuilding its navy in 1936 with the battleships *Bismarck* (right) and *Tirpitz*. With their high speed, armour, and 15in (380mm) guns, these were among the most advanced ships of World War II.

Arado 196 floatplane on catapult

Conning tower

Main 15in gun turrets

20mm gun

5.9in guns

Twin 60mm gun

Main 15in gun turrets

Twin rudders

Radio office

Double 5.25in gun turret

Searchlight platform

Bridge

Anti-aircraft rocket

Anti-aircraft rocket

>> **BATTLESHIP (1939)** Britain's King George V-class battleships were built with 14in guns because of the restrictions imposed by the naval treaties. They were faster and better armoured than previous Royal Navy battleships, but were outgunned by *Bismarck* and *Tirpitz*.

Quadruple 14in gun turret

Supermarine Walrus reconnaissance plane

Catapult to launch aircraft

Armour belt

Double 14in gun turret

Quadruple 14in gun turret

1 torpedo tube in stern

Aft diving planes

>> **DESTROYER (1920)** 156 Clemson-class destroyers were mass-produced for the US Navy from 1919. Many of the destroyers were decommissioned as part of the naval treaties but others, including USS *Bainbridge* (right) served through World War II.

4in gun

3in gun

Searchlights

Bridge

4in gun

Rudder

246

Triple 18in torpedo tubes

Four funnels gave Clemson class the nickname "four pipers"

4in guns

3in gun

MAJOR NAVIES entered World War II still preoccupied with developing bigger and better battleships. Ships under construction when the war started included the German *Tirpitz* and *Bismarck*, the American *Iowa*, and the Japanese *Yamato* and *Musashi*, the two largest battleships ever built. Capable of speeds of around 30 knots and with a main armament of 15in to 18.1in guns, these capital ships were extraordinary fighting machines. But although big-gun ships played an important part in the war, they were upstaged by the rise of air power.

Warships were fitted with ever greater numbers of anti-aircraft guns, but proved painfully vulnerable to land- and

carriers had been under development since World War I, and during World War II naval air power came to maturity. Equipped with a mix of dive-bombers, torpedo, and fighter aircraft, fleet carriers proved a dominant force especially in the Pacific theatre, where some naval battles were fought exclusively between carriers. Smaller escort carriers provided air cover for convoys.

Explosive paravane
This underwater glider was an anti-submarine device which was towed behind a ship. It exploded on impact with a submarine.

SUBMARINE WARFARE

Powered by diesel engines on the surface and electric motors under the sea, submarines remained relatively primitive "submersibles" until relatively late in the war, when the Germans introduced U-boats capable of sustained underwater operations. Yet even these unsophisticated boats had a critical impact in both the Pacific and the Atlantic theatres. A whole new range of anti-submarine weaponry was deployed aboard destroyers, frigates, sloops, and corvettes. Radar and sonar detection technologies became integral to naval warfare, particularly in detecting enemy aircraft or submarines. The importance of amphibious operations in World War II also drove the development of a broad spectrum of landing craft

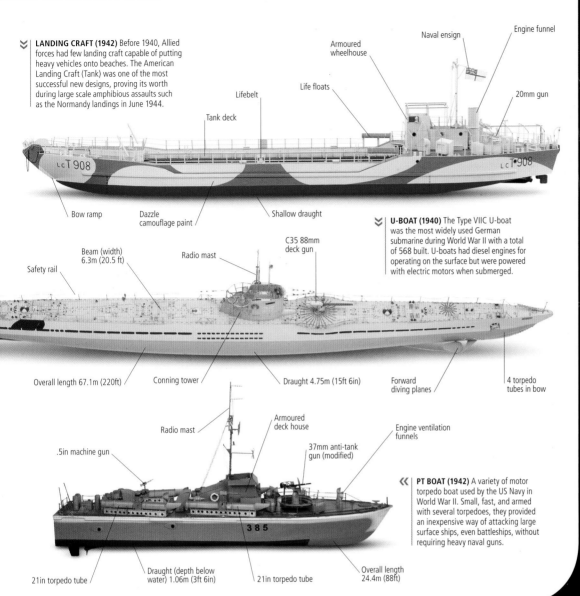

LANDING CRAFT (1942) Before 1940, Allied forces had few landing craft capable of putting heavy vehicles onto beaches. The American Landing Craft (Tank) was one of the most successful new designs, proving its worth during large scale amphibious assaults such as the Normandy landings in June 1944.

Naval ensign

Engine funnel

Armoured wheelhouse

20mm gun

Life floats

Lifebelt

Tank deck

Bow ramp

Dazzle camouflage paint

Shallow draught

U-BOAT (1940) The Type VIIC U-boat was the most widely used German submarine during World War II with a total of 568 built. U-boats had diesel engines for operating on the surface but were powered with electric motors when submerged.

C35 88mm deck gun

Beam (width) 6.3m (20.5 ft)

Radio mast

Safety rail

Overall length 67.1m (220ft)

Conning tower

Draught 4.75m (15ft 6in)

Forward diving planes

4 torpedo tubes in bow

Radio mast

Armoured deck house

Engine ventilation funnels

.5in machine gun

37mm anti-tank gun (modified)

PT BOAT (1942) A variety of motor torpedo boat used by the US Navy in World War II. Small, fast, and armed with several torpedoes, they provided an inexpensive way of attacking large surface ships, even battleships, without requiring heavy naval guns.

21in torpedo tube

Draught (depth below water) 1.06m (3ft 6in)

21in torpedo tube

Overall length 24.4m (88ft)

GLOSSARY

PORT The left side of the ship, looking forward.

POWER PROJECTION A state's ability to deploy naval and other military forces far from its own territory. This threat of force can be used as a political weapon.

PRIZE REGULATIONS Rules governing the taking of enemy merchant ships as prizes with regard to treatment of prisoners and profits made from the sale of the ship and its cargo.

PRAM Shallow-hulled Swedish sailing ship used as gunboat in naval warfare in the Baltic.

PRE-DREADNOUGHT Battleship built or ordered before HMS *Dreadnought* set new standards for armament, armour, and speed when she was launched in 1906.

PRESS To conscript sailors to serve on a warship.

PROW, GIVING THE Tactic employed in the 16th century of firing first with guns in the bow then delivering a broadside.

PT BOAT Patrol torpedo boat. Small, fast US craft of World War II, usually with four torpedo tubes.

QUARTERDECK The deck at the rear of a sailing ship below the poop, where the ship's wheel and binnacle are located.

QUINQUEREME Large warship of the Hellenic and Roman eras.

Q-SHIP Merchantman with concealed guns used by the British to trick U-boats in World War I.

RAM Projecting armoured beak at the front of an Ancient Greek or Roman galley. Ramming was revived as a tactic in 19th century when early ironclads were fitted with reinforced bows for ramming.

RATING Classification of sailing warships according to the number of cannon they carried.

REEF To reduce the area of sail when a strong wind is blowing.

RIGGING All the ropes, etc. that support masts and yards or are used to hoist, lower, or trim sails.

SCREEN To sail ahead of a fleet for reconnaissance and to act as protection for the other ships.

SCUTTLE To sink one's own ship deliberately, often to avoid capture.

SEXTANT Nautical instrument for measuring the angle of the sun or a star to the horizon.

MODERN WARSHIPS

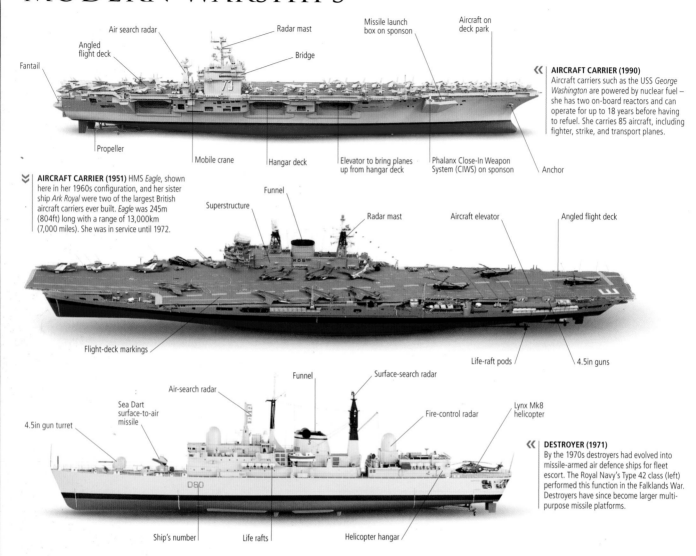

Air search radar

Angled flight deck

Fantail

Radar mast

Bridge

Missile launch box on sponson

Aircraft on deck park

Propeller

Mobile crane

Hangar deck

Elevator to bring planes up from hangar deck

Phalanx Close-In Weapon System (CIWS) on sponson

Anchor

« AIRCRAFT CARRIER (1990)
Aircraft carriers such as the USS *George Washington* are powered by nuclear fuel – she has two on-board reactors and can operate for up to 18 years before having to refuel. She carries 85 aircraft, including fighter, strike, and transport planes.

AIRCRAFT CARRIER (1951) HMS *Eagle*, shown here in her 1960s configuration, and her sister ship *Ark Royal* were two of the largest British aircraft carriers ever built. *Eagle* was 245m (804ft) long with a range of 13,000km (7,000 miles). She was in service until 1972.

Funnel

Superstructure

Radar mast

Aircraft elevator

Angled flight deck

Flight-deck markings

Life-raft pods

4.5in guns

Sea Dart surface-to-air missile

Air-search radar

Funnel

Surface-search radar

Fire-control radar

Lynx Mk8 helicopter

4.5in gun turret

D80

« DESTROYER (1971)
By the 1970s destroyers had evolved into missile-armed air defence ships for fleet escort. The Royal Navy's Type 42 class (left) performed this function in the Falklands War. Destroyers have since become larger multi-purpose missile platforms.

Ship's number

Life rafts

Helicopter hangar

SINCE THE END of World War II, naval warfare has been dominated by the aircraft carrier, the submarine, and the guided missile. The age of the battleship was over, even if big guns still served a purpose for shore bombardment. Aircraft carriers began to grow in size so that they could operate jet aircraft. By the 1970s, however, only the United States could afford to operate a fleet of full-size carriers – these were virtual floating cities, with enough air power to sustain an independent air campaign and were driven by nuclear powerplants that allowed them to stay at sea almost indefinitely. Smaller carriers were still deployed by some of the less affluent countries, and by the US Navy as "assault ships", operating helicopters and vertical/short take-off and landing (V/STOL) jet aircraft.

Nuclear-powered submarines, capable of phenomenal submerged endurance and speed, were equipped with intercontinental ballistic missiles as part of the nuclear armoury of major powers. Hunter-killer submarines were also built, chiefly designed to hunt down enemy submarines. The days of pitched battles between surface fleets seemed over, replaced by a game of underwater cat-and-mouse between nuclear-armed or powered submarines.

GUIDED MISSILES

The development of guided missiles dramatically altered the nature of surface warfare at sea. Guns were reduced to a subsidiary role, with most surface vessels retaining only a single automatic cannon on the foredeck. By this point in time warships effectively became floating electronics

and missile platforms. The destroyer ceased to have a role as a torpedo-attack ship, assuming a range of roles including fleet defence against air attack using anti-aircraft missiles. Frigates tended to specialize in anti-submarine warfare. Both vessels were driven by gas-turbine engines and were designed to be able to carry at least one helicopter. The offensive role of naval guns, meanwhile, was largely taken over by ship-killing missiles – which could be carried even by quite small patrol boats – and by Cruise missiles that were used for the bombardment of land targets. To defend against attack, warships began to deploy a range of electronic countermeasures designed to confuse missile guidance systems. Control rooms on modern naval vessels became vastly complex suites of electronic equipment, including links to surveillance satellites.

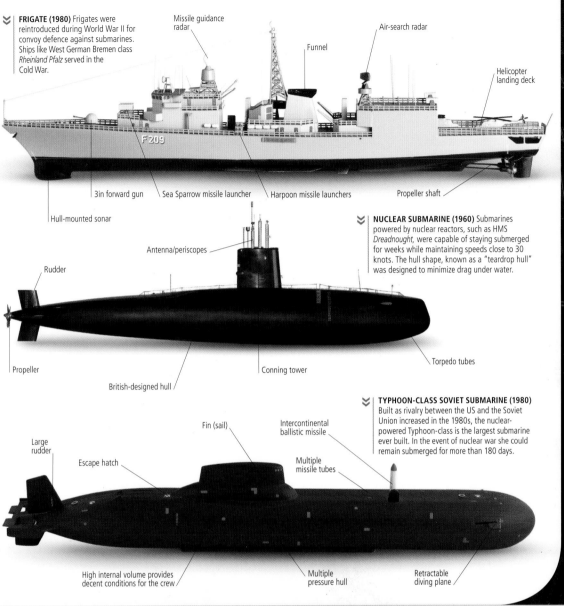

FRIGATE (1980) Frigates were reintroduced during World War II for convoy defence against submarines. Ships like West German Bremen class *Rheinland Pfalz* served in the Cold War.

Missile guidance radar

Funnel

Air-search radar

Helicopter landing deck

F 209

3in forward gun

Sea Sparrow missile launcher

Harpoon missile launchers

Propeller shaft

Hull-mounted sonar

NUCLEAR SUBMARINE (1960) Submarines powered by nuclear reactors, such as HMS *Dreadnought*, were capable of staying submerged for weeks while maintaining speeds close to 30 knots. The hull shape, known as a "teardrop hull" was designed to minimize drag under water.

Antenna/periscopes

Rudder

Propeller

British-designed hull

Conning tower

Torpedo tubes

TYPHOON-CLASS SOVIET SUBMARINE (1980) Built as rivalry between the US and the Soviet Union increased in the 1980s, the nuclear-powered Typhoon-class is the largest submarine ever built. In the event of nuclear war she could remain submerged for more than 180 days.

Fin (sail)

Intercontinental ballistic missile

Large rudder

Escape hatch

Multiple missile tubes

High internal volume provides decent conditions for the crew

Multiple pressure hull

Retractable diving plane

GLOSSARY

SHIP OF THE LINE A well-armed sailing warship between the 17th and 19th centuries, built to fight in the line of battle, exchanging broadsides with the enemy's line.
SHROUDS Strong supporting ropes on either side of a mast.
SLOOP Single-masted sailing vessel with a fore-and-aft rig.
SPAR Wooden pole, part of the rig of a ship, for example a yard from which a sail is suspended.
SQUARE RIG Arrangement on a sailing ship where the principal sails are carried on horizontal spars.
STRIKE COLOURS To lower a ship's flag to signal surrender.
STARBOARD The right-hand side of the ship.
STERNCASTLE Raised structure at the stern of medieval ships that served as a platform for archers, spearmen, and other soldiers.
TACK To turn ship's bow through the wind, to follow a zigzag course in order to sail into the wind.
TENDER Supply ship for bringing food, fuel, crew, etc. to another ship.
TOPMAST Extension to the mast of a ship that carried the topsail.
TREBUCHET Medieval catapult that used a counterweight system to propel missiles.
TRIERARCH Man who raised the crew for, and was responsible for the running of a Greek trireme.
TRIREME Ancient Greek galley with three banks of oars.
TURTLE SHIP *see* PANOKSEON
UNRATED Term that described small British warships with fewer than 20 guns.
VAN The leading ships at the head of a fleet or squadron.
WEATHER GAGE To have the weather gage means to be upwind of another sailing ship, a favourable position for an attack.
WEAR To turn ship's stern through the wind, so that wind direction changes from one side of the ship to the other.
WINDWARD Position of one ship relative to another in terms of which way the wind is blowing, i.e. upwind of the other.
XEBEC Small, fast Mediterranean galley, favoured by Barbary corsairs.
YARD Horizontal spar tapered at the end, used to support and spread a sail.

INTRODUCTION

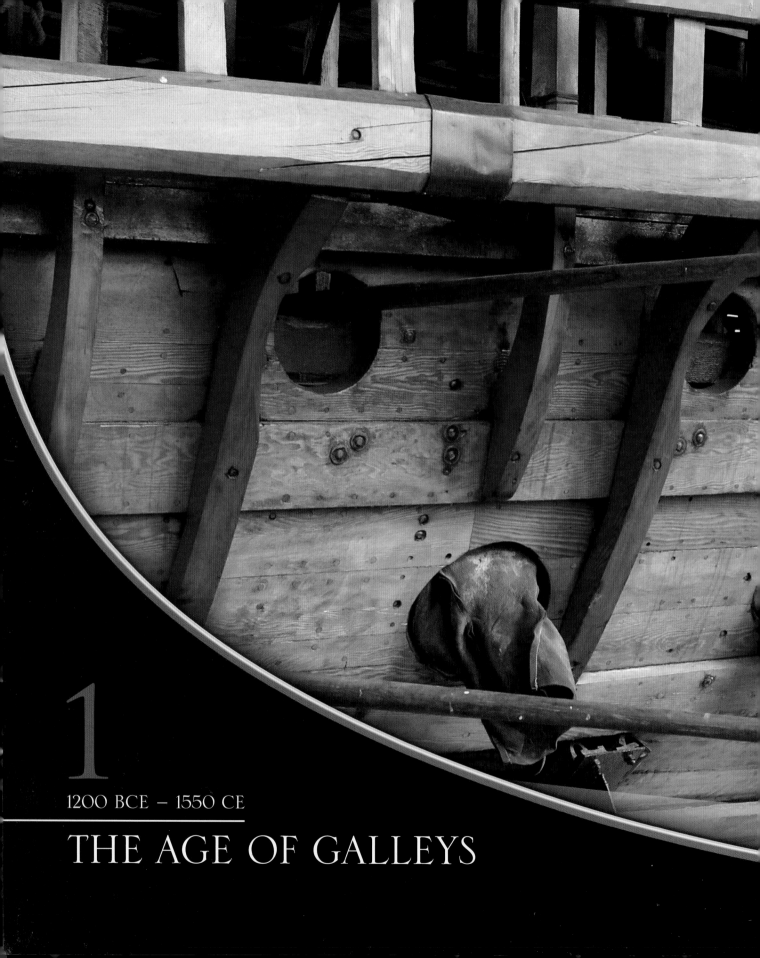

1

1200 BCE – 1550 CE

THE AGE OF GALLEYS

THE GALLEY WAS INVENTED in the eastern Mediterranean in the early 3rd millennium BCE. Although galleys had a sail or sails, they were distinguished by the fact that they could be propelled by oars alone if required. Oars were used either when the wind was absent or contrary, or when faster propulsion was required or tighter manoeuvre – as in battle. These extraordinary war machines, propelled by their great gangs of oarsmen, held their place, with variations of design and tactics, as the prime warships of Europe for around 3,000 years. From the 15th century onward galleys were gradually supplanted by ocean-going sailing ships, capable of year-round operation in all weathers and providing a superior platform for heavy cannon.

Minoan galley
A fresco found on the Greek island of Akrotiri, dating from c.1700 BCE, shows a procession of galleys from one coastal port to another. In this detail, the man standing at the back of the boat holds a steering oar, a feature of all Egyptian, Greek, and Roman ships.

EARLY GALLEY WARFARE

The first recorded use of a warship was an Egyptian sortie into Lebanon and Palestine around 2450 BCE, when troops were landed by sea, presumably ferried from the Nile delta. By the reign of the great pharaoh Thutmose III a thousand years later, seaborne movement of troops was standard Egyptian practice. By this time another warlike use of galleys was emerging. In Egyptian sources around 1500–1300 BCE there is a record of sea raiders seizing merchant ships, attacking coastal settlements, and blockading ports. There are reckoned by this time to have been galleys that carried marines – including archers and javelin-throwers – and others in which the rowers doubled as fighting men, as they would later in the era of the Vikings.

Actual battles at sea emerge in shadowy form in the historical record around the 12th century BCE. At first there was no evidence of naval manoeuvres –

these were simply fights between soldiers on water. But the seagoing peoples of the eastern Mediterranean, especially the Phoenicians and the Greeks, developed skills as sailors that could be applied to warfare, using the first specialist warships, the penteconter and the trireme.

PERSIA AND THE GREEEKS

Some of the basics of naval warfare became evident very early on. To become a naval power a state needed a population with seafaring skills and the resources to finance a fleet – it has always been very expensive to build and man a body of ships. The Persian Empire was the first state to develop a fleet as an element in large-scale power-projection, buying the services of Phoenician and Greek sailors to provide the necessary expertise. Faced with a Persian invasion in the 5th century BCE, the Greek

Early Greek battle at sea
Many images of naval warfare appear on Greek ceramics. On this *krater* (a vessel used for mixing wine and water) from the 7th century BCE the ship on the left is a penteconter with a ram at the prow.

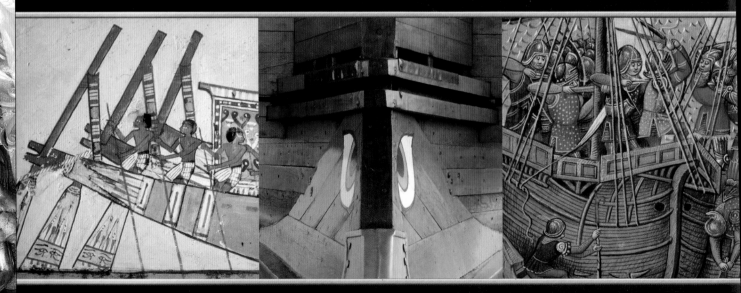

the enemy's ships with firepower and boarding them with bodies of soldiers. When the rising Roman Republic came into conflict with the greatest naval power in the western Mediterranean, Phoenician Carthage, in the First Punic War in the 3rd century BCE, the stage was set for some of the largest naval battles ever fought, involving hundreds of thousands of men. Eventually Rome's willpower and resources made up for lack of naval experience and it was left as the sole dominant power in the Mediterranean.

CONTINUING THE GALLEY TRADITION

In galley warfare there was no sharp transition from the "ancient" to the "medieval" world. Rome's eastern successor state, the Byzantine Empire, fought Arab fleets from the 7th century in battles whose chief novelty was the use of "Greek fire" as an incendiary weapon. The tradition of galley warfare was maintained in the second millennium above all by the Italian city-states – chiefly Venice and Genoa – which financed fleets from the profits of trade with the Black Sea and the Levant and from selling their services to larger powers. As well as fighting pitched battles, their war galleys also engaged in regular commerce raiding. The Catalans and the sailors of Provence were also involved in wars fought for control of trade routes and for possession of islands and coastal bases.

city-state of Athens used the silver produced by its richest mine to pay for a countering fleet. Victorious against Persia, Athens became the greatest naval power in the eastern Mediterranean, creating the world's first maritime empire. It was in the wars between the Greeks and Persians and between Athens and other Greek city-states that naval battles were for the first time fought on a large scale.

BUILDING BIGGER

The success of the Athenians was based upon the ramming power of the swift manoeuvrable trireme – the galley itself used as a weapon to sink enemy ships. This was a tactic that exploited the superior skills of Athenian oarsmen. States with more powerful armies and less skilled sailors opted for different tactics using different kinds of galley. From the 4th century BCE rulers such as Dionysius of Sicily, the Ptolemies in Egypt, and the Seleucids in Syria built larger vessels that were powered by vast numbers of less skilled oarsmen. These quinqueremes and even larger polyremes carried artillery in the form of siege machines, capable of hurling rocks at an enemy, and were packed with troops. Instead of the rapier thrusts of the trireme's ram, battles were won by bludgeoning

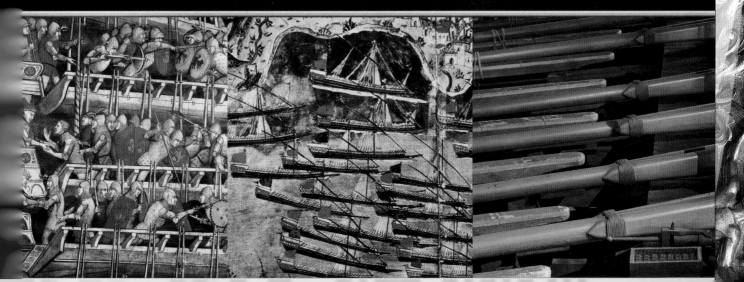

Explorers and raiders
The Vikings of Scandinavia were the most intrepid sailors of medieval Europe, braving the Atlantic to reach Greenland and North America. The horn (*left*) was used for signalling between ships at night and in foggy weather. The settled populations of Europe lived in constant dread of their destructive raids.

LIMITED WAR

Through the rise and fall of Mediterranean naval powers, there were inevitably changes in galley construction, tactics, and weaponry. But what was most remarkable was perhaps the conservatism of combat between galleys: advance to battle in line abreast; a preliminary exchange of missiles; ramming or grappling, followed by boarding of enemy ships. Such tactics served for 2,000 years. The limitations of galley warfare were considerable. Relatively small ships with a large complement of oarsmen and marines, galleys could not carry supplies to stay at sea for periods longer than a few days. Nor were they suited to sailing in heavy seas.

Galley warfare was thus restricted to coastal waters, and almost always ceased in the winter months when the weather was too rough. These limitations did not matter much until the rise of the sailing warship in northern and western Europe presented a direct challenge to the reign of the war galley and to the central importance of the Mediterranean as a theatre of naval warfare.

NORTHERN WATERS

Galleys were never confined exclusively to the Mediterranean. The Viking longships that terrorized northern Europe in the 9th century, with their mix of oars and sails, were a kind of galley. Oared ships played an important part

in warfare in the Baltic into the 18th century. In medieval times merchant galleys sailed in convoys from the Mediterranean to England and Flanders, and war galleys were used by the kings of France and Castile in battles against English kings in the English Channel and the Bay of Biscay. But countries with Atlantic shorelines had their own shipbuilding and ship-fighting traditions more suited to rougher, wider waters. The round ships known as cogs, developed initially as merchant vessels, became warships, because navies took over merchant ships in times of war. They provided a high platform for bowmen and men-at-arms in battles such as Sluys, fought between the English and French in 1340 – essentially a land battle fought on water. By the end of the 15th century, ships relying on oars for even part of their propulsion had only a subsidiary role to play in warfare in most northern waters, supporting larger sailing ships such as carracks and caravels.

ASIAN DEVELOPMENTS

Asia and the Indian Ocean, meanwhile, had their own traditions of naval warfare. Most of this took place in coastal or inland waters and was a direct adjunct to land warfare. By the time a permanent Chinese navy was founded by the Song dynasty in 1132, China had an array of diverse vessels including paddle-wheel ships, galleys, and sailing ships. Exploiting the resources of a prosperous and populous state, China became the world's greatest naval power, although Europeans knew little or nothing about it. In the early 15th century the Ming dynasty embarked on naval power-projection on a vast scale with the voyages of Admiral Zheng He, who took a fleet of massive war junks around southeast Asia and across the

---

1210
First recorded sea battle, between the Hittites and the Cypriots

800
Foundation of Carthage by the Phoenicians, the leading maritime power in the Mediterranean

500
Greek city-states such as Corinth and Athens develop the trireme, powered by three banks of oars and designed for ramming

Corinthian helmet
One of Athens' chief rivals as a sea power, Corinth fought with the Spartans in the Peloponnesian War.

31
Battle of Actium: Octavian's defeat of Antony and Cleopatra gives Rome mastery of the Mediterranean

1200 BCE   **900 BCE**   **600 BCE**   **300 BCE**   **1 CE**

1190
Egyptians win sea battle against the "Sea Peoples"

Stone anchors
Simple anchors consisting of stones with holes drilled in them have been found in all parts of the Mediterranean.

480
Battle of Salamis: decisive naval victory of the Greeks over the invading Persians

431–404
Peloponnesian War: Athens defeated by alliance of rival Greek city-states led by Sparta

264–241
First Punic War: Romans build fleet to challenge Carthaginians for control of the western Mediterranean

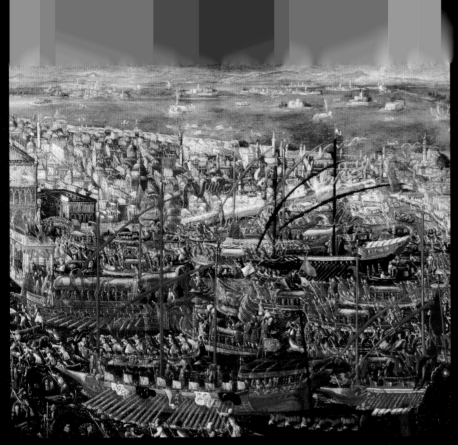

GALLEY SWANSONG

As this fundamental change took place, however, an intense power struggle developed in the Mediterranean that brought the age of galley warfare to an epic climax. The rapid rise of the Muslim Ottoman Empire, which conquered the Byzantine capital Constantinople in 1453, confronted the Christian states of the Mediterranean with a formidable new enemy. The Ottomans possessed impressive resources, great organizational skills, and an apparently unstoppable will to power. While the Ottoman sultans created a large galley fleet to support military operations against Christian-ruled Mediterranean islands, their vassals and allies, the Barbary corsairs of North Africa raided and pillaged the coasts of Italy and preyed upon merchant shipping. The vast battle of Lepanto, fought in 1571 between an alliance of Christian states and the Ottomans and the Barbary corsairs, was the last great engagement of the long age of galley warfare in Europe.

Although the ramming, grappling, and boarding at Lepanto would have been familiar to many earlier generations of galley sailor, cannon and firearms had now become crucial elements in combat between galleys. Oared ships could never be as successful a platform for cannon as the much larger sailing ships. War galleys remained in use until the end of the 18th century, but their role in naval warfare became increasingly specialized and localized. The age of the sailing ship had arrived.

Indian Ocean as far as east Africa. The decision of the Ming to withdraw from such maritime adventures after the 1430s was one of the turning points of world history.

NEW OCEAN-GOING POWERS

As Ming China turned inward, the states along Europe's Atlantic seaboard sought to exploit their maritime skills to capture the wealth of the luxury trade that previously had always passed through the Mediterranean from Asia

to Europe. At the end of the 15th century the Portuguese found their way around southern Africa into the Indian Ocean, while Christopher Columbus, sailing in the name of the Spanish crown, accidentally landed in the West Indies. The result was a total shift in the European – and global – balance of power. The future lay with the ocean-going sailing ships of northern and western Europe, armed with cannon to make them impressive fighting machines engaging in a new kind of naval warfare.

8 CE
tle of Red Cliffs: cisive battle ght on the river gtze during the clining years of Han Dynasty

440–476
As Roman control collapses, Vandals use large fleet to dominate western Mediterranean

674–678
Arab siege of Constantinople. Byzantines employ Greek fire to defeat invasion fleet

1095
Launch of First Crusade: Italian maritime republics – Venice, Genoa, and Pisa – grow rich by shipping men and supplies to Holy Land

1204
Fourth Crusade: Constantinople sacked by Crusader forces

1340
Battle of Sluys: major battle between England and France at start of Hundred Years War

1453
Constantinople falls to the Ottomans

1492
Columbus crosses the Atlantic in search of India. Spain embarks on creation of empire in the New World

300 CE	600 CE	900 CE	1200 CE	1500 CE

Roman anchor
The use of metal for anchors began some e around 600 BCE. By man times most were ade of a combination of wood and iron.

655
Battle of the Masts: Arabs win first naval victory over the Byzantines

793
First recorded Viking raid – on Lindisfarne in northern England

1185
Battle of Dan-no-Ura: decisive victory of Minamoto clan over their rivals the Taira for control of Japan

1282–87
War of the Sicilian Vespers: Aragon emerges as major sea power under Italian admiral Roger di Lauria

1379–80
War of Chioggia: Venice defeats its principal rival Genoa

1571
Battle of Lepanto: coalition of Christian powers led by Spain and Venice inflicts first major defeat on Ottomans at sea

EARLY NAVAL BATTLES AND THE RISE OF THE GREEKS

ALTHOUGH THERE WERE other seafaring peoples, notably the Phoenicians, around the coasts of the Mediterranean in ancient times, the development of early naval warfare is especially associated with the Greek city-states. Their wars against the Persians in the 5th century BCE and then against one another in the Peloponnesian War (431–404 BCE), generated sea battles large and small. The trireme, a powerful but nimble war galley armed with a ram at its prow, made naval combat into a contest of manoeuvre between teams of skilled oarsmen. The Greek cities – especially Athens – put impressive resources of money and manpower into their navies. At the battle against the Persians at Salamis there may have been as many as 34,000 oarsmen on the Greek side.

Battle of Salamis
This fanciful picture of the battle captures the spirit of the chaotic close-quarters duels that developed between pairs of ships. The ships' sails, however, would not have been raised during a Greek sea battle; all the propulsion was provided by the oars.

War galleys under sail
The oarsmen in a galley naturally took full advantage of winds and tides to make their task easier when travelling long distances. Even so, they never ventured far from shore.

EARLY SEA POWER
The first sea battle of which record exists occurred in 1210 BCE off the island of Cyprus. Nothing is known about it but the bare fact that the fleet of Hittite king Suppiluliumus II defeated the Cypriots. The earliest known depiction of naval forces in action comes from two decades later, in 1190 BCE, when the Egyptians fought the invaders known as the Sea People in the Nile Delta. The Sea People's naval force was apparently ambushed, for an Egyptian text states: "Those who entered the river mouths were like birds ensnared in a net." Egyptian archers on oared river vessels and on shore deluged the invaders' packed ships

Phoenician bireme
The war galley shown on this Phoenician silver shekel of the 4th century BCE is a bireme – powered by two banks of oars rather than the three of a trireme.

with arrows, before the pharaoh's galleys closed to allow soldiers with shields and spears to board them. There is no evidence that the vessels involved were specifically designed for warfare. This was a battle that could have been fought in similar fashion on land – except that on land it was always possible to run away. Other early seagoing peoples in the eastern Mediterranean, such as the Minoans and Mycenaeans, probably fought their sea battles in much the same manner.

The most skilled seafarers of ancient times were the Phoenicians and the Greeks. Their gifted boat-builders and sailors developed specialist warships that depended upon highly experienced crews to operate successfully.

In the 6th century BCE the Phoenicians and Greeks came into conflict. The Phoenicians had established a colony at Carthage in North Africa and sought to dominate the western Mediterranean. Various Greek cities challenged this dominance, notably Phocaea, which founded a colony that would become Marseilles.

RAMMING AND TRIREMES

The encounters between the Carthaginians and Phocaeans – notably the battle of Alalia fought off Corsica around 540 BCE – were ramming combats. Both sides used 50-oar penteconters, purpose-built warships with rams, although the Carthaginians may also have fielded larger biremes. The contest was a draw: the Phocaeans maintained a toehold in southern France and the eastern part of Sicily, while the Carthaginians retained overall superiority in the western Mediterranean.

The penteconter was the first true warship, but it was surpassed in performance by the trireme, made famous by the Athenian-led Greek victory at Salamis in 480 BCE. The trireme was a fast stripped-down vessel packed with oarsmen for maximum rowing power. There was no room to eat or sleep on board, or to carry substantial supplies. The crew went ashore every day, buying food from coastal towns and villages, and eating and sleeping beside their beached ships.

In battle, the trireme was designed to crush the hull of an enemy ship with its ram after

Votive offering of a trireme
This small bronze model of an Athenian trireme dates from the time of the Persian Wars, around 500 BCE. It was probably made to appeal to Gods – or thank them – for victory in battle.

manoeuvring for superior position – the blow would not actually "sink" the ship, since the waterlogged wreck of a galley would stay afloat to be towed away by the victor. Sails were not used in battle – the mainmast was usually left behind on shore when expecting combat, although a smaller mast might be carried so a sail could be hoisted to flee the field if worsted. Expert oarsmanship was required to find a way through or around the enemy line. The ideal was to ram from the side, then the trireme had to back oars to disengage from the ship it had rammed – always a tricky performance. The rowing benches were manned by free citizens or hardened professionals from abroad. Even well motivated oarsmen tired easily, so exhaustion was often a major factor in galley warfare.

The Athenians rarely used boarding as a tactic in trireme combat. A handful of hoplite soldiers and archers were carried on board to bombard the enemy with missiles and to cope with a situation in which two galleys accidentally became locked together. Fleets with less skilled crews, however, often carried more marines and hoped to seize a chance to board that would compensate for their shortcomings in manoeuvre.

END OF AN ERA

During the 4th century BCE much larger galleys packed with infantry and carrying artillery were introduced into Mediterranean warfare. The trireme, which had been both the emblem and the instrument of the naval dominance of Athens and the other Greek city-states, was relegated to a secondary role in major battles.

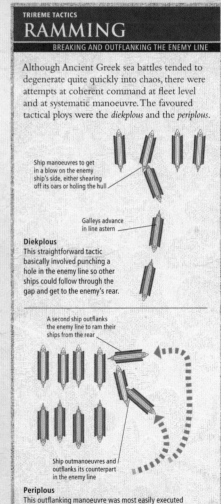

TRIREME TACTICS

RAMMING
BREAKING AND OUTFLANKING THE ENEMY LINE

Although Ancient Greek sea battles tended to degenerate quite quickly into chaos, there were attempts at coherent command at fleet level and at systematic manoeuvre. The favoured tactical ploys were the *diekplous* and the *periplous*.

Ship manoeuvres to get in a blow on the enemy ship's side, either shearing off its oars or holing the hull

Galleys advance in line astern

Diekplous
This straightforward tactic basically involved punching a hole in the enemy line so other ships could follow through the gap and get to the enemy's rear.

A second ship outflanks the enemy line to ram their ships from the rear

Ship outmanoeuvres and outflanks its counterpart in the enemy line

Periplous
This outflanking manoeuvre was most easily executed when one fleet was larger than its enemy's. As with the *diekplous*, its aim was to reach the enemy's rear.

THE PERSIAN WARS

THE FIRST OF THE WARS between the Greek city-states and Persia was provoked by the Ionian revolt in 499 BCE, a rebellion of the Greek cities of Asia Minor, which were under Persian rule. After suppressing this revolt, the Persians embarked on two unsuccessful invasions of Greece itself. The Persian fleets were initially superior at sea, but by 480, under the inspired leadership of Themistocles, Athens had built a formidable force of triremes. This enabled the Greek allies to crush the invaders at Salamis. The Greeks then took the offensive, using their command of the sea to carry out operations in Asia Minor, Cyprus, and Egypt.

480 BCE: Persians dig canal for fleet to cross Athos peninsula, thus avoiding danger of storms

492 BCE: Persian fleet dispersed by violent storm and invasion called off

Black Sea

THRACE

Sea of Marmara

Pella

MACEDONIA

Xerxes Canal

Abydus

Lemnos

Larissa

Aegean Sea

Greece

Thermopylae 480 BCE

Artemisium 480 BCE

Lesbos

Plataea 479 BCE

Delphi

Marathon 490 BCE

Chios

IONIA

Sardis

Corinth

Athens

Salamis

Mycale 479 BCE

Peloponnese

Lade 494 BCE

Miletus

Sparta

N

Eurymedon 466 BCE

Rhodes

PERSIAN EMPIRE

THE PERSIAN WARS c.499–448 BCE

The Persian Empire, founded by Cyrus the Great in the 6th century BCE, expanded westward into the Middle East, Egypt, and Asia Minor, rapidly becoming the dominant power in the eastern Mediterranean. Under Cyrus's successor Darius, it even extended into Europe. The revolt of the Greek city-states on the Aegean coast of Asia Minor led to the invasions of Greece mounted by Darius (492 BCE) and his son Xerxes (480 BCE).

KEY
- Persian Empire and vassals c.500 BCE
- Greek opponents of Persia
- Route of Xerxes' army 480 BCE
- Route of Xerxes' fleet 480 BCE
- Greek victory
- Persian victory
- Inconclusive battle

0 km 50 100
0 miles 50 100

GRECO–PERSIAN WARS

LADE

Date 494 BCE
Forces Persian fleet (mainly Phoenicians): 600 ships; Greeks: 353 triremes
Losses Persians: 57 ships; Greeks: 234 triremes

Location Off Miletus, western Turkey

During the Ionian revolt of the early 5th century BCE, Persia laid siege to the city of Miletus by land and sea. The Greeks assembled a substantial fleet, mainly from the islands of Chios, Lesbos, and Samos. According to the historian Herodotus, their commander, Dionysius, berated the crews for their slackness, subjecting them to a tough training routine that led to mutinous discontent.

The Greeks sailed to confront the Persian fleet at Lade, Miletus's port. The Phoenicians drew up their ships in a defensive formation, while the triremes from Samos led the Greek attack, rowing towards their enemy in line ahead. The aim of the Greek tactics, carefully rehearsed by Dionysius, was to punch a hole in the Phoenician line by ramming. But the Samians, disaffected after their experience in training, had no stomach for the fight. Forty-nine of their 60 triremes never engaged the enemy, instead raising sails and heading for home. The 70 galleys from Lesbos followed suit. Vastly outnumbered, the remaining Greek triremes engaged the enemy, inflicting substantial losses, but were eventually overwhelmed and annihilated. This defeat condemned the Ionian revolt to failure.

WEAPONS AND TECHNOLOGY

THE RAM OF A TRIREME

The bow of an Athenian trireme was equipped with a bronze-sheathed ram just below the waterline. Weighing around 200kg (440lb), its function was to smash the hull of an enemy vessel from the side. The ram was designed to avoid locking into the hull it had penetrated. The trireme crew were expected to reverse fast after ramming, pulling back to disentangle their ship from the enemy's and then attack another victim. Rams may have been deliberately designed to detach if they were subjected to substantial strain, thus preventing attacking ships from being dragged under water by a sinking opponent.

Bronze beaked ram
The ram on the reconstructed trireme *Olympias* is based on depictions in Greek art and on a well preserved example from the seabed near Haifa, Israel.

GRECO–PERSIAN WARS

TWIN BATTLES OF EURYMEDON

Date c.466 BCE
Forces Delian League: c.350 ships; Persians: c.350 ships
Losses Delian League: c.30 ships; Persians: c.240 ships

Location Eurymedon River, southern Turkey

The Athenian-led Delian League mounted a campaign to drive the Persians out of Asia Minor and establish firm control of the Aegean. After most coastal towns had fallen to the League, a fleet under the command of Cimon of Athens sought to bring the Persian fleet to battle. Cimon's naval force consisted of some 250 Athenian triremes plus 100 other ships supplied by allies. The Persians had a similar number of ships commanded by Tithrafstes, an illegitimate son of Xerxes. They were anchored in the mouth of the Eurymedon River, close to a force of Persian soldiers camped on the coast. According to the Greek historian Plutarch, the Persian fleet was expecting Phoenician reinforcements to arrive from Cyprus, so Cimon attacked as soon as he could. The Persians tried to row away but were trapped and many of their ships were captured. The survivors joined the soldiers ashore. Landing with his sailors and marines, Cimon then won a second battle, attacking the Persian camp under cover of darkness. These "twin battles" were followed by another naval encounter, in which the Delian League pursued and destroyed the Phoenician reinforcements.

---

c.523–c.458 BCE

THEMISTOCLES

ATHENIAN POLITICIAN AND NAVAL COMMANDER

A prominent Athenian political leader, Themistocles takes credit for founding the city's naval power by persuading the popular assembly in 482 to spend the wealth from a newly discovered vein of silver on building a fleet of triremes. The following year he proposed the detailed measures adopted to organize the fleet to meet the Persian invasion, which were codified in the "Decree of Themistocles". During the key battles of Artemisium and Salamis he showed tactical ingenuity and political subtlety. He held together a fragile alliance with Sparta and his other Peloponnesian allies while discreetly exercising personal command of tactics and strategy. After the threat of Persian invasion had passed, Themistocles was involved in the rebuilding of Athens, which had been sacked by Xerxes, and in the development of Piraeus as the city's port. Always a controversial figure, he was later ostracized and expelled from Athens, ironically ending his life in the service of his old enemies, the Persians.

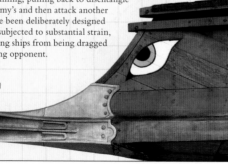

THE BATTLE OF ARTEMISIUM

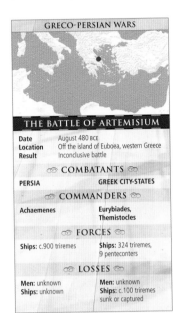

THE BATTLE OF ARTEMISIUM

Date	August 480 BCE
Location	Off the island of Euboea, western Greece
Result	Inconclusive battle

☙ COMBATANTS ❧

PERSIA	GREEK CITY-STATES

☙ COMMANDERS ❧

Achaemenes	Eurybiades, Themistocles

☙ FORCES ❧

Ships: c.900 triremes	Ships: 324 triremes, 9 penteconters

☙ LOSSES ❧

Men: unknown	Men: unknown
Ships: unknown	Ships: c.100 triremes sunk or captured

The Persian Emperor Xerxes invaded Greece in 480 with a massive army accompanied by an impressive fleet. While the Spartans confronted the Persian army at Thermopylae, a fleet of 271 triremes, about half of them Athenian, was sent to Artemisium at the northern end of the island of Euboea. The Greek fleet was commanded by a Spartan, Eurybiades, with Themistocles, the mastermind of Athenian naval expansion, as his second-in-command.

As the Persian fleet sailed down the Greek coast, it was hit by a particularly violent storm which, according to Herodotus, cost them 400 ships. But the force that reached the harbour of Aphetae, on the mainland north of Artemisium, in mid-August still far outnumbered the Greeks. Sensing the possibility of a crushing victory, the Persian commander Achaemenes sent 200 of his ships down the east coast of Euboea, hoping to sail around the south of the island and cut off the Greek fleet's line of withdrawal.

The fighting at Artesium began with a late afternoon sortie by the Greeks, apparently designed to test their enemy's mettle. The Greeks had by far the better of the resulting skirmish. With skilful rowing they succeeded in ramming and capturing 30 ships before nightfall.

The following day was a fortunate one for the Greeks. Another sudden storm wrecked the fleet of 200 Persian ships travelling along the exposed east coast of Euboea. Meanwhile, the Greek fleet was reinforced by the arrival of 53 more Athenian triremes. The Persians decided to seek a conclusive combat.

The next morning their fleet closed in on Artemisium in a sickle formation designed to block any escape from the bay. The Greeks rowed out vigorously, hoping to smash a way through the Persian line, but, by the time the fleets broke off combat, almost a third of their triremes had been sunk or captured.

Although the Persian fleet had also suffered heavy losses, the news of the Persian victory on land at Thermopylae persuaded the Greek commanders to withdraw. They pulled back to the island of Salamis, where the decisive battle of the war would be fought.

> ❝ THE BODIES OF THE SLAIN AND BROKEN PIECES OF THE DAMAGED SHIPS DRIFTED IN THE DIRECTION OF APHETAE, AND FLOATED ABOUT THE PROWS OF THE VESSELS THERE, DISTURBING THE ACTION OF THE OARS. ❞
>
> **HERODOTUS**, DESCRIBING THE AFTERMATH OF THE FIRST CLASH OFF ARTEMISIUM

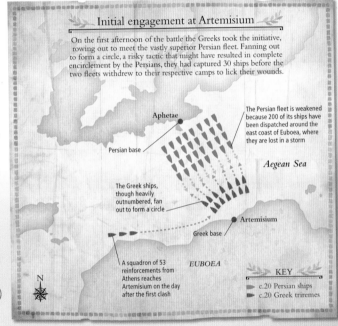

Initial engagement at Artemisium

On the first afternoon of the battle the Greeks took the initiative, rowing out to meet the vastly superior Persian fleet. Fanning out to form a circle, a risky tactic that might have resulted in complete encirclement by the Persians, they had captured 30 ships before the two fleets withdrew to their respective camps to lick their wounds.

Aphetae

The Persian fleet is weakened because 200 of its ships have been dispatched around the east coast of Euboea, where they are lost in a storm

Persian base

Aegean Sea

The Greek ships, though heavily outnumbered, fan out to form a circle

Artemisium

Greek base

A squadron of 53 reinforcements from Athens reaches Artemisium on the day after the first clash

EUBOEA

KEY

N

c.20 Persian ships
c.20 Greek triremes

Sea around the island of Euboea
The Persian and Greek fleets clashed in the narrow straits that divide the Greek mainland from Euboea. The battle of Artemisium was fought at the northern end where the straits open out into the Aegean Sea.

THE BATTLE OF SALAMIS

In September 480 BCE the Greek city-states resisting invasion by the Persian Emperor Xerxes were facing defeat. As the Persian army pressed southward, Athens evacuated its population to the island of Salamis, where the Greek fleet assembled in Paloukia Bay. Athens duly fell to Xerxes, who felt confident that the conquest of Greece was close to being accomplished.

FAITH IN THE ORACLE

The Greek fleet's Spartan commander, Eurybiades, favoured withdrawal, but the Athenian Themistocles argued they should stand and fight. He invoked a recent prophecy by the Delphic oracle, that Greece would be saved by a "wooden wall". He claimed that this referred to the Greek ships and, since he controlled the Athenian triremes, around half of the entire Greek naval force, his voice prevailed. Xerxes, meanwhile, was bent upon finishing off the Greeks as quickly as possible. He was only worried that their fleet might slip away before he could crush it.

To stand a chance of victory, Themistocles needed to negate the Persians' numerical advantage – perhaps three ships to one. He planned to induce Xerxes to divide his fleet. An agent was sent to the Persian emperor, pretending to be a deserter. He told Xerxes that the Greeks were on the point of withdrawing. Xerxes responded exactly as Themistocles would have wished. One squadron of Persian ships was dispatched to block the western end of the Megarian Strait, another sent to patrol the southern coast of Salamis. His other two squadrons were sent out during the night to patrol the eastern end of the strait.

At dawn these two Persian squadrons headed into the strait toward Paloukia Bay, but their oarsmen were tired after their night's exertions. The Greeks, who had slept soundly on shore, pushed off from the beach, fresh and ready for battle. The Persians heard them approaching before they saw them, a cacophony of war songs and bugles echoing out from the sheltered bay. The Greeks emerged from behind the island at the mouth of the bay a little too quickly. Wanting to stay close to shore, where the Persians could not use their numbers to outflank them, the Greeks had to back oars momentarily – giving an impression of hesitation or flight that drew the Persians forward.

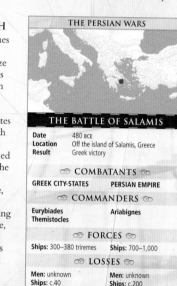

Saviours of Greece
This amber seal is carved with a striking image of a trireme with a row of armed hoplites on its deck. It dates from the time of the battle of Salamis.

JARRING CLASH

The Greek triremes manoeuvred to smash their bronze rams into the hulls of the larger Persian ships. Where galleys became entangled, armoured Greek hoplites fought face to face with Persian soldiers, while arrows and spears rained down on both sides. The sea was littered with broken oars, wreckage, and the bodies of the slain. To the dismay of Xerxes, watching the battle from a hilltop on the shore, his right wing gave way under the battering from the Athenian triremes on the Greek left. His commander, Ariabignes, was killed and central control rapidly disintegrated. As the Athenians swung round to attack the Persian centre and right from the flank and rear, the battle turned into a rout, with surviving Persian ships escaping as best they could. Salamis ended Xerxes' attempt to conquer Greece. It was the first decisive naval battle in history.

THE PERSIAN WARS

THE BATTLE OF SALAMIS

Date	480 BCE
Location	Off the island of Salamis, Greece
Result	Greek victory

∞ COMBATANTS ∞

GREEK CITY-STATES	PERSIAN EMPIRE

∞ COMMANDERS ∞

Eurybiades	Ariabignes
Themistocles	

∞ FORCES ∞

Ships: 300–380 triremes	Ships: 700–1,000

∞ LOSSES ∞

Men: unknown	Men: unknown
Ships: c.40	Ships: c.200

Serried ranks of galleys
In the narrow straits where the battle of Salamis was fought, the smaller Greek triremes proved far more manoeuvrable than the larger galleys employed by the Persians.

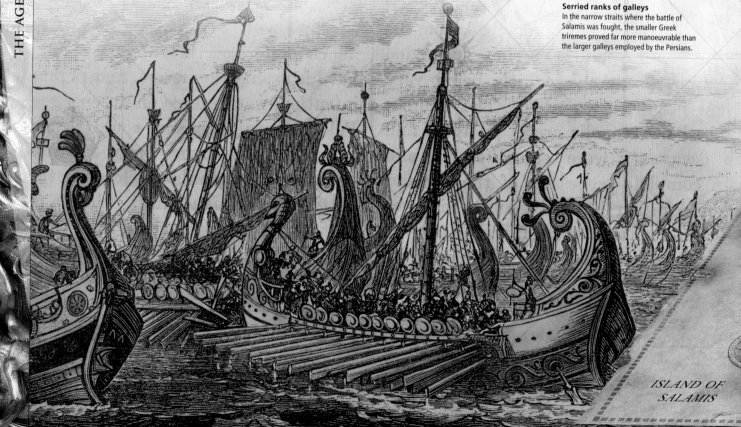

ISLAND OF SALAMIS

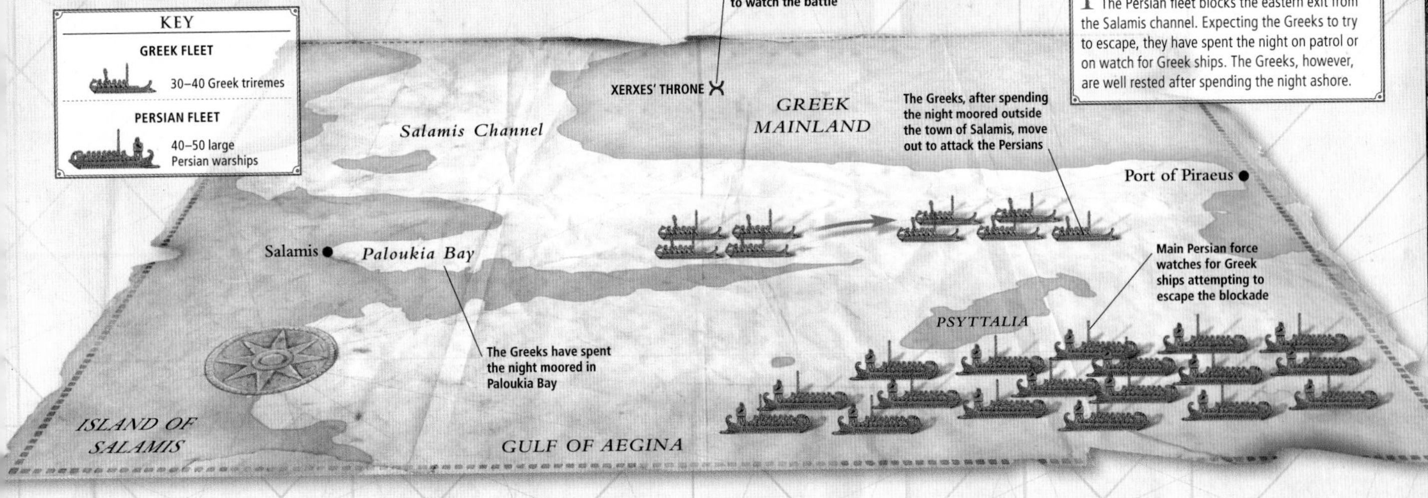

1200 BCE – 1550 CE

KEY

GREEK FLEET

30–40 Greek triremes

PERSIAN FLEET

40–50 large
Persian warships

Xerxes sets up his throne
on slopes of Mount Aegaleos
to watch the battle

XERXES' THRONE ✕

GREEK MAINLAND

Salamis Channel

The Greeks, after spending
the night moored outside
the town of Salamis, move
out to attack the Persians

Port of Piraeus ●

1 EARLY MORNING

The Persian fleet blocks the eastern exit from
the Salamis channel. Expecting the Greeks to try
to escape, they have spent the night on patrol or
on watch for Greek ships. The Greeks, however,
are well rested after spending the night ashore.

Salamis ● *Paloukia Bay*

Main Persian force
watches for Greek
ships attempting to
escape the blockade

PSYTTALIA

The Greeks have spent
the night moored in
Paloukia Bay

**ISLAND OF
SALAMIS**

GULF OF AEGINA

---

2 THE PERSIAN PURSUIT

The Persians are lured into the narrow strait
between the island of Salamis and the mainland.
Despite their overwhelming numerical superiority,
the size of their ships is now a handicap and they
are at the mercy of the nimbler Greek triremes.

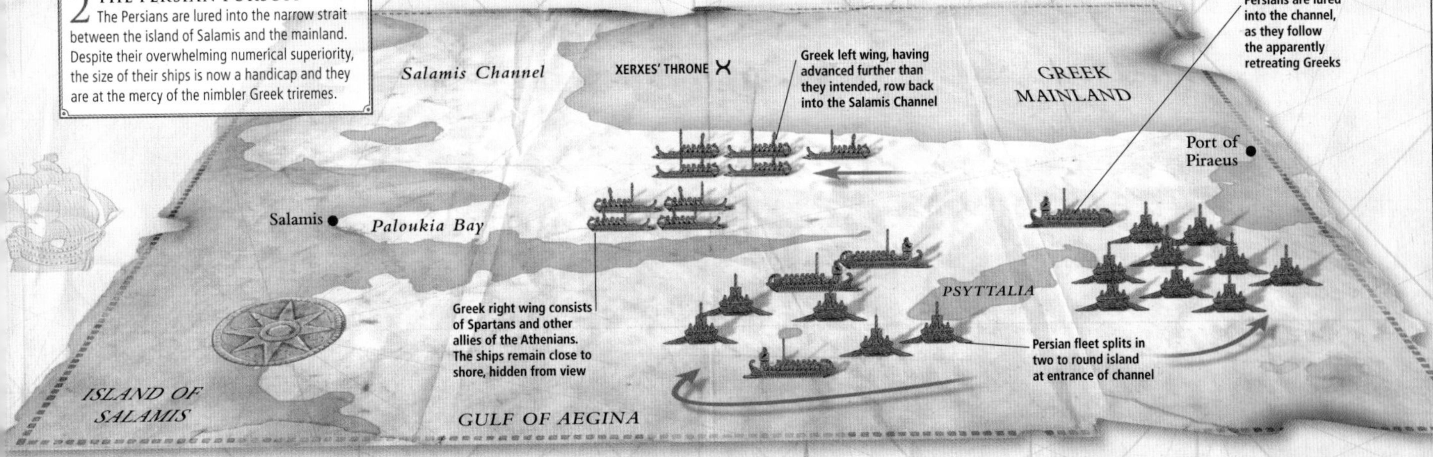

Salamis Channel

XERXES' THRONE ✕

Greek left wing, having
advanced further than
they intended, row back
into the Salamis Channel

**GREEK
MAINLAND**

Persians are lured
into the channel,
as they follow
the apparently
retreating Greeks

Port of
Piraeus ●

Salamis ● *Paloukia Bay*

Greek right wing consists
of Spartans and other
allies of the Athenians.
The ships remain close to
shore, hidden from view

PSYTTALIA

Persian fleet splits in
two to round island
at entrance of channel

**ISLAND OF
SALAMIS**

GULF OF AEGINA

---

3 GREEK COUNTERATTACK

In the narrow channel, the smaller Greek
triremes outmanoeuvre the Persians, making
devastating use of their rams. At least
200 Persian warships are sunk, while
the Greeks lose only 40 of their triremes.

Salamis Channel

XERXES' THRONE ✕

**GREEK
MAINLAND**

Port of Piraeus ●

Greek left wing draws
leading Persian ships into
narrow part of the strait,
then turns to engage in
fierce battle of ramming
and boarding. Persian
commander is killed and
right wing crumbles

Greek right wing attacks
Persian flank as the enemy ships
row up the channel, successfully
sinking many of them by ramming

PSYTTALIA

Very few Persian ships
are able to withdraw

The narrow channels on
either side of the island of
Psyttalia become clogged
with Persian ships

GULF OF AEGINA

THE PELOPONNESIAN WAR

IN THE SECOND HALF of the 5th century BCE Sparta, Corinth, and other city-states of the Peloponnese fought to throw off the dominance of Athens. While the Spartans were superior on land, the Athenians' superior seamanship generally gave them the upper hand in battles fought at sea. It was only after the disastrous failure of the Athenian expedition to Syracuse in Sicily (415–413 BCE) that the Peloponnesians were able to make a serious bid for naval superiority. When their fleet was destroyed at Aegospotami in 405, the Athenians had lost the war.

THE PELOPONNESIAN WAR 431–404 BCE

In response to the threat of Persia, many Greek city-states on the islands and coastline of the Aegean formed themselves into the Delian League. The dominant member was Athens, whose wealth and naval power transformed the league into an Athenian empire, incurring the enmity of Sparta, Corinth, and other cities outside the league.

KEY

- Athenian Empire and allies of Athens c.431 BCE
- Sparta and allied states
- → Athenian expedition to Sicily 415 BCE
- Athenian victory
- Spartan victory
- Inconclusive battle

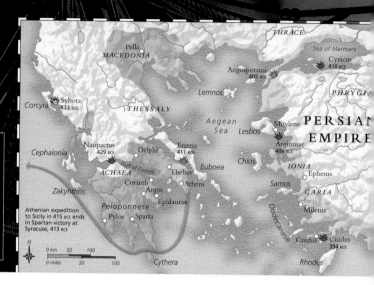

CORINTHIAN WAR WITH CORCYRA

SYBOTA

Date 433 BCE
Forces Corcyraeans and Athenians: 140 ships; Corinthians: 150 ships
Losses Corcyraeans: c.70 ships; Corinthians: c. 30 ships

Location Between Corfu and Sybota

In 433 BCE Corinth assembled a fleet to subdue its restive colony Corcyra (Corfu). Following a similar conflict two years earlier the Corcyraeans had agreed a treaty with Pericles, the Athenian leader, and now appealed to Athens for help. At first the Athenians sent only 10 triremes to give moral support. According to Thucydides, the Corinthians and Corcyraeans fought "in the old-fashioned way", using their ships for boarding with soldiers rather than for a ramming contest. The Corinthians came close to routing their enemy, but late in the day 20 more Athenian triremes arrived on the scene, deterring the Corinthians from attempting a landing on Corcyra itself. The inconclusive battle was the prelude to the Peloponnesian War.

Pericles
Athenian leader during the city's "golden age", Pericles was unable to avert the deterioration of relations with Sparta and Corinth that led to the Peloponnesian War.

PELOPONNESIAN WAR

CYZICUS

Date 410 BCE
Forces Athenians: 80–100 ships; Spartans: 60–80 ships
Losses Athenians: few; Spartans: 60–80 ships

Location The Hellespont, northern Turkey

The Athenians, with Alcibiades as their principal commander, launched an amphibious operation to recapture the city of Cyzicus from the Spartans. Despite an unfortunate tendency to defect to the other side, Alcibiades was one of Athens's most talented military leaders. He had just been reinstated as a general after a political coup in 411 BCE. Sailing from a forward base on the island of Proconnesus, Alcibiades first landed a body of soldiers south of Cyzicus. He then led a squadron of 40 triremes toward the city, while two other squadrons under generals Thrasybulus and Theramenes followed some distance behind, keeping close to shore. When they sighted Alcibiades with such a weak force, the Spartans sensed an easy victory. Mindarus, the Spartan general, led his triremes out of Cyzicus harbour. As Alcibiades's ships appeared to flee, they pursued.

The Athenian trap now closed. Thrasybulus and Theramenes appeared inshore of the Spartans, cutting them off from the harbour, and Alcibiades turned to attack. Many Spartan ships were sunk; the remainder succeeded in reaching a beach. A fierce land battle ensued, which the Athenians won.

PELOPONNESIAN WAR

NAUPACTUS

Date 429 BCE
Forces Athenians: 20 ships; Peloponnesians: 77 ships
Losses Athenians: 1 ship; Peloponnesians: 6 ships

Location Off Naupactus, Gulf of Corinth, Greece

In the winter of 430, a small squadron of Athenian triremes under Phormio established a base at Naupactus on the Corinthian Gulf. The following summer the Peloponnesian League sent a convoy of 47 ships carrying troops through the gulf. Phormio ambushed the convoy, which was forced into a defensive circle, then attacked and routed.

The Peloponnesians swiftly sought revenge, dispatching a fleet of 77 ships with the bold Spartan general Brasidas among its commanders. Phormio had received no reinforcements, meaning the Athenians were outnumbered by almost four to one. The two fleets moored opposite one another at the mouth of the gulf. Faster and more skilful at manoeuvre, the Athenians wanted to fight in open waters; Brasidas was determined to force them to fight in a confined space, where manoeuvre would be impossible.

The Peloponnesians headed into the gulf, moving in column toward Naupactus. Obliged to defend his base, Phormio shadowed them on a parallel course close to the land. Choosing their moment, the Peloponnesians turned and bore down on the Athenian line. Nine of the Athenian triremes – the rear of the force – were trapped and forced to the shore, where fierce hand-to-hand fighting took place. The others fled for Naupactus pursued by some 20 enemy ships. As they reached the base, the rearmost trireme turned in a tight circle around a merchant vessel anchored offshore and rammed its nearest pursuer. Thrown into confusion, the Peloponnesians lost formation. An Athenian counterattack scattered them and put them to flight.

WITNESS TO WAR

THUCYDIDES

GREEK HISTORIAN

ACTION BEFORE THE BATTLE OF NAUPACTUS

"… the enemy's ships were now in a narrow space, and what with the wind and the small craft dashing against them, at once fell into confusion: **ship fell foul of ship***, while the crews were pushing them off with poles, and by their* **shouting, swearing, and struggling** *with one another, made captains' orders and boatswains' cries alike inaudible, and through being unable for want of practice to clear their oars in the rough water,* **prevented the vessels from obeying their helmsmen** *properly. At this moment Phormio gave the signal, and the Athenians attacked."*

THE FOURTH BATTLE OF SYRACUSE

In 415 the Athenians dispatched a seaborne expedition to attack the city of Syracuse in Sicily. In the spring of the following year they laid siege to the city, with their ships in the Grand Harbour. By fighting the Athenians in the enclosed waters of the harbour, the Syracusans could deny them the room to manoeuvre their light, agile triremes in the manner that had won so many naval battles. Also, the Syracusans had reinforced the bows of their galleys – following the example set by the Corinthians at Naupactus – so they could smash the hulls of the lighter Athenian vessels in a head-on collision.

While the Athenians had the worse of naval encounters within the harbour, they were also defeated in their efforts to enforce a blockade of the city by land. By late summer 413 Syracuse had become a trap for the Athenians from which they needed to escape either by land or sea. Their commander Nicias fatally hesitated, influenced by bad omens. By the time he had decided to abandon the siege, the Syracusans had already blocked the harbour exit with a line of galleys and smaller craft, leaving only a narrow passage clear.

Having decided on a breakout, the Athenians packed their remaining ships with infantry and headed for the passage out of the harbour. The Syracusans had warships covering the passage and others in an arc to both sides. As the Athenians tried to smash through the blockade, the Syracusans fell on them from all sides and

Hoplite helmet
Soldiers in the Greek city-states of southern Italy and Sicily wore helmets in the ornate so-called "Chalcidian" style.

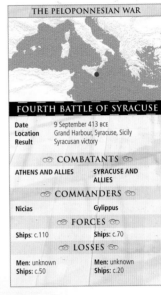

a general mêlée ensued. According to Thucydides, "never did so many ships fight in so small a space". As triremes rammed and counter-rammed, they became inextricably entwined; javelins, arrows, and stones showered down onto decks; soldiers clashed in hand-to-hand combat. The Athenians tried to use grappling hooks but the Syracusans had covered the prows and other upper parts of their ships with hides so the hooks would not grip. After a long, hard fight the Athenians broke. Many of their galleys were lost and the rest driven back to shore. They still had more ships than their enemies, but their sailors were demoralized and a further breakout was not attempted. Instead, their troops tried to escape overland, but the entire force was captured. Those who were not executed were sold into slavery.

THE PELOPONNESIAN WAR

FOURTH BATTLE OF SYRACUSE

Date	9 September 413 BCE
Location	Grand Harbour, Syracuse, Sicily
Result	Syracusan victory

⟡ COMBATANTS ⟡

ATHENS AND ALLIES	SYRACUSE AND ALLIES

⟡ COMMANDERS ⟡

Nicias	Gylippus

⟡ FORCES ⟡

Ships: c.110	Ships: c.70

⟡ LOSSES ⟡

Men: unknown	Men: unknown
Ships: c.50	Ships: c.20

Beached triremes
Fighting a sea battle in Syracuse harbour ended in disaster for the Athenian ships. When forced to disembark, sailors and soldiers alike were easy prey for the Syracusan troops on the shore.

THE BATTLE OF ARGINUSAE

In 406 BCE Sparta and its Peloponnesian allies assembled a large fleet of triremes. Under the command of the Spartan navarch Callicratidas, it caught up with the Athenian general Conon near Mytilene on the island of Lesbos, and sank 30 of his ships. When Callicratidas blockaded the Athenians in Mytilene harbour, Conon sent a message to Athens detailing his plight. The Athenians reacted by building a new fleet – paid for by melting down the gold statue of Nike – and recruiting slaves and foreigners in the city to serve as oarsmen, since the supply of experienced free rowers was exhausted.

Placed under the command of eight generals, this inexperienced fleet was sent to the relief of Mytilene. Leaving a squadron of 50 ships to maintain the blockade, Callicratidas sailed to meet the Athenians, making camp at Cape Malea, from where he could observe his enemies beached on the Arginusae Islands an hour's rowing away. The Spartan navarch planned a surprise night attack but this was abandoned because of a squall. Instead, it was at dawn that Callicratidas, positioned in the place of honour on the right wing, led his ships across the channel toward the enemy camp.

The Athenians scrambled to launch their ships, each general leading his own squadron. The Peloponnesians approached with groups of galleys in line ahead, intending to break though gaps in the Athenian line or outflank it, the classic manoeuvres for victory in trireme contests. The inexperienced Athenian crews could not match Callicratidas for speed or nimbleness, so they adopted a novel defensive formation, each Athenian general organizing his triremes into a compact group several lines deep.

The fighting was prolonged, but at some point Callicratidas's galley was rammed and he disappeared into the sea. The Spartan right then collapsed and fled, leaving the left to sustain the full weight of the Athenian onslaught before it also broke. Athens had a naval victory to celebrate – in fact, its last – and the grateful city granted citizenship

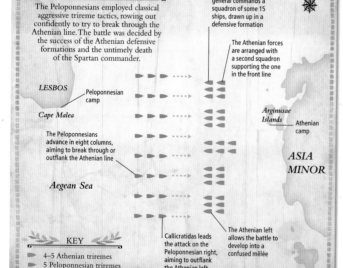

Arginusae

The Peloponnesians employed classical aggressive trireme tactics, rowing out confidently to try to break through the Athenian line. The battle was decided by the success of the Athenian defensive formations and the untimely death of the Spartan commander.

Each Athenian general commands a squadron of some 15 ships, drawn up in a defensive formation

The Athenian forces are arranged with a second squadron supporting the one in the front line

LESBOS

Peloponnesian camp

Cape Malea

The Peloponnesians advance in eight columns, aiming to break through or outflank the Athenian line

Aegean Sea

Arginusae Islands — Athenian camp

ASIA MINOR

Callicratidas leads the attack on the Peloponnesian right, aiming to outflank the Athenian left

The Athenian left allows the battle to develop into a confused mêlée

KEY

◄ 4–5 Athenian triremes
► 5 Peloponnesian triremes

Spartan ship
Sparta's power depended on its soldiers rather than its sailors. This ivory relief of a warship shows Spartan hoplites on its deck.

❝

AS HIS VESSEL DASHED HER BEAK INTO HER ANTAGONIST, HE WAS HURLED OFF INTO THE SEA AND DISAPPEARED.

XENOPHON, DESCRIBING THE DEATH OF SPARTAN COMMANDER CALLICRATIDAS AT ARGINUSAE

❞

Triremes in the Aegean

Triremes could either move forward with their sails raised, sailing with the wind, or under oar power alone. Once two fleets had met and battle was joined, the sails – and often the masts as well – would be lowered.

AEGOSPOTAMI

Date 404 BCE
Forces Spartans: unknown; Athenians: 170 ships
Losses Spartans: none; Athenians: 160 ships

Location
The Hellespont

The Hellespont was crucial to Athens, for grain convoys passed through it on their way from the Black Sea and without them Athens would starve. The Spartans were able to threaten this lifeline in 404 BCE because of an alliance with the Persians, which gave them the resources to revenge the losses at Arginusae. They recalled their most successful naval commander, Lysander, to lead the new fleet.

Lysander entered the Hellespont and captured the town of Lampsacus. The Athenian fleet, under the collective command of six generals, came after him and beached at Aegospotami opposite Lampsacus. It was a wild location that lacked adequate supplies for the thousands of sailors and marines, forcing the Athenians to bring the Spartans immediately to battle. On four consecutive days the Athenian fleet sortied toward Lampsacus, but each time Lysander refused to be drawn and remained in harbour.

What happened on the fifth day is a matter of dispute. According to the most likely version, Philocles, the Athenian general commanding that day, sent a small force of triremes toward Lampsacus to lure Lysander out. The Athenians were then to launch swiftly from their beach and crush the Spartans. But the plan misfired. The Spartan fleet swiftly smashed the triremes at sea and then destroyed the main force before it could get off the beach and into formation. Only 10 Athenian ships escaped. Lysander had Philocles and 3,000 other Athenian prisoners executed. With its fleet destroyed and no resources to build a new one, Athens surrendered the following year.

LYSANDER

SPARTAN GENERAL AND NAVAL COMMANDER

Having risen from poor origins, Lysander was appointed nauarch, or admiral-in-chief, of Sparta in 407 BCE. It was a post that could be held only for one year and never twice by the same individual. Lysander cultivated close relations with Cyrus, wealthy son of the Persian emperor Darius II, and thus obtained funds to strengthen the Spartan fleet, creating a naval force capable of challenging Athenian naval might. He defeated an Athenian fleet under Alcibiades at Notium, before his term of office came to an end. After the Spartan defeat at Arginusae Lysander was restored to command, although not accorded the official post of nauarch. His victory at Aegospotami allowed Lysander to make himself the most powerful man in Greece. He was an arrogant and cruel individual, but also an inspired naval leader.

to the slave and foreign oarsmen. But the aftermath of the battle was less than satisfactory. Most of the Athenian force was to sail to Mytilene to destroy the Spartan blockading force, while the rest would rescue crews clinging to the 25 wrecked Athenian triremes. But a sudden storm prevented either of these plans being put into effect. The failure to save the shipwrecked crews caused such outrage in Athens that six of the victorious generals were executed.

THE BATTLE OF ARGINUSAE

Date	406 BCE
Location	East of the island of Lesbos
Result	Athenian victory

⚔ COMBATANTS ⚔

ATHENS	SPARTA AND ALLIES

⚔ COMMANDERS ⚔

Eight generals	Callicratidas

⚔ FORCES ⚔

Ships: 143 triremes	**Ships:** 120 triremes

⚔ LOSSES ⚔

Men: unknown	**Men:** unknown
Ships: 25 triremes	**Ships:** 70 triremes

CREW PROFILE

GREEK TRIREME

5TH CENTURY BCE

A TRIREME REQUIRED A CREW of around 200 men. In Athens responsibility for recruiting them fell to a trierarch, a wealthy individual who had this task imposed upon him as one of his duties as a citizen. Since the trierarch was unlikely to have much seagoing experience, once at sea he was heavily dependent upon his four naval officers – the helmsman, rowing master, purser, and bow officer – who between them effectively ran the ship. The men on board most similar to the trierarch in social status were the ship's 10 hoplite soldiers.

THE OARSMEN

The oarsmen, who made up the majority of the crew, were usually free men hired from among the poorest citizens. Foreigners were sometimes employed when local oarsmen could not be found in sufficient numbers. Only experienced rowers skilled and hardened to the job were really useful, and they could command a good wage. Rowing manoeuvres were practised relentlessly once a crew was assembled. The oarsmen were seated in three rows, the thalamites at the bottom close to the waterline, the zygites in the middle, and the thranites in the highest row at the top. Thranites had the hardest job, because of the angle at which their oars struck the water. They tended to command higher wages than the others. As free men, the oarsmen were generally decently treated. Although they were occasionally expected to take part in fighting with hand weapons, they were normally considered too valuable to risk losing in close combat. Desertion was often a problem, as oarsmen would leave to join a ship offering higher pay, especially if their trierarch's money ran out, as sometimes happened.

Trireme oarsmen
By the time of the Peloponnesian War, Athens had increased her fleet to 200 triremes, each requiring 170 oarsmen seated in 3 tiers on each side.

OLYMPIAS

NO ORIGINAL EXAMPLE of a trireme, the key warship of Ancient Greece, has survived from antiquity. *Olympias*, built at Piraeus, Athens, between 1985 and 1987, is a scrupulous reconstruction based on the best available historical evidence. It did well in sea trials, confirming that a galley with three tiers of oars could perform impressively in action.

A GREEK TRIREME was a lightweight, shallow-draught vessel some 35m (115ft) long and less than 6m (20ft) wide. Although it cruised under sail, it was propelled in battle by 170 oarsmen in three tiers: 62 thranites highest, 54 zygians in the middle, and 54 thalamians at the bottom. With 30 other men completing the crew, including soldiers and archers, it was a crowded vessel. There was no room for carrying more than a few basic supplies and insufficient space for the whole crew to sleep on board. The trireme proved itself capable under oar of speeds in excess of eight knots and was highly manoeuvrable.

In sea trials *Olympias* was turned about at speed in two-and-a-half times its own length. A fast-manoeuvring trireme

did not provide a stable platform for its fighting men – marine hoplites had to learn to throw their spears while sitting down. Even when its hull was smashed by an enemy ram, a trireme would not actually sink, as its wreckage would float.

Trireme under sail and oar power
In this artist's impression of a trireme, the arrangement of the three banks of oars is more or less accurate, but other details, such as the lateen sails, are incorrect.

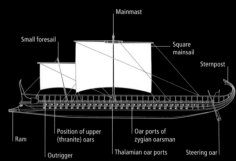

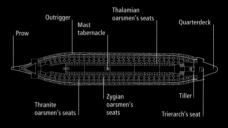

Olympias
The side view of *Olympias* (top) gives an idea of the arrangement of the sails and the three levels of oar ports. The overhead view (bottom) shows the exact location of each individual oarsman's seat. The oarsmen's positions are covered by a protective deck.

⌄ **Prow and ram**
The business-end of the trireme was the prow with its heavy bronze-sheathed ram for holing the hulls of enemy galleys. The weight of the ram on the *Olympias* is 200kg (440lb).

66

THE ATHENIANS ... LEARN TO USE THE OAR AS SECOND NATURE ... WHEN A MAN IS OFTEN AT SEA HE MUST OF NECESSITY TAKE AN OAR HIMSELF ... AND LEARN THE LANGUAGE OF THE SEA.

ANONYMOUS ATHENIAN WRITING IN THE 5TH CENTURY BCE

99

》 **Ear and anchor**
Projecting on either side of the galley were the *epotides* (ears). These served both as protection for the outriggers and oarsmen behind them and as platforms for sailors to drop and weigh anchor.

》 **Outrigger**
This projection was built out from the sides of the galley, supported by brackets. It allowed the upper tier of oarsmen to row from a position outboard of the other two tiers.

Mainmast tabernacle
When the crew of the *Olympias* is required to hoist the galley's masts and sails, the foot of the mainmast is slotted into this solid base.

View from the stern
The helmsman's position overlooks the central slot between the decks covering the oarsmen, where the mast is stowed when not in use.

Trierarch's seat
At the stern of the galley beneath the ornamental sternpost sat the trierarch, the man responsible for fitting out and crewing the ship. In front of his chair the handles of the two tillers are visible.

Central gangway
The narrow gangway that runs the length of the ship also serves as a storage area for the masts and spare spars, oars, ropes, and sails.

Tiller
The two tillers can be controlled by a single helmsman, but if extra force is needed, one man can pull on one, while a second man pushes the other.

Thranites' benches
The topmost tier of oarsmen, the thranites, whose oars passed through the outrigger, were the only ones who could actually see their oars entering the water.

The oarsman's seats
This view of the seats shows the extremely cramped positions occupied by the three tiers of oarsmen: the thranites above, the zygians below them, and the thalamians at the bottom.

Oar handles
The handle and inner part of the oar, the loom, are thick and heavy, giving the oarsman greater control when raising the blade from the water and moving it back for the next stroke.

The three banks of oars
At any point on the *Olympias* the oars are of the same length for each of the three banks of oarsmen. Where the ship narrows, however, at the bow and the stern, slightly shorter oars are used.

Steering oar
The *Olympias* is fitted with a pair of steering oars (rudders) on either side of the ship's stern. These can be lowered into the water and used as brakes to the ship's foreward movement on one side or the other. They are controlled from a pair of tillers on the quarterdeck.

Protective sleeve
The lowest bank of oars, that of the thalamian rowers, was much closer to the waterline than the other two. In order to prevent water from splashing through the holes, they were fitted with protective leather sleeve

Foot stretcher
The oarsmen crewing the reconstructed *Olympias* have experimented with various methods of rowing, including this means of securing one foot on the stretcher.

ROMAN NAVAL WARFARE

IN THE THIRD CENTURY BCE the Mediterranean was host to a diversity of naval powers large and small. The western part was dominated by Carthage, a North African city founded by the Phoenicians, which continued their great seafaring tradition in trade and war. In the eastern Mediterranean the wealthy Hellenic states of Antagonid Macedonia and Ptolemaic Egypt maintained imposing fleets of outsized warships appropriate to their notions of royal prestige and large-scale warfare. The island of Rhodes, a major maritime trading centre, had an efficiently organized fleet of lighter ships, used to suppress piracy and deter the predatory ambitions of larger states. But all of these diverse maritime powers, along with Seleucid Syria, were ultimately subjected to the naval power of Rome, a state with no tradition of shipbuilding or seafaring that created a navy out of nothing in 260 BCE.

Roman port
This detail from a Roman fresco of the 1st century CE shows the port at Castellammare di Stabia in the Gulf of Naples. During the first two centuries of the Empire ports like this ringed the entire Mediterranean, which the Romans justifiably called *Mare Nostrum* (Our Sea).

Sailing from Alexandria
A trireme carrying a large force of legionaries is rowed out of the port of Alexandria, one of the main centres of Roman naval power in the east. Many Egyptians served as oarsmen and sailors in the imperial Roman navy.

INSTANT NAVAL POWER

Rome's progress to naval dominance began with the defeat of Carthage in the First Punic War (264-241 BCE), continued with the rapid extension of Roman power to the eastern Mediterranean in the 2nd century BCE, and was completed in 67 BCE with the suppression of piracy by Pompey the Great. These successes were not achieved through any radical naval innovations, although Roman technical ingenuity did play its part. Rome's first fleet – 100 quinqueremes and 20 triremes built in 60 days – was created partly by copying a galley captured from the Carthaginian enemy.

The Roman quinqueremes were smaller than the huge ungainly warships of some of the Hellenic states, but they still probably had five men operating each oar and 28 oars to a side. This made them better suited to the largely inexperienced crews that Rome had available than the one-man-per-oar trireme. On these heavier and less manoeuvrable vessels, oarsmen needed muscle power rather than skill. Most important, the quinqueremes could carry some 120 soldiers, enabling the Romans to transfer their proven supremacy in land warfare to the sea. Although most of their ships were still fitted with rams, the Romans' prime aim in naval warfare was to board the enemy's galleys. They would first soften them up by bombarding them with missiles from wooden towers that stood at the prow and stern of their ships.

Ram shaped as boar's head
The ship's ram (*rostrum*) was very important in Roman iconography. The beaks of Carthaginian ships captured at Mylae in 260 BCE were used to decorate the raised platform used by speakers in the Roman forum, hence the word "rostrum" meaning a speaker's podium.

WEAPONS ON BOARD

In their first war against Carthage the Romans introduced the spiked corvus as an aid to grappling and boarding. Later the extraordinary arpax was invented, a catapult used to propel grappling tackle onto an enemy ship. Most of the Romans' on-board military technology, however, was identical to that used on land. Shipborne artillery consisted of catapults and ballistas, mostly firing darts and stones as anti-personnel munitions, although they could be used to propel heavier rocks to bombard city walls during the siege of a port. Roman success at sea cannot be put down to technological superiority. Rather it was a triumph of willpower and organization. When Rome lost an entire fleet to shipwreck during the Punic Wars, it simply built and manned another to replace it. Pompey's suppression of piracy was achieved by the systematic application of ruthless force, clearing the entire Mediterranean area by area, leaving no hiding place for the pirates.

Rome's battles against Carthage were fought on a vast scale. In terms of the sheer numbers of men involved – probably more than 300,000 –

the battle of Ecnomus ranks as one of the largest naval encounters ever. By the 1st century BCE, however, the only major battles were between Roman forces engaged in civil wars. Sea power proved decisive at Actium in 31 BCE, the battle that enabled Octavian to become sole ruler of the Roman world as the Emperor Augustus.

DOMINANCE AT SEA

Since the Roman world encompassed the entire coastline of the Mediterranean, Augustus and his successors faced no major enemies at sea. But they still had need of a navy. Ships provided military supply and transport, as in the invasion of Britain in 43 CE. They also gave river support for the long series of military campaigns waged in Germany and Dacia. In the Mediterranean they pursued pirates and protected merchant shipping. Some 10,000 men were stationed at a great naval base on the bay of Naples, with another fleet in the Adriatic based at Ravenna, and provincial squadrons deployed elsewhere – for example in the Black Sea and at Alexandria. Without major enemies the Romans were able to rely for the most part on smaller galleys – triremes and liburnians. The navy was manned by volunteers who signed up for 26 years' service, many recruited from among the Phoenicians, Greeks, and Egyptians with their long tradition of seafaring.

A riverine navy
Part of the frieze on Trajan's Column in Rome shows Roman ships on the Danube. In the first two centuries CE the Danube and Rhine formed the Roman Empire's eastern border and were patrolled by squadrons of warships.

DECLINE AND FALL

The navy participated in the general decline of the Roman Empire from the 3rd century CE. Shipborne Germanic Goths rampaged through the Aegean and British rebels challenged Roman shipping in northern seas. Meanwhile, the Mediterranean saw the revival of widespread piracy as a weakening Roman navy lost its grip.

The 5th century brought a general collapse of Roman authority in the west. Another invading Germanic tribe, the Vandals, took to the sea and took control of the western Mediterranean from Carthage and other naval bases in North Africa. In 455 the Vanadal king, Geiseric sailed his fleet across to Italy and sacked the city of Rome itself. The Roman navy's inheritance was to survive, however, in the eastern half of the empire. The Byzantine Empire, centred on Constantinople, would rely on a powerful navy to uphold Rome's imperial tradition.

THE FIRST PUNIC WAR

THE ROMAN REPUBLIC fought the First Punic War against Carthage for control of the island of Sicily. The Romans were dominant on land, but initially the Carthaginians controlled the seas. To challenge this well-established maritime power the Romans had to build a fleet from scratch and teach themselves the skills of naval warfare. They were so successful that the Carthaginians scored only one sizeable naval victory in the course of the war – at Drepana – while suffering many defeats, including at Mylae and the huge battle of Ecnomus. The Romans used sea power to carry the war into Carthaginian territory in North Africa, although they suffered catastrophic losses when fleets were sunk by storms in 255, 253, and 249. After a final defeat at the Aegates Islands in 241 the Carthaginians could no longer supply their troops on Sicily by sea and were forced to make peace on Roman terms.

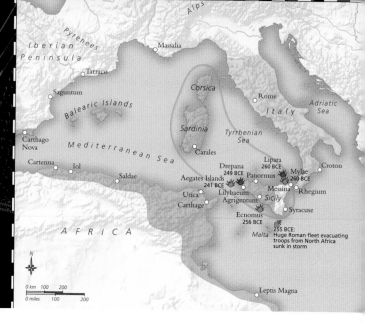

THE FIRST PUNIC WAR 264–241 BCE

In the mid-3rd century BCE territory under Roman control was limited to the Italian mainland. By the terms of the treaty at the end of the war with Carthage, they gained not only Sicily – the original cause of the conflict and scene of most of the fighting – but the islands of Sardinia and Corsica as well.

KEY

- Area controlled by Carthage 264 BCE
- Area controlled by Rome 264 BCE
- Roman gains at end of war
- Carthaginian victory
- Roman victory
- Roman fleet lost in storm

255 BCE: Huge Roman fleet evacuating troops from North Africa sunk in storm

---

FIRST PUNIC WAR

MYLAE

Date 260 BCE
Forces Romans: c.130 ships; Carthaginians: 130 ships
Losses Romans: unknown; Carthaginians: c.45 ships

Location Off northern Sicily

The Romans built a fleet of 100 quinqueremes and 20 triremes in 60 days and somehow found the men to crew them. This inexperienced navy went to sea in 260 and soon lost 17 ships in a skirmish at the Lipari Islands. This inauspicious start led to a swift change at the top, the consul Gaius Duilius taking control of the navy. The Romans realized that their green sailors were no match for the seasoned Carthaginians in a battle of manoeuvre. On the other hand, no one was better at close-quarters fighting than a Roman soldier. Seeking to exploit their strength, they came up with the corvus as a way of boarding enemy ships and sailed to meet the Carthaginians at Mylae.

Carthaginian commander Hannibal Gisco was puzzled by the Roman ships with the strange-looking devices at their prows. Nonetheless, he led the way as the Carthaginian ships surged forward in loose formation to engage the enemy. The Romans kept their prows turned toward the Carthaginians and at the right moment brought their corvuses crashing downward. Thirty of the Carthaginians' leading ships were pinned, including Hannibal's. Roman soldiers then began to pour across the boarding bridges, slaughtering efficiently with sword and spear. Hannibal had to make his escape in a small rowing boat.

The Carthaginian ships following behind realized they had to keep away from the Roman prows. They manoeuvred around the Roman fleet and attacked with their rams from the rear, but still the balance of losses went against them.

When the surviving Carthaginian ships broke off the battle, the Romans did not attempt a pursuit. After the battle, the speakers' platform in the Roman forum was decorated with prows cut from enemy ships to celebrate Rome's first naval triumph. Hannibal was crucified by his own captains.

A hero remembered
This inscription in the Roman forum honoured Duilius, commander at Rome's victory at Mylae.

WEAPONS AND TECHNOLOGY

CORVUS

The corvus ("raven" in Latin) was an ingenious boarding device adopted by the Romans before the battle of Mylae. Attached by a cable to a pole at the prow of a ship, it was raised and lowered by pulleys. On its underside was a sharp beak-shaped metal spike. When an enemy ship drew near, the corvus was lowered so the spike smashed into its deck. This locked the two ships together, providing a bridge over which Roman soldiers swarmed. Unfortunately ships with a corvus proved dangerously unstable and the device probably contributed to heavy losses in storms. Its use was abandoned before the end of the First Punic War.

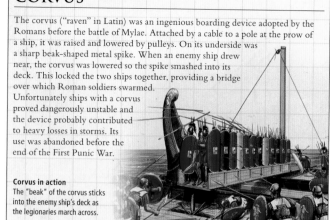

Corvus in action
The "beak" of the corvus sticks into the enemy ship's deck as the legionaries march across.

FIRST PUNIC WAR

AEGATES ISLANDS

Date 10 March 241 BCE
Forces Romans: c.200 ships; Carthaginians: c.250 ships
Losses Romans: c.30 ships; Carthaginians: c.120 ships

Location Off coast of western Sicily

In 241 the Carthaginians sent a large fleet to carry grain from North Africa to feed their hard-pressed army in Sicily. The fleet sailed to the Aegates Islands and awaited a favourable wind that would carry it to the Sicilian mainland. But the Romans were well informed of their movements and had a fleet under Caius Catullus ready to intercept. On 10 March a strong breeze blew from the west and Carthaginian commander Hanno ordered the dash for Sicily. The Romans had to row against a heavy swell to get into position, but their now experienced crews coped magnificently and formed a line blocking their enemy's path. The Carthaginians had no choice but to take down their masts, take up their oars, and prepare to fight. They rowed boldly into battle, their crews shouting encouragement to one another from ship to ship, but they were severely overburdened with the supplies they were carrying and short on marines.

The Romans had the better of the contest both in ramming and boarding, sinking 50 enemy ships and capturing another 70. Carthage could no longer deny Rome command of the sea.

THE BATTLE OF DREPANA

When a Roman fleet was sent to support the army in a siege of the coastal stronghold of Lilybaeum, the Carthaginians sailed reinforcements to the fortress right under the noses of the Romans, repeatedly running ships into Lilybaeum from their nearby base at Drepana. The Romans eventually managed to seal the blockade, but they wanted to avenge these humiliations.

One of the consuls for 249, Publius Claudius Pulcher, decided to launch a surprise raid on Drepana with ships and marines. The Roman fleet sailed up the coast at night, but this led to its losing formation. Dawn found a straggling line of galleys approaching Drepana, with Claudius's flagship well to the rear. Fearing he would be pinned in harbour, the Carthaginian admiral, Adherbal, boldly set to sea as soon as the Romans were sighted.

Meanwhile Claudius performed one of the most important functions of any Roman leader: he sought evidence of the support of the gods. Sacred chickens were carried on board for the purpose. If they were happy, divine support in battle could be expected. Ominously, when offered grain, the birds sulkily refused to eat. Instead of cancelling the battle, Claudius had the chickens

thrown into the sea, explaining with an irreverent quip that if they would not eat, perhaps they would drink.

CARTHAGINIAN TRIUMPH

Adherbal skilfully led his ships out to sea, rounding two islands at the northern end of the harbour mouth as the first Roman ships were entering the harbour from the south. Claudius realized what they were doing, but had difficulty communicating with his leading galleys. After a period of confusion, in which several ships collided, the Romans were organized into a line with their sterns to the coast, facing the Carthaginians who had swiftly rowed round to attack shoreward. The Punic crews used their rams with deadly efficiency against the cornered Roman ships, many of which ran aground trying to avoid being sunk. Claudius escaped with around 30 ships; the rest were lost. When he returned to Rome Claudius was put on trial and exiled, with his cavalier treatment of the sacred chickens topping the list of his misdemeanours.

A moment of pride and folly
Publius Claudius Pulcher commits the sacrilege of ordering the drowning of the sacred chickens. These were carried aboard Roman ships so their behaviour could be analysed by the priests.

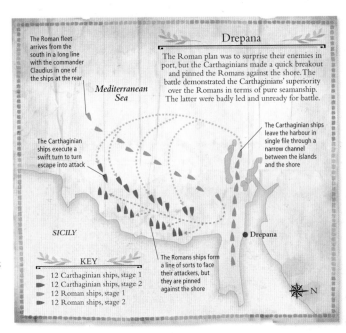

Drepana

The Roman plan was to surprise their enemies in port, but the Carthaginians made a quick breakout and pinned the Romans against the shore. The battle demonstrated the Carthaginians' superiority over the Romans in terms of pure seamanship. The latter were badly led and unready for battle.

The Roman fleet arrives from the south in a long line with the commander Claudius in one of the ships at the rear

The Carthaginian ships execute a swift turn to turn escape into attack

The Carthaginian ships leave the harbour in single file through a narrow channel between the islands and the shore

The Romans ships form a line of sorts to face their attackers, but they are pinned against the shore

Mediterranean Sea

SICILY

Drepana

KEY
- 12 Carthaginian ships, stage 1
- 12 Carthaginian ships, stage 2
- 12 Roman ships, stage 1
- 12 Roman ships, stage 2

N

> ## HE ONLY RIDICULED THE GODS IN JEST, BUT THE MOCKERY COST HIM DEAR, FOR HIS FLEET WAS UTTERLY ROUTED ...
> **CICERO** ON PUBLIUS CLAUDIUS PULCHER'S TREATMENT OF THE SACRED CHICKENS

THE FIRST PUNIC WAR

THE BATTLE OF DREPANA

Date	249 BCE
Location	Off Trapani, western Sicily
Result	Carthaginian victory

COMBATANTS

ROME	CARTHAGE

COMMANDERS

Publius Claudius Pulcher	Adherbal

FORCES

Ships: c.120	Ships: c.120

LOSSES

Men: unknown	Men: unknown
Ships: 93 ships sunk or captured	Ships: no losses

A violent clash
Cape Ecnomus was the largest and fiercest sea battle fought between Rome and Carthage. The Carthaginians were fighting to prevent the Romans from invading their North African homeland.

KEY

ROMAN FLEET

16–20 Roman warships

12–15 Roman horse transports

CARTHAGINIAN FLEET

20–22 Carthaginian warships

20–22 Carthaginian warships, under sail

1 CARTHAGINIAN SUBTERFUGE
As the Roman fleet sets sail for Africa, the Carthaginians are there to block their path. But as the Romans sail along the coast to try and force their way through, the Carthaginian centre turns and pretends to flee away from the battle.

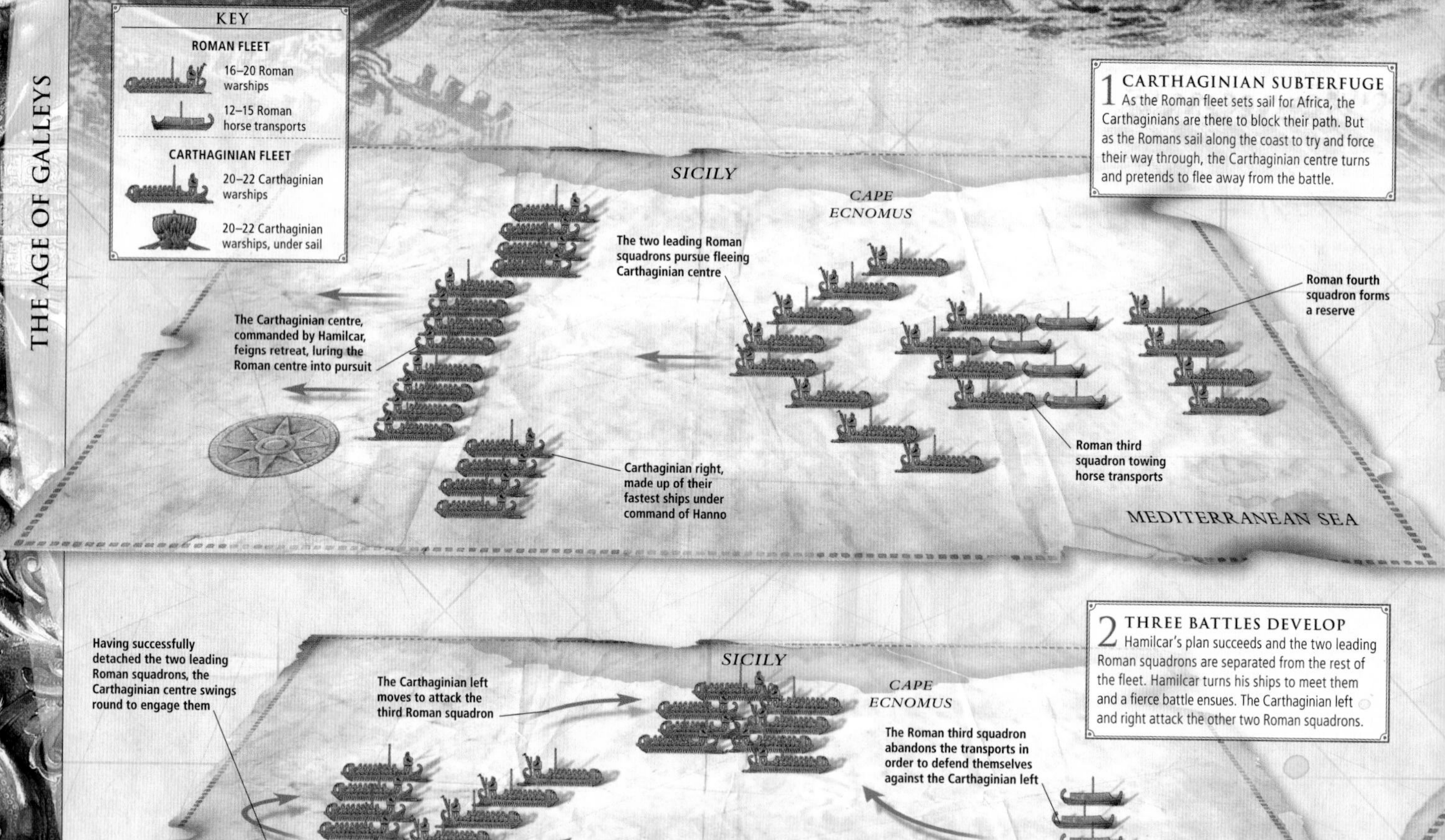

SICILY

CAPE ECNOMUS

The two leading Roman squadrons pursue fleeing Carthaginian centre

Roman fourth squadron forms a reserve

The Carthaginian centre, commanded by Hamilcar, feigns retreat, luring the Roman centre into pursuit

Carthaginian right, made up of their fastest ships under command of Hanno

Roman third squadron towing horse transports

MEDITERRANEAN SEA

2 THREE BATTLES DEVELOP
Hamilcar's plan succeeds and the two leading Roman squadrons are separated from the rest of the fleet. Hamilcar turns his ships to meet them and a fierce battle ensues. The Carthaginian left and right attack the other two Roman squadrons.

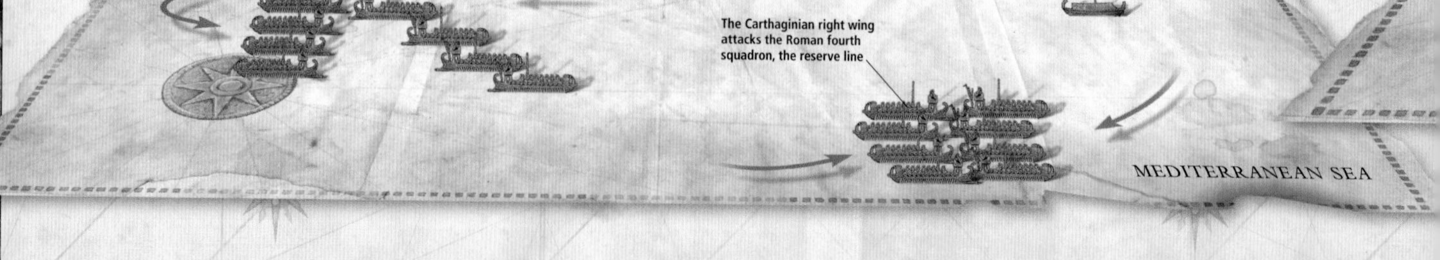

Having successfully detached the two leading Roman squadrons, the Carthaginian centre swings round to engage them

SICILY

CAPE ECNOMUS

The Carthaginian left moves to attack the third Roman squadron

The Roman third squadron abandons the transports in order to defend themselves against the Carthaginian left

The Carthaginian right wing attacks the Roman fourth squadron, the reserve line

MEDITERRANEAN SEA

THE BATTLE OF CAPE ECNOMUS

By 256 BCE the Roman Republic had been fighting Carthage for control of Sicily for eight years. Increasingly confident of their power to challenge Carthaginian dominance at sea, the Romans decided to mount an invasion of North Africa, sailing across the Mediterranean from Sicily to put Carthage itself under threat. They assembled a vast fleet which, according to the historian Polybius, numbered 330 ships. Most were quinqueremes with around 100 rowers. For the invasion attempt each ship also carried about 150 soldiers. The Roman consuls Lucius Manlius Vulso and Marcus Atilius Regulus led the expedition. The Carthaginians were well aware of Roman plans and determined to stop the invasion taking place. They assembled a fleet of broadly similar size, also in Sicily at Heraclea Minoa, under the command of the generals Hanno and Hamilcar. The scene was set for one of the largest battles in the history of naval warfare.

HAMILCAR'S STRATAGEM

As the Roman fleet set out for Africa, the Carthaginians spread theirs out in a line across its path, with its left wing close to the Sicilian shore. Hamilcar was in the centre and Hanno on the right. The Romans advanced in a compact formation. In the van were two squadrons, each commanded by a consul. Behind these a third squadron

Frieze of a Roman warship
Despite the success of the corvus against the Carthaginians, it was subsequently abandoned in favour of a tower for launching missiles.

towed horse transports. A fourth squadron protected the rear. Assuming that the Romans would attempt simply to smash through the Carthaginian line, Hamilcar ordered his captains in the centre to withdraw as the Romans approached. This would draw the Roman van forward, allowing the Carthaginian wings to outflank them.

At first Hamilcar's plan worked. The leading Roman squadrons surged forward and a gap opened up between them and the rest of the fleet to the rear. At a signal from Hamilcar, the ships in the Carthaginian centre turned back to face the Roman quinqueremes. The ships on the left turned inward to engage the Roman third squadron, whose warships were forced to cast the transports adrift in order to defend themselves. Meanwhile Hanno's right

wing, with the Carthaginians' fastest ships, fell fiercely upon the fourth squadron in the rear.

Both sides sought to exploit their strengths. The Romans had the better soldiers and, in the spiked corvus, a superbly effective method of grappling and boarding an enemy ship. The Carthaginians, as the more skilled sailors, hoped to outmanoeuvre the Romans. Their aim was to avoid being boarded and to sink ships by ramming them from the side or rear.

CRUCIAL TURNING POINT

Hamilcar's plan fell apart in the centre, where the two Roman squadrons had the advantage. The Carthaginian galleys found it difficult to manoeuvre in a dense mêlée. A number of them were captured – a corvus spike smashed into their deck and Roman legionaries swarming across to board – and the rest fled. Vulso secured the captured vessels while Regulus led a force of quinqueremes back to aid the rear squadron. This had suffered serious losses, but the arrival of Regulus's ships drove Hanno off. The Roman third squadron, hemmed in against the shore, had adopted a defensive formation with their prows facing outward, holding off the Carthaginians, who thus found themselves trapped as both Vulso and Regulus came up behind them. The Romans succeeded in capturing 50 Carthaginian ships.

The Roman fleet was in no condition to pursue the scattered Carthaginian survivors and retired to Sicily for a refit before proceeding with the planned invasion of North Africa. After some initial success, the invasion itself resulted in disaster, but from this point on the Carthaginians could never again hope to achieve dominance at sea.

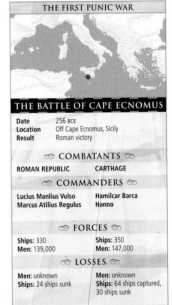

THE FIRST PUNIC WAR

THE BATTLE OF CAPE ECNOMUS

Date	256 BCE
Location	Off Cape Ecnomus, Sicily
Result	Roman victory

∞ COMBATANTS ∞

ROMAN REPUBLIC	**CARTHAGE**

∞ COMMANDERS ∞

Lucius Manlius Vulso	**Hamilcar Barca**
Marcus Atilius Regulus	**Hanno**

∞ FORCES ∞

Ships: 330	**Ships:** 350
Men: 139,000	**Men:** 147,000

∞ LOSSES ∞

Men: unknown	**Men:** unknown
Ships: 24 ships sunk	**Ships:** 64 ships captured, 30 ships sunk

1200 BCE – 1550 CE

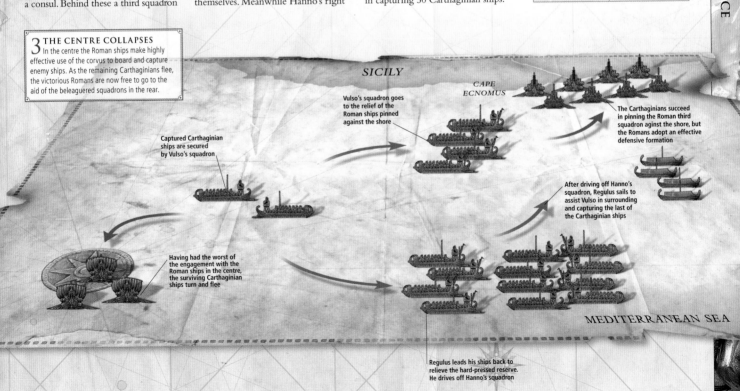

3 THE CENTRE COLLAPSES
In the centre the Roman ships make highly effective use of the corvus to board and capture enemy ships. As the remaining Carthaginians flee, the victorious Romans are now free to go to the aid of the beleaguered squadrons in the rear.

SICILY

CAPE ECNOMUS

Vulso's squadron goes to the relief of the Roman ships pinned against the shore

The Carthaginians succeed in pinning the Roman third squadron against the shore, but the Romans adopt an effective defensive formation

Captured Carthaginian ships are secured by Vulso's squadron

After driving off Hanno's squadron, Regulus sails to assist Vulso in surrounding and capturing the last of the Carthaginian ships

Having had the worst of the engagement with the Roman ships in the centre, the surviving Carthaginian ships turn and flee

MEDITERRANEAN SEA

Regulus leads his ships back to relieve the hard-pressed reserve. He drives off Hanno's squadron

ROME ACHIEVES MASTERY OF THE MEDITERRANEAN

AFTER THE DEFEAT OF CARTHAGE, Rome turned its attention to the eastern Mediterranean, where regional powers were engaged in their own struggles for dominance. Macedonia and Seleucid Syria possessed imposing fleets, while the island of Rhodes was a major naval power. The mauling of the Macedonian fleet at Chios in 201 BCE opened the way for Roman involvement in the region as an ally of Rhodes. Macedonia and the Seleucids were defeated and Egypt occupied, leaving the Romans with no one to fight at sea except pirates – and one another.

The civil wars in the second half of the 1st century BCE, as Rome made the transition from republic to empire, brought major sea battles that had a crucial impact on the outcome of the struggle for power. The defeat of Sextus Pompeius at Naulochus left Octavian and Mark Antony the only contenders for leadership of the Roman world. The issue between them was settled at Actium in 31 BCE. With Octavian installed as the Emperor Augustus, Roman naval mastery of the Mediterranean was established. It remained virtually unchallenged for the next two centuries.

THE AGE OF GALLEYS

SECOND MACEDONIAN WAR

CHIOS

Date 210 BCE
Forces Macedonians: 53 large ships, c.150 others; Rhodians and allies: 65 large ships, 12 others
Losses Macedonians: 42 ships; Rhodians and allies: 9 ships

Location Off Chios, Aegean Sea

Philip V of Macedon was fighting for control of the eastern Mediterranean. Rhodes and Pergamon formed an alliance against him, aided by Cyzicus and Byzantium. Philip had landed an army on the island of Chios when he was surprised by a fleet under the Rhodian admiral Theophiliscus and the Pergamonese ruler Attalus.

Some of the ships engaged in the ensuing battle were huge polyremes with eight or ten oarsmen to each column of oars. One of these monsters, the Macedonian flagship, was sunk early in the battle when its ram stuck inextricably in a smaller vessel, leaving it exposed to ramming from both sides. The small, nimble Rhodian galleys attacked from the flank, ramming Philip's ships from the rear or slicing off their oars. But the Macedonians made good use of smaller galleys to protect their larger ships from ramming and held off their attackers with catapults mounted on the high decks.

Both allied commanders were in the thick of the contest. Theophiliscus was wounded three times coming to the aid of one of his quinqueremes that was sinking surrounded by enemy ships – he later died of his injuries. Attalus was forced to run his flagship ashore to escape enemy pursuit. Philip escaped with the majority of his ships, but his losses had been extremely heavy.

ROMAN–SELEUCID WAR

MYONESSUS

Date 190 BCE
Forces Romans and Rhodians: 83 ships; Seleucids: 90 ships
Losses Romans and Rhodians: 3 ships; Seleucids: 29 ships

Location Off west coast of Turkey

Between 192 and 188 Rome, in alliance with Rhodes and Pergamon, fought a war against the Seleucid ruler Antiochus III of Syria. The Seleucid admiral Polyxenidas, based at Ephesus, came out to give battle to a combined fleet of Roman and Rhodian ships off Myonessus. Control of the Aegean was at stake. The Rhodians under Eudoras skilfully manoeuvred their lighter, faster galleys, blocking an attempted outflanking move by Polyxenidas by swiftly transferring from one wing to the other. They broke up the Seleucid formation through the aggressive use of incendiary devices. The heavier Roman ships under Lucius Aemilius Regillus punched through the centre of the enemy line. In places, with opposing ships locked together, crews and marines fought hand-to-hand. Once the Seleucids realized there were Roman ships to their rear, they turned and fled. This victory gave Rome command of the sea, enabling its armies to carry the war to a successful conclusion on land.

PIRACY IN THE MEDITERRANEAN

POMPEY'S CAMPAIGN AGAINST THE PIRATES

Date 67 BCE
Forces Pompey: 500 ships; Pirates: unknown
Losses Pompey: unknown; Pirates: 846 ships surrendered

Location Mediterranean

Despite Rome's nominal sovereignty over the Mediterranean Sea, the seafaring inhabitants of port cities and coastal areas were inevitably tempted to make an easy living preying on merchant vessels, especially during the periods when Rome was preoccupied with its regular civil wars.

Coin of Pompey the Great
Issued by Pompey's son Sextus Pompeius, this silver coin shows Pompey's head with a trident in honour of his achievement of ridding the Mediterranean of pirates.

The unpoliced waters became too hazardous for trade, while the pirates grew ever richer and bolder, raiding Rome's port of Ostia and kidnapping Roman officials on the Italian coast.

After several ineffectual attempts to crack down on piracy, in 67 BCE the politician and general Pompey, known as "the Great", was given wide-ranging powers and large-scale resources for a war on the pirates. He divided the Mediterranean into 13 zones, each under a legate with army and naval forces at his command. Pompey himself kept a roving brief, leading 60 ships in pursuit of the most troublesome and persistent offenders.

In a mere 40 days during the spring Pompey swept the entire western Mediterranean clear of pirates, most submitting virtually without a fight. He then turned to the eastern Mediterranean, the heartland of piracy. On Crete and along the coast of Cilicia in

Legionary helmet
The sight of Pompey's well-equipped legions was enough to make most pirates surrender. This replica helmet is of a kind widely used in the 1st century BCE.

Asia Minor pirate chiefs held many ports and strongholds. Pompey went after them in person, taking with him a large quantity of siege equipment in the expectation of hard fighting to subdue fortified pirate bases. But as in the west, a show of strength usually sufficed. According to Roman historian Florus, at the approach of Pompey's galleys the pirate crews would throw down their weapons, relinquish their oars and clap their hands as a gesture of surrender.

Pompey is reported to have taken just 71 pirate ships in combat, out of 846 captured in the campaign. Pirates were resettled where the Romans could keep an eye on them and there was more chance of making an honest living.

> **THERE WERE OF THESE CORSAIRS ABOVE A THOUSAND SAIL, AND THEY HAD TAKEN NO LESS THAN 400 CITIES …**
>
> **PLUTARCH**, GREEK HISTORIAN OF THE 1ST CENTURY CE IN HIS *LIFE OF POMPEY*

THE BATTLE OF NAULOCHUS

In the course of the civil wars that succeeded the assassination of Julius Caesar in 44 BCE, Sextus Pompeius, son of Pompey the Great, attempted to grab a share of the spoils. In command of the Roman fleet, he captured Sicily, a vital source of grain supplies. Octavian, a member of Rome's ruling triumvirate, entrusted Marcus Vipsanius Agrippa with creating a fleet to retake Sicily.

Agrippa established a naval base, Portus Julius, near modern-day Naples. There he built ships and trained their crews in the latest fighting techniques. They learned to use not only the rock-hurling artillery now standard upon warships, but also a new device known as the arpax, a catapult that projected grappling irons onto an enemy galley. Agrippa also had his ships' hulls reinforced with beams around the waterline to resist ramming.

THE POMPEIANS CRUSHED

In summer 36 BCE, Octavian launched an invasion of Sicily with armies from Italy and North Africa. Agrippa, who was to cover the movement of troops and keep their supply lines open, moved to a forward base on the Lipari islands. From there he made a successful but inconclusive attack on part of Sextus's fleet at Mylae. Sextus then sent his entire naval force to confront Agrippa in a desperate bid to regain command of the sea, which alone offered him a chance of resisting Octavian's invasion.

Almost equal in number, the two forces approached each other in line abreast along the Sicilian coast. Agrippa's ships were, however, slightly more widely spaced. This enabled them to turn Sextus's flank on the seaward side and press their enemy in to the shore. As the battle developed into a close-packed mêlée, Agrippa's well-trained force gained the upper hand. His archers, mounted on towers, shot fire arrows down onto the enemy. His catapults battered hulls and carved deadly paths through crowded decks. The arpax allowed his men to grapple and board ships weakened by the missile barrage.

When the fighting stopped, 28 of Sextus's ships had been sunk and almost all the rest had been captured. Only 17 ships escaped out of a fleet of around 300 vessels. Sicily fell to Octavian. Sextus slipped away to the east, but the following year fell into the hands of one of Mark Antony's followers and was summarily executed.

ROMAN CIVIL WARS

BATTLE OF NAULOCHUS

Date	3 September 36 BCE
Location	Off north coast of Sicily
Result	Crushing victory for Octavian

∾ COMBATANTS ∾

OCTAVIAN	**SEXTUS POMPEIUS**

∾ COMMANDERS ∾

Marcus Vipsanius Agrippa	**Sextus Pompeius**

∾ FORCES ∾

Ships: c.300	**Ships:** c.300

∾ LOSSES ∾

Men: unknown	**Men:** unknown
Ships: 3	**Ships:** 28 sunk, c.255 captured

---

c.63–12 BCE
MARCUS VIPSANIUS AGRIPPA
ROMAN NAVAL COMMANDER

Agrippa was a friend of Julius Caesar's adopted son Octavian from childhood, and became the future emperor's right-hand man during his rise to power. He made a reputation as a general on land before, in 37 BCE, Octavian made him consul and gave him responsibility for creating a fleet to defeat Sextus Pompeius. His victories over Sextus at Naulochus and Mark Antony at Actium showed a firm grasp of naval tactics as well as great powers of organization and leadership. Much of his later life was spent on campaign in Gaul, Spain, Germany, and Rome's eastern provinces.

Mosaic of Roman war galley
The mosaic shows the helmsman in the stern, the commander standing in the galley's bow, and armed soldiers ready to board an enemy ship.

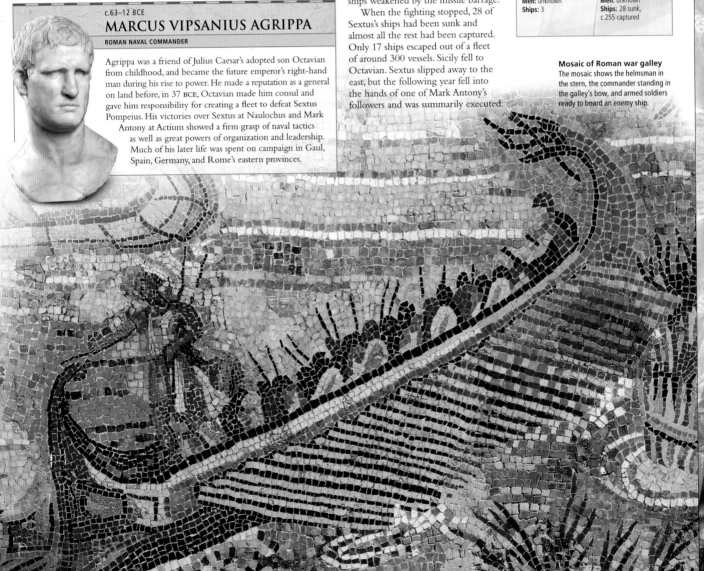

THE BATTLE OF ACTIUM

The Battle of Actium was the climax of the great power struggle between Mark Antony and Octavian for the leadership of the Roman world following the assassination of Julius Caesar in 44 BCE. In the summer of 31 BCE the forces of Antony and his Egyptian ally Cleopatra were cornered by Octavian at Actium, a Roman colony on the Greek coast. Octavian's admiral, Marcus Vipsanius Agrippa, who commanded a battle-hardened Roman fleet, pinned Antony's fleet in harbour with a close blockade and cut his supply line from Egypt. This allowed Octavian to ferry an army from Italy across the Adriatic unchallenged and to confront Antony on land.

DESPERATE MEASURES

By August, Antony's soldiers and seamen had run desperately short of food and other supplies, their ranks decimated by desertion and disease. Antony and Cleopatra devised a plan for a breakout by sea, hoping to escape back to Egypt with their army and as much as possible of their treasure. Many of their ships were in poor condition and, even after sending out press-gangs to round up able-bodied locals, they were short of oarsmen. Although the least seaworthy ships were burned, the rest were still undermanned.

The breakout was planned for 29 August, but four days of storms delayed the operation until the morning of 2 September. Antony led his war galleys out of harbour, while transport vessels loaded with treasure remained in the rear under Cleopatra's command. Most unusually, all of Antony's galleys had their masts and sails on board – normally these were never carried into battle. The plan was to exploit the expected offshore breeze from the north in order to sail off to Egypt and safety.

Throughout the morning there was a stand-off, Antony's fleet staying inshore and waiting for the wind. Then, as Agrippa's ships attempted to outflank their enemy, battle was joined. The squadron that included Antony's flagship, on the right of his line, was especially hotly engaged.

AN UNEQUAL CONTEST

Agrippa's host of small warships, mostly liburnians, were far nimbler than Antony's hefty quinqueremes, however these larger galleys provided a high platform for catapults and for soldiers with bows, spears, and slingshots. Ships grappled closely, many set aflame by incendiary devices such as fire arrows. In the afternoon the long-awaited breeze got up and Cleopatra seized the opportunity to sail her ships through the centre of the blockading line, which had thinned as battle raged on the flanks. Deserting his flagship, which had been grappled by the enemy, for a lighter vessel, Antony sped after the Egyptian queen. Few of his warships were able to follow. The leaderless fleet fought on for a while until, heavily battered, it surrendered. Antony and Cleopatra reached Alexandria with around 60 vessels, but, the following summer, abandoned by almost all his troops, and facing defeat, Antony committed suicide. A week later Cleopatra did the same.

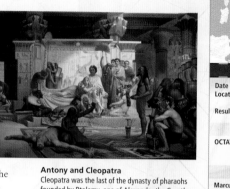

Antony and Cleopatra
Cleopatra was the last of the dynasty of pharaohs founded by Ptolemy, one of Alexander the Great's generals. In order to prevent Egypt from falling to Rome, she used her legendary charms to seduce first Julius Caesar, then Mark Antony.

Cleopatra's escape
This fanciful representation of the battle shows Cleopatra fleeing treacherously – a version of Actium no longer widely accepted. The escape of the Egyptian queen was rather a pre-planned manoeuvre.

ROMAN CIVIL WARS	

THE BATTLE OF ACTIUM

Date	2 September 31 BCE
Location	Ionian Sea, off the Gulf of Abracia, western Greece
Result	Decisive victory for Octavian

∞ COMBATANTS ∞

OCTAVIAN	MARK ANTONY CLEOPATRA VII

∞ COMMANDERS ∞

Marcus Vipsanius Agrippa	Mark Antony

∞ FORCES ∞

Ships: 400 warships, mostly liburnians and triremes	Ships: 230 warships, mostly quinqueremes

∞ LOSSES ∞

Men: unknown	Men: 5,000 dead
Ships: unknown	Ships: 300 vessels of all types – warships and transports

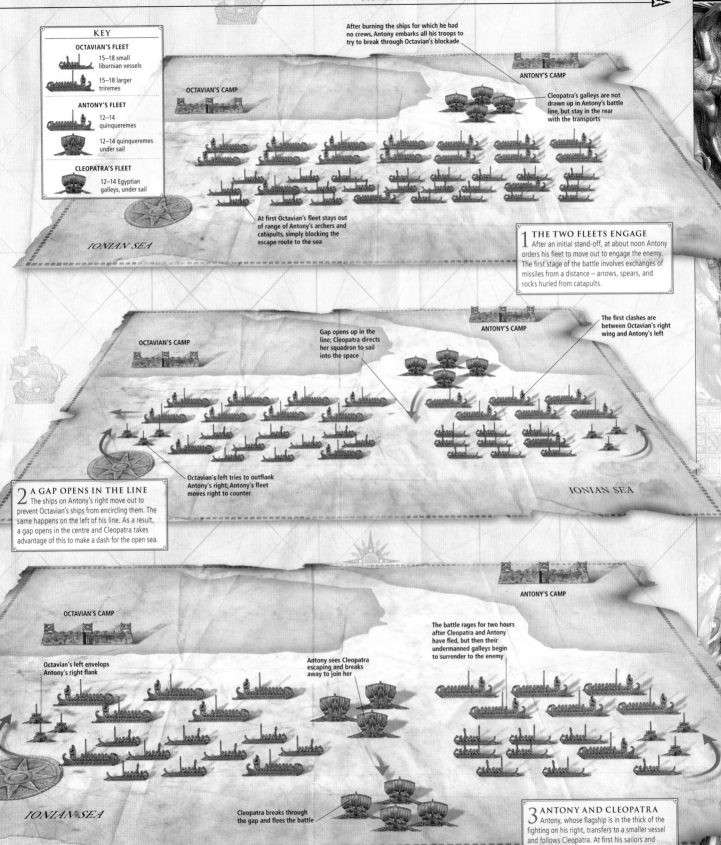

KEY

OCTAVIAN'S FLEET
15–18 small liburnian vessels

15–18 larger triremes

ANTONY'S FLEET
12–14 quinqueremes

12–14 quinqueremes under sail

CLEOPATRA'S FLEET
12–14 Egyptian galleys, under sail

OCTAVIAN'S CAMP

ANTONY'S CAMP

IONIAN SEA

After burning the ships for which he had no crews, Antony embarks all his troops to try to break through Octavian's blockade

Cleopatra's galleys are not drawn up in Antony's battle line, but stay in the rear with the transports

At first Octavian's fleet stays out of range of Antony's archers and catapults, simply blocking the escape route to the sea

1 THE TWO FLEETS ENGAGE
After an initial stand-off, at about noon Antony orders his fleet to move out to engage the enemy. The first stage of the battle involves exchanges of missiles from a distance – arrows, spears, and rocks hurled from catapults.

OCTAVIAN'S CAMP

ANTONY'S CAMP

The first clashes are between Octavian's right wing and Antony's left

Gap opens up in the line; Cleopatra directs her squadron to sail into the space

Octavian's left tries to outflank Antony's right; Antony's fleet moves right to counter

IONIAN SEA

2 A GAP OPENS IN THE LINE
The ships on Antony's right move out to prevent Octavian's ships from encircling them. The same happens on the left of his line. As a result, a gap opens in the centre and Cleopatra takes advantage of this to make a dash for the open sea.

OCTAVIAN'S CAMP

ANTONY'S CAMP

Octavian's left envelops Antony's right flank

Antony sees Cleopatra escaping and breaks away to join her

The battle rages for two hours after Cleopatra and Antony have fled, but then their undermanned galleys begin to surrender to the enemy

Cleopatra breaks through the gap and flees the battle

IONIAN SEA

3 ANTONY AND CLEOPATRA
Antony, whose flagship is in the thick of the fighting on his right, transfers to a smaller vessel and follows Cleopatra. At first his sailors and legionary marines fight on despite their leaders' desertion, but after a while are forced to surrender.

NAVAL WARFARE IN ASIA

THE DEVELOPMENT OF NAVAL WARFARE in East Asia was in some ways similar to that of Europe. At the time of the Roman Empire, Chinese warships fought using the tactics of ramming or grappling and boarding just as fleets did in the Mediterranean. The Chinese even had an equivalent to the corvus, the Romans' boarding bridge. Naval warfare in Japan, where samurai contested land battles on water fought with bows and swords, at times resembled the battles fought between seaborne medieval European knights and archers. Yet Asian navies developed a distinctive range of ships, including large numbers of vessels with paddlewheels, a form of propulsion that did not catch on in Europe until the steam era. The Chinese in particular were at the cutting edge of technology, using gunpowder, crossbows, and the compass earlier than Europeans, and by the 15th century building the world's largest sailing ships.

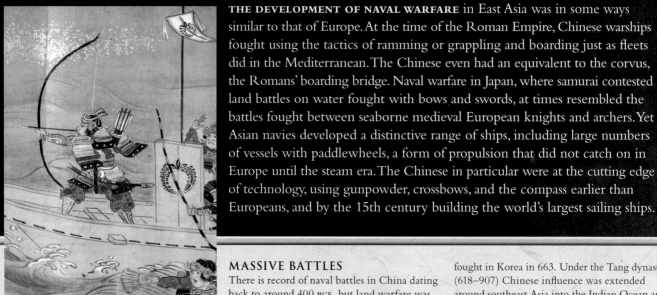

Samurai warriors at sea
Samurai sailed out on fast, light boats to harass the invasion fleets of Kublai Khan's Mongols. Two attempts to invade Japan from China failed, the second in 1281 when the invasion fleet was destroyed by a typhoon.

Legends of the Three Kingdoms
Three Chinese leaders competing for the fragmented Han Empire fought a decisive river battle at Red Cliffs in 208 ce. This illustration shows legendary events from the period, including "borrowing" arrows by sailing boats manned with straw scarecrows past the enemy's camp.

MASSIVE BATTLES

There is record of naval battles in China dating back to around 400 BCE, but land warfare was understandably the major preoccupation of the Chinese emperors, given their country's barely defensible western frontier. Land operations were, however, often accompanied by battles fought on rivers and lakes. Japan and Korea also developed naval forces at an early stage of their history. The Koreans largely outfought the Chinese in the Yellow Sea during the wars between the Korean Goguryeo and Chinese Sui dynasties from 598 to 614. The Chinese navy was more successful against Japan in the Baekje War,

fought in Korea in 663. Under the Tang dynasty (618–907) Chinese influence was extended around southeast Asia into the Indian Ocean and across to the east coast of Africa. This brought the Chinese into contact with Arab sailors and with Indian fleets such as that of the southern Indian Chola dynasty in the 11th century.

By the time the Song dynasty founded China's first permanent navy in 1132, southern China almost certainly possessed the world's largest concentration of naval forces. The Song fought massive naval battles against Jurchen Jin and Mongol Yuan assailants from the north. After the Mongols triumphed over the Song under Kublai Khan in the 1270s, Chinese naval power was asserted from the Indian Ocean to Japan – although Yuan attempts at a seaborne invasion of Japan failed. The Japanese, meanwhile, were feared as pirates raiding the coasts of the Asian mainland. They also undertook major naval battles during the civil conflict known as the Gempei Wars, fought in the 12th century, when the movement of troops around Japan's Inland Sea became strategically crucial. It was their naval victory at Dan-no-Ura that ensured that the Minamoto clan would take power in Japan as shoguns in 1185.

SHIPS AND WEAPONRY

The Chinese developed a range of different types of warship, each with a specific tactical role. These included large multi-deck war junks and "tower ships" with portholes through which crossbows could be fired and lances thrust, and often carrying varieties of catapult. Smaller vessels included "covered swoopers", fast assault ships covered with thick hides to protect against missiles and incendiary devices, which were designed for aggressive "swoops" on the enemy. "Flying barques" were fast moving galleys that

had more oarsmen than other ships and a smaller complement of soldiers – comparable to the Greek trireme in concept. Paddle-wheel craft, initially introduced in the 8th century, became of paramount importance under the Song dynasty. The wheels were driven by treadmills inside the hull typically operated by the leg-power of crews of 28 to 42 men. Large vessels might have 23 wheels – 11 on each side and one at the stern – and measure up to 110m (360ft) in length. One type, known as a "sea-hawk" ship, had a low bow and a high stern, a ram at the prow and iron plates for armoured protection. Used on rivers and lakes, the paddle-wheel craft were extremely manoeuvrable, capable of travelling forward or backward with equal ease.

The weaponry carried on board ship ranged from crossbows and lances to catapults and, later, primitive cannon. Gunpowder became an important element of missile warfare in the Song period. It could be wrapped in small packages around arrowheads to make fire-arrows, or used as fuel for a fire-lance, a kind of proto-flamethrower – or made into explosive grenades or bombs. Many Chinese naval battles were decided by ships being set on fire.

MING SEA POWER

Naval conflict played a critical role in the warfare that ended in the establishment of the Ming dynasty in China in the 14th century.

Samurai helmet
Most battles at sea are won by selfless teamwork, but the medieval samurai warrior was able to show off his individual prowess, especially his skill as an archer, just as well on water as on land.

There were engagements between probably some of the numerically largest fleets ever assembled. Once in power, the Ming at first devoted vast resources to shipbuilding. Since they also had the magnetic compass at their disposal, there was nothing to stop them embarking upon oceanic voyages. Between 1405 and 1433 fleets led by the eunuch Admiral Zheng He cruised around southeast Asia and across the Indian Ocean, entering the Red Sea and voyaging down the east African coast as far as Mozambique. The greatest of the Chinese fleets comprised 63 large war junks – the largest more than 120m (390ft) long and almost 50m (160ft) broad – plus more than 200 support vessels and nearly 30,000 men. This constituted a thoroughly intimidating assertion of imperial suzerainty. On the few occasions when he encountered resistance, Admiral He did not hesitate to use force to impose respect – for example arresting and executing a Sumatran ruler who objected to paying tribute. But from the 1430s the Ming emperors turned instead to a policy of inward-looking development that rejected all overseas ventures. The maintenance of an ocean-going navy was abandoned. By the time European mariners arrived in Asian waters in the 16th century, they encountered no serious competitors in the bid for control of the world's ocean trade routes.

WEAPONS AND TECHNOLOGY

SONG CATAPULT SHIP

A trebuchet is a sling for hurling missiles, using the principle of the lever to give greater power and accuracy than a torsion device such as a ballista. The Chinese are credited with the invention of the first trebuchets around the 5th century BCE. The power for these traction trebuchets was supplied by teams of men pulling on ropes attached to the shorter arm of the device, the sling being at the end of the longer arm. The more powerful counterweight trebuchet was introduced to China from Muslim west Asia in the 13th century, first playing a crucial role in the Mongols' siege of Xiangyang in 1273. In the Song dynasty navy trebuchets were habitually deployed as shipborne artillery, mounted on the larger "tower ships" both as a weapon for ship-to-ship combat and as a siege weapon for bombarding land fortifications from the water. When attacking ships, the trebuchets would often hurl explosive incendiary devices, an effective tactic against highly flammable vessels. Many of the Song catapult ships were driven by paddlewheels, but they could also be propelled by oars.

River ship with trebuchet
This 13th-century drawing shows a trebuchet with the counterweight on the shorter arm and the longer throwing arm on the right.

CHINA, JAPAN, AND KOREA

NAVAL POWER played an important part in East Asian warfare, as a sometimes crucial ancillary to land campaigns. As early as the 3rd century CE, the battle of Red Cliffs established a consistent theme in Chinese history: the ability of the southern Chinese to defend themselves against invaders from the north by resort to river and sea warfare. This pattern was repeated against the Jurchen at Tangdao and initially against the Mongols in the 13th century. The Mongol Yuan dynasty eventually conquered the Song after adapting to naval warfare. The period of Yuan rule was framed by two naval battles: a Mongol victory at Yamen in 1279 and a defeat at Lake Poyang in 1363. Sea battles were also crucial in the histories of Korea and Japan. The Japanese failed to extend their influence into Korea in the 7th century, repulsed by the Chinese navy, and the Mongols made equally unsuccessful attempts to invade Japan. The outcome of Japan's civil wars was affected by fighting on water, notably at Dan-no-Ura in 1185.

SILLA–BAEKJE WARS

BAEKGANG

Date 27–28 August 663
Forces Japanese: 800 ships; Chinese: 170 ships
Losses Japanese: 400 ships; Chinese unknown

Location Geum River, Korea

China's Tang dynasty occupied the Baekje kingdom of southern Korea in alliance with another Korean kingdom, Silla. Japan's Yamato government sent a fleet and an army of more than 40,000 men to aid Baekje forces under siege at Churyu. They intended to ferry the troops up the Geum River, but found the river blocked by a Chinese fleet. The Chinese were heavily outnumbered but their ships held a disciplined line from bank to bank. In two days of repeated attacks the Japanese failed to break through. Seeing the Japanese tired and disorganized, the Chinese then launched a counterattack, outflanking and encircling the Japanese fleet. Many of the Japanese ships were burned and thousands of soldiers drowned. Baekje was defeated and, with Chinese aid, the Silla kingdom unified Korea.

JURCHEN–SONG WARS

TANGDAO

Date 16 November 1161
Forces Song: 120 ships; Jurchen: 600 ships
Losses Unknown

Location Near Shandong peninsula, East China Sea

In 1161 the Jurchen of northern China were attempting to conquer southern China, ruled by the Song dynasty. An invasion force of warships and troop transports was intercepted by the Song navy among the islands of the East China Sea. The Song had developed ingenious paddle-wheel craft powered by treadmills, which moved swiftly into the attack. On their decks they had trebuchets that could hurl primitive incendiary bombs to explode on the wooden enemy ships. Soon much of the great Jurchen armada was ablaze. Its commander, Zheng Jia, jumped into the sea and was drowned. The following month another Jurchen fleet was defeated by the Song at the battle of Caishi on the Yangtze River, ensuring the survival of the southern Song as an independent state for another century.

THE BATTLE OF RED CLIFFS

The Battle of the Red Cliffs, or Chibi as it is sometimes known, was a crucial point in the transition from the Han Dynasty to the Three Kingdoms period in Chinese history. The all-powerful Han minister Cao Cao had embarked on a campaign to unify China under his rule. His army was enormous and initially victorious. But in order to conquer southern China, he needed to gain command of the Yangtze River. This ambition was opposed by the warlords Liu Bei and Sun Quan, who formed an alliance to resist Cao Cao.

FIGHT OR SURRENDER

The warlords looked doomed when Cao captured a powerful river fleet and the Yangtze naval port of Jiangling. Cao loaded his men onto the boats and set off downstream toward Sun Quan's power base at Chaisang. The majority of Sun's advisers advocated

Unleashing the fire ships
Having ignited the flammable materials aboard the fire ships, Huang Gai's men escape in rowing boats as the ships drift downriver to collide with their targets.

surrender, but his military commander Zhou Yu argued that Cao's forces were less formidable than they seemed. Exhausted after conducting a long, hard campaign and unaccustomed to naval warfare, they would be outfought by fresher troops that were skilled in the techniques of river fighting. What is more, he anticipated correctly that Cao's northerners would fall sick as soon as they were exposed to the disease environment of the south.

Zhou Yu led the combined forces of Sun and Liu up river. The precise location of their encounter with Cao's fleet is uncertain. The battle opened with indecisive skirmishing, after which the two sides broke off to rest. Cao was concerned about the spread

Cao Cao on the eve of Red Cliffs
In this atmospheric 14th-century painting, the great general ponders the wisdom of confronting his enemies in a river battle.

of disease in his army and the difficulty his soldiers experienced in fighting on water. To provide a more stable platform for his troops, he had his boats lashed together in large groups. This made it impossible for them to manoeuvre and vulnerable to incendiary weapons, such as fire arrows, that were a feature of Chinese warfare.

It appears that a veteran soldier, Huang Gai, offered to sail fire ships, loaded with dry reeds and inflammable wax, into Cao's tethered fleet. To confuse the enemy, Huang approached Cao's boats pretending he wanted to surrender. Then the crews set the ships on fire, disembarked into small boats, and watched as the blazing vessels drifted down on to their immobile target.

Enough of Cao's fleet was destroyed to discourage him from any further naval adventures. His army set off overland on a retreat that turned into a rout. The defeat ended Cao's chances of unifying China, which entered a period of warfare between conflicting kingdoms.

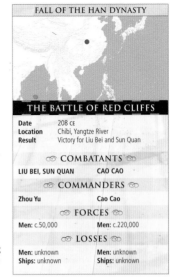

FALL OF THE HAN DYNASTY

THE BATTLE OF RED CLIFFS

Date	208 CE
Location	Chibi, Yangtze River
Result	Victory for Liu Bei and Sun Quan

◈ COMBATANTS ◈

LIU BEI, SUN QUAN	CAO CAO

◈ COMMANDERS ◈

Zhou Yu	Cao Cao

◈ FORCES ◈

Men: c.50,000	Men: c.220,000

◈ LOSSES ◈

Men: unknown	Men: unknown
Ships: unknown	Ships: unknown

GEMPEI WARS

MIZUSHIMA

Date 17 November 1183
Forces Minamoto: unknown;
Taira: unknown
Losses Unknown

Location Between
Honshu and Shikoku

Beginning in 1180, the Gempei Wars pitted the Minamoto samurai clan against the rival Taira clan in a struggle for control of Japan. In the summer of 1183 the Minamoto seized the upper hand in the civil war. Minamoto no Yoshimaka defeated the Taira at the battle of Kurikara and surrounded the imperial capital, Kyoto. The Taira were forced to flee and take refuge in their traditional power base in western Honshu and Shikoku, where they had a number of fortresses around the shores of the Inland Sea.

Taking the offensive, Minamoto no Yoshimaka sent an army to attack the Taira fortress at Yashima, a small island off the coast of Shikoku. The army was put under the command of a general, the unsophisticated Yada Yoshiyasu, since Yoshimaka himself was preoccupied with power struggles in his own clan.

The Minamoto army embarked at Mizushima on Honshu to cross the Inland Sea, but was surprised by a Taira fleet sent to intercept them. This force was commanded by Taira no Tomomori and Taira no Noritsune, experienced fighters with victories to their name. They ordered their ships to be tied together with hawsers at the stem and stern, and planks laid across them, so the whole fleet was a level surface for the samurai and their followers to fight on. The Taira then drew their bows and deluged the Minamoto ships with a rain of arrows. When the fighting came to close quarters, men attacked one another with swords and daggers, while some infantry with long rakes tried to pull enemy warriors into the water.

As the battle turned against him, Yada Yoshiyasu led a desperate foray forward with a few followers in a small boat, but the vessel was overturned and all aboard drowned. Desperate Minamoto soldiers splashed to shore through the shallows, but they were pursued by the Taira, who had horses on board their ships. The Taira horsemen rode down upon the Minamoto remnants and scattered them in flight. This spectacular victory could not prevent Yoshimaka from seizing Kyoto for the Minamoto the following year.

GEMPEI WARS

YASHIMA

Date 22 March 1185
Forces Minamoto: unknown;
Taira: unknown
Losses Unknown

Location Yashima,
off Shikoku

By 1185 Japan's Gempei Wars between the Minamoto and Taira clans were approaching their climax. Minamoto no Yoshitsune was pursuing the Taira in their last fortresses in Shikoku. While crossing the Inland Sea, however, Yoshitsune ran into a storm and much of his fleet was lost. Although he was resupplied by his ally Kajiwara Kagetoki, he no longer had a clear advantage. By lighting hundreds of fires around the fortress of Yashima, Yoshitsune tricked the Taira into thinking that he had a large army. They abandoned the fortress, embarking on ships with their most precious possessions, the child emperor Antoku and the imperial treasure. As the Taira fled, Minamoto samurai Nasu no Yoichi rode into the sea and shot a fan off the masthead of one of the ships – a famous feat of archery.

Aftermath of Yashima
Although most of the Taira escaped with the child emperor, some fell into the hands of the enemy. Here a Taira lady is discovered by Yoshitsune.

1152–1185

TAIRA NO TOMOMORI

COMMANDER OF THE FORCES OF THE TAIRA CLAN

The son of a famous father – the clan leader Taira no Kiyomori – Tomomori was the most successful of the Taira military commanders in the Gempei Wars. He won notable victories over the Minamoto on land at Uji in 1180 and Sunomata in 1181 and on the sea at Mizushima in 1183. Although Tomomori was primarily a soldier, he also seems to have possessed considerable experience in the use of ships in war. He committed suicide after the final defeat of the Taira at the sea battle of Dan-no-Ura, jumping into the water with an anchor tied to his feet.

MONGOL–SONG WARS

XIANGYANG

Date 1268–1273
Forces Mongol Yuan: 5,000
ships; Song: unknown
Losses Unknown

Location Xiangfan,
Hubei province, China

The Mongol warrior Kublai Khan made himself ruler of northern China in 1260, establishing the Yuan dynasty. The wealthy and populous lands of southern China, however, remained under the rule of the Song dynasty.

The Mongols were steppe horsemen with no knowledge of naval warfare, but in order to conquer the south they had to learn to fight on rivers and lakes. The lengthy struggle to reduce the fortified city of Xiangyang, held by the Song, was in effect a battle for control of the Han river, a major tributary of the Yangtze. Xiangyang was surrounded on three sides by mountains and on the fourth by the river. The Mongols had already realized the need for naval power if they were to conquer the Song and had recruited a vast fleet of river craft. This enabled them to impose a river blockade on Xiangyang, as well as besieging the city by land. One Song flotilla managed to break through the blockade to resupply the city's defenders, but this was not enough to save Xiangyang. Once it fell, the Yuan fleet could sail down the river system to capture the major Song cities.

MONGOL–SONG WARS

YAMEN

Date 19 March 1279
Forces Mongol Yuan: unknown;
Song: unknown
Losses Unknown

Location Guangdong,
South China Sea

After years of stubborn resistance, in 1278 southern China, ruled for 300 years by the Song dynasty, was finally overrun by the armies of Kublai Khan, Mongol founder of the Yuan dynasty. The surviving officials and members of the Song imperial family became fugitives, seeking a base from which to begin organizing resistance. In March 1279 they were on board ship in a bay at Yamen, on the Guangdong coast, when they were

Mongol bowcase
The Mongols learned to use siege weapons to conquer the Song, but they still relied on the bows that brought them such success on the Asian steppe.

located by a Yuan fleet under the command of Kublai's general Zhang Hongfan. The Song fleet and soldiers were commanded by grand general Zhang Shijie. Instead of advancing his ships to defend the mouth of the bay, which would have left the option of fleeing in case of defeat, Zhang Shijie adopted a passive formation inside the anchorage. He had his ships tied together and awaited the Yuan attack.

Zhang Hongfan first sent fire ships into the bay, but the Song coped successfully with this timeworn tactic. So the Yuan divided their fleet in order to attack from three directions. They were apparently heavily outnumbered by the Song, but their ships were equipped with primitive gunpowder weapons and stone-hurling catapults.

The Song soon lost heart. Zhang Shijie attempted to stage a breakout with a few ships carrying the seven-year-old emperor and the imperial entourage. When this failed, a senior official picked up the emperor and jumped overboard with the boy in his arms. Other officials and concubines followed his example. Zhang Shijie himself survived the battle but was drowned in a storm shortly after.

FAILED MONGOL INVASION OF JAPAN

Date June–August 1281
Forces Mongols: 4,400 ships;
Japanese: unknown
Losses Mongols: c.3,000 ships

Location
Tsushima Strait

The Mongol emperor of China, Kublai Khan, demanded that the Japanese acknowledge his suzerainty. In 1274 he raided Japan, sending a substantial force across from Korea to land in Hakata Bay. The attack failed to cow the Japanese, but it did stimulate them to organize new coastal defences. In 1281 Kublai

mounted a full-scale invasion, assembling more than 4,000 ships from China and Korea to carry some 150,000 troops. The 900 Korean ships were thoroughly seaworthy vessels, but the Chinese ones were mostly flat-bottomed river or coastal craft. Kublai's fleet formed two squadrons, the smaller sailing from Korea and the larger from northern China. The force from Korea arrived first, but was unable to land its soldiers because of the coastal fortifications built and manned by the Japanese since 1274.

Anchored offshore, the Mongols were harassed by Japanese samurai in small craft, who set fire to ships and killed crew and soldiers. The Mongols withdrew to Iki island to rendezvous with the squadron from China. They then attacked Takashima island, while the Japanese awaited an assault on the mainland. The invasion never came, however, for a typhoon – known to the Japanese as the "divine wind" or "kamikaze" – struck the Mongol fleet, sinking most of the Chinese ships.

Hit-and-run tactics
Before the Mongol invasion fleet was struck by a typhoon, it was attacked by waves of attacks by samurai archers in fast, light boats.

LAKE POYANG

Date 30 August–
2 September 1363
Forces Ming: unknown;
Han: unknown
Losses Unknown

Location
Lake Poyang, China

By the mid-14th century the rule of the Mongol Yuan dynasty in China was disintegrating. Rebel peasant bands known as the Red Turbans took control of the Yangtze River region, and two of their leaders, Chen Youliang and Zhu Yuanzhang, became rivals for power. Chen declared himself emperor and founder of the Han dynasty. Zhu, leader of the Ming, ruled a large area of southern China from his capital city, Nanjing. The war between them lasted from 1360 to 1363, climaxing in a large-scale naval battle on China's largest freshwater lake, Lake Poyang.

Zhu Yuanzhang voyaged up the Yangtze from Nanjing with a large number of ships to confront the Han fleet blockading Ming forces in the lakeside town of Nanchang. Some sources claim that a million men were present in the two fleets, making this possibly the largest naval battle in history, although such immense figures

have to be doubted. Chen Youliang had the largest vessels, three-decked "tower ships" propelled by sails and oars, with high sterns and iron-armoured turrets. The Ming ships were smaller but more numerous and manoeuvrable, many of them treadmill-powered paddle ships.

The lake battle lasted four days. The initial Ming attack came close to disaster. Zhu's flagship ran aground on a sandbank and was set on fire by incendiary weapons. His other ships rescued him, but Ming attempts to close and board Han vessels failed. On the second day, Zhu exploited a favourable wind to send in fire ships – small boats packed with straw and gunpowder. These had considerable success against the tower ships, whose deep draught limited mobility in the shallow lake waters. After a day spent on repairs, battle was resumed on 2 September. This time the Ming ships penetrated the weakened Han formation and a number of ships were boarded and taken.

The battle ended inconclusively and there followed a month-long stand-off between the two fleets. In a skirmish on 4 October, Chen Youliang was shot through the head with an arrow and killed. The Han cause collapsed without its leader. Zhu Yuanzhang went on to overthrow the Yuan and founded the Ming dynasty four years later.

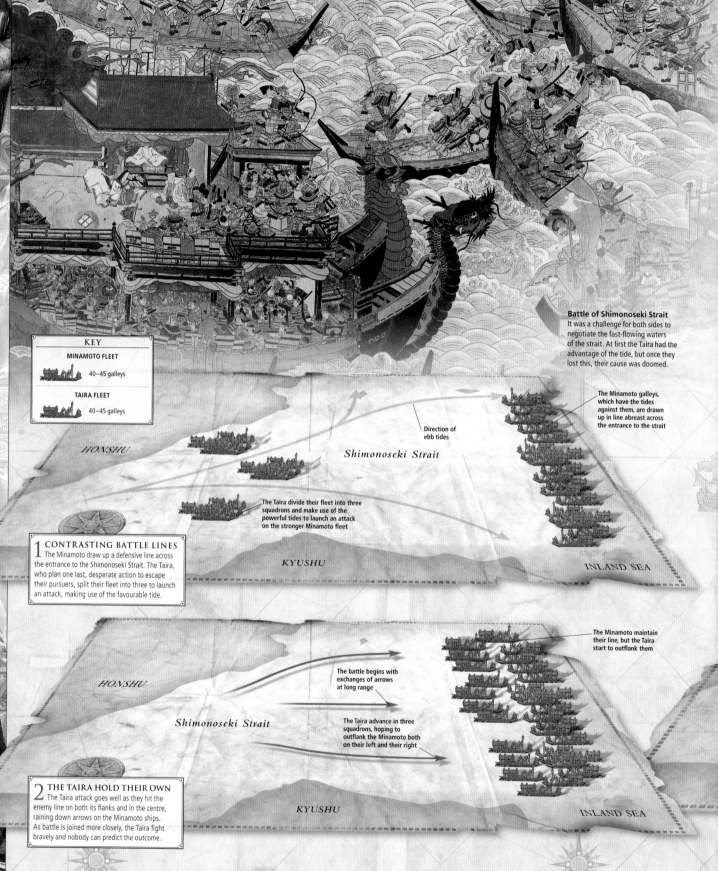

KEY

MINAMOTO FLEET

40–45 galleys

TAIRA FLEET

40–45 galleys

Battle of Shimonoseki Strait
It was a challenge for both sides to negotiate the fast-flowing waters of the strait. At first the Taira had the advantage of the tide, but once they lost this, their cause was doomed.

The Minamoto galleys, which have the tides against them, are drawn up in line abreast across the entrance to the strait

Direction of ebb tides

Shimonoseki Strait

HONSHU

The Taira divide their fleet into three squadrons and make use of the powerful tides to launch an attack on the stronger Minamoto fleet

KYUSHU

INLAND SEA

1 CONTRASTING BATTLE LINES
The Minamoto draw up a defensive line across the entrance to the Shimonoseki Strait. The Taira, who plan one last, desperate action to escape their pursuers, split their fleet into three to launch an attack, making use of the favourable tide.

The Minamoto maintain their line, but the Taira start to outflank them

The battle begins with exchanges of arrows at long range

HONSHU

The Taira advance in three squadrons, hoping to outflank the Minamoto both on their left and their right

Shimonoseki Strait

KYUSHU

INLAND SEA

2 THE TAIRA HOLD THEIR OWN
The Taira attack goes well as they hit the enemy line on both its flanks and in the centre, raining down arrows on the Minamoto ships. As battle is joined more closely, the Taira fight bravely and nobody can predict the outcome.

THE BATTLE OF DAN-NO-URA

By 1185 the Gempei Wars, in which the Minamoto and Taira clans fought for control of Japan, had turned decisively in favour of the Minamoto. The Taira had possession of the child emperor Antoku and the sacred imperial treasure, but they were on the run from the samurai Minamoto Yoshitsune after being driven from their fortress of Ichi-no-Tani in March 1184. The Taira only escaped massacre at Ichi-no-Tani by taking to their boats. Yoshitsune pursued them by sea, driving them from an anchorage at Yashima later in the same year. In April 1185 he caught up with them again in the strait of Shimonoseki between Honshu and Kyushu.

The vessels employed by both sides in the battle were oared galleys, carrying samurai armed with bows, swords, and daggers. The Taira were outnumbered but had the advantage of familiarity with local weather and tides. They adopted a well-organized formation in three squadrons, while the Minamoto came forward in a single line abreast. Like a Japanese land battle at this period, the combat began with a long-range archery duel, in which the splendidly armoured samurai competed to show off their prowess with the bow – then the most prestigious samurai weapon rather than the sword.

Taira commander Tomomori was waiting for an ebb tide to flow in mid-morning, which would aid his oarsmen. With the help of the tide, his three

squadrons manoeuvred to surround the Minamoto fleet on three sides and engage at close quarters. Soon ships were grappled and samurai fought samurai with sword and dagger. Men armed with hooks or rakes – perhaps grappling implements – used them to pull enemy warriors into the water. Archers targeted helmsmen and rowers, hoping to immobilize ships or put them out of control by disabling the crew.

THE TAIRA BETRAYED

The battle was evenly poised until two events – one predictable, the other not – swung the balance. The tide turned, giving the advantage formerly enjoyed by the Taira to their opponents. And one of the Taira commanders, Taguchi Shigeyoshi, suddenly defected and attacked his own side. More important than his contribution to the fighting

Suicide of Taira no Tomori
Tomomori (centre) has tied himself to an anchor before throwing himself into the sea, accompanied by one of his retainers (left) and his mistress (right).

was information he brought with him. The Taira had concealed the child emperor, his female relatives, and the sacred treasure on an unremarkable ship. Shigeyoshi indicated which vessel this was. The Minamoto closed in to capture this most valuable of prizes.

The end of the battle is the stuff of legend. Facing certain defeat, the Taira apparently chose mass suicide rather than captivity. Taira no Tomomori set the example in spectacular fashion, jumping into the sea tied to an anchor, which carried him to the bottom. The emperor's grandmother Taira no Tokiko took her six-year-old grandson in her arms and leapt into the sea. The Taira

also tried to throw the imperial crown jewels overboard, but the ultimate fate of the sacred treasures – a sword, a mirror, and a necklace – remains a mystery. The sea was red with blood and, we are told, with dye from the Taira banners.

The battle of Dan-no-Ura brought the Gempei Wars to an end, enabling the Minamoto to establish a shogunate, a form of military government that was to persist in Japan in various forms until the mid-19th century.

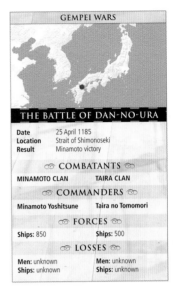

GEMPEI WARS

THE BATTLE OF DAN-NO-URA

Date	25 April 1185
Location	Strait of Shimonoseki
Result	Minamoto victory

∞ COMBATANTS ∞

MINAMOTO CLAN	TAIRA CLAN

∞ COMMANDERS ∞

Minamoto Yoshitsune	Taira no Tomomori

∞ FORCES ∞

Ships: 850	Ships: 500

∞ LOSSES ∞

Men: unknown	Men: unknown
Ships: unknown	Ships: unknown

1200 BCE – 1550 CE

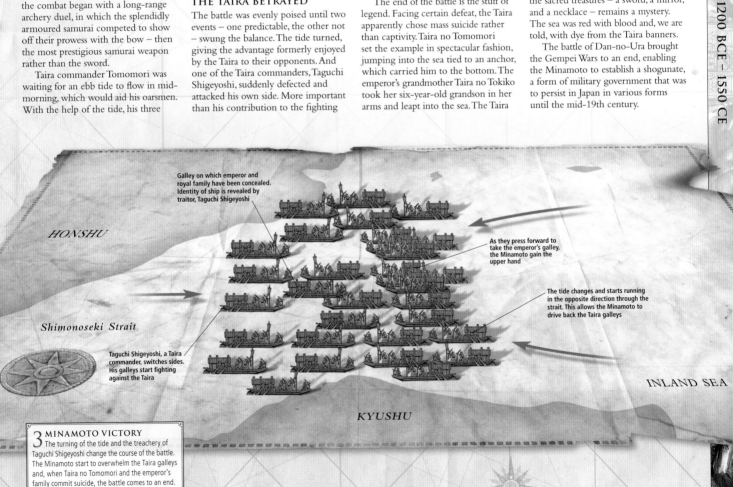

HONSHU

Galley on which emperor and royal family have been concealed. Identity of ship is revealed by traitor, Taguchi Shigeyoshi

As they press forward to take the emperor's galley, the Minamoto gain the upper hand

Shimonoseki Strait

The tide changes and starts running in the opposite direction through the strait. This allows the Minamoto to drive back the Taira galleys

Taguchi Shigeyoshi, a Taira commander, switches sides. His galleys start fighting against the Taira

INLAND SEA

KYUSHU

3 MINAMOTO VICTORY
The turning of the tide and the treachery of Taguchi Shigeyoshi change the course of the battle. The Minamoto start to overwhelm the Taira galleys and, when Taira no Tomomori and the emperor's family commit suicide, the battle comes to an end.

THE GEMPEI WARS
The wars fought in medieval Japan between the rival Minamoto and Taira clans became the subject of a popular epic sung by blind musicians. In this detail from a screen that shows the last great battles, the Taira ships are being attacked by the mounted warriors of Minamoto. The Taira managed to escape their pursuers for a time, but were defeated at the decisive naval battle of Dan-no-Ura in April 1185.

BATTLES FOR THE MEDITERRANEAN

DURING THE THOUSAND YEARS between 500 and 1500 CE maritime powers rose and fell in the Mediterranean. The initial dominance of the Byzantine Empire, the successor state to Rome, was first challenged by the Muslim Arabs, then supplanted by the Italian maritime republics, Venice, Genoa, and Pisa, and by the Catalan galleys of the kingdom of Aragon. With no single state capable of achieving command of the sea, outbreaks of naval warfare were inevitable. Innovative weaponry, from Greek fire to the crossbow, produced important changes in combat at sea, as did variation in ship design and rowing systems. But galleys still predominated and boarding the enemy remained the essential goal in battle, as it had been in Roman times.

The sack of Constantinople
Venice contracted with the organizers of the Fourth Crusade to ship their army to Egypt. When the crusaders were unable to pay the full sum, the fleet was diverted to the Byzantine capital, Constantinople, where, in 1204 the Venetians and crusaders ended up capturing and sacking the city.

TACTICS AND TECHNOLOGY

The dominant warship of the naval battles between the Byzantines and the Arabs was the dromon. This was a formidable platform for marines, catapults, and flamethrowers, heading into battle propelled not only by up to 100 oarsmen but also by sails – a radical departure from the practice of the ancient world. The raised beak at the prow of the dromon would smash through an opponent's oars and provide a bridge for boarding soldiers to swarm across. Oarsmen were expected to take up arms and join the fighting once the enemy was engaged at close quarters. From the 12th century the crossbow was introduced as an important element in Mediterranean sea battles. The Genoese and the Aragonese were especially famed for their use of this weapon. It added a deadly new element to the array of missiles hurled against an enemy as galleys closed for combat – which included incendiary grenades, darts, containers filled with soap thrown onto the opponent's deck to make it slippery under foot, and lime dust intended to blind the enemies' eyes. Galleys entered battle in line abreast, each ship protecting its neighbour's vulnerable flank. Maintaining formation was considered of far greater importance than manoeuvre – galleys were sometimes loosely linked together with cables, to keep them in line and prevent an enemy penetrating between them.

SHIFTING POWER

Similar tactics and technology were used by all the combatants in medieval Mediterranean naval conflicts. For example, the dromon and its style of warfare – including the use of Greek fire – was invented by the Byzantines but was over time adopted by the Arabs as well. Relative success in naval warfare depended upon material resources and seafaring and fighting skills. Once the Byzantine Empire had resisted the initial Arab onslaught in the 7th and early 8th centuries, which briefly threatened to overrun its capital Constantinople, it remained a dominant presence at sea in the eastern Mediterranean because it could afford a large fleet and dockyards.

From the end of the 11th century the balance of naval power shifted as maritime trade brought wealth to relatively small states further west. The Italian republics of Venice and Genoa had populations of only a few hundred thousand, but their involvement in the Crusades in the 12th and 13th centuries enabled them to gain a dominant position in the trade of the Levant and the Black Sea. Their profits provided them with the funds

---

WEAPONS AND TECHNOLOGY

GREEK FIRE

The inflammable liquid known as "Greek fire" was reportedly invented by an engineer called Callanicus in Constantinople around 670 CE. It was used chiefly in incendiary grenades and flamethrowers. A small catapult on deck propelled clay jars containing the substance onto enemy ships; the jar broke apart and the fire ignited. Alternatively, a bronze tube was mounted at the prow of a ship, through which the Greek fire was pumped, projecting a stream of flame. For psychological effect, the tube of the flamethrower often stuck out from the mouth of a carved dragon's or lion's head. It was known as a "siphon". The composition of Greek fire was a carefully guarded secret and can still only be guessed at. It was employed in Byzantine naval warfare for five centuries.

Greek fire in action
The few contemporary illustrations of ships using Greek fire in battle give little clue as to its composition or how it was propelled.

Portolan chart
From the 13th century Mediterranean sailors used a distinctive kind of map, the portolan. Coasts and ports were well charted and the maps were criss-crossed with a network of lines projecting from compasses.

VENETIAN EMPIRE

Of the many medieval Mediterranean states, Venice was the quintessential naval power. The shipbuilding and repair facilities of the Venetian Arsenal, founded around 1200, grew into the biggest industrial enterprise in Europe – it was said they could build and fit out a galley in a single day. Venetian galleys were rowed "alla sensile" – with oarsmen grouped in threes, each with a single oar – and proved successful, highly manoeuvrable warships. The Venetians were generally reckoned the first to adopt such innovations as the compass, the stern rudder, and the lateen sail. Their oarsmen – volunteers or conscripts – were honoured seamen rather than galley slaves, some earning promotion through long careers to captain. By the 15th century Venice had created a Mediterranean empire based on sea power, as Athens had done in ancient times. But by the end of that century profound changes were under way, both in the naval balance of power with the rise of the Ottoman Empire, and in technology with the introduction of cannon into naval warfare.

to develop powerful navies to defend their trade routes and fight their competitors – chiefly one another. There was in this period only relatively minor conflict between Christians and Muslims at sea, but intense rivalry between Christian states, much of it fought out around the coasts of Italy and Sicily between galleys from Catalonia and Provence as well as various Italian ports.

Provisioning the Crusades
The larger items of cargo are being loaded aboard a cog, while the galley in front of it is filled with armed men. Among the banners of the various crusading states involved, those of England and France are most prominent, along with the crossed keys of the papacy.

BYZANTINE–ARAB WARS

WHEN THE ARABS, inspired by the newly founded religion of Islam, embarked upon their campaigns of conquest around 630 CE, the dominant naval power in the Mediterranean was the Byzantine Empire. This status was swiftly challenged by the crushing victory of an Arab fleet at the battle of the Masts in 655. Although the technologically innovative use of Greek fire helped the Byzantines drive back Arab ships from under the walls of Constantinople two decades later, the fall of

Carthage to the Muslims at the end of the 7th century extended Arab sea power into the western Mediterranean. Fierce naval battles were fought over the following two centuries in struggles for control of major islands such as Sicily, Cyprus, and Crete. In the 11th and 12th centuries the strategic situation began to shift, with Turks replacing Arabs as the major power in the Muslim world and the Byzantines becoming increasingly dependent upon the navies of the Italian city-states of Genoa and Venice.

THE MEDITERRANEAN WORLD c.650–950

Following the conquest of Egypt in 639–646, it took Arab armies just 70 years to extend the lands of the Caliphate across North Africa into the Iberian Peninsula. Since the Arabs had no experience of seafaring, their conquests by sea were less spectacular. In the east the Byzantine Empire remained a powerful block to Arab expansion, but in the 9th century the Byzantines were ejected from Sicily, and Arab raids extended into Italy and the South of France, where Arab corsairs established bases.

KEY

- Abbasid Caliphate c.850
- Other Islamic states
- Byzantine Empire
- → Arab invasion/ raid
- Arab victory
- Byzantine victory

ARAB EXPANSION IN THE MEDITERRANEAN

BATTLE OF THE MASTS

Date 655
Forces Byzantines: c.500 ships; Arabs: c.200 ships
Losses Byzantines: c.400 ships; Arabs: unknown

Location Off Lycia, southern Turkey

The Arab conquests of the 7th century gave them control of ports and seafaring populations on the coasts of Egypt and Syria. Muawiyah, the governor of Syria, urged the development of naval warfare but Caliph Omar, a man bred in the Arabian desert, was unconvinced, describing people on board ship as like "a worm in a log of wood". When Uthman succeeded to the caliphate in 644, however, Muawiyah was authorized to develop a fleet, as was the governor of Egypt, Abdullah bin Saad bin Abil Sarh. This took two years, after which

the Arabs began conquering or raiding Byzantine-ruled islands throughout the eastern Mediterranean.

With the fall of Rhodes in 654, the young Byzantine Emperor Constans II woke up to the threat and sought to organize a counter-offensive. The following year he sailed south in command of an imperial fleet possibly numbering 500 ships. At the same time, the

combined Egyptian and Syrian fleets, under the command of Abdullah bin Saad, were advancing along the coast of Asia Minor, intending to raid the shores and islands of the Aegean. The Arabs came upon the Byzantine fleet anchored off southwest Turkey.

The Arabs were probably outnumbered by more than two to one, but after some hesitation they decided to attack.

Both fleets carried archers and as the distance between the ships closed, showers of arrows

fell upon both sides, causing substantial casualties. The Byzantine were more skilled in naval manoeuvre and this, together with their superior numbers, at first gave them the advantage. At one point the Arab flagship was grappled by a Byzantine dromon and almost captured. But soon ships became so packed together that men fought with swords and daggers from deck to deck. The forest of masts gave the battle its name – in Arabic, *That al-Sawari*.

The tide of battle turned in favour of the Arabs. Amid scenes of terrible carnage, many Byzantine dromons were boarded and captured. Constans himself escaped after prudently changing clothes with one of his men. The Byzantine navy was shattered. But fortunately for the empire, the following year the Arab world was thrown into political turmoil, ending any further naval ventures until the establishment of Muawiyah as caliph in 661.

Byzantine dromon
The word "dromon", meaning "swift runner", was applied to a range of ships, from small galleys to large biremes like the one shown here.

THE SIEGE OF CONSTANTINOPLE

The establishment of the Umayyad Caliphate in Damascus, Syria, in 661 was followed by a reinvigoration of Arab efforts to conquer the Byzantine Empire. The first Umayyad caliph, Muawiyah, understood the importance of sea power and in 672 sent a fleet through the Dardanelles into the Sea of Marmara, where it established a base at Cyzicus, about 80km (50 miles) from Constantinople. Four years later Muawiyah's son Yazid led a full-scale naval attack on the Byzantine capital.

A FOUR-YEAR CAMPAIGN

The Byzantine ruler, Constantine IV, was a vigorous leader who ensured the city's defences were in excellent repair. The Arabs used their ships as artillery platforms, sailing up to the city walls and bombarding them with rocks from giant catapults mounted on deck. The Byzantines responded with harassing sorties by small, fast-moving galleys, some of them probably employing the newly invented Greek fire as a shock tactic. The Byzantine fleet also prevented

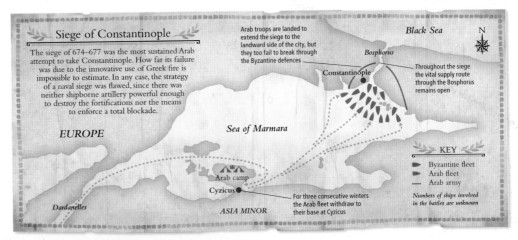

Siege of Constantinople

The siege of 674–677 was the most sustained Arab attempt to take Constantinople. How far its failure was due to the innovative use of Greek fire is impossible to estimate. In any case, the strategy of a naval siege was flawed, since there was neither shipborne artillery powerful enough to destroy the fortifications nor the means to enforce a total blockade.

Arab troops are landed to extend the siege to the landward side of the city, but they too fail to break through the Byzantine defences

Throughout the siege the vital supply route through the Bosphorus remains open

EUROPE

Sea of Marmara

Black Sea

Bosphorus

Constantinople

N

Arab camp

Cyzicus

For three consecutive winters the Arab fleet withdraw to their base at Cyzicus

Dardanelles

ASIA MINOR

KEY
- Byzantine fleet
- Arab fleet
- Arab army

Numbers of ships involved in the battles are unknown

the Arabs sailing into the Bosphorus, which remained a lifeline for grain supplies from across the Black Sea.

The Arab attacks on Constantinople were maintained through the summer of 674 without much effect on the impressive fortifications. In October the Arab fleet withdrew to Cyzicus, where they refitted their ships and rested their crews, ready to renew the fight in the spring. This pattern was repeated stubbornly through to autumn 677, before the Arabs finally gave up. In that year they suffered two disasters. They were defeated by a Byzantine fleet at Syllaeum, a site probably in the Sea of Marmara, and a large part of a force returning to Syria was sunk in a storm.

The walls of Constantinople
When the Arabs attacked Constantinople in 674, the city was protected by the Theodosian Walls, built in the 5th century ce. Restored stretches of the land wall still stand, though the original sea wall has long since disappeared.

BYZANTINE—ARAB WARS

SIEGE OF CONSTANTINOPLE

Date	674–677
Location	Sea of Marmara, near Istanbul, Turkey
Result	Byzantine victory

COMBATANTS

BYZANTINE EMPIRE	UMAYYAD CALIPHATE

COMMANDERS

Emperor Constantine IV	Caliph Muawiyah I

FORCES

Ships: unknown	Ships: unknown

LOSSES

Men: unknown	Men: unknown
Ships: unknown	Ships: unknown

BYZANTINE—ARAB WARS

CARTHAGE

Date	698
Forces	Byzantines: unknown; Arabs: unknown
Losses	Unknown

Location Carthage, near present-day Tunis

When the port of Carthage was lost in the Arab advance across North Africa, Byzantine Emperor Leontius sent a large fleet under Ioannes the Patrician to retake the city. Caught by surprise, the Arabs were defeated at sea and Carthage returned to Byzantine rule – but not for long. The Arabs mounted a siege by sea and land. The city held out while resupplied by sea, but the Arab fleet eventually broke through the line of ships defending the harbour. Carthage fell but Ioannes escaped with much of the fleet, only to be murdered by his second-in-command, a German called Apsimarus. With the support of his mutinous crews, Apsimarus then sailed to Constantinople and seized the throne as Emperor Tiberios III.

BYZANTINE—ARAB WARS

CALABRIA

Date	964
Forces	Byzantines: unknown; Arabs: unknown
Losses	Unknown

Location Off Calabria, southern Italy

In 827 Arabs and Berbers invaded Byzantine-ruled Sicily from North Africa. The struggle for control of the island lasted for more than a century, during which time Byzantine naval forces based in southern Italy fought a number of battles with an Arab fleet based in Palermo. By 964 Byzantine resistance was at an end and Patriarch Nicetas organized a squadron of ships to evacuate the last Byzantine forces from eastern Sicily. Unfortunately the squadron was intercepted by a superior Arab force off the coast of Calabria. The Arabs reportedly used swimmers to attack the Byzantine ships with incendiary devices, an unconventional tactic that contributed to the total destruction of the patriarch's squadron.

THE RISE OF THE ITALIAN MARITIME REPUBLICS

THE ITALIAN CITY-STATES of Venice, Genoa, and Pisa grew rich on seaborne trade and providing transport and naval support for the Crusades. Their rivalry for control of trade routes from the Levant and the Black Sea led inevitably to conflict. Pisa was knocked out of the competition by defeat at the hands of Genoa in 1284, while Venice and Genoa fought one another to exhaustion in four inconclusive wars between 1253 and 1381. The battles between Venetian and Genoese galley fleets often resulted in crushing losses for one side or the other, but defeat had little long-term effect as new galleys were built and fresh crews were recruited. Losses of merchant convoys to commerce raiders often had more strategic significance. By the 15th century Genoa was becoming exhausted while Venice faced the task of defending its scattered possessions in the eastern Mediterranean against the rising power of the Ottoman Empire.

THE ITALIAN MARITIME REPUBLICS c.1050–1400

Although their territorial possessions were negligible, the Italian maritime republics gained extraordinary wealth through trade with the east – especially in silks and spices. Venice acquired a string of ports on the Adriatic and the coasts of Greece, while Genoa had trading posts in Greece and even on the Black Sea.

KEY
- Venetian Republic and possessions c.1270
- Republic of Genoa
- Republic of Pisa
- Genoese victory
- Venetian victory
- Inconclusive battle

NORMAN–BYZANTINE WAR
DURAZZO

Date June 1081
Forces Venetians: 59 ships; Normans: 150 ships
Losses unknown

Location Adriatic, off modern-day Albania

When Norman adventurer Robert Guiscard conquered Sicily and southern Italy, threatening Venetian shipping in the Adriatic, Venice agreed an alliance with the Byzantines. In spring 1081 Guiscard sailed with 30,000 men from Brindisi, captured Corfu, and besieged the city of Durazzo. A Venetian fleet under Doge Silvio arrived to confront the Normans anchored in the city's harbour. During the night the doge had his largest ships anchor in a line, with cables looped from ship to ship, making an impassable barrier described as a "sea harbour". Behind this he positioned his war galleys.

In the morning the Normans, led by Guiscard's son Bohemond, attacked. The Venetians had built towers on their ships, which were manned by soldiers armed with heavy timbers studded with iron spikes. When the Norman ships were halted by the Venetian barrier, the soldiers hurled the timbers down to smash holes in their hulls. Bohemond's ship was one of those sunk. Retreating from this bombardment, the Normans were pursued to shore by the Venetian galleys and routed. The battle marked a significant step in the rise of Venetian maritime power.

FIRST VENETIAN–GENOESE WAR
TRAPANI

Date June 1266
Forces Genoese: 27 ships; Venetians: 24 ships
Losses Genoese: entire fleet; Venetians: none

Location Off western Sicily

During the first war between Genoa and Venice, Venetian admiral Jacopo Dandolo's galleys sailing round Sicily met Lanfranco Borbonino's Genoese fleet sailing south from Corsica. Aware that most of his crews were Lombards with no seafaring skills and no battle experience, Borbonino adopted a static defensive formation, cabling his galleys together with their sterns to the shore. The Venetians, experienced sailors inspired by patriotic fervour, launched a vigorous and noisy attack, exciting terror in the Lombards who abandoned ship in droves, making for the nearby shore. Three of the Genoese galleys were burned and the rest captured.

PISAN–GENOESE WAR
MELORIA

Date 6 August 1284
Forces Genoese: 93 galleys; Pisans: 72 galleys
Losses Genoese: unknown; Pisans: c.40 galleys, c.10,000 casualties and prisoners

Location Off Livorno, Italy

Genoa and Pisa went to war in 1282 over control of the islands of Corsica and Sardinia. In the summer of 1284 the Genoese sent part of their fleet to Sardinia under the command of Benedetto Zaccaria. Seeing an opportunity to catch their enemy at a disadvantage, the Pisans dispatched their entire fleet to attack Genoa. Unfortunately for them, Zaccaria returned just as their ships reached the city. The outnumbered Pisans fled for home, with the Genoese, under the overall command of Oberto Doria, in pursuit. The Pisans reached the safety of Porto Pisano, at the mouth of the Arno, but were lured out by a ruse. Doria drew up his own 63 galleys in a line offshore; Zaccaria's 30 galleys lurked behind with their masts lowered. Believing they had the numerical advantage, the Pisans' Venetian commander Alberto Morosini and his second-in-command Ugolino della Gherardesca led their 72 galleys out to sea. By the time they saw Zaccaria's galleys coming up to join Doria, it was too late to retreat.

The Pisans fought fiercely against the odds. The opening exchange of missiles – bolts fired from crossbows, stones hurled by mangonels – was followed by boarding and murderous hand-to-hand combat. Many of the Pisans wore armour, which exposed them to heat exhaustion under the summer sun; the Genoese fought stripped to their shirts and lasted better. Morosini's flagship, eventually under simultaneous attack from Doria and Zaccaria, was overcome and the standard cut down. Ugolino escaped with a handful of galleys.

After this catastrophic defeat, Pisa lacked the resources to build and crew a new fleet. It never regained its status as a naval or commercial power.

Survivor of Meloria
Ugolino later starved to death in captivity with his sons and grandsons, an event narrated in Dante's *Inferno*.

THE BATTLE OF CURZOLA

An indirect legacy of the battle
It is said that Marco Polo began dictating his famous memoirs while in Genoese captivity after the battle of Curzola. He is seen here departing from Venice with his father and uncle on his journey to China.

The battle of Curzola occurred during the Second Venetian-Genoese War (1294–99). In 1298 Genoa mounted a bold raid into Venetian home waters. Sailing from La Spezia on the west coast of Italy, a fleet of Genoese galleys made its way round to the Adriatic via Tunisia and Sicily. It was commanded by the veteran Admiral Lampa Doria, younger brother of the Doria who had triumphed over the Pisans at Meloria 14 years earlier. Entering the Adriatic Doria's galleys were scattered by a storm, but most of them reassembled and proceeded up the coast of Dalmatia, burning and plundering the Venetian-ruled towns of the mainland and offshore islands. On the afternoon of 6 September they were busy pillaging the island of Curzola when a large Venetian fleet suddenly appeared on the scene.

Venice had been caught off guard by the attack on its Dalmatian possessions. A squadron of galleys commanded by Maffeo Querini was brought back from the Ionian islands and joined with freshly equipped and crewed galleys from Venice and Dalmatia to form the largest war fleet the Venetians had ever assembled. Quality had, however, been sacrificed to

Deadly crossbow
The principal Genoese weapon both on land and at sea was the crossbow. The highly trained Genoese crossbowmen were feared across Europe and the Middle East.

quantity. The hastily conscripted soldiers and sailors did not have the skills usually expected of Venetian galley crews. The fleet was commanded by Andrea Dandolo, son of a former Doge.

The Venetians found the Genoese galleys in a sheltered bay near the eastern tip of the island late on 6 September. Battle was joined early the following morning and lasted through to evening. It was a savage combat. The Genoese suffered heavy casualties, including Lampa Doria's son Octavian, killed by an arrow while fighting on the forecastle of his father's flagship. Seeing his men waver, the admiral had his son's body thrown unceremoniously into the sea

and ordered the fight to continue. The Venetians, however, came off worse. At a crucial moment, 16 Genoese galleys that had become detached from the main body in the earlier gale returned to attack the Venetians from the flank. Only Querini's experienced crews had the skills to manoeuvre out of the ensuing debacle, but led back into the mêlée in an attempt to rescue Dandolo, they too were overcome.

Only a handful of galleys returned to Venice to report the disaster.

Taken prisoner and bound in chains, Dandolo committed suicide by dashing his head against one of the rowing benches. Among other prisoners taken by the Genoese was Marco Polo, who had commanded one of the Venetian galleys.

The battle had little political consequence. The war ended the following year with no significant advantage to the Genoese.

1200 BCE – 1550 CE

THIRD VENETIAN–GENOESE WAR

BOSPHORUS

Date 13 February 1352
Forces Venetians, Aragonese, Byzantines: 78 ships; Genoese: 64 ships
Losses Unknown

Location Near Constantinople

In its third war with Genoa, Venice was allied with Aragon, which included Catalonia, and the Byzantine Empire. In February 1352, Paganino Doria's Genoese fleet was wintering on the Bosphorus when a fleet of mostly Venetian and Catalan galleys under Niccolo Pisani appeared. The Genoese came out to give battle and a fierce action ensued, fought beyond nightfall in strong winds and rough seas. Next day Pisani judged his fleet no longer in fit shape to continue and withdrew.

THIRD VENETIAN–GENOESE WAR

ALGHERO

Date 29 August 1353
Forces Venetians and Aragonese: unknown; Genoese: unknown
Losses Venetians and Aragonese: unknown; Genoese: 33 galleys

Location Off Sardinia

After the battle of the Bosphorus the Byzantines made peace with Genoa, but the war continued. In summer 1353 the Aragonese were fighting for control of Sardinia, supported by a force of Venetian and Catalan galleys under Niccolo Pisani. The Genoese, without their inspired admiral Paganino Doria, were defeated in another fierce battle. Pisani took 4,500 prisoners, most of whom were executed. Genoa was then forced to accept rule by Milan as the price for financing a new fleet.

THIRD VENETIAN–GENOESE WAR

MODON

Date 3 November 1354
Forces Venetians: unknown; Genoese: unknown
Losses Unknown

Location Gulf of Sapienza, Peloponnese

In 1354 Niccolo Pisani anchored his fleet for the winter at Porto Longo, near Modon. The Genoese had rebuilt their fleet with Milanese money after the defeat at Alghero, so Paganino Doria sailed to Porto Longo to challenge the Venetians to fight. Outnumbered, Pisani refused, so the Genoese penetrated the harbour and overwhelmed the Venetians, capturing Pisani and many others. Venice made peace shortly afterward.

THE WAR OF CHIOGGIA

The conflict known as the War of Chioggia (1378–81) was the last fling in the long series of confrontations between Venice and Genoa. In alliance with Hungary and Padua, the Genoese came close to inflicting a humiliating defeat on their Venetian enemies.

Venice's problems began in the spring of 1379. A fleet commanded by Vettor Pisani – nephew of the Niccolo Pisano defeated at Modon and one of Venice's most successful admirals – had wintered at Pola in the northern

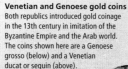

Venetian and Genoese gold coins
Both republics introduced gold coinage in the 13th century in imitation of the Byzantine Empire and the Arab world. The coins shown here are a Genoese grosso (below) and a Venetian ducat or sequin (above).

Adriatic. The galleys were still there on 7 May, refitting and taking on supplies, when a Genoese squadron appeared at the harbour mouth. Pisani had only 16 galleys ready for action, but this seemed enough since there were only 14 Genoese galleys in sight. When the Venetians sailed out to attack, however, 10 more enemy galleys appeared from behind a headland. After fierce fighting the majority of the Venetian galleys were captured along with their crews. Pisani survived but, on his return to Venice, was permanently banned from holding a command and, for a time, clapped in irons.

The destruction of its galleys at Pola put Venice at great risk. Its other major fleet, commanded by Carlo Zeno, was far away, commerce raiding in the eastern Mediterranean. Doge Andrea Contarini hastily improved the defences of the city, but could do nothing to prevent a reinforced Genoese fleet of 47 galleys under Pietro Doria entering the Venetian lagoon in early August. With the aid of the land forces of Francesco da Carrara, lord of Padua, Doria seized the port of Chioggia at the southern end of the lagoon.

Pisani was immensely popular with his sailors – he was known as the "chief and father of all the seamen of Venice".

At this moment of crisis, many men refused to serve under anybody else. The Venetian authorities had to give in to popular pressure and reinstated the sacked admiral, placing him in control of the defence of the city.

VENICE STRIKES BACK

The Genoese did not attempt a direct attack on Venice, relying on a blockade by land and sea to reduce the city to surrender. Doge Contarini did in fact seek peace terms, but found the price too high to pay. Pisani had no intention of surrendering. On 21 December he launched an operation to turn the tables on the Genoese. Under cover of darkness he sank stone-filled hulks in the channels leading from Chioggia to the open sea. The original besiegers

66

TAKE BACK YOUR PRISONERS ... I SHALL BE AT VENICE IN A FEW DAYS TO RELEASE THEM ... FROM YOUR DUNGEONS.

FRANCESCO DA CARRARA RULER OF PADUA, REFUSING THE VENETIAN PEACE OFFER

99

now found themselves besieged. It still seemed possible that the hungry and demoralized Venetians would give up the fight when, on 1 January 1380, Carlo Zeno's ships were sighted on the horizon. This tipped the balance of forces decisively in favour of Venice. A Genoese relief fleet led by Matteo Marufo arrived on 12 May, but could find no way through to Chioggia.

On 24 June, the Genoese and their allies inside Chioggia surrendered. When a peace treaty was signed the following year, the terms were equable, but in reality Genoa's attempt to win control of the priceless trade routes through the eastern Mediterranean had failed. Venetian naval power would not be challenged again until the rise of the Turkish Ottoman Empire.

Venetian galleys outside Chioggia
In this triumphalist painting celebrating Venice's victory over the Genoese in 1380, the galleys depicted are typical 16th-century vessels rather than those in use two centuries earlier.

FOURTH VENETIAN–GENOESE WAR

THE WAR OF CHIOGGIA

Date	16 August 1379–24 June 1380
Location	Venice lagoon
Result	Venetian victory

☞ COMBATANTS ☜

VENICE	GENOA, PADUA, HUNGARY

☞ COMMANDERS ☜

Vettor Pisani	Pietro Doria
Carlo Zeno	

☞ FORCES ☜

Ships: unknown	Ships: unknown

☞ LOSSES ☜

Men: unknown	Men: unknown
Ships: unknown	Ships: unknown

THE WAR FOR SICILY

WHEN THE PEOPLE OF SICILY rose in rebellion against their hated ruler Charles of Anjou in 1282, King Peter III of Aragon landed troops in Sicily to fight the Angevins. The complex conflict that followed the uprising known as the "Sicilian Vespers" brought a number of naval engagements, from the battle of Malta in 1283 to Ponza in 1300, in which Aragonese admiral Roger di Lauria proved himself a ruthless master of galley warfare. The war ended in 1302 with the Aragonese in control of Sicily and the Angevins ruling Naples and southern Italy.

WAR OF THE SICILIAN VESPERS 1282–1302

Southern Italy and Sicily had been part of the domains of Holy Roman Emperor Frederick II. When he died in 1250, the papacy was determined that the kingdom should not pass to his heirs and in 1265 gave it to Charles of Anjou, brother of Louis IX of France (St Louis).

KEY

- Kingdom of Sicily (to House of Anjou) 1282
- Kingdom of Aragon
- Route of Aragonese invasion
- Aragonese victory over the Angevins
- Aragonese–Angevin victory over Sicily

WAR OF THE SICILIAN VESPERS

GULF OF NAPLES

Date 5 June 1284
Forces Aragonese: 36 galleys; Angevins: c.30 galleys
Losses Aragonese: unknown; Angevins: c.12 galleys captured

Location Gulf of Naples, Italy

The crushing victory of the Aragonese fleet at Malta in 1283 gave Admiral Roger di Lauria a temporary naval superiority he was keen to exploit. Charles of Salerno, son and heir of Charles of Anjou, was in command in Naples, capital of the mainland half of the kingdom of Sicily. In spring 1284 Charles of Anjou was preparing to send powerful naval reinforcements to Naples. Di Lauria took his fleet to blockade the city, hoping to provoke Charles of Salerno into sending his galleys out to fight before reinforcements arrived.

Charles of Anjou had given his son strict instructions to avoid a sea battle, but the young man was impetuous and eager to demonstrate his courage and

fighting prowess. He was humiliated to stand by passively as di Lauria's fleet captured incoming ships and carried out raids around Naples. On 5 June the Aragonese admiral succeeded in luring Charles of Salerno out of harbour with the apparent offer of an easy victory. Making a conspicuous show of sending a dozen of his galleys away to the south, di Lauria approached the harbour with a weakened force. Charles could not resist the temptation to engage with a numerically inferior enemy and led his

Neapolitan and Provencal galleys out to attack. Di Lauria turned and fled southward with Charles in pursuit.

As the Angevin galleys approached Castellammare on the Gulf of Naples, the trap was sprung. The group of Aragonese galleys that had sailed southward rejoined the main body of di Lauria's ships. The opposing forces were now roughly equal in numbers, but the Aragonese were far superior in organization and fighting experience. Forming a crescent in line abreast,

they turned and bore down on Charles's galleys, which had been pursuing in no particular formation. The Neapolitan galleys had lagged behind the others and were thus able to flee in disorderly fashion back to the harbour. The leading group of Provencal galleys, including Charles's own ship, was outflanked and attacked from the sides and rear. Outnumbered and outfought, all these galleys were captured after a short, sharp action. Charles's ship was the last to surrender, deluged with the bolts of di Lauria's Catalan crossbowmen and assailed by combat swimmers.

The capture of Charles was the crucial outcome of a victory otherwise lacking in strategic significance. He was carried off to Aragon, where he was held prisoner until 1288. He was then released after swearing that he would cede Sicily to the Aragonese, but this was a promise he felt free to renounce once he had returned to Naples.

Coronation of Charles of Anjou
This French manuscript illumination shows Charles arriving in Rome by sea in 1265 and being crowned king of Naples and Sicily by Pope Clement IV.

The Gulf of Naples
The spectacular bay dominated by Mount Vesuvius was the scene of three of Roger di Lauria's great naval victories, the first being over Charles of Anjou's son Charles of Salerno in 1284.

WAR OF THE SICILIAN VESPERS

LAS HORMIGAS

Date 4 September 1285
Forces Aragonese: 40 galleys; French: 30 galleys
Losses Aragonese: unknown; French: 13 galleys captured

Location
Off Catalonia, Spain

In 1285 Philip III of France invaded the kingdom of Aragon, a rapacious enterprise declared a crusade by a partisan pope. French troops advanced down the coast of Catalonia, supported by a force of Provencal and Genoese galleys. Roger di Lauria's fleet sailed from Sicily to help resist the invasion.

Arriving in Barcelona at the end of August, di Lauria led his own 40 galleys from Sicily and 10 Catalan galleys north toward Gerona, which was under siege. At the same time, unaware of di Lauria's arrival, the French fleet advanced south toward Barcelona, hoping to annihilate the small Catalan galley force. The two fleets met, to their mutual surprise, some time before daybreak on 4 September. Chroniclers disagree about almost every detail of the battle that followed. In the darkness the action must have developed into a confused close-quarters mêlée, with boarding the only effective tactic.

A lucky dozen of the outnumbered French galleys escaped back to Aigues-Mortes. The rest fell into the hands of a vengeful enemy. The wounded were tied to cables behind galleys and left to drown. Fit prisoners were blinded and sent back to the French king, led by one of their number left with a single eye. The invasion failed.

WAR OF THE SICILIAN VESPERS

THE COUNTS

Date 23 June 1287
Forces Aragonese: 44 galleys; Angevins: c.70 galleys
Losses Aragonese: unknown; Angevins: 40 galleys captured

Location
Bay of Naples, Italy

By 1287 the original contenders for the throne of Sicily had disappeared from the scene. Charles of Anjou died in 1285, leaving southern Italy to his son Charles of Salerno, still a prisoner of the Aragonese after his defeat at the battle of the Gulf of Naples. In 1286 Peter III of Aragon also died. He left his Aragonese kingdom to his eldest son Alfonso III, but Sicily to his second son James II. In the absence of the imprisoned Charles II, the Angevin cause was led by Count Robert II of Artois. He assembled substantial land and naval forces in Naples for an invasion of Sicily, hoping to prevent James II's succession.

The Aragonese defence of the island still lay primarily in the hands of Roger di Lauria and his experienced fleet. In the spring of 1287 he sailed to relieve Augusta.

Catalan astrolabe
Many of the Catalans' naval skills were inherited from Spain's Muslims, as was the use of the astrolabe as an astronomical aid. This one is from the late 13th century.

c.1245–1305

ROGER DI LAURIA

ADMIRAL OF THE ARAGONESE FLEET

Roger di Lauria was born into the nobility of Calabria, southern Italy, but was driven into exile at the court of Peter III of Aragon when the Angevins seized his family's lands in 1266. He proved his worth as a soldier before his appointment as admiral at the start of the War of the Sicilian Vespers in 1282. His energy and administrative skill were demonstrated in strengthening the Aragonese fleet, but he is respected above all for his leadership in combat. He never lost a single sea battle, showing a cunning, good judgement, and boldness that have earned him a reputation as the finest of medieval naval commanders. Ruthless toward his enemies, he remained unswervingly loyal to the Aragonese throne.

in eastern Sicily, which had been seized by Angevin troops, leaving the west of the island vulnerable to invasion. But the Angevins failed to act and di Lauria had time to sail back around the south of Sicily to seek battle with their fleet. In June he found them in harbour at Naples.

The Count of Artois was willing to send his galleys out to fight. He had a far more substantial galley force than the one defeated by di Lauria off Naples three years before. There was also an impressive array of military leaders at his side, including Reynald III Quarrel, Count of Avella; Hugh, Count of Brienne, who was ruler of the Principality of Taranto; and Guy de Montfort, Count of Nola, son of the Simon de Montfort who had once ruled England. But these counts, for whom the battle is named, were no match for di Lauria in a sea fight. Far superior at manoeuvre, his experienced and highly motivated Sicilian galley crews attacked their opponents from the beam, destroying their oars and leaving them immobilized, to be massacred by the Catalan crossbowmen and boarding parties of fierce Spanish light troops, the *almogavers*.

More than half the Angevin galleys were captured, along with some 5,000 crew and soldiers. Those taken prisoner included Hugh of Brienne, and Guy de Montfort, who did not survive his captivity. The planned invasion of Sicily was abandoned, enabling James II to confirm his hold on the throne.

WAR OF THE SICILIAN VESPERS

CAPE ORLANDO

Date 4 July 1299
Forces Aragonese and Angevins: 56 galleys; Sicilians: 48 galleys
Losses Aragonese and Angevins: unknown: Sicilians: 36 galleys captured

Location
Off northern Sicily

In the 1290s the struggle for Sicily took on a radically altered shape. James II inherited the throne of Aragon, leaving Sicily to his brother Frederick. But James then made an alliance with his old enemy, Charles II of Anjou, and led an expedition to regain Sicily for the Angevins. Roger di Lauria stayed loyal to Aragon and found himself fighting against his old Sicilian fleet, now led by Frederick and admiral Conrad d'Oria.

In summer 1299 King James and di Lauria sailed from Naples for northern Sicily, the war galleys escorting a convoy of troop transports. Frederick sailed from Messina to intercept, but moved too slowly. James was able to land his troops and horses at Cape Orlando.

When the Sicilians arrived, an onshore breeze made it hard for di Lauria to leave the bay where he was moored. Instead he adopted a tight defensive formation, his galleys drawn up in line close to the shore and linked by cables.

Frederick entered the bay on the morning of 4 July, also placing his fleet in a cable-linked line. The galleys exchanged missiles at distance until a Sicilian captain, tiring of the punishment his crew was taking from the Catalan crossbowmen, cut his cables and plunged forward to engage the enemy at close quarters. Others followed suit and the battle became a mêlée. In the heat and exhaustion of combat Frederick, in the centre

Prisoners of war
Angevin prisoners are escorted onto a Sicilian galley. Sicilian soldiers and sailors captured by di Lauria were not so lucky – they were often executed on the spot.

of the Sicilian line, fainted and was rowed from the battle. Di Lauria got some of his galleys behind the Sicilians, who were gradually ground down in fierce fighting. Only 12 Sicilian galleys escaped. As at Las Hormigas, di Lauria was savage in victory, slaughtering the crews of captured galleys out of hand.

WAR OF THE SICILIAN VESPERS

PONZA

Date 14 June 1300
Forces Aragonese and Angevins: 59 galleys; Sicilians 32 galleys
Losses Aragonese and Angevins: 1 galley captured; Sicilians: c.20 galleys captured

Location Gulf of Gaeta, north of Naples, Italy

Despite his crushing victory at Cape Orlando, James II failed to seize Sicily for the Angevins from his brother Frederick. The following year a rebuilt Sicilian fleet boldly entered the Bay of Naples, challenging Roger di Lauria's Angevin galleys to come out and fight. Di Lauria prudently chose to wait for reinforcements from Genoa and Apulia before accepting the challenge. The one-sided engagement took place off the island of Ponza. The Sicilians' admiral Conrad d'Oria bravely attacked di Lauria's flagship, but despite inflicting some damage, was obliged to surrender, along with more than half his force. Frederick nonetheless retained Sicily in the peace treaty signed two years later.

THE AGE OF GALLEYS

THE BATTLE OF MALTA

The outbreak of the War of the Sicilian Vespers in 1282 set Charles of Anjou, Count of Provence and ruler of Naples and Sicily, against King Peter III of Aragon, whose domains included Catalonia. Initially the Aragonese had the better of the Angevins at sea, so Charles ordered the creation of a new galley fleet at Marseille – to be manned by Provencal crews and soldiers, and commanded by two Marseillais admirals, Guillaume de Cornut and Bartolomé Bonvin. In June 1283 these Provencal galleys arrived in Malta to aid an Angevin garrison besieged in Fort St Angelo on the Grand Harbour.

In the Sicilian port of Messina, Aragon's newly appointed admiral Roger di Lauria was informed of the Angevin move and set off in pursuit. The Aragonese fleet was considered the best in the western Mediterranean. Its oarsmen were Sicilians in revolt against Angevin rule, and therefore highly motivated. Each galley carried 30 or 40 Catalan crossbowmen and some 50 *almogavers* – tough fighters recruited from wild areas of Spain bordering on Muslim territory.

GIVE THE ENEMY A CHANCE

Di Lauria reached Malta on 7 June. That night, under cover of darkness, he slipped an armed boat into the harbour to reconnoitre. It found the Angevin galleys beached with oars unshipped in a narrow inlet under the castle walls. Di Lauria decided to draw them out into the open harbour to fight. Sacrificing the chance to surprise a sleeping enemy, he announced his presence with a blast of trumpets. While the startled Angevins rushed to man and launch their galleys, di Lauria organized his fleet in line abreast across the harbour. Heavy cables were strung from galley to

Valletta harbour
The harbour today is still dominated by Fort St Angelo. It retains its medieval appearance, but has been completely rebuilt since the time of Roger di Lauria.

galley, making it impossible for enemy ships to pass between them.

At daybreak the Angevin galleys emerged into the harbour, their complement of marines augmented by a hundred armoured knights from the castle. They deluged the Aragonese galleys in a hail of missiles – crossbow bolts, stones, javelins, darts, and pots containing a variety of substances from burning pitch to lime (intended to blind its victims). Di Lauria told his men to take cover and return fire only with crossbows. Ranging from heavy winched machines to light hand-held weapons spanned using a foot-stirrup, these were cruelly effective. A chronicler says the Catalan archers "did not discharge a shot without killing or disabling the man they attacked".

When the Angevins had exhausted most of their supply of missiles, di Lauria ordered his galleys forward. They crashed into the prows of the enemy ships with a splintering shock. Then Aragonese missiles rained down on the enemy decks, including pots filled with soap that shattered, making

the pitching decks treacherous for armoured soldiers. The fierce *almogavers*, nimble and lightly clad in leather, sure-footedly stormed the Angevins' galleys. The Sicilian oarsmen joined in the fight, leaving their benches to take up sword and shield.

The Angevins were overwhelmed and slaughtered. Only a handful of their galleys evaded capture. Bonvin was among those who escaped, but de Cornut was killed along with the majority of those he commanded. Roger di Lauria had laid the foundations of his reputation as the greatest naval commander of his age.

Medieval Catalan galleys
This romantic image shows the ships crammed with *almogavers*, the troops that played such a vital role in the Aragonese victory at Malta.

WAR OF THE SICILIAN VESPERS

THE BATTLE OF MALTA

Date	8 July 1283
Location	Grand Harbour, Valletta, Malta
Result	Aragonese victory

☞ COMBATANTS ☜

PETER III OF ARAGON	CHARLES OF ANJOU

☞ COMMANDERS ☜

Roger di Lauria	Bartolomé Bonvin Guillaume de Cornut

☞ FORCES ☜

Ships: 18 galleys	Ships: 19 galleys

☞ LOSSES ☜

Men: 300	Men: 3,500
Ships: none	Ships: 14 galleys

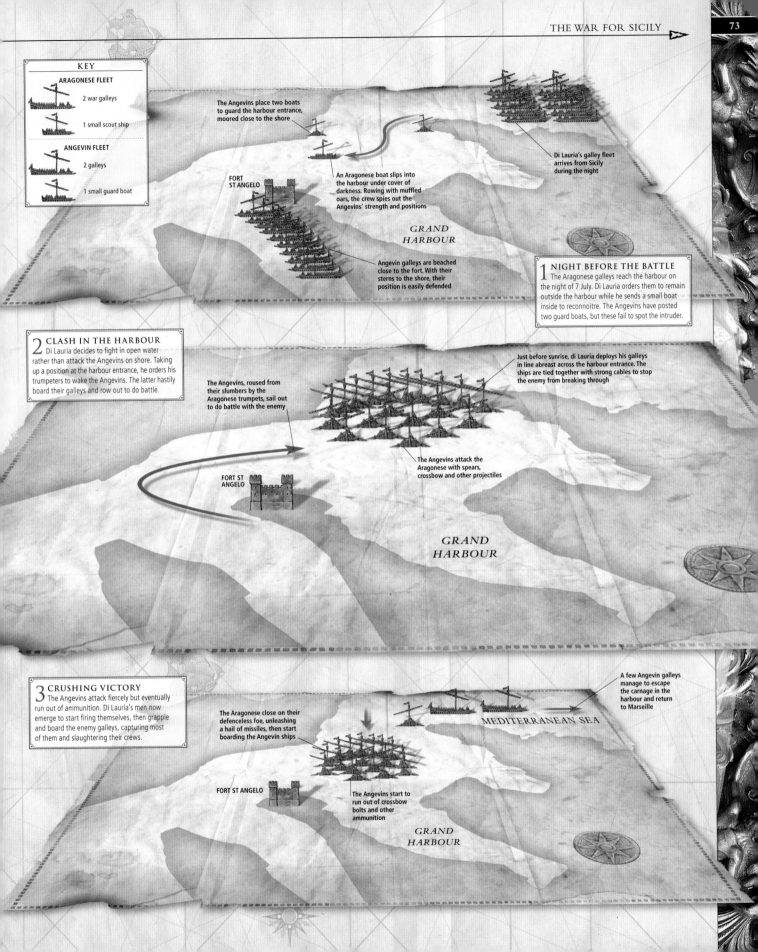

KEY

ARAGONESE FLEET

2 war galleys

1 small scout ship

ANGEVIN FLEET

2 galleys

1 small guard boat

The Angevins place two boats to guard the harbour entrance, moored close to the shore

An Aragonese boat slips into the harbour under cover of darkness. Rowing with muffled oars, the crew spies out the Angevins' strength and positions

Di Lauria's galley fleet arrives from Sicily during the night

FORT ST ANGELO

Angevin galleys are beached close to the fort. With their sterns to the shore, their position is easily defended

GRAND HARBOUR

1 NIGHT BEFORE THE BATTLE
The Aragonese galleys reach the harbour on the night of 7 July. Di Lauria orders them to remain outside the harbour while he sends a small boat inside to reconnoitre. The Angevins have posted two guard boats, but these fail to spot the intruder.

2 CLASH IN THE HARBOUR
Di Lauria decides to fight in open water rather than attack the Angevins on shore. Taking up a position at the harbour entrance, he orders his trumpeters to wake the Angevins. The latter hastily board their galleys and row out to do battle.

Just before sunrise, di Lauria deploys his galleys in line abreast across the harbour entrance. The ships are tied together with strong cables to stop the enemy from breaking through

The Angevins, roused from their slumbers by the Aragonese trumpets, sail out to do battle with the enemy

The Angevins attack the Aragonese with spears, crossbow and other projectiles

FORT ST ANGELO

GRAND HARBOUR

3 CRUSHING VICTORY
The Angevins attack fiercely but eventually run out of ammunition. Di Lauria's men now emerge to start firing themselves, then grapple and board the enemy galleys, capturing most of them and slaughtering their crews.

A few Angevin galleys manage to escape the carnage in the harbour and return to Marseille

MEDITERRANEAN SEA

The Aragonese close on their defenceless foe, unleashing a hail of missiles, then start boarding the Angevin ships

The Angevins start to run out of crossbow bolts and other ammunition

FORT ST ANGELO

GRAND HARBOUR

Warship fit for a king
Henry VIII's trip to France in 1520 to meet with French King François I was a chance to show off the largest ship in his navy – possibly in all Europe – the *Henry Grace à Dieu*. Launched in 1514, the "Great Ship" was armed with 21 heavy bronze cannons and scores of smaller iron ones.

Catching the wind
Many later Viking longships were equipped with a bronze weather vane that was attached to the prow. These were often decorated with grotesque animals.

THE EVOLUTION of the three-masted sailing ship in the 15th century was a turning point in history. Armed with cannon, it was to give Europe global reach and maritime dominance. It also brought a fundamental change to naval warfare within Europe. Large sailing ships rendered manoeuvrable by a combination of square and lateen sails could outfight galleys, providing a superior platform for large numbers of cannon. These ocean-going ships began to shift the focus of European seapower from the Mediterranean to the Atlantic. Portugal showed the way in voyages down the African coast in the 15th century, but Spain was best placed to take the lead in ocean sailing because it was both a Mediterranean and an Atlantic power. Northern Europe had a long sailing tradition but its states rarely had the resources and political organization to maintain substantial fleets of warships until the 16th century.

LONGSHIP RAIDERS

The first distinctive contribution of northern Europe to naval history was provided by the Viking warriors of Scandinavia from the 8th century. Their longships used sails and oars, like Mediterranean galleys, but were better able to function in heavier seas. Warriors doubled as oarsmen. Viking raiders devastated coastal settlements around the British Isles, besieged Paris, and even sailed into the Mediterranean and penetrated the Black Sea via the river systems of the Ukraine. Raiding parties grew into fleets as political consolidation created powerful Scandinavian kingdoms.

Viking longships were mostly employed in amphibious operations – in which the fighting took place on land – but occasionally crude sea battles took place with exchange of missiles and boarding with hand weapons. Although Anglo-Saxon England in particular tried to develop naval strength, there was little that any country – at least any as undeveloped as the states of northern Europe were at this time – could do to stop the Vikings landing forces or settlers whenever they wanted. England was invaded twice in 1066, by Scandinavians and their Frenchified descendants the Normans, without succeeding in mounting a response at sea.

ANGLO-FRENCH RIVALRY

The development of England and France as naval powers was slow. Medieval English fleets were improvised from a few king's ships, vessels provided by port towns and merchant cogs – round sailing ships – pressed into service for the purpose. Under French King Philip le Bel in the late 13th century the "clos des galées" for a while functioned as a kind of royal dockyard at Rouen, but there was nothing in northern waters that was remotely comparable with the

Sea battle at La Rochelle
During the Hundred Years War sieges of ports often led to clashes at sea. In 1372 an English convoy taking supplies and reinforcements to their troops in La Rochelle lost all its ships to a Castilian squadron fighting for the French.

size and sophistication of the great arsenals at Venice and Genoa. Henry VII finally established a permanent dock for the English king's ships at Portsmouth at the end of the 15th century.

Nevertheless, Anglo-French rivalry ensured that the English Channel became a focal point of naval operations from the 13th century onward. Large numbers of ships were sent sailing in both directions to land troops, horses, and supplies, and to embark on coastal raids, as Southampton endured when it was sacked by French galleys in 1338. During the Hundred Years War, English military operations in northern France and Aquitaine would have been impossible without maritime support. Sea battles as such, however, were infrequent, and when they did take place, consisted mostly of fights between knights, men-at-arms, and archers on board ships.

COGS AND CARRACKS

The French used galleys for cross-Channel raiding and in the battles of the Hundred Years War – the oared vessels were often supplied by Genoese mercenaries. The Castilians also used galleys successfully against the English, who for their part had balingers, small singled-masted vessels powered by a combination of oars and sails. But vessels powered by sails alone were becoming increasingly important in northern wars. Sturdy single-masted cogs were the trusty workhorses of maritime trade in the Baltic and North Sea. With high castles added fore and aft, these merchant ships provided excellent platforms for the archers who played a major role in combat at sea, as well as spacious holds for the purposes of military transport.

The carrack emerged in the 15th century as a large hybrid of the cog and the sleeker Mediterranean lateen-sailed ships. The Genoese brought carracks into the Channel in support of the French fighting England's Henry V in 1416. Henry himself built the massive *Grace Dieu*, a carrack as large as a first-rate ship of the line of the Nelson era. Such "Great Ships" appealed to monarchs for their prestige value. Initially, their fighting advantage lay primarily in how difficult they were to board, with their high inward-sloping hull. But by the start of the 16th century they were being equipped with cannon in large numbers, with gun ports cut into the hull. Purpose-built warships such as England's *Mary Rose* were a new kind of fighting machine whose firepower would make most earlier forms of naval warfare redundant.

Portuguese carracks
Having explored the entire west coast of Africa, the Portuguese reached their true goal when Vasco da Gama completed his historic voyage to India in 1498. Carracks were the mainstays of their long-distance voyages of exploration.

THE VIKINGS

DURING THE LATE 8th and 9th centuries Viking sea warriors from Scandinavia terrorized much of Europe, devastating sites along coasts and up rivers. At first small-scale hit-and-run raids mounted by single war bands, these attacks grew into sustained operations involving hundreds of longships, and led to permanent Viking settlement in France and the British Isles. From around 980 a new wave of Viking expansion, led by warriors such as Olaf Trygvasson, struck in particular at Anglo-Saxon England, which came under the rule of the Danish King Canute from 1017. In Scandinavia the kingdoms of Norway, Denmark, and Sweden were consolidated and their warrior kings, or claimants to their thrones, fought one another repeatedly in shifting alliances. Longships were central to Viking invasions and raids, but actual battles on water were rare. When forces clashed at sea, the style of fighting differed little from a battle on land, with an exchange of missiles followed by close combat with axe, sword, and spear.

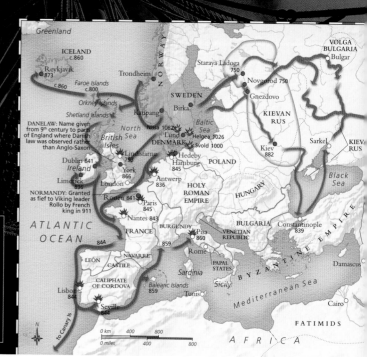

THE VIKING WORLD c.793–1050 CE

The Viking raids of the late 8th and early 9th centuries were followed by a period of conquest and settlement, with Vikings settling in Iceland as well as in conquered areas of France, Britain, and Ireland. As the regions ruled by the Vikings grew to become powerful states, wars between rival Viking leaders became increasingly frequent as they quarrelled over their inheritance.

KEY

- Area settled by Vikings
- Area of Viking influence
- → Viking voyage, trade route, or raid
- ● Major Viking settlement
- 866 Date of Viking voyage, battle, raid, or settlement
- ⚔ Viking sea battle
- ⚔ Viking raid

VIKING ATTACKS ON NORTHERN ENGLAND

RAID ON LINDISFARNE

Date June 793
Forces Vikings: unknown
Losses Unknown

Location Lindisfarne
Island, off Northumbria

In the 8th century the monastery on Lindisfarne was a famed centre of Christian learning. Its remote coastal location showed the security felt by a people unsuspecting of seaborne attack. The Viking raiding party that crossed the North Sea and beached its longships near the monastery in 793 met little or no resistance. According to the Anglo-Saxon Chronicle, the raiders "devastated God's church on Lindisfarne island by looting and slaughter". The Vikings stole the treasures of the church and either killed the monks or carried them off in chains to be sold as slaves. Only a hit-and-run attack by a small war band, the raid was a profound shock to Christian Europe. The scholar Alcuin wrote that "never before has such terror appeared as we have suffered from a pagan race".

Viking leader's helmet
Elaborate bronze helmets contributed to the terrifying spectacle of sudden landings of groups of Viking raiders.

VIKING ATTACKS ON NORTHERN FRANCE

RAID ON PARIS

Date November 885–October 886
Forces Vikings: c.300 longships; Franks: 200 men-at-arms
Losses Unknown

Location Paris

In 885 a vast Viking fleet, led by the chieftain Sigfrid, sailed up the River Seine, bent upon pillaging inland France and Burgundy. The Frankish town of Paris, built on the Ile de la Cité, was joined to each bank of the Seine by bridges, one of wood and one of stone. To the surprise of the Vikings, the handful of Frankish warriors in the town, led by Count Odo, defended the bridges, blocking the raiders' progress up the river. A prolonged siege ensued. The Vikings were determined not to be thwarted by a few Frankish warriors: they used siege engines to bombard the fortifications; they attempted to burn the wooden bridge with fireships; they filled moats with dead bodies. After the timber bridge was destroyed by winter floods, some of the Vikings sailed on to plunder elsewhere. The rest were eventually bought off by the Frankish emperor, Charles the Fat, with 60 pounds of silver.

NORWEGIAN-DANISH WAR

SVOLD

Date September 1000
Forces Norwegians: 11 ships; Coalition: c.70 ships
Losses Norwegians: 11 ships; Coalition: unknown

Location Baltic Sea

Olaf Trygvasson, king of Norway, was opposed by a coalition of Danish king Svein Forkbeard, Swedish king Olaf Eiriksson, and the Earl of Lade, Eirik Hakonarson, a pretender to the Norwegian throne. Olaf was sailing home from Wendland when his small fleet was intercepted by a far superior coalition force. The battle that followed is best described by Icelandic chronicler Sonni Sturluson in his sagas of the Norwegian kings, the *Heimskringla*.

King Olaf was travelling on board *Long Serpent*, a ship 50m (165ft) long, powered by 70 oars and carrying 200 warriors. As the opposing fleets closed for battle,

Presumed death of Olaf Trygvasson
The king throws himself overboard to avoid capture at Svold, an event that passed into Norse folklore.

raining spears and arrows upon one another, he had smaller longships lashed to each side of his large warship, to provide a stable platform on which he and his followers could fight.

Earl Eirik led the attack on Olaf's floating fortress. Sailing alongside and grappling the smaller ships, Eirik's warriors boarded them and cleared their decks in tough hand-to-hand fighting. They then cut the hawsers holding the smaller ships to *Long Serpent*. Earl Eirik brought his longship *Barthi* directly alongside *Long Serpent*, but his first boarding party was repelled with heavy losses. Despite desperate resistance, Olaf's men were gradually worn down, until they held only the aft of their ship, grouped around their king. To avoid being taken, Olaf leaped into the sea and was never seen again. The victors divided Norway between them, with Earl Eirik taking the lion's share.

> THE PAGANS ... CAME WITH A NAVAL FORCE TO BRITAIN LIKE STINGING HORNETS AND SPREAD ON ALL SIDES LIKE FEARFUL WOLVES, ROBBED, TORE, AND SLAUGHTERED ...

SIMEON OF DURHAM, *HISTORIA REGUM*, 1129

Viking longship
This reconstruction of a Viking longship of the 11th century, created at Roskilde in Denmark, has demonstrated its ability to sail long distances in open water without resort to oar power.

WARS OF KING CANUTE

HELGEÅ

Date 1026
Forces Danish and English: c.600 ships; Swedes and Norwegians: c.400 ships
Losses Unknown

Location
Coast of Sweden

While Canute, king of England and Denmark, was ruling his English domains, Swedish King Anund Jacob and Norwegian King Olaf Haraldsson ravaged his Danish territories. In search of revenge, Canute led a large fleet in pursuit of the marauders. Olaf and Anund devised a trick to counter their enemy's superior force. Landing at the mouth of the Helgeå River – a site located on the Swedish coast – they had a dam constructed upstream. When Canute's war fleet was sighted, the

Swedes and Norwegians hastily took to their ships and rowed out of the harbour, taking up a defensive formation offshore. Since it was late in the day and his fleet was widely dispersed, Canute sailed into the now empty harbour to spend the night. As there was limited space, most of his ships remained in open sea. The following morning his enemies breached the dam, releasing a cascade of water. Some of Canute's men were drowned. The king's own ship rode the surge out into the sea, where it was surrounded by the enemy. But Canute's vessel was so large and well defended that it could not be boarded. There was some fierce fighting before Olaf and Anund, sure that they would lose heavily once Canute's ships were properly organized for battle, decided to withdraw. Their flight confirmed Canute's dominance of Scandinavia. He replaced Olaf as king of Norway two years later.

c.990–1035

CANUTE

KING OF ENGLAND, DENMARK, AND NORWAY

Canute accompanied his father Svein Forkbeard, king of Denmark, on an invasion of England in 1013. The following year his father died and the Danish army elected him king of England, although it was only after a second seaborne invasion and much hard fighting that the Anglo-Saxons submitted to his rule. Canute succeeded his brother as king of Denmark in 1018 and, after the battle of Helgeå in 1026, also affirmed his claim to be "king of the Norwegians and some of the Swedes". He ruled his North Sea empire wisely but failed to create any political structure that could maintain it after his death.

NORWEGIAN-DANISH WAR

NISSA

Date 9 August 1062
Forces Norwegians: 150 ships; Danes: 300 ships
Losses Norwegians: unknown; Danes: more than 70 ships captured

Location
The Kattegat

Harald III Sigurdsson, also known as Harald Hardrada, was one of the most celebrated of Viking warriors. He served in the elite Varangian Guard of the Byzantine Empire before returning to become king of Norway in 1047. He also claimed the throne of Denmark, held by Svein Estridsson, a nephew of Canute. There was warfare between the two for 15 years. In summer 1062 Harald sailed south to seek battle with the Danes. He laid waste the Danish coast to draw Svein out to fight. The Danish king appeared with a far larger

fleet than Harald's, but many of his followers seem to have been lacking in confidence. On either side of Svein's own vessel ships were tied together with cables, but many other Danish ships were loose and disorganized, some hanging back while others pressed forward to fight.

The battle was joined late in the day and continued through the night. Enemies assailed one another with stones and arrows, as well as closing to clash with swords and shields. The loose Danish vessels were mopped up by aggressively-led groups of Norwegian longships. Svein's ship and those tied to it in the centre were finally overrun after savage fighting, although the king escaped capture. Despite the scale of the Norwegian victory, Harald made peace with Svein in 1064. Instead he pursued a flimsy claim to the English throne. Harald was killed leading an invasion of England at Stamford Bridge in 1066.

LIFE ON BOARD

RELIGION AND SUPERSTITION

THE HAZARDOUS AND UNPREDICTABLE nature of any seaman's life, subject to the vagaries of weather and waves, is compounded in naval service by the uncertainties of warfare creating fertile ground for superstition of all kinds. Religious belief at sea has in some of its aspects been hard to distinguish from superstition, although religion has often developed a very different role as a motivating and bonding force, and a source of spiritual comfort on board.

OMEN AND SACRIFICE

In ancient times any enterprise, whether in peace or war, would be preceded by animal sacrifice and the consultation of omens, often by examination of burned entrails. On important occasions renowned professionals were employed for the purpose, like Euphrantides the Soothsayer who allegedly advised Themistocles to sacrifice three Persian prisoners to the gods before the battle of Salamis. When Roman consul Publius Claudius infamously refused to heed the omen presented by sacred chickens before the defeat at Drepana, Rome was in uproar and it nearly cost him his life. The Viking warriors, worshippers of Odin and Thor, practised human sacrifice and divination from examining the remains of the victims. Omens could also be accidental, however. At Lepanto a number of crows were seen over the Turkish fleet before the battle, and their admiral had great difficulty persuading his men to enter the fight.

APOLLO Ancient Greek galley crews sang specific hymns, or paeans, to the god Apollo as they rowed into battle. Battlefield paeans were accompanied by pipes and instruments called *kitharas*, like the one Apollo is seen holding here.

SACRED CHICKENS Roman leaders would consult sacred chickens, specially brought on board for the purpose, for signs of divine support prior to battle. A chicken that refused to eat the grain it was offered could prove ominous.

SILVER COIN In deference to Charon, ferryman of the underworld in Greek legend who was paid with a coin, shipbuilders once placed a silver coin under the masthead.

EX-VOTO These works were a display of gratitude to God for sparing the mariner, fulfilling part of the deal they made with God in a time of difficulty. The painting by a Spanish sailor opposite depicts the moment of peril.

Now Friday came. Your old wives say,
Of all the week's the unluckiest day.

RICHARD FLECKNOE, *Diarum* (1656) on the belief preventing ships launching on Fridays

SUPERSTITIONS

Sailors maintained into modern times many beliefs that are widely though to be pagan in origin. For example, death was believed to come with the ebb tide. If a dying man survived one ebb tide, he would live until the next. Possessing a caul from a newborn baby was believed to ensure a man against drowning – sailors were still known to buy cauls into the 20th century. It was also unlucky to kill a seagull or, especially, an albatross, since they embodied the souls of lost mariners. This prohibition was not universally observed – sailors were known to make tobacco pouches out of albatrosses' webbed feet. It was bad luck to carry a corpse on board. If unavoidable, it should always be carried sideways onto the ship, not end on. Whistling was generally disapproved of as likely to cause a storm, although soft whistling might be indulged in a dead calm as a way of summoning a wind. Placing a silver coin under the mast might ensure good fortune, while it was taboo to launch a ship on a Friday.

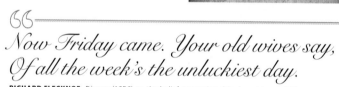

ORTHODOX CHAPEL Many ships had their own chapels, where a chaplain could perform services and rites. This Orthodox chapel from the Greek WWII-era battleship *Georgius Averof* came with its own icons.

PRAYER SERVICE Sailors often attended services before and after battle. Here British officers and men pray for their fallen comrades after the battle of the Nile (1798).

> *May the great God …grant to my country and … Europe in general, a great and glorious victory: and may no misconduct, in anyone, tarnish it …*

HORATIO NELSON Prayer written before battle of Trafalgar on 21 October 1805

RELIGION ON BOARD

Clergymen, monks, or nuns on board were traditionally regarded as unlucky. In the 16th century Spanish royal galleys, which operated close to shore and were never at sea for long periods, had clergy assigned to them, but the ocean-going sailing fleet did not. The celebration of mass on board was banned because the consecrated wafer or wine might be spilt in the sea. The ship's master led services on board and the ship's boys sang the Ave Maria at sunset. Spanish sailors wore medallions of the saints and Virgin around their necks as charms, and made ex-voto offerings in churches to give thanks for a safe voyage. English sailors of Francis Drake's time, affected by Protestantism, would sing hymns on deck, while denouncing their Catholic enemies as merely superstitious. Religious services on board Royal Navy ships in the 18th century were mostly conducted by the captain. The growth of Christian evangelicalism in the early 19th century affected Royal Navy officers, who were more likely to take their religious duties seriously. From 1812 the official policy of the Royal Navy was that every ship from a sixth-rate upward should have a chaplain, but until the mid-19th century there were never enough chaplains to fulfil this aspiration. Eventually, in the course of the 19th century, religious personnel on board were generally provided by navies around the world as part of a concept of a well-run ship caring for its sailors.

BLESSING CEREMONY Clergy inspect a submarine after a ceremony. Another maritime tradition views a priest on board as bad luck.

ORGAN Specially built organs for submarines, such as this WWII model, were issued for religious services until the 1980s.

SEA BATTLES IN NORTHERN EUROPE

DURING THE PERIOD of almost half a millennium between the Norman invasion of England in 1066 and the loss of the English "Great Ship" *Mary Rose* in the Solent in 1545, naval warfare in northern Europe underwent decisive technological changes. The Normans crossed the Channel in vessels resembling Viking longships; by the 16th century war fleets included large three- and four-masted carracks armed with cannon. But the place of sea power in north European warfare remained relatively constant. It enabled states to conduct coastal raids or to land troops and horses for larger scale military incursions. Naval matters were most important to the English kings, who needed to ferry armies to the European mainland where they possessed or claimed substantial territories, and also depended on the Channel to protect them from attack by continental armies. Rivalry between the kings of France and England, at its fiercest during the Hundred Years War (1337–1453), was at the root of most naval conflicts in the region. Permanent navies were slow to emerge, however, limiting the scale and frequency of sea warfare.

THE NORMAN INVASION OF ENGLAND

In 1066 Anglo-Saxon England was the target of no less than three seaborne attacks, all concerned with contesting the accession to the Anglo-Saxon throne of Harold Godwinson at the start of the year. In May Harold's exiled brother Tostig landed on the Isle of Wight with a fleet from Flanders and went on to raid Harold's main naval base at Sandwich. In early September a fleet of some 300 ships commanded by Norwegian King Harald Hardrada, with Tostig as his ally, landed an army in northern England. This invasion

The invasion fleet
The Bayeux Tapestry includes a fairly faithful representation of William's ships, especially the sails, stays, and steering oars. Less realistic is the method shown of transporting horses.

failed because King Harold defeated Harald Hardrada's land forces at Stamford Bridge. The third seaborne operation, mounted by William Duke of Normandy, was a resounding success.

DAUNTING LOGISTICS

Whatever the merits of William's claim to the English throne, his preparations were thorough and determined. William had to transport an army of 7,000 men or more, along with some 2,000 horses, and military equipment that included the components for a prefabricated wooden fort. At Dives-sur-Mer on the Normandy coast he assembled a fleet that has been estimated at around 700 ships. Some of these were built from scratch, a process shown in the Bayeux Tapestry. Most of the ships were

probably much broader in the beam and deeper in draught than a Viking longship. It has been estimated that one such ship would have taken a team of 12 shipwrights three months to build. Given the scale of the enterprise, most vessels must surely have been existing craft supplied by the duke's seagoing subjects.

The invasion fleet was ready by 12 August, but the weather would not cooperate and a north wind kept the ships firmly bottled up in harbour for a month. On 12 September, the fleet moved to St Valéry-sur-Somme, losing several ships en route through

Norman helmet
Standard equipment of the Normans who crossed the Channel in 1066 was chainmail armour and an iron helmet with a distinctive nose guard.

stormy weather. This placed William's invasion force much closer to the English coast and enabled him to target a landing site nearer London. Harold, meanwhile, was well informed of William's preparations and waited with his own ships and army on England's south coast. The long delay worked against Harold, however. Firstly, on 8 September, most of his forces were sent home. Then the sudden invasion by Harald Hardrada required a hasty

*"... but I have heard my father say – I remember it well, although I was but a lad – that there were **seven hundred ships, less four**, when they sailed from St Valéry; and that there were besides these ships, **boats and skiffs** for the purpose of carrying the **arms and harness**. I have found it written (but I know not whether it be true) that there were in all three thousand vessels bearing sails and masts. Any one will know that there must have been a great many men to have furnished out such vessels ... The duke placed **a lantern on the mast of his ship**, that the other ships might see it, and hold their course after it."*

march northward. When a southerly wind finally set in that could carry the Norman fleet to England, coastal defences were almost non-existent.

Soldiers and horses boarded the ships on 27 September – probably 10 horses to each transport ship – and at high tide around 3pm they rowed out to an assembly point at sea. There, sails were raised and the fleet set off with the duke's ship in the lead. When night fell there was no moon, so lanterns were hoisted to keep the ships in formation. A few became detached, but the main body came ashore – unopposed – on the pebble beach at Pevensey on the morning of 28 September. Such ships as Harold had on duty were stationed in the Solent, far to the west.

William went on to defeat Harold at Hastings and replace him on the English throne, an event that radically altered the structure of English society and England's relation to mainland Europe.

NORMAN CONQUEST

NORMAN INVASION OF ENGLAND

Date	28 September 1066
Location	Pevensey, southern England
Result	Norman victory

COMBATANTS

NORMANS	ANGLO-SAXONS

COMMANDERS

William Duke of Normandy	King Harold II of England

FORCES

Ships: c.600–700	Ships: c.200

LOSSES

Men: none	Men: none
Ships: none	Ships: none

KING JOHN'S WAR WITH FRANCE

DAMME

Date	30–31 May 1213
Forces	English: c.500 ships; French: c.1,700 ships
Losses	English: none; French: c.400 ships

Location Scheldt estuary, Flanders

In 1213 French King Philip Augustus was threatening an invasion of England. He assembled a large fleet at the mouth of the Seine, but when English King John made a number of concessions that undermined the justification for an invasion, Philip instead turned his forces against England's ally, the Count of Flanders. The French fleet sailed to the area of the Scheldt estuary known as the Zwyn and came ashore at Damme, threatening the important Flemish cities of Bruges and Ghent.

c.1176–1226
WILLIAM DE LONGESPEE
ENGLISH NOBLEMAN AND MILITARY COMMANDER

An illegitimate son of King Henry II, de Longespee, Third Earl of Salisbury, was also known as William Longsword. Holding the post of warden of the Cinque Ports may have given him some knowledge of naval affairs, but he commanded the English fleet at Damme in 1213 as a leader of fighting men, not as a sailor. He subsequently fought the French on land at the battle of Bouvines in 1214 and later in Gascony. In 1225 he was shipwrecked in the Bay of Biscay while en route to England. He eventually reached home but died shortly after, possibly poisoned by the victor of the battle of Dover, Hubert de Burgh.

King John assembled his own fleet, under the command of William de Longespee. It comprised some 500 ships carrying 700 knights and large numbers of mercenaries. Whether the plan was for a preemptive strike to prevent a French invasion is not clear. Leaving England on 28 May, the ships reached the Zwyn two days later. The French were totally unprepared for an attack from the sea. Hundreds of their ships lay at anchor or beached on mudflats outside the port, with few men aboard. The English seized these vessels almost without a fight, taking 300 as prizes and burning a hundred more.

The following day de Longespee attacked the port of Damme itself. The fighting moved onto land and there was some sharp combat as the French organized a counterattack. The English force had to reembark in some haste, but sailed happily back to England with its prizes and a wealth of booty.

FRENCH INVASION OF ENGLAND

DOVER

Date	24 August 1217
Forces	English: c.40 ships; French: c.80 ships
Losses	English: none; French: 65 ships

Location English Channel, off Dover

The barons' revolt against King John enabled the French to invade England in 1215 and occupy a large part of the country. After John's death in 1216, they wanted to install the Dauphin Louis on the throne of England in place of the nine-year-old Henry III. William Marshal and Hubert de Burgh led the

Arms of the Cinque Ports
The Cinque Ports were Dover and four other nearby ports, entrusted with defending England from invasion.

resistance to the French and tried to prevent reinforcements and supplies reaching England from France.

In summer 1217 Marshal and de Burgh were besieged in Dover. On 24 August, 70 French supply vessels approached the coast escorted by 10 warships under the command of Eustace the Monk, a famed sea warrior from Boulogne. De Burgh reacted swiftly, setting sail with some 40 ships. At first the English sailed past the incoming convoy, but then came about to attack from the rear and grappled the enemy ships for boarding. They captured almost all the French vessels and towed them into Dover. Eustace was found hiding in the bilges of his ship and summarily executed. This defeat forced the French to abandon their invasion of England. The battle can probably be counted as the first fought between sailing ships in open sea.

TRAN   S[

THE BATTLE OF SLUYS

On 22 June 1340 King Edward III of England set sail across the North Sea from the Orwell estuary on board *Cog Thomas*, bound for the Scheldt in Belgium. His large fleet of round ships, balingers, galleys, and barges was packed with troops, although a party of high-born English ladies was also on board, being carried to the court of Edward's Flemish wife at Ghent. Joined by the English North Sea squadron under Sir Robert Morley, Edward arrived off the Flanders coast to find a large French fleet anchored in the Scheldt estuary.

DEPLOYMENTS BEFORE THE BATTLE

According to the French chronicler Jean Froissart, the king was astonished when he first saw the vast fleet of French ships, whose "masts resembled a forest". Under the command of Admiral Hugues Quiéret and lawyer Nicolas Béhuchet, the French force had been assembled for an invasion of England. It included a contingent of Genoese galleys under the experienced mercenary naval commander Egidio Bocanegra, known as Barbavara. While the English waited for a favourable wind and tide to enter the estuary, the French placed their ships in a defensive formation, anchored in lines tied together with cables. The idea was to create a stable floating platform to be defended by the crossbowmen and men-at-arms. The *Christopher*, one of five large English ships recently captured by the French, was stationed in front of this mass, with Genoese crossbowmen manning her high castles. Barbavara, a true sailor, kept his own ships separate and manoeuvrable.

The English fleet was arranged with one ship packed with men-at-arms between each two ships of longbowmen. Manoeuvring to approach with the sun and wind behind them, they attacked at around noon on 24 June. Both sides sounded trumpets, horns, and drums to encourage resolve as battle was joined. According to Froissart's account, "fierce fighting broke out on every side, archers and crossbowmen shooting arrows and bolts at each other pell-mell, and men-at-arms struggling and striking in hand-to-hand combat". Iron grappling hooks were used to hold the enemy fast for boarding. The *Christopher* was one of the first ships to be taken, all her defenders killed or captured.

CONTROL OF THE SEA

According to a letter written by King Edward after the battle, the fighting continued "all that day and the night after". The French clearly had the worst of it, possibly because of the rapid rate of fire and accuracy of the English king's longbowmen, or because the English ships were free to move around their anchored adversaries. It is no doubt significant that Barbavara's galleys were the only ships on the French side to escape the debacle, taking two prizes into the bargain.

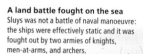

Commemorative coin
This gold noble was issued by Edward III in the year of the battle of Sluys. It shows the king standing in a ship with a sword and shield.

Both Quiéret and Béhuchet were killed. The latter was possibly executed after the battle on Edward's orders, though for what reason is not known. The sea was red with blood and thick with the bodies of French soldiers and sailors who had sought vainly to escape. The English victory, establishing naval dominance at the outset of the Hundred Years War, was strategically decisive, ensuring that the conflict would be fought in France, with little risk of a counter-invasion of England.

A land battle fought on the sea
Sluys was not a battle of naval manoeuvre: the ships were effectively static and it was fought out by two armies of knights, men-at-arms, and archers.

> ❝ THE FRENCH SHIPS WERE ALL CHAINED TOGETHER, SO THAT THEY COULD NOT BE SEPARATED FROM ONE ANOTHER; THUS ONLY A FEW ENGLISH SHIPS WERE NEEDED TO GUARD ONE GROUP OF THOSE WHICH HAD BEEN ABANDONED. ❞
>
> **GEOFFREY LE BAKER DE SWYNEBROKE**, ENGLISH CHRONICLER

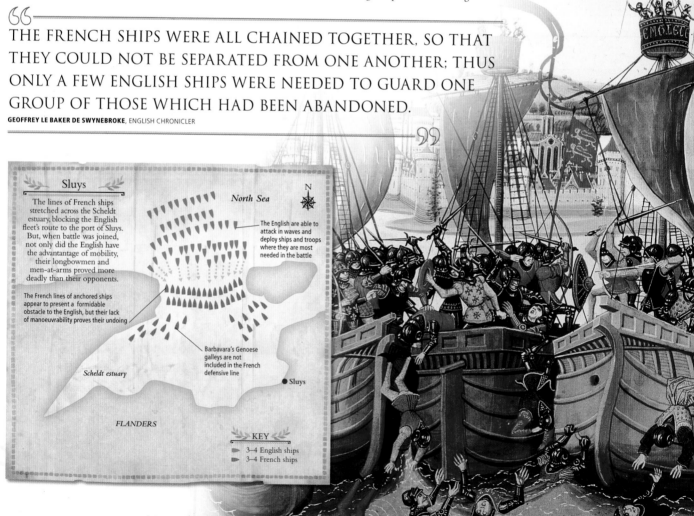

Sluys

The lines of French ships stretched across the Scheldt estuary, blocking the English fleet's route to the port of Sluys. But, when battle was joined, not only did the English have the advantantage of mobility, their longbowmen and men-at-arms proved more deadly than their opponents.

The French lines of anchored ships appear to present a formidable obstacle to the English, but their lack of manoeuvrability proves their undoing.

North Sea

N

The English are able to attack in waves and deploy ships and troops where they are most needed in the battle

Barbavara's Genoese galleys are not included in the French defensive line

Scheldt estuary

• Sluys

FLANDERS

KEY
➤ 3–4 English ships
➤ 3–4 French ships

HUNDRED YEARS WAR

BATTLE OF SLUYS

Date	24 June 1340
Location	Flanders coast, Belgium
Result	English victory

⚔ COMBATANTS ⚔

ENGLAND — FRANCE

⚔ COMMANDERS ⚔

King Edward III — Admiral Hugues Quiéret
Nicolas Béhuchet
Egidio Bocanegra
(Barbavara)

⚔ FORCES ⚔

Ships: c.210 — Ships: c.190

⚔ LOSSES ⚔

Men: 4,000–9,000 — Men: c.20,000–30,000
Ships: 2 captured — Ships: c.170 lost

HUNDRED YEARS WAR

LES ESPAGNOLS SUR MER

Date 29 August 1350
Forces English: 50 ships; Castilians: 40 ships
Losses English: 2 ships; Castilians: 14 ships sunk or captured

Location Off Winchelsea, S. England

English King Edward III decided to intercept a fleet of France's ally Castile, as it sailed from Flanders for Spain. He assembled a naval force at Winchelsea under his personal command aboard *Cog Thomas*. Carlos de la Cerda, the Castilian commander, was only too happy to give battle. He had larger ships, their fighting tops crammed with soldiers armed with various missiles, including crossbowmen. The English sallied forth to meet the Castilians as they sailed into the Channel. King Edward ordered the master of his own ship to sail directly into one of the enemy ships. Damaged by the impact, *Cog Thomas* began to founder. Edward successfully grappled another Castilian vessel and transferred his men across before his cog sank. Although the king's son, the Black Prince, also lost his ship, the English generally had far the better of a hot engagement.

HUNDRED YEARS WAR

LA ROCHELLE

Date 22–23 June 1372
Forces English: unknown; Castilians: 12 galleys
Losses English: entire fleet, 8,400 captured; Castilians: none

Location La Rochelle

The Earl of Pembroke led a large convoy of round ships carrying troops, horses, and money to reinforce the English army at La Rochelle, which was under siege by the French. France called upon its ally Castile to intercept the English convoy. A Castilian squadron of 12 galleys commanded by Genoese mercenary Ambrosio Bocanegra, met the English convoy in the mouth of La Rochelle harbour.

The first encounter was indecisive, but on the second day the Spanish galleys were able to exploit their greater manoeuvrability and ability to operate in shallow water. Many of the English ships were grounded. The Castilians sprayed their decks with oil and set them ablaze with burning arrows. The Earl of Pembroke and all his men were captured, along with £20,000. It was a striking example of a victory for galleys over sailing ships. The English had now clearly lost the control of the sea, which had been theirs since their victory over the French at Sluys in 1340.

TACKING AND WEARING

SAILING INTO THE WIND

The obvious disadvantage of a sailing ship is that it cannot move directly into the wind. To make progress against the wind a ship has to follow a zig-zag course toward its ultimate destination. When the ship turns with its bow into the wind to change direction, this is known as "tacking": when it turns with its stern facing the wind, this is called "wearing". Wearing required more sea room, so in a confined space – for example, when leaving port – it was often essential to tack.

Tacking
To follow its zig-zag course into the wind, the ship turns its bow through the direction of the wind before setting off in the other direction – the "opposite tack".

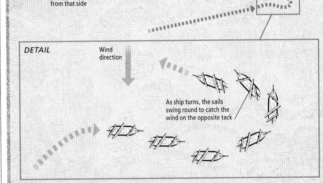

Port tack: the ship's port (left) side is now to windward and its sails fill with wind from that side

Starboard tack: the ship's starboard (right) side is to windward and its sails are adjusted to fill with wind from that side

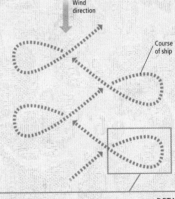

DETAIL — Wind direction

As ship turns, the sails swing round to catch the wind on the opposite tack

Wearing
In contrast to tacking, the ship goes about (changes direction) by turning its stern through the wind rather than its bow. As a result the ship will sail for a time with the wind – in the opposite direction to the way it is trying to go. Progress is slower than with tacking.

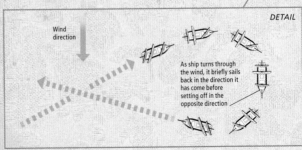

DETAIL

As ship turns through the wind, it briefly sails back in the direction it has come before setting off in the opposite direction

WAR OF THE LEAGUE OF CAMBRAI

BREST

Date	10 August 1512
Forces	English: 25 ships; French: 22 ships
Losses	English: 1 ship; French: 2 ships

Location Off Brest, Brittany, France

In 1512 England went to war with France. Edward Howard took a fleet to sea and harassed French shipping. To put a stop to these depredations, French King Louis XII ordered a fleet of warships to be assembled at Brest under Vice-Admiral René de Clermont.

On 10 August the English surprised the French at anchor off the Pointe de St Mathieu. Many Breton gentry were on board the ships to celebrate the Feast of St Lawrence. The French cut their cables and many fled for the safety of the Brest roadstead. De Clermont's flagship was assailed by Howard aboard the newly commissioned *Mary Rose* and had his mainmast shot away before drifting out of the battle. The largest English ship, the 1,000-ton *Regent*, commanded by Sir Thomas Knyvet, grappled *Cordelière*, whose captain Primauget was a noted Breton seaman. Knyvet was cut in two by a cannonball, but *Cordelière* seemed sure to be taken when it exploded, destroying both ships and killing more than a thousand men. Despite the loss of *Regent*, it was a clear English victory. In reward, King Henry VIII appointed Howard Admiral of England.

THE BATTLE OF THE SOLENT

In 1543 the English king Henry VIII went to war with France as an ally of Emperor Charles V. After the English seized Boulogne, French king François I planned an invasion of England. He assembled a fleet at Le Havre in the summer of 1545, bringing 25 of his Mediterranean galleys north to join his Channel ships. In June English admiral John Dudley attempted to deliver a pre-emptive strike against the French

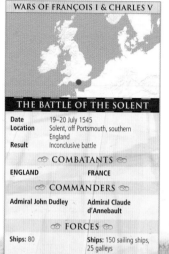

WARS OF FRANÇOIS I & CHARLES V

THE BATTLE OF THE SOLENT

Date	19–20 July 1545
Location	Solent, off Portsmouth, southern England
Result	Inconclusive battle

⚓ COMBATANTS ⚓

ENGLAND	FRANCE

⚓ COMMANDERS ⚓

Admiral John Dudley	Admiral Claude d'Annebault

⚓ FORCES ⚓

Ships: 80	Ships: 150 sailing ships, 25 galleys

⚓ LOSSES ⚓

Men: unknown Ships: unknown	Men: unknown Ships: unknown

invasion fleet but failed to cause any significant damage. Dudley arrived back at Portsmouth on 13 July with his ships in need of resupply and repair. The English fleet was far from ready when the French invasion force arrived.

AN INAUSPICIOUS START

The man appointed admiral in charge of the French expedition was Claude d'Annebault, a soldier with great experience of land warfare but no experience at sea. He suffered an early setback when his flagship

Relic of the Mary Rose
Among the many weapons, personal effects, and nautical instruments found in the wreck of the *Mary Rose* was the ship's bronze bell.

Carraquon caught fire before leaving harbour and had to be abandoned. He then shifted his flag to *La Grande Maîtresse*, which subsequently ran aground as the invasion fleet left the French coast on 15 July. The *Maîtresse* continued across the Channel but was shipping water, and had to be sent home before battle was joined.

The French reached the Sussex coast on 18 July and sailed west to the mouth of the Solent, off the Isle of Wight. The English were distracted by the presence of their king, who had come to visit his fleet and inspect the defences of Portsmouth.

Sunday, 19 July was a fine, still day. With sailing ships becalmed, some French

> 66
>
> ## WHEN SHE HEELED OVER WITH THE WIND, THE WATER ENTERED BY THE LOWEST ROW OF GUN PORTS WHICH HAD BEEN LEFT OPEN AFTER FIRING.
>
> **VAN DER DELFT,** IMPERIAL AMBASSADOR, REPORTING THE ACCOUNT OF A SURVIVOR FROM THE *MARY ROSE*
>
> 99

galleys rowed into the Solent toward Portsmouth. When they were sighted, the king was dining on board the great ship *Henry Grace à Dieu* with various officers, including Sir George Carew, Dudley's newly appointed vice admiral. The king departed to view events from the ramparts of Southsea Castle, while his fleet prepared to fight.

The English ships had enormous difficulty extricating themselves from their crowded anchorage with scarcely a breath of wind to assist them. In the afternoon, however, a wind arose and they began to emerge, sailing out toward the French galleys in the Solent. The large but aged carrack *Mary Rose*, with Vice Admiral Carew on board, took the lead. The vice admiral's wife Lady Mary Carew was among the spectators alongside King Henry who were watching the action from Southsea Castle.

THE MARY ROSE SINKS

Witnesses to the battle saw the *Mary Rose* fire her starboard broadside at the galleys and come about to bring the guns on the port side to bear. As she did so, a gust of wind caused the ship to heel over, plunging her open gun ports below

water. The *Mary Rose* sank with awesome swiftness. The cries of the trapped crew were momentarily audible to the onlookers on the castle ramparts, before they were stifled by the waves. Lady Carew

fainted, while King Henry cried out in anguish at the sight. All but 30 of the 415 people on board the *Mary Rose* were drowned. Sir George Carew was not among the survivors. The French failed to capitalize upon this shocking disaster. There were some long-range exchanges of fire between the two fleets

the following day and French soldiers briefly went ashore on the Isle of Wight. But while the English vainly attempted to salvage the sunken *Mary Rose*, the French then withdrew eastward along the coast. Dudley eventually came out in pursuit, but d'Annebault had had enough of the sea and tamely headed for home, to the great displeasure of his king. The battle, like the war of which it formed part, was entirely inconsequential.

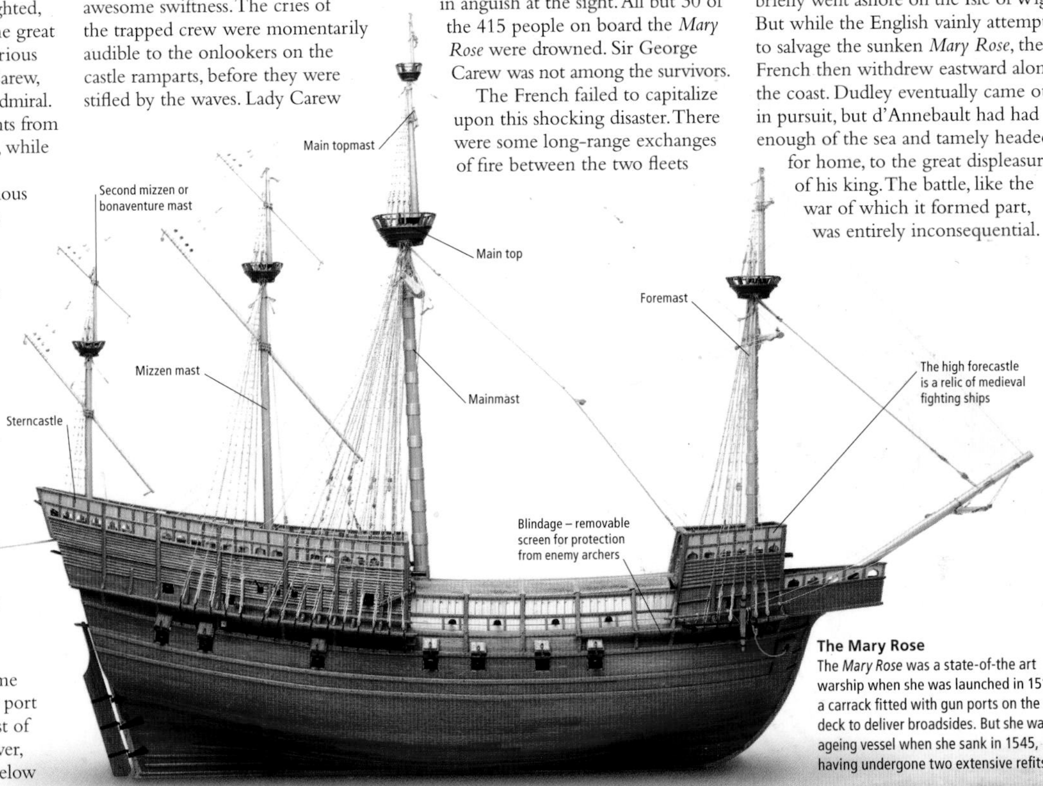

Main topmast

Second mizzen or bonaventure mast

Main top

Mizzen mast

Foremast

Sterncastle

Mainmast

The high forecastle is a relic of medieval fighting ships

Blindage – removable screen for protection from enemy archers

The Mary Rose
The *Mary Rose* was a state-of-the art warship when she was launched in 1511 – a carrack fitted with gun ports on the main deck to deliver broadsides. But she was an ageing vessel when she sank in 1545, having undergone two extensive refits.

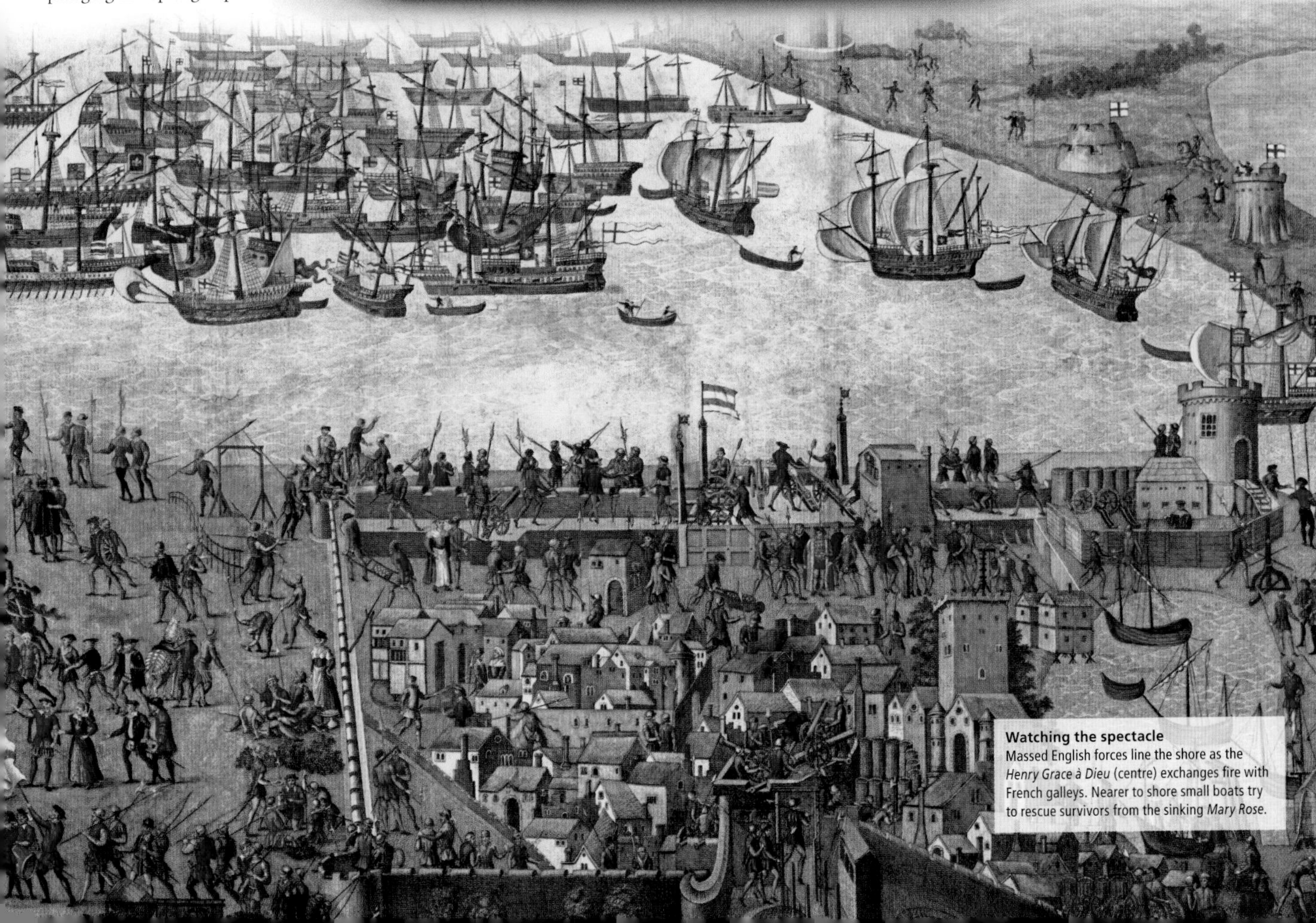

Watching the spectacle
Massed English forces line the shore as the *Henry Grace à Dieu* (centre) exchanges fire with French galleys. Nearer to shore small boats try to rescue survivors from the sinking *Mary Rose*.

THE OTTOMANS

AT THE BEGINNING of the 14th century the Ottoman Turks were a small band of Muslim warriors in northern Anatolia. In a remarkably short time they made themselves rulers of a great land empire and a major naval power. The capture of Constantinople in 1453 completed their conquest of the Byzantine Empire. This was followed by expansion westward and southward that gave them control of the eastern Mediterranean, coastal areas of North Africa, and the Red Sea. Through most of the 16th century the Christian states of the Mediterranean could do little to counter Ottoman naval operations, which threatened Italy and Provence with invasion and filled the slave markets of the Islamic world with Christians carried off by Muslim privateers. Victory at Lepanto in 1571 gave the Christian powers a breathing space, but the Ottoman navy remained a major force into the 18th century.

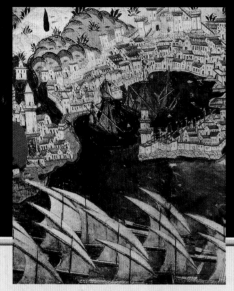

A constant menace
An Ottoman fleet commanded by Kheir-ed-Din sails past the entrance to the harbour at Genoa. No port in the Christian Mediterranean was safe from his raids. At times the Ottomans were allied with the French, as when Kheir-ed-Din joined forces with François I to sack Nice in 1543.

---

c.1478–1546
KHEIR-ED-DIN

OTTOMAN NAVAL COMMANDER AND PRIVATEER

Kheir-ed-Din, known to Europeans as Barbarossa, was born on the island of Lesbos, probably to a family of Albanian origin. He went to sea at an early age and became a corsair, a role in which he was initially overshadowed by his elder brother Oruç Reis. Kheir-ed-Din succeeded Oruç as ruler of Algiers in 1518, swearing allegiance to the Ottoman sultan. Like his brother, he helped large numbers of mudejars, Spanish Muslims, to escape from Andalusia to North Africa. He was also extraordinarily active as a corsair, appearing off the coast of Spain, the Balearic Islands, southern France, and Italy, to launch lightning raids that made him both feared and admired. In 1534 he was appointed Fleet Admiral of the Ottoman navy, winning a great victory over the Christian Holy League at Preveza four years later. He retired to Istanbul in 1545, shortly before his death.

FIGHTING CORSAIRS

The Ottoman navy was a hybrid force that drew strength from its diversity. The empire was run by a well organized bureaucracy and had impressive financial resources. Once these were devoted to the construction, equipping, and manning of a navy in the late 15th century, a formidable fleet was the almost inevitable result. But the Ottomans also relied heavily upon the skills and initiative of privateers. The Barbary corsairs of Algiers and other North African ports, officially sanctioned by the Ottoman sultans, not only preyed upon Christian merchant shipping and raided the coasts of Christian states, but also provided a considerable percentage of the galleys found in Ottoman war fleets. The aggression and daring of their commanders was a vital adjunct to the more formal fighting style of the official Ottoman navy. The Ottoman sultan and his military authorities always tended to regard sea power as a support to land operations, best employed for transporting large armies such as the 100,000 soldiers employed in the successful siege of Rhodes in 1523, or the 40,000 used in the failed siege of Malta in 1565.

Ottoman war galley
This 16th-century depiction of an Ottoman galley bristles with cannons. This was more typical of a Venetian galleass of the period – Ottoman ships were usually more lightly armed.

CHRISTIAN DISUNITY

The Christian states around the Mediterranean struggled to mount a unified response as the Ottomans pressed westward. No country alone was sufficiently strong to stand up to the Turks. Venice suffered first and worst. After they had suffered defeat at the hands of the Ottoman navy at the end of the 15th century, the Venetians found all their possessions and trade in the eastern Mediterranean under threat. The Knights of St John, who operated as Christian predators upon Muslim shipping, were driven out of their stronghold on Rhodes but survived precariously in a new base at Malta. Emperor Charles V and subsequent Habsburg rulers of Spain fought, with little success, to contest Ottoman control of the Muslim states of North Africa. Even when the Christians achieved sufficient unity to send out a combined fleet, they were defeated at Preveza in 1538 and Djerba in 1560, before a victory for the Holy League in the great galley battle of Lepanto in 1571 sent the whole of Christendom delirious with relief.

FIREPOWER REVOLUTION

The rise of Ottoman naval power coincided with the introduction of cannon and handguns into naval warfare. On land Turkish armies were not at all backward in the deployment of the latest gunpowder weapons, but their Christian opponents were definitely more thoroughgoing in their use at sea. Even the Venetians' low and nimble galleys would have a bow gun firing

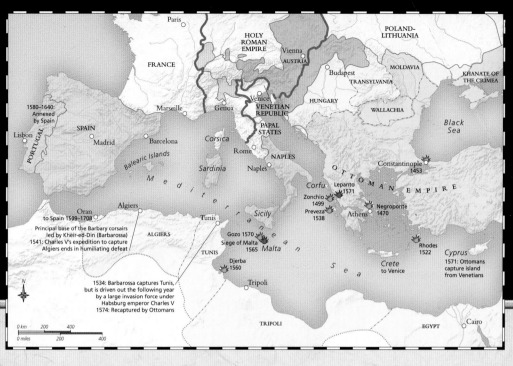

1200 BCE – 1550 CE

THE OTTOMAN EMPIRE

The great period of Ottoman expansion was in the reigns of Selim the Grim (1512–20) and Suleiman the Magnificent (1520–66). The former conquered Egypt and much of the Middle East, the latter extended Ottoman rule far into southeastern Europe and along the coast of North Africa. During this time the Ottomans also became the dominant naval power in the eastern Mediterranean and threatened to do the same in the western half.

KEY

▪ Ottoman Empire 1512
▪ Ottoman conquests by 1639
▪ Austrian Habsburg possessions
▪ Spanish Habsburg possessions
— Frontiers 1600
— Holy Roman Empire
⚔ Ottoman victory
⚔ Ottoman defeat

---

straight ahead – aimed by pointing the galley directly at the target – augmented by swivel guns to rake the enemy decks. Other Christian vessels might carry a much heavier weight of armament. Large galeasses – converted merchant ships – were even capable of delivering broadsides. Christian fighting men often wore armour and fired arquebuses instead of crossbows, while the Muslims remained lightly clad and equipped with traditional missile weapons. An Ottoman fleet usually had the advantage of superior manoeuvrability, however. In the course of the 16th century most Christian states resorted to *a scaloccio* rowing – very large oars, each pulled by four, five, or even more rowers. These were operated mostly by slaves and criminals condemned to the galleys. Venice alone managed to maintain a predominance of free oarsmen. The *a scaloccio* system militated against deft and skilful manoeuvre, as did the increasing size of galleys viewed as gun platforms. Christian fleets typically advanced in line abreast to defend their flanks and maximize forward fire. Handled aggressively, Ottoman galleys could break up the Christian line and win in a pell-mell battle.

AFTER LEPANTO

Lepanto, the last major battle in which galleys overwhelmingly predominated, was a major Ottoman defeat. But it was far from ending Ottoman naval efforts, because the empire had the resources to build a new

fleet to replace the one it had lost. For a long time the Ottomans were able to hold their own against Christians in the eastern Mediterranean, beating Venice in a war for control of Crete in the mid-17th century and besting a combined Christian fleet at Matapan in 1717. Meanwhile, the Barbary corsairs extended their activities

into the Atlantic, their nifty xebecs even raiding the coasts of the British Isles – almost the entire population of the Irish village of Baltimore was carried off by the North African raiders in 1631. The depredations of the Barbary pirates continued largely unchecked until the early years of the 19th century.

The Crescent and the Cross
In this clash of galleys of the Lepanto era, the Christians fire their foredeck cannons on the Ottoman foe.

CHRISTIAN NAVIES AGAINST THE TURKS

THE FIRST CHRISTIAN STATE to feel the effects of Ottoman naval power was Venice, thoroughly defeated in a war fought between 1499 and 1503. From then until the battle of Lepanto in 1571, the Christians were unable to challenge Ottoman command of the eastern Mediterranean. However, the galleys of Malta, commanded by the Knights of St John, harassed Turkish communications, and the failure of the Ottoman siege of the island in 1565 was a major relief for Christian Europe. Efforts to wrest control of North Africa from the Muslims repeatedly failed and

the Barbary corsairs of Algiers, Tunis, and Tripoli, operating as Ottoman privateers, were a constant threat in the central and western Mediterranean. The Ottoman cause was aided by the lack of unity between the Christian powers, with Venice and the Habsburgs fixed enemies, and the French mostly allied with the Turks. The battle of Diu, which extended Christian-Muslim conflict into the Indian Ocean, was a reminder that the Mediterranean powers were fighting for control of a backwater, as oceanic voyages opened up new trade routes and ocean-going ships transformed naval warfare.

THE AGE OF GALLEYS

VENETIAN–OTTOMAN WAR

ZONCHIO

Date 12–25 August 1499
Forces Ottomans: 87 galleys and galliots, c.200 other ships; Venetians: 64 galleys and galliots, c.100 other ships
Losses Unknown

Location Cape Zonchio, Lepanto, Greece

In spring 1499 a Venetian force under Antonio Grimani met an Ottoman fleet under Kemal Reis off Lepanto. Both fleets had a number of great galleys and carracks that provided a high platform for breach-loading iron cannon and primitive handguns, as well as troops armed with bows and other traditional missiles. Kemal Reis's flagship, *Göke*,

could reputedly carry 700 soldiers. In the first engagement on 12 August *Göke* was grappled and boarded by two large Venetian carracks, one of them commanded by Andrea Loredano. A fire broke out on *Göke* and all three vessels were burnt. Grimani was accused of failing to come to Loredano's aid.

Further actions were fought between the two fleets on 20, 22, and 25 August. The overall result was a clear defeat for the Venetians. Grimani was arrested on his return to Venice, but survived to become doge later in life.

Grappling and boarding
This contemporary woodcut shows the central event of the battle of Zonchio, when two Venetian ships grappled the Ottoman flagship, resulting in hand-to-hand fighting and deadly exchanges of arrows.

PORTUGUESE–OTTOMAN WAR

DIU

Date February 1509
Forces Portuguese: 18 ships; Egyptian-Gujerati force: 12 ships
Losses Unknown

Location Diu, western India

After Vasco da Gama's voyage to India in 1498, the Portuguese set out to take over the spice trade between the Indian Ocean and Europe. This was a threat to Egypt, Venice, and the Ottoman Empire, which all profited from the trade. The Ottomans

Portuguese naval artillery
The swivel-gun was a small anti-personnel weapon with a a wide arc of fire, fired at the enemy's deck as one closed to board.

gave the Egyptians galleys to send into the Indian Ocean. The Egyptian squadron joined with the dhows of Gujerati Sultan Mahmud Begada and, in March 1508, intercepted a Portuguese convoy. In the action Lourenço de Almeida, son of Portuguese viceroy Dom Francisco de Almeida, was killed.

Officially replaced as viceroy in December 1508, de Almeida refused to give up command and took his

carracks and caravels to seek revenge. He found the Egyptian-Gujerati force in port at Diu. The Portuguese first used their cannon to bombard the enemy, then closed to board. The many prisoners taken were vilely mistreated by de Almeida, incensed at his son's death. The battle established the absolute superiority of European ocean-going sailing ships in naval warfare.

AS LONG AS YOU MAY BE POWERFUL AT SEA, YOU WILL HOLD INDIA AS YOURS; AND IF YOU DO NOT POSSESS THIS POWER, LITTLE WILL AVAIL YOU A FORTRESS ON THE SHORE.

FRANCISCO DE ALMEIDA IN A LETTER TO KING MANUEL OF PORTUGAL AFTER THE VICTORY AT DIU

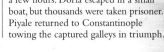

OTTOMAN–HABSBURG WARS

DJERBA

Date May 1560
Forces Ottomans: 86 galleys or galliots; Christians: 54 galleys, 66 other vessels
Losses Ottomans: none; Christians: 30 ships captured

Location Off coast of Tunisia

In 1560 panic at Muslim raids in the western Mediterranean led various Christian powers, including Genoa, the Knights of Malta, and Savoy, to support an expedition mounted by Philip II of Spain against North Africa. Led by the Genoese Giovanni Andrea Doria, they captured the island of Djerba. With Djerba and Malta in their hands, they would control access to the western Mediterranean. The Ottomans dispatched a fleet under Grand Admiral Piyale Pasha, who arrived off Djerba to find the Christian ships scattered and half their crews ashore. He attacked immediately and captured half the Christian galleys in a few hours. Doria escaped in a small boat, but thousands were taken prisoner. Piyale returned to Constantinople towing the captured galleys in triumph.

THE BATTLE OF PREVEZA

In 1537 the Ottoman admiral-in-chief Kheir-ed-Din (Barbarossa) launched a campaign to annexe Venetian possessions around the coasts of Greece. He also raided the Italian coast, ravaging the Papal States and the domains of the Spanish Habsburgs. In desperation the Christian states united to face a common enemy, forming a Holy League under the leadership of Pope Paul III. In summer 1538 they assembled a large fleet under the overall command of the Habsburgs' admiral, the Genoese Andrea Doria.

Barbarossa, who was in the Aegean when he learnt that the Christian fleet had appeared in the Ionian Sea, sailed around Greece to confront it. The Holy League decided to attack Preveza, an important Ottoman base on the Greek mainland at the mouth of the Gulf of Arta. The attack failed and Barbarossa reinforced Ottoman control of the coast by seizing the fortress of Actium

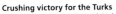

Crushing victory for the Turks
Barbarossa and his captains exploited the speed and mobility of their galleys to outmanoeuvre the heavier Christian ships, inflicting heavy material losses.

on the opposite shore of the gulf. With the guns of these two strongholds under his command, he was able to shelter his fleet inshore while the Christian ships were forced to keep out to sea.

The Ottomans were greatly inferior in numbers and firepower. Their 122 galleys and light fustas faced more than 130 Christian galleys with a host of other vessels in support. The Holy League may have had as many as 60,000 fighting men, outnumbering the Ottomans by three to one. Yet Barbarossa had not the slightest intention of avoiding battle. The Ottomans attacked at dawn on 28 September, a still day that virtually immobilized the sailing ships that made up a substantial part of the Christian fleet. Much of the fighting consisted of lightweight Ottoman galleys and fustas manoeuvring deftly around relatively static but heavily armed Christian ships in order to board them.

Doria's conduct both during and after the battle was controversial. He chose to organize his fleet in depth rather than exploiting the

Terracotta grenades
The Ottomans were very innovative in their use of gunpowder weapons. As well as powerful cannons, they used arquebuses and exploding grenades made of terracotta.

opportunity for outflanking that his numerical superiority presented. He also failed to engage the Ottoman centre with any vigour, manoeuvring to avoid close contact. The Papal and Venetian galleys on the flanks were meanwhile heavily engaged and the sailing ships exposed to capture. By the end of the day the Ottomans had suffered substantial casualties but had taken 36 ships as prizes and some 3,000 prisoners.

HIDDEN AGENDA

The Venetians wanted to continue the fight the following day, but Doria insisted on withdrawal to Corfu. He may have been influenced by financial considerations, since he owned many of the galleys under his command. But he was probably obeying secret orders from his Habsburg masters, who were not at all sorry to see Venice lose territory, the immediate consequence of the battle.

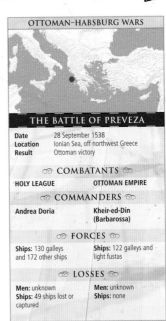

OTTOMAN–HABSBURG WARS

THE BATTLE OF PREVEZA

Date	28 September 1538
Location	Ionian Sea, off northwest Greece
Result	Ottoman victory

COMBATANTS

HOLY LEAGUE	OTTOMAN EMPIRE

COMMANDERS

Andrea Doria	Kheir-ed-Din (Barbarossa)

FORCES

Ships: 130 galleys and 172 other ships	Ships: 122 galleys and light fustas

LOSSES

Men: unknown	Men: unknown
Ships: 49 ships lost or captured	Ships: none

1466–1560

ANDREA DORIA

GENOESE ADMIRAL

The most famous Christian admiral of his day, Andrea Doria was admired and distrusted in equal measure. Born into one of Genoa's most distinguished families, he earned his reputation fighting for the French in the 1520s before changing sides and selling his services to the Habsburgs. A military entrepreneur who rented out his galleys to his employer, he was always suspected of putting his business interests first in the struggle against the Turks. He did not retire from fighting until the age of 89. His great nephew Giovanni Andrea Doria inherited his role as Habsburg admiral.

THE CAPTURE OF TUNIS
Holy Roman Emperor Charles V, who was also king of Spain, organized regular campaigns against the Muslim states of North Africa to try to curb the depredations of Christian shipping by Kheir-ed-Din and other Barbary corsairs. In 1535, Charles led a force of 60,000 soldiers, with a Genoese fleet commanded by Andrea Doria, to take the port of Tunis. The Spanish held on to a base at Tunis until 1574, when it was recaptured by the Ottomans.

OTTOMAN EXPANSION

SIEGE OF MALTA

Date 18 May–11 September 1565
Forces Ottomans: c.180 ships; Knights of Malta: unknown
Losses Unknown

Location
Malta

In spring 1565 the Ottoman sultan Suleiman the Magnificent sent an expedition to capture Malta. The navy was commanded by Grand Admiral Piyale Pasha, aided by the Barbary corsair Turgut Reis and an Egyptian fleet under Uluç Ali. Some 40,000

Ottoman landings on Malta
The Ottoman army disembarks at Marsascirocco on the east coast of Malta south of Grand Harbour. The distinctive white headgear of the janissaries is conspicuous among the Turkish forces.

soldiers were landed, including at least 6,000 janissaries, the Ottomans' crack troops. Cannon and gunpowder was shipped to the island in enormous quantities to besiege the Knights of Malta in their fortresses around the Grand Harbour. A relief force gathered in Sicily, but Spanish commander Don Garcia de Toledo knew his fleet was not strong enough to take on the Turks.

The first Maltese fortress to suffer the onslaught of the Turkish artillery was Fort St Elmo at the entrance to Grand Harbour. The defenders held out valiantly for over a month, but Turgut Reis was killed during the siege. An attempt to attack St Michael fort across the Grand Harbour failed, the Turkish ships blocked by a boom and blasted by cannon at water level.

In September the Ottomans admitted defeat and headed for home. The failed siege was the first significant reverse for the Ottomans in the Mediterranean.

CREW PROFILE

RENAISSANCE GALLEY

16TH CENTURY

THE CREW OF A RENAISSANCE WAR GALLEY was typically assembled by a captain of high social status, appointed to his command by the state. On the other hand, a galley might also be the private venture of a mercenary or corsair. The captain did not necessarily have any nautical experience, relying on a team of experienced seamen to navigate and run the ship. Spanish royal galleys had a chaplain to look after the crew's spiritual welfare and a governor to maintain order and discipline. Although sailors and even oarsmen might at a push take part in combat, the fighting force was a separate body of men – a land army at sea that included gentleman volunteers, infantry, and specialist artillerymen.

CONVICTS AND SLAVES

Oarsmen made up the majority of the crew. Some were free men, either signing on as volunteers or recruited by conscription – the latter common in Ottoman and Venetian fleets. But in the 16th century free oarsmen became increasingly rare, especially in the Spanish galley fleet, partly because they were too expensive to employ. Their place was taken by convicts or slaves. A spell in the Spanish galleys was the punishment for offences such as murder, robbery, bigamy, rape, and vagrancy, with sentences ranging from a few months to life.

CONDITIONS ON BOARD

The slaves were usually prisoners of war, although more likely to have been seized by marauding privateers than taken prisoner in battle. Thus slaves in Christian galleys were chiefly Muslims, and vice versa. Free oarsmen were not chained and might have a weapon so they could fight if needed.

But convicts and slaves were shackled to their benches. Life below deck on a crowded galley was miserable. A drum was beaten to give the rhythm for their strokes, but the lash was often used freely on any man thought to be slacking. An oarsman was a valuable item and intelligent captains kept their ships clean and the crew well fed. But often sanitary arrangements were poor, ships stank, disease was rife, and gross ill-treatment common. Average life expectancy for a convict in a Spanish galley has been estimated at two years.

Venetian galley slave
As the Venice lost its possessions in the Ionian and Aegean to the Ottomans, there were fewer free men to recruit as oarsmen, so it relied more and more on slaves and convicts.

OTTOMAN EXPANSION

GOZO

Date 15 July 1570
Forces Knights of Malta: 4 galleys; Ottomans: 19 galliots
Losses Knights of Malta: 3 galleys captured; Ottomans: none

Location Off Cape Passaro, Sicily

In June 1570 the Knights of Malta sent four galleys under the command of French knight François de St Clément to join a Christian fleet in Sicily that had assembled for a campaign against the Turks. As things turned out, this campaign, did not come to fruition until the following year, when the fleet of the Holy League defeated the Ottomans at Lepanto. Since there was little prospect of action in Sicily, St Clément decided to return to Malta, setting sail on the evening of 14 July.

The following morning, some 30km (20 miles) off the island of Gozo, the Knights' galleys were spotted by a squadron of galliots that Uluç Ali, the recently appointed Beylerbey of Algiers, was taking to Constantinople. St Clément turned back for Sicily with the Muslims in hot pursuit. The galliots were faster under oars than the large Maltese galleys, whose Muslim slave oarsmen had no incentive to make haste. Two galleys, *Santa Anna* and *San Giovanni*, were surrounded by galliots and boarded after heavy fighting that left their decks strewn with the dead and dying. The other two galleys managed to reach the Sicilian coast, where St Clément's flagship ran aground. As the knights fled ashore, the slave oarsmen took over the galley and handed it over to Uluç Ali. Returning to Malta, St Clément was condemned to death by strangulation and his body thrown into the sea in a sack.

Dardanelli

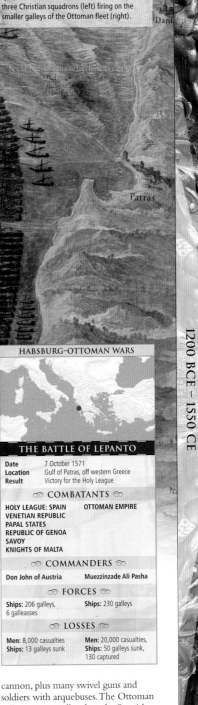

The opposing lines at Lepanto
This painting, completed in 1581, gives a spectacular aerial view of the battle. It depicts three Christian squadrons (left) firing on the smaller galleys of the Ottoman fleet (right).

Patras

Dard

THE BATTLE OF LEPANTO

On 16 September 1571 a large Christian fleet set sail from Sicily on an expedition to relieve Venetian-owned Cyprus, then under attack by the Ottoman Empire. Most of the men and galleys had been supplied by Venice and Habsburg Spain, but Genoa, the Papacy, Savoy, and Malta's Knights of St John had all made contributions. In command was the Habsburg prince Don John of Austria.

As his fleet drew near to where the Ottomans lay at Lepanto in western Greece, Don John organized the galleys into four squadrons, that on the right commanded by Genoese Giovanni Andrea Doria, the left under Venetian Agostino Barbarigo, the centre under Don John himself. Spanish admiral Santa Cruz was placed in reserve.

Facing the Christian fleet, the Ottoman forces advanced in a crescent, with the admiral Ali Pasha in the centre, the right wing under Suluc Mehmed Pasha, and the left under the feared corsair Uluç Ali, an Italian-born convert to Islam. As the moment for combat approached Don John had the Holy League's banner of Christ crucified raised above his flagship, *Real*. Ali Pasha sailed under a banner embroidered 29,800 times with the name of Allah.

CANNON AND ARQUEBUS

The Christians placed their faith solidly in firepower. Most of their galleys had a centreline cannon or culverin in the bows firing up to a 25kg (60lb) iron shot, flanked by up to four smaller cannon, plus many swivel guns and soldiers with arquebuses. The Ottoman galleys were smaller than the Spanish ones, but similar to the Venetian. They had fewer – and less powerful – cannon and their soldiers depended more on composite bows than on firearms. The Ottomans hoped to manoeuvre, ram, and board the Christian vessels. Both sides hoped to maintain formation and avoid being attacked on the flank where the galleys were most vulnerable.

1547–1578
DON JOHN OF AUSTRIA
COMMANDER OF SPAIN'S MEDITERRANEAN GALLEY FLEET

The illegitimate half-brother of Philip II of Spain, John of Austria was named commander of the Spanish galley fleet at the age of 18, with more experienced admirals to advise him. He developed a reputation for reckless courage during Spain's suppression of the Moriscos revolt in Andalusia, before his appointment to lead the fleet of the Holy League. Victory at Lepanto was followed by the capture of Tunis from the Muslims in 1573. Philip then sent him to deal with a rebellion in Flanders, where he died aged 31.

HABSBURG–OTTOMAN WARS

THE BATTLE OF LEPANTO

Date	7 October 1571
Location	Gulf of Patras, off western Greece
Result	Victory for the Holy League

∞ COMBATANTS ∞

HOLY LEAGUE: SPAIN VENETIAN REPUBLIC PAPAL STATES REPUBLIC OF GENOA SAVOY KNIGHTS OF MALTA	OTTOMAN EMPIRE

∞ COMMANDERS ∞

Don John of Austria	Muezzinzade Ali Pasha

∞ FORCES ∞

Ships: 206 galleys, 6 galleasses	Ships: 230 galleys

∞ LOSSES ∞

Men: 8,000 casualties Ships: 13 galleys sunk	Men: 20,000 casualties, Ships: 50 galleys sunk, 130 captured

Hol. de Curzolari

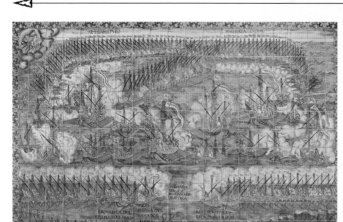

Commemorating the victory
Lepanto became a favourite subject for art all over Catholic Europe. This colourful Spanish version is painted on tiles. Between the Christian fleet (below) and the Ottomans (above), the huge Christian galleasses open fire at the start of the battle.

Crucially, the Venetians also provided six galleasses – large transport galleys turned into floating gun platforms. These were so unwieldy they had to be towed into position, but their massed guns packed a formidable punch. The presence of the galleasses was a surprise to the Ottomans. They were unsure of their tactical function, but soon found out as the thunder of the galleasses' guns sent a savage hail of iron balls lashing into the galleys of the Ottoman centre.

Although his fleet was thrown into disorder and two galleys had been sunk, Ali Pasha pressed on past the galleasses and through the fire from the galleys behind to engage the Christian centre at close quarters. On the flanks a desperate battle was joined as the horns of the Turkish crescent attempted to outflank the Christian line. The Venetian galleys on the Christian left were close to shore, but some of Suluc's ships succeeded in rowing through shallow

water beyond the edge of their line. Barbarigo's galleys skilfully backed to turn outward facing toward the shore and presenting their bow guns to the Ottoman ships, which were forced to turn to face them. A brutal close-quarter mêlée ensued, in which Barbarigo was hit in the eye by an arrow and killed.

On the Christian right there was open water. Uluç Ali tried to outflank Doria's squadron, and Doria shifted further to the right to block him. This stretched the line between the Christian right and centre. Choosing his moment, the wily Uluç Ali turned swiftly back to attack the straggling Christian galleys left behind by Doria's rightward move.

CHAOS AND BLOODSHED

By this stage, cloaked in a fog of gunpowder smoke, the battle was a scene of brutal slaughter. Everywhere galleys were locked together, soldiers fighting hand-to-hand on the decks with sword and pike. At the heart of the battle, Don John's flagship was boarded by janissaries – elite Ottoman infantry – from Ali Pasha's *Sultana*.

The key to the outcome was the use of the reserve squadron made by Santa Cruz. Feeding his galleys into the action where and when they were needed, he enabled the Venetians on the left to hold and then put to flight their adversaries – many Ottoman troops escaping through the shallow water onto land.

Santa Cruz then decisively intervened in the struggle in the centre. The *Sultana* was stormed and taken. Ali Pasha's severed head was displayed on a pike and the Ottoman standard struck from the mast. As the Ottoman centre collapsed, fighting turned to massacre and plunder. Only Uluç Ali was able to extricate his galleys from the debacle, leading perhaps a sixth of the original force back to Constantinople.

The Ottomans quickly built a new fleet – their grand vizier bragged that the Christians had merely shaved the Ottoman beard that "would grow all the better for the razor". But Christian jubilation at victory in one of the largest sea battles ever fought was justifiable, for it stemmed the tide of Ottoman expansion that had threatened to engulf the whole Mediterranean.

Detailed contemporary record
The individual ships engaged in the centre are clearly identifiable by their banners. At this early stage of the battle several of the Christian galleys have been boarded by Ottoman troops.

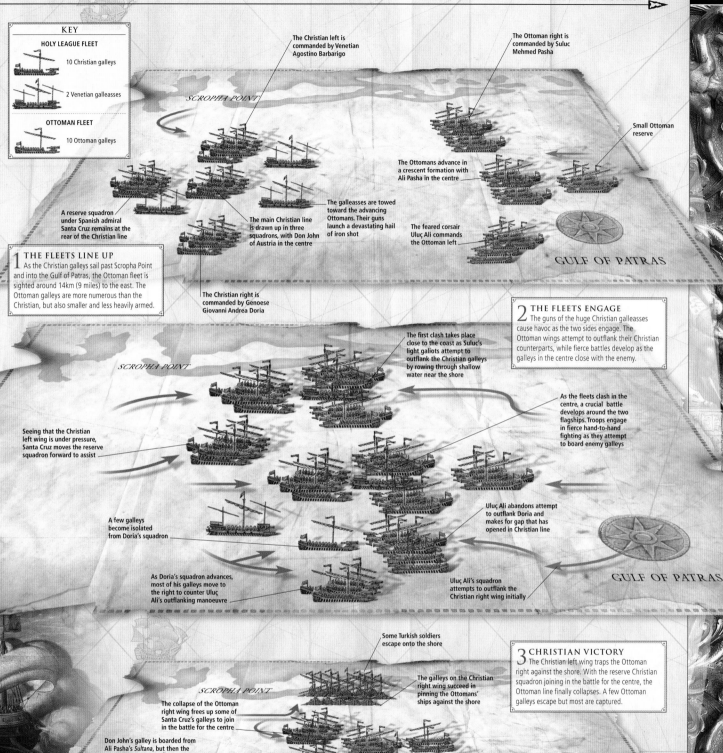

KEY

HOLY LEAGUE FLEET

10 Christian galleys

2 Venetian galleasses

OTTOMAN FLEET

10 Ottoman galleys

The Christian left is commanded by Venetian Agostino Barbarigo

The Ottoman right is commanded by Suluc Mehmed Pasha

SCROPHA POINT

Small Ottoman reserve

The Ottomans advance in a crescent formation with Ali Pasha in the centre

A reserve squadron under Spanish admiral Santa Cruz remains at the rear of the Christian line

The galleasses are towed toward the advancing Ottomans. Their guns launch a devastating hail of iron shot

The main Christian line is drawn up in three squadrons, with Don John of Austria in the centre

The feared corsair Uluç Ali commands the Ottoman left

GULF OF PATRAS

1 THE FLEETS LINE UP

As the Christian galleys sail past Scropha Point and into the Gulf of Patras, the Ottoman fleet is sighted around 14km (9 miles) to the east. The Ottoman galleys are more numerous than the Christian, but also smaller and less heavily armed.

The Christian right is commanded by Genoese Giovanni Andrea Doria

2 THE FLEETS ENGAGE

The guns of the huge Christian galleasses cause havoc as the two sides engage. The Ottoman wings attempt to outflank their Christian counterparts, while fierce battles develop as the galleys in the centre close with the enemy.

SCROPHA POINT

The first clash takes place close to the coast as Suluc's light galiots attempt to outflank the Christian galleys by rowing through shallow water near the shore

As the fleets clash in the centre, a crucial battle develops around the two flagships. Troops engage in fierce hand-to-hand fighting as they attempt to board enemy galleys

Seeing that the Christian left wing is under pressure, Santa Cruz moves the reserve squadron forward to assist

A few galleys become isolated from Doria's squadron

Uluç Ali abandons attempt to outflank Doria and makes for gap that has opened in Christian line

As Doria's squadron advances, most of his galleys move to the right to counter Uluç Ali's outflanking manoeuvre

Uluç Ali's squadron attempts to outflank the Christian right wing initially

GULF OF PATRAS

3 CHRISTIAN VICTORY

The Christian left wing traps the Ottoman right against the shore. With the reserve Christian squadron joining in the battle for the centre, the Ottoman line finally collapses. A few Ottoman galleys escape but most are captured.

Some Turkish soldiers escape onto the shore

The galleys on the Christian right wing succeed in pinning the Ottomans' ships against the shore

SCROPHA POINT

The collapse of the Ottoman right wing frees up some of Santa Cruz's galleys to join in the battle for the centre

Don John's galley is boarded from Ali Pasha's *Sultana*, but then the tables are turned, the Ottoman flagship captured, and Ali Pasha killed

Two galleasses move up to help prevent threatened breakthrough on the Christian right

Seeing the Ottoman standard cut down from the flagship's mast, the Turkish centre collapses

A few Ottoman galleys escape, chiefly those of Uluç Ali

Doria's right wing turns to assist the isolated galleys that had been under attack from Uluç Ali

GULF OF PATRAS

THE AGE OF GALLEYS

GALERA REAL

THE GALERA REAL was no ordinary war galley, but a luxury vessel made for Don John of Austria, commander-in-chief of the fleet of the Holy League assembled to fight the Ottoman Turks. A gift from his half-brother, King Philip II of Spain, the galley was built in the shipyards of Barcelona in 1568, then decorated and gilded in Seville.

THE PALATIAL ROYAL FLAGSHIP was 60m (197ft) long and 6.2m (24ft) wide and carried a crew of as many as 400 men. Of these, 236 were required simply to row the galley, with four men manning each oar. In addition, there were a number of skilled sailors to steer and manage the two lateen sails, as well as a large detachment of soldiers. The galley was armed with a large central cannon in the bow, flanked by four medium-sized guns. There were also four much smaller guns sited between the oarsmen's stations, two on each side of the ship.

This replica of the galley was made for the Maritime Museum in Barcelona to mark the 400th anniversary of the Holy League's victory at the battle of Lepanto on 7 October 1571. The ship's most striking feature is the sheer richness of its decoration, from the figurehead of Neptune to the paintings, statues, and reliefs on the stern. These were painstakingly recreated from a description written at the time. Many of them feature the Classical heroes Hercules and

Jason. The choice of these two figures was significant: in his quest for the Golden Fleece Jason sailed with the Argonauts to Colchis on the Black Sea, while legend placed the Pillars of Hercules at the Strait of Gibraltar – the two extremes of the vast length of coastline controlled by the Ottoman Empire.

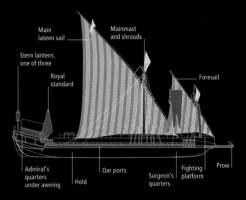
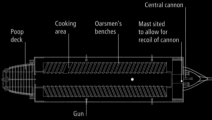

Galera Real
The galley raised its sails when crossing open sea with a favourable wind, but in battle relied on its 236 oarsmen. The main battle tactic was to board and capture enemy ships.

In action at Lepanto
Don John's galley fought a close-quarters duel with the Ottoman flagship *Sultana*. Turkish soldiers boarded the galley, but were driven back.

> **THE GREAT BANNER OF THE LEAGUE, DISPLAYING CHRIST CRUCIFIED, ... THE COATS OF ARMS OF HABSBURG SPAIN, THE POPE, AND THE REPUBLIC OF VENICE, WAS HOISTED ON THE REAL'S MAINMAST.**
> **NICCOLÒ CAPPONI** DESCRIBING THE OPENING OF THE BATTLE OF LEPANTO

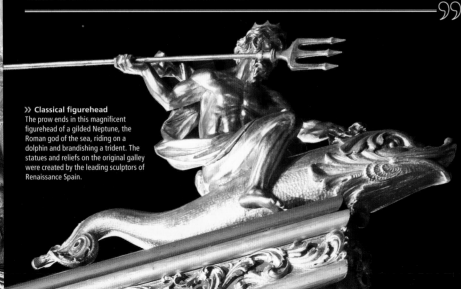

» Classical figurehead
The prow ends in this magnificent figurehead of a gilded Neptune, the Roman god of the sea, riding on a dolphin and brandishing a trident. The statues and reliefs on the original galley were created by the leading sculptors of Renaissance Spain.

» Prow
The galley's long prow is decorated with the coat of arms of Philip II of Spain, supported by two mermen. Before Lepanto Don John had the end of the prow cut off so that the central cannon could be depressed to shoot down on the Ottoman ships.

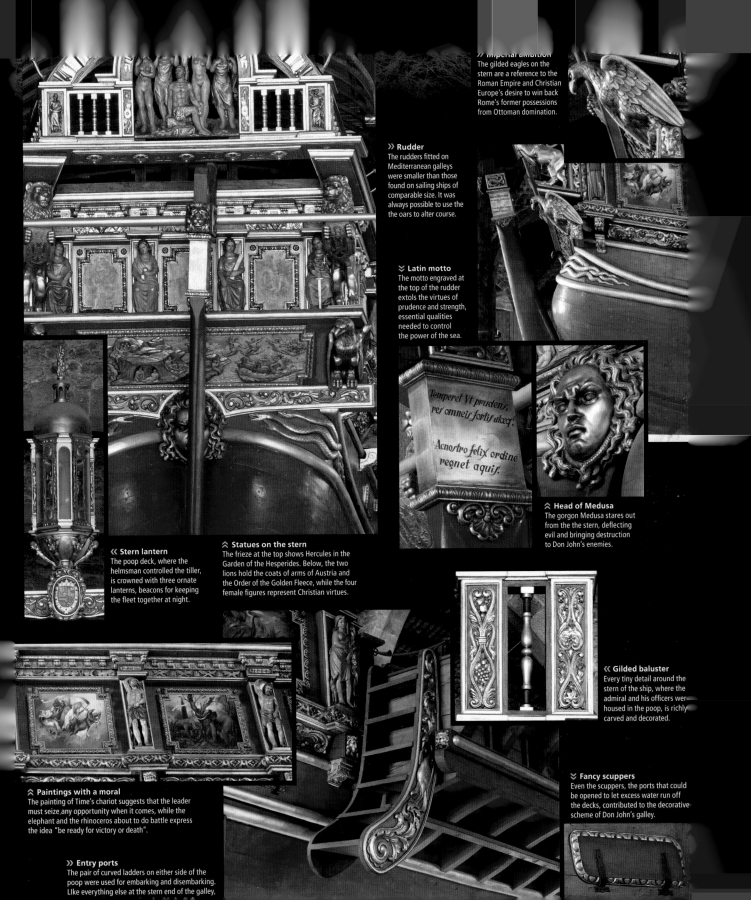

» Imperial ambition
The gilded eagles on the stern are a reference to the Roman Empire and Christian Europe's desire to win back Rome's former possessions from Ottoman domination.

» Rudder
The rudders fitted on Mediterranean galleys were smaller than those found on sailing ships of comparable size. It was always possible to use the the oars to alter course.

⌄ Latin motto
The motto engraved at the top of the rudder extols the virtues of prudence and strength, essential qualities needed to control the power of the sea.

Temperet Vt prudens, res omneis fortis vlceq?

Acnostro felix ordine regnet aquis.

⌃ Head of Medusa
The gorgon Medusa stares out from the the stern, deflecting evil and bringing destruction to Don John's enemies.

« Stern lantern
The poop deck, where the helmsman controlled the tiller, is crowned with three ornate lanterns, beacons for keeping the fleet together at night.

⌃ Statues on the stern
The frieze at the top shows Hercules in the Garden of the Hesperides. Below, the two lions hold the coats of arms of Austria and the Order of the Golden Fleece, while the four female figures represent Christian virtues.

« Gilded baluster
Every tiny detail around the stern of the ship, where the admiral and his officers were housed in the poop, is richly carved and decorated.

⌃ Paintings with a moral
The painting of Time's chariot suggests that the leader must seize any opportunity when it comes, while the elephant and the rhinoceros about to do battle express the idea "be ready for victory or death".

⌄ Fancy scuppers
Even the scuppers, the ports that could be opened to let excess water run off the decks, contributed to the decorative scheme of Don John's galley.

» Entry ports
The pair of curved ladders on either side of the poop were used for embarking and disembarking. Like everything else at the stern end of the galley,

ABOVE DECK

THE GALERA REAL mounted five cannon on the raised fighting platform or forecastle at the prow and four lighter artillery pieces. Going into battle, soldiers were stationed around the galley from the bow to the stern, many of them armed with arquebuses. The galley was rowed *a scaloccio*, with four men to a single oar. Although elaborately decorated, the poop functioned as the centre of armed resistance if the galley was boarded in battle, fighting men clustering there to defend their flag and their commmander. At Lepanto the galley was rammed by the Turkish flagship, the enemy prow penetrating as far inboard as the fourth oarsman.

Position of principal oarsman · Deck · Oarsmen's bench
Outrigger · Outrigger
Thole pin · Oars
Hull
Keel · Waterline
Hold

Cross-section of galley
The galley has 30 oars on the starboard (right) side and 29 on the port (left) side, with four oarsmen to each oar. As the men rowed the inside oarsman had to move further than the others, rising to his feet as he pressed on the foot brace in front of him to pull the oar through the water.

⩔ **Interior of the poop**
The poop deck, where Don John and his officers spent most of their time, was richly decorated with marquetry. The scenes on the backrest of the bench are episodes from Greek mythology, most having a nautical angle as well as a moral point to make.

≫ **Canopy and awning**
The admiral's quarters on the poop deck did not have a permanent roof. When necessary the canopy would be covered with a large cloth to keep out the sun or the wind and rain.

« Auxiliary gun
Unlike the cannon in the prow, the small breech-loading guns on either side of the galley could swivel. They would be loaded with small shot and used as anti-personnel weapons against the crew on the deck of an enemy galley.

« The binding of the oars
The oars are made of beechwood and 11.4m (37ft) long. Oars were sometimes made from a single piece of wood, but these broke easily and more often they were made of two lengths bound together.

« Renaissance rowlock
This peg, known as a thole pin, was the point at which the oar pivoted as the oarsmen drove the blade into the water. The oar was simply tied to the pin with a loop of rope.

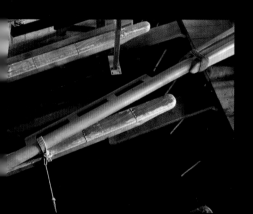

⌃ Rowing bench and oar
The most experienced and trusted oarsman took the position on the inside, from where he dictated the timing of the stroke to the other three oarsmen, who were normally less skilled. These each grasped one of the three handhold battens.

⌃ Range on the deck
One of the luxury extras on Don John's galley was a fire for cooking. On the replica of the *Galera Real* one of the oarsman's benches on the port side has been removed and the space created used for a fire with a metal bar above it for suspending cooking pots. This leaves the ship with 30 oars on one side and only 29 on the other.

BELOW DECKS

THE GALERA REAL had a wider and deeper hold than ordinary war galleys, and although there was not much headroom, there was plenty of space for stores. Below the poop deck were the armouries and the majordomo's pantry, where food and drink were prepared for Don John and his advisers and officers. Foreward of this were storerooms for bread and fresh vegetables, which would be taken on board whenever possible. Then there were the basic stores of water, wine, and grain for the oarsmen. More or less amidships was the gunpowder room and beneath the mainmast an extensive area given over to spare sailcloth, spars, and ropes. At the front of the hold was the surgeon's dispensary and a cramped surgery where he could set the bones or amputate the limbs of the wounded.

« Stores in the hold
Besides food, the spacious hold contained spare clothing, armour, and weapons. This recreated scene includes a selection of rapiers and a lockable chest of the kind that would have been used by the gentlemen on Don John's staff.

⌄ Essential kit
Buckets were in constant use on the galley: for carrying food and water, for washing the filth from the decks and the oarsmen's benches, and on occasions for putting out fires during battle.

⌃ Basic stores
The hold contained sacks of grain and barrels of wine and water. The oarsmen were fed on simple gruel and given wine and water to drink. When fighting in the heat of summer, it was essential to keep the crew well watered.

THE AGE OF GALLEYS

DISCIPLINE AND PUNISHMENT

A SHIP IS AN ENVIRONMENT in which problems of order and discipline are naturally acute. Men are crammed together for long periods of time, in boredom, danger, and discomfort. The lower orders always outnumber the officers, who are poorly placed to call for help in case of trouble. Crews also need to be drilled to work together as a tight-knit team in case of combat or to face crises such as storms at sea. The danger of their situation made most sailors favour good discipline, which would contribute to their survival.

STICKING TOGETHER

At best a ship's crew became its captain's bonded followers – a self-sufficient band owing allegiance primarily to one another and to their leader. Divisions between officers and men, normally rigid in class terms, were often less sharp in practice once at sea, simply because crew were so clearly all in it together. But a badly run ship with a sadistic captain was a hell-hole in any age. Naval warfare is studded with stories of desertion and mutiny – the latter often a systematic, almost formalized response to bad practice by a captain or officers, or to perceived breaches of customary law. Yet even in a good ship, where officers and men practised mutual respect, there was a need for punishment to enforce discipline.

> *It is (the captain's) indispensable duty to see that the poor seaman be not wronged of his due, nor the service carried on by noise, stripes or blows.*
>
> **CAPTAIN CHRISTOPHER O'BRIEN,** *Advice on Sea-Discipline & from a Father to his Son in Naval Tactics*

KIT INSPECTION The armed services take appearance very seriously as a reflection of personal discipline. These American sailors are waiting to have their kit inspected.

BEATING TO QUARTERS Drums, such as this 18th-century British example, were historically used to "beat to quarters", preparing the men for action. Sailors were exptected to clear the main gun deck and prime the cannons in preparation for battle.

PECULIAR PRACTICES

Some ingeniously cruel punishments have been unique to navies. At the time of the Ancient Greek galleys, a malefactor might be lashed with his head sticking out of one of the lower oar ports – an uncomfortable public humiliation in port, but torture if at sea. Keel-hauling was a practice particularly associated with the Dutch navy from the 16th century, although also occasionally practised by others. A man was tied to a rope slung under a ship and dragged from one side of the vessel to the other under the hull. Keel-hauling was not officially abolished in the Dutch navy until 1853. Ducking was a nautical punishment much practised by the French: a man was tied to a rope attached to one of the mainmast cross-trees and dropped into the sea, then heaved up again to repeat the exercise. There is little evidence of "walking the plank".

LEG IRONS Also known as bilboes, these were fixed to the deck, and could be used either for punishment or to hold a man awaiting trial. The prisoner, who was locked in for several days, was fed on bread and water.

FLOGGING Public flogging was the most widespread form of corporal punishment for breaches of the naval code, with the number of lashes dependant on the severity of the crime.

> *At an anchor in Leghorn Road ... were three seamen whipped from ship to ship ...*
>
> **POWELL,** *Weale Journal,* 1654 on "flogging round the fleet"

CORPORAL AND CAPITAL

In general, though, punishments at sea have always tended to reflect the norms of the society from which the navy is drawn. For example, Britain's 18th-century navy used public corporal and capital punishment just as Britain did on land – but with less capital punishment because one could not afford to lose the men. Mutiny, treason, desertion, and sodomy were capital offences for which a man could be hanged from the yard-arm. Flogging with the cat-o'-nine tails was the punishment for many other serious offences. It was carried out with formal ceremony, the ship's crew drawn up to watch and a roll of drums to add drama. Boys were exempt from flogging, instead made to "kiss the gunner's daughter" – they were tied over a gun and caned on their bare behinds. Theft from shipmates was usually punished by running the gauntlet, with the crew themselves whipping the offender in turn. Much resented by sailors was casual "starting" – bosun's mates hitting a man with a rope or cane when he was felt not to be working hard enough. Starting was banned in the Royal Navy in 1809.

⌃ **HANGING** In Nelson's navy death by hanging was the most serious punishment, usually for sodomy or mutiny. Like flogging, it was always inflicted in public with great theatricality to ensure the maximum deterrence. The crew would be formed up on deck, with the officers separated from the seamen.

« **CORPORAL DISCIPLINE** The cane (far left) was used on the boys, the starter (centre) was used to motivate the men as they performed their duties, while wayward crew members were punished by a lashing with the whip or cat-o'-nine tails (left).

CLEANING UP THE ACT

During the 19th century social norms altered away from corporal to custodial punishment. These changes were inevitably reflected at sea, although navies have often lagged behind reforms on shore. The last man in the US Navy hanged on board ship was Midshipman Philip Spencer, son of the secretary for war, allegedly guilty of mutiny in 1842. Britain's Royal Navy suspended flogging in 1881. At the same time there was more formality on board, with emphasis on saluting and minutiae of uniform. And punishments could still be harsh. The imprisonment routines of the US Navy in the "brig", including confinement on bread and water, were notoriously tough into the second half of the 20th century. The emphasis is now on "correction" rather than punishment, in line with current prison theory. Easier conditions have generally made naval service in the contemporary era a more mellow experience.

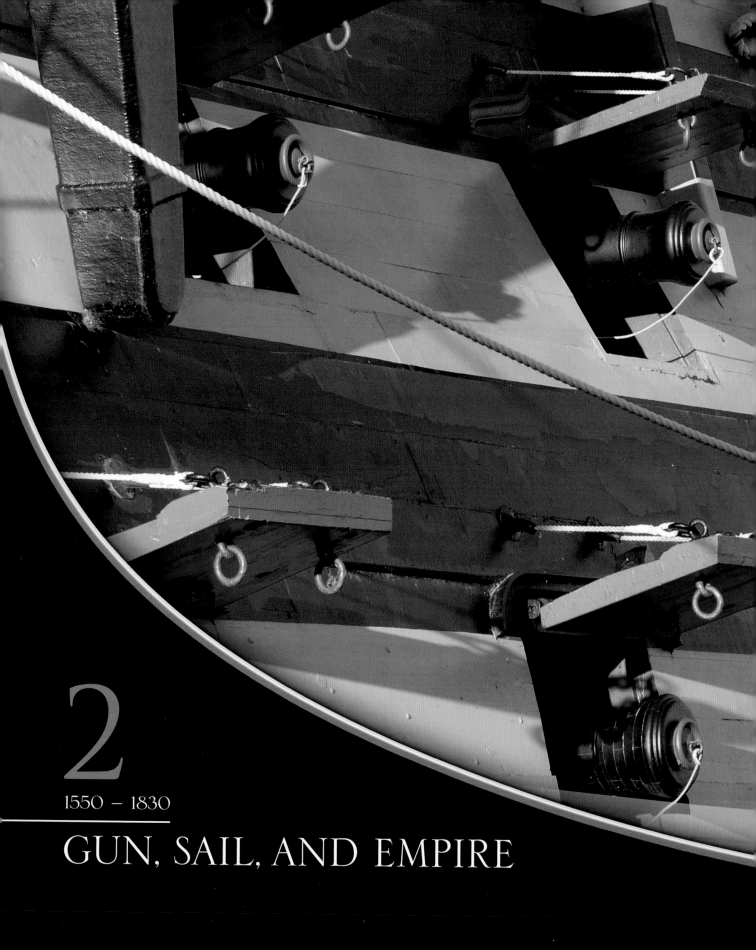

2

GUN, SAIL, AND EMPIRE

For approximately three centuries, from the early 1500s through to the 1830s, naval warfare was dominated by three-masted ocean-going sailing ships, armed with cannon. Although the tactics of grappling and boarding continued to hold their place in war at sea, from the 17th century the dominant mode of combat became the exchange of broadsides – volleys of cannon fire designed to bring down masts and rigging, hole the hull, and kill or wound the crew of an enemy vessel. European navies fought battles in the East Indies, the Caribbean, and the mid-Atlantic, as well as in Mediterranean and north and west European coastal waters. Sea power grew from an adjunct to land operations into a major source of imperial dominance in its own right.

The Golden Hind
The *Golden Hind* was the Elizabethan galleon Sir Francis Drake used to circumnavigate the globe (1577–80) and launch numerous raids on the Spanish. It carried an armament of 22 guns and had a top speed of 8 knots (15kph). This full-size replica was launched in 1973.

ships needed large crews packed into their decks because of the number of hands required to sail the vessel and to man the cannon in battle. In order to stay at sea for long periods they also had to carry substantial supplies of all essentials.

MANNING SHIPS

Fleets of sail were extremely expensive to build, maintain, and supply. Any country that wanted to have a dominant navy needed an extensive organization of dockyards for repair and shipbuilding, an administrative system to supply munitions and food, and a pool of sailors to draw on, since only experienced seamen were really useful on board. No country could afford to maintain a full navy in peace and war. Until the mid-17th century, merchant ships, under their peacetime captains, were pressed into frontline service when war broke out. This practice was discontinued because of the superior performance of purpose-built warships

FIGHTING MACHINES

The design of warships and combat tactics evolved subtly rather than dramatically through the age of sail. During the course of the 16th century ungainly carracks, conceived as large floating fortresses, were supplanted by sleeker galleons. The need to bring guns to bear in broadsides led to the adoption of the line of battle, and by the late 17th century the dominant warships were "ships of the line", graded into first-, second-, and third-rate by their weight of cannon. These were extraordinary fighting machines. Even in the 16th century there were "great ships" – large vessels built for prestige as much as combat – carrying more than 50 guns, but by the late 18th century a three-deck first-rate ship of the line would carry from 100 to 130 guns. Such

under military command, but sailors remained a general body of men who might sail in naval ships or merchant ships, or as privateers. Every sea power had to have a system for transferring its seagoing population into naval service in wartime. The Dutch banned merchant ships from sailing, forcing seamen to opt for naval employment. France registered its sailors, who were called up in "classes" and served their share of conscription. Britain used "press-gangs" to forcibly recruit sailors on shore and at sea, or tried to attract volunteers by offering bonuses

to those who signed on. In a crisis, landsmen had to be accepted as extra muscle on board, a dilution of seafaring expertise that became acute for Britain during the Napoleonic Wars. Permanent bodies of naval officers developed very gradually. Until the late 17th century senior commanders were usually not seamen and the senior seamen on board were often merchant captains or privateers. A career structure for naval officers emerged only slowly.

PRIVATEERS

The expense of maintaining navies encouraged states to turn to private enterprise as a way of financing sea warfare. Privateering ranged from the authorization of individual captains to prey upon the commerce of an enemy nation, to the mounting of major operations in which rulers, from England's Elizabeth I to France's Louis XIV, took a financial stake along with other

The Spanish Armada
Various events in the defeat of the Spanish Armada in August 1588 are combined in this painting: the English fireship attack off Calais, columns of smoke from the warning beacons lit in England, and even the appearance of Queen Elizabeth I on a white horse.

wealthy individuals. At times, the marauding of privateers amounted to what we would now call state-backed terrorism. The exploits of Jean Bart, Piet Heyn, Francis Drake, and other famous "sea dogs" made them national heroes, but they were understandably denounced as pirates by the victims of their depredations. The distinction between privateer and naval vessels was not always clear, not only because they might fight alongside one another – as in the English resistance to the Spanish Armada in 1588 – but because naval ships also operated with a profit motive, most navies offering prize money for the capture of enemy vessels and their cargoes.

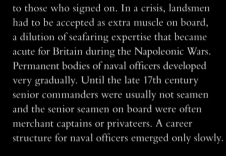

Armada medal
Silver medals, depicting English naval galleons, were cast to commemorate the defeat of the Spanish Armada in 1588.

PEACE AND WAR

In the age of sail, life on board ship was harsh as a matter of course. Crews suffered heavy losses, even in peacetime, to disease, accident, fire, and weather. In many ways life on ships was chaotic. Often, for example, there were children on board, as well as farm animals to provide food. Ratings had no uniforms and on many ships neither did officers. Yet by the 18th century, a well-run warship could equally be regarded, by contemporary standards, as a model of organization and efficiency – the regular processes of navigation, the handling of the sails, the keeping of watches, the maintenance of cleanliness, and frequent gunnery drill. The experience of sea combat, although infrequent, was intense by any standards. Broadside duels were bloody affairs, ships battering one another at close range with their cannon while sailors and marines with muskets fired down onto the enemy's deck from the rigging. Amid scenes of unutterable carnage, traditional principles of honourable conduct were maintained. Officers disdained to take cover, standing at great risk on the exposed quarterdeck. The convention of striking colours – lowering the flags – to signal surrender put a limit to the sufferings of a defeated crew, although honour dictated that a captain should not "strike" until his ship was a shambles. Surrender was usually conducted with great ceremony, the defeated commander handing his sword to his victorious opponent who would formally return it to its owner with a few polite words of respect. Such ceremonies took place on blood-spattered decks strewn with the dead.

BATTLE TACTICS

Naval engagements fought by sail were always subject to the influence of the wind, which could change direction, rise, or drop altogether in the course of a battle, confounding planned manoeuvres. A contrary wind might trap a fleet in harbour or prevent an entire division from joining a combat in which their comrades were hotly engaged within sight of them. The ships that held the weather gage were well situated to attack – it was the position the British always preferred. The slow movement of the ships meant that hours passed between sighting an enemy and opening fire. Once an engagement started, the fighting was usually quite static for long periods, with opposing ships sometimes locked together or even anchored opposite one another. Rowing boats might be sent from ship to ship around a fleet in battle carrying messages. Until the mid-17th century, tactics involved little more than a scrimmage in which fleets might show a greater or lesser inclination for boarding or for reliance on firepower. The adoption of the line of battle brought more order into naval combat, but no less savagery as each ship chose an enemy to set alongside and duel with. Although its formality could appear stultifying, fighting in line allowed for aggressive manoeuvres such as sailing around the enemy van to trap ships between two fires. In the 18th century more adventurous commanders used variants on line tactics such as the "general pursuit" and "breaking the line". But even the famous Admiral Horatio

Saluting the flagship
A 17th-century Dutch states yacht (right) fires a salute to the admiral's flagship (left), possibly belonging to the popular Admiral Michiel de Ruyter. Following naval tradition, a salute usually consists of an odd number of shots. An even number denotes a death. A 21-gun salute is reserved for heads of state.

1568
Start of 80 Years War, Dutch struggle for independence from Spain

1588
Defeat of the Armada prevents invasion of England by Philip II of Spain

1628
Dutch privateer Piet Heyn succeeds in capturing Spanish silver fleet at Matanzas in northern Cuba

1652–73
Anglo-Dutch Wars: series of three wars fought for control of the English Channel and North Sea

1653
Line-of-battle tactics used at the battle of the Gabbard, between England and the United Provinces

Cat-o'-nine tails
This rope whip was used aboard ship for administering corporal punishment.

1550   **1580**   **1610**   **1640**   **1670**

Musketeer's powder flask
The matchlock musket was the standard firearm of marines in the 17th century.

1572
Group of privateers, known as the Sea Beggars, capture port of Brielle (Brill) from the Spanish

1592–98
Japanese invasion of Korea thwarted by naval victories of Yi Sunshi

1628
The *Vasa*, pride of Sweden's navy, sinks on maiden voyage

1639
Dutch under Maarten Tromp defeat Spanish fleet at battle of the Downs

1690
War of the League of Augsburg: newly built French navy defeats Dutch and English at the battle of Beachy Head

Nelson, whose pursuit of the "pell-mell" battle gave a less formal and more decisive quality to naval warfare, for the most part adhered to the broad principles of the line of battle.

RISE AND FALL

Their sailing ships guaranteed European powers dominance in the oceans of the world and the ability to found overseas empires. Korea triumphed in an intensive naval war with Japan in the late 16th century, but even the Koreans could not begin to challenge the Europeans as oceanic sailors. Different European countries rose and fell in the naval pecking order through the resources they had available for – or were prepared to devote to – their navies and the quality of the seamen they had available to man their ships. Spain was the first dominant naval power of the sailing ship era, especially after incorporating Portugal in 1580. England was one of the first countries to organize a naval infrastructure and bureaucracy, but at first could not match the resources of the Spanish Empire. The Dutch proved themselves superb seamen and built a trading empire in the early 17th century, but they were slow to build a naval administration, relying for too long on merchantmen and privateers. France devoted major resources to naval power under the Sun King Louis XIV, but the counter demands of land warfare always militated against French concentration on sea power.

By the late 17th century Britain had established itself as the world's leading naval power, a status it maintained – not without serious challenges from the French – through the 18th century, but then triumphantly reaffirmed in the Napoleonic Wars. The

The Battle of the Nile (1798)
In 1798 Nelson's British fleet defeated the French fleet at the Battle of the Nile. The 80-gun French ship of the line *Tonnant* had its mast blown away, but fought on heroically, only surrendering after the death of its captain.

United States, founded in 1776, showed signs of naval potential but was still a minor sea power when the age of sail ended.

PROGRESS AND CHANGE

Many changes occurred over the 300 years of the sailing ship era. There were enormous improvements in navigation and nautical charts, in sailors' nutrition and health, and in the design of ships – copper bottoms in

US navy cutlass
The American navy played a minor role on the world's stage, but men such as Stephen Decatur performed heroic deeds with cutlass and pistol, boarding the ships of the Barbary pirates in the wars of 1804 and 1815.

particular vastly increased the time wooden sailing ships could stay at sea. By the later part of the period navies fought almost exclusively in purpose-built warships and privateering had been supplanted by the marauding of naval frigates. There was an increasingly formal structure of naval careers and hierarchies. Yet the era holds together in retrospect as a time of extraordinary conflicts and exploits that made naval battles central to the historical identity of European seagoing nations.

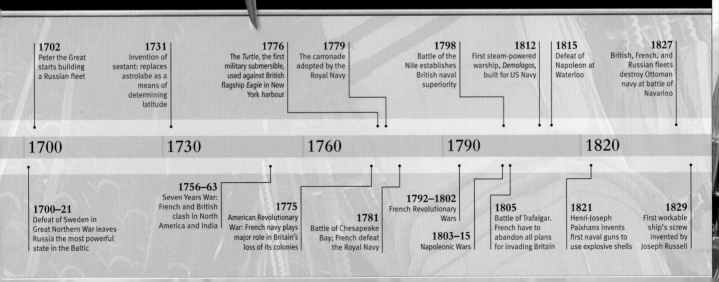

1702
Peter the Great starts building a Russian fleet

1731
Invention of sextant: replaces astrolabe as a means of determining latitude

1776
The *Turtle*, the first military submersible, used against British flagship *Eagle* in New York harbour

1779
The carronade adopted by the Royal Navy

1798
Battle of the Nile establishes British naval superiority

1812
First steam-powered warship, *Demologos*, built for US Navy

1815
Defeat of Napoleon at Waterloo

1827
British, French, and Russian fleets destroy Ottoman navy at battle of Navarino

1700   **1730**   **1760**   **1790**   **1820**

1700–21
Defeat of Sweden in Great Northern War leaves Russia the most powerful state in the Baltic

1756–63
Seven Years War: French and British clash in North America and India

1775
American Revolutionary War: French navy plays major role in Britain's loss of its colonies

1781
Battle of Chesapeake Bay; French defeat the Royal Navy

1792–1802
French Revolutionary Wars

1803–15
Napoleonic Wars

1805
Battle of Trafalgar. French have to abandon all plans for invading Britain

1821
Henri-Joseph Paixhans invents first naval guns to use explosive shells

1829
First workable ship's screw invented by Joseph Russell

JAPAN INVADED KOREA TWICE in the late 16th century, precipitating epic naval conflicts between two countries with very different seafaring traditions. Since the 1220s Japanese pirates had plagued the Korean coasts. This forced Korea to organize a naval defence system, with large, well-armed ships, to protect merchant convoys and coastal settlements. In Japan, by contrast, despite a thriving population of fishermen, pirates, and sea traders, naval development was limited. Accounts of Japan's long drawn out civil wars of the 16th century include very few references to fighting on water. When Japan's warrior leader Toyotomi Hideyoshi mounted a large-scale invasion of Korea in 1592, he saw ships merely as troop transports. But for the Koreans their naval strength proved to be a trump card, allowing them to achieve decisive victories at sea that forced the Japanese invaders to withdraw in 1593 and again in 1598.

Building a turtle ship
Admiral Yi Sunshin himself inspects the progress and plans of the shipbuilders. The extraordinary armoured turtle ships captured the Koreans' imagination, despite the fact that Yi's navy probably never had more than three of four of them at any one time.

CHINESE ABSENCE

The naval war between Japan and Korea in the 1590s was fought without the intervention of the major regional power, China. Ming China was the most sophisticated, technologically advanced society in the world, but its decision, taken in the 15th century, to get rid of large warships and abandon long-distance voyages left a naval vacuum in Asian waters. Japanese pirates – known as *wako* ("dwarf raiders") to their victims – were free to raid China's defenceless coasts, while the Portuguese,

once they were well established in the Indian Ocean, sought further trading opportunities in China and Japan. When Japan invaded Korea, the Chinese sent an army to support the Koreans, but, because of their naval weakness, intervened on a relatively small scale in the conflict at sea.

JAPANESE SEA POWER

The Japanese were able to assemble a fleet large enough to transport 160,000 soldiers to Korea in 1592. The fleet consisted chiefly of pirate or merchant vessels turned to military use. For sea

---

WEAPONS AND TECHNOLOGY

TURTLE SHIP

The turtle ship, or *kobukson,* was a variant on the *panokseon,* the Korean cannon-armed warship, comparable to a Mediterranean galleass. Admiral Yi Sunshin is credited with reviving the design, which had been tried out experimentally almost two centuries earlier. The first of Admiral Yi's turtle ships was launched in March 1592, just as the Japanese invasion of Korea began. Its most original feature was the covered upper deck, shielded with iron plates and spikes – thought to resemble a turtle's shell. This protected the crew from missiles and, more importantly, made the ship impossible to take by boarding. The impressive array of cannon fired out of portholes, with two at the prow, one at the stern, and possibly 10 along each side. A cannon may also have been placed to fire from the dragon's head. The oars, each pulled by eight men, permitted rapid manoeuvre in combat. The turtle ships' role in the war between Korea and Japan has often been exaggerated – only three were built at the time, possibly because iron was in short supply.

Replica turtle ship
Korea's Naval Academy Museum houses this life-sized replica of a turtle ship, one of a number that have been built in the country. There is even one replica that is regularly sailed on a lake.

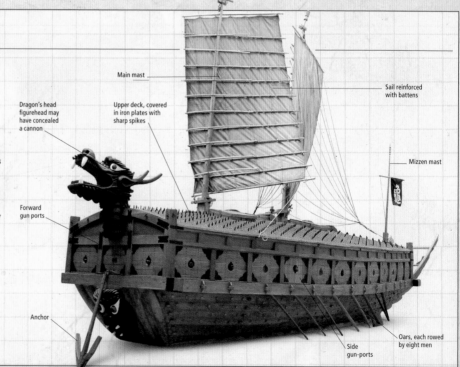

Main mast

Dragon's head figurehead may have concealed a cannon

Upper deck, covered in iron plates with sharp spikes

Sail reinforced with battens

Forward gun ports

Mizzen mast

Anchor

Side gun-ports

Oars, each rowed by eight men

Japanese leader Toyotomi Hideyoshi's first step toward fulfilling his ambition of conquering China was to invade Korea. In 1592 he shipped a large army to Pusan, the port closest to Japan across the Tsushima Strait. Japanese land forces made rapid progress northward, but their seaborne supply lines were always vulnerable and the invasion was called off in 1593. When the Japanese returned in 1597, they conquered less territory on land and again suffered crucial defeats at the hands of Yi Sunshin's navy.

KEY

- Japan
- Korea
- Area of Korea occupied by Japanese forces
- Japanese invasion route
- Korean victory
- Japanese victory

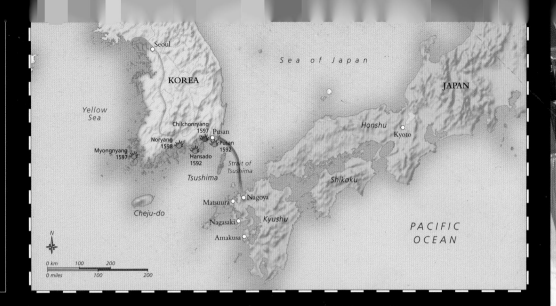

Korean naval cannon
Usually mounted on wheeled wooden carriages, Korean cannons fired a range of projectiles, including solid shot, fragmentation bombs, and incendiary "fireballs". Some longer cannons fired giant arrows with iron tips.

fighting, Japanese raiders traditionally employed swift-moving boats crammed with warriors, who would board and overwhelm their enemy's larger, slower-moving craft. The larger Japanese ships would also be packed with fighting men, armed with missile weapons to soften up the enemy, prior to boarding and fighting with sword and spear. One striking advantage the Japanese held over the Koreans was the possession of firearms. The arquebus, the precursor of the matchlock musket, which had been introduced by the Portuguese, was enthusiastically adopted by the Japanese during their 16th-century civil wars. Deployed at sea, it proved to be a highly effective complement to traditional bows. But the Japanese lacked larger gunpowder weapons. They had lagged behind China and Korea in the development of cannon, and their ships were in any case too flimsy and unstable to provide a good platform for guns.

KOREAN VICTORY

The Koreans had learned the use of gunpowder weapons from Ming China, but they had quickly surpassed the Chinese in the manufacture of cannon for naval use. By the late 16th century they had the most advanced shipborne artillery in Asia. Their key warship, the *panokseon*, was a robustly constructed ship that functioned as a

stable gun platform. It carried cannon capable of delivering a variety of missiles, including gunpowder-based incendiary devices known as "fireballs". Whereas Japanese ships had only square sails, the *panokseon* could be propelled by oars in combat, giving it impressive speed and manoeuvrability. With an admiral of genius in charge, Yi Sunshin, the Koreans repeatedly outmanoeuvred and outfought the Japanese. Yi Sunshin used local knowledge of currents, tides, and winds to gain a huge advantage for his ships, even in situations where they were vastly outnumbered by the enemy.

JAPAN TURNS INWARD

Although its invasions of Korea were defeated at sea, it still seemed that Japan might emerge as an Asian naval power. The Japanese had galleons built under European influence in the early 17th century, one of which carried a Japanese embassy to Europe. But like Ming China before it, Japan then turned its back decisively on oceanic travel. It is said that, by order of the Japanese shoguns, all ships had to be built with a hole in the hull so they could not survive an ocean voyage. Japan's next emergence into naval history would not come until the 19th century.

Korean turtle ship in action at Hansando
Yi Sunshin's most spectacular victory over the Japanese was at Hansando in August 1592. Cannon and fire arrows wrought incredible destruction among the enemy ships, of which 47 were destroyed, while the Koreans lost none.

JAPANESE INVASION OF KOREA

AFTER UNIFYING war-torn Japan in 1590, warrior leader Toyotomi Hideyoshi then devised a megalomanic plan to conquer Ming China and India. When the Koreans refused to allow his army free passage through their country, in 1592 Hideyoshi embarked upon the conquest of Korea as a prelude to an invasion of China. Japanese troops were largely successful on land, advancing north as far as Pyongyang, but the Korean Admiral Yi Sunshin organized a naval campaign that severely disrupted Japan's supply lines. The Japanese suffered a crushing defeated at Hansando, but avoided total catastrophe in a defensive sea battle at Pusan. Hideyoshi was put under so much pressure, however, that he was forced to withdraw his troops in 1593. A second invasion in 1597 was no more successful. Although Japan scored a naval victory at Chilchonryang – in the absence of Yi Sunshin – the subsequent defeat at Myongyang was a setback from which Hideyoshi's project of conquest never recovered. The Japanese leader had died by the time Yi Sunshin inflicted the final humiliation on Japanese naval forces at Noryang in 1598, a battle that cost the Korean admiral his life.

GUN, SAIL, AND EMPIRE

JAPANESE INVASION OF KOREA

PUSAN

Date 1 September 1592
Forces Koreans: c.250 ships; Japanese c.470 ships
Losses Unknown

Location
Pusan, Korea

In spring 1592 a vast Japanese fleet set off from Naguya on northern Kyushu island carrying an army some 160,000 strong for the invasion of Korea. The first 700 boats landed their troops near the fortified port of Pusan on 13 April. The Koreans were caught unprepared. Their warships stationed in the Pusan area, commanded by Won Kyun, simply fled when confronted by the Japanese armada. Toyotomi Hideyoshi's soldiers, battle-hardened after years of civil war in Japan, swiftly took Pusan by assault. As the Japanese fought their way up the Korean peninsula, Pusan became the gateway for supplies and reinforcements brought by sea from Japan.

Fortunately for Korea, Admiral Yi Sunshin, commander of the Cholla Left Naval District at Yosu, to the west of Pusan, was better prepared to react to the Japanese invasion. He had a force of cannon-armed warships, known as

1545–1598

YI SUNSHIN

ADMIRAL OF THE KOREAN FLEET

Yi Sunshin pursued a successful career in the army until disgraced as a result of political machinations. In 1590, suddenly returned to favour, he was appointed naval commander of the Cholla District. His outstanding performance in a series of naval battles during the Japanese invasion of 1592 to 1593 did not save him from being once more disgraced and demoted to a lowly rank. Returned to command after the Korean defeat at Chilchonryang, he again trounced the Japanese at Myongyang and Noryang, dying in the hour of victory. Yi Sunshin is deservedly one of Korea's greatest national heroes.

panokseon, and had recently completed construction of three iron-armoured "turtle ships" or *kobukson*. With these ships he mounted a counterattack in the offshore islands between his base at Yosu and Pusan. In a five-day period in early May at and around Okpo, he sank 44 Japanese ships without loss. Further successes followed at Sachon, Tangpo, and Tanghangpo. When the Japanese attempted a major naval counterattack against Yi in August, their fleet was shattered at the battle of Hansando.

After Hansando, Yi felt strong enough to attempt an attack on the Japanese base at Pusan. He was joined by the fleet of Won Kyun, creating a formidable force with more than 70 substantial warships. Pusan Bay was crowded with Japanese ships, which were landing a second wave of troops. Yi hoped to destroy the Japanese fleet and recapture or at least blockade Pusan. He was not successful. Although the Japanese lost many ships, they held off the attack using cannon captured from the Koreans. The Korean fleet was forced to withdraw but, with its supply lines insecure, the first Japanese invasion was doomed.

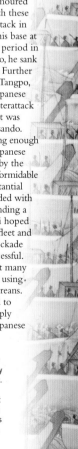

Multiple rocket-launcher
The Koreans possessed an array of ingenious artillery weapons. These included the *hwacha*, a rocket-launcher used with great success both against Japanese land forces and for firing volleys of incendiaries at enemy ships.

Japanese capture of Pusan
The main Japanese landing was at Pusan at the southern tip of the Korean peninsula. The invaders were able to repel all attempts to retake the port, but convoys to and from Pusan were always vulnerable.

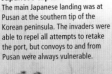

JAPANESE INVASION OF KOREA

CHILCHONRYANG

Date 16 July 1597
Forces Koreans: 166 ships; Japanese: c.500 ships
Losses Koreans: 153 ships; Japanese: unknown

Location Chilchonryang, off southern Korea

In 1597, command of the Korean navy was entrusted to Won Kyun, promoted in place of the disgraced Yi Sunshin. Urged by the royal court to take an aggressive stance, Won Kyun led the entire Korean fleet to attack the Japanese at Pusan.

The Japanese appeared in overwhelming strength and brought the Koreans to battle on their own terms. As the Korean fleet was ill-coordinated, the Japanese were able to impose a close-quarters mêlée in which the Koreans could not use their cannon, while the Japanese were able to grapple and board the ships of their enemies. Korean ships that attempted to flee were pursued and captured. Those who sought to escape to shore on nearby Kojedo Island, including Won Kyun, were massacred by the island's Japanese garrison. Only 13 Korean warships, which had prudently fled before the fighting began, survived the debacle.

JAPANESE INVASION OF KOREA

MYONGYANG

Date 16 September 1597
Forces Koreans: 13 ships; Japanese: 133 ships
Losses Koreans: none; Japanese: 31 ships

Location Myongyang Strait, southwest Korea

Encouraged by their overwhelming victory at Chilchonryang, the Japanese sought to destroy the remnants of the Korean navy and to take control of the Yellow Sea, opening up a maritime supply line along the west coast of Korea to their armies, which were advancing to the north. There was no time to rebuild the Korean navy, but on the advice of his counsellors the king belatedly reinstated Yi Sunshin to the command of what was left of it. On his way to resume his duties as admiral, Yi wrote to the Korean royal court: "As I am alive, the enemies will never gain the Western Seas."

Korean quiver
Archers played a major role in Korea's naval victories over Japan, making extensive use of fire arrows to attack the flimsy Japanese ships.

Admiral Yi had only 13 serviceable *panokseons* with which to confront the Japanese, but he took advantage of his knowledge of local conditions to even the odds. After fighting a holding action at Oranpo he withdrew to the Myongyang Strait, which separates Jindo Island from the mainland. The strait has strong currents that change direction every three hours. Yi Sunshin correctly anticipated that the Japanese fleet would enter the strait when the current was flowing in the direction to carry them toward the Yellow Sea.

MIRACULOUS VICTORY

Yi placed his ships across the western end of the strait so that the Japanese were borne toward his cannon on the current. A well-coordinated barrage of shot combined with fire arrows, threw the Japanese van into confusion. The admiral in command of the van, Kurushima Michifusa, was blown overboard and his body drifted to the Korean line. Yi had the admiral's head cut off and stuck on a masthead. When the current changed the Korean ships were carried down at speed upon the demoralized and disorganized Japanese, who left 31 blazing or sinking vessels behind them as they fled in disorder. The battle is known to Koreans as the "miracle of Myongyang" because of the unlikely balance of forces between the victors and the defeated.

JAPANESE INVASION OF KOREA

NORYANG

Date 19 November 1598
Forces Koreans and Chinese: 150 ships; Japanese: c.500 ships
Losses Koreans and Chinese: 1 ship lost; Japanese: c.200 ships sunk, 100 captured

Location Noryang Strait, southern Korea

In the autumn of 1598, with their leader Toyotomi Hideyoshi dead and with the Chinese having now entered the war in support of Korea, the Japanese were hastening to extricate themselves from their ill-judged Korean adventure.

On 18 November some 200,000 Japanese troops had embarked on a large fleet of transport ships, their aim to join up with other Japanese forces and return to Japan. A combined fleet of Korean and Chinese warships was blockading the Japanese-held fortresses along the southern coast of Korea. Chen Lin, commanding the Chinese squadron of 65 warships, favoured making a deal to let the Japanese go. But Yi Sunshin, with 85 Korean *panokseons* and turtle ships, was not prepared to allow the

Death of Yi Sunshin
Like Nelson, Yi was killed in his hour of triumph, struck by a stray shot fired by an enemy arquebusier. The captain on his flagship had been lucky to escape with his life when an arquebus ball hit his helmet.

enemy to escape unmolested, and his view prevailed. The combined fleet waited at the entrance to the narrow Noryang Strait.

The vast Japanese convoy was commanded by Shimazu Yoshihiro. It approached the strait at night and blundered into the Korean and Chinese ships in the early hours of the morning. With large numbers of ships clashing in darkness in confined waters, the conflict was inevitably confused. The Japanese fought desperately to open a passage through the strait; the Koreans and Chinese struggled to stop them. The mêlée favoured the Japanese, who

could bring their arquebus fire to bear at close quarters. One Chinese ship was taken by the Japanese and all on board slaughtered. Chen Lin's flagship was boarded and only narrowly saved from capture. Yet dawn revealed that the allied fleet had triumphed, with hundreds of Japanese transports captured or sunk.

Yi led the pursuit of the Japanese ships that had broken through and were heading for Pusan, but in the course of the action, he was shot dead. This fact was concealed until the combat was over. One week after the battle, the Japanese army sailed from Pusan back to Japan, and the war came to an end.

Korean panokseons at Hansando
The workhorse of Yi Sunshin's navy at all his famous victories over the Japanese was the *panokseon*, a reliable, manoeuvrable platform for the Korean archers and artillery.

KEY

JAPANESE FLEET

 4–5 Japanese war galleys (*sekibune* or *atakebune*)

 4–5 Japanese scout ships

KOREAN FLEET

 4–5 Korean *panokseons* (unless otherwise stated)

1 Korean *kobukson* (turtle ship)

1 THE LURE AND THE TRAP

Yi Sunshin sends six ships forward to lure the Japanese fleet into following them into open water, where he carefully deploys his fleet in a "crane's wing" formation. The Japanese commander Wakizaka obliges by taking the bait.

A number of *panokseons* are held in reserve

MIRUK ISLAND

The six ships sent forward by Yi Sunshin race back to the main fleet with the Japanese in hot pursuit

KOREAN MAINLAND

The Korean "turtle ships" are deployed in the centre

The Japanese fleet, led by the scout ships, pursues the decoy ships into open water

HWADO ISLAND

The main fleet is still unaware of the size of the Korean fleet waiting in ambush

The majority of the Korean ships deploy in a "crane's wing" formation. This allows interlocking fields of fire – they can fire on the enemy ships from several angles

HANSANDO ISLAND

MIRUK ISLAND

Cannon fire keeps the Japanese at a distance so their soldiers have no chance to grapple and board the Korean ships

KOREAN MAINLAND

The "turtle ships" hold the Korean centre, their spiked decks making it impossible for the Japanese to board them

Kyonnaeryang Strait

The impetuous Japanese commander Wakizaka orders his ships straight into the waiting Korean trap

As the Korean "crane's wing" formation encircles the Japanese, reserve ships move up to plug the gaps in the expanding line

The wings close in around the Japanese fleet, causing their ships to collide with each other, making it harder and harder for them to manoeuvre

HWADO ISLAND

HANSANDO ISLAND

2 CLOSING THE TRAP

The Japanese rush headlong into the Korean trap to be met by a withering barrage of cannon fire and fire arrows from three sides. Many Japanese ships are soon set on fire or sunk and many of their soldiers are killed.

THE BATTLE OF HANSANDO

When Japanese shogun Toyotomi Hideyoshi embarked upon the invasion of Korea in May 1592, he seems to have anticipated little resistance from the Koreans at sea. His mistake was soon evident, as Korean ships inflicted heavy losses on the Japanese in a series of encounters through June and July, of which those at Okpo and Sacheon were the most notable.

As Korean naval power threatened Japanese supply and reinforcement of its land army on the Korean peninsula, Hideyoshi called on one of his boldest warlords, Wakizaka Yasuharu, to lead a counter-offensive. Wakizaka sailed from the Japanese base at Pusan with 73 ships, in search of the Korean fleet. The Koreans were equally keen on a battle. Their inspired admiral Yi Sunshin had also assembled a large fleet and was confident of victory.

Using information from local people, Yi located the Japanese fleet at anchor in Kyonnaeryang strait. He sent six ships into the strait, hoping to lure the Japanese into more open water. The stratagem worked. An impulsive, aggressive commander, Wakizaka

Yi Sunshin's war diary
Yi recorded all the events of his career in his diary. Despite the unfair treatment he received as a result of intrigues at court, his loyalty to his king and the Korean people never faltered.

ordered his captains to pursue the Korean ships as they fled, leading him to Yi's main fleet waiting off Hansan island. Yi had adopted a "crane's wing" formation – a U-shape designed to envelop an approaching enemy on both flanks. Wakizaka obligingly thrust his ships forward into the open trap.

Half the Japanese ships were multiple-decked *atakebune*, the rest smaller vessels, but all were packed with fighting men, armed with bows, swords, and arquebuses. Their aim was to board Korean ships. But Yi planned to keep the fighting at a distance. Most of his ships were *panokseons*, stoutly-built galleys mounting 10 to 20 cannon on

their upper decks. There were also two or three *kobuksons*, the iron-spiked vessels known as "turtle ships", that deployed even more firepower and were almost impossible to board.

FALLING INTO THE TRAP

As the Japanese advanced into the "crane's wing", they became targets for ships to the front and on both sides. The Korean cannon were slow to reload, but the oarsmen kept their ships turning so that both broadsides and guns at the stem and stern were brought to bear in succession, maintaining a constant fire. The *panokseons* also carried large complements of archers, whose composite reflex bows had greater range than Japanese bows or arquebuses. Wakizara himself was hit several times by arrows, his life saved by the quality of his armour.

Inexorably the Koreans drew their formation tighter around the Japanese fleet, driving the enemy ships closer together so they could no longer manoeuvre and offered a dense-packed target for the gunners and archers.

Incendiary weapons were also apparently used – a Japanese source speaks of "fireballs shot at our ships, which were burned and destroyed". The carnage was awesome. Several Japanese commanders committed ritual suicide aboard their sinking ships. Wakizaka was on board one of only 14 Japanese vessels to escape the scene of destruction.

The annihilation of the Japanese fleet had a decisive effect on the invasion. Unable to guarantee the seaborne supply of his army, Hideyoshi had to scale back his plans and the Japanese eventually evacuated Korea in 1593 – although Admiral Yi would be called upon to save his country from invasion again before the century's end.

JAPANESE INVASION OF KOREA

THE BATTLE OF HANSANDO

Date	14 August 1592
Location	Off Hansan Island, Korea
Result	Korean victory

COMBATANTS

JAPAN	KOREA

COMMANDERS

Wakizaka Yasuharu	Yi Sunshin

FORCES

Ships: 73	Ships: 56

LOSSES

Men: 9,000	Men: 123
Ships: 47 destroyed, 12 captured	Ships: none

> THE REMAINING JAPANESE BOATS … SEEING FROM AFAR THE HORRIBLE SIGHT OF BURNING VESSELS AND FALLEN HEADS, ROWED THEIR BOATS FAST AND FLED IN ALL DIRECTIONS.

YI SUNSHIN, DESCRIBING THE END OF THE BATTLE IN HIS WAR DIARY

3 VICTORY IS COMPLETE
Yi Sunshin's plan works to perfection. The "crane's wing" encircles the Japanese fleet and concentrated cannon fire completes the destruction. Only 14 Japanese ships, including Wakizaka's flagship, manage to escape.

MIRUK ISLAND

KOREAN MAINLAND

The few Japanese ships that can flee the destruction

Kyonnaeryang Strait

As the "crane's wing" formation tightens around the Japanese ships, Korean artillery and archers combine to destroy a total of 47 Japanese ships

HWADO ISLAND

HANSANDO ISLAND

THE OCEANIC VOYAGES of European sailors wrought fundamental changes in world trade and power politics in the 16th century. The Portuguese played a leading part in the initial voyages of exploration, establishing bases in Africa, Brazil, and India, and reaching as far as Japan by the 1540s. Trade in Asian spices and other luxury goods brought wealth flooding into the coffers of the Portuguese monarchy. But it was Spain that emerged as the first oceanic imperial power. After backing Christopher Columbus's transatlantic voyage of 1492, the Spanish took control of areas of Central and South America rich in precious metals. Silver from mines in Peru, carried across the Atlantic by an annual treasure fleet, financed a bid by the Spanish monarchy to achieve dominance in Europe. Resistance to Spanish power bred wars in which Dutch and English sailors proved themselves doughty sea fighters against the odds.

Battle of Gibraltar
After the Dutch had gained the upper hand in their own home waters, they extended their naval operations to attack Spanish shipping in its overseas colonies and even off the coast of Spain, as here at Gibraltar in 1607, where they destroyed an entire Spanish fleet of 21 ships.

c.1540–1596
SIR FRANCIS DRAKE
ENGLISH PRIVATEER AND NAVAL COMMANDER

Born in Tiverton, Devon, England, Francis Drake went to sea at an early age. Fearless, arrogant, and quarrelsome, he built a reputation as a peerless privateer, ravaging the Spanish colonies around the Caribbean. In 1577, with the covert backing of Elizabeth I, he sailed around Cape Horn to attack Spain's possessions on the Pacific coast of the Americas. Returning home in 1580 he was knighted as the first Englishman to circumnavigate the globe. His raid on Cadiz in 1587 confirmed his status as Spain's "most wanted" enemy. During the resistance to the Spanish Armada the following year Drake was vice admiral of the English fleet, a subordinate role he accepted with ill grace. He died of dysentery during a final disastrous expedition to the Caribbean in 1596.

SPANISH ASCENDANCY
In the second half of the 16th century Spain was unquestionably the strongest European naval power, especially after it annexed Portugal in 1580. Despite having simultaneously to maintain a Mediterranean galley fleet to fight the Ottomans, the Spanish monarchy had the resources and the bureaucratic organization to build and supply a fleet of sail on a scale beyond the reach of any other European state of the time. The Dutch, in revolt against Spanish rule, and the English, determined to remain free of it, had relatively puny resources. What they did possess, however, was a large number of adventurous, independent-minded seamen. The foundations of a permanent English Royal Navy were laid under Henry VIII (reigned 1509–47) and the later Tudors, especially Elizabeth I (reigned 1558–1603), maintained a royal interest in the navy that, by contrast, was only intermittently present in France. But even the English were far from achieving the level of naval organization and funding present in Spain – England typically could not afford to pay the sailors who fought off the Spanish Armada in 1588. Both the Dutch and English depended to a large degree on privateers to wage war upon the Spanish Empire. Men such as Francis Drake and Piet Heyn operated sometimes as licensed pirates or maritime guerrilla fighters, sometimes as conventional naval commanders.

GUNS AND GALLEONS
During the second half of the 16th century the galleon replaced the carrack as the premier purpose-built warship in European fleets. A leaner, sleeker vessel, it was built for speed,

Heart of the empire
This view of Cadiz shows Spanish ships preparing to sail to the West Indies. Despite raids by the English and Dutch at the end of the 16th century, Cadiz and Seville remained immensely wealthy commercial centres.

especially in the low-hulled version favoured by the English. How best to use these ships in combat was still a matter for experiment. The English, who had the best cannon, favoured prolonged gun duels, chiefly targeting the opponent's hull. The Spanish, although fully aware of the importance of guns in naval warfare, regarded cannon fire as a prelude to boarding – their galleons carried large numbers of soldiers. The English, in their smaller, nimbler ships, hoped to avoid being boarded by holding the weather gage and thus dictating the range at which the encounter was fought. The battles of the Spanish Armada campaign showed that, on the whole, English guns were not powerful enough to inflict serious damage upon large Spanish galleons. It is worth noting that the Dutch, using even smaller ships than the English, generally favoured boarding as a tactic.

DUTCH GLORY

Spanish naval predominance survived the maritime disaster of the 1588 Armada. Further expeditions were planned against England and magnificent ships built for new Armadas. But in the 17th century, as Spanish financial and military resources began to decline, the Dutch seized the opportunity not only to win their independence but to become a global sea power.

Dutch privateers and irregular coastal forces had performed well against the Spanish in the 16th century, but the Dutch flowering in the first half of the 17th century was on an altogether different scale. The ships of the Dutch East India Company ruthlessly supplanted the Portuguese in much of Asia, most profitably in Indonesia, creating a fabulously wealthy trading empire.

In the Americas the Dutch attacked Portuguese and Spanish colonies and their privateers stole a fortune in Spanish silver.

By the 1630s Spain could no longer communicate with its forces fighting in the Netherlands by sea, having to send arms, supplies, and pay for their troops overland from Italy. Dutch dominance of their home waters was confirmed in spectacular fashion by their total annihilation of a Spanish fleet at the Downs in 1639, an event from which Spain did not recover, and marked the end her time as a major naval power.

Galleon against galley
In a clash off the coast of the Netherlands in the early years of the 17th century, a Dutch galleon gets the better of two Spanish galleys, sinking one of them by ramming.

1550 – 1830

SPANISH WARS

THE DUTCH REVOLT of 1568 against the rule of Spanish Catholic king, Philip II, started a war that would last for 80 years. With William of Nassau, Prince of Orange, as their leader, the Dutch fought a desperate struggle for survival against the might of Spain, greatly aided by the skill and courage of their sailors, whose small ships fought a seaborne guerrilla campaign against Spanish naval might. The English queen, Elizabeth I, tried to avoid war with Spain, but she could not resist backing privateers preying on Spanish colonies in the New World. England was also drawn into support for the Dutch rebels. By 1585 Philip had decided that the heretical English queen must be subdued. Victory over French-backed mercenaries in the Azores in 1583 encouraged him to believe that he could defeat the English navy with an oceanic fleet. The Spanish Armada operation of 1588, intended to allow an invasion of England by Spanish troops from the Netherlands, was an ambitious but ill-conceived exercise in the use of naval power. The skill and courage of English sailors ensured its failure, although the subsequent destruction of the Armada by storms was fortuitous.

⬡ ENGLISH PRIVATEERING EXPEDITION

SAN JUAN DE ULÚA

Date 24 September 1569
Forces English: 5 ships; Spanish: 13 ships
Losses English: 3 ships: Spanish: none

Location Veracruz, New Spain (Mexico)

After two years' illegal trading and piracy around the coasts of Spain's American colonies, in September 1569 English privateer John Hawkins and his cousin Francis Drake entered the port of Veracruz, with the reluctant permission of the Spanish authorities. They were anchored in the harbour off San Juan de Ulúa island when a fleet from Spain arrived, bringing a new viceroy. At first the viceroy pretended to accept the English presence, but on 24 September he ordered a surprise night attack. Hawkins and Drake made their escape on board two small ships, *Minion* and *Judith*. After much hardship, they reached home the following year.

⬡ DUTCH REVOLT

ZUIDERZEE

Date 5–12 October 1573
Forces Spanish: 18 ships; Dutch: 24 ships
Losses Spanish: 6 ships captured; Dutch: none

Location Zuiderzee, near Hoorn, Netherlands

In 1569 William of Nassau, Prince of Orange, issued letters of marque to a motley assembly of sea captains prepared to offer their services to the Dutch revolt. As the rebels in the Netherlands had adopted the ironic nickname of "the Beggars", these privateers became known as the Sea Beggars. Operating out of safe havens provided by the Protestant French in La Rochelle and Queen Elizabeth in southern England, they raided the Netherlands coast and inhibited the seaborne trade of the Spanish-ruled provinces. The Sea Beggars' indiscriminate plunder of merchant shipping led Elizabeth to ban them from English ports in spring 1572, whereupon they seized new bases on the Dutch coast.

The Spanish fought back and in the summer of 1573 retook the rebel city of Haarlem. They then planned to regain control of the Zuiderzee, the inland water between Spanish-held Amsterdam and the North Sea. Maximilien de Henin, Count of Bossu, assembled a war fleet at Amsterdam. In October he sailed out aboard his provocatively named 34-gun flagship, *Inquisition*. The Sea Beggars emerged from their bases around the Zuiderzee to give battle, with Cornelis Dirkszoon, mayor of Monnickendam, in command.

The Spanish were superior in firepower, but Dirkszoon hoped to close with them with his smaller ships and take them by boarding. The first encounter, on 5 October, went badly for the Sea Beggars. In adverse winds they were unable to board the enemy ships and suffered heavily from cannon fire. There followed a stand-off until 11 October, when the wind shifted in Dirkszoon's favour. His ships bore down upon the Spanish, three of them engaging *Inquisition*, which ran aground. The fighting was fierce. Dirkszoon was wounded, command passing to his captain Jan Floor. Several Spanish ships were taken, while the rest fled back to Amsterdam. *Inquisition* held longest but was captured after more than 24 hours' combat. Bossu was taken prisoner.

Sea Beggars in action
The Sea Beggars make a surprise landing in a coastal town, putting the Spanish and the Catholics among the local residents to flight.

WAR OF THE PORTUGUESE SUCCESSION

AZORES

Date 26 July 1582
Forces French: 56 ships; Spanish: 32 ships
Losses French: 11 ships; Spanish: none

Location Terceira island, Azores

In 1580 the Spanish king, Philip II, took over Portugal. His claim to the throne was contested by Don Antonio, Prior of Crato. Basing himself in the only remaining independent Portuguese territory, the Azores, Don Antonio won the backing of France. Filippo Strozzi, a Florentine who had been commander-in-chief of the French army, recruited a multinational mercenary force that sailed from France for the Azores in June 1582.

Philip II reacted by sending the Marqués de Santa Cruz with a fleet of galleons and armed merchantmen, which reached the Azores on 22 July. The Spanish were outnumbered, but their ships were larger. For four days the fleets manoeuvred in light winds.

On the morning of 26 July they were sailing in opposite directions a few miles apart when Don Lope de Figueroa, commander of the galleon *San Matteo*, made a death-or-glory dash toward the enemy. Five of Strozzi's ships surrounded the isolated galleon, battering it with cannon fire for two hours, but were unable to board the high-sided vessel. Meanwhile, the rest of the Spanish fleet manoeuvred to come to Figueroa's aid. The armed merchantmen of their rear squadron arrived first and soon disabled Strozzi's flagship with their powerful guns. A confused mêlée ensued. Santa Cruz, on board *San Martin*, sought out Strozzi's limping ship and bombarded it until most of those on board were dead or wounded. The Spanish boarded the vessel and took Strozzi off, but he was badly injured and soon died. The survivors of his fleet fled in all directions, bringing the battle to a close. Victory in the Azores convinced Santa Cruz that a Spanish Armada could defeat the English.

Spain's takeover of Portugal
The Spanish fleet under Santa Cruz sails into Lisbon to back up Philip II's claim to the Portuguese throne in 1580. Santa Cruz sailed on to defeat the only pocket of resistance to Spanish rule in the Azores in 1582.

1526–1588

MARQUÉS DE SANTA CRUZ

SPANISH ADMIRAL, VICTOR AT LEPANTO AND THE AZORES

Don Álvaro de Bazán was born in Granada, southern Spain. He followed in the footsteps of his father, who was commander of Spain's Mediterranean galleys. Bazán was created Marqués de Santa Cruz in reward for his outstanding performance as a galley commander at Lepanto in 1571. Appointed Admiral of the Ocean in 1583, he showed equal aptitude for warfare under sail at the battle of the Azores. The original idea of sending a fleet to attack England was his, and he would have led the Armada but for his death in February 1588.

ANGLO–SPANISH WARS

CADIZ

Date 29 April–1 May 1587
Forces English: 21 ships; Spanish: 8 galleys
Losses English: 1 ship captured; Spanish: 24

Location Cadiz, southern Spain

In spring 1587 Spain was preparing an Armada to invade England. Sir Francis Drake, on board *Elizabeth Bonaventure*, sailed from Plymouth with a force of warships and armed merchantmen to carry out a pre-emptive strike against the Spanish. On the afternoon of 29 April Drake's ships appeared off Cadiz and immediately entered the harbour. Brushing aside the galleys defending the port and sinking a Genoese merchant ship that had the audacity to put up a fight, the English settled in among the crowd of ships at anchor, emptying them of their cargoes and setting them on fire. The Spanish galleys harassed the English with hit-and-run attacks and succeeded in capturing one ship that had become isolated. The next day Drake explored further reaches of the harbour, in particular destroying a large galleon belonging to the Marqués de Santa Cruz. But the Spanish brought up heavy guns on shore and began to fire on the English ships. *Golden Lion*, commanded by Drake's vice admiral, William Borough, had to manoeuvre briskly to avoid serious damage. An unfavourable wind confined Drake's ships in the harbour for another night, but they skilfully fended off attacks by Spanish fireships, as well as the persistent attentions of the galleys. Drake sailed out of Cadiz the following day, claiming to have "singed the king of Spain's beard". In practical terms, perhaps the expedition's greatest achievement was the destruction of thousands of barrel staves, making it hard for the Spanish to make sufficient barrels for the food and water required for the Armada.

> ## THE LOSS WAS NOT VERY GREAT, BUT THE DARING OF THE ATTEMPT WAS VERY GREAT INDEED.
> **KING PHILIP II OF SPAIN**, COMMENTING ON DRAKE'S RAID ON CADIZ

MAN-OF-WAR TACTICS

GIVING THE PROW

MAKING MAXIMUM USE OF THE WIND

Guns on 16th-century ships were very slow to reload. A ship would typically sail toward an enemy, firing the powerful guns mounted in the prow, and then turn to allow the broadside and stern guns to be fired. If the manoeuvre was possible, the captain might turn his ship about to fire the other broadside. The ship would withdraw to a safe distance to reload. The guns in the prow were considered the prime armament, rather than the broadside cannon.

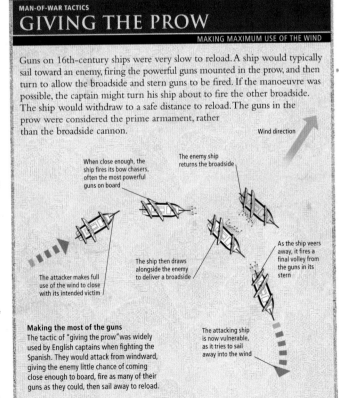

Wind direction

When close enough, the ship fires its bow chasers, often the most powerful guns on board

The enemy ship returns the broadside

The ship then draws alongside the enemy to deliver a broadside

As the ship veers away, it fires a final volley from the guns in its stern

The attacker makes full use of the wind to close with its intended victim

The attacking ship is now vulnerable, as it tries to sail away into the wind

Making the most of the guns
The tactic of "giving the prow" was widely used by English captains when fighting the Spanish. They would attack from windward, giving the enemy little chance of coming close enough to board, fire as many of their guns as they could, then sail away to reload.

1550 – 1830

CREW PROFILE

GALLEON

1550–1650

A LATE 16TH-CENTURY GALLEON might typically have 200 to 300 men on board. The normal social hierarchy continued to function at sea, with those of higher standing relatively privileged, but life aboard was hard for everyone. Men slept on the wooden deck unless they had brought their own bed with them – hammocks were not yet in common use and no specific areas were designated for sleeping. Food was often poor due to storage problems, and beer, wine, and water was sometimes sour and undrinkable. Outbreaks of disease were a constant threat, taking a heavy toll of galleon crews at all times. Pay was low and uncertain, but there was always the chance the crew might profit from seizing a prize.

CAPTAIN AND OFFICERS

The captain of a galleon would be at least a gentleman and very often a nobleman. Many were experienced soldiers but were in no sense men of the sea. In the Spanish navy the captain might be supported by a hierarchy of commissioned officers, but on board an English galleon he held command alone. The only other officer on board was likely to be the commander of the body of soldiers carried in the forecastle. The captain's only social equals on board were likely to be gentleman adventurers who pressed forward to serve in pursuit of glory. Regarded as rank amateurs who drove admirals to despair, many were nonetheless taken on board with varying degrees of usefulness.

PROFESSIONAL SEAMEN

The captain was not necessarily expected to know anything about sailing a ship, a job which fell to his most important subordinate, the master, an experienced mariner, along with the pilot and the boatswain. The bulk of the crew – some of them volunteers but most pressed into service – were in theory experienced seamen. The Spanish used convicts to row galleys but not to man galleons. Crew were taken in time of war from the population of fishermen, merchant seamen, and privateers in port towns. However, Sir Walter Raleigh complained of men being taken on "so ignorant in sea service, as they know not the name of a rope". There was always a flock of ship's boys on board learning their trade. One of their duties on the ships of the Armada was to sing out the changes of the watch.

Sir James Lancaster
A typical captain of the era, Lancaster was part merchant, part privateer. In 1588 he commanded an armed merchantman in the battle against the Armada.

The crucial battle
There were a number of small engagements as the English ships followed the Armada up the Channel. The fleets did not fully engage until the Spanish reached Calais, when the English launched a full-scale attack.

THE DEFEAT OF THE SPANISH ARMADA

On 28 May 1588 Spanish king Philip II's "Invincible Armada" sailed from Lisbon on the "Enterprise of England". Goaded by English privateers' attacks on his colonial possessions and treasure fleets, and by Queen Elizabeth's support for Dutch rebels in the Netherlands, King Philip had decided that England must be taught a lesson. The Armada was due to sail through the English Channel and escort a Spanish army from the Netherlands across the North Sea to land in Kent. The original leader of the enterprise was the Marqués de Santa Cruz, Spain's most distinguished admiral, but on his untimely death in February 1588 command had been most reluctantly assumed by the Duke of Medina Sidonia – who, by his own account, "did not understand it and knew nothing about it".

The assembly, equipping, and supply of this vast fleet had been a long and arduous task, rendered more difficult by English raids on Spanish ports. It took the Armada a further three weeks to reach Coruña in northern Spain, and it did not weigh anchor again until 21 July. The English were not inclined to wait for the slow-moving Spanish to arrive. The fiery vice admiral Francis Drake persuaded his commander-in-chief, Lord Howard of Effingham, to attempt the destruction of the Armada before it sailed, but three times ships sent to Spain were driven back by bad weather. The English commanders then resolved to base their main force in Plymouth, ready to tackle the Armada as soon as it approached the Channel.

THE COUNTRY ALERTED

The Spanish were spotted off the Lizard on 29 July, news conveyed by the lighting of a string of beacons along the coast from Devon to the Scottish border. The Armada was an awesome sight – some 130 ships carrying possibly 18,000 soldiers as well as their usual complement of sailors. But it was a heterogeneous collection of vessels. Less than 50 of them could be described as fighting ships, the rest being transports. The fleet's Spanish and Portuguese galleons were state-of-the-art warships, but they were slower and considerably less manoeuvrable than their English equivalents. The English had about 65 galleons and armed merchantmen at Plymouth, with another contingent waiting at the eastern end of the Channel.

On the day the alarm was raised Howard and Drake were pinned in Plymouth Sound by the wind, but the following morning the wind turned off shore. For most of the next eight days, while they shadowed the Spanish along the Channel, the English held the weather gage. The Armada advanced in a well-disciplined crescent, the fighting ships sheltering the transports in the centre. The nimble English ships

Armada medal
This silver medal was made for Dutch prince Maurice of Nassau. The inscription reads "He (Jehovah) blew and they were scattered".

buzzed tirelessly around the Spanish flanks, harassing them with largely ineffective long-range cannon fire. Whereas the English saw their galleons as gun platforms, the Spanish regarded cannon as ancillary weapons, useful for softening up an enemy ship prior to grappling and boarding. Keeping the advantage of the wind, however, the English had no intention of letting their enemies come close enough to board.

By the time the Armada anchored off Calais on 6 August, Howard was thoroughly satisfied with his fleet's performance. "We have so daily pursued them at heels," he wrote, "that they never had leisure to stop at any place along our English coast."

Route of the Armada
The map shows the course taken by the Armada, the skirmishes and battles fought with the English in the Channel, and the routes taken by the scattered Spanish ships after their defeat at Gravelines.

KEY
→ Route of English ships
→ Route of Spanish ships
✳ Battle or skirmish

N

Atlantic Ocean

SCOTLAND

North Sea

IRELAND

Gravelines 8 August 1588

ENGLAND

London

Plymouth

Calais

English Channel

FRANCE

Yet Medina Sidonia had lost only two major ships in the course of the Channel run. *Nuestra Senora del Rosario* was damaged in a collision and snapped up by the indisciplined Drake as his personal prize, and *San Salvador* was destroyed by an unexplained explosion. Philip's great "Enterprise of England" fell apart not because of the efforts of the English sailors, but because the intended coordination with the Duke of Parma's army in the Netherlands never happened. The Duke informed Medina Sidonia on arrival that he did not have the barges ready with which to ferry his troops to England.

With no suitable harbour at its disposal, the Armada was left waiting in the exposed Calais roads. At a council on board Howard's flagship *Ark Royal*, the English captains agreed

Relic of an Armada wreck
This Spanish mariner's astrolabe was found on Valentia Island off the west coast of Ireland, where three Armada ships are known to have been wrecked.

upon a night attack using fireships. It was a familiar tactic and the Spanish had a screen of boats with grapnels – barbed anchors – prepared to haul the burning hulks off course. The British, however, were helped that night by a stiff wind and a following tide, and most of the eight blazing ships bore down into the anchorage.

Although not a single Spanish ship was set on fire, panic seized the fleet and ships slipped their cables, fleeing in disorder in the darkness.

The following morning, 8 August, found the ships of the Armada scattered northward off Gravelines, between Calais and Dunkirk, and pressed toward dangerous shoals by an onshore wind. The English, led by Drake's squadron, sailed into the attack while Medina Sidonia gallantly marshalled a defensive formation. The cannon fire was,

according to one observer, "the greatest that was even seen or imagined". The Spanish could not match their opponents' rate of fire and were again given no chance to board, although the fighting was often within musket range. The flagship *San Martin* was especially hard hit, with shot tearing the rigging and sails, holing the hull, and killing and wounding many on board. The galleons *San Mateo* and *San Felipe* were so badly shot up that they had to be run aground. Most of the other Spanish front-line fighting ships were damaged, although only the armed merchantman *Maria Juan* was actually sunk by cannon fire.

AFTERMATH OF THE BATTLE

The English broke off the battle after about nine hours, because they were running low on ammunition and confident that the battered Spanish were facing imminent catastrophe, as a rising gale drove them inexorably toward the shoals. The following morning, however, the wind veered as if by miracle and blew the Armada clear into the North Sea. Howard shadowed them as far as

the Firth of Forth before turning back, short of supplies and with rapidly sickening crews. Medina Sidonia decided to return to Spain by sailing around the north of Scotland and down the west coast of Ireland.

For English sailors the aftermath of the fighting was a disillusioning experience. Kept in service in case the Armada returned, they were unpaid and short of food, adequate clothing, and shelter. Thousands of them died of epidemic diseases. The fate of the Spanish was worse. Freak storms turned their voyage home into a naval catastrophe. Scattered ships disappeared without trace in the Atlantic Ocean or were wrecked upon the wild north and west coasts of Ireland. Those men who survived experienced extremes of deprivation and exhaustion. Just 67 ships out of the original fleet of 130 succeeded in making it back to Spanish shores, most of them limping to the port of Santander, where they were repaired and refitted.

Gravelines
This dramatic representation of the battle was painted in 1796, at a time when England again faced the threat of invasion by sea, this time from Revolutionary France. It shows the scene in the early morning after the English fireship attack, with the prow of a Spanish ship silhouetted against the flames.

KEY

ENGLISH FLEET

5–6 galleons or armed merchant vessels

1–2 fireships

SPANISH AND PORTUGUESE FLEET

5–6 galleons or armed merchant vessels (unless otherwise stated)

1 THE FIRESHIP ATTACK

Following a series of inconclusive engagements in the English Channel, the Armada anchors off Calais, waiting to be joined by the Duke of Parma's invasion force. During the night of August 7 the English attack the Spanish with eight fireships.

The Spanish ships scatter away from their anchorage

The Spanish ships are riding at anchor. During the fireship attack they cut their cables and flee. From now on they are at the mercy of winds and tides

The English fireships are carried by the tide toward the Spanish ships, but the Spanish are ready for them and use grapnels to prevent them from hitting their targets

ENGLISH CHANNEL

● Calais

Gravelines ●

SPANISH NETHERLANDS

2 THE POSITION AT DAWN

The English close in to exploit the confusion caused by the fireship attack. A few galleons under the command of Medina Sidonia manage to hold off the attacks of Sir Francis Drake's squadron, while the other Spanish ships struggle to regroup.

The Spanish flagship *San Martin* and four other galleons fight a brave rearguard action to gain time for the rest of the fleet to reorganize

Drake's squadron batters the Spanish galleons with shot, scoring around 200 hits on the *San Martin*

After two hours, *San Martin* and the other ships escape to join the rest of the fleet

An onshore wind places the Spanish ships in danger of running aground on the shoals and sandbanks around Gravelines

The *San Lorenzo*, damaged in the confusion following the fireship attack, attempts to row to the safety of Calais harbour, but runs aground and is captured

ENGLISH CHANNEL

● Calais

Gravelines ●

SPANISH NETHERLANDS

1550 – 1830

3 THE BATTLE OF GRAVELINES

Many Spanish ships are damaged, a few run aground, but only one ship is sunk. After nine hours' fighting, bad weather forces the English, who are low on ammunition, to break off the action. The wind changes and forces the Spanish northward.

Later in the day the wind changes and forces the Spanish northward, making it impossible for them to rendezvous with the invasion force in Dunkirk to the east

The Spanish ships suffer considerable damage, but few are lost. Their own guns prove ineffective in the battle

The English guns inflict damage on the enemy, but they seldom get within close range for fear of boarding attempts by Spanish soldiers

Lord Howard sends to England for more ammunition, but it never reaches the fleet

ENGLISH CHANNEL

● Calais

Gravelines ●

SPANISH NETHERLANDS

DEFEAT OF THE SPANISH ARMADA
Philip II of Spain's "Invincible Armada" sailed up the English Channel in order to ship an army across from the Spanish Netherlands to conquer England. In the end it was defeated in this battle, fought off Gravelines, and failed to rendezvous with the army. The Spanish fleet consisted of all kinds of ships, including galleons, armed merchantmen, and even Mediterranean galleasses, heavy oar-powered galleys, like the one shown in the centre of the foreground.

AFTER THE ARMADA

THE SPANISH ARMADA of 1588 was both a military fiasco and a maritime disaster, but in the 1590s Spain reasserted its status as the leading oceanic naval power. The English "Counter-Armada" of 1589 failed to exploit Spain's temporary weakness, and after that the willpower and resources of the Spanish state were marshalled to restore the strength of the Spanish navy. The overwhelming force sent to attack an English fleet off the Azores in 1591 was indicative of Spanish recovery, even as the resistance put up by Sir Richard Grenville and the *Revenge* exemplified the best of English fighting spirit. The Spanish were capable of sending further Armadas to attack England in 1596 and 1597. Although both were defeated by the weather before reaching their objective, they were a more serious threat to England than the English raid on Cadiz in 1596 was to Spain. For England, the deaths of Sir John Hawkins and Sir Francis Drake on a vain expedition to the Caribbean symbolized the end of an era. The accession of James I to the English throne in 1603 led to peace with Spain and a period of decline for the English navy.

ANGLO–SPANISH WARS

THE COUNTER-ARMADA

Date April–June 1589
Forces English: c.120 ships;
Spanish: unknown
Losses Unknown

Location Coruña, Spain
and Lisbon, Portugal

Flush with victory over the Armada, England sought to strike a decisive blow against a weakened Spain. An expedition was mounted with three ambitious goals: to destroy the Spanish ships refitting in northern Spain; to seize Lisbon and restore Portugal's independence; and to capture the Spanish treasure fleet from the Americas. Since the English state was broke, the expedition was financed as a joint-stock venture, with Queen Elizabeth as one of the investors.

After endless delays a large fleet carrying 20,000 troops set out from England in April, with Sir Francis Drake and Sir John Norreys in command. Also on board, against the Queen's wishes, was her courtier the Earl of Essex.

The Counter-Armada was a fiasco from start to finish. It failed to attack the port of Santander, where most of the refitting Spanish fleet lay defenceless, instead taking Coruña, where the most notable prize was a damaging quantity of wine. The attempt to take Lisbon failed dismally: the population refused to rise against the Spanish and the expedition had no siege engines with which to breach the city's walls. The interception of the Spanish treasure fleet was foiled by Atlantic storms. Decimated by disease – as many as 10,000 men may have died – the fleet straggled home, to the special distress of its disappointed financial backers.

1532–1595

SIR JOHN HAWKINS

ENGLISH PRIVATEER AND ADMIRAL

Born in Plymouth, Hawkins was a privateer who pioneered English participation in the Atlantic slave trade in the 1560s. In 1577 he was appointed treasurer to the queen's navy. He was a fine administrator, making improvements in ship design and showing an admirable concern for sailors' welfare. Hawkins fought against the Armada as a vice admiral on board *Victory*, a service for which he was knighted. In the 1590s he was a leading advocate of an offensive strategy in the war with Spain. He died of disease on an expedition to the Caribbean in 1595.

The port of Lisbon
The Portuguese capital, under Spanish rule since 1580, was one of the main targets of the Counter-Armada, but the English failed to cause any damage.

ANGLO–SPANISH WARS

AZORES

Date 30–31 August 1591
Forces Spanish: 53 ships;
English: c.20 ships
Losses Spanish: 1 ship sunk;
English: 1 ship captured

Location Off Flores
island, Azores

In spring 1591 an English fleet under
Lord Thomas Howard set sail for the
Azores, hoping to intercept the annual
Spanish treasure fleet. Lord Howard's
second-in-command was Sir Richard
Grenville, a soldier and privateer of an
arrogant and violent disposition, feared
by his enemies and his own men alike.
Grenville was on board *Revenge*, widely
respected as one of the finest galleons
in the world. While Howard waited at
the Azores for a treasure fleet that never
came, a large force of warships assembled

Defying the odds
The last stand of the *Revenge*
was the kind of heroic tale
told again and again to inspire
patriotism in generations of
English schoolboys.

in the Spanish port of
Ferrol, commanded
by Don Alonso de
Bazán, a brother of
the deceased Marqués
de Santa Cruz.

Bazán reached the
Azores in late August.
The English were now
weary from waiting,
many of their crew struck down by
disease. They had landed their sick on
Flores island and were taking on water
and cleaning out their bilges when
they learned that a Spanish fleet was
approaching. Bazán had cleverly split
his force in two, sending ships around

both sides of the island to catch his
enemy in a pincer movement. The
English were just ready to make sail
when the Spanish appeared around a
headland at 5pm. Howard led a dash
to open sea between the pincers of
Bazán's trap. One ship lagged behind:
Grenville's *Revenge*. As the trap closed,
Grenville attempted to break through
the mass of Spanish ships. Rammed
by the galleon *San Felipe*, he was
trapped, while Howard led the rest
of the English fleet away to safety.

The struggle that followed was an
epic of resistance by Grenville's crew.
Grappled by another galleon, the *San
Barnabe*, and surrounded by four others,
she fought off repeated attempts to
board, even succeeding in sinking one
Spanish ship. Wounded in the head,
Grenville insisted on continuing
resistance, although it was evidently
hopeless. The following morning his
crew disobeyed his order to blow up
the ship and surrendered. Grenville
died of his wounds; *Revenge* sank
in a gale two weeks later.

WITNESS TO WAR

SIR WALTER RALEIGH
ENGLISH NAVAL COMMANDER

LAST FIGHT OF THE REVENGE IN THE AZORES

*"Sir Richard finding himself in this distress, and unable any longer
to make resistance, having endured in this **fifteen hours fight**, the
assault of fifteen several Armadoes, all by turns aboard him, and by
estimation **eight hundred shot of great artillery**, besides many
assaults and entries … commanded the Master Gunner, whom he
knew to be a most resolute man, to split and sink the ship; that thereby
nothing might remain of glory or victory to the Spaniards: seeing
in so many hours fight, and with so great a Navy they were not able
to take her, having had fifteen hours time, **fifteen thousand men**,
and **fifty and three sail of men of war** to perform it withal."*

ANGLO–SPANISH WARS

CARIBBEAN

Date August 1595–
January 1596
Forces English: 26 ships;
Spanish: unknown
Losses Unknown

Location
The Caribbean

In 1595 the ageing Sir Francis Drake
and Sir John Hawkins planned a return
to privateering. They would raid the
Spanish colonies in the Caribbean,
combining private profit with damage
to the Spanish war effort. The two
leaders of the expedition, strong-willed
contrasting characters, soon succumbed
to arguing. Drake insisted on attacking
Grand Canary island en route, but an
attempted landing failed in the face of
stiff resistance. They then crossed the
Atlantic to attack the port of San Juan
in Puerto Rico, hoping to capture a
disabled Spanish treasure ship which
was sheltering in the harbour. When
they arrived off San Juan, Hawkins
died of a fever. The Spanish authorities
on the island had been warned of their
approach and the defences were too
strong for Drake's force to overcome.
In search of easier prey they shifted to
the mainland, going ashore at Nombre
de Dios, but when the expedition's land
commander, Sir Thomas Baskerville,
led a march on Panama he met stiff
resistance and had to turn back. Drake
still refused to give up, saying: "We must
have gold before we reach England".
He died of dysentery off Puerto Bello
on 28 January 1596. The expedition was
a complete fiasco, although Baskerville
brought most of the ships home.

ANGLO–SPANISH WARS

CADIZ

Date 20 June–5 July 1596
Forces English and Dutch:
120 ships; Spanish: unknown
Losses English: none; Spanish:
2 ships sunk, 2 captured

Location
Cadiz, Spain

On 3 June 1596 a fleet set sail from
Plymouth to attack the Spanish port
of Cadiz. Its commanders were Elizabeth
I's favourite Robert Devereux, Earl of
Essex, and her experienced lord admiral,
Lord Howard of Effingham. Also on
board was Sir Walter Raleigh, with
the post of rear admiral. The queen
regarded the expedition as a hopefully
self-financing pre-emptive strike against
Spanish preparations for a new Armada,
but Essex had a much more ambitious
objective – to seize and hold the port
with a permanent garrison. Arriving
at Cadiz, the English fought a sharp,
successful naval engagement during
which competition for glory between

the rival English commanders was as
prominent as hostility to the enemy.
Two Spanish galleons were destroyed
and two were captured. Essex then
stormed the town walls and seized
control of Cadiz. His soldiers ransacked
the town for valuables – one account
describes common soldiers "with their
arms full of silk and cloth of gold".
But the English failed to seize the rich
merchant ships in the inner harbour,
which the Spanish were able to scuttle.
Howard refused to go along with Essex's
plan for a permanent occupation of
Cadiz. The English were in any case
keen to get their treasure back home.
They left on 5 July with the city in
flames. The raid was a severe blow to
Spanish prestige, but it did not prevent
the dispatch of an Armada four months
later that was, fortunately for England,
forced back by bad weather.

Anglo-Dutch attack on Cadiz
This Dutch engraving of the 1596 attack on Cadiz
shows buildings around the port in flames. The Dutch
published many such propaganda images of Spain's
discomfiture at the hands of its Protestant enemies.

THE RISE OF DUTCH SEA POWER

IN THE FIRST HALF of the 17th century the sailors of the Dutch United Provinces, in rebellion against the rule of mighty Habsburg Spain, were the world's most formidable sea fighters. Their best commanders – men such as Piet Heyn and Maarten Tromp – showed a combination of seamanship and ruthless aggression that their enemies, although sailing in larger warships, could not match. Dutch naval victories helped force the Spanish to conclude a 12-year truce in 1609. Meanwhile the fleet of the Dutch East India Company supplanted the Portuguese in

the Indian Ocean and East Asia, forcibly seizing control of the valuable spice trade. By the time the war with Spain resumed, the Dutch had used increasing wealth to finance naval expansion. The Dutch West India Company, established in 1621, harassed the Spanish and Portuguese in the New World, occupying part of Brazil and, in 1628, capturing the entire Spanish treasure fleet. A stunning victory over the Spanish at the Downs in 1639 confirmed the naval supremacy of the Dutch and rendered inevitable Spain's eventual acknowledgement of Dutch independence.

GUN, SAIL, AND EMPIRE

DUTCH–PORTUGUESE WAR

BANTAM BAY

Date 27 December 1601–1 January 1602
Forces Dutch: 3 ships, 2 yachts; Portuguese: 8 galleons, 22 other vessels
Losses Dutch: none; Portuguese: 3 fustas captured

Location Sunda Strait, western Java

On 23 April 1601 five ships sailed from the Netherlands for Indonesia – then known as the East Indies or simply the Spice Islands. Calling itself the Moluccan Fleet, this flotilla was commanded by Admiral Wolphert Harmensz and consisted of three armed merchantmen and two yachts – fast lightly armed ships used as scouts. The Moluccan Fleet was intended to help break the Portuguese monopoly of the spice trade. Portuguese sailors had dominated the Indian Ocean for almost a century, but they were ill-prepared to meet a ruthless challenge from an aggressive European arrival. Harmensz's ships appeared off the Javanese port of Bantam, a major centre for the export of pepper, at Christmas 1601. The

Portuguese had an apparently superior force of galleons and fustas – light galleys – in harbour, but when skirmishing began they soon had the worst of it. On New Year's Day the Portuguese abandoned the port, which became the Indian Ocean headquarters of the newly formed Dutch East India Company.

Horary quadrant
Used for telling the time by the angle of the sun, the quadrant has a scale that is adjusted for every day of the year.

EIGHTY YEARS WAR

GIBRALTAR

Date 25 April 1607
Forces Dutch: 26 ships; Spanish: 21 ships
Losses Dutch: none; Spanish: 21 ships destroyed

Location Bay of Gibraltar

In early April 1607 a fleet of 26 small but well-armed Dutch warships set sail for the Iberian peninsula, accompanied by four supply ships. In command was the audacious and experienced Jacob van Heemskerk on board *Aeolus*. Arriving off Lisbon, he learned that a Spanish war fleet was in the Strait of Gibraltar and headed south to engage it. The Dutch found ten large Spanish galleons – far bigger ships than any of their own – and a number of lesser vessels anchored in Gibraltar Bay. Van Heemskerk decided to attack. He knew his ships would have no chance to withdraw if the battle went against them – there would be, he told his captains, "no choice between triumph and destruction".

The Spanish fleet was under the command of Admiral Don Juan Álvarez de Ávila, a veteran of Lepanto. He was astonished by the presumption of the small Dutch ships, which sailed

fearlessly into the bay, drifting slowly toward his galleons in a faint wind. Van Heemskerk's plan was for two ships to place themselves alongside each galleon, firing point-blank broadsides into both sides of the hull. His *Aeolus* was to engage the Spanish flagship *San Augustin*, with *Tiger* on the other side. During the long slow approach the Dutch held their fire, the gunners ordered to wait until the ships were hull-to-hull. In the first broadsides

van Heemskerk was fatally wounded, his leg torn off by a cannonball. De Ávila was also killed immediately. The carnage as the Dutch ships fired into galleons packed with soldiers was appalling. Several galleons were set ablaze and reduced to burning hulks, drifting out of control onto shore. Other Spanish ships were sunk. One exploded as a shot ignited its powder store, showering blazing debris across the smoke-darkened bay. *San Augustin*

was the last to succumb, boarded from both sides. The fighting ended toward sunset, but not the slaughter. The Dutch sailors rowed boats around the wreckage-strewn bay shooting or stabbing Spaniards who had leaped into the water from their burning ships. Around 4,000 Spanish sailors and soldiers are reckoned to have lost their lives; the Dutch dead numbered about one hundred. Van Heemskerk was awarded a hero's funeral in Amsterdam.

Death by fire and water
The battle of Gibraltar saw the total destruction of the Spanish fleet. Here, one of the Spanish galleons explodes as it is hit in the powder magazine.

EIGHTY YEARS WAR

MATANZAS BAY

Date 8 September 1628
Forces Spanish: 4 galleons, 11 merchantmen; Dutch: 35 ships
Losses Spanish: all ships captured; Dutch: none

Location
Matanzas Bay, Cuba

Every year a treasure fleet sailed across the Atlantic carrying silver, gold, and valuable exotic goods to Spain from its American colonies, riches used to finance Spain's wars in Europe. In 1628 the Dutch West India Company sent warships to capture the treasure fleet, a feat never before achieved. They were led by Admiral Piet Heyn on board the 50-gun *Amsterdam*, with Witte de With as his flag captain. The Spanish treasure ships sailed from Cartagena in Venezuela and Vera Cruz in Mexico, rendezvousing in Havana, Cuba, before crossing the Atlantic. Heyn waited off Havana for the ships to arrive. Warned of the Dutch presence the Cartagena squadron did not sail, but the Vera Cruz ships – four large galleons stuffed with bullion and 11 lesser merchantmen – approached Cuba on 7 September.

The convoy was led by Juan de Benavides y Bazan, a man with influence at court but little personal merit. One of Heyn's ships ran into the fleet during the night and at dawn, firing a quick broadside, hastened away to report the contact. Although the Dutch ships were much smaller than the galleons, their collective firepower was formidable. Benavides did not rate his chances in a fight. Abandoning the merchantmen to capture, the galleons sought refuge in Matanzas Bay. But they

were too heavily laden with cargo and passengers, and all four ran aground. The Dutch ships fired a few broadsides and then sent in boats that received the surrender of the galleons – from which senior officers had fled ashore – with hardly a shot fired. The captured treasure included 90 tons of silver and gold and was valued at 11.5 million guilders.

1577–1629

PIET HEYN

DUTCH NAVAL COMMANDER AND PRIVATEER

Born in Delftshaven, Heyn was a seafarer from boyhood. Twice captured by the Spanish, he served four years as a galley slave before joining the Dutch East India Company in 1607. He rose to captain and then, in the 1620s, vice admiral in the Dutch West India Company. He raided Spanish and Portuguese settlements and shipping in Africa, South America, and the West Indies, famously seizing the Spanish treasure fleet in 1628. Made Lieutenant Admiral of Holland in March 1629, he died fighting Dunkirk privateers three months later.

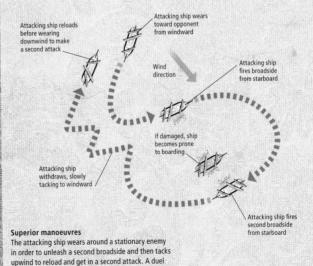

EIGHTY YEARS WAR

SLAAK

Date 12–13 September 1631
Forces Dutch: 50 boats; Spanish: 90 boats
Losses Dutch: unknown; Spanish: c.60 boats

Location Slaak channel, Scheldt estuary

The Spanish mounted an amphibious operation to seize strongpoints on the border between rebel Holland and Zeeland, embarking soldiers, under the Marquis of Aytona, on shallow-draught boats and sailing from Antwerp into the Scheldt. Forewarned of the incursion, the Dutch assembled 50 boats under Marinus Hollaer to intercept the convoy. Their attack, on the evening of 12 September, took the Spanish by surprise. The Dutch were able to use superior knowledge of the narrow channels and sandbanks to outmanoeuvre their enemy. Hundreds of Spanish drowned, jumping into the water in an attempt to escape. Aytona was among the few to return to Antwerp. The Admiralty of Amsterdam wanted the Spanish prisoners killed, but Dutch stadtholder Frederick Henry would not allow it.

PRIVATEER ACTION

DUNKIRK SORTIE

Date 14 August–8 September 1635
Forces Dunkirkers: 21 ships; Dutch: 35 warships
Losses Dunkirkers: unknown: Dutch c.120 fishing boats

Location
North Sea

Through most of the Dutch war of independence Dunkirk was controlled by the Spanish. They authorized the Dunkirkers to sail as privateers raiding Dutch merchant convoys and fishing fleets. The Dutch attempted to blockade Dunkirk to stop these attacks, but failed to prevent the privateers inflicting heavy losses. Jacob Collaart, vice admiral of the Dunkirk privateers, succeeded in running the blockade with 21 ships

on 14 August 1635. Over the following five days he savaged two Dutch fishing fleets, driving off their armed escorts and sinking more than 120 herring boats. The Dutch sent every available warship in pursuit of the marauders. On 21 August a squadron of 20 Dutch ships under Lieutenant Admiral Filips van Dorp engaged the Dunkirkers near the Dogger Bank. They inflicted little damage and four of them were crippled by the Dunkirkers' guns. When 15 more Dutch warships arrived, Collaart skilfully disengaged. Taking advantage of poor weather, he slipped back into Dunkirk on 8 September carrying 975 Dutch fishermen as prisoners.

Dunkirk harbour
Throughout the 17th century Dunkirk was a hotbed of privateers, encouraged – first by the Spanish, then by the French – to attack Dutch and English convoys.

MAN-OF-WAR TACTICS

MÊLÉE TACTICS

MAKING MAXIMUM USE OF THE WIND

Before Europe's navies all started to adopt line-of-battle tactics in the mid-17th century, a naval battle in the open sea was a disorderly affair that could easily degenerate into a series of duels between individual ships. A skilful captain and crew would use their superior seamanship to outmanoeuvre an opponent, using the wind to wear and tack around the enemy, getting in as many shots as possible while avoiding the enemy's fire. The Dutch were particularly formidable opponents when this kind of mêlée developed.

Attacking ship reloads before wearing downwind to make a second attack

Attacking ship wears toward opponent from windward

Wind direction

Attacking ship fires broadside from starboard

If damaged, ship becomes prone to boarding

Attacking ship withdraws, slowly tacking to windward

Attacking ship fires second broadside from starboard

Superior manoeuvres
The attacking ship wears around a stationary enemy in order to unleash a second broadside and then tacks upwind to reload and get in a second attack. A duel between two ships could last a long time, sometimes a matter of hours if the crews were evenly matched.

THE BATTLE OF THE DOWNS

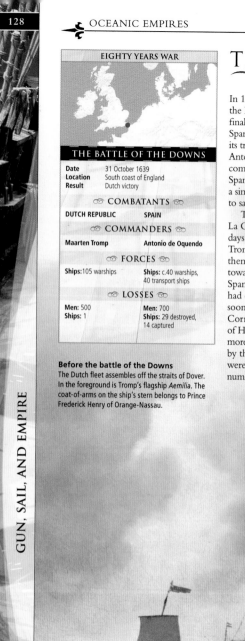

THE BATTLE OF THE DOWNS

Date	31 October 1639
Location	South coast of England
Result	Dutch victory

∞ COMBATANTS ∞

DUTCH REPUBLIC	SPAIN

∞ COMMANDERS ∞

Maarten Tromp	Antonio de Oquendo

∞ FORCES ∞

Ships: 105 warships	Ships: c.40 warships, 40 transport ships

∞ LOSSES ∞

Men: 500	Men: 700
Ships: 1	Ships: 29 destroyed, 14 captured

Before the battle of the Downs
The Dutch fleet assembles off the straits of Dover. In the foreground is Tromp's flagship *Aemilia*. The coat-of-arms on the ship's stern belongs to Prince Frederick Henry of Orange-Nassau.

GUN, SAIL, AND EMPIRE

In 1639 Spain's long struggle to suppress the Dutch revolt was in its desperate final phase. At war with France, the Spanish could only reinforce and pay its troops in the Netherlands by sea. Antonio de Oquendo was put in command of a fleet of around 40 Spanish and Portuguese warships and a similar number of troop transports to sail from Spain to Flanders.

The Spanish fleet sailed from La Coruña on 16 September. Nine days later Dutch Admiral Maarten Tromp, on board *Aemilia*, spotted them heading along the Channel towards the Catholic (i.e. pro-Spanish) port of Dunkirk. Tromp had only 13 ships, one of which he soon lost. He was joined by Witte Corneliszoon de With, vice admiral of Holland and West Frisia, with five more, but was still heavily outgunned by the Spanish, whose men-of-war were much larger as well as more numerous than the Dutch. Yet Tromp

engaged his enemy in a running duel, adopting a line of battle and firing broadsides. Many of Oquendo's ships took damage. Concerned above all for the safety of his transports, the Spanish commander took refuge in the Downs, an anchorage on the English coast. He expected the protection of the English, who were officially neutral but covertly pro-Spanish.

SPAIN IN ECLIPSE

Tromp established a blockade of the Downs and gathered reinforcements. The Dutch authorities increased the blockade force to over 100 ships. English vice admiral John Pennington was sent with a squadron to observe proceedings, and English merchant ships began ferrying Spanish troops and treasure to Flanders. Tromp

Grappling hook
A ship attempting to board an enemy would throw grappling hooks aboard, usually hoping to snag them in the rigging.

ordered English ships to be stopped and searched. The situation was delicate, for the Dutch did not want to go to war with England but wanted to destroy the Spanish fleet. With winter drawing near, Tromp knew he could not sustain the blockade indefinitely.

On 31 October, with an easterly wind in their favour, the Dutch decided to attack. Leaving one squadron to deter Pennington from intervening, Tromp sailed into the Downs. By accident or design, some of the Spanish ships ran ashore, where they were plundered by the gleeful English crowds that had gathered to see the fighting. Others followed

Oquendo's flagship *Santiago* in an attempted dash for Dunkirk. The release of Dutch fireships into the crowded waters spread panic. The Portuguese ship *Santa Teresa*, the largest vessel in the battle, was set ablaze and destroyed with heavy loss of life. Only a dozen ships, including *Santiago*, eventually reached Dunkirk and safety.

The battle of the Downs was a landmark in the precipitous decline of Spanish imperial power. In 1648 Spain was obliged to acknowledge Dutch independence after an 80-year conflict. The battle also triggered an uprising against Spanish rule in Portugal. In the meantime, England had been humiliated by its failure to react to a violation of its coastal waters. The desire to avenge this insult contributed to the outbreak of the first Anglo-Dutch War in May 1652.

1598–1653

MAARTEN TROMP

DUTCH ADMIRAL

Dutch admiral Maarten Tromp was born into a seagoing family in Briel. Twice in his early years he was captured by pirates – the first time at the age of 12 – but on both occasions he regained his freedom. He proved his worth as a naval officer serving under Piet Heyn in the 1620s, and was appointed lieutenant admiral commanding the Dutch fleet in 1637. His victory at the Downs in 1639 made him a Dutch national hero. He was, however, too independent-minded to suit the States-General, which dismissed him from office in the summer of 1652. By the end of the year he was reinstated, only to be killed by musket fire on 10 August at the battle of Scheveningen.

 DUTCH-PORTUGUESE WAR

PERNAMBUCO

Date 12–15 January 1640
Forces Dutch: 41 ships; Portuguese and Spanish: c.90 ships
Losses Dutch: 3 ships; Portuguese and Spanish: c.11 ships

Location Off coast of northeast Brazil

A large Spanish-Portuguese fleet commanded by Admiral Fernão de Mascarenhas tried to retake Pernambuco, Brazil, which the Dutch had seized from Portugal. A smaller Dutch fleet under Admiral Loos gave battle near the island of Itamaraca. Loos was killed during the first day's fighting, but the Dutch continued the battle under James Huyghens. On the fourth day of the action a number of Portuguese ships were driven aground on coastal shoals. After this, the Spanish-Portuguese force limped home. The Dutch held Pernambuco until 1654.

 EIGHTY YEARS WAR

PUERTO DE CAVITE

Date June 1647
Forces Dutch: 12 ships; Spanish: coastal batteries
Losses Dutch: 1 ship; Spanish: 1 fort destroyed

Location Manila Bay, Philippines

Manila was the eastern end of the Spanish cross-Pacific trade route plied by galleons which were carrying silver from Acapulco in Mexico. For the Dutch this was a tempting target. On 10 June 1647, a fleet of 12 Dutch ships sailed into Manila Bay and laid siege to Puerto de Cavite. The Spanish defended the port vigorously with shore guns and sank the Dutch flagship. Although the Dutch destroyed a fort at Porta Vaga, they could not take Cavite.

> ## TOO GREAT FOR SEA ALONE, HE HAS CARVED HIMSELF AN IMAGE IN THE HEARTS OF ALL MORE LASTING THAN GRAVE'S SPLENDOUR AND ITS MARBLE STONE.

JOOST VAN DEN VONDEL, DUTCH POET, ON ADMIRAL TROMP

WEAPONS AND TECHNOLOGY

CULVERIN

The culverin was a long-barrelled cannon typically firing a solid round shot of 17–18 pounds weight. A muzzle-loader, it was the longest-range gun on a 16th–17th century warship. Demi-culverins, firing roughly half the weight of shot, were also common. Culverins and demi-culverins were much favoured by the Dutch and English, whereas the Spanish tended to prefer heavier guns with shorter range. A long-barrelled gun posed problems for loading in a confined space, but the small truck carriage made the culverin relatively easy to handle. The stepped side of the carriage provided a fulcrum for the lever used to raise and lower the barrel.

English culverin
This 18-pounder culverin, dating from the English Civil War, has a calibre of 13.2cm (5.2in) and a range of some 3,000m (3,280yds).

RIVALRY ACROSS THE NORTH SEA

IN THE THIRD QUARTER of the 17th century the English and the Dutch fought one another in three wars that rank among the most intensive naval struggles of all time, with many large fleet encounters and heavy loss of life on both sides. The toll of casualties was partly a result of the massive firepower deployed, with a single ship carrying a larger weight of cannon than an entire 17th-century land army, but also a consequence of the close proximity of the opposing fleets, facing one another across the southern North Sea. The Anglo-Dutch Wars forced both sides to improve their navies at every level. The wars established the importance of fighting in line and made reliance on armed merchantmen, rather than purpose-built warships, obsolescent.

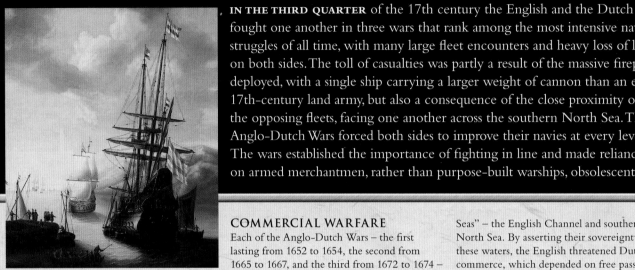

Dutch men-of-war in harbour
The ship in the foreground is anchored at the entrance to a harbour, with small boats going alongside to deliver supplies. Another man-of-war is entering the harbour under sail. The scene was painted in the early 1650s about the time of the First Anglo-Dutch War.

Battle of Scheveningen
The last battle of the First Anglo-Dutch War was fought off the Dutch coast in 1653. The Dutch succeeded in lifting the blockade that the English had imposed on them, but their great admiral, Maarten Tromp, lost his life in the process.

COMMERCIAL WARFARE

Each of the Anglo-Dutch Wars – the first lasting from 1652 to 1654, the second from 1665 to 1667, and the third from 1672 to 1674 – had its own specific origins. The third war also involved France, this time in a rare alliance with England. But the common root of this series of conflicts lay in commercial and colonial rivalry between two maritime nations.

The Dutch were regarded as the leading naval power of Europe, and their prowess at sea had enabled them to accumulate enormous wealth through the control of trade and their colonies. English governments and merchants envied Dutch success and hoped by war to steal trade and the colonies for themselves. Despite raiding and small-scale fighting in Africa, Asia, and the Americas, however, the decisive battles between them were all fought in the "Narrow

Seas" – the English Channel and southern North Sea. By asserting their sovereignty over these waters, the English threatened Dutch commerce, which depended on free passage through the Narrow Seas. England had the geographical advantage in the wars, being better placed to block Dutch trade, although the conflict cut England off from essential nautical supplies from the Baltic. On the other hand, one geographical advantage that the Dutch enjoyed over the English was that their coastline was protected by shoals and sandbanks that provided a safe haven for their ships.

IMPROVEMENTS IN GUNNERY AND COMMAND

After the clear superiority of English guns and gunnery had been demonstrated in the First Anglo-Dutch War, the Dutch had to build

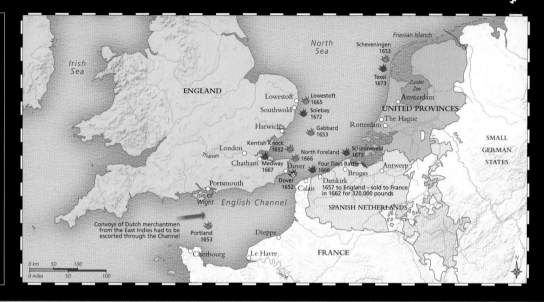

THE ANGLO-DUTCH WARS

Although the theatre sometimes switched to the Mediterranean, the coast of West Africa, and even North America, the most destructive fleet engagements of the Anglo-Dutch Wars all took place in the North Sea and the English Channel. The three costly wars that England and the United Provinces fought between 1652 and 1674 were forgotten when the two states allied to face the threat of the expansionist policies of Louis XIV's France.

KEY

- England
- United Provinces
- Spanish Netherlands
- Borders 1650
- Dutch convoy route
- Dutch victory
- English victory
- Inconclusive battle

Badge of wealth
The Dutch East India Company, the Vereenigde Oost-Indische Compagnie, founded in 1602, controlled the highly lucrative trade routes to the Spice Islands of Indonesia. VOC, the company's monogram, appears on this 17th-century seal.

bigger, more heavily armed ships. It was a sign of the inflation of firepower that the cannonade in the Four Days Battle, fought off the North Foreland during the Second Anglo-Dutch War in 1666, was audible to strollers in London's Hyde Park, at a distance of some 120km (80 miles) from the battle.

Command and control needed improvement as well as armament. The top commanders on the English side, such as Robert Blake and George Monck, were land officers sent to sea, while Dutch commanders were seamen born and bred – Michiel de Ruyter and the Tromps, for example, began their careers as cabin boys. But both sides initially depended heavily on merchant captains forced to bring their ships into temporary naval service. These not surprisingly often proved unreliable in the heat of battle. Thus there was swift progress toward creating a body of dedicated senior ratings and naval officers – in England a mix of "tarpaulins" bred to the sea and "gentleman commanders" – to man fleets ideally consisting entirely of warships.

In 1653 the English navy's famous Articles of War were first instituted, prescribing severe punishments for officers who failed to obey orders or who hung back from a fight. The systematic adoption of the line of battle, initially by the English, was intended to improve

discipline and organization in combat, as well as making it less likely ships would be hit by "friendly fire". Although battles still tended to disintegrate into general mêlées, the line of battle gave commanders some chance of effecting coherent manoeuvres.

ESCALATING DEMANDS OF WAR

Both sides struggled to meet the material and financial demands of naval warfare. The docks at Chatham were by far the largest industrial enterprise in England, and a sea battle used up shot and powder at a phenomenal rate. A fleet of ships contained as many people as a major contemporary town – Norwich in England or Haarlem in Holland, for example – posing daunting problems of supply of food and water.

Racked by political conflicts, both states struggled to keep up with these demands. England had just been torn apart by civil war, the king executed and replaced by the Lord Protector, Oliver Cromwell. The Restoration of the monarchy under Charles II came

between the First and the Second Anglo-Dutch Wars. When the monarchy's money ran out during the second war, sailors were not paid and supplies could not be bought. Sustaining warfare was made even more difficult because it interrupted trade, both through enemy commerce raiding and the transfer of seamen from merchant to naval service, thus cutting into the revenues available.

The difficulties experienced by both sides in financing the war effort helped make these conflicts, despite their savagery, totally indecisive. Yet a fundamental shift in the naval balance of power was under way. Before the end of the century, the once dominant Dutch would become the junior partner of the English in their joint wars against the French.

Holmes's Bonfire
In August 1666 the British fleet lay off the Dutch coast and watched as a small squadron of frigates and fireships under Sir Robert Holmes raided the town of Terschelling. They not only burned the town, but also destroyed 140 merchantmen.

1550 – 1830

FIRST ANGLO-DUTCH WAR

IN 1651 THE PARLIAMENT of the Commonwealth of England, just emerging from a civil war, passed the first Navigation Act. Stating that all goods brought to England must be carried either in English vessels or those of the country of origin, the act was a deliberate challenge to Dutch domination of maritime trade. The Dutch responded to England's search and seizure of merchant ships by assembling an imposing war fleet to protect merchant convoys and to intimidate the English in the Channel and North Sea. War broke out unintentionally through a naval clash at Dover in May 1652. After an initial setback at the battle of the Kentish Knock, the Dutch scored victories at Dungeness in winter 1652 and at Leghorn in the Mediterranean in spring 1653. But the English improved the organization of their fleet and had the better of a series of fierce encounters at Portland, Gabbard Bank, and Scheveningen. The war exhausted both countries and was ended in April 1654 with a peace treaty that resolved nothing. Unsurprisingly, the Anglo-Dutch contest for maritime supremacy was resumed in the following decade.

FIRST ANGLO-DUTCH WAR

DOVER

Date 29 May 1652
Forces English: 25 ships; Dutch: 47 ships
Losses English: none; Dutch: 2 ships captured

Location Goodwin Sands, off Dover

The English provocatively asserted the right to be saluted by foreign ships in the Channel and the North Sea. Admiral Maarten Tromp, escorting a Dutch merchant convoy down the Channel in May 1652, had been authorized by his government to dip his flag in salute if necessary. On 29 May, Tromp met an English squadron commanded by General-at-Sea Robert Blake, whose warning shots hit Tromp's flagship *Brederode*. Tromp gave answer with a broadside and a general fight ensued. After five hours nightfall brought an end to the exchanges and Tromp escorted his convoy onward. A formal declaration of war followed six weeks later.

FIRST ANGLO-DUTCH WAR

KENTISH KNOCK

Date 8 October 1652
Forces English: 68 ships; Dutch: 62 ships
Losses English: none; Dutch: 1 ship sunk, 1 captured

Location North Sea, off Thames estuary

By October 1652 Admiral Maarten Tromp had fallen out of favour with the Dutch States-General. He was replaced with Vice Admiral Witte de With, whose instructions were to seek out and destroy the English fleet. With *Prins Willem* as his flagship, de With led a fleet of 62 ships to attack the English at their anchorage in the Downs.

Under the overall command of General-at-Sea Robert Blake, the English came out to fight, but bad weather delayed the start of the battle. The two fleets finally met near the sandbank of the Kentish Knock late in the afternoon of 8 October. Blake held the weather gage and chose to attack,

but the battle started badly for the English when two of their largest ships, *Sovereign* and *James*, ran aground in the shallow channels. While Blake, on board *Resolution*, led an onslaught against de With, the rear English squadron under Rear Admiral Nehemiah Bourne was surrounded by a superior force of Dutch ships commanded by Michiel de Ruyter. Bourne's ships were "very much maimed" before Blake came to their rescue. But the Dutch suffered worse. One ship, *Burgh van Alkmaar*, exploded, and another, *Maria*, was captured. De With was obliged to move his flag after *Prins Willem* lost two masts.

Darkness brought the fighting to a close and saved the Dutch from an even worse defeat. De With failed to convince his captains to continue the battle on the following day, and both he and de Ruyter succeeded in withdrawing without further loss.

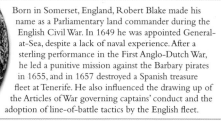

1599–1657
ROBERT BLAKE
GENERAL-AT-SEA

Born in Somerset, England, Robert Blake made his name as a Parliamentary land commander during the English Civil War. In 1649 he was appointed General-at-Sea, despite a lack of naval experience. After a sterling performance in the First Anglo-Dutch War, he led a punitive mission against the Barbary pirates in 1655, and in 1657 destroyed a Spanish treasure fleet at Tenerife. He also influenced the drawing up of the Articles of War governing captains' conduct and the adoption of line-of-battle tactics by the English fleet.

FIRST ANGLO-DUTCH WAR

PORTLAND

Date 28 February–2 March 1653
Forces Dutch: c.80 warships; English: c.80 warships
Losses Dutch: 10 warships; English: 1 warship

Location The English Channel

On 10 December 1652, reinstated in command of the Dutch fleet, Admiral Maarten Tromp inflicted a significant defeat on the English at Dungeness. As a result, he was able to escort a large convoy of merchant vessels down the Channel to the Atlantic. Tromp then waited at La Rochelle to gather more ships and shepherd them back to the Netherlands – a delay that gave the English time to recover.

The English and Dutch sighted one another at dawn on 28 February. Tromp had the weather gage and chose to attack, rather than passively shield his merchant convoy. The English were scattered and General-at-Sea Robert

Blake at first had to engage around 30 Dutch ships with only a dozen of his own. Blake's flagship *Triumph* was battered at close range by broadsides from Tromp's *Brederode*, suffering over 100 casualties. But only one English frigate was sunk, while the Dutch lost eight ships as the main body of the English fleet joined the combat.

Over the following days a running battle ensued. Though short of powder, the Dutch saved most of their warships and more than half the merchant convoy from capture or destruction.

Running battle
In defence of its merchant convoy, the Dutch fleet descended on the English in the Channel. By the third day, the battle had drifted as far as Kent.

FIRST ANGLO-DUTCH WAR

SCHEVENINGEN

Date 8–10 August 1653
Forces Dutch: 106 ships; English: c.120 ships
Losses Dutch: 15 ships; English: none

Location Off the Netherlands

In August 1653 Admiral Maarten Tromp attempted to break a blockade of the Dutch coast by the English fleet under General-at-Sea George Monck. Tromp's ships in the Maas needed to link up with Witte de With's squadron in the Texel. With a brilliant manoeuvre, on 8 August Tromp drew Monck southward, allowing de With to sortie. With Tromp and de With united, battle was joined. Crossing and recrossing the enemy fleet in line, the English devastated the Dutch ships with their heavy guns. The battle ended with the Dutch in disorganized flight, but they had inflicted enough damage for the English to abandon the blockade.

THE GABBARD

Date 12–13 June 1653
Forces English: 110 ships;
Dutch: 98 ships
Losses English: none;
Dutch: 10 ships sunk,
11 captured

Location Off Suffolk,
eastern England

The spring of 1653 found both sides in the Anglo-Dutch War still keen for battle. The English had improved the discipline of their navy by the adoption of the Articles of War, which imposed strict rules of

Close quarters
This contemporary grisaille drawing shows the *Brederode* (left) engaged with the *Resolution* (right).

conduct upon captains. They had also laid down the principles of fighting in an orderly line of battle that would maximize the impact of their broadsides. Dutch Admiral Maarten Tromp, however, was still confident that his lighter ships could outmanoeuvre the English with superior seamanship and force them into a mêlée in which the firepower of his marines would be crucial.

The two fleets met near the Gabbard Bank, some 40km (25 miles) east of the Suffolk coast on 12 June 1653. The battle opened disastrously for the English when Richard Deane, one of their two commanding Generals-at-Sea, was killed by almost the first shot fired. But a light wind made it hard for the Dutch to manoeuvre and so exposed them to steady attrition by broadsides fired by the disciplined English line at medium range. Late

Matchlock musket
Though lethal at 90m (100yds) or less, the matchlock musket was a cumbersome weapon that often failed to fire in wet conditions.

in the day Tromp succeeded in trapping part of the English fleet between two of his squadrons, but the balance of damage in the day's fighting was very much in England's favour.

ENGLISH VICTORY

The English fleet was strengthened on the evening of 12 June by the arrival of Admiral Robert Blake with 18 more ships. Tromp nonetheless attacked the next day, which proved unwise. Many Dutch ships were running low on powder and some of Tromp's captains were far keener to escape than to fight. Tromp's flagship *Brederode* was badly holed but avoided capture, its withdrawal covered by the lieutenant admiral's more devoted captains. Eleven Dutch ships were taken by the English, however, and probably as many as 11 destroyed. The survivors found refuge from a pursuing enemy in the shoals off the Dutch coast, where they were put under blockade. Morale on board Tromp's ships was so poor that he did not dare send them into port for repair, for fear of mass desertion. Nonetheless, with trade stopped, Tromp would have to challenge the English again.

MAN-OF-WAR TACTICS
THE LINE OF BATTLE

MAXIMIZING THE USE OF BROADSIDES

Although casually used on earlier occasions, notably by the Dutch in the prelude to the battle of the Downs in 1639, line-of-battle tactics were first adopted systematically by the English in 1653, during the First Anglo-Dutch War. The line usually consisted of three squadrons, with the senior admiral commanding the centre, and vice and rear admirals commanding the van and the rear. It soon became an assumption of naval warfare that both sides would use essentially the same formation. Typically the fleet to windward would approach in line abreast, and then wear together with each ship placing

itself alongside an enemy. In a perfect battle, the two lines would sail on the same tack exchanging broadsides, with ships matched to opponents from the lead ship of the van to the rearmost vessel. Only warships from fourth-rate upward were reckoned powerful enough to act as ships of the line. These tactics could be a straitjacket for captains, with more attention focused on keeping alignment than on attacking the enemy. Yet they enabled commanders to keep some control of their fleets and execute coherent manoeuvres such as doubling the enemy line if there were spare ships in the van.

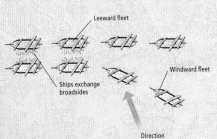

Leeward fleet

Ships exchange broadsides

Windward fleet

Direction of wind

Engaging the enemy
The attacking fleet sails from the windward side to attack the enemy. Each ship singles out one of the enemy with which to engage. The windward fleet has many advantages, including being clear of gun smoke, but it cannot easily withdraw.

Firing on the downward roll
This tactic was especially associated with the English. By firing shot into the enemy's hull, they spread death and destruction through the gun decks.

Firing on the upward roll
Some navies preferred directing chain-shot and canister upward to sails and rigging and to kill men on the upper decks. The disabled ship would then be open to boarding.

SECOND ANGLO-DUTCH WAR

THE RESTORATION OF THE English monarchy under Charles II in 1660 did nothing to improve relations with the Dutch. A faction at the English court associated with Charles's brother James, Duke of York, was determined to challenge Dutch dominance of world trade. In 1664 the English attacked Dutch slave trading posts on the west coast of Africa, captured New Amsterdam in North America, which they renamed New York, and seized Dutch merchant ships. War was formally declared in March 1665. The Dutch were building a new navy with larger warships, although this was still incomplete. Hostilities opened with a stunning defeat for the Dutch at Lowestoft. Vigorous action by Dutch leader Johan de Witt and the return of Admiral Michiel de Ruyter from colonial duties then shifted the balance in favour of the Dutch. England was struck by the disasters of the Plague and the Fire of London, while royal finances collapsed. The bold Dutch raid on the Medway in 1667 was a final humiliation for England's rulers, who hastily signed a peace that left them no gains but the little-valued possession of New York.

LOWESTOFT

Date 13 June 1665
Forces English: 109 ships; Dutch: 103 ships
Losses English: 1 ship lost; Dutch: 17 ships lost

Location Off Suffolk, eastern England

When war broke out the Dutch government had great confidence in the strength of its new navy. Admiral Jacob van Wassenaer Obdam was sent to seek out the English fleet and give battle. Aware of Dutch intentions, the English were waiting for Obdam when he appeared off East Anglia.

There was little tactical coherence to a battle fought in shifting winds. The English commander James, Duke of York, struggled to keep his ships in formation but the Dutch engaged pell-mell. The combat grew in ferocity. James, on his flagship *Royal Charles*, narrowly escaped death when chain-shot decapitated several courtiers who were standing alongside him. Obdam was less fortunate. After a lengthy duel with *Royal Charles*, his flagship *Eendracht* exploded, killing almost all those on board. After Obdam's death, which occurred at around 3pm, the Dutch had no overall commander. Panicking Dutch captains began to flee back across the North Sea piecemeal. Several ships became tangled together in the confusion and were set ablaze by English fireships. Vice Admiral Cornelis Tromp distinguished himself by organizing a rearguard action to cover the withdrawal.

The English botched the pursuit through the following night, allowing most of the Dutch ships to regain the safety of the Texel shallows. Still, the Dutch had lost two ships sunk, six burned, and nine captured, plus some 6,000 men killed or taken prisoner. It was the heaviest Dutch defeat of the three Anglo-Dutch Wars.

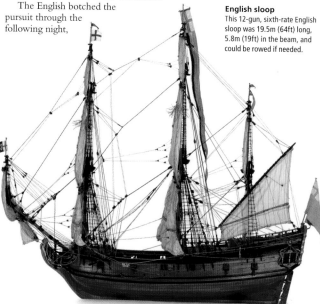

English sloop
This 12-gun, sixth-rate English sloop was 19.5m (64ft) long, 5.8m (19ft) in the beam, and could be rowed if needed.

1607–1676
MICHIEL DE RUYTER
DUTCH ADMIRAL

Spending more than six decades at sea and fighting in over 40 maritime battles, Michiel Adrianzoon de Ruyter was the greatest Dutch naval commander of the 17th century. Going to sea as a boy, he worked his way up to merchant captain before proving his worth as a naval commander in the First Anglo-Dutch War. He fought the English in West Africa and the Caribbean, and liberated some 2,500 Christian slaves from the Barbary pirates in the Mediterranean, before returning to take command of the Dutch navy in August 1665. He led his fleet to a hard-fought victory in the Four Days Battle, but only held nominal command in the raid of the Medway. His finest hour came fighting against the odds in the Third Anglo-Dutch War. He was fatally wounded in a battle with the French off Sicily in 1676.

BERGEN

Date 13 August 1665
Forces English: 14 warships; Dutch: 60 merchant ships
Losses English: none; Dutch: none

Location Bergen, Norway

After the English victory at Lowestoft, a Dutch merchant fleet took shelter at Bergen in Norway, then ruled by the king of Denmark. On attempting to capture the fleet, the English, under the command of Rear Admiral Thomas Teddiman, failed to win the Danes' cooperation and were battered by the guns of a fortress commanding the bay. The Dutch also kept up a brisk fire, forcing the English to withdraw.

FOUR DAYS BATTLE

Date 11–14 June 1666
Forces English: 79 ships; Dutch: 84 ships
Losses English: 10 ships; Dutch: 4 ships

Location Between England and Flanders

By June 1666, France had gone to war with England and the Dutch had strengthened their navy with a substantial shipbuilding programme. So when George Monck, Duke of Albemarle, came upon the Dutch fleet anchored off Dunkirk on 11 June, he had only 56 ships to Michiel de Ruyter's 84. Monck nonetheless attacked, precipitating the bloodiest battle of the Anglo-Dutch Wars.

In the first day's fighting English Vice Admiral William Berkley was killed by a musket ball in the throat as he resisted the boarding of his ship, *Swiftsure*. Dutch Lieutenant Admiral Cornelis Evertsen was cut in half by a shot from Rear Admiral John Harman's flagship *Henry*, which had refused to strike despite being on fire and part of its crew jumping overboard in panic. By the end of the second day, with only 29 ships in fighting condition, Monck was desperately trying to disengage. Late on the third day Prince Rupert's ships tardily arrived to even the odds, but when Rupert's flagship *Royal James* was dismasted the following morning his squadron left Monck to face de Ruyter unaided. After further heavy losses (totalling 2,000 killed) the English disappeared into a fog bank and de Ruyter abandoned the pursuit.

THE RAID ON THE MEDWAY

In the winter of 1666–67, with peace negotiations with the Dutch under way, King Charles and his advisers decided to keep the fleet laid up in dockyards when spring came. Meanwhile, the Dutch political leader Johan de Witt wanted to inflict a humiliating defeat on England that would enable him to dictate peace terms. He ordered an expedition to raid the Thames and the Medway, placing his brother Cornelis in charge to ensure bold aggressive action. The Dutch fleet appeared in the Thames estuary on 7 June. Overcoming the objections of his cautious sea captains, Cornelis de Witt ordered his ships into the mouth of the Thames, where they failed to capture 20 merchantmen that took refuge in the direction of London. An attack on Sheerness three days later was more successful, Dutch marines capturing the poorly defended fort without difficulty.

A clutch of English commanders, including George Monck (Duke of Albermarle), gathered at Chatham to organize the defence of the dockyards. Blockships were hastily sunk at various points in the Medway's navigable channels. The chain was defended by the frigate *Unity*, two captured Dutch merchantmen renamed *Matthias* and *Charles V*, and the ship of the line *Monmouth*. When the Dutch ships advanced into the Medway on 12 June they made short work of these defences. The *Unity*'s crew rapidly jumped ship, leaving their vessel to be taken. Fireships daringly sailed over the chain and set *Charles V* and *Matthias* ablaze. Dutch engineers set to work dismantling the chain and worked to haul off the blockships, soon clearing the passage upriver.

The 80-gun first-rate *Royal Charles* had been left in an exposed position manned with a skeleton crew and was easily taken. Numerous other English vessels – including the great ships *Loyal London*, *Royal James*, and *Royal Oak* – were scuttled to prevent them too being captured. Half sunk, the three great ships were set on fire by the Dutch to complete the scene of destruction. Only *Monmouth* escaped. The Dutch took some casualties from the fire of shore batteries and guns in Upnor Castle. On 14 June they decided to withdraw, without having destroyed the dockyard stores. *Royal Charles* was towed back to the Netherlands, to be shown off to foreign visitors over the following years. Peace was soon made on terms highly favourable to the Dutch. But, rather like the United States after Pearl Harbor in 1941, England was soon able to rebuild its fleet and plot its revenge.

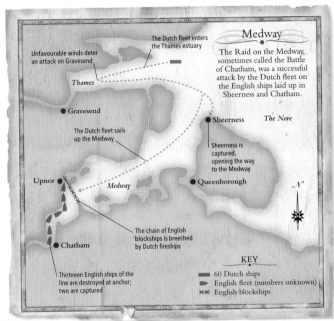

Commemorative medal
This Dutch medal remembers the day "the ships of war ... were attacked, burnt, and sunk".

Medway
The Raid on the Medway, sometimes called the Battle of Chatham, was a successful attack by the Dutch fleet on the English ships laid up in Sheerness and Chatham.

Unfavourable winds deter an attack on Gravesend

The Dutch fleet enters the Thames estuary

Thames

● Gravesend

The Dutch fleet sails up the Medway

● Sheerness   *The Nore*

Sheerness is captured, opening the way to the Medway

Upnor ●

Medway

● Queenborough

The chain of English blockships is breeched by Dutch fireships

● Chatham

Thirteeen English ships of the line are destroyed at anchor; two are captured

KEY
▬ 60 Dutch ships
► English fleet (numbers unknown)
✕✕ English blockships

Destruction at Chatham
Some of the English navy's best ships were destroyed at Chatham, where they were laid up some 48km (30 miles) east of London.

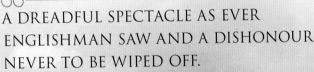

> A DREADFUL SPECTACLE AS EVER ENGLISHMAN SAW AND A DISHONOUR NEVER TO BE WIPED OFF.
>
> **JOHN EVELYN**, WRITER AND DIARIST, JUNE 1667

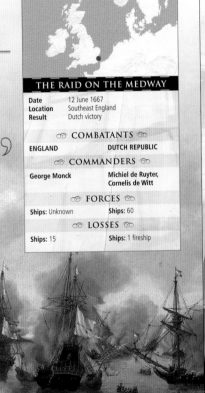

SECOND ANGLO-DUTCH WAR

THE RAID ON THE MEDWAY

Date	12 June 1667
Location	Southeast England
Result	Dutch victory

COMBATANTS

ENGLAND	DUTCH REPUBLIC

COMMANDERS

George Monck	Michiel de Ruyter, Cornelis de Witt

FORCES

Ships: Unknown	Ships: 60

LOSSES

Ships: 15	Ships: 1 fireship

1550 – 1830

FIRESHIP ATTACK

Fireships, which played a major role during the Anglo-Dutch Wars, are known to have been used in Classical times, and remained in use well into the 19th century. Here, French fireships attack the British fleet off Quebec in June 1759, during the Seven Years War. Though spectacular, the attack was largely ineffective, most of the fireships being towed away before they could cause any damage.

THIRD ANGLO-DUTCH WAR

ENGLAND'S KING CHARLES II made a secret alliance with France's King Louis XIV in 1670 to attack the Dutch Republic. However, a declaration of war was delayed until April 1672, giving Dutch Lieutenant-Admiral Michiel de Ruyter time to train the Dutch fleet in disciplined battle tactics. The combination of the English fleet and the French navy, recently strengthened and expanded by Louis's chief minister, Colbert, gave the allies an overwhelming superiority of numbers. But they cooperated poorly and quarrels disrupted their naval operations. De Ruyter fought an inspired campaign with inadequate resources, tempering aggression with a necessary concern to preserve his fleet. He came under political attack at home after his friend Johan de Witt was expelled from office and lynched by a mob, but at sea his performance was impeccable. His successes in defensive battles at Scheveningen and Texel led to recriminations between the allies and fuelled anti-war feeling in England, where the alliance with Catholic France was deeply unpopular. Under pressure from his own people, King Charles made peace with the Dutch in 1674.

THIRD ANGLO-DUTCH WAR
THE BATTLE OF SOLEBAY

Date	7 June 1672
Location	Off Southwold, eastern England
Result	Dutch victory

⚓ COMBATANTS ⚓
ENGLAND FRANCE	DUTCH REPUBLIC

⚓ COMMANDERS ⚓
Duke of York, Comte d'Estrées	Michiel de Ruyter

⚓ FORCES ⚓
Ships: English: 63, French: 30	**Ships:** 75

⚓ LOSSES ⚓
Ships: 1	**Ships:** 3

Friesland
This model of the Dutch second-rater *Friesland* shows the shallow draught characteristic of Dutch warships. It was needed for sailing in Holland's coastal waters.

THE BATTLE OF SOLEBAY

At the outset of the war, the Dutch planned to attack the English fleet before it could join with its French allies, but they delayed too long. By early June 1672 the allied fleets, under the overall command of King Charles's brother James, Duke of York, had met up and were anchored in Solebay, careening hulls and taking on supplies. They heavily outnumbered the Dutch, but de Ruyter decided to attack, with the advantage of surprise and an onshore wind behind him.

At 2:30 on the morning of 7 June, a French frigate reported sighting the Dutch approaching Solebay. The allies were totally unprepared, moored in no particular order and with many sailors sleeping ashore. Ships hastily made ready for battle and strove to get out to sea against the breeze. Whether through a misunderstanding or a deliberate decision, the Comte d'Estrées, in command of the French fleet, steered to the south, despite a signal from the Duke of York to follow him northward. The allied line was thus split in two. De Ruyter detached the 15 ships of his rear squadron to keep d'Estrées' 30 ships occupied in a long-range duel, while his centre and van went for the English fleet, now deprived of their numerical advantage.

Putting to sea in haste, the English ships were spread out in a ragged formation, and thus poorly placed to support one another. The Dutch concentrated on attacking the English flagships, easily identifiable by their array of large ensigns. The Duke of York's *Royal Prince* was engaged at close range by de Ruyter's flagship *Zeven Provincien* and the 76-gun *Eendracht*. The power of *Royal Prince's* guns kept the Dutch at bay, but after two hours' battering the Duke was forced to shift his flag from the crippled ship. A worse fate befell *Royal James*, the 100-gun flagship of the Earl of Sandwich. She was grappled by the 60-gun *Groot Hollandia*, which raked her with broadsides point blank until she was disabled. The Earl refused to strike his colours and got away from the Dutch ship, but as *Royal James* drifted out of control it was struck by a fire ship. In the panic to abandon the blazing vessel, the Earl of Sandwich was drowned, his body washing ashore a few weeks later, identifiable only by his badge of the Order of the Garter.

Battle of Solebay medal
This French medal depicts a horse-drawn Neptune threatening Holland with his trident.

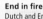

End in fire
Dutch and English sailors shoot at each other with pistols as men-of-war engage with broadsides. To the right, *Royal James* burns after a Dutch fireship attack.

SCHOONEVELD

Date 7 and 14 June 1673
Forces English: 54 ships; French: 27 ships; Dutch: 55 ships
Losses English and French: 2 ships; Dutch: 1 ship

Location Off the Scheldt estuary

In 1673 the French army was invading the Dutch Republic. The English intended to land troops to support the French, but first needed to defeat de Ruyter or blockade him in port. In May, the Dutch moored in the Schooneveld, an anchorage protected by shoals.

Prince Rupert led an Anglo-French fleet to confront them but did not dare take his ships into the narrow channels.

On 7 June de Ruyter surprised the allies by coming out to fight against the odds. Seizing the weather gage, he broke up the French formation in the allied centre and then turned to support Admiral Cornelis Tromp's squadron hard-pressed by Rupert. At nightfall the allies were happy to disengage. De Ruyter made a second sortie a week later, once again surprising the allies who had believed the Dutch fleet to be badly mauled. By the end of the second engagement the allies were in no condition to continue at sea and returned to England for repairs.

The Dutch had also suffered losses and towards nightfall de Ruyter broke off the engagement. The following day the Duke of York ordered a pursuit as the Dutch headed for home. The French, in the van, overtook the Dutch rear but unaccountably failed to engage and the pursuit was soon abandoned. Both sides had suffered heavy casualties, yet the moral victory clearly lay with the Dutch. Allied officers indulged in bitter recriminations, even between opposing factions within the national fleets, and the Comte d'Estrées' second-in-command Abraham Duquesne refused to serve under him again.

> ## THE FIGHTING WAS SO STUBBORNLY CONTESTED BY BOTH SIDES THAT ONE COULD NOT COUNT EITHER SIDE AS HAVING THE ADVANTAGE ...
>
> **MARCUS GJOE**, DANISH OBSERVER, REPORTING ON THE BATTLE OF SOLEBAY

TEXEL

Date 21 August 1673
Forces English and French: 92 ships; Dutch: 75 ships
Losses English and French: none; Dutch: none

Location Between Kamperduin and Texel

De Ruyter remained in his safe haven at Schooneveld until August 1673, when concerns for the safety of the incoming Dutch spice fleet made him sail north to the Texel and contest the Anglo-French blockade. As in the previous battles in this war, the tactical dexterity of the Dutch and the failure of coordination between different divisions of the allied fleet negated the Anglo-French numerical superiority.

The opposing rear divisions were commanded by Admiral Sir Edward Spragge and Lieutenant Admiral Cornelis Tromp. Spragge had developed a feud with Tromp and had given King Charles his word that he would kill the Dutch admiral. Pursuing his vendetta with no regard for the overall shape of the battle, he allowed his squadron to

Royal Prince dismasted
English and Dutch sailors fight each other with oars, daggers, and cutlasses. In the background, Tromp's flagship *Gordon Leeuw* sails to the right of *Royal Prince*, Spragge's dismasted flagship.

become detached from the centre under Prince Rupert. Spragge and Tromp fought their personal duel with such ferocity that both had to shift their flags twice from corpse-strewn, dismasted ships. Transferring for the second time, Spragge was killed when a cannonball struck his boat.

Meanwhile, the French in the van became totally detached from the fight. De Ruyter initially sent a handful of ships under Adriaen Banckert to take on the Comte d'Estrées' division. At a chosen moment, Banckert disengaged and turned to join the battle in the centre, where de Ruyter was engaged with Prince Rupert. Either unable or unwilling to follow Banckert, the French were left with no one to fight. At the end of the day the Dutch disengaged and returned to safe anchorage. The allied naval command subsequently disintegrated in a storm of accusations of cowardice and treachery, focused chiefly upon the Comte d'Estrées' failure to come to Prince Rupert's aid.

WITNESS TO WAR
ENGLISH OFFICER, BLUE SQUADRON
IN A REPORT ON THE BATTLE

AT THE BATTLE OF TEXEL

"I went aboard Sir Edward Spragge ... and found his ship extremely disabled, and as we set our boat from his ship, **down fell his main mast** within a yard of our boat ... after this, Sir Edward Spragge came on board the St George where **he put up his flag** ... at two of the clock St George was so disabled too that Sir Edward Spragge took boat to go on board the Royal Charles ... **but a bullet came through the St George and broke his boat**; they made back again as fast as they could ... but the boat sunk, and **Sir Edward Spragge drowned** being taken up dead, his head and shoulders above water having taken so dead hold of the boat, they could hardly disengage him from it."

GUN, SAIL, AND EMPIRE

REST AND RECREATION

OFF-DUTY SAILORS have often had a deserved reputation for excess and disorder. Naval towns were known for their drinking establishments, brothels, gambling dens, and tattoo parlours, where seamen could be relieved of their hard-earned pay during a brief spell of shore leave, ending back on board with empty pockets and a severe hangover. But sailors, of course, have not all been drinkers and brawlers in their leisure time. They might be as likely to spend their free hours making music, sketching caricatures, or even writing poetry.

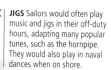

《《 | JIGS Sailors would often play music and jigs in their off-duty hours, adapting many popular tunes, such as the hornpipe. They would also play in naval dances when on shore.

LEISURE AT SEA

At sea in the age of sail, the forecastle was the place where sailors relaxed in their off-duty hours during the week, and on Sundays after a religious service and the reading of the Articles of War. Sailors sprawled on the deck in fine weather, combing and plaiting one another's hair. They also danced and sang songs – known as fo'c'sle songs. These were distinct from sea shanties that were sung to relieve the tedium and keep rhythm while working. Younger sailors might indulge in skylarking, playing and chasing in the rigging high above the deck, a dangerous sport generally disapproved of. In a calm, the captain might have a sail let down over the side to make a swimming pool. Gambling games with dice and cards were always popular, although usually officially banned as counter to religious principle and a potential source of disorder – many fights on board were caused by gambling disputes.

⌃ | PLAYING MAH JONG The Chinese game of Mah Jong was popular with sailors who were responsible for its introduction to Britain.

》 | UCKERS BOARD A more complex form of Ludo, Uckers has a long tradition in the Royal Navy and is still played widely below decks today.

DRUNKENNESS

Drinking alcohol to excess was always a favourite off-duty activity for sailors. While navies of the sailing-ship era issued men with alcohol as part of their daily rations, they clamped down with a heavy hand on men who drank any more than their ration on board – drunkenness was a major cause of accidents and was incompatible with the good running of a ship. Official disapproval and severe punishments did not prevent men going to extreme lengths to procure drunkenness, either illegally saving up their ration for a binge or smuggling drink on board. The ban on excessive drinking never applied to officers, who were often the most flagrant offenders, indulging in spectacular drinking bouts involving the consumption of extraordinary quantities of wine and brandy.

》 | HORN OF PLENTY Alcohol has often fuelled sailors' lives both on board and off. Beer, wine, and rum have been served by many navies as part of regular rations, although the authorities at the same time have attempted to suppress outright drunkenness.

⌃ | RELAXING ON DECK Off-duty German sailors in the late 1800s are permitted some time off on a Sunday afternoon to take advantage of the fine weather and take in the fresh air before disappearing back below deck to their service.

WOMEN

In the age of sail the need of hundreds of young men crowded on ships to find sexual relief once in harbour was widely – though not universally – accepted by their officers. Port towns were notorious sites of debauchery and it is no surprise that venereal diseases were commonplace in all navies. When captains were reluctant to let men ashore for fear of desertion, they frequently allowed women to come on board while in port. Officially tolerated as "wives", sometimes hundreds would be accommodated on a warship's gun deck at one time. In the absence of privacy, this lead to scenes that shocked more religious consciences.

» **PORT OF PLEASURE** The expansion of London's maritime trade during the 18th century, and the presence of two Royal Navy dockyards, created an increasing demand for prostitution in the capital.

MODERN TIMES

In the 20th century the maritime authorities made increasing efforts to regulate leisure activities. They encouraged more salubrious games by organizing official competitions – racing ship's boats was a favourite of the pre-World War I Royal Navy. The US Navy tried to clean up its act by, for example, banning all alcohol consumption on ships along with indecent tattoos – an edict that sent many sailors scurrying to tattoo parlours to "dress up" their naked ladies. During World War II the ban on alcohol was subverted on some US ships by the operation of illegal stills, refining alcohol from various cleaning substances or fuels. Gambling also flourished unchecked by official disapproval. Radios and gramophones replaced group singing, while increasing literacy made reading a favourite pastime.

≥ **SHIP'S LOUNGE** This lounge room on the American destroyer USS *Donald Cook* combines a dining area with a plasma TV, a DVD player, and easy chairs.

Many a man of war hath been her willing prisoner, and paid a proper ransom … [she] loves to fight yard arm … and be briskly boarded.

HARRIS'S LIST OF LONDON LADIES (1758), John Harris's popular list of ladies was updated annually until the 1790s

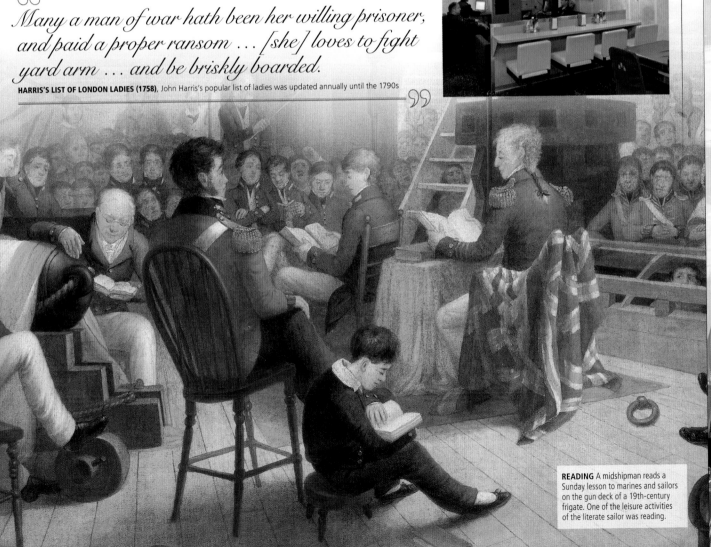

READING A midshipman reads a Sunday lesson to marines and sailors on the gun deck of a 19th-century frigate. One of the leisure activities of the literate sailor was reading.

THE SUN KING'S NAVY

IN THE COURSE of the 17th century the kings of France made their country the dominant land power in Europe, but maritime affairs traditionally had less importance for the French than for the English or the Dutch. It was not until the reign of the "Sun King" Louis XIV that a thoroughgoing effort was initiated to turn France into an oceanic power. From the 1660s the Sun King's principal minister, Jean-Baptiste Colbert, embarked on a programme of naval expansion that went hand in hand with the development of overseas colonies and maritime commerce. France had a sufficient population of seamen, greater resources than any other contemporary European state, and a powerful centralized administration. What it turned out to lack was the political will to sustain world-beating naval forces. After promising beginnings, the Sun King's navy in effect conceded command of the seas to the British.

GUN, SAIL, AND EMPIRE

Battle of La Hogue
The disastrous series of actions in 1692 resulted in the burning of 12 French ships of the line. It put an end to Louis XIV's plan to give naval support to an invasion of England by the deposed Catholic monarch James II.

COLBERT'S ACHIEVEMENT

Cardinal Richelieu, principal minister of King Louis XIII, had made an initial move to build up French naval forces in the 1620s, but both ships and shore facilities had subsequently fallen into disrepair. Colbert thus had to start almost from scratch. His aim was to create a formidable force of warships with highly efficient crews and officers, supported by an effective infrastructure. To build the ships he at first brought in expertise from abroad, chiefly employing Dutch master shipwrights, but also the Englishman Anthony Deane and the Neapolitan Biagio Pangallo. Through this transfer of technology the French soon became fine shipbuilders in their own right. They favoured large three-deck ships of the line, decorated with magnificent figureheads and carvings by noted artists such as sculptor Pierre Puget. France's great military engineer Vauban was entrusted with the building and fortification of naval bases. Toulon was developed as the main Mediterranean port and Brest as the principal Atlantic naval base. These were backed up by less satisfactory facilities at Rochefort and Le Havre, and by Dunkirk, sold to France by the English in 1662. Colbert also promoted improvements in navigation and hydrography. Appearing after Colbert's death in the 1690s, the *Neptune Français* charts produced by French maritime surveyors were the best in Europe.

MEN AND OFFICERS

In 1668 Colbert instituted a rational system for the conscription of sailors into the navy. All seamen in France had to register – the "Inscription Maritime" – and men from the register were called up by rotation in "classes". Each class performed naval service for a fixed number of years. To make this compulsory service more palatable there were social benefits. The children of seamen on naval duty were educated free and there was also provision for sick pay. The sailors' wages were sent to their homes rather than paid on ship, preventing the men from spending it all on drink and loose women. Some officers were transferred from the army to the navy; others were recalled from

Shipbuilding in the reign of Louis XIV
Colbert aimed to create a merchant marine to rival that of the Dutch, so that French trade would always be carried in French ships. A strong navy was essential to protect merchant shipping from Dutch, English, and other raiders.

service with the galley fleet of the Knights of St John in Malta, where many French gentlemen had gained naval experience. A path for the sons of the well-born to enter naval service was opened by the creation of the Garde de Marine, training them to become commissioned officers. The structure of French society required senior commanders to be noble, but merit was usually rewarded. Abraham Duquesne had been born into a Dieppe merchant family, but was ennobled so that he could hold a high command. French officers' seamanship was not always faultless – Admiral Jean d'Estrées lost an entire fleet through bad navigation, running onto rocks in the West Indies in 1678 – but they usually showed a high level of courage and fighting spirit.

TEST OF BATTLE

The Sun King's fleet was blooded as an ally of the English in the Third Anglo-Dutch War of 1672-74. It fought the Dutch and Spanish in the Mediterranean, and then took on the English and Dutch together in the War of the League of Augsburg from 1689. The English and Dutch were ill-prepared for this conflict and at first the French scored notable successes. An army was landed in Ireland and victory at Beachy Head in 1690 gave France temporary command of the sea. Yet a major war soon put the structure that Colbert had created under severe strain. Orderly conscription failed to deliver sufficient sailors and soon press-gangs were in action, although ships still remained undermanned.

Abraham Duquesne
One of Louis XIV's most able naval commanders, Duquesne won significant victories over the Spanish and Dutch in the Mediterranean. His Protestant faith prevented him from reaching the rank of full admiral.

As France was both a Mediterranean and an Atlantic power, concentrating all its naval forces to fight for control of the English Channel proved impossible. A major defeat at the twin battles of Barfleur and La Hogue in 1692 convinced Louis that major fleet engagements were a costly and fruitless indulgence.

COMMERCE RAIDING

Renouncing the struggle for command of the sea, the king ordered his sailors to focus on commerce raiding. This they did very successfully, with bold captains such as René Duguay-Trouin from St Malo and Jean Bart from Dunkirk sailing at the head of small hunting packs. By the time the war ended in 1697 some 4,000 English and Dutch ships had been captured, including the immensely valuable Smyrna convoy ambushed by the French Mediterranean fleet in 1693. When fighting resumed in 1702, in the War of the Spanish Succession, French commerce raiding was again effective, but there was no disguising the overall decline of the French navy. Increasingly short of money, Louis was reduced to fitting out fleets of privateers by sharing the cost and the profits with wealthy businessmen. In truth, as a continental land power, France logically had to give priority to its army in the allocation of resources. Colbert's vision of France as the hub of a maritime trading empire was never more than partially realized.

1619–1683

JEAN-BAPTISTE COLBERT

FRENCH MINISTER OF FINANCE AND THE NAVY

Born in Reims, eastern France, Colbert learned his trade as an administrator in the service of Cardinal Mazarin, the effective ruler of France during the minority of Louis XIV. Soon after Louis took power into his own hands in 1661, Colbert was appointed Intendant of Finance, in control of taxation, trade, and manufactures. Two years later he was also styled Intendant of the Navy. Colbert saw that a strong navy was essential to protect maritime trade and to enable France to expand its empire. His financial reforms vastly increased tax revenues, making funds available for the building of ships and naval facilities. In his later years Colbert was unpopular, blamed for the high taxation that financed Louis' wars. He never convinced the king of the overriding importance of naval power and overseas trade. Yet by 1683, when he died, the French navy was the largest in Europe, with 117 ships of the line, 1,200 officers, and over 50,000 men.

THE FRENCH WARS

THE AMBITIONS OF French King Louis XIV generated a series of wars in which to test his freshly expanded navy. After England made peace with France in 1674, Louis remained at war with the Dutch, who allied themselves with their former enemies the Spanish. A series of sharp sea battles were fought in the Mediterranean, which ended in a notable success for the French navy under Admiral Duquesne. However, the War of the League of Augsburg (1688–97) brought France into conflict with England, which was supported by the Dutch, now fielding a distinctly inferior naval force. An early victory at Beachy Head, under the excellent Admiral de Tourville, gave the French navy command of the sea, but this was soon reversed by a disastrous defeat at the twin battles of Barfleur and La Hogue. For the rest of the war, and through the subsequent War of the Spanish Succession (1701–14), the French made no further serious attempt to contest the dominance of the English fleet, although France's seamen demonstrated their skill and boldness in commerce-raiding and other small-scale actions.

GUN, SAIL, AND EMPIRE

FRANCO-DUTCH WAR

ALICUDI

Date 8 January 1676
Forces Dutch and Spanish: 19 ships of the line; French: 20 ships of the line
Losses Dutch and Spanish: 1 ship; French: none

Location
Aeolian islands, Sicily

In 1674 the people of Messina in Sicily rose up in revolt against Spanish rule and invited the French to come to their aid. King Louis XIV sent a squadron to Messina, installing a viceroy to rule the island. When the Spanish fleet attempted to intercept a troop convoy sent to Sicily in February 1675, it was roundly defeated off Stromboli. The Spanish called on the Dutch for help and Dutch Admiral Michiel de Ruyter was sent with a weak squadron of 18 ships to link up with the Spanish fleet. He found the Spanish to be in a hapless state of disorganization, however, and sailed for Sicily with only a single Spanish ship of the line to augment his squadron, plus a handful of galleys.

De Ruyter encountered a French force under Admiral Duquesne off the island of Alicudi. The French had a similar number of ships but far superior firepower and de Ruyter was reluctant to give battle, but once the wind shifted to Duquesne's advantage the French attacked. Approaching the Dutch line obliquely, the French van took a pounding and several ships were forced to withdraw. Nonetheless, once the two lines were closely engaged the French guns did their work. After six hours the fighting ceased. The Spanish galleys towed off the most badly damaged Dutch ships, one of which sank during the night. The French had suffered the heavier casualties, however, in a thoroughly inconclusive encounter.

> **THE DUTCH FLEET UNDER DE RUYTER CAN ENTER A MOONLESS NIGHT IN HEAVY WIND AND FOG AND EMERGE THE NEXT DAY IN PERFECT LINE AHEAD.**
>
> FRENCH ADMIRAL ABRAHAM DUQUESNE, REPORT TO KING LOUIS XIV, 1676

FRANCO-DUTCH WAR

AGOSTA

Date 22 April 1676
Forces Dutch and Spanish: 27 ships of the line; French: 29 ships of the line
Losses Dutch and Spanish: none; French: none

Location Off Agosta, eastern Sicily

After the battle of Alicudi, Michiel de Ruyter's Dutch squadron was belatedly joined by a further eight Spanish ships under Admiral Don Francisco de la Cerda. Admiral Duquesne entered Messina. The total French strength still exceeded that of the combined Spanish and Dutch fleet, but they allowed themselves to be blockaded in harbour by de Ruyter, so little confidence did they have in their ability to defeat the legendary Dutch admiral.

In April, despairing of the French ever coming out, the Spanish and Dutch sailed to threaten the French-controlled harbour of Agosta. Duquesne felt bound to respond and the two fleets met on 22 April. The haughty

Matchlock musket
Muskets were brought to bear when ships came within 200m (220yds) or so of each other. Matchlocks remained in use in Europe until about 1700.

Eendracht
The Dutch ship *Eendracht* was de Ruyter's flagship at Agosta when the admiral was mortally wounded by the French guns.

Admiral de la Cerda insisted on being recognized as overall commander of the combined fleet and thus holding the position of honour in the centre of the line. He also insisted that his Spanish squadron remain together under his command. Thus the Dutch vessels were split, de Ruyter leading half of their ships in the van and the rest of the Dutch ships making up the rear division.

De Ruyter closely engaged the French van, but the Spanish held off, limiting themselves to some token long-range exchanges with the French centre. The Dutch in the rear, under Admiral den Haen, mostly focused on the Spanish, although they did succeed in engaging the rearmost French ships. At first the Dutch van had the better of the fighting, but once Duquesne realized the Spanish were not going to fight he began moving ships forward from his centre. Isolated and outgunned, the Dutch van suffered grievously. De Ruyter was wounded in the leg, and his flagship was shattered.

Both sides were happy to break off the fight at the end of the day. De Ruyter died a week later of gangrene; a sad end for an admiral who deserved to fall in a more distinguished combat.

FRANCO-DUTCH WAR

PALERMO

Date 2 June 1676
Forces Dutch and Spanish: 27 ships of the line; French: 28 ships of the line
Losses Dutch and Spanish: 7 ships; French: none

Location
Palermo, Sicily

The combined Dutch and Spanish fleet was in poor shape after the battle of Agosta. Demoralized by the loss of Admiral de Ruyter, they anchored in a defensive line across Palermo harbour. The French, largely at the inspiration of the Comte de Tourville, conceived a bold plan of attack. The Marquis de Preuilly took nine ships to attack one end of the enemy line at close quarters. The rest of the French fleet maintained a barrage from longer range while sending fireships down on the harbour.

In panic the Dutch and Spanish ships cut their cables, drifting into shore. Three Dutch ships and four Spanish ships were destroyed by fire, including both flagships. Satisfied with this triumph, the French fleet subsequently withdrew from Sicily, allowing the island to return to Spanish rule.

Destruction of the Soleil Royal
The French ships *Soleil Royal*, *Triomphant*, and *Admirable* are set on fire by English fireships at Cherbourg. Only one crew member on board the French flagship *Soleil Royal* survived the raid.

WAR OF THE LEAGUE OF AUGSBURG

BARFLEUR AND LA HOGUE

Date	29 May–4 June 1692
Location	Off northern France
Result	Anglo-Dutch victory

COMBATANTS

ENGLAND AND DUTCH REPUBLIC	FRANCE

COMMANDERS

Edward Russell	Anne Hilarion de Tourville

FORCES

Ships: 82 ships of the line	**Ships:** 44 ships of the line

LOSSES

Ships: none	**Ships:** 15

BARFLEUR AND LA HOGUE

Encouraged by the French victory over the English and Dutch fleets at Beachy Head in 1690, French King Louis XIV planned an invasion of England in 1692 to reinstate the deposed King James II. Admiral de Tourville was to concentrate the French fleet at Brest, then sail on to Le Havre where French and Jacobite soldiers would embark in transports to be escorted across the Channel.

The project was from the outset plagued by delays. Originally planned for April, it had to be postponed because the transports were not ready in time.

Even with an extra month, the French Mediterranean fleet, held up by bad weather, never arrived to join Tourville, who also had to sail without 20 of his own ships for lack of crews to man them. His fleet was thus woefully inadequate to confront the combined forces of the English and Dutch, who had been given ample time to gather in the Channel.

Tourville sighted the allied fleet off Cape Barfleur on the morning of 29 May. Although it was twice his strength, he opted to give battle, perhaps hoping that English captains of Jacobite sympathies would change sides. None did. Holding the weather gage, Tourville no doubt hoped to exploit skilful seamanship and gunnery to inflict damage on a superior force and disengage at will.

BROADSIDES AND FIRESHIPS

Tourville laid his centre, including his superb flagship *Soleil Royal*, alongside the allied centre and a brutal exchange of broadsides began. The French van avoided envelopment by the Dutch ships of the allied van by continually giving way until at right-angles to the centre. Tourville's attempt to control the battle was undermined by the caprice of the wind, which first shifted to deny him the advantage, and then dropped altogether. In a flat calm, ships of the line manoeuvred under tow

from their boats, sailors straining at the oars, or were carried by the tide if they opted not to anchor. The French centre, unable to disengage, heroically fought a prolonged gunnery duel against the odds, while the allied rear strove to bring them under fire from both sides.

Fighting continued in an increasingly confused mêlée after nightfall. The English sailed fireships towards the enemy on the tide but the French coped with them efficiently. Sheer exhaustion brought the battle to an end around 10pm.

Heavy casualties were suffered by both sides, but no ship was sunk or taken. If the French had escaped the following day, they could have celebrated a fine performance against a superior force. But too long was spent trying to save the crippled *Soleil Royal* and it was evening before Tourville ordered a general flight. Twenty-two ships used local knowledge to navigate a dangerous channel past Alderney to safety. Several escaped further afield, including two ships that took the Armada route around the north of Scotland. But 15 ships did not escape. The *Soleil Royal* and two others were beached at Cherbourg, where the English destroyed them with fireships. The rest beached at La Hogue. Despite the presence of shore batteries, the English attacked with long boats and fireships, and burned them all. The invasion plans were abandoned.

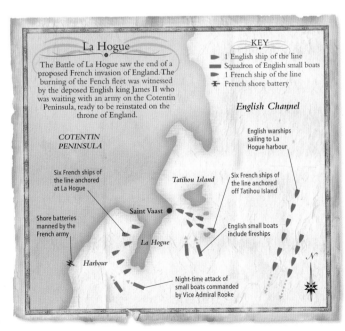

La Hogue

The Battle of La Hogue saw the end of a proposed French invasion of England. The burning of the French fleet was witnessed by the deposed English king James II who was waiting with an army on the Cotentin Peninsula, ready to be reinstated on the throne of England.

KEY

- ➡ 1 English ship of the line
- ■ Squadron of English small boats
- ➡ 1 French ship of the line
- ⚓ French shore battery

COTENTIN PENINSULA

Tatihou Island

Saint Vaast

La Hogue

Harbour

English Channel

Six French ships of the line anchored at La Hogue

Shore batteries manned by the French army

English warships sailing to La Hogue harbour

Six French ships of the line anchored off Tatihou Island

English small boats include fireships

Night-time attack of small boats commanded by Vice Admiral Rooke

Fireships at La Hogue
This Dutch delftware plaque depicts French sailors at La Hogue escaping from their burning ships, all 12 of which were destroyed.

THE BATTLE OF BEACHY HEAD

The War of the League of Augsburg, sparked by the Protestant William of Orange's accession to the English throne in 1688, set the navy of Louis XIV's Catholic France against the formidable maritime power of the English and the Dutch. On 21 June 1690 the French Mediterranean fleet commanded by the Marquis de Châteaurenault sailed into Brest to join the Atlantic fleet commanded by

the Comte de Tourville. This combined fleet had a local numerical advantage over its enemies, for the English had dangerously dispersed their forces, with detachments in the Mediterranean and the Irish Sea, as well as numerous ships on convoy escort duties.

Tourville entered the English Channel with 70 magnificent ships of the line, intending to attack the depleted English in their anchorage at Spithead. But English admiral Arthur Herbert, the 1st Earl of Torrington, did not wait to be attacked, advancing cautiously westward along the south coast of England, where he was joined by a squadron of 22 Dutch ships under Cornelis Evertsen. Encountering the French off the white cliffs of Beachy Head, Torrington held the weather gage and at first used it to avoid battle with a superior force. But the English royal council rejected this negative posture and ordered Torrington to attack.

Battle was joined on the morning of 10 July. The two fleets formed up conventionally in line ahead. Since the French ships of the line outnumbered the English and the Dutch, their line was longer, a problem the allies failed to address. The Dutch squadron forming the allied van boldly sailed forward

to engage the enemy but failed to reach the front of the French line, the foremost Dutch ship exchanging broadsides with the eighth French ship. Châteaurenault, commanding the French van in the 110-gun *Dauphin Royal*, ordered the Marquis de Villette-Mursay to double back with the seven front ships down the lee side of the Dutch, who were caught between two lines of fire. When Tourville, commanding the centre division in his three-decker flagship *Soleil Royal*, succeeded in slipping some of his ships into a gap that had opened up between the hesitant Torrington's centre and the vanguard, the Dutch ships were surrounded.

The French rear squadron, vigorously attacked by the third English squadron under Sir Ralph Delaval, took some heavy punishment. Three French ships had to withdraw from the line, one with its poop blown off when cartridges exploded on deck. But their losses were as nothing to those suffered by the Dutch. Only one ship, *Friesland*,

Victory at Bévéziers
This French medal commemorating the Battle of Beachy Head (Bévéziers, in French) depicts Louis XIV as Neptune ruling the seas.

struck and was sunk, but all were shattered, their decks littered with the dead and wounded. In the afternoon the wind dropped and the ships drifted with the current. As the tide began to ebb, Torrington gave the signal to anchor. Caught unawares, the French drifted away from the allied ships, bringing the day's fighting to an end.

The aftermath brought controversy on both sides. Torrington fled for the Thames, abandoning any ships too badly damaged to follow (all but one of them Dutch). Tourville contented himself with finishing off these defenceless wrecks and then, after sacking the port of Teignmouth, returned to France to unload his wounded men and to refit his mauled ships. Torrington was imprisoned in the Tower of London. Although a court martial cleared him of treachery, he was dismissed from the service. Tourville was also criticized for failing to pursue the defeated English. His great victory failed to have any decisive consequence.

WAR OF THE LEAGUE OF AUGSBURG

BATTLE OF BEACHY HEAD

Date	10 July 1690
Location	Off Sussex, southern England
Result	French victory

∞ COMBATANTS ∞

FRANCE	ENGLAND DUTCH REPUBLIC

∞ COMMANDERS ∞

Comte de Tourville	Earl of Torrington

∞ FORCES ∞

Ships: 70 ships of the line	**Ships:** 56 ships of the line

∞ LOSSES ∞

Men: none **Ships:** none	**Men:** unknown **Ships:** 17 ships of the line

Dutch ship ablaze
A Dutch ship catches fire after sustained bombardment from the French. The close of the battle saw the complete destruction of the Dutch fleet that formed the van.

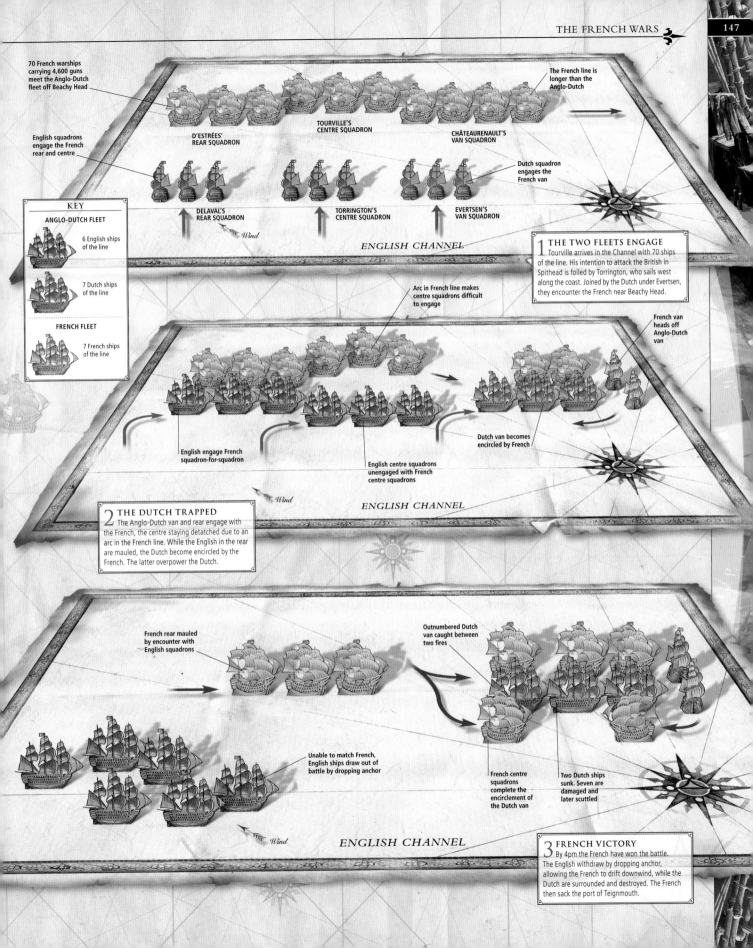

70 French warships carrying 4,600 guns meet the Anglo-Dutch fleet off Beachy Head

The French line is longer than the Anglo-Dutch

D'ESTRÉES' REAR SQUADRON

TOURVILLE'S CENTRE SQUADRON

CHÂTEAURENAULT'S VAN SQUADRON

English squadrons engage the French rear and centre

Dutch squadron engages the French van

DELAVAL'S REAR SQUADRON

TORRINGTON'S CENTRE SQUADRON

EVERTSEN'S VAN SQUADRON

Wind

ENGLISH CHANNEL

KEY

ANGLO-DUTCH FLEET

6 English ships of the line

7 Dutch ships of the line

FRENCH FLEET

7 French ships of the line

1 THE TWO FLEETS ENGAGE
Tourville arrives in the Channel with 70 ships of the line. His intention to attack the British in Spithead is foiled by Torrington, who sails west along the coast. Joined by the Dutch under Evertsen, they encounter the French near Beachy Head.

Arc in French line makes centre squadrons difficult to engage

French van heads off Anglo-Dutch van

English engage French squadron-for-squadron

Dutch van becomes encircled by French

English centre squadrons unengaged with French centre squadrons

Wind

ENGLISH CHANNEL

2 THE DUTCH TRAPPED
The Anglo-Dutch van and rear engage with the French, the centre staying detatched due to an arc in the French line. While the English in the rear are mauled, the Dutch become encircled by the French. The latter overpower the Dutch.

French rear mauled by encounter with English squadrons

Outnumbered Dutch van caught between two fires

Unable to match French, English ships draw out of battle by dropping anchor

French centre squadrons complete the encirclement of the Dutch van

Two Dutch ships sunk. Seven are damaged and later scuttled

Wind

ENGLISH CHANNEL

3 FRENCH VICTORY
By 4pm the French have won the battle. The English withdraw by dropping anchor, allowing the French to drift downwind, while the Dutch are surrounded and destroyed. The French then sack the port of Teignmouth.

ACTION OF 29 JUNE 1694

Date 29 June 1694
Forces French: 6 warships;
Dutch: 8 warships
Losses French: none;
Dutch: 3 warships captured

Location Off Texel,
North Sea

With the French facing starvation after a year of bad harvests, Jean Bart was dispatched to escort a large grain convoy that was crossing the North Sea. He met the convoy off Texel – in the possession of a Dutch flotilla that had captured it. Bart held the weather gage and, although outnumbered, attacked the Dutch ships fiercely. His flagship *Maure* was almost disabled by the guns of the Dutch flagship *Prins Friso*, but he nonetheless boarded and captured her. Two other Dutch ships were also taken and the rest fled. Bart brought the 120 ships of the convoy with their invaluable cargo safely to port in France.

1651–1702

JEAN BART

FRENCH PRIVATEER AND ADMIRAL

The son of a Dunkirk fisherman, Jean Bart proved from an early age to be an outstanding sailor and fighter. He was the leader of the Dunkirk privateers by 1676 and rose to the rank of admiral in the French navy despite his lack of noble birth. In 1689 he was captured by the English but escaped after three days and crossed from Plymouth to Brittany in a rowing boat. He was ennobled after saving France from starvation by the rescue of a grain convoy captured by the Dutch in June 1694. A supreme commerce raider, Bart repeatedly defied English efforts to blockade him in port and is credited with capturing over 300 ships in his career. His exploits made him a French national hero.

DOGGER BANK

Date 17 June 1696
Forces French: 7 warships;
Dutch: 5 warships
Losses French: none;
Dutch: 5 warships, 25 merchant ships

Location Dogger Bank,
North Sea

Blockaded inside Dunkirk by an English squadron under Admiral John Benbow, Jean Bart slipped out of harbour on a misty night in June 1696 and headed for the North Sea, fruitful ground for commerce raiding.

On 17 June the French happened upon a Dutch convoy of a large number of merchant vessels escorted by five frigates. Since Bart had under his command seven naval warships mounting from 36 to 54 guns, supported by two privateers, it was an unequal contest. Bart's flagship

Maure and the other naval ships engaged the Dutch escorts, while the privateers set about pursuing and overtaking the merchant ships. The fight began at 7pm and was hotly contested. The Dutch flagship *Raadhuis van Haarlem* duelled valiantly with *Maure*, which lost 15 of her crew, killed before forcing her opponent to surrender. The rest of the escorts also struck their colours and the entire convoy was captured.

However, Bart was being searched for by Benbow's blockade squadron and a group of Dutch warships, and their arrival on the scene forced the French to depart in haste. They set fire to most of the ships they had captured and fled, carrying some 1,200 prisoners with them. Dodging the English and Dutch ships pursuing them, they sailed along the Norwegian coast to Denmark. Bart eventually slipped back into Dunkirk in late September. The loss of the convoy was a serious blow to Dutch merchants and a demonstration of the limitations of Anglo-Dutch command of the sea.

VIGO BAY

Date 23 October 1702
Forces English and Dutch: 28 ships of the line; French and Spanish: 17 ships of the line
Losses English and Dutch: none; French and Spanish: all ships destroyed or captured

Location Vigo Bay,
northern Spain

An Anglo-Dutch fleet commanded by Admiral Sir George Rooke was sent to attack the Spanish port of Cadiz. At the same time French Vice Admiral Louis Rousselet de Chateau-Renault was

escorting a Spanish treasure fleet across the Atlantic from Cuba. Hearing of the presence of enemy ships at Cadiz, the treasure fleet prudently diverted to Vigo, where the unloading of its silver bullion got under way.

Rooke's raid on Cadiz was a failure, but on his way home he learned of the arrival of the treasure ships in Vigo and seized the opportunity to redeem himself. The harbour was well defended, its entrance blocked by a boom of masts chained together, covered by the fire of shore batteries and the guns of ships anchored inside. Rooke landed troops to attack the Spanish forts and ordered the British and Dutch vice

admirals Thomas Hopsonn and Philip van der Goes to sail in and break through the boom. The Allied ships came in for very heavy punishment. Hopsonn's *Torbay* was especially hard hit and he was obliged to shift his flag to *Monmouth*. But the boom was breached and the Allies broke into the harbour. Believing he had no chance in a fight, Chateau-Renault ordered his captains to fire their ships. The harbour was soon an amazing spectacle of

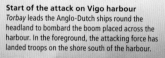

Commemorative medal
Hercules seizes a French soldier holding the Golden Fleece – a reference to Spanish treasure.

blazing and exploding vessels. The Allies succeeded in capturing some of the ships before fire took hold, including galleons that still had bullion and other valuables worth £14,000 on board. Apart from ships and treasure, the disaster cost the French and Spanish some 2,000 casualties. English and Dutch dead and wounded numbered around 800.

Start of the attack on Vigo harbour
Torbay leads the Anglo-Dutch ships round the headland to bombard the boom placed across the harbour. In the foreground, the attacking force has landed troops on the shore south of the harbour.

Heat of the action at Malaga
On the left, the French flagship, *Foudroyant*, commanded by the Comte de Toulouse, an illegitimate son of Louis XIV, is closely engaged with Admiral Rooke's flagship, *Royal Katherine*.

 WAR OF THE SPANISH SUCCESSION

MALAGA

Date 24 August 1704
Forces English and Dutch: 53 ships of the line; French: 50 ships of the line
Losses None

Location South of Malaga, Spain

In early August 1704 an Anglo-Dutch fleet under Admiral Sir George Rooke captured Gibraltar from the Spanish. A French fleet under the Comte de Toulouse sailed from Toulon to retake it. Rooke met the French south of Malaga. The action was an indecisive slaughter, two powerful forces in formal line of battle battering one another with broadsides. Occasionally a ship withdrew because of the scale of the damage and casualties suffered, but no vessel had been lost by either side when they disengaged at the day's end. The Anglo-Dutch fleet was overall in worse shape and desperately short of powder and shot. But the French did not renew the battle next morning, instead sailing back to Toulon. Both sides claimed victory, even though the English retained Gibraltar.

 WAR OF THE SPANISH SUCCESSION

LIZARD

Date 21 October 1707
Forces English: 5 ships of the line; French: 13 ships of the line
Losses English: 1 ship of the line sunk, 3 captured, 60 transport ships captured; French: none

Location Off Cornwall, southwest England

An English convoy of 80 transport ships sailed from Plymouth, bound for Portugal with men and supplies for the war then being fought in Spain. On the following day the convoy was seen and intercepted off the Lizard by two French squadrons, one of them led by the Saint-Malo privateer Captain René DuGuay-Trouin and the other by Admiral Claude de Forbin.

With only five ships of the line to his opponents' 13, the commander of the English convoy escort, Commodore Richard Edwards, stood little chance. The English ships nonetheless formed up in line of battle and mounted a spirited resistance, hoping this would allow at least some of the transports to escape. Edwards' flagship, the 80-gun *Cumberland*, was captured after being attacked by DuGuay's 74-gun *Lys* and two smaller ships. The other 80-gun English ship, *Devonshire*, defended herself against overwhelming odds until dusk, when the ship exploded, killing more than 800 men on board. *Royal Oak* was the sole English warship to escape, reaching Kinsale in southern Ireland with a handful of transports.

 WAR OF THE SPANISH SUCCESSION

CARTAGENA

Date 8–9 June 1708
Forces English: 3 ships of the line; Spanish: 4 galleons, 13 other vessels
Losses English: none; Spanish: 2 ships destroyed, 1 captured

Location Isla de Baru, Cartagena, Colombia

Admiral Charles Wager with three English ships of the line – *Expedition*, *Kingston*, and *Portland* – intercepted a Spanish treasure fleet bound for Cartagena from Porto Bello. The two largest and most heavily armed galleons, *San José* and *San Joaquín*, were carrying most of the silver and gold bullion. The fight began late in the afternoon. Wager's flagship *Expedition* engaged *San José* in a lengthy exchange of broadsides. Darkness had fallen when the Spanish galleon suddenly exploded, showering *Expedition* with burning splinters of wood. In moonlight *Expedition* then engaged a smaller galleon *Santa Cruz*. Both *Kingston* and *Portland* joined him, allowing *San Joaquín* to steal away. *Santa Cruz* surrendered during the night and Wager sent *Kingston* and *Portland* to pursue *San Joaquín*. They found the galleon the following morning but failed to stop her entering Cartagena harbour. Wager was furious at the failure to capture the bullion and the captains of *Kingston* and *Portland* were court-martialled. Still, his share of *Santa Cruz*'s valuable cargo made Wager a rich man.

Explosion of the galleon San José
The Spanish treasure ship, which still lies at the bottom of the Caribbean, is thought to have been carrying a fortune in silver, gold, and jewels.

BALTIC CONFLICTS

THE BALTIC WAS A STRATEGICALLY crucial region of Europe in the Age of Sail, for it was a source of vital nautical supplies – timber, tar, flax and hemp – as well as of other important trade goods. Yet the naval conflicts in the region fought in the 17th and 18th centuries were almost exclusively contests between the countries around the Baltic shores. The Dutch intervened in Baltic warfare to protect their naval supplies and trading interests in the 17th century, as the British later did during the Napoleonic Wars, but mostly the combatants were Sweden, the kingdom of Denmark-Norway and, in the 18th century, Russia. The battles they fought often took place in the shallow waters around the inlets and islands of the Baltic coast. Thus in Baltic navies large sailing ships were often less decisive in combat than shallow-draught oared galleys and flat-bottomed boats.

Battle of Fredrikshamn
On 15 May 1790, the Swedish fleet under the command of King Gustavus III engaged and destroyed a Russian fleet off Fredrikshamn (now Hamina, Finland) in the Gulf of Finland.

Running the gauntlet
After two disastrous attacks on the Russian fleet, the 400-strong Swedish fleet found itself blockaded in Vyborg Bay on 3 July 1790 by 150 Russian ships. Thanks to a lucky change in wind direction, they were able to escape, but lost 10 ships.

POWERFUL SWEDES

Sweden established its independence from Denmark and Norway in the 1520s. A navy was founded under King Gustav Vasa (ruled 1523–60), but when his famous grandson Gustavus Adolphus came to the throne in 1611 it consisted only of small and ageing vessels.

To serve both his military ambitions and sense of personal prestige, in the 1620s the king had a new fleet built at the Royal Dockyard in Stockholm, under the direction of Dutch master shipwright Henriks Hybertszoon. This included some of the largest warships in the world, but was far from a total success. The mighty *Vasa*, intended to be the pride of the new navy, sank ignominiously in Stockholm Harbour on her maiden voyage in August 1628. This was not untypical of the general performance of the Swedish navy.

The Danes benefited from the income generated by the tolls on the straits they controlled at the mouth of the Baltic. They were also aided by the formidable

Dutch and generally had the better of naval combat in the Baltic during the 17th century.

RUSSIAN ASCENDANCY

The rise of Russia under Tsar Peter the Great fundamentally altered the power balance in the Baltic. The Great Northern War in the first two decades of the 18th century brought victories not only for Russian armies but also for the newly created Russian navy at the battles of Ezel and Grengam. Peter's absolute power in Russia enabled him to build fleets

Backstaff
The backstaff, or English quadrant, was one of the main instruments of navigation until the development of the octant in the 1730s.

and naval facilities in the Baltic and Black seas. The lack of a Russian seafaring tradition was more difficult to overcome. For many decades the officers of the Russian navy were recruited abroad. Like the Swedes, the Russians maintained two separate forces in the Baltic, a conventional sailing ship fleet for open waters and a fleet of galleys and prams – flat-bottomed ships carrying a heavy gun – to serve in coastal waters.

SWEDEN'S LAST THROW

Russia replaced Sweden as the major power in the Baltic after the Great Northern War, but through the 18th century Sweden put substantial effort into upgrading its navy, especially the coastal fleet. The traditional galley and prams were augmented by various types of gun sloop and coastal frigate – udemas, turumas, and hemmemas – the largest capable of mounting up to 48 guns. Sailing ships that were designed to be rowed when necessary, these innovative British-designed vessels performed well when Sweden went to war with Russia again in 1788–90. There were large-scale battles, ending with the mighty but indecisive encounter known as Second Svensksund. It was Sweden's most impressive naval performance, but the size and population of Russia inevitably meant it would dominate the Baltic in the future.

1672–1725
PETER THE GREAT
LIEUTENANT-ADMIRAL OF THE UNITED PROVINCES

Tsar Peter the Great was the ruler who turned Russia into a major military power. An absolute monarch and ruthless modernizer, he looked to western Europe for examples to follow and for expertise to import. Peter created the Russian navy out of nothing. Fascinated by boats from an early age, he travelled to the Netherlands and England in the 1690s to study shipbuilding and navigation. He worked at the East India Company shipyard in Amsterdam and at the Royal Dockyard in London to gain first-hand experience of maritime technology. He took back with him shipwrights, experienced seamen, and designs for ships. Peter's conquests on land gave Russia access to the Black Sea and the Baltic, where he founded the city of St Petersburg in 1703 with the naval base of Kronstadt alongside. By the time of his death in 1725 the Russian navy had 48 ships of the line and some 800 galleys.

Peter the Great
Emperor Peter I was physically imposing, loud, violent, and a keen learner. He transformed Russia into a modern European state.

SWEDEN FIGHTS FOR DOMINATION

DURING THE 17th century Sweden established itself as a major power in Europe, especially through its wars with Poland and its prominent participation in the Thirty Years War (1618-48) in Germany. Swedish monarchs wanted a navy to match their great power status, but despite spending heavily on warship construction they found success at sea elusive, repeatedly depending upon the triumphs of their land forces to compensate for maritime failings. Denmark and Norway, united under the Danish crown since 1537, struggled to resist Swedish domination of the Baltic on land and at sea. The Dutch United Provinces at times gave support to Denmark because the Baltic was a prime source of trade and naval supplies to which they needed secure access. Their principle was to support whichever of the Scandinavian states was weakest, to prevent a naval power emerging that might control the Baltic at their expense. Despite the severe setbacks of the Scanian War (1675-78), which brought humiliating defeats for the Swedish navy at Öland and Kjöge Bay, Sweden remained the dominant power in the Baltic until the early 18th century.

GUN, SAIL, AND EMPIRE

THE BATTLE OF THE SOUND

DUTCH-SWEDISH WAR

BATTLE OF THE SOUND

Date	29 October 1658
Location	The Oresund, off Copenhagen
Result	Dutch victory

⚓ COMBATANTS ⚓

DUTCH UNITED PROVINCES, DENMARK	**SWEDEN**

⚓ COMMANDERS ⚓

Jacob van Wassenaer	Karl Gustav Wrangel

⚓ FORCES ⚓

Ships: Dutch 35, Danes 7	**Ships:** 45

⚓ LOSSES ⚓

Men: 450 **Ships:** 2	**Men:** c.1,000 killed or wounded **Ships:** 5

For the Dutch United Provinces access to the Baltic for naval supplies and trade was commercially and militarily crucial. Sweden wished to exclude the Dutch from the Baltic by forcing the Danes to block their passage through the Oresund, the narrow sound between Denmark and Sweden. In 1658 Sweden's king Karl X Gustav put the Danish capital Copenhagen under siege by land and naval blockade. The Dutch sent a fleet to prevent the Swedes from defeating the Danes.

On the morning of 29 October a north wind allowed the Dutch commander Lieutenant Admiral Jacob van Wassenaer to sail into the Oresund and confront the Swedish blockade squadrons. There were seven Danish warships in Copenhagen, but they were unable to join the fighting at all because the wind that filled the Dutch sails kept them pinned in port. This left the Dutch substantially outgunned, with around 1,300 cannon to the Swedes' 1,600, although they could claim the advantage of being upwind.

A DISORDERED CONFLICT

Strong currents prevented ships maintaining much order on either side and a savage piecemeal battle ensued. Wassenaer's flagship *Eendracht* was surrounded by Swedish ships and took some heavy punishment, but was rescued by Dutch captains coming to their admiral's aid. Four Swedish ships were boarded and taken in the close-quarters fighting, while one ran ashore.

In the course of battle the Dutch lost one of their most famous – and controversial – admirals, the choleric and notoriously insubordinate Witte Cornelizoon de With. His flagship *Brederode* ran aground and, lying defenceless, was battered for two hours by enemy fire before being boarded. De With was injured by musket fire and died of his wounds – his embalmed body was exhibited by the Swedes as a battle trophy, before being returned to the Dutch for burial.

At around 2pm the Dutch broke contact to sail into Copenhagen. The Swedes withdrew to the southern Swedish port of Landskrona to refit. Both fleets claimed a victory. But the Dutch had achieved their strategic objective, for the blockade and the siege of Copenhagen was lifted, and instead a Dutch and Danish squadron blockaded the Swedes in Landskrona.

Dutch double-barrelled flintlock
Double-barrelled flintlocks, like this, would have been used for sniping from the rigging, once the enemy ships came in range.

Close of battle
In this contemporary drawing by an eyewitness, a 60-gun Swedish ship (fourth from left) fires back at the Dutch 76-gun *Eendracht* as she passes by.

POLISH-SWEDISH WAR

OLIWA

Date 28 November 1627
Forces Swedish: 6 ships;
Polish: 10 ships
Losses Swedish: 1 ship
captured, 1 destroyed; Polish:
none

Location Off Danzig
(Gdansk), Poland

In 1627 Sweden was at war with the Polish-Lithuanian Commonwealth. In May the Swedish navy sent 15 ships to blockade the Polish port of Gdansk. Outbreaks of disease and wear and tear to the ships took its toll on the blockading squadron. By November only six ships were left on station. Poland had no naval tradition, but it had assembled a scratch naval force under the command of a Dutch merchant captain resident in Gdansk, Arend Dickmann. On 28 November Dickmann attacked the Swedish squadron with four galleons and six smaller vessels. His flagship *Sankt Georg* tackled the Swedish flagship *Tigern*. Swedish commander Nils Stjernskjold was killed; *Tigern* was captured. Another Swedish galleon, *Sol*, was blown up by her captain to avoid capture. The rest of the Swedish squadron fled. Dickmann, however, was killed, his legs shot away by a cannonball on Tigern's deck. It was the Polish navy's most famous victory.

THIRTY YEARS WAR

COLBERGER HEIDE

Date 1 July 1644
Forces Swedish: 34 ships;
Danish: 40 ships
Losses None

Location Near Femern
Island, off Germany

In 1644 Sweden and Denmark were on opposite sides in the Thirty Years War. A Swedish fleet under Finnish admiral Klas Fleming landed troops on the Danish island of Femern. Danish king Christian IV responded by leading a fleet out from Copenhagen. The Danes had more ships but were significantly outgunned by the Swedes. Fleming had the best of the initial manoeuvres. His flagship *Scepter* led an attack by several ships upon Danish admiral Jorgen Wind's *Patientia* heading the Danish van. King Christian's *Trefoldighed* came to Wind's aid but was also battered. The king suffered a head wound, which would cost him the sight of one eye, but stayed on deck. Wind was mortally injured and *Patientia* withdrew. Overall, however, the Danes had the better of the action, which ended with sunset. The badly mauled Swedish fleet was blockaded in Kiel Fjord for a month, during which time Fleming was killed.

Under fire
A Swedish man of war in the foreground exchanges fire with ships bearing the red Danish ensign. In the background more ships, possibly enemy reinforcements, approach to join the engagement.

SCANIAN WAR

ÖLAND

Date 1 June 1676
Forces Swedish: 26 ships
of the line, 12 frigates; Dutch
and Danish: 25 ships of the line,
10 frigates
Losses Swedish: 3 ships
of the line, 4 other vessels;
Dutch and Danish: none

Location Off Öland
Island, the Baltic

The decision of Swedish king Charles XI to ally himself with French king Louis XIV in his struggle against the Dutch United Provinces eventually led to the Scanian War, in which the Dutch combined forces with Denmark against Sweden. Off Bornholm Island in late May 1676 a Danish and Dutch squadron commanded by Danish admiral Niels Juel had the better of an encounter with a numerically superior Swedish force, which withdrew toward Stockholm. The allies were then reinforced by the arrival of nine ships under Dutch admiral Cornelis Tromp. Tromp immediately gave pursuit and caught up with the Swedes off the island of Öland. The Swedish commander, Admiral Lorens Creutz, was on board *Kronan*, one of the largest and most heavily armed warships of its day. The lower gun ports were opened on the flagship's leeward side as the Danish-Dutch fleet approached holding the weather gage. In a moment of confusion, Creutz ordered a sharp change of tack without reefing the sails. The open gun ports went under water as the ship heeled over. With sea pouring into the ship there was an explosion in the gunpowder store. *Kronan* sank rapidly, taking 801 of the 842 men on board to their deaths. Despite this catastrophe, some Swedish ships fought bravely. The 94-gun *Svärd* held out for two hours before striking its colours. After surrender she was hit by a Dutch fireship, causing a fire and explosion in which most of the 670 crew were killed. Scattered Swedish ships fleeing were pursued and a few captured. With this comprehensive defeat, Sweden decisively lost naval control of the Baltic.

SCANIAN WAR

KJÖGE BAY

Date 1–2 July 1677
Forces Swedish: 31 ships;
Danish: 25 ships
Losses Swedish: 8 ships;
Danish: none

Location Kjöge Bay,
south of Copenhagen

In spring 1677 the Swedish navy sought to attack the Danes in the absence of their Dutch allies, who were slow to send ships to the Baltic that year. Danish admiral Niels Juel was also keen to fight in the absence of the Dutch, since the arrival of Admiral Cornelis Tromp would mean that he was superseded in overall command.

Juel deliberately offered the Swedes a chance to attack him in Kjöge Bay. The Swedish fleet was led by Henrik Horn, a field marshal who had no experience at sea. Juel unsurprisingly outmanoeuvred him. On the morning of 1 July the Swedes attacked with the advantage of an offshore wind. The Danes skilfully fended off some Swedish fireships and then squeezed the Swedes against the coast. The 64-gun *Drake* ran aground at Stevns Point. Six Swedish ships remained behind to defend the exposed ship, while the rest broke for more open seas. *Drake* was forced to strike colours, lowering the ensign in surrender, while two of the ships left to protect her were also captured.

Juel pursued the remainder of the Swedish force and a fierce engagement ensued, during which the Danish admiral was forced to transfer his flag from the damaged *Christianus V*. The Dutch presented themselves for the second day of the battle and captured three Swedish ships, but the honour went to the Danish navy for their fine defeat of a numerically superior force.

Three victories
A medal commemorates Öland, Langeland, and Kjöge triumphs. The Swedish flagship is shown as she strikes her flag to the Danish.

THE GREAT NORTHERN WAR

FOUGHT BETWEEN 1700 and 1721, the Great Northern War was a contest between Sweden and a coalition of other countries determined to end Swedish domination of the Baltic region. Russia under Tsar Peter the Great and Denmark-Norway – at that time united under the Danish crown – were Sweden's major opponents at sea. The naval battles, which were contested by a mix of deep-sea sailing fleets and inshore galley fleets, mostly centred on the need for both sides to reinforce and resupply land forces fighting around the shores of the Baltic and North Sea. Through roughly the first decade of the war Sweden had the upper hand, but a series of defeats inflicted both by the Russians and by Denmark-Norway decisively turned the tide in the second half of the conflict. The overall outcome of the war was to establish Russia as a significant European naval and land power at the expense of Sweden.

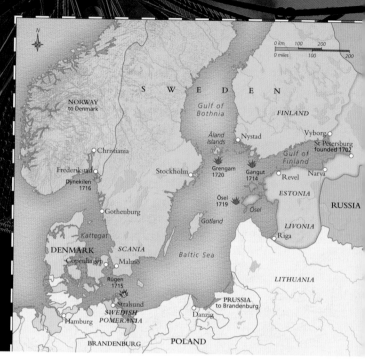

THE GREAT NORTHERN WAR 1700-1721

Sweden's chief rival was Peter the Great's Russia, which gained a toehold in the Baltic with the founding of the city of St Petersburg in 1702. By the end of the war a newly confident Russia was well established in the region with significant territorial gains around the Baltic coast. Sweden also lost all its possessions in Germany, mainly to another emergent power, Brandenburg-Prussia.

KEY

- Sweden
- Russia
- Denmark
- Borders 1700
- Russian gains from Sweden by 1721
- ⚔ Russian victory over Sweden
- ⚔ Danish victory over Sweden
- ⚔ Inconclusive action

THE GREAT NORTHERN WAR

GANGUT

Date 7 August 1714
Forces Russians: c.100 galleys; Swedish: 1 pram, 6 galleys, 3 smaller boats
Losses Russians: 1 galley captured; Swedish: all ships lost

Location Hanko Peninsula, Finland

In summer 1714 Russian tsar Peter the Great's army was campaigning in Finland. The Russians wanted to open a line of supply and reinforcement to their land forces by sea, but the presence of the Swedish fleet off southern Finland blocked the passage of Russian vessels out of the Gulf of Finland.

In July Admiral Fyodor Apraksin led a strong force of galleys packed with soldiers as far as the Hanko Peninsula – known as Gangut to the Russians – where Swedish Vice Admiral Gustav Wattrang was waiting with 15 ships of the line supported by galleys and other smaller vessels. The Russians also had a sailing fleet commanded by the Tsar himself, but Peter shifted to a galley, intending to mastermind the outflanking of the Swedish ships. The Russians planned to drag their galleys overland across the peninsula and refloat them behind the Swedish line, thus slipping through to join the army to the northwest. Gaining intelligence of this plan, Wattrang sent Rear Admiral Nils Ehrenskjold with the pram *Elefant* – a shallow-draught ship with heavy guns – and a few galleys and skerries (rowing boats) to attack the Russian galleys as they reached the northern shore of the peninsula.

MAIDEN VICTORY

Unfortunately for Ehrenskjold, the Russians changed their plan. Taking advantage of a dead calm, Apraksin rowed his galleys past the flanks of the line of Swedish sailing ships, which were unable to move or bring guns to bear. Only one Russian galley ran aground and was captured. The swarm of galleys then fell upon Ehrenskjold's isolated squadron. The Swedish admiral arranged his ships across a narrow channel with *Elefant* in the centre, broadside on to the enemy, and his galleys on the flanks. In the limited space the Russians could not bring all their galleys into the battle at once and *Elefant*'s guns drove off two attacks. On the third occasion, however, the Russians focused on the flanks, boarding the Swedish galleys with so many men that one was swamped and sank. Isolated and surrounded, *Elefant* was on fire with her admiral wounded. She surrendered as Russians swarmed aboard from all sides.

The Swedish lost 361 men killed on the spot, and about 400 more died of their wounds in Russian captivity. Russian dead and wounded numbered 466. Gangut was the first victory of the Russian Navy and allowed the tsar's fleet to operate freely in support of the land forces in Finland.

Closing in for the kill
Among the islands and narrow straits of the Baltic coast, oared galleys could often get the better of large sailing ships. At Gangut the Russian galleys scored a notable victory, even though it was against a much smaller and isolated Swedish force.

DYNEKILEN

Date 8 July 1716
Forces Danish-Norwegians:
2 prams, 2 frigates, 3 galleys;
Swedish: 1 pram, 4 galleys, 10
other armed boats
Losses Danish-Norwegians:
none; Swedish: 1 pram, 3 galleys,
5 other armed boats,
19 transports captured

Location Dynekilen
Fjord, western Sweden

King Charles XII of Sweden invaded
Norway in 1716, besieging the citadel
of Frederikstad. A squadron of Danish-
Norwegian ships of the line in the
Kattegat was unable to prevent the
Swedish ferrying men and supplies from
Gothenburg to their army, as transports
and their escorts hugged the coast where
the water was too shallow for the big
sailing ships. Peter Tordenskjöld was

sent from Copenhagen with a flotilla
of Norwegian-crewed, shallow-draught
vessels to break the Swedish supply line.
On his way Tordenskjöld learned that
a Swedish convoy was sheltering in
Dynekilen fjord. He entered the narrow
fjord on the morning of 8 July and
found the Swedish sheltering under
the protection of the 12-pounder guns
of an island fort. Tordenskjöld's flotilla
anchored and opened fire at around
7.30am. After a lengthy exchange the
fort was captured in the early afternoon.
The Swedish pram *Stenbock* surrendered
and the crews of her accompanying
galleys fled. As Tordenskjöld secured his
prizes he came under heavy fire from
Swedish land forces. He made his escape
late in the evening and anchored next
day off Frederikstad. Sweden soon
abandoned the siege and the invasion.

1691–1720
PETER TORDENSKJÖLD
DANISH NAVAL COMMANDER

Born Peter Wessel in Trondheim, Norway,
Tordenskjold ran away to sea as a boy and
was a merchant seaman and privateer
before becoming an officer in the Danish
navy in 1711. He attracted the favour
of Danish king Frederick IV through
the boldness of his attacks on Swedish
shipping, although his unorthodox
style alienated his conservative naval
superiors. He was ennobled with the title
Tordenskjöld ("thundershield") shortly
before his great victory at Dynekilen in
1716. His capture of the Swedish fortress
at Marstrand in 1718 was another notable
feat. He was killed in a duel with a Livonian
colonel he had accused of cheating at cards.

GRENGAM

Date 7 August 1720
Forces Swedish: 2 ships of the
line, 6 frigates, 10 other vessels;
Russians: 61 galleys, 25 other
vessels
Losses Swedish: 4 frigates
captured; Russians: 43 galleys

Location Åland
Islands, Baltic Sea

The newly built Russian deep-sea
sailing fleet recorded its first victory
at Ezel on 24 May 1719, when it
captured three Swedish warships. The
galley fleet, however, continued to play
a leading role in Russia's Baltic war.

In summer 1720 General Mikhail
Golitsyn was commanding a large
force of galleys in operations around
the Åland Islands. Admiral Karl
Wachtmeister, the Swedish commander-
in-chief, sent a squadron under Erik
Sjoblad to the islands with orders to
cover the withdrawal of Swedish ships
from the area. However, Sjobald chose
instead to attack Golitsyn's galleys near
Grengam Island. Confronted by Swedish
ships of the line and frigates, the galleys
hastily withdrew toward the shallow
waters of Flisesund. There they formed
up in line abreast and turned to face
their pursuers. The Swedish cannon
inflicted heavy damage on the Russian

galley fleet but, manoeuvring in the
treacherous sound, two of the Swedish
frigates soon ran aground. Russian
galleys swarmed around the grounded
ships and boarded them. Two other
Swedish frigates were also chased and
captured as the Russians took the
offensive. Sjoblad's flagship,
the 52-gun *Pommern*, had
a narrow escape, saved
only by the outstanding
seamanship of its crew.

More than two-
thirds of the Russian
galleys were so badly
damaged they had to
be scuttled, leading

Sweden to claim victory in the battle.
However, there was no question that
the Swedish had been put to flight,
leaving Golitsyn in possession of the
four frigates as prizes. The balance
of casualties was also in Russia's favour,
with the Swedish losing 103 men
killed and 407 captured,
compared with Russia's
82 killed and 236
wounded.

Triumphal medallion
The capture of the Swedish
frigates is commemorated on
this copper medallion from the
workshops of Peter the Great.

1550 – 1830

Moment of victory
The battle of Grengam ended with the
Swedish sailing ships overwhelmed
by the sheer numbers of Russian galleys.

THE RUSSO-SWEDISH WAR

KING GUSTAV III OF SWEDEN was an unpopular ruler who hoped to drum up support for his rule by success in war. Seeking to profit from the involvement of Russia's empress Catherine II in a conflict with Ottoman Turkey in the Black Sea, he peremptorily demanded that Russia hand over Finland. When the Russians refused, in June 1788 he faked a Russian attack on Sweden and declared a war of self-defence. As usual in the Baltic the conflict that ensued was fought both by coastal fleets, including galleys, and by deep-sea sailing ships. Foreign naval officers,

especially British, played a prominent role in the conflict. Gustav hoped to seize St Petersburg, the Russian capital, in a swift campaign, but a setback for his ships of the line at Hogland dashed hopes of a quick victory. Despite a success at Svensksund in 1798, Sweden mostly had the worse of the war and narrowly escaped total disaster at Vyborg Bay in July 1790. Yet a stunning victory at Second Svensksund unexpectedly restored Swedish fortunes, allowing them to negotiate a peace without gains on either side. King Gustav was assassinated two years later.

THE RUSSO-SWEDISH WAR

HOGLAND

Date 17 July 1788
Forces Russians: 17 ships of the line; Swedish: 15 ships of the line
Losses Russians: 1 ship captured; Swedish: 1 ship captured

Location Off Hogland Island, Gulf of Finland

Early in the war a Swedish sailing fleet commanded by King Gustav III's brother, Prince Karl, entered the Gulf of Finland. The Russians hastily sent out their own ships of the line from Kronstadt, commanded by Scottish-born admiral Samuel Greig. The two

fleets met off Hogland Island on a day of light winds that made manoeuvre painfully slow. The Russians were somewhat superior in firepower. Fighting in traditional line of battle, the two sides inflicted considerable losses on one another to little decisive effect. The 70-gun *Prince Gustav*, flagship of Swedish vice admiral Gustav Wachtmeister, was so battered that it surrendered to Greig's 100-gun *Rostislav*. The Russian 74-gun *Vladislav* was surrounded by Swedish ships and taken. After six hours night fell and the battle ended. Russian casualties were heavier – 1,800 against the Swedes' 1,200 – but the Swedish force withdrew, allowing Russia to claim a strategic victory.

THE RUSSO-SWEDISH WAR

FIRST BATTLE OF SVENSKSUND

Date 24 August 1789
Forces Russians: 86 ships; Swedish: 49 ships
Losses Russians: 2 ships; Swedish: 8 ships

Location Svensksund, Gulf of Finland

Admiral Carl August Ehrensvärd, commanding a Swedish squadron of small sailing ships, gunboats, and galleys, was trapped in Svensksund harbour by two squadrons of Russian coastal vessels. Prince Charles of Nassau-Siegen, in

overall command of the Russian forces, attacked from the north with 66 vessels, while a much smaller squadron attacked from the south. Ehrensvärd blocked the northern entrances to the harbour with sunken ships and, posting a few gunboats to cover them, concentrated his forces against the Russian southern squadron. The Russians failed to coordinate their movements, the northern squadron starting far too late, so Ehrensvärd was able to rout the southern squadron before turning to engage Nassau-Siegen. But the Swedes ran low on ammunition and had to retreat under hot pursuit, losing a number of ships in the process. The way was open for the Russian fleet to support land operations in Finland.

THE BREAKOUT FROM VYBORG BAY

Swedish king Gustav III began the third year of his war with Russia boldly, with a bid to land troops on the Russian coast at Vyborg and to establish naval dominance of the Baltic. However, a Swedish attack on part of the Russian fleet in its anchorage at Reval in May

misfired, and, in a further action in early June, the Swedes failed to prevent the junction of the main Russian fleet from Kronstadt with the Reval squadron. As a result, the Swedish battle fleet under Grand-Admiral Prince Karl was bottled up in Vyborg Bay with the galley flotilla and troop transports commanded by King Gustav – around 400 ships and 30,000 men under naval siege.

Dangerously short of food and water, and fearing a Russian attack, the Swedish forces needed to break out of the bay. Both feasible channels through the shallow seas were blocked by Russian ships anchored broadside-on with mortar vessels in support. The Swedes decided to break out through the western channel by Krysserort after a feint toward Björkö in the east. It was not until early July that the wind shifted to the east and the attempt could be made.

On the morning of 3 July the ship of the line *Dristigheten*, commanded by Colonel Johan af Puke, led the Swedish

battle fleet toward the line of Russian blockade ships, accompanied by the flotilla of coastal galleys inshore to the west. Braving the Russian broadsides, Puke sailed through the blockade between the ships of the line *Selsav* and *St Peter*, raking them with his cannon as he passed. Overwhelmed by the number of ships bearing down upon them, the Russian blockade vessels were badly shot up as the Swedish ships of the line and oared gunboats came through.

The shallowness of the waters was the worst hazard, one ship of the line and four galleys soon running aground.

Around 10am the Swedes suffered a spectacular mishap. The rearmost ship of the line, *Enigheten*, was towing a fireship, *Postiljonen*. This was ignited at the wrong moment and collided with *Enigheten*'s stern. The two ships ablaze ran into a third, the frigate *Zamine*, and the whole tangled mass was destroyed in a massive explosion. As smoke blocked visibility, several more Swedish

THE RUSSO-SWEDISH WAR

BREAKOUT FROM VYBORG BAY

Date	3 July 1790
Location	Near St Petersburg, Russia
Result	Swedish victory

∞ COMBATANTS ∞

RUSSIA	SWEDEN

∞ COMMANDERS ∞

| Vasili Chichagov | King Gustav III
Prince Karl, Duke of Sodermanland |
|---|---|

∞ FORCES ∞

Ships: 50 sailing ships 80 galleys	Ships: 400, including 21 ships of the line

∞ LOSSES ∞

| Men: unknown
Ships: none | Men: unknown
Ships: 6 ships of the line, 3 frigates, 4 galleys |
|---|---|

Russian medal
This medal was awarded to the seamen and marines who fought for Russia at Vyborg Bay. Galleys and ships of the line are depicted engaging the Swedes.

SECOND BATTLE OF SVENSKSUND

Date 9–10 July 1790
Forces Swedish: 6 sailing ships, 18 galleys, 172 other vessels; Russians: 30 sailing ships, 23 galleys, 88 other vessels
Losses Swedish: 1 sailing ship, 4 smaller ships; Russians: 10 sailing ships, 16 galleys, 17 other vessels

Location Svensksund, Gulf of Finland

The Second battle of Svensksund was an immediate sequel to the battle of Vyborg Bay. The Russians under Prince Charles of Nassau-Siegen pursued the Swedish galley flotilla, commanded by King Gustav, to Svensksund. There the king's force was joined by a squadron under Colonel Carl Cronstedt and anchored in a strong defensive position. They spread out in a crescent formation blocking the entrance to Svensksund harbour, with their gunboats on the two wings and their sailing ships and galleys in the centre.

Nassau-Siegen prepared to attack on 9 July and went ahead with his plan on the

Swedish naval reward medal
Inscribed to King Gustav III, this medal depicts Victory standing on a two-masted galley with a wreath in each hand.

day, despite the fact that a fresh wind and choppy sea created conditions that were far from ideal for galley warfare. He arranged his ships in four squadrons, one on each flank and two in the centre. The battle was hard fought but soon turned in Sweden's favour. On both flanks the Russians were met with determined fire from the Swedish gunboats, supported by shore batteries, and were gradually pushed back. By the afternoon the Swedes, first on the left and then also on the right, had achieved a position from which to turn inward and rake the Russian galleys and sailing ships in the centre from both sides. The galleys were soon in desperate trouble, taking damage and being swamped by waves. As rowers left their benches to man the pumps,

Russian ships of the line
Prince Charles of Nassau-Siegen arrives with the Russian fleet to face the Swedish force anchored at Svensksund harbour.

some vessels drifted aground or sank. Around 7pm Nassau-Siegen ordered a withdrawal. Many of his sailing ships could not get away and were boarded – either taken as prizes or burned.

Night ended the day's combat but fighting resumed the following morning, this time with the Swedes on the attack and the battered Russians

striving to escape. Several more Russian ships were lost in the confused flight. Although exact figures for losses and casualties are hard to establish, the Swedes had unquestionably inflicted a major defeat on a numerically superior enemy. Unable to crush Sweden, Russia accepted the need to make peace the following month.

ships ran aground, King Gustav's British naval adviser Sidney Smith needing to be rescued from one of them.

Despite these losses, both the Swedish battle fleet and galley flotilla broke out into the Baltic; the former sailed for Sveaborg in Finland for repairs; the latter took shelter at Svensksund, where it anchored in a strong defensive position. Russian admiral Chichagov mounted a tentative and tardy pursuit of the battle fleet, succeeding in capturing *Retvisan*, one of Duke Karl's ships of the line. Within days the Swedish galleys were the target for a determined Russian attack in the Second Battle of Svensksund.

> ## CAPTAIN DENISON ... HAD HIS HEAD SHOT OFF BY A CANNONBALL ... CAPTAIN AIKEN HAD HIS THIGH-BONE SHATTERED SO AS TO RENDER AMPUTATION NECESSARY ...
>
> **WILLIAM TOOKE**, HISTORIAN, WRITING IN 1798 OF BRITISH OFFICERS IN RUSSIAN SERVICE AT VYBORG BAY

The gauntlet of Vyborg Bay
Swedish oared gunboats run the gauntlet of Russian ships blockading Vyborg Bay. The Swedish ship *Enigheten* explodes as she accidentally becomes entangled with a Swedish fireship.

Vyborg Bay

On 3 July 1790 two squadrons of the Swedish coastal fleet joined the main Swedish battle fleet and broke through the Russian blockade of Vyborg Bay.

Russian fleet guarding western channel

Lovisa Ulrica
Omheten

Charlotta

Enigheten

Finland

Johan af Puke leads the Swedish attack on the Russians in the shallow western channel

Squadron of Swedish coastal fleet

Swedish coastal fleet squadrons head for the main Swedish battle fleet

Surviving Swedish ships head for Sveaborg and Svensksund

Biskopso

Chichagov's ships in eastern channel, broadsides to the Swedes

Björkö sound

Swedish coastal fleet attacks Russian unit west of Björkö sound

Unit of Russian coastal fleet

Bay of Finland

KEY
- Swedish battle fleet
- Swedish coastal fleet
- Russian battle fleet
- Russian coastal fleet
- Burnt Swedish ships
- Grounded Swedish ships of the line
- Grounded Russian ships of the line
- Russian battery

MAINTAINING BRITISH NAVAL POWER

BY THE START of the 18th century, Britain had established itself as the world's dominant naval power. But maintaining this status was at times a close-run thing. France and Spain pushed Britain hard, especially when they fought together. The French in particular had the potential to challenge British naval supremacy, although they were usually distracted by land wars in Europe. The responsibilities the Royal Navy had to shoulder in war – defence of overseas colonies, protection of merchant shipping, prevention of an invasion of the British Isles – meant resources were thinly spread. The British rarely fought battles with any great numerical advantage, but in the last resort no one could match them for bold aggressive leadership allied to seamanship of a high order.

Capture of Porto Bello
A typical exploit of the Royal Navy that caught the imagination of the British public was the capture of Porto Bello on the Isthmus of Panama. Vice Admiral Vernon had claimed in the House of Commons that he could take the Spanish port with just six ships of the line. A few months later in November 1739 he duly made good his boast.

GUN, SAIL, AND EMPIRE

1719–1792
GEORGE RODNEY
BRITISH ADMIRAL

The son of a marine officer, George Rodney joined the navy aged 13 and saw action as a captain under Admiral Hawke at Cape Finisterre in 1747. Rodney distinguished himself during the Seven Years War, especially in the capture of Martinique in 1762. Despite being made Rear Admiral of Great Britain, in the subsequent peace he fell heavily into debt and fled to France to escape his creditors. He was able to return to fight in the American Revolutionary War only because a French aristocrat settled his debts. Although ageing and ill, he was appointed to command the West Indies squadron. Victories over the Spanish at Cape St Vincent in 1780 and the French at the Saints in 1782, both displaying aggressive, unorthodox tactics, crowned his career.

PRACTICAL KNOWLEDGE

The administration of the Royal Navy was efficient for the time but the system of recruitment was far from ideal. The use of press-gangs to forcibly transfer seamen from merchant ships in time of war was clumsy and haphazard compared with the French system of "classes" – the conscription of registered seamen. The training of British officers by taking young boys on board as midshipmen meant their formal education was minimal, whereas the French developed a body of well-educated officers with a scientific knowledge of navigation and gunnery. Yet the British officers' practical knowledge of the sea was incomparable.

Ship's steering wheel
A major innovation of the late 17th century was the wheel, which allowed the helmsman to stand on the quarterdeck and control the tiller via a system of ropes and pulleys.

Although promotion in the Royal Navy was governed by a mix of personal patronage and strict seniority, men of talent were able to rise to the top by merit – outstanding commanders such as Edward Hawke, Edward Boscawen, and George Rodney.

MAJOR WARS
Between the death of French king Louis XIV in 1715 and the outbreak of the French Revolution in 1789, Britain and France fought on opposite

Opening exchange of broadsides
The battle of Negapatam (1782) was one of five actions fought by the French and British East Indies squadrons during the American Revolutionary War. The British line, commanded by Sir Edward Hughes, is on the left.

sides in three major wars: the War of the Austrian Succession (1740–48), the Seven Years War (1756–63), and the American Revolutionary War (1775–83). After a shaky start, Britain's navy was clearly superior in the first of these. The Seven Years War was a hard-fought but overwhelming triumph of British naval power, allowing a major expansion of Britain's colonial empire. Nevertheless, the French navy achieved a remarkable recovery in the 1760s under the direction of Louis XV's chief minister the Duc de Choiseul, with a shipbuilding programme funded by the French public and inspired by patriotic enthusiasm. During the American Revolutionary War, facing a coalition of European powers supporting the rebellious American colonists, Britain suffered a crucial naval defeat at the hands of the French at

Chesapeake Bay in 1781, although Rodney's victory at the Saints the following year redeemed the Royal Navy's reputation.

TECHNOLOGY AND TACTICS
During the 18th century two-deck 74-gun or 80-gun warships became established as the key ships of the line alongside 100-gun three-deckers. The French introduced a new breed of sleek frigate that became crucial to naval warfare, both as scouts and raiders. Cannon became more reliable, with a range of different shot, and experiments were made with replacing

linstocks by flintlocks. The introduction of carronades by the Royal Navy in the 1770s – a lightweight upper deck gun potent at short range – increased the deadliness of close combat, as did improved muskets. The tactics employed in naval battles remained broadly unchanged, with broadsides forced by ships sailing in line, but some British commanders chafed at the formality of established rules and introduced the "general pursuit", allowing captains, when appropriate, to chase and engage the enemy in a free-for-all. Rodney's breaking of the French line at the Saints pointed forward to the Nelson era.

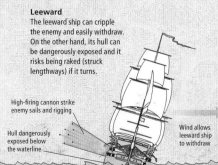

MAN-OF-WAR TACTICS
THE WEATHER GAGE
GUNNERY AND WIND DIRECTION

The British preferred to hold the weather gage in battle – that is, to fight from the windward side of the enemy. When they prevented the Spanish Armada from closing to board in 1588, they used the weather gage defensively, but it was above all an attacking position. While the French held a defensive line to leeward, the British would approach aggressively with the wind to engage them. During the approach they were exposed to French fire without being able to respond. On the other hand, the windward position meant smoke from cannon fire blew toward the enemy, giving the windward fleet better visibility. Lying to windward also favoured the British lethal tactic of firing into the enemy's hull.

Windward
The windward ship can fatally strike the enemy in the hull and blind the latter with gun smoke. Its disadvantage is its inability to withdraw.

Leeward
The leeward ship can cripple the enemy and easily withdraw. On the other hand, its hull can be dangerously exposed and it risks being raked (struck lengthways) if it turns.

Wind commits windward ship to battle

Low-firing cannon strike enemy hull

Lower gun ports potentially awash

High-firing cannon strike enemy sails and rigging

Hull dangerously exposed below the waterline

Wind allows leeward ship to withdraw

ROYAL NAVY BATTLES

AT THE END of the War of the Spanish Succession in 1713 Britain was indisputably Europe's dominant naval power. In a brief war with Spain from 1718 to 1720, it crushed the Spanish navy almost effortlessly. British merchants urged their government to use sea power aggressively to advance the nation's trade. The severing of the ear of Captain Robert Jenkins, master of the trading brig *Rebecca*, by Spanish coast guards in the Caribbean in 1731 provided ammunition for those arguing for action against Spain's empire in the Americas. The War of Jenkins' Ear,

launched by Britain on a tide of jingoistic enthusiasm in 1739, began well with the capture of Porto Bello, but soon ran into disaster in the failed expedition against Cartagena de Indias. This ignominious defeat severely dented British prestige. The war of the Austrian Succession (1740–48) brought Britain once more into conflict with its old enemy France, as well as with Spain. The French navy was in no condition to challenge British supremacy, and the British found themselves fighting, with varying degrees of competence, engagements in which they held a clear superiority.

WAR OF THE QUADRUPLE ALLIANCE

CAPE PASSARO

Date 11 August 1718
Forces British: 21 ships of the line; Spanish: 18 ships of the line
Losses British: none; Spanish: 11 ships of the line captured or burned

Location Cape Passaro, southeast Sicily

In 1718 Britain sent a fleet to the Mediterranean under Admiral Sir George Byng to oppose Spanish ambitions in Sicily. Although Britain and Spain were not officially at war, Byng pursued a Spanish squadron

under Vice Admiral Don Antonio Castaneta down the east coast of Sicily. At daybreak on 11 August battle was joined. Byng's 90-gun *Barfleur* and the other largest British ships overcame one Spanish division, including Castaneta's flagship *Real San Felipe*, while Captain George Walton led the chase of another, laconically reporting: "We have taken or destroyed all the Spanish ships which were upon this coast the number as per margin."

The British Mediterranean squadron
British ships of the line under Admiral Byng stop at Naples en route to Sicily. They engaged the Spanish near Cape Passaro, south of Messina.

WAR OF JENKINS' EAR

PORTO BELLO

Date 21–22 November 1739
Forces British: 6 ships of the line; Spanish none
Losses none

Location Porto Bello, Panama

The desire of British merchants wanting access to the markets of the Spanish Empire in the Americas reached fever pitch in 1738 when Captain Jenkins exhibited his ear, severed by Spanish coast guards, to the House of Commons. Naval officer and Member of Parliament Edward Vernon boasted that he could take Porto Bello, a Caribbean port used for the export of silver, "with six ships only". Succumbing to the pressure for war, in 1739 the British government made Vernon a vice

admiral with orders to do just that. Vernon appeared off Porto Bello on 20 November with seven ships, one of which he sent away so he could fulfil his promise. The following day, with his flag on board the 64-gun *Hampton Court*, he led his ships in line into Porto Bello. The assortment of coast-guard vessels and warships present could offer no resistance to the British squadron, but the fort of San Felipe, with some 100 guns manned by 300 soldiers, had to be overcome. A failing wind for a time left *Hampton Court* immobilized and alone under the fort's guns, although her broadsides were easily a match for the shore batteries. When the other ships came up the balance of firepower swung heavily against the fort, which surrendered after the landing of marines. Thomas Arne composed "Rule Britannia" for the celebrations and areas of London, Dublin, and Edinburgh were named Portobello.

WAR OF JENKINS' EAR

CARTAGENA

Date 14 March–20 May 1741
Forces British: 29 ships of the line, c.150 other vessels; Spanish: 6 ships of the line
Losses British: 50 ships of all kinds; Spanish: 6 ships of the line

Location Cartagena de Indias, Colombia

The success at Porto Bello in 1739 inspired the British to prey further upon Spain's colonial possessions. A massive force, requiring a quarter of the entire strength of the Royal Navy, was sent to the Caribbean the following year. The death of the expedition's overall commander, Lord Cathcart, en route left the naval force under Vice Admiral Edward Vernon, victor of Porto Bello, and the troops under Major-General Thomas Wentworth, with no one to arbitrate if they disagreed.

Victory medal
The Vernon medal was struck by the British to celebrate the taking of Cartagena – which in fact never happened.

Britain's target was Cartagena de Indias, the major port in Spanish-ruled New Grenada. Leading its defence was Admiral Bas de Lezo, one of Spain's most gallant naval commanders, who had lost a leg, an arm, and an eye in a distinguished fighting career. He had only six ships of the line to face the British armada, but had no intention of giving in. The British arrived off the city in mid-March and settled down to a bombardment of its walls. The entrance to the harbour was defended by shore batteries and the guns of de Lezo's six ships anchored inside. On 15 April the British attempted a combined sea and land assault on these defences. After a sharp fight de Lezo scuttled his ships to keep them out of British hands and fell back on the port's inner fort. As time passed and tempers frayed, cooperation between Vernon and Wentworth broke down. Land assaults proved to

be costly failures, while Vernon's ships bombarding the walls came under damaging fire from shore guns. Caribbean epidemic diseases raged, decimating naval crews and troops. After 67 fruitless days the British sailed away on 20 May, burning some of their ships because they had no crews left to man them. De Lezo did not enjoy his triumph for long, dying of a wound

sustained in the siege. The British government was especially embarrassed by this ignominious defeat because the operation had been prematurely hailed as a triumph and victory medals struck.

Spanish fortifications
The fort of Cartagena, where the British attack of 1741 was repulsed. As a result, Spain retained control of its highly lucrative colony.

TOULON

Date 22–23 February 1744
Forces British: 30 ships of the line; French and Spanish: 28 ships of the line
Losses British: none; Spanish: 1 ship of the line burned

Location Off Cape Sicié, southern France

In February 1744 Britain was at war with Spain and Spain was an ally of France, but France was not at war with Britain. This complicated background prepared the way for a confused and unsatisfactory naval encounter. Twelve Spanish ships of the line commanded by Admiral Don José Navarro were trapped in the French port of Toulon by a far superior British fleet under Vice-Admiral Thomas Mathews. The French government ordered the 16 ships of its fleet in Toulon to escort the Spanish out of harbour, but not to seek a fight with the British. The French admiral entrusted with carrying out these difficult instructions was 78-year-old Admiral de Court la Bruyère.

The Allied fleet sailed out of Toulon with French ships making up the van and most of the centre and the Spanish in the rear. Holding the weather gage, Mathews brought his line down upon the enemy, but with his van opposite their centre, and his centre opposite the Spanish in the rear. The British rear, under Vice Admiral Richard Lestock, totally failed to engage the enemy. The choleric Mathews, feeling his ships were holding off, took his flagship *Namur* out of the line to engage the Spanish more closely, but few of his captains followed his example. There was much damaging fire exchanged between *Namur* and Admiral Navarro's *Real Felipe*. One Spanish ship, *Poder*,

Breech-loading swivel gun
This 18th-century swivel gun was attached to a ship's bulwark by an iron yoke. It has a removable breech chamber that was filled with gunpowder.

was captured by Captain Edward Hawke, although she was too badly shattered to be a manageable prize and was later abandoned for the Spanish to scuttle. The battle ended inconclusively with an impression on both sides that it had been conducted incompetently. A score of British officers faced court-martials, including Mathews and Lestock. Remarkably, Lestock was acquitted on a technicality while Mathews was dismissed from service.

THE BATTLE OF CAPE FINISTERRE

BATTLE OF CAPE FINISTERRE

Date 23 May 1747
Location Off Cape Finisterre, Bay of Biscay
Result British victory

⚓ COMBATANTS ⚓

BRITAIN	SPAIN

⚓ COMMANDERS ⚓

George Anson	Jacques-Pierre de la Jonquière

⚓ FORCES ⚓

Ships: 14 ships of the line, 1 frigate	**Ships:** 5 ships of the line, 2 frigates, 7 others

⚓ LOSSES ⚓

Men: 520 casualties **Ships:** c.50	**Men:** c.800 casualties **Ships:** 4 ships of the line, 2 frigates, 13 others captured

Recently appointed governor-general of French Canada, Admiral Jacques-Pierre de la Jonquière set sail from France with 24 transport ships and an escort of three ships of the line and two frigates. He was joined by a convoy sent out by the French East India Company with two ships of the line and a number of armed merchantmen. A strong British squadron commanded by Vice Admiral George Anson, sent out to intercept French shipping in the Bay of Biscay, spotted the French ships off northern Spain. De la Jonquière formed all his warships and some of the armed merchantmen into a line of battle, hoping to hold the British off for long enough to allow the slow-moving transports to escape. On his flagship *Prince George* Anson also signalled his ships to form a line, but, at the urging of Rear Admiral Sir Peter Warren, changed the order to a general chase.

> ❝
> I CAN WITHOUT VANITY SAY THAT OUR SHIPS WERE BETTER DISCIPLINED AND MADE A MUCH HOTTER FIRE ON THEM.
> **ADMIRAL GEORGE ANSON,** IN A LETTER TO THOMAS NEWCASTLE, SECRETARY OF STATE, 1747
> ❞

The British thus came down upon the outnumbered French led by the 50-gun *Centurion*, which engaged the French rear while other ships came up.

Although hopelessly outgunned, the French fought valiantly in a battle that lasted five hours. La Jonquière's flagship *Sérieux* had every officer wounded. The 40-gun *Gloire* held out for three hours, until her captain was dead and most of her crew injured, before surrendering. But the weight of British broadsides battered the French into submission before nightfall. Through their brave resistance most of the transport ships escaped, only six being taken. The East Indiamen yielded £300,000 in booty for the victors.

A second, broadly similar, battle of Cape Finisterre was fought later in the same year. On 25 October a British squadron of 14 ships of the line under Admiral Edward Hawke intercepted a French convoy bound for the Caribbean with an escort of eight ships of the line under the Marquis Desherbiers de l'Etanduère. Again the British admiral ordered a general chase; once more the French fought against overwhelming odds; and again the convoy was saved at the expense of its escorts. Six French ships of the line were taken.

Overwhelming odds
British and French ships engage off Cape Finisterre. Lord Anson's flagship *Prince George* opens fire in the centre.

SEVEN YEARS WAR

THE SEVEN YEARS WAR of 1756 to 1763 has been described as the first true "world war" because it was contested on three continents. The British fought colonial campaigns against the French in North America, the West Indies and India, while a major land war took place in Europe. Britain's Royal Navy began the conflict in some disarray and suffered an initial setback at the battle of Minorca on 20 May 1756. With Admiral George Anson installed as First Lord of the Admiralty in 1757, however, British naval fortunes soon revived. A close blockade

of French ports executed by superb admirals such as Edward Hawke and George Boscawen inhibited France from defending its colonies. British naval victories at Lagos Bay and Quiberon Bay in 1759 scotched French plans for an invasion of Britain and put the Royal Navy in such a dominant position that it was in no way disturbed by the entry of Spain into the war alongside France in 1761. The peace that was reached in 1763 left Britain as clearly Europe's leading colonial and commercial power, with the French effectively driven out of North America and India.

⬡ SEVEN YEARS WAR

MINORCA

Date 20 May 1756
Forces British: 13 ships of the line; French: 12 ships of the line
Losses none

Location Off Minorca, Balearic Islands

Minorca, a British possession from 1708, had a splendid harbour that was considered a key asset for the British navy in the Mediterranean. In spring 1756 French troops landed on the island, quickly overrunning all but Fort St Philip in Port Mahon. The landings were covered by a French squadron under the Marquis de la Galissonière. Admiral John Byng sailed from Gibraltar with orders to relieve the fort. His squadron of 11 ships was numerically comparable to that of la Galissonière, but many of his ships were in poor repair and undermanned.

Execution of Admiral Byng
Admiral Byng is executed by firing squad aboard HMS *Monarch* in the Solent on 14 March 1757. He had been accused of "failing to do his utmost".

The opposing squadrons sighted one another on 19 May. The French admiral aimed only to prevent the British interfering with the land operations, and thus adopted a purely defensive stance. Byng sought to attack and on 20 May, having gained the weather gage, came down upon the French line. The British approached at an angle, a tactic known as "lasking", designed to reduce the time during which the attacking line was exposed to enemy fire it could not return. But the approach went disastrously wrong. While the five ships of Byng's van engaged the enemy closely, the rest of his line fell behind, its progress hampered by a ship dismasted by French fire. Byng, on board *Ramillies*, lacked the flexibility to revise his plan on the spot. The French came close

to surrounding the isolated ships in the British van, but mindful of his defensive responsibilities la Galissonière exploited the British confusion to withdraw from contact. Demoralized, with heavy casualties and half his ships badly damaged, Byng headed for Gibraltar

to refit. Fort St Philip fell to the French and the need for a scapegoat led to the court-martial and execution of the hapless Byng the following year. His death prompted Voltaire's famous remark; "In this country, it is wise to kill an admiral from time to time to encourage the others".

Embarking for Minorca
French ships embark for Minorca in May 1756. When they arrived, the French took all the British bases except for Fort St Philip in Port Mahon.

LAGOS BAY

Date 18–19 August 1759
Forces British: 14 ships of the line; French: 7 ships of the line
Losses British: none; French: 3 ships of the line destroyed, 2 ships of the line captured

Location Off the Algarve, Portugal

In the summer of 1759 France was preparing for an invasion of Britain. Admiral Jean-François de la Clue-Sabran was ordered to bring the French Mediterranean fleet from Toulon to join the Atlantic fleet at Brest. The combined force would then escort troops to landing places in Scotland and England. A British squadron under Admiral Edward Boscawen was maintaining a blockade of Toulon, but in late July Boscawen was forced to sail to Gibraltar to refit damaged ships and take on supplies. La Clue seized the opportunity to set sail with 12 ships of the line on 5 August.

Reaching Gibraltar on 17 August, the French squadron was spotted by a British observation ship. Boscawen gave chase while La Clue raced through the night into the Atlantic. Daybreak revealed that the French squadron had become divided, only seven ships remaining with their admiral while the others made for Cadiz. Boscawen had ordered a general pursuit and his ships engaged the enemy as they came up. The 74-gun *Centaure*, in the French rear, attempted to hold off the pursuit and give the other French ships a chance to escape. She fought for five hours before surrendering, half shot to pieces. La Clue's flagship *Océan* fought fiercely against Boscawen's *Namur* but by nightfall she had suffered some 200 casualties, the wounded including la Clue himself.

During the night two French ships escaped, dawn revealing the remainder at Boscawen's mercy. La Clue sailed the remnant of his squadron into a bay to the west of Lagos in neutral Portugal, hoping that a shore battery might scare the British off. But Boscawen followed the French into the bay regardless and opened fire. The French crews got ashore as best they could, abandoning their ships into British hands. The three worst damaged were set ablaze and the other taken back to Gibraltar as a prize.

Gunner's quadrant
A quadrant was used to determine the elevation of a gun's barrel. A spirit level attached to the pivot arm marked the horizontal, while a plum bob measured the required angle.

1704–1759
JOHN BYNG
BRITISH ADMIRAL

John Byng was the son of a distinguished admiral, Viscount Torrington. He made comfortable peacetime progress in a naval career, progressing from lieutenant at age 19 to rear admiral in his 40s. Byng had never held command in battle before being sent into action against the French at Minorca in 1756. His withdrawal to Gibraltar after that indecisive encounter led to a court-martial. The British navy's Articles of War obliged officers to do their utmost to engage the enemy, which Byng had failed to do. He was found guilty, the offence carrying a mandatory death penalty. The court recommended royal clemency, which was normal when men of high birth were condemned to execution. However, the loss of Minorca had caused a popular outcry in Britain, and a scapegoat was needed. Byng was executed by firing squad on the quarter-deck of the ship of the line *Monarch* at Portsmouth on 14 March 1757.

CREW PROFILE
SHIP OF THE LINE
1700–1800

THE MAJORITY OF THE CREW of an 18th-century Royal Navy ship of the line were ordinary seamen and able seamen, the latter being trained up to skilled tasks such as working aloft or steering the ship. Sailors usually first went to sea as boys – it was reckoned that a grown man could never learn to work high above the deck without dying in the attempt. In peacetime naval vessels were manned largely by volunteers, but in wartime sailors had to be pressed into naval service from merchant vessels or other maritime occupations. Though subject to harsh discipline, seamen on a well-run ship would feel a bonded part of a skilled team, and, in battle, would enthusiastically man the guns or take up arms to repel boarders.

WARRANT OFFICERS
The master, although still a significant figure on the ship, had lost importance compared with a century earlier, because commissioned officers were now trained in seamanship and rivalled the master for knowledge of navigation and sailing. The purser and the surgeon were the other warrant officers of wardroom rank. Below them came the boatswain, carpenter, sailmaker, and gunner, solid characters of lower-class origin traditionally attached to a single ship in which they served for long periods. They were sometimes unofficially allowed their wives on board.

COMMISSIONED OFFICERS
Although in the Royal Navy progress from warrant officer or even able seaman to commissioned rank was not unknown, officers were usually gentlemen. The sons of socially respectable families were taken into naval service as boys, usually recommended to a captain by a relative or family friend. When old enough they became midshipmen, hoping to pass the examination required for appointment as lieutenant, probably after six years at sea. The next step was to be made post-captain, with command of their own ship, after which promotion to admiral was strictly by seniority. A captain's authority was absolute, although his own behaviour was subject to the Articles of War.

Gun crew at battle stations
Each gun was manned by up to six sailors. A gunner was in charge of all the cannons, while a quarter gunner was in charge of four.

THE BATTLE OF QUIBERON BAY

BATTLE OF QUIBERON BAY

Date	20 November 1759
Location	Quiberon Bay, Brittany, France
Result	British victory

❧ COMBATANTS ❧

BRITAIN	FRANCE

❧ COMMANDERS ❧

Edward Hawke	Herbert de Brienne, Comte de Conflans

❧ FORCES ❧

Ships: 27	Ships: 21

❧ LOSSES ❧

Men: 300	Men: 2,500
Ships: 2	Ships: 7

In 1759 France hoped to reverse the course of the Seven Years War by launching an invasion of the British Isles. An army of 20,000 men and troop transports were assembled at Quiberon Bay. The Comte de Conflans, then the commander the French fleet in Brest, was to escort the army to Scotland. The Royal Navy was maintaining a close blockade of Brest, a feat of seamanship, organization, and endurance. But in November a westerly Atlantic gale forced Admiral Edward Hawke to withdraw his blockading squadron to shelter in Torbay. Conflans seized the opportunity to sail for Quiberon Bay.

Hawke returned to Brest as soon as the weather permitted and, finding Conflans gone, pursued him southward. Delayed by erratic winds, the French were approaching the bay when the British hove into view. Conflans was not greatly outnumbered – 27 ships of the line to 21 – but he knew his officers and crews were far inferior. His sole advantage was possession of local pilots with an intimate knowledge of the reefs and shoals of the treacherous coast. With a gale rising from the northwest, he formed a line and sailed for the shelter of the bay. Conflans assumed Hawke would not dare to follow him in. But the British admiral signalled a "general chase" and his ships, crowding on all the sail they could bear in the howling wind, tailed the French into the narrow mouth of the bay.

THWARTED INVASION

The risk Hawke took was astonishing. Caught in a gale off a lee shore, his ships could have been shattered on the jagged rocks, leaving Britain defenceless against invasion. Instead, it was the French squadron that met disaster. The British van, commanded by Viscount Howe aboard *Magnanime*, savaged the ships of the French rear before the rest of the squadron came up to join in a mêlée made even more chaotic by the heavy seas. The captain of the French 74 *Thésée* opened his lower gun ports to bring his heaviest battery into action, only for a sudden squall to plunge the ports under water, the ship sinking instantly under full sail. Another French ship, *Superbe*, also foundered, its hull shattered by a broadside from Hawke's flagship *Royal George*. *Formidable* and *Héros*, battered into submission, struck their colours, although the raging seas prevented the British getting a prize crew aboard the latter, which was later

Quiberon Bay

The most decisive battle of the Seven Years War, and one of the Royal Navy's greatest victories, the battle of Quiberon Bay saw the destruction of the French fleet off the coast of Brittany. The fleet was making ready for an invasion of England.

Atlantic Ocean   *Quiberon Bay*

Houat Island

Belle Isle   *Hoëdic Island*

Thésée, sunk

Twenty-seven British ships force the French into the shallows of Quiberon Bay

British flagship *Royal George*

Superbe, sunk

Formidable, captured

Resolution, run aground

Essex, run aground

Seven French ships escape up the Vilaine estuary

Vilaine River

Inflexible, destroyed

Héros, run aground

Soleil Royal, run aground

Juste, destroyed

Eight French ships escape to Rochefort

KEY

→ 1 French ship, stage 1
→ 1 French ship, stage 2
→ 1 British ship, stage 1
→ 1 British ship, stage 2

N

run aground. The French fleet was only saved from destruction by the early nightfall on a dark November day. At around 5pm firing ceased and ships anchored where they lay.

Dawn brought a renewal of the battle with the elements, but not between the fleets. Two British ships had been dragged onto a shoal and could not be saved. The French ship *Juste*, badly damaged in the fighting, was wrecked fleeing towards the Loire. Surrounded by the enemy, Conflans ran his flagship *Soleil Royal* aground and fired it to save it from falling into British hands. Seven other French ships

exploited the effect of the high tide and an onshore gale to attempt to cross the usually impassable sandbar at the mouth of the river Vilaine. To do so, the sailors had to throw their cannon overboard to reduce their draught. Six ships made it to the shallow water beyond, thus escaping the British ships but trapping themselves in the estuary for the following year.

Hawke's victory shattered the French navy, ended the prospect of an invasion of the British Isles, and exposed French colonies and merchant shipping to the depredations of the Royal Navy for the rest of the war.

> ## HAD WE BUT TWO HOURS MORE DAYLIGHT, THE WHOLE [ENEMY FLEET] HAD BEEN DESTROYED OR TAKEN.
>
> **ADMIRAL HAWKE**, DESCRIBING HIS VICTORY AT QUIBERON BAY, 1759

Decisive victory
Admiral Hawke's *Royal George* (left) is shown engaging with *Soleil Royal* (right). The latter is erroneously portrayed as a three-decker; she was in fact an 84-gun third-rater, with two decks.

WEAPONS AND TECHNOLOGY

BOARDING WEAPONS

Despite the reign of the cannon in the age of sail, boarding was still an essential tactic, whether to seize a valuable prize or to end the resistance of a battered enemy. Either men crossed between two vessels side by side or boats were sent out with a boarding party to swarm up the hull of an enemy ship. Although musket-armed marines took part in boarding and repelling boarders, sailors bore the brunt of the action. They were issued with a range of weapons from pistols and blunderbusses to swords and axes. The cutlass was favoured over longer-bladed, more refined swords, as a robust and compact weapon suitable for use by unpractised swordsmen fighting in a confined space. The boarding axe, or tomahawk, could be driven into the hull of an enemy ship to provide a step for climbing up – as well as being used to smash skulls. Boarding pikes were especially handy for holding off boarders from a defensive position.

CUTLASS

Thin iron hand guard

BOARDING AXE

Sharpened axe blade also useful for clearing fallen rigging or wreckage

Spike could be driven into enemy hulls, making a step for climbing up

BOARDING PIKE

Pikes were handy for keeping the enemy at a distance

Flat steel blade

Tools of combat
In addition to edged weapons, sailors often wore boarding pistols, which usually came in pairs. This gave the sailor at least two shots at the enemy; there was rarely time to reload.

1705–1781
EDWARD HAWKE

BRITISH ADMIRAL

Joining the Royal Navy at the age of 15, Hawke took 27 years to reach the rank of Rear Admiral, his progress inhibited by a shortage of naval warfare. Establishing his reputation at Cape Finisterre in 1747, he was an advocate of individual initiative and the "general chase" in preference to formal line tactics. Victory at Quiberon Bay made him a national hero, and the taking of Spanish treasure ships made him rich. Retired from seagoing, he was First Lord of the Admiralty from 1766 to 1771.

THE AMERICAN REVOLUTIONARY WAR

THE REVOLT OF 13 North American colonies in 1775 led to war with Britain and the founding of the United States. The American rebels created a Continental Navy that lacked the resources to challenge the might of the Royal Navy, but did found a naval tradition. Its most significant action was the lake battle at Valcour Island in 1776, which at heavy cost delayed a British advance from Canada. Raiding and harrying actions by enterprising captains such as John Paul Jones raised spirits but had limited effect. Major naval conflict developed only when France, Spain,

and the Dutch Republic entered the war against Britain. Battles were then fought in the West Indies, in European waters, and in the Indian Ocean, as well as off the United States. In the end naval power was crucial, for the British army in North America was dependent on supply by sea. The French victory at Chesapeake Bay in 1781 caused the surrender of the British at Yorktown and hence American triumph in the war. Yet Admiral Rodney's tactically innovative victory at the battle of the Saints was a reminder that the era of British naval dominance was very far from over.

Engagement on Lake Champlain
British ships fire broadsides at the American line in a firefight lasting several hours. The American squadron was largely destroyed, but the battle did successfully delay the British advance.

THE AMERICAN REVOLUTIONARY WAR

VALCOUR ISLAND

Date 11–13 October 1776
Forces British: 30 ships; Americans: 16 ships
Losses British: 3 gunboats; Americans: 11 ships

Location Lake Champlain, New York

By the summer of 1776 the British had repulsed an American invasion of Canada and planned to counterattack by taking troops across Lake Champlain to the Hudson. A naval race began, with the Americans under Benedict Arnold improvising a naval squadron on the southern shore of the lake while the British did the same in the north.

The two forces met on 11 October. The British, commanded by Captain Thomas Pringle, had the three-masted 18-gun *Inflexible*, the schooners *Maria* and *Carleton*, plus an array of small gunboats and other craft. Arnold had a force of about half the size including three schooners and a sloop, plus row galleys and gondolas built on the spot. Hoping to avoid the need to manoeuvre

with his inexperienced crews, Arnold anchored the American squadron in a line across the channel between Valcour Island and the shore.

The battle started badly for the Americans when their schooner *Royal Savage* ran onto rocks, but the *Carleton*, advancing to board the disabled ship, was itself battered by the concentrated fire of the American line. With half her crew and her captain killed, the *Carleton* made a fighting withdrawal under the command of 19-year-old midshipman Edward Pellew – a future admiral. The Royal Navy's small gunboats bore the brunt of the fighting. The Americans sank one and disabled two others, but themselves took heavy punishment.

By nightfall the gondola *Philadelphia* was sinking and the British expected to finish off the rest of the American ships the following day. During the night, however, the Americans slipped away undetected. The British gave chase and overhauled the more damaged American ships. One was sunk, one captured, and others deliberately run aground. Five vessels reached the fort at Crown Point, though these were eventually burned to keep them out of British hands.

WEAPONS AND TECHNOLOGY

TURTLE SUBMERSIBLE

American patriot David Bushnell (1742–1824) of Saybrook, Connecticut, devised a submersible vessel to counter the Royal Navy's coastal blockade. His egg-shaped *Turtle* had ballast water tanks that were filled to make it dive, then emptied with a hand pump to return to the surface. It carried an underwater gunpowder charge to be attached to the hull of a ship at anchor and detonated by a time fuse. The *Turtle* went into action on 7 September 1776 with volunteer Sergeant Ezra Lee at the controls. It was launched into New York harbour to attack the British flagship, HMS *Eagle*. Lee brought the *Turtle* up against the underside of *Eagle's* hull undetected, but failed to attach the explosive charge to the ship's copper-sheathed bottom. The *Turtle* made three attempts to sink British ships but never achieved a successful attack.

Revolutionary submersible
Seated in the cramped interior, the operative manoeuvred the *Turtle* underwater using screw propellers, operated by foot pedals and a handle.

USHANT

Date 27 July 1778
Forces British: 30 ships of the line; French: 27 ships of the line
Losses none

Location
Bay of Biscay

The Royal Navy's Western Squadron, commanded by Admiral Augustus Keppel aboard the newly commissioned first-rate *Victory*, met the French Atlantic fleet under the Comte d'Orvilliers about 160km (100 miles) off Ushant. Keppel attacked against the wind and the two lines cannoned each other on the same tack. The French began to draw ahead, so d'Orvilliers then wore to pass the British on the opposite tack. The British rear, under Admiral Sir Hugh Palliser, was hard hit by excellent French gunnery and lucky not to be doubled. Keppel wanted to turn to follow the French but Palliser was apparently in no state to perform the manoeuvre. The inconclusive engagement ended in bitter dispute between Keppel and Palliser, the Royal Navy having failed to fulfil Britain's high expectations.

FLAMBOROUGH HEAD

Date 23 September 1779
Forces Americans: 5 ships; British: 2 ships
Losses Americans: 1 ship sunk; British: 2 ships captured

Location Off Flamborough Head, Yorkshire

In August 1779 American captain John Paul Jones led a small squadron to raid shipping around the British Isles. Jones was on board the 42-gun converted merchant ship *Bonhomme Richard*, accompanied by the frigates *Alliance* and *Pallas*, both under French captains, and two smaller vessels.

On 23 September Jones surprised a convoy of 50 merchant ships escorted by the 44-gun frigate *Serapis* and a 20-gun escort ship, *Countess of Scarborough*. The first broadside was fired at around 7pm,

French medallion
This commemorative bronze medal depicts the clash between *Serapis* and *Bonhomme Richard* off Flamborough Head.

with *Serapis* and *Bonhomme Richard* within hailing distance. The British frigate's guns were more effective and it was the nimbler ship. Jones' only chance was to grapple *Serapis*. Carnage ensued, *Bonhomme Richard* scouring *Serapis*'s deck with grapeshot and musket fire while the frigate's heavy guns battered her hull. *Alliance* and *Pallas* forced the *Countess*

to strike, but they could find no way to support Jones effectively – when *Alliance* fired a broadside at *Serapis*, it caused equal damage to *Bonhomme Richard*.

Darkness fell but the fight continued by moonlight. *Bonhomme Richard* was on fire and near sinking; *Serapis* was also ablaze after a grenade ignited powder below decks. As Jones refused to surrender – apparently saying "I may sink, but I'll be damned if I strike" – *Serapis*'s captain decided to give in and end the slaughter. Jones transferred his crew to the more seaworthy British frigate to return triumphantly to port.

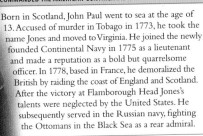

1747–1792
JOHN PAUL JONES
COMMANDED THE AMERICAN CONTINENTAL NAVY AT FLAMBOROUGH

Born in Scotland, John Paul went to sea at the age of 13. Accused of murder in Tobago in 1773, he took the name Jones and moved to Virginia. He joined the newly founded Continental Navy in 1775 as a lieutenant and made a reputation as a bold but quarrelsome officer. In 1778, based in France, he demoralized the British by raiding the coast of England and Scotland. After the victory at Flamborough Head Jones's talents were neglected by the United States. He subsequently served in the Russian navy, fighting the Ottomans in the Black Sea as a rear admiral.

CAPE ST VINCENT

Date 16–17 January 1780
Forces British: 18 ships of the line, 9 frigates; Spanish: 9 ships of the line, 2 frigates
Losses British: none; Spanish: 1 ship sunk, 6 ships captured

Location Off the Algarve, southern Portugal

Spain's chief war aim in the American Revolutionary War was to regain Gibraltar from Britain. They placed the Rock under siege and naval blockade. In January 1780 British admiral Sir George Rodney was sent to relieve Gibraltar with a strong force of ships of the line and frigates. Commodore Don

The moonlight battle
The *Santo Domingo* explodes during the battle of Cape St Vincent. The ship to the foreground is the HMS *Sandwich*, flagship of Admiral Rodney.

Juan de Lángara, a strikingly brave and competent Spanish officer, was at sea to the west of Gibraltar, hoping to intercept a merchant convoy bound for the West Indies. A winter storm blew two of his ships of the line off station, leaving him with a weakened squadron of nine ships of the line when he had the misfortune to encounter Rodney's superior British force. As the British bore down upon him, De Lángara had no choice but to run for Cadiz, the nearest safe port.

Rodney ordered a general chase and within two hours, at around 4pm, the fastest British ships had got among the fleeing Spanish. The 70-gun *Santo Domingo* exploded, killing all on board, but the rest of de Lángara's outclassed ships fought on with notable

> ## HE NEVER LET SLIP AN OPPORTUNITY TO BRING OPPONENTS TO ACTION, OR BEING HIMSELF IN THE THICKEST OF THE FIGHT
>
> **ADMIRAL RODNEY,** *DESCRIBED BY JOHN KNOX LAUGHTON*

courage. The battle continued long after night fell. With a strong westerly blowing and a treacherous rocky coast to the lee, there was a serious risk of ships running ashore, but Rodney had no intention of allowing the Spanish to escape and stuck tenaciously to the pursuit. De Lángara's battered flagship *El Felix*

was the last of six to be taken, striking its colours in the early hours of the morning. In the aftermath of the battle two of the prizes taken were lost, for in stormy weather off an unfamiliar coast the British could not sail them without using the captured Spanish crews, who eagerly seized back their ships and joined the other escapees in Cadiz.

GUN, SAIL, AND EMPIRE

THE BATTLE OF THE SAINTS

Buoyed by their success at Chesapeake Bay, by 1782 the French were on the offensive in the West Indies, hoping to seize control of valuable British colonies. In early April the Comte de Grasse, with 33 ships of the line and two 50-gun ships, escorted a large convoy of merchant ships from Martinique. His mission was to deliver the merchantmen safely to Havana and join with the fleet of France's ally Spain to capture Jamaica. De Grasse was shadowed by the 36 ships of the line of the British fleet under Admiral Sir George Rodney.

On 9 April the two fleets clashed off Dominica. Straining ahead to snap at the heels of the French, the British van, commanded by Admiral Samuel Hood, found itself briefly exposed to attack by de Grasse's entire force. It was an opportunity the French failed to exploit and the exchange ended with one French ship badly shot up. De Grasse's misfortunes continued as he sailed between Dominica and the rocky islets known as the Saintes.

On the night of 11 April the 74-gun *Zélé* collided with de Grasse's flagship *Ville de Paris*. The next morning, seeing Hood launch in pursuit of the crippled *Zélé,* de Grasse came about and gave the order to clear for action.

BREAKING THE LINE

Since Hood needed time to recall his ships, Rodney formed a battle line with his rear division in the van and Hood's division in the rear. Despite this hasty reorganization, the British line was more compact than the straggling and gappy line formed by the French. At around 7:45am the exchange of broadsides began, ships passing in opposite directions within musket range. The French came off worst, partly because many of the British guns had been newly equipped with flintlocks.

The decisive moment of the battle came around 9am. As the wind shifted southerly, Rodney sailed

"The Glorious Action"
This gold badge, which belonged to a daughter of King George III, shows the captured French flagship *Ville de Paris* flying the British ensign above the French.

Commemorative gold ring
The gold and glass intaglio ring bears Rodney's name and the date of the battle of the Saints.

his flagship, the 100-gun *Formidable*, through a gap in the French line, blasting two French ships as he went. As other British ships followed their admiral's example, de Grasse's centre division was split into incoherent fragments. The French van, badly knocked about by British broadsides, had sailed clear of the battle and showed little inclination to return. This left Hood free to plunge into the mêlée in the centre. The French rear under the Marquis de Vaudreuil made an effort to aid de Grasse, but in vain. The slaughter on the French admiral's flagship was extreme, with some 400 men dead by the time de Grasse struck at 6pm. His was the fifth French ship to be taken. As darkness fell one of the captured vessels, *César*, was destroyed by a massive explosion.

Rodney controversially failed to order a pursuit of the beaten enemy, although two more French ships of the line were taken in the following week. Still, the revenge for the British defeat at Chesapeake was sweet. French aspirations to control the Caribbean were crushed and Rodney's bold breaking of the line – which may not even have been intentional – initiated a new phase in naval tactics.

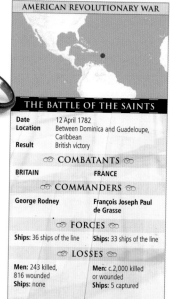

AMERICAN REVOLUTIONARY WAR

THE BATTLE OF THE SAINTS

Date	12 April 1782
Location	Between Dominica and Guadeloupe, Caribbean
Result	British victory

∞ COMBATANTS ∞

BRITAIN	FRANCE

∞ COMMANDERS ∞

George Rodney	François Joseph Paul de Grasse

∞ FORCES ∞

Ships: 36 ships of the line	**Ships:** 33 ships of the line

∞ LOSSES ∞

Men: 243 killed, 816 wounded	**Men:** c.2,000 killed or wounded
Ships: none	**Ships:** 5 captured

Exchange of broadsides
Admiral Hood's 90-gun ship *Barfleur*, centre, engages the 104-gun French flagship *Ville de Paris*, right. Badly damaged in the mêlée, the *Ville the Paris* surrendered shortly afterwards.

1550 – 1830

AMERICAN REVOLUTIONARY WAR

PROVIDIEN

Date 12 April 1782
Forces French: 12 ships of the line; British: 11 ships of the line
Losses None

Location Off east coast of Sri Lanka

French admiral Pierre André de Suffren appeared off southeast India in February 1782 commanding a squadron of 12 ships. His mission was to contest the British takeover of French colonial outposts by cooperating with Indian Prince Hyder Ali. After an indecisive encounter with a British force under Vice Admiral Sir Edward Hughes at Sadras, Suffren sailed for Trincomalee in Ceylon (Sri Lanka), which he hoped to seize as a naval base. Vice Admiral Hughes intercepted him with 11 ships near the islet of Providien.

Suffren held the weather gage and pinned the British against a rocky coast. He closed with the British in line abreast, turning to line ahead to begin firing broadsides. But some of his captains, lacking stomach for a fight, hung back on the approach and only Suffren's flagship *Héros* and four other ships in the French centre engaged at close range. In fierce fighting the British 64-gun *Monmouth* was disabled while *Héros* lost her foretopmast and the French 74-gun *Orient* caught fire. The onset of a violent rainstorm brought a general ceasefire as both sides strove to avoid running ashore or colliding in the crowded seas. The French ships withdrew the next day in serious need of repair, but after an improvised refit resumed operations.

1729–1788

PIERRE ANDRÉ DE SUFFREN

FRENCH ADMIRAL

Suffren de St Tropez took part in all France's wars against Britain from the 1740s to the 1780s, fighting at Toulon in 1744, Minorca in 1756, and Lagos Bay in 1759, as well as in many lesser actions. He was twice taken prisoner by the British. A fiery, impetuous character, he was critical of French naval tradition, believing lack of energy and initiative was responsible for repeated poor performances. Taking command in the Indian Ocean in 1782, he resolved to redeem his navy's honour with a display of fighting spirit. Although he won no outright victories, he kept his ships committed to combat under most difficult circumstances, earning the praise of friend and foe alike.

AMERICAN REVOLUTIONARY WAR

TRINCOMALEE

Date 3 September 1782
Forces French: 14 ships of the line; British: 12 ships of the line
Losses None

Location Off east coast of Sri Lanka

In August 1782 Suffren captured the port of Trincomalee from the British. Hughes sailed his squadron offshore, inviting the French to come out. Reinforced, Suffren now had clearly superior numbers, so he gave battle hoping for a crushing victory. As at Providien, many of Suffren's captains did not share his enthusiasm. Only Suffren's flagship *Héros*, along with *Ajax* and *Illustre*, initially engaged at closest range. In three hours' savage combat these ships suffered heavy losses. At one point *Héros'* flag was shot away, but Suffren bellowed: "Flags, flags, hoist them all around the ship." More French ships belatedly joined the fighting and the British suffered enough damage to feel the need to disengage, leaving the French in possession of Trincomalee.

AMERICAN REVOLUTIONARY WAR

CUDDALORE

Date 20 June 1783
Forces French: 15 ships of the line; British: 18 ships of the line
Losses None

Location Off Coromandel coast of India

In 1783 French army reinforcements arrived in India. The soldiers were soon trapped at Cuddalore, besieged by land and under naval blockade. Suffren sailed to contest the blockade, though his ships were in poor shape, undermanned, and outnumbered. He cleverly manoeuvred to draw the British out of the Cuddalore roadstead and occupy it himself. Then, taking on board sepoys to help man his guns, he boldly went out to attack the superior British force. Both sides maintained a steady line through several hours' broadsides, ended by nightfall. The moral victory went to the French, still ready to take the offensive despite their patched sails and depleted crews. The news arrived shortly after that peace had already been declared.

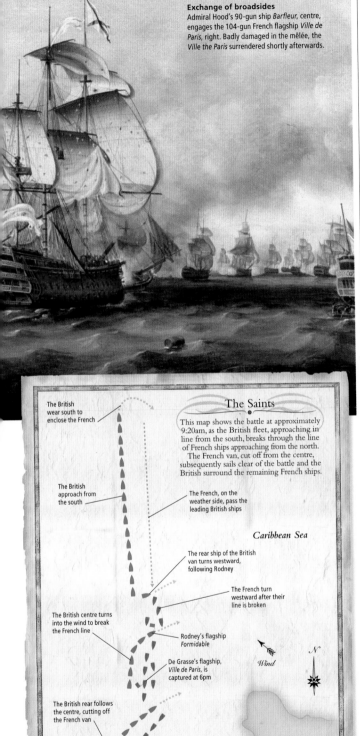

The Saints

This map shows the battle at approximately 9:20am, as the British fleet, approaching in line from the south, breaks through the line of French ships approaching from the north. The French van, cut off from the centre, subsequently sails clear of the battle and the British surround the remaining French ships.

The British wear south to enclose the French

The British approach from the south

The French, on the weather side, pass the leading British ships

Caribbean Sea

The rear ship of the British van turns westward, following Rodney

The French turn westward after their line is broken

The British centre turns into the wind to break the French line

Rodney's flagship *Formidable*

De Grasse's flagship, *Ville de Paris*, is captured at 6pm

Wind

N

The British rear follows the centre, cutting off the French van

The French withdraw to the west, where they are decimated by the British

DOMINICA

Ten French ships off-map to southwest

KEY
➤ 1 English warship
➤ 1 French warship

Exchange of fire
The vans of the French (left) and British (right) fleets engage at Chesapeake Bay. The centre and rear squadrons remain unengaged due to the angle at which the two lines approached.

1 THE BRITISH FLEET ARRIVES

After finding the Chesapeake unoccupied by the French, the British under Rear Admiral Hood set sail for New York to report to Admiral Graves. When they return, they find the French blockading the bay. De Grasse immediately attacks.

CHESAPEAKE BAY

French fleet blockading Chesapeake Bay

British miss opportunity of attacking isolated French van. Hood currently in British van

British form line ahead and bear down on French from the north

Wind

"Promiscuous" line of French ships sets sail to engage British fleet. Van pulls ahead of centre and rear squadrons

ATLANTIC OCEAN

KEY

FRENCH FLEET

2 French ships of the line

BRITISH FLEET

2–3 British ships of the line

> SIR SAMUEL WOULD BE GLAD TO SEND AN OPINION, BUT KNOWS NOT WHAT TO SAY IN THE TRULY LAMENTABLE STATE WE HAVE BROUGHT OURSELVES.
>
> **REAR ADMIRAL SIR SAMUEL HOOD,** IN A COMMUNICATION TO ADMIRAL GRAVES

THE BATTLE OF CHESAPEAKE BAY

In the summer of 1781 the heads of the French and American land forces fighting the British in North America appealed for support from the French fleet in the West Indies. The fleet's admiral, the Comte de Grasse, set off with 28 ships of the line for Chesapeake Bay, where a British army under Cornwallis was besieged at Yorktown. Part of the British West Indies fleet, 14 ships of the line commanded by Sir Samuel Hood, was sent in search of de Grasse, but arrived at Chesapeake Bay ahead of him. Finding no French ships, Hood then continued north to report to Admiral Thomas Graves in New York. Hood's ships had barely disappeared over the horizon when, on 29 August, de Grasse arrived and anchored inside Cape Henry, blockading Cornwallis from supply or evacuation by sea.

Underestimating the size of de Grasse's fleet, Graves added five ships of his own to Hood's 14 and sailed for the Chesapeake. On the morning of 5 September a lookout spotted the French fleet at anchor, revealing to Graves that he was outgunned and outnumbered. Nonetheless the British cleared for action and, in the words of a French officer "came down on us with … an assurance that made us

British surrender
British troops led by General Cornwallis surrender at Yorktown on 21 October 1871, after the failure of the British fleet to secure Chesapeake Bay. French ships fill the bay.

think they did not know our strength". The French showed equal spirit. De Grasse had 24 of his ships available for battle, although he was short of some officers and crew who were currently ashore. Slipping their anchors, they emerged from behind the cape barely 45 minutes after sighting their enemy.

De Grasse ordered his captains to form a "promiscuous" line; whoever had his ship ready first would lead the van, the rest following when they could. Competing for the honour of leading the fleet, five of the fieriest captains had their ships well ahead of the rest. But Graves let slip the opportunity to attack this isolated van. He sought a formal battle in line. In order to sail

in the same direction as the French (which was essential for a prolonged exchange of broadsides) Graves had to wear his ships together, a manoeuvre that reversed the sailing order. Hood, previously commanding the van, now found himself in the rear, while the former rear, composed of the least seaworthy ships, became the van.

It was around 4pm before Graves signalled for close action, though he also maintained a signal to hold the line ahead. The British and French columns met at an angle, which meant that the ships in the van were fiercely engaged, while the centre and rear stayed well apart. The boldest French commanders with the best trained crews duelled with British ships, some of which were having trouble staying afloat. In an hour of close fighting, the British suffered the worst of the damage. The captain of *Shrewsbury*, the

lead ship, lost a leg, and *Intrepid*, the next ship in line, had 65 holes shot in her hull, as well as her rigging cut and masts shattered.

With Graves and Hood bickering over the way the battle had been fought, the British fleet went back to New York, missing a chance to intercept French transport ships bringing siege guns to the Chesapeake. By the time Graves returned with a relief expedition in October, the blockaded General Cornwallis had surrendered, ensuring the independence of the United States. Tactically indecisive, Chesapeake Bay was strategically one of the most decisive sea battles in history.

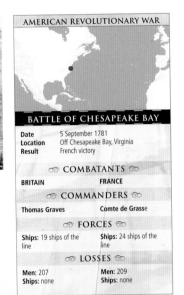

AMERICAN REVOLUTIONARY WAR

BATTLE OF CHESAPEAKE BAY

Date	5 September 1781
Location	Off Chesapeake Bay, Virginia
Result	French victory

⚓ COMBATANTS ⚓

BRITAIN	FRANCE

⚓ COMMANDERS ⚓

Thomas Graves	Comte de Grasse

⚓ FORCES ⚓

Ships: 19 ships of the line	Ships: 24 ships of the line

⚓ LOSSES ⚓

Men: 207	Men: 209
Ships: none	Ships: none

1550 – 1830

Boatswain's call
Whistles such as this are used for conveying orders aboard ship. The design has changed little from medieval times to the present day.

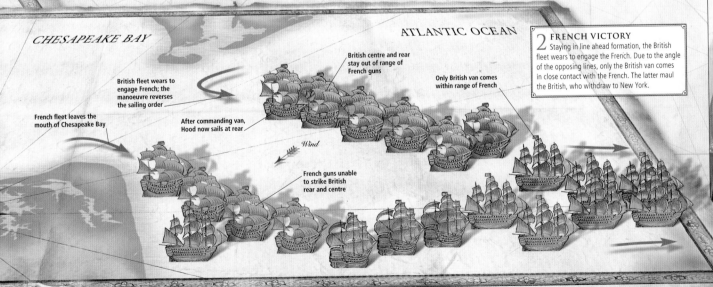

CHESAPEAKE BAY

ATLANTIC OCEAN

French fleet leaves the mouth of Chesapeake Bay

British fleet wears to engage French; the manoeuvre reverses the sailing order

After commanding van, Hood now sails at rear

British centre and rear stay out of range of French guns

Only British van comes within range of French

Wind

French guns unable to strike British rear and centre

2 FRENCH VICTORY
Staying in line ahead formation, the British fleet wears to engage the French. Due to the angle of the opposing lines, only the British van comes in close contact with the French. The latter maul the British, who withdraw to New York.

LIVING CONDITIONS

LIFE ON BOARD a warship has at times been compared unfavourably with life in prison – both involving large numbers of men confined in a very restricted space with no privacy and primitive facilities, but prison offering better chances of escape and less risk of death. In the age of galley warfare, although living conditions could be appalling in terms of sanitation and overcrowding, the problem was mitigated by the shortness of voyages and frequent landfall. But in the age of sail men would live on board for months at a time. To man their guns and handle their sails, the ships required large crews relative to their size. Work was hard, food often poor (though also poor ashore), and comforts few – a naval tradition maintained into the 20th century.

DITTY BOX Wooden boxes, such as this one, were part of every sailor's kit during both World Wars. They used them to store their personal possessions, such as photographs, letters, and wash kit.

SLEEPING CONDITIONS

Through most of history ships had few or no special spaces for the crew to sleep. On an ancient galley the density of crew and soldiers made it impossible to sleep on board with any comfort, and men slept ashore if they could. By the early modern period, with longer voyages in sailing ships, men usually slept on the deck on rolled-up bedding. Hammocks were a Native American invention encountered by European sailors at the end of the 15th century, although they were still not widely adopted on ships until the 17th century. Their many advantages, including comfort and ease of stowage, were eventually appreciated. On an 18th-century ship of the line men slept in hammocks slung from the roof of the gun deck. The hammock hooks were around 38cm (15in) apart, so in harbour the men's bodies were in contact while sleeping. At sea the situation was improved by the watch system, which meant that only half the crew was sleeping at the same time. Still, the state of the air in such a crowded, unventilated space, especially when in the tropics, can easily be imagined.

GUN-DECK ACCOMMODATION Space was at a premium in Napoleonic-era warships, so sailors slept in storable canvas hammocks among the cannon. Half worked while the others slept.

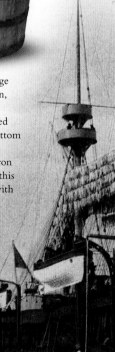

TUB This wooden tub, situated in the sick berth of an 18th-century ship of the line, was large enough for a man to bathe in.

FIGHTING DIRT

The need for cleanliness and hygiene was appreciated by navies in the age of sail. Sailors were required to keep themselves and their clothes clean, but this was hard to achieve. The use of the heads, opening over the sea, as toilets was strictly enforced, yet men, whether wilfully or accidentally, failed to reach them on many occasion. The shingle ballast in the bilges at the bottom of the hull collected detritus from the decks above, turning over time into a cesspool that infected the ship with stinking fumes. The substitution of iron pigs for shingle as ballast in the early 19th century largely solved this problem. Humidity was a plague below deck on wooden ships, with no sunlight to dry out the water that seeped in. Dampness was often worsened by the pursuit of cleanliness which led to the decks being over-frequently washed down.

SUBMARINE TOILET Underwater toilets had to be designed differently to prevent the external water pressure from flinging the contents straight back. A flooded airlock ejected the waste safely.

STEAM ERA

The era of steam and steel changed living conditions, not always for the better. With no gun ports there was even less air below deck than previously, and the heat, noise, and fumes from the engines could become intolerable. Artificial ventilation was only slowly introduced. Many men found the motion of a steamship cutting through the waves more upsetting than the subtler movement of an old sailing ship, with the result that seasickness became a worse problem. The introduction of bunks took a while. It was still common in World War II for hundreds of men to sleep in hammocks hanging in the mess halls and perform their morning ablutions, including cleaning teeth and shaving, in a single bucket of cold water.

BUNK BEDS The African American Corps of Engineers being transported in 1942 temporarily experience the same crowded conditions the average sailor endured, bunking "on the shelf" on canvas beds.

OFFICER'S ROOM This officer's room aboard the 277m (910ft) long WWII-era aircraft carrier, the USS *Lexington*, afforded some privacy and had its own sink.

In the cockpit of a line of battle ship, where all the gentlemen mess, they never have any daylight ... dirty screens, cots and hammocks hanging in all directions ...

JAMES LOWRY, *Fiddlers and Whores* A surgeon in Nelson's fleet gives his first impressions of his living quarters

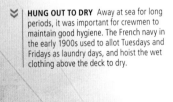

HUNG OUT TO DRY Away at sea for long periods, it was important for crewmen to maintain good hygiene. The French navy in the early 1900s used to allot Tuesdays and Fridays as laundry days, and hoist the wet clothing above the deck to dry.

UNDERWATER

Submarines always presented special problems, being by their nature claustrophobic and cramped. Some early World War I types had no toilet facilities except a bucket. German U-boat crews in World War II normally shared bunks, one man rising for his watch as the other occupant turned in. The boats spent most of their time on the surface, where they pitched and rolled mercilessly – diving often came as a sweet relief, both from seasickness and the clattering of the diesel engine. With only seawater available, most men did not bother to wash their clothes or themselves, and no one shaved. The smell of unwashed bodies and diesel fuel was masked by generous application of eau de cologne. On modern nuclear submarines showers are obligatory – although carried out with the minimum use of water – and bunks are individual, but with nine men sleeping in a room sometimes shared with a missile tube, the sailor's life remains short on the luxuries of space and privacy.

SLEEPING QUARTERS Launched in 1954, the *Nautilus* was the world's first nuclear-powered submarine. In contrast with the cramped crew's quarters on the lower deck, with their three-tiered bunks, the officers' quarters on the upper deck, has a single bed and a table.

THE AGE OF NELSON

THE FIGURE OF HORATIO NELSON, Britain's greatest admiral, dominates the period of the French Revolutionary and Napoleonic Wars. Nelson embodied the principles that had been instilled into the Royal Navy by its best admirals over previous generations: attack at all costs, seizing the initiative, and pursuing decisive victory. But he carried these principles to unsurpassed extremes. Building on the new tactics pioneered by Admiral Sir George Rodney at Les Saintes in 1782, Nelson set out to break the enemy line and create a "pell-mell" battle in which superior gunnery would carry the day and the enemy would be as far as possible annihilated. His two greatest victories, at the Nile and Trafalgar – the battle in which he died – not only contributed to the eventual defeat of France but ensured British domination of the world's oceans for the rest of the 19th century.

Glorious First of June
The French flagship *Montagne* (right) and the British flagship *Queen Charlotte* (left) are locked in a fierce gunnery duel. The battle, fought far out in the Atlantic in 1794, ended in a notable British victory. A British boat is shown picking up survivors from French ships.

Britain's greatest national hero
Horatio Nelson's personal bravery and bold, innovative tactics had already made a him a legend in his lifetime. Death in his hour of victory at Trafalgar ensured the legend would never become tarnished.

NELSON

NAVIES UNDER STRAIN

Between 1793 and 1815 Britain's Royal Navy was almost continuously at war, fighting not only the French but, at various times, the Spanish, Dutch, Danes, and Americans as well. The triumph of British sea power in this long period of conflict was in no sense predictable or easily gained. The Royal Navy frequently fought against numerically equal or superior enemy forces. If the British were widely recognized as best at gunnery, the French generally had better ships, and the Spanish bigger ones.

The British were greatly aided by the impact of the French Revolution of 1789 upon their most dangerous opponent. The French navy never fully recovered from the chaos of the revolutionary period, when mutinies were commonplace and many experienced naval commanders were lost, either fleeing into exile or persecuted as counter-revolutionaries. Yet the British navy was also operating under great strain. The authorities' fear of revolution made issues of discipline on board ship acute. Simmering discontent spilled over into large-scale fleet mutinies at Spithead and the Nore in 1797. The lack of shore leave – denied for fear of desertion – the unfair allocation of prize money, poor food and pay, and excessive punishments were the mutineers' main grievances. To the relief of the British government the mutinies were suppressed through punishment and concessions, and never recurred on a similar scale. Yet the sheer extent and duration of the conflict threatened traditional systems of recruitment and discipline. Britain's policy of permanent blockade of French ports meant sailors remained at sea for unprecedented periods of time. The pressing of men into

service, usually a workable system of conscription, became oppressive because of the massive demand for crew. Too many landsmen, including convicts, were recruited.

DISCIPLINE AND INITIATIVE

The Royal Navy overcame its problems, largely through finding the right leadership at the right time. Admiral Sir John Jervis – ennobled as Earl St Vincent after his victory over the Spanish at Cape St Vincent in 1797 – was a major influence as commander of the Mediterranean and Channel fleets, then First Lord of the Admiralty. Jervis was a severe disciplinarian, but his insistence on daily gunnery practice, smartness, and cleanliness sharpened the navy considerably.

Royal Navy cutlass
This basic, utilitarian sword was what the British sailor usually had to rely on when boarding an enemy ship.

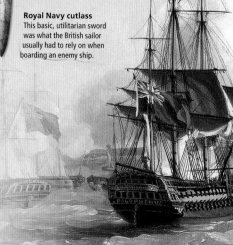

NAPOLEONIC EUROPE

While Napoleon's armies swept all before them in mainland Europe, the war at sea was a different matter. The Royal Navy blockaded the major ports such as Toulon and Brest, restricting trade and keeping the French from bringing their own naval forces out to do battle. On the few occasions they succeeded, they were defeated.

KEY

- French territory ruled directly from Paris 1812
- Dependent states 1812
- Britain and British occupied territories
- British naval blockade
- British victory
- British defeat
- Inconclusive battle
- Movement of British fleet
- Movement of French fleet

He was most demanding of his officers, believing that captains should lead by example to form well-drilled, motivated crews.

Nelson was in a sense a product of the Jervis school of leadership, forming his officers into a "band of brothers" who could be trusted to take the initiative in battle. Nelson himself sometimes went further, acting directly counter to orders. This regularly earned him official disapproval, but in general officers were rewarded for showing offensive spirit. Apart from decisive victories in battle, the Royal Navy's permanent blockade of the French ports was an astonishing feat of seamanship and organization. The French often fought well – their frigates were especially feared and admired – but they were up against a navy that was rising to an unprecedented dominance of the world's oceans.

Map labels:

North Sea
Dublin
SWEDEN
1801
Copenhagen 1801, 1807
Baltic Sea
Copenhagen
BRITAIN
DENMARK
Camperdown 1797 British defeat Dutch
Bristol
London
Hamburg
PRUSSIA
RUSSIAN EMPIRE
Portsmouth
Boulogne
Berlin
Warsaw
ATLANTIC OCEAN
Brussels
GRAND DUCHY OF WARSAW
Glorious First of June 1794
Brest
Lorient
Paris
CONFEDERATION OF THE RHINE
Belle Isle 1795
Basque Roads 1809
FRANCE
Vienna
Ferrol
Rochefort
HELVETIA
AUSTRIAN EMPIRE
Bay of Biscay
Genoa
PORTUGAL
Marseille
Toulon
Madrid
Barcelona
Iles d'Hyères 1795
Corsica
Black Sea
Lisbon
SPAIN
Balearic Islands
Rome
OTTOMAN EMPIRE
Cape St Vincent 1797
Minorca 1798–1800: to Britain
KINGDOM OF SARDINIA
Naples
Constantinople
Seville
Cádiz
Gibraltar to Britain
KINGDOM OF NAPLES
Trafalgar 1805
Algeciras Bay 1801
Mediterranean Sea
Palermo
MOROCCO
ALGIERS
Tunis
KINGDOM OF SICILY
Crete
Malta Jun 1798: occupied by Napoleon Sep 1800: French surrender after blockade; occupied by British
AFRICA
Jun 1798
Battle of the Nile 1798
Jun 1798
EGYPT
Alexandria
Cairo

0 km 200 400
0 miles 200 400
N

Battle of Copenhagen

In 1801 a fleet under Admiral Sir Hyde Parker with Nelson as his second-in-command was sent to Copenhagen to deal with the threat posed to Britain by the Russian-led League of Armed Neutrality. Nelson disobeyed Parker's orders, opening fire on the Danish fleet, sinking three ships and capturing 12.

FRENCH REVOLUTIONARY WARS

REVOLUTION IN 1789 PLUNGED France into a political crisis that led to the abolition of the French monarchy and war with most of Europe. The French navy suffered grievously in this upheaval, with most of its officers either resigning or dismissed and indiscipline rampant. At war with France from 1793, the British at first comfortably had the upper hand at sea. When the Spanish and Dutch became France's allies, however, British complacency was shattered. The threat of a French invasion of England was averted in 1797 by the defeat of the Spanish at Cape St Vincent, followed by the crushing of the Dutch at Camperdown. But in the same year as these triumphs, mutinies at Spithead and the Nore temporarily paralysed the Royal Navy, exposing the strain on morale in a long drawn out conflict. Evading a slack British blockade, the French were able to make landings in Ireland and Wales. Britain found its saviour in Admiral Horatio Nelson, whose stunning victory over a French fleet at the Nile in 1798 ruined General Napoleon Bonaparte's military expedition to Egypt and heralded a new era of British naval supremacy.

THE FIRST OF JUNE

FRENCH REVOLUTIONARY WARS	
THE FIRST OF JUNE	
Date	1 June 1794
Location	Atlantic Ocean, west of Ushant
Result	British victory
☞ **COMBATANTS** ☜	
BRITAIN	FRANCE
☞ **COMMANDERS** ☜	
Richard Howe	Louis Thomas Villaret de Joyeuse
☞ **FORCES** ☜	
Ships: 25	Ships: 26
☞ **LOSSES** ☜	
Men: 1,200 casualties Ships: none	Men: 4,000 casualties, 3,000 captured Ships: 7

On 17 May 1794 the French Atlantic Fleet commanded by Louis Thomas Villaret de Joyeuse sailed from Brest. Its mission was to ensure the safe arrival in France of a food convoy from the United States, desperately awaited by a hungry people. The Royal Navy's Channel Fleet under Lord Howe had been sent to intercept the food convoy, but Howe was more concerned with seizing an opportunity to engage the French navy. He sighted Villaret's ships on 25 May and gave chase.

On 28 May Howe caught up with the French rear, which was defended by the 110-gun *Révolutionnaire*. The next day a more substantial skirmish ended with damage to ships on both sides. Thick fog then interrupted the engagement, but 1 June dawned clear. Villaret could no longer evade battle.

Howe, holding the weather gage, adopted a bold and unconventional plan that envisaged the annihilation of the enemy fleet. Each of his ships was to pass individually through the French line and come up in the lee of an opponent. The French ships would be raked as their line was crossed, and then blocked from escape to leeward. Superior British gunnery would do the rest. But Howe's attack did not go to smoothly, for he apparently failed to persuade his captains to follow his plan. Only seven of his ships in fact crossed the French line, some making no attempt to do so. This was sufficient, however, to break up the French formation and ensure a brutal pell-mell battle. Howe's flagship *Queen Charlotte* passed behind Villaret's *Montagne* and simultaneously engaged the French flagship and the 90-gun *Jacobin*. *Brunswick*, captained by John Harvey, collided with *Vengeur du Peuple* and the two ships became entangled, firing broadsides hull-to-hull. Harvey was

Blunderbuss pistol
With its bell mouth ensuring a wide spread of shot at close range, the blunderbuss pistol was a perfect boarding weapon. This example has a spring-loaded bayonet, operated by the rear trigger.

CAMPERDOWN

Date 11 October 1797
Forces British: 16 ships of the line, 8 others; Dutch: 16 ships of the line, 9 others
Losses British: none; Dutch: 11 ships captured

Location Off Kamperduin, Netherlands

In 1795 the Dutch were driven into an alliance with revolutionary France. Britain responded by blockading the Dutch coast with a naval force under the command of Admiral Adam Duncan. In summer 1797 the difficult operation of maintaining a permanent close blockade was rendered almost impossible as mutinies spread through the Royal Navy, leaving Duncan with only two loyal ships under his command. Meanwhile the Dutch assembled a fleet off

Fouled anchor
This badge honouring the battle of Camperdown features a "fouled anchor" (wrapped in its chain), the traditional symbol of the British Admiralty.

the island of Texel; its purpose was to escort troops across the Noth Sea for an invasion of the British Isles.

Fortunately for the British nothing came of these plans. By October all thought of invasion had been abandoned for the year, but the Dutch government unwisely instructed Vice Admiral Jan Willem de Winter to stage a sortie from Texel. By this time order had been restored in the British fleet. Most of Duncan's ships were taking on supplies in Yarmouth when news arrived that the Dutch had come out. Duncan immediately set sail for the Dutch coast. He found de Winter around 9am on 11 October.

The Dutch sailed towards Texel in line ahead. Desperate to catch them before they reached the shallows off the Dutch coast, Duncan ordered a general pursuit. In two ragged groups, one led by Duncan in *Venerable* and the other by Vice-Admiral Richard Onslow in *Monarch*, the British bore down upon the Dutch line. Onslow's group engaged and broke the Dutch rear, but Duncan's had a

far tougher fight with the centre and van. *Venerable* was engaged by three Dutch ships and nearly overwhelmed. Duncan was saved by British ships sailing forward from the rear to help their hard-pressed colleagues – one captained by William Bligh, later to face mutiny on the *Bounty*.

1775–1831

JACK CRAWFORD

SAILOR HERO OF CAMPERDOWN

Born in Sunderland, northern England, Jack Crawford worked at sea from boyhood. In 1796 he was pressed into the Royal Navy to serve on board *Venerable*, the flagship of Admiral Adam Duncan. At Camperdown he distinguished himself when *Venerable* was surrounded by enemy ships, including the Dutch flagship *Vrijheid*, and the top of its main mast was shot off, bringing down the admiral's flag. It was imperative to restore the flag aloft, for a failure to do so would be taken as a signal of surrender. Under intense gunfire, at great risk to his life, Crawford climbed the broken mast under fire and nailed the flag to the top of the shattered stump. On his return home Crawford was awarded a silver medal by the people of Sunderland. He was later presented to King George III, who gave him a pension of £30 a year. He died of cholera in 1831.

Eventually, superior British gunnery prevailed. The Dutch were subdued after more than two hours' battering. De Winter was taken prisoner on his flagship *Vrijheid*, the surrender of his sword graciously refused by Duncan. The defeat ended Dutch pretensions to be a major naval power.

---

mortally wounded amid the general carnage, but lived long enough to force *Vengeur* to strike. There were many other examples of furious close combat.

Villaret exhibited excellent coolness and judgement. Despite his flagship having by far the worse of the exchange with *Queen Charlotte*, the French admiral succeeded in disengaging and reforming a diminished line to leeward. With a number of the British ships disabled, the French were allowed to escape with a clutch of shattered ships under tow. Howe concentrated on securing the seven French ships that had struck. *Vengeur* proved too badly holed to be saved, sinking with several hundred of its crew still aboard.

When the convoy reached France safely on 12 June, the revolutionary government hailed the naval operation as a triumph. Yet the British were surely justified in celebrating the First of June. Fighting an equal force, they had taken seven ships for the loss of none and inflicted three times the casualties they suffered.

Engagement off Ushant
The *Brunswick* (centre) is seen in action with the *Vengeur du Peuple* (right) and the *Achille*, left. The *Achille* has lost her masts, and the *Vengeur* is soon to sink having been holed beneath the waterline.

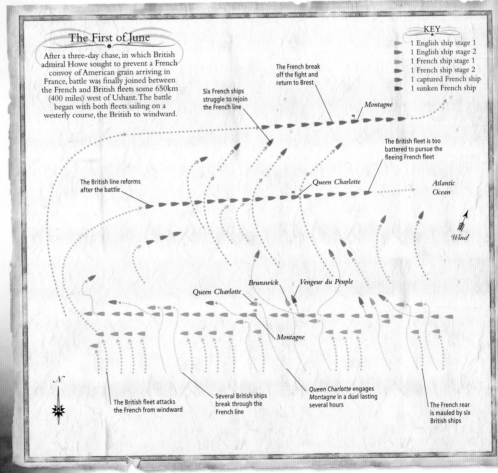

The First of June

After a three-day chase, in which British admiral Howe sought to prevent a French convoy of American grain arriving in France, battle was finally joined between the French and British fleets some 650km (400 miles) west of Ushant. The battle began with both fleets sailing on a westerly course, the British to windward.

KEY
- 1 English ship stage 1
- 1 English ship stage 2
- 1 French ship stage 1
- 1 French ship stage 2
- 1 captured French ship
- 1 sunken French ship

Six French ships struggle to rejoin the French line

The French break off the fight and return to Brest

Montagne

The British fleet is too battered to pursue the fleeing French fleet

The British line reforms after the battle

Atlantic Ocean

Queen Charlotte

Wind

Brunswick   *Vengeur du Peuple*

Queen Charlotte

Montagne

N

The British fleet attacks the French from windward

Several British ships break through the French line

Queen Charlotte engages *Montagne* in a duel lasting several hours

The French rear is mauled by six British ships

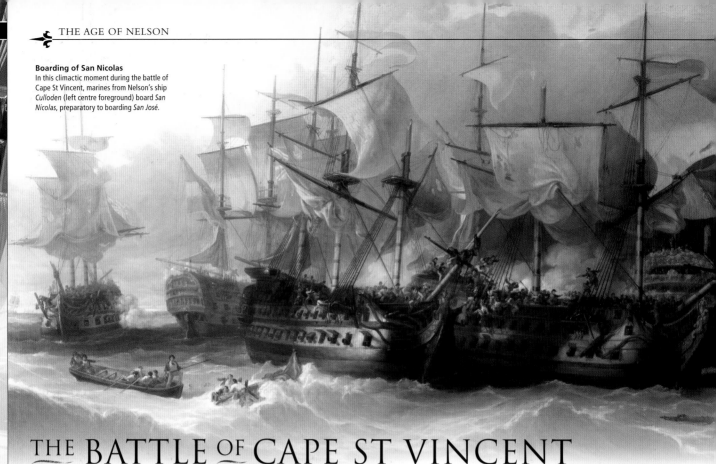

Boarding of San Nicolas
In this climactic moment during the battle of Cape St Vincent, marines from Nelson's ship *Culloden* (left centre foreground) board *San Nicolas*, preparatory to boarding *San José*.

THE BATTLE OF CAPE ST VINCENT

In early 1797 the Spanish fleet sailed from its Mediterranean harbour at Cartagena, aiming to join the French fleet in Brest. This would create a combined naval force powerful enough to cover a French invasion of Ireland. At the time, British admiral Sir John Jervis was stationed off Cape St Vincent to intercept the Spanish on their way north to France. Spanish admiral Don José de Córdoba intended to pause at Cadiz, but as he left the Mediterranean an easterly gale blew his fleet out into the Atlantic. When the wind permitted he turned his fleet back toward Cadiz on a course that brought him into sight of the British fleet early on the misty morning of 14 February.

THE DIE IS CAST

Jervis had 15 ships of the line, and when the count of Spanish ships sighted rose to 27 he reportedly said: "Enough of that; the die is cast and if there are 50 sail I will go through them." The Spanish, despite their large numerical advantage, had no desire to fight. Their ships were large but their crews included few experienced sailors. Jervis had ensured that his men were superbly trained and led by able captains keen for action. The British ships formed a line ahead and astern of Jervis's flagship *Victory*. With Captain Thomas Troubridge's *Culloden* in the lead, they sailed into a gap between two columns of the approaching Spanish fleet, firing broadsides as they passed through the enemy formation. Once they were beyond the rearmost Spanish ship they

tacked around in succession to pursue de Córdoba's fleet still keeping course for Cadiz. This manoeuvre was complicated by the intervention of ships from the Spanish column to leeward, which briefly attempted to break through the British line to join their colleagues to windward.

THE PATENT BRIDGE

Commodore Horatio Nelson had only joined Jervis's fleet the night before the battle, transferring from a frigate to Captain Ralph Miller's 74-gun *Captain*. He was near the rear of the British line. As his turn approached to tack in succession he instead ordered Miller to wear ship, reversing direction out of the line. This was contrary to orders, but a justifiable intiative, since Nelson could see that the Spanish were threatening to reassemble their split force and escape

to Cadiz. *Captain* boldly engaged the centre of the Spanish windward column, which included the 130-gun *Santisima Trinidad*, fighting alone until joined first by *Culloden* and then by Captain Cuthbert Collingwood's *Excellent*. At the climax of the battle the Spanish first-rate *San José* and the second-rate *San Nicolas*, both with shattered masts and corpse-strewn decks, became inextricably entangled. Although *Captain* was by this time uncontrollable, with its foretopmast over the side and wheel shot away, the ship's marines (and Nelson himself) boarded first *San Nicolas* and from there took *San José* – the dramatic double-boarding becoming known as "Nelson's patent bridge for boarding first rates". The slaughter ended with the ceremonious surrender of swords by Spanish officers.

Jervis's ships were in no fit shape to prevent the main part of the Spanish fleet reaching Cadiz. But four Spanish ships had been taken by a numerically inferior enemy and France's hopes of combining its naval forces with those of Spain were dashed. It was a fine victory that brought Jervis an earldom and Nelson a knighthood.

FRENCH REVOLUTIONARY WARS

BATTLE OF CAPE ST VINCENT

Date	14 February 1797
Location	Off the Algarve, southern Portugal
Result	British victory

COMBATANTS

BRITAIN	SPAIN

COMMANDERS

Sir John Jervis	Don José de Córdoba

FORCES

Ships: 15 ships of the line	Ships: 27 ships of the line

LOSSES

Men: 300 casualties	Men: c.1,000 casualties
Ships: none	Ships: 4 ships captured

Carronade
The carronade was a short smoothbore cannon used by the Royal Navy from the 1770s to the 1860s.

GRAPESHOT

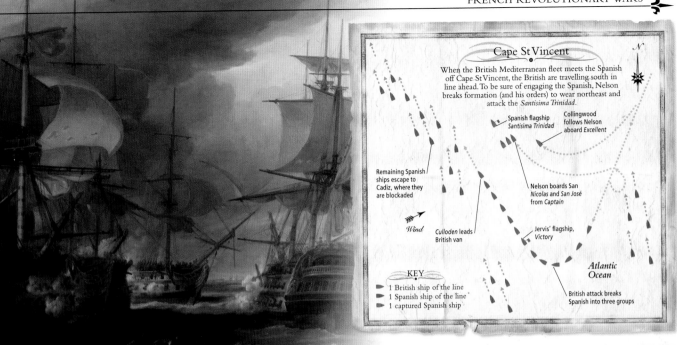

Cape St Vincent

When the British Mediterranean fleet meets the Spanish off Cape St Vincent, the British are travelling south in line ahead. To be sure of engaging the Spanish, Nelson breaks formation (and his orders) to wear northeast and attack the *Santisima Trinidad*.

Spanish flagship *Santisima Trinidad*

Collingwood follows Nelson aboard *Excellent*

Remaining Spanish ships escape to Cadiz, where they are blockaded

Nelson boards San *Nicolas* and San José from *Captain*

Jervis' flagship, *Victory*

Wind

Culloden leads British van

Atlantic Ocean

KEY
➤ 1 British ship of the line
➤ 1 Spanish ship of the line
➤ 1 captured Spanish ship

British attack breaks Spanish into three groups

MAN-OF-WAR TACTICS

BREAKING THE LINE

TACTICS IN THE AGE OF NELSON

The line of battle used by fleets in combat from the 17th century was intended to ensure that each ship came alongside an enemy for a broadside duel. By the late 18th century many British naval commanders had become convinced that breaking the enemy line offered better opportunities for a decisive victory. First used by Admiral George Rodney at the Saints in 1782, breaking the line was brought to perfection by Admiral Nelson at the battle of Trafalgar and Duncan at Camperdown. Although this tactic exposed the attacking ships to fire they could not return during the approach, they could rake enemy vessels from stem to stern as they passed through and also prevent enemy ships withdrawing by engaging them from the leeward side. The attacking fleet would hope to outnumber the ships in the sections of the enemy line that they attacked, while the rest of the enemy ships were left out of the fight. Nelson favoured breaking the line above all as a way of precipitating a "pell-mell" battle in which captains could use individual initiative to take on and destroy their opponents.

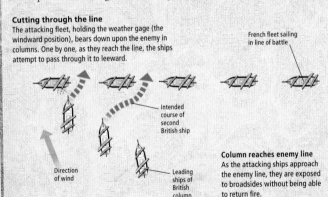

Cutting through the line
The attacking fleet, holding the weather gage (the windward position), bears down upon the enemy in columns. One by one, as they reach the line, the ships attempt to pass through it to leeward.

French fleet sailing in line of battle

Intended course of second British ship

Direction of wind

Leading ships of British column

Column reaches enemy line
As the attacking ships approach the enemy line, they are exposed to broadsides without being able to return fire.

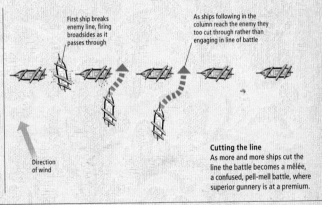

First ship breaks enemy line, firing broadsides as it passes through

As ships following in the column reach the enemy they too cut through rather than engaging in line of battle

Direction of wind

Cutting the line
As more and more ships cut the line the battle becomes a mêlée, a confused, pell-mell battle, where superior gunnery is at a premium.

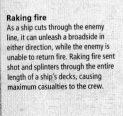

Raking fire
As a ship cuts through the enemy line, it can unleash a broadside in either direction, while the enemy is unable to return fire. Raking fire sent shot and splinters through the entire length of a ship's decks, causing maximum casualties to the crew.

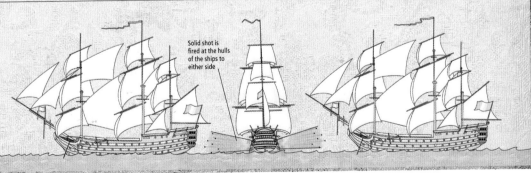

Solid shot is fired at the hulls of the ships to either side

THE BATTLE OF THE NILE

FRENCH REVOLUTIONARY WARS

THE BATTLE OF THE NILE

Date	1–2 August 1798
Location	Near Alexandria, Egypt
Result	British victory

⚓ COMBATANTS ⚓

BRITAIN	FRANCE

⚓ COMMANDERS ⚓

Horatio Nelson	François-Paul Brueys

⚓ FORCES ⚓

Ships: 14 ships of the line	**Ships:** 13 ships of the line, 4 frigates

⚓ LOSSES ⚓

Men: 800	**Men:** 2,000–5,000
Ships: none	**Ships:** 11 ships of the line, 2 frigates

The start of the action
The French fleet lies at anchor in Aboukir Bay at 6:30pm. The British fleet sails into position from right to left, *Goliath* rounding the head of the French line. Four French frigates lie to the left, with Aboukir Fort in the background.

On 19 May 1798, General Napoleon Bonaparte set sail from Toulon for Egypt, his army transports escorted by 13 ships of the line and four frigates commanded by Admiral François-Paul Brueys. Bonaparte was fortunate to avoid interception by a Royal Navy force under Admiral Horatio Nelson, which was vainly criss-crossing the Mediterranean in search of the French convoy. Bonaparte landed his army in Aboukir Bay at the start of July, and it was there, a month later, that Nelson at last came upon Brueys.

Nelson found the French ships anchored in line in the sandy bay with their port side to the shore. Although it was dusk he signalled an immediate attack. His captains were ordered to concentrate on the French van and centre; because of the wind direction, the ships at the French rear would find it impossible to join the fight and could be rolled up later. The British ships, all 74s except the 50-gun *Leander*, entered the bay with *Goliath* leading. Probably on his own initiative, Captain Thomas Foley took *Goliath* round the head of the French line and into the shallow inshore water; four others followed him. This was a manoeuvre for which the French were wholly unprepared. The gun ports on their landward sides were closed and the decks uncleared.

As darkness fell a savage fight was joined. Thirteen British ships (one, *Culloden*, having run aground on a reef) anchored to hold position alongside the French. The five 74s of the French van were battered by broadsides from both port and starboard. The larger ships in the centre of the French line, including Brueys's three-decker 120-gun flagship *L'Orient*, at first fared better. The *Bellerophon* took terrible punishment from the flagship's guns, drifting dismasted out of the fighting.

The horrors and heroism of that night were to become legendary. The captain of *Le Tonnant*, Dupetit-Thouars, with one arm and both legs shot away, had himself propped up in a barrel of bran to continue the fight. *Le Guerrier*, first in the French line, went on fighting with only one gun left firing, until the British sent a boat across to the shattered ship to persuade her captain to strike. Nelson, aboard his flagship *Vanguard*, had his forehead cut open by grapeshot and, temporarily blinded,

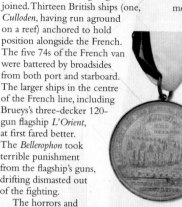

Nile victory medal
Dedicated to John Lewes of HMS *Defence*, this medal shows the British fleet going into action and the French fleet at anchor.

thought he was dying. The climactic moment came at around 10pm.

Battered by broadsides from *Alexander* and *Swiftsure*, *L'Orient* caught fire. When the flame spread to her magazine, she was destroyed by a gigantic explosion. The hundred survivors from *L'Orient* did not include Brueys or his flag captain Casabianca, whose son, refusing to leave the ship, would later be immortalized in verse as "the boy who stood on the burning deck".

The ships in the rear of the French line, under Villeneuve, were impotent spectators of this immense carnage. When the sun rose on a bay floating with dead bodies and wreckage, the futility of continuing resistance by the French was apparent. Villeneuve seized a chance to slip away, thereby saving two ships of the line and a couple of frigates, only to face unfair accusations of cowardice that he would seek to efface seven years later at the battle of Trafalgar. Nelson's phenomenal victory (nine French ships of the line taken, two destroyed) made him a national hero.

> ❝ THE WHOLE BAY WAS COVERED WITH DEAD BODIES, MANGLED, WOUNDED, AND SCORCHED, NOT A BIT OF CLOTHES ON THEM EXCEPT THEIR TROUSERS. ❞
>
> **JOHN NICOL**, A SAILOR ABOARD HMS *GOLIATH*

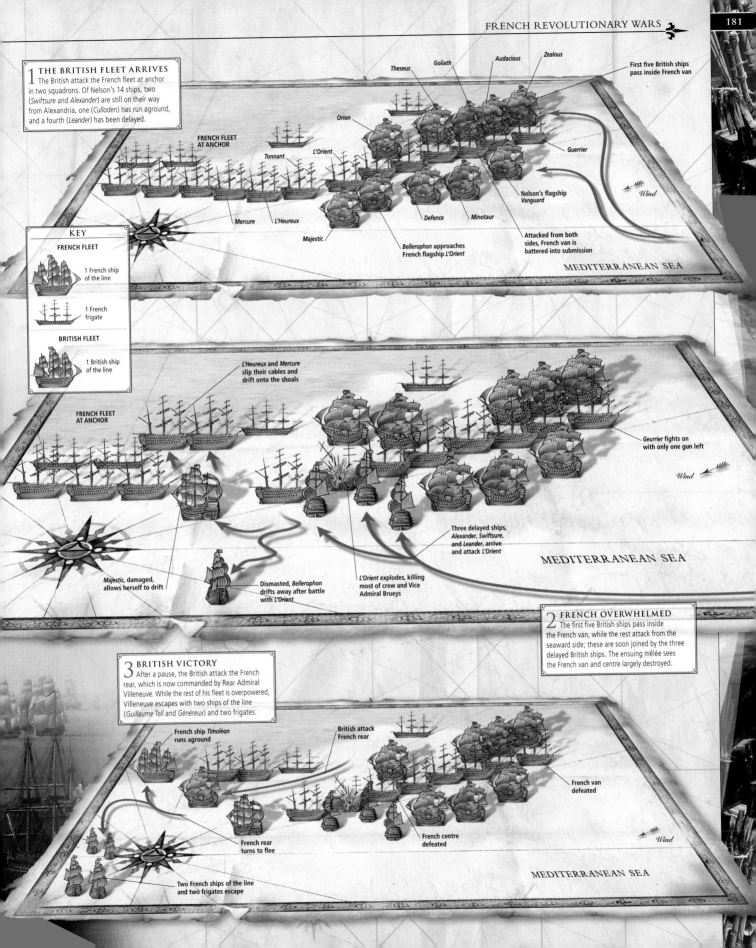

1 THE BRITISH FLEET ARRIVES
The British attack the French fleet at anchor in two squadrons. Of Nelson's 14 ships, two (*Swiftsure* and *Alexander*) are still on their way from Alexandria, one (*Culloden*) has run aground, and a fourth (*Leander*) has been delayed.

FRENCH FLEET AT ANCHOR

Theseus

Goliath

Audacious

Zealous

First five British ships pass inside French van

Orion

Tonnant

L'Orient

Guerrier

Mercure

L'Heureux

Majestic

Defence

Minotaur

Nelson's flagship *Vanguard*

Bellerophon approaches French flagship *L'Orient*

Attacked from both sides, French van is battered into submission

Wind

MEDITERRANEAN SEA

KEY

FRENCH FLEET

1 French ship of the line

1 French frigate

BRITISH FLEET

1 British ship of the line

FRENCH FLEET AT ANCHOR

L'Heureux and *Mercure* slip their cables and drift onto the shoals

Geurrier fights on with only one gun left

Wind

Majestic, damaged, allows herself to drift

Dismasted, *Bellerophon* drifts away after battle with *L'Orient*

L'Orient explodes, killing most of crew and Vice Admiral Brueys

Three delayed ships, *Alexander*, *Swiftsure*, and *Leander*, arrive and attack *L'Orient*

MEDITERRANEAN SEA

2 FRENCH OVERWHELMED
The first five British ships pass inside the French van, while the rest attack from the seaward side; these are soon joined by the three delayed British ships. The ensuing mêlée sees the French van and centre largely destroyed.

3 BRITISH VICTORY
After a pause, the British attack the French rear, which is now commanded by Rear Admiral Villeneuve. While the rest of his fleet is overpowered, Villeneuve escapes with two ships of the line (*Guillaume Tell* and *Généreux*) and two frigates.

French ship *Timoléon* runs aground

British attack French rear

French van defeated

French rear turns to flee

French centre defeated

Two French ships of the line and two frigates escape

Wind

MEDITERRANEAN SEA

DESTRUCTION OF L'ORIENT

The French warship *L'Orient* explodes during the battle of the Nile, on 19 May 1798, killing most of her crew. Both sides were so shocked by the explosion that firing ceased for several minutes. In the centre, the British warship *Swiftsure* is rocked by a wave caused by the blast, her sails billowing. In the foreground sailors cling to wreckage, while others are hauled from the water.

NAVAL CANNON

CANNON WERE FIRST used at sea in the 14th century, and evolved through wrought iron, cast bronze, and cast iron production methods. The very earliest of these were breech-loaders, but muzzle-loaders quickly took over and held sway for four centuries until the advent of shell-firing breech-loaders in the 19th century. Naval cannon varied enormously in terms of calibre and size, the largest being the "cannon royal" that fired a 66lb shot, down to smaller guns such as the culverin, which had a shot of around 17lb.

Rammer

Gun sponge

Damp sheepskin sponge for "swabbing" the barrel

Wooden stave

«| SALT BOX This held two ready powder charges stored side by side, and had leather straps and fittings to prevent sparks. Salt inside the box kept the charges dry.

⌃⌃ ROPE WADDING Coils of old rope were beaten into shape to make wadding. These were then used to hold powder and ball firmly in place in the barrel of the cannon.

Matches were lit at the start of battles and then placed in the match tub

Concave ramming head

Iron corkscrew to remove wadding

«| CASE OF WOOD These wooden cylinders were used for holding and carrying a single cartridge safely. As with gun carriages, elm was the preferred wood because of its anti-splinter properties.

⌃⌃ CARTRIDGE Fabric sheets were sewn into cylinders as containers for powder charges, each bag being filled with a precise amount of powder to suit a particular gun.

«| MATCH TUB This small wooden keg was used to hold slow matches, which were kept burning behind the gun, to ignite it if the gun lock failed in some way. Made from hemp, the matches were boiled in wine spirits and saltpetre solution, which caused the matches to burn slowly.

Vent for igniting the powder charge

GUN, SAIL, AND EMPIRE

GUN DRILL

Naval cannon were usually mounted on wheeled wooden carriages, allowing them to run backward under recoil. The backward motion was controlled by restraining ropes running around the breech or the carriage. The ropes were critical – a 32-pounder gun could fly up to 15m (50ft) across a deck if allowed to freewheel. Carriages were often made of elm, which produced less splinters than other woods if struck by an enemy shell. Despite such precautions, being a gunner was a dangerous job, with recoil and accidental explosions just two of the hazards.

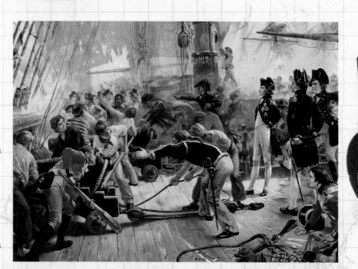

Wooden gun carriage, usually made from elm

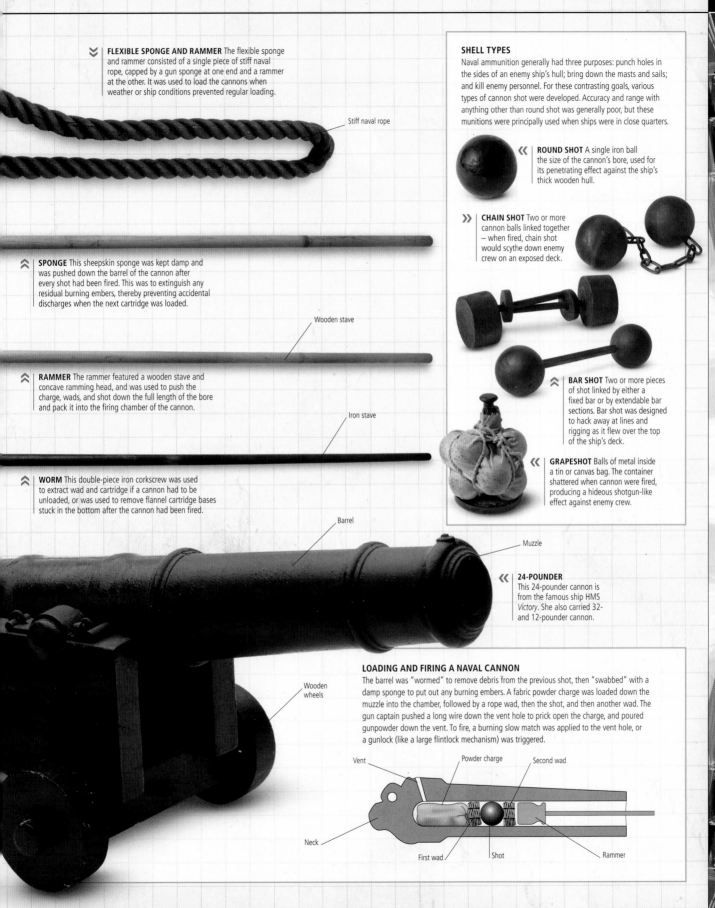

FLEXIBLE SPONGE AND RAMMER The flexible sponge and rammer consisted of a single piece of stiff naval rope, capped by a gun sponge at one end and a rammer at the other. It was used to load the cannons when weather or ship conditions prevented regular loading.

Stiff naval rope

SPONGE This sheepskin sponge was kept damp and was pushed down the barrel of the cannon after every shot had been fired. This was to extinguish any residual burning embers, thereby preventing accidental discharges when the next cartridge was loaded.

Wooden stave

RAMMER The rammer featured a wooden stave and concave ramming head, and was used to push the charge, wads, and shot down the full length of the bore and pack it into the firing chamber of the cannon.

Iron stave

WORM This double-piece iron corkscrew was used to extract wad and cartridge if a cannon had to be unloaded, or was used to remove flannel cartridge bases stuck in the bottom after the cannon had been fired.

Barrel

Muzzle

Wooden wheels

SHELL TYPES

Naval ammunition generally had three purposes: punch holes in the sides of an enemy ship's hull; bring down the masts and sails; and kill enemy personnel. For these contrasting goals, various types of cannon shot were developed. Accuracy and range with anything other than round shot was generally poor, but these munitions were principally used when ships were in close quarters.

ROUND SHOT A single iron ball the size of the cannon's bore, used for its penetrating effect against the ship's thick wooden hull.

CHAIN SHOT Two or more cannon balls linked together – when fired, chain shot would scythe down enemy crew on an exposed deck.

BAR SHOT Two or more pieces of shot linked by either a fixed bar or by extendable bar sections. Bar shot was designed to hack away at lines and rigging as it flew over the top of the ship's deck.

GRAPESHOT Balls of metal inside a tin or canvas bag. The container shattered when cannon were fired, producing a hideous shotgun-like effect against enemy crew.

24-POUNDER
This 24-pounder cannon is from the famous ship HMS Victory. She also carried 32- and 12-pounder cannon.

LOADING AND FIRING A NAVAL CANNON

The barrel was "wormed" to remove debris from the previous shot, then "swabbed" with a damp sponge to put out any burning embers. A fabric powder charge was loaded down the muzzle into the chamber, followed by a rope wad, then the shot, and then another wad. The gun captain pushed a long wire down the vent hole to prick open the charge, and poured gunpowder down the vent. To fire, a burning slow match was applied to the vent hole, or a gunlock (like a large flintlock mechanism) was triggered.

Vent · Powder charge · Second wad · Neck · First wad · Shot · Rammer

NAPOLEONIC WARS

RETURNING FROM HIS ILL-FATED expedition to Egypt, Napoleon made himself ruler of France as First Consul in 1799, and declared himself Emperor in 1804. He continued France's Revolutionary Wars, but with megalomanic ambition replacing ideological aspirations. Britain had no hope of resisting Napoleon's armies, which dominated in Europe, and was thus utterly dependent upon its naval strength. The French could not hope to contest this on their own, but could challenge in alliance with other naval powers. In 1800 the formation of an anti-British League of Armed Neutrality by the Scandinavian countries under Russian leadership threatened to block Britain's access to essential naval supplies from the Baltic. Decisive action by Nelson at Copenhagen successfully averted this threat. A greater peril for Britain arose when Napoleon assembled an invasion force on the Channel coast in 1805. Nelson's famous victory at Trafalgar both scotched the invasion plans and ended the naval war as a contest of fleets. Through the last decade of the Napoleonic Wars there were many notable smaller actions fought, but the Royal Navy's command of the sea was unshakeable.

THE BATTLE OF COPENHAGEN

Hoping to detach Denmark from the Russian-led League of Armed Neutrality, Britain assembled a fleet at Yarmouth in eastern England under Admiral Sir Hyde Parker, with Vice Admiral Nelson as second-in-command. Parker's orders were to see if the Danes would agree to abandon the league and, if not, open

Pocket telescope
Legend relates that Nelson lifted his telescope to his blind eye at Copenhagen, allowing him to ignore Admiral Parker's signal to withdraw. The story is almost certainly apocryphal.

hostilities. Once Denmark was overcome, he was to enter the Baltic and attack the Russians. Nelson was for speedy and decisive action; Parker prevaricated. Even he was aware, though, that the question of Denmark must be settled before the winter ice melted, releasing the Russian fleet from its ports.

On 30 March the British fleet sailed through the narrows between Sweden and Denmark to confront the Danish fleet in front of Copenhagen. The Danes took up a strong defensive position with

a line of ships and floating batteries anchored in the King's Channel in front of Copenhagen. The attackers would have to sail through shallow waters and past treacherous shoals, and would also come under fire from the powerful Trekroner shore battery at the northern end of the channel. This mission was entrusted to Nelson with 12 ships of the line – those with the shallowest draught – supported by frigates, sloops, and bomb-ketches. Nelson's plan was simple. His ships would sail in line and each would anchor opposite an opponent to blast it with broadsides. When enough of the Danish guns were

silenced, the bomb-ketches would move forward and threaten Copenhagen with mortars, obliging the Danes to cede.

"DOWNRIGHT FIGHTING"
The operation began on the morning of 2 April. Initially it was a disaster. Captain Hardy had spent the previous night in a rowing boat taking soundings of the channel, but to no avail. One of Nelson's ships of the line ran aground immediately and two more were stuck on the shoal known as the Middle Ground. Nelson pressed on regardless. His flagship *Elephant* and the other ships duly anchored a cable's length from their

ALGECIRAS BAY

Date 8–12 July 1801
Forces British: 7 ships of the line; French and Spanish: 8 ships of the line
Losses British: 1 ship captured; French and Spanish: 2 ships sunk, 1 ship captured

Location Off southern Spain

Admiral Charles-Alexandre Durand-Linois, bound for Cadiz with three ships of the line and a frigate, found the port under blockade by a superior British force. He moored in Algeciras Bay, under the protection of shore batteries. On 8 July British rear admiral Sir James Saumarez led six third-rates to attack the French, but lack of wind and tricky shoals made it difficult to engage. The British suffered damage from the shore guns and Spanish gunboats as well as Linois' broadsides. The 74-gun *Hannibal* ran aground at the northern end of the bay and stuck. After five punishing hours Saumarez withdrew to nearby Gibraltar, with his damaged flagship *Caesar* under tow, leaving *Hannibal* to be captured. While Linois refitted, one French and four Spanish ships of the line arrived to help him escape from the bay.

On 12 July Linois headed for Cadiz with Saumarez in pursuit. The British admiral had been joined by the 74-gun *Superb*. Fresh and undamaged, *Superb* pulled ahead and, during the night, got between two Spanish first-rates, firing broadsides against both. In the darkness the Spanish ships went on firing long after *Superb* had gone, pouring shot into one another. Both sank with heavy loss of life. One French ship was captured, but Captain Aimable Troude's *Formidable* distinguished itself by fighting off four British pursuers to reach Cadiz.

Volley gun
Multi-shot firearms such as this seven-barrelled volley gun, produced for the Royal Navy in 1795, allowed marines to fire several balls at once.

opponents and exchanged fire with the usual murderous results – "downright fighting" Nelson called it. The Danes fought courageously, reinforcing their ships from the shore as casualties rose.

Admiral Parker was meanwhile stationed to the north with eight ships of the line. Seeing Nelson's ships in trouble, he signalled for him to withdraw – apparently intending it as a permission rather than an order. Nelson chose to ignore the signal, though most likely without the theatrical gesture of placing a telescope to his blind eye.

Although the British ships took heavy punishment, their superior gunnery gradually overcame Danish resistance. By 2:30pm the firing had subsided, but the Danes had not surrendered. Nelson threatened to use fire ships; he also had his bomb-ketches in position to bombard the city. The Danes agreed to a general ceasefire on humanitarian grounds.

Subsequent negotiations were tricky, but eventually Denmark agreed to terms acceptable to the British. Nelson was made a viscount and went on to lead a demonstration against the Russians in the Baltic, but the League of Armed Neutrality was already disintegrating.

Close action
Nelson's ships are depicted anchored and in action against the Danish line. Bomb vessels behind the lines fire shells over both fleets towards Copenhagen.

> ❝ IT IS WARM WORK, AND THIS DAY MAY BE THE LAST TO ANY OF US AT A MOMENT. ❞
> **HORATIO NELSON**, AT THE BATTLE OF COPENHAGEN, 1801

THE BATTLE OF COPENHAGEN

Date	2 April 1801
Location	Copenhagen, Denmark
Result	British victory

COMBATANTS

BRITAIN	DENMARK

COMMANDERS

| Hyde Parker | Olfert Fischer |
| Horatio Nelson | |

FORCES

| **Ships:** 20 ships of the line, 5 frigates, 4 sloops, 7 bomb-ketches | **Ships:** 7 ships of the line, 28 other ships |

LOSSES

| **Men:** 264 | **Men:** c.790 |
| **Ships:** none | **Ships:** 2 sunk, 12 captured |

THE BATTLE OF TRAFALGAR

NAPOLEONIC WARS

THE BATTLE OF TRAFALGAR

Date	21 October 1805
Location	Off Cape Trafalgar, southern Spain
Result	British victory

☙ COMBATANTS ☙

BRITAIN	FRANCE AND SPAIN

☙ COMMANDERS ☙

Horatio Nelson	Pierre-Charles Villeneuve
	Federico Gravina

☙ FORCES ☙

Ships: 27 ships of the line	**Ships:** 33 ships of the line

☙ LOSSES ☙

Men: 449 killed, 1,246 wounded **Ships:** none	**Men:** 4,500 killed, 2,400 wounded, c.7,000 taken prisoner **Ships:** 1 sunk, 17 captured

In summer 1805 Emperor Napoleon was encamped with his Grande Armée at Boulogne, ready to invade Britain. He required the French navy and its Spanish allies to guarantee the non-intervention of the Royal Navy for sufficient days to get his army across the Channel. The French Mediterranean squadron under Vice Admiral Pierre-Charles Villeneuve succeeded in joining up with the Spanish under Admiral Federico Gravina, but failed to help France's Atlantic squadron escape the British blockade at Brest. Pessimistic about his chances of victory against the Royal Navy, Villeneuve took refuge with the Spanish at Cadiz. Napoleon abandoned his invasion plan. Furious with Villeneuve, he ordered another admiral take over his command.

Through September the British assembled a fleet off Cadiz. Admiral Nelson arrived to take command of this blockade force on 29 September. His frigates kept watch on the Spanish port while his ships of the line waited beyond sight of shore. Despite having an inferior force by any count of ships, guns, or men, Nelson planned a battle of annihilation. He intended to attack in two columns, cutting the French-Spanish line so the centre and rear squadrons were isolated from the van. His captains would then use their initiative to win a "pell-mell" battle.

Meanwhile, Villeneuve decided to sail before his replacement arrived, hoping to redeem his honour. On 19 October, with much delay and confusion, the 33 French and Spanish ships of the line began to leave Cadiz. The following day, they headed for Gibraltar with Nelson's ships in pursuit. After some confused manoeuvring, daybreak on 21 October found the two fleets near Cape Trafalgar. At around 7:30am Villeneuve ordered his fleet to wear together and turn back for Cadiz. He did not in fact intend to

> **❝ I WAS AWAKENED BY THE CHEERS OF THE CREW AND THEIR RUSHING TO GET A GLIMPSE OF THE HOSTILE FLEET. ❞**
>
> **BRITISH OFFICER,** DESCRIBING THE JOY OF ARRIVING AT TRAFALGAR

avoid a battle, but to fight closer to a friendly port. Nelson, however, was worried that his prey was going to escape him and so he urgently sought to engage the combined fleet.

Through the morning the British sorted themselves into two groups, one (to windward) led by Nelson on *Victory* and the other (to leeward) led by Vice Admiral Collingwood on the 100-gun *Royal Sovereign*. They bore down at a right-angle to the line of the combined fleet. It was a day of light wind and the British ships, painted with a yellow and black chequer pattern to distinguish them from the enemy, made slow progress.

As the fleets closed Nelson hoisted a series of signals, including the famous "England expects that every man will do his duty." Once the fighting finally started, the terrifying risks involved in Nelson's battle plan became plainly evident. Aiming to cross the line behind Villeneuve's flagship *Bucentaure* in the French-Spanish centre, *Victory* was under fire from enemy broadsides for

40 minutes during its agonizingly slow approach, able to reply only with its few forward guns. Collingwood's faster *Royal Sovereign* took less punishment approaching the enemy line but was then isolated, fighting five enemy ships at once while slower British ships came up to join her. Yet both flagships made excellent use of the opportunity presented by cutting the line. *Victory* raked *Bucentaure* with a devastating broadside through its stern that killed almost 200 men. *Royal Sovereign* did the same to *Santa Anna*, flagship of Spanish admiral Alava, causing some 400 casualties at a stroke.

As more British ships came up, the pell-mell battle Nelson had envisaged developed in the centre and rear of the French-Spanish line. In a series of savage close engagements the British used their superior gunnery to batter the French and Spanish ships, causing massive casualties and silencing their guns. The French and Spanish fired their cannon high to dismast British ships, which they then tried to board.

Santisima Trinidad surrenders
The Battle of Trafalgar at 3pm: on the left, with all her masts destroyed, the Spanish flagship *Santisima Trinidad* (painted orange) surrenders to *Neptune*. At the time she was the largest warship in the world.

1758–1805
HORATIO NELSON
BRITISH ADMIRAL

Although Nelson's father was an undistinguished Norfolk clergyman, the family had excellent connections in British naval administration. After going to sea at the age of 12, Nelson became the youngest captain in the Royal Navy in 1779 – aged just 20. He saw service in the Caribbean during the American Revolutionary War, but it was his performance during the French Revolutionary and Napoleonic Wars that brought him undying fame. Nelson was particularly recognized for employing the radical battle tactic of cutting through the enemy's lines, which although not entirely novel, had never been adopted to such successful effect. Always leading from the front, he lost the sight of his right eye in the siege of Calvi, Corsica, in 1793 and his right arm in a raid on Tenerife four years later.

BIRTH OF A LEGEND
He first won renown for his initiative at the battle of Cape St Vincent in 1797, and his stunning victory at the battle of the Nile in 1798 made him a national hero. Nelson's tendency to obey orders only when it suited him, displayed most famously at Copenhagen in 1801, was not to everyone's taste, and his very public liaison with Lady Emma Hamilton damaged his reputation, but he could always count on the loyalty and devoted admiration of the captains who served under him. After his death at Trafalgar, he was accorded a state funeral of unparalleled splendour.

Death of Nelson
Nelson dies below decks aboard HMS *Victory*, three hours after being mortally wounded by a French sniper.

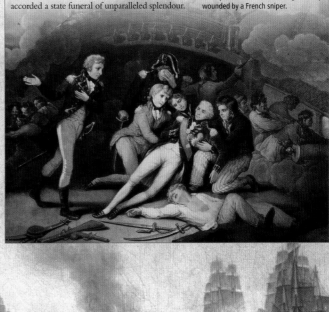

Men on both sides fought with the utmost courage amid the indescribable carnage of the battle.

In the attempt to cross the line, *Victory* became entangled with the 74-gun *Redoutable*, commanded by the able Captain Jean-Jacques Lucas. *Redoutable's* rigging was swarming with infantry armed with muskets and grenades, intent on clearing *Victory's* upper decks preparatory to boarding. At about 1:15pm a musket ball struck Nelson, who was standing in full view on the quarterdeck, overseeing the battle. It passed down through his shoulder and lodged alongside his spine. He was carried below, where he would die more than three hours later. *Victory* was saved from being taken by the arrival of the 98-gun *Temeraire*, which hit *Redoutable* with a broadside that killed or wounded 200 men. *Temeraire* then drifted into *Redoutable*, while disabling *Fougueux* with a broadside from its disengaged side. Both *Redoutable* and *Fougueux* struck to *Temeraire*. A similar pattern of hard-fought

Spanish shot
This iron cannonball was found embedded in *Victory's* bow. It was fired from a Spanish 40-pounder, the heaviest cannon used at Trafalgar.

combat and eventual surrender was being played out everywhere in the French-Spanish centre and rear. Some of the first British ships to engage took severe punishment. *Belleisle*, which followed *Royal Sovereign*, was engaged at different times by seven French and Spanish ships and left as a dismasted hulk with 126 men dead or wounded. The captain of *Mars*, George Duff, had his head struck off by a cannonball,

one of 300 casualties the ship suffered. But the French and Spanish were overwhelmed as fresh British ships came up. *Santa Anna* struck to *Royal Sovereign* after an engagement that also left Collingwood's flagship disabled. The Spanish giant *Santisima Trinidad* surrendered after losing all her masts. Although barely able to fight from the moment it was raked by *Victory*, *Bucentaure* held out for three hours before Villeneuve struck his colours. Amid the slaughter, the surrenders were conducted with dignity and exchange of compliments.

Meanwhile 10 ships in the French-Spanish van had been left out of the fight, as Nelson planned. By 2:30pm they had with difficulty manoeuvred back against the wind and were approaching the scene of combat. By then seven ships of the combined fleet had already surrendered, but the fighting had left many of the British ships in poor shape. If Dumanoir had

led a determined counterattack it might have turned the battle around. But after a half-hearted exchange of fire the French admiral fled southward with four ships. Two other ships from the van were captured by the British, while the rest were among a small band of survivors led by Spanish admiral Gravina back to Cadiz.

Before Nelson died *Victory's* captain was able to inform him that his final battle had been a triumphant success. Nelson's final words were: "Now I am satisfied. Thank God, I have done my duty." By the end of the day eight French and nine Spanish ships had been captured – more than half the entire fleet. One French ship, the *Achille*, had exploded. No British ships had been lost.

The victory won at the Battle of Trafalgar was a great one for the Royal Navy, establishing as it did a dominance over the world's oceans that would last virtually unchallenged for over a century.

Desperate fight
Marines and gun crews aboard *Victory* fight desperately as the ship is trapped between the French *Bucentaure* and *Redoutable* after crossing the Allied line. Shot by a French sniper on *Redoutable*, Nelson lies mortally wounded on the right.

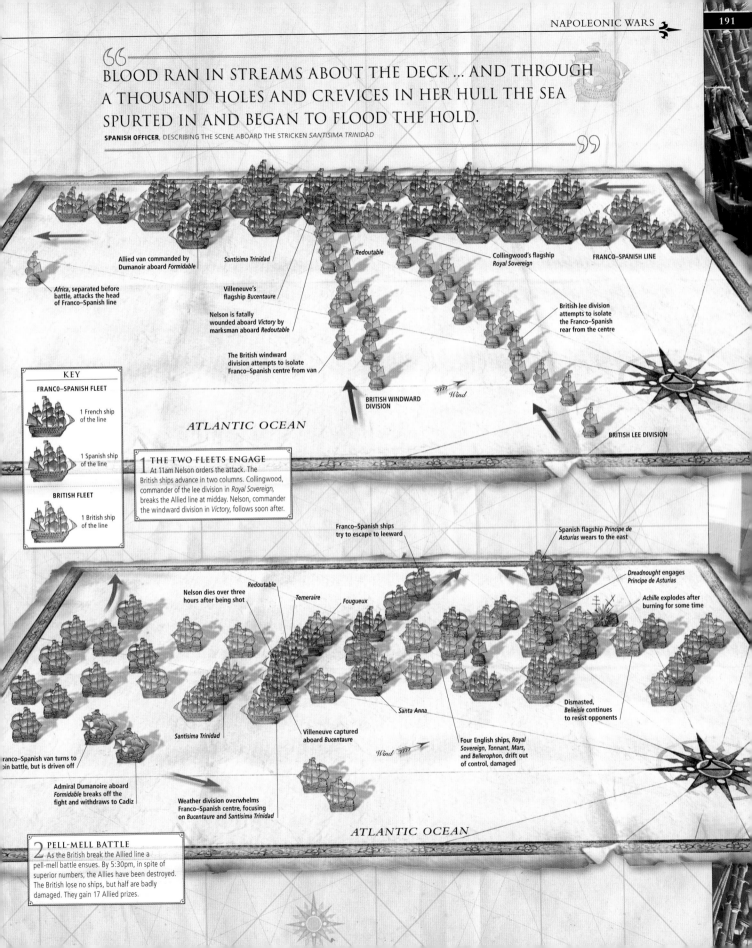

> **"** BLOOD RAN IN STREAMS ABOUT THE DECK ... AND THROUGH A THOUSAND HOLES AND CREVICES IN HER HULL THE SEA SPURTED IN AND BEGAN TO FLOOD THE HOLD. **"**
>
> **SPANISH OFFICER**, DESCRIBING THE SCENE ABOARD THE STRICKEN *SANTISIMA TRINIDAD*

Map 1 labels

Allied van commanded by Dumanoir aboard *Formidable*

Santisima Trinidad

Redoutable

Collingwood's flagship *Royal Sovereign*

FRANCO–SPANISH LINE

Africa, separated before battle, attacks the head of Franco–Spanish line

Villeneuve's flagship *Bucentaure*

Nelson is fatally wounded aboard *Victory* by marksman aboard *Redoutable*

British lee division attempts to isolate the Franco–Spanish rear from the centre

The British windward division attempts to isolate Franco–Spanish centre from van

BRITISH WINDWARD DIVISION

Wind

ATLANTIC OCEAN

BRITISH LEE DIVISION

KEY

FRANCO–SPANISH FLEET

1 French ship of the line

1 Spanish ship of the line

BRITISH FLEET

1 British ship of the line

1 THE TWO FLEETS ENGAGE
At 11am Nelson orders the attack. The British ships advance in two columns. Collingwood, commander of the lee division in *Royal Sovereign*, breaks the Allied line at midday. Nelson, commander the windward division in *Victory*, follows soon after.

Map 2 labels

Franco–Spanish ships try to escape to leeward

Spanish flagship *Principe de Asturias* wears to the east

Dreadnought engages *Principe de Asturias*

Nelson dies over three hours after being shot

Redoutable

Temeraire

Fougueux

Achille explodes after burning for some time

Franco–Spanish van turns to join battle, but is driven off

Santisima Trinidad

Santa Anna

Villeneuve captured aboard *Bucentaure*

Four English ships, *Royal Sovereign, Tonnant, Mars,* and *Bellerophon*, drift out of control, damaged

Dismasted, *Belleisle* continues to resist opponents

Admiral Dumanoire aboard *Formidable* breaks off the fight and withdraws to Cadiz

Weather division overwhelms Franco–Spanish centre, focusing on *Bucentaure* and *Santisima Trinidad*

Wind

ATLANTIC OCEAN

2 PELL-MELL BATTLE
As the British break the Allied line a pell-mell battle ensues. By 5:30pm, in spite of superior numbers, the Allies have been destroyed. The British lose no ships, but half are badly damaged. They gain 17 Allied prizes.

NAPOLEONIC WARS
SANTO DOMINGO

Date 6 February 1806
Forces British: 7 ships of the line, 2 frigates; French: 5 ships of the line, 2 frigates
Losses British: none; French: 2 ships wrecked, 3 captured

Location Off Santo Domingo, Dominican Republic

On 13 December 1805 the best part of the French fleet at Brest profited from bad weather to slip past the British close blockade. One squadron, commanded by Rear Admiral Leissegues on board the magnificent 130-gun *Impérial*, had orders to sail to Santo Domingo in the West Indies. A month later, Vice Admiral Duckworth, commanding the British squadron blockading Cadiz, learned that the French ships had been sighted heading for the Caribbean. He promptly set off across the Atlantic in pursuit. On 1 February 1806 Duckworth's squadron was taking on water at St Kitts when a sloop reported seeing French ships of the line at Santo Domingo.

At daybreak on 6 February the British squadron surprised Leissegues's ships at anchor in the Santo Domingo roads. The French had been making preparations to sail, and although many men were ashore, including Admiral Leissegues, the crews on board were able swiftly to weigh anchor and make a dash for the open sea.

French marine's sword
Short swords, such as this French example, were used by marines in close combat when boarding enemy vessels. Pistols were also carried.

Duckworth formed his ships into windward and leeward divisions and raced to bar the French escape. The three ships in the van of the windward line (*Superb*, *Northumberland,* and *Spencer*) made far better speed than the rest and engaged the French in a running battle. *Northumberland* in particular took heavy punishment from *Impérial's* thundering broadsides, before the rest of the British ships came up and overwhelmed the fierce and stubborn French resistance. Harried by *Superb* and *Canopus* (the latter captained by Francis Austen, the brother of the novelist Jane Austen), *Impérial* deliberately ran on to the shore, as did the 74-gun *Diomède*. The other three French ships of the line, *Alexandre, Jupiter,* and *Brave*, were all disabled and obliged to strike their colours. British casualties were 74 killed and 264 wounded; the French lost some 1,500 men. *Impérial* and *Diomède* were burned two days later to prevent them falling into British hands.

NAPOLEONIC WARS
COPENHAGEN

Date 2–5 September 1807
Forces British: 17 ships of the line, 21 frigates
Losses British: none; Danish: 18 ships of the line, 11 frigates surrendered

Location Copenhagen, Denmark

In July 1807 Britain feared that neutral Denmark was about to ally itself with Napoleon, giving France control of the Danish fleet and of the entrance to the Baltic Sea. Such a situation would be intolerable as it would prove ruinous to British trade and block the Royal Navy's access to two of its allies against France – Sweden and Russia. In response, on 26 July, a British fleet sailed from Yarmouth for Copenhagen under Admiral James Gambier aboard the 98-gun *Prince of Wales*. After the Danes refused to hand over their fleet to Britain for the duration of the war,

British troops landed and laid siege to Copenhagen, while the warships stayed out of range of shore batteries.

On the night of 2 September, Gambier began a bombardment of the city to intimidate the population into surrender. Newly introduced Congreve rockets were among the weapons used to rain destruction upon the Danes. An eyewitness in the city described how "bombs, grenades, fireballs … rockets and shells flew about our ears." The bombing continued for three nights, flattening a third of Copenhagen and killing thousands of civilians. Powerless to resist, the Danes surrendered both the city and their fleet. Denmark became an ally of France but the British took the Danish ships and were able to maintain access to the Baltic.

Trekroner fort
Part of the formidable coastal defences faced by Nelson in the Battle of Copenhagen in 1801, the Trekroner fort could do nothing to prevent the bombardment of 1807.

NAPOLEONIC WARS
BASQUE ROADS

Date 11–13 April 1809
Forces British: 11 ships of the line, 1 frigate; French: 11 ships of the line, 4 frigates
Losses British: none; French: 4 ships of the line, 1 frigate

Location Off Rochefort, Bay of Biscay

In February 1809 Admiral Jean-Baptiste Willaumez sailed from Brest with eight ships of the line, eluding the blockading squadron of Admiral James Gambier. Willaumez reached the Rochefort roads, where three more ships awaited him, but delays allowed Gambier to catch him up. Since the British admiral refused to risk his ships in the narrow channels of the roads, and Willaumez would not come out to fight, a stalemate ensued. The aggressive Captain Thomas Cochrane, agitating for more positive action, arranged for himself to be sent from Britain to join Gambier with a score of fireships – a move the admiral did not welcome. In the roads the French were prepared for a fireship attack, anchoring their ships in two lines between the islands of Aix and Oléron, behind

a defensive boom of spars and chains. Cochrane launched his attack on the night of 11 April. He packed four vessels with explosives and took them in first to blow holes in the boom. The explosions were so spectacular that they also destroyed French morale. In utter panic the French captains cut their cables and fled for the safety of the Charente River. In the darkness and confusion many ships collided and all but two of them ran aground. The fireship attack itself proved to be a damp squib, but morning broke to reveal French ships grounded at the mercy of British guns. But Gambier was in no hurry to enter the roads and proceeded with great caution. As a result, seven of the French ships were refloated and managed to escape upriver. Two ships of the line were destroyed by the British and two were scuttled by their crews.

NAPOLEONIC WARS
GRAND PORT

Date 23–24 August 1810
Forces British: 4 frigates; French: 5 frigates
Losses British: 2 ships destroyed, 2 captured; French: none

Location Grand Port, Mauritius

French frigates based on Mauritius were preying upon British merchant ships crossing the Indian Ocean. In response, in the summer of 1810 British frigates launched an attack on the island's east coast, capturing the Ile de la Passe at the entrance to the lagoon off Grand Port. On 20 August the French frigates *Bellone, Minerve,* and *Victor*, under the command of Commodore Guy-Victor

Duperré, arrived at Grand Port, unaware of the British presence, and broke through to the lagoon. Three days later, largely on the initiative of Nesbit Willoughby, captain of *Néréide*, the four British frigates sailed into the lagoon to engage the French at anchor. Two of the British ships, *Sirius* and *Magicienne*, quickly ran aground. *Néréide* was left exposed to the full force of the French broadsides. In a static encounter at close range the frigate was reduced to a shambles. Willoughby had an eye torn out of its socket by a splinter. More than 220 of *Néréide's* 280 crew were killed or wounded before she struck the following morning. The immovable *Magicienne* and *Sirius* were scuttled and the surviving British frigate, *Iphigenia*, was trapped by the arrival of two more French frigates as she made to escape. It was the only defeat of a British squadron during the Napoleonic Wars.

Flintlock swivel gun
This bowsprit swivel gun was mounted on the front of the ship to guard against boarders. It was loaded and fired in the same way as a musket or pistol.

NAVAL COMMUNICATION

BEFORE THE INTRODUCTION OF RADIO, visual signals were the prime means of fleet communication. Sailing-era navies chiefly relied upon flags, although these had many drawbacks. The admiral's flags could only be seen by ships close to him, and had to be passed on by others raising the same signal. Complex instructions could not be easily conveyed, and once in battle, smoke rendered flags invisible.

FLAG SYSTEMS

During the 17th-century Anglo-Dutch Wars, Britain's Royal Navy introduced a system using five large flags to convey 25 possible signals. The number of signals had grown to 45 by the 1690s, but there was no substantial progress until the mid-18th century, when the French introduced number flags. These allowed hundreds of different signals to be conveyed and were belatedly adopted by the Royal Navy in 1799, which was employing a telegraphic system of communication by the early 1800s. Flags representing letters, and also specific messages, permitted almost unlimited communication.

» **DISTRESS SIGNAL** Flare pistols were developed in World War I to be used by ships in distress.

Nelson's signal
Admiral Nelson signals "England expects every man to do his duty" aboard Victory before the battle of Trafalgar

» **CURRENT MERCANTILE CODES** In the International Code of Signals each flag stands for a letter as well as a message.

 **A** KEEP WELL CLEAR AT LOW SPEED

 B I AM CARRYING DANGEROUS GOODS

 C YES (AFFIRMATIVE)

 D I AM MANOEUVRING WITH DIFFICULTY

 E I AM DIRECTING MY COURSE TO STARBOARD

 F I AM DISABLED; COMMUNICATE WITH ME

 G I REQUIRE A PILOT

 H I HAVE A PILOT ON BOARD

 I I AM DIRECTING MY COURSE TO PORT

 J I AM FINE; KEEP CLEAR OF ME

 K I HAVE SOMETHING TO COMMUNICATE

 L YOU SHOULD STOP YOUR VESSEL

 M MY VESSEL IS STOPPED

N NO (NEGATIVE)

O MAN OVERBOARD

 P ALL PERSONS TO REPORT ON BOARD

 Q I REQUEST FREE PRATIQUE

 R NO MEANING

 S MY ENGINES ARE GOING FULL SPEED ASTERN

 T KEEP CLEAR OF ME

 U YOU ARE RUNNING INTO DANGER

 V I REQUIRE ASSISTANCE

 W I REQUIRE MEDICAL ASSISTANCE

 X STOP CARRYING OUT YOUR INTENTIONS

 Y I AM DRAGGING MY ANCHOR

 Z I REQUIRE A TUG

MORSE CODE

The code invented by American Samuel Morse in the 1840s allowed any letter to be represented by two symbols, for example a dot and a dash, in different combinations. Morse was adopted by navies using flashing signal lights for communication and then for wireless telegraphy at the end of the 19th century. The most famous Morse code message is SOS, adopted as an agreed international distress signal in 1908.

Dots and dashes
A "straight key" (below right) is used to transmit the code. The operator controls the timing of the dots and dashes.

1	.————
2	..———
3	...——
4	....—
5	.....
6	—....
7	——...
8	———..
9	————.
0	—————

A .—	J .———	S ...
B —...	K —.—	T —
C —.—.	L .—..	U ..—
D —..	M ——	V ...—
E .	N —.	W .——
F ..—.	O ———	X —..—
G ——.	P .——.	Y —.——
H	Q ——.—	Z ——..
I ..	R .—.	1 .————

» **PENNANTS** The tapered type of flag known as a pennant is used primarily to indicate numbers.

 1

2

3

 4

5

6

7

8

9

0

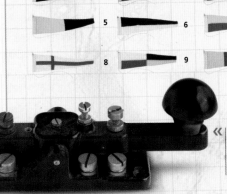

« **STRAIGHT KEY** When sending a message, the signal is "on" when the knob is pressed, and "off" when it is released.

HMS VICTORY

HER ROLE AS HORATIO NELSON'S FLAGSHIP at the battle of Trafalgar in 1805 made *Victory* the world's most famous first-rate ship of the line. Preserved as a museum ship at Portsmouth, England, she is now also the oldest commissioned naval vessel. *Victory* was a typical warship of its time, although one of the largest in the Royal Navy.

MORE THAN 6,000 trees, mostly oak, were felled for *Victory*'s construction. She cost £63,175 to build, probably equivalent to US $100 million today. This expensive ship was launched in 1765, but was not commissioned until war with France broke out in 1778. She saw her first action as the flagship of Admiral Keppel at the battle of Ushant in that year and was notably Admiral John Jervis's flagship at the battle of Cape St Vincent in 1797. By that time *Victory* was showing her age and was retired to serve as a hospital ship for prisoners of war. This decision was, however, soon reconsidered. After extensive repair and reconstruction, *Victory* was recommissioned as Nelson's flagship in 1803, remaining in active service until 1812.

Victory was operated by a crew of 850 men and mounted 104 smoothbore, muzzle–loading cannon (including four carronades). Even with solid shot, this was formidable firepower – for comparison, at the great battle of Austerlitz in the same year as Trafalgar, the entire French Army fielded 139 cannon.

Sailing for the Downs
HMS *Victory* sails past Dover on her way to the Downs. Sailors can be seen high in the rigging lowering topgallant sails, while lower down a course sail is unfurled on the mainmast.

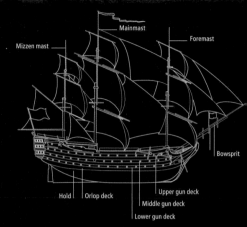

Mizzen mast · Mainmast · Foremast · Bowsprit · Hold · Orlop deck · Middle gun deck · Lower gun deck · Upper gun deck

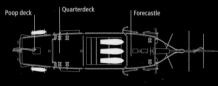

Poop deck · Quarterdeck · Forecastle

HMS Victory
Launched on 7 May 1765, *Victory* was a first-rate ship of the line with three gun decks. The decks were 57m (186ft) long and the ship was 16m (52ft) wide at its broadest point. The masts and spars supported a total of 37 sails.

⌃ Stern galleries
The rear of the ship housed the cabins of the admiral, the captain, and other senior officers. The stern of *Victory* was less decorated than earlier ships of her kind.

⟫ Figurehead
Victory's figurehead shows two cupids supporting the royal coat of arms (then featuring the escutcheon of Hanover) surmounted by a crown. The arms are surrounded by the motto of the Order of the Garter, "Honi soit qui mal y pense" ("Shame on he who thinks evil of it").

⌄ Ship's name
Nelson's flagship at Trafalgar was the sixth Royal Navy ship to bear the name *Victory*. The first was a 42-gun ship originally called *Great Christopher* and purchased by the Royal Navy in 1569.

VICTORY

66
THE DEAD LAY ALONG THE DECKS IN HEAPS ... MORE THAN FOUR HUNDRED HAD BEEN KILLED AND WOUNDED ... AN EXTRAORDINARY PROPORTION HAD LOST THEIR HEADS.

CAPTAIN JAMES ATCHERLY, DESCRIBING THE CARNAGE ABOARD *BUCENTAURE* AFTER HER ENGAGEMENT WITH *VICTORY* AT TRAFALGAR
99

Standing rigging
The ropes which hold the masts in place are known as standing rigging. Of these, "shrouds" are tied to the sides of the ship, forming a ladder up the masts.

Rigging
A total of 42km (26 miles) of rope (or "cordage") was used to rig *Victory*, along with 768 blocks, or pulleys. All sailors learned how to mend rope, which easily frayed at the ends.

Main mast
Victory's main mast reaches 67m (220ft) above sea level. Halfway up is a platform; this was used by musketeers in battle, and by the crew when access to sails was needed.

Running rigging
The ropes which raise, lower, and manipulate sails are known as running rigging.

Heavy anchor and gun ports
Victory had seven anchors, the heaviest weighing more than 4.5 tons. Raising the latter required the effort of 144 men turning two interlinked capstans. The anchor was hung above the upper gun deck.

Carronade
Victory had two carronades mounted on her forecastle. They were lethal at close range, as shown by their contribution to the mauling of the French ship *Bucentaure* at Trafalgar.

Skylight
A skylight (here covered) stood in the middle of the poop deck, allowing light to enter the great cabin below.

Double wheel and binnacle
Located under the poop deck, the double wheel was operated by four men in calm weather, and up to eight men in a storm. The binnacle in front of the wheel contains two compasses and a lantern for taking readings at night. The copper flue on top of the binnacle allowed smoke from the lantern to escape, keeping the binnacle clean.

Belfry
The bell in the belfry was rung every half hour. Two sandglasses kept the time, one lasting half an hour, one lasting four hours. Both were set at the beginning of each four-hour watch, at which the bell was rung eight times.

BELOW DECKS

AS WELL AS THREE GUN DECKS, *Victory* had, below the waterline, the orlop deck and the hold. To keep the ship stable, the heaviest guns were toward the bottom of the ship. There were 32-pounder guns on the lower gun deck, 24-pounders on the middle gun deck, and 12-pounders on the upper gun deck. The gun decks also provided living quarters for most of the crew, in airless, damp, and overcrowded conditions. The orlop deck was safe from enemy fire, and thus the chosen site for the powder magazines and the surgeon's operating room.

≫ Day cabin
The day cabin was the admiral's private study. It was here that he wrote letters and kept his most valuable personal effects

≫ Gun decks
The *Victory* had 88 guns arranged on its three gun decks, the lowest of which contained the heaviest Blomfield 32-pounder guns. Other lighter guns (including carronades) were arranged on the poop deck and the forecastle.

≫ Great cabin
Situated at the rear of the upper gun deck, the great cabin served as the admiral's quarters. The most comfortable part of the ship, it was divided into a day cabin, a dining cabin, and a bed space.

≫ Admiral's cot
The admiral and other high-ranking officers slept in box-like cots that hung from the deckhead. The cot also served as a coffin in the event of the officer's death.

≫ Capstan
Victory had two capstans, one for raising and lowering anchors, and another for lifting stores. Over a hundred men could be needed to haul in a cable, which wrapped around a drum on the deck beneath.

≫ Gun lock
On *Victory* flintlock mechanisms were used to fire the guns. Pulling the cord made the flint strike a spark, which ignited a primer, in turn igniting the main charge in the barrel.

≫ Marines' quarters
The middle gun deck was home to *Victory*'s 146 Royal Marines, who, like the sailors who occupied the other decks, all ate and slept between the guns. They were the ships soldiers, and were trusted to protect the ship's officers in the event of a mutiny.

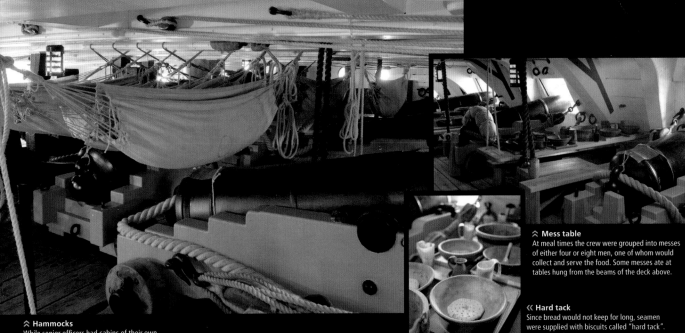

⌃ Hammocks
While senior officers had cabins of their own, most of the crew slept in hammocks which were no more than 71cm (28in) in width. They were slung above the guns on all three gun decks.

⌃ Mess table
At meal times the crew were grouped into messes of either four or eight men, one of whom would collect and serve the food. Some messes ate at tables hung from the beams of the deck above.

≪ Hard tack
Since bread would not keep for long, seamen were supplied with biscuits called "hard tack". They were often home to maggots.

⌄ Galley
The ship's galley, on the middle gun deck, had a cast-iron Brodie stove and a copper distiller that could produce 2 gallons (9 litres) of water a day. Its two copper kettles could produce 250 gallons (1,135 litres) of stew.

⌃ Bosun's storeroom
The boatswain (or bosun) was a warrant officer in charge of the ship's anchors, cordage, rigging, colours, boats, and deck crew. His storeroom contained all the stores necessary for the repair and upkeep of the ship, including plenty of spare rope.

⌃ Elm tree pumps
Two elm pumps located by the mainmast drew water up from the sea when it was needed for fighting fires and for washing down the decks. Two or three men manned the pump handle, while another caught the water in a bucket.

≫ Storage and ballast
The hold was the largest storage area of the ship and contained up to six months worth of food and drink. The floor was lined with 457 tons of ballast, which was needed to keep the ship level and upright. The ballast was made of iron ingots and shingle.

≫ Shot lockers
There were four shot lockers in the hold, each containing 80 tons of shot; a further 40 tons were stored near the grand magazine, also in the hold. At the battle of Trafalgar, *Victory* fired 2,667 rounds of shot, weighing a total of 27 tons.

⌃ Hanging magazines
Two hanging magazines were situated on the orlop deck above the hold. The 24lb gunpowder cartridges were kept towards the bow, the 12lb cartridges towards the stern. They were located beneath the waterline to protect them from enemy fire, and suspended from the deckhead to keep them from being damaged by water.

DISEASE, MEDICINE, AND SURGERY

THROUGHOUT MOST OF the history of naval warfare, disease took a far heavier toll on sailors' lives than actual combat. Until the 18th century there was little any navy could do about it, because medical knowledge remained too primitive. Gradually common-sense application of principles of hygiene and nutrition by good captains became systematized to good effect. Treatment of those injured in battle also remained a crude business until modern times.

MEDICINE A supply of medicines, ointments, and instruments was to hand in the sick berth on board a British ship like *Victory*. A larger lockable dispensary was situated on the orlop level where the surgeon, as a professional man, had his own cabin.

SICKLY SAILING SHIPS

Although conditions on board galleys were often unhygenic and overcrowding chronic, galleys stayed at sea for only short periods at one time. They suffered epidemics like any accumulation of men in pre-modern times – the Venetians lost 20,000 crew in their fleet, probably to typhoid fever, in June 1570. But once sailing ships started going to sea for long periods death rates regularly soared. It was common for ships on oceanic voyages to lose a third to a half of their crew to disease. A lengthy operation such as a blockade was virtually impossible because disease inevitably decimated the crews after a time. Large numbers of men were cooped up together in overcrowded conditions, in humid, unventilated spaces between decks, with food supplies short on freshness and variety. Scurvy was a typical sailor's disease. Typhus – often brought on board by recruits from jails – and tuberculosis were great killers, as was yellow fever in the tropics.

LEMONS
During the Napoleonic Wars the Royal Navy began to systematically carry citrus fruit on board ship to prevent scurvy, a disease caused by lack of vitamin C.

When a patient dies from a local injury, with the limb on, we are apt to blame ourselves … but it does not follow that the operation would have saved him.

Lancelot Haire, *Remarks on Mr Lucas's practical observations on amputations, 1786*

SHIPS' DOCTORS

Medical staff on ships were rarely properly trained. A barber surgeon on a sailing ship would be expected to deal in a rough-and-ready way with a steady stream of fractures and hernias gathered through the heavy and hazardous nature of the work on board, as well as venereal disease after a spell in port. His real challenge, of course, came in battle. Men who might survive mostly had limbs shattered by solid shot or gouge wounds caused by flying splinters of wood. Amputations were performed in two minutes, the limbs collected in a basket by the surgeon's assistant, the loblolly man. Speed was the most appreciated quality as there were no anaesthetics except alcohol. Surgery was performed below the waterline, if the ship was big enough to permit it, so as to be safe from shot. Wounds almost always became infected, but various primitive techniques ensured reasonable survival rates.

OPERATING TABLE The surgeon's operating theatre in HMS *Victory* was in the cockpit, an open area near his cabin, located on the orlop deck well below the waterline.

SURGEON'S TOURNIQUET The 19th-century Petit type of screw tourniquet (the strap is missing) was used to stem bleeding as patients waited for the surgeon to operate.

SURGEON'S SAW Tenon saws, such as this one, were used for amputation on British ships, since the stout blades were less likely to break. Amputation was a last resort, and speed and efficiency were required from a good surgeon.

MEDICAL PROFESSIONALS

In the 18th century health at sea increasingly became a subject of systematic inquiry and naval medicine was slowly professionalized. Theories of disease were still woefully inadequate – the fumes from smelly cheese were thought a serious health risk by the Royal Navy. But systematic studies by ships' surgeons such as James Lind, whose *Treatise on Scurvy* was published in 1753, encouraged action by captains and administrators to improve cleanliness and nutrition. The role of citrus fruit and fresh vegetables in preventing scurvy was known from at least the early 17th century, but organizing a general policy to eradicate the disease was a slow business. Still, by 1800 the British fleet blockading Brest could keep 24 ships at sea all through a summer without crippling death rates.

SURGEON'S INSTRUMENTS A typical naval surgeon's chest contained instruments for amputation, trephination, draining, dentistry, probing wounds, and bleeding, as well as copious bandages and cloth for tourniquets.

SUNRAY TREATMENT Submariners back from patrol in the 1950s take sunray treatment in the depot ship to compensate for their lack of exposure to daylight when on active duty. They wear goggles to protect their eyes.

SICK BERTH Located far away from living quarters to prevent the spread of disease, the sick berth on an 18th-century sailing ship was constructed out of canvas screens. During battle the screens were taken down and patients moved to the orlop level for safety.

> *I shall here only observe that the result of all my experiments was that oranges and lemons were the most effectual remedies for this distemper at sea.*
>
> **James Lind,** *A Treatise of the Scurvy,* 1753

HOSPITAL SHIP Wounded US marines lie in their bunks in close quarters aboard the USS *Bolivar* which transferred casualties in the course of its service during World War II.

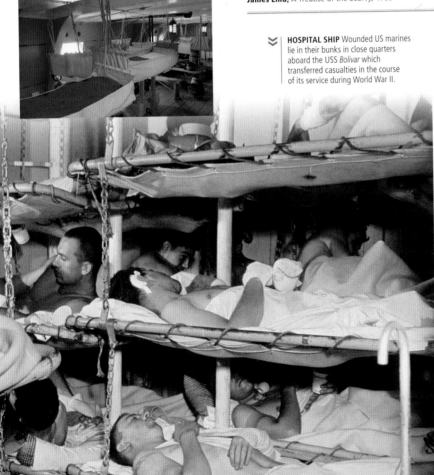

CUTTING THE DEATH RATE

The introduction of steamships was a boon. They were healthier above all because they cut voyage times. Food on board improved sharply through the 19th century, and water quality was ameliorated by storage in iron tanks. The general progress of medicine and provision of properly qualified medical staff reduced deaths from disease and wounds radically by the 20th century. The nature of wounds in battle altered, with the treatment of flash burns an unexpected problem for ships' medical staff in World War I. But as in the wider body of society, epidemic disease became a radically diminishing threat.

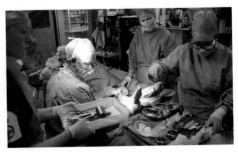

ONBOARD OPERATION Today, cooperation between navies means that an injured American sailor can be taken 480km (300 miles) to a British aircraft carrier where surgeons perform damage control surgery on his fractured ankle in an onboard operating theatre.

EARLY 19TH-CENTURY BATTLES

GUN, SAIL, AND EMPIRE

THE EARLY DECADES of the 19th century were the final years of the age of sail. Up to 1815 this was a time of major warfare – not only the Napoleonic Wars in Europe but also a stiff contest between the United States and Britain in the three-year 1812 War. After 1815, however, a period of comparative peace ensued, especially at sea. The position of superiority enjoyed by Britain's Royal Navy on the world's oceans was overwhelming and unchallenged. The French, still with the world's second largest navy, had neither the power nor the inclination to stop Britannia ruling the waves. The destruction of an Ottoman fleet at Navarino in 1827 was the last major fleet engagement of the 19th century, because a full-scale challenge to British hegemony was impossible.

The Battle of Navarino
The destruction of the Turkish-Egyptian fleet at Navarino by the French, British, and Russian allies was the last battle under sail. Here, an exploding Turkish frigate illuminates the approaching allied vessels. The 84-gun French ship *Breslau* (left) fires a broadside into the Turks.

FOUNDING A TRADITION

The United States founded a naval tradition by fits and starts in this period. Anti-militarist instincts, which had seen the Continental Navy disbanded after the Revolutionary War, were overcome in 1794 when Congress agreed to build six frigates, which were soon supported by more warships as threats to American merchant shipping began to mount. The US Navy saw action against France in the undeclared Quasi War of 1798 to 1800 (responding to French attacks on American merchant ships trading with France's enemy Britain) and against the Barbary pirates in the Mediterranean. War with Britain in 1812 was a challenge on a quite different scale. It gave the American heavy frigates a chance to show their fighting qualities in a series of successful duels with British warships, while American victories in lake battles played an important role in inhibiting British military operations inland.

Inevitably the power of the Royal Navy

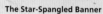

The Star-Spangled Banner
This is the original flag seen by Francis Scott Key flying over Fort McHenry during a British bombardment in 1814. The sight inspired him to write *The Star-Spangled Banner*.

ROYAL NAVY AT PEACE

The advent of peace with France and the United States in 1815 inevitably brought sharp cutbacks in Britain's war-swollen Royal Navy. By 1817 Royal Navy officers in active service stood at below a quarter of wartime numbers, and naval seamen at around a sixth of the full wartime complement. The number of British naval ships in commission fell from 713 in 1814 to 121 in 1818. This was still considered sufficient muscle for Britain to undertake the role of policeman of the oceans, in which capacity it attempted to impose a unilaterally declared ban on slave trading and took action to suppress piracy, most famously in the bombardment of Algiers, a nest of Barbary pirates, in 1816.

LIBERATION WARS

Much of the warfare in the aftermath of the Napoleonic Wars arose from the birth of national liberation movements that sought freedom from foreign rule. In South America, a series of wars was fought, firstly to establish independence from the colonial rule of Spain, and subsequently to define the frontiers of the new states. In Europe the Greeks fought a liberation war against the Ottoman Turks from 1821 to 1828. The independence movements could only assemble makeshift naval forces, placed under the command of imported officers such as the ubiquitous British admiral Thomas Cochrane, who served

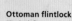

Ottoman flintlock
Flintlock firearms had rendered the matchlock obsolete by 1700. By the early 19th century they had reached a pinnacle of sophistication, as shown by this silver-inlaid Ottoman example.

predominated by the end of the conflict, but the United States emerged with a valuable stock of naval heroes, such as Stephen Decatur and Oliver Hazard Perry, and tales of derring-do to provide inspiration for the future. The US Navy remained a small force to the end of the age of sail – it never commissioned a ship of the line – but it had won acceptance as a necessary and respected institution.

in Chile, Brazil, and Greece. The fact that such improvised forces performed with considerable success in the independence wars was powerful evidence of the decline of those once-great naval powers, Spain and the Ottoman Empire. The weakness of Ottoman sea power had been exposed by a series of defeats at the hands of Russia in the late 18th century. This process of humiliation was completed at Navarino in 1827.

ON THE BRINK OF CHANGE

Navarino was still a battle from the age of sail. But the transition to a new era of naval warfare was already under way. The introduction of steam ships into warfare was slow because their usefulness was at first limited. In 1814 the United States had embarked on construction of the first steam-powered warship, *Demologos*, designed by the prolific inventor Robert Fulton, but it was only suitable for use as a floating gun battery in harbour. The British adopted steamships as tugs, initially only to tow sailing ships in and out of harbour, but later as armed support vessels for use in combat. By 1829 the Royal Navy had built eight armed paddle steamers. The steamship *Karteria*, built and manned by the British, saw

action with the Greeks in their independence war. Meanwhile, in 1824, French general Henri-Joseph Paixhans demonstrated the effectiveness of a naval gun firing explosive shells. Between them, steam power and the exploding shell would spell the end of the era of battle between wooden sailing ships. The latter would soon be replaced by ironclads.

Bombardment of Algiers
Dutch and British ships bombard Algiers in 1812, in an operation that broke the power of the Barbary pirates.

THE UNITED STATES AT WAR

DURING THE OPENING DECADES of the 19th century, the United States fought a major war against Britain and two lesser conflicts against the Barbary pirates. These wars had in common a concern to maintain the freedom of the seas. The Barbary pirates were the naval forces of rogue North African Muslim states that preyed upon shipping in the Mediterranean. The United States was one of the countries that paid protection money to these states until President Thomas Jefferson threw doubt upon the practice, provoking Tripoli to declare war on America in 1801. An American squadron fought Tripoli until a compromise was reached in 1805, but a second round in 1815 was required to finish off the pirate menace. The war with Britain was largely the result of the high-handed actions of the Royal Navy during the Napoleonic Wars. When the conflict began the United States had 17 warships to Britain's 719. The Americans distinguished themselves in battles on Lake Erie and Lake Champlain and in frigate actions at sea, although the Royal Navy was able to blockade the American coast, burn Washington, and bombard Baltimore.

FIRST BARBARY WAR

TRIPOLI HARBOUR

Date 3 August, 1804
Forces Americans: 1 frigate, 6 gunboats, 2 bomb-ketches; Libyans: 11 gunboats
Losses Americans: none; Libyans: 3 boats sunk, 3 captured

Location Tripoli harbour, Libya

In June 1803, Commodore Edward Preble was put in command of the squadron of ships sent by the United States to the Mediterranean to deal with the problem of piracy promoted by North African Barbary states. Where previous US naval commanders had concentrated on protecting American ships, Preble was determined to take the fight to the most obdurate of the pirate cities, Tripoli, which had declared war on the United States.

In the autumn an American frigate, *Philadelphia*, ran aground off Tripoli while in hot pursuit of two pirate ships. It was captured and taken into the harbour for use as a floating battery. On 16 February 1804 a young lieutenant, Stephen Decatur, took a raiding party into the harbour at night and stormed *Philadelphia*, setting it ablaze so that it could be of no further use to the enemy. This action, hailed by Lord Nelson as "the most bold and daring act of the age", made Decatur an American national hero.

On 3 August 1804, Preble launched his most determined assault on Tripoli. He sent Decatur, now a captain, with a small force of gunboats and bomb-ketches (borrowed from the Bourbon Kingdom of the Two Sicilies) to enter the shallow waters of the harbour, while the frigate *Constitution* bombarded Tripoli's shore batteries and castle at long range. In the event only three of Decatur's six gunboats succeeded in entering the harbour, where they were

Close-quarters fight
During the fight in Tripoli harbour, Decatur shot a Libyan in the back with a pistol, the spent ball lodging in the American captain's clothes.

met by 11 Tripolitan gunboats. Fierce hand-to-hand fighting developed as boats were boarded. Decatur was fortunate to escape with his life. The Libyans suffered by far the heavier losses, but no decisive advantage was gained and the blockade and occasional bombardment of the port continued.

An end to the conflict came in 1805 after US Marines were put ashore to threaten Tripoli by land. A compromise agreement saw the United States pay $60,000 for the release of all hostages.

1779–1820
STEPHEN DECATUR
AMERICAN NAVAL COMMANDER

Born in Maryland, Decatur became a naval midshipman in 1798. After his bold action in Tripoli Harbour in 1804 he was made a captain, the youngest ever in the US Navy. Commanding the frigate *United States*, he captured the British frigate *Macedonian* in October 1812. Three years later, as commodore of a squadron in the West Indies, he was overcome by a British force and taken prisoner. After the war he commanded the American Mediterranean squadron and secured a final peace treaty with the Barbary pirates. He was killed in a duel with Commodore James Barron.

WAR OF 1812

CONSTITUTION VS GUERRIERE

Date 19 August, 1812
Forces Americans: 1 frigate; British: 1 frigate
Losses Americans: none; British: 1 frigate

Location Off Halifax, Nova Scotia

Early in the Anglo-American war, on 2 August 1812, Captain Isaac Hull took the American heavy frigate *Constitution* out of Boston to harass British shipping around the Gulf of St Lawrence. Seventeen days later, sailing back southward, he ran into the smaller 38-gun British frigate *Guerriere*. With full confidence in British naval superiority, *Guerriere*'s captain, James Dacres, was happy to fight, even though *Constitution* mounted 52 guns and had 476 men on board to the British frigate's 280.

The *Guerriere* opened fire first, but her solid shot bounced off the *Constitution*'s live oak hull – earning the American frigate the nickname "Old Ironsides". When the two ships came to close action, *Guerriere*'s mizzen mast was quickly brought down, lying over the side of the ship. Partially out of control, the British frigate was raked by the American heavy guns and her deck

Victory medal
This medal, commemorating the battle, shows a starboard-quarter view of the *Guerriere* dismasted (left), and a port broadside view of the *Constitution* firing (right).

swept by grapeshot. The *Guerriere*'s fallen mizzen mast snagged on *Constitution* and the two ships tangled together but, despite their greater numbers, the Americans failed to board, driven back by British musket fire. Casualties were heavier on *Guerriere*'s decks, however, with Dacres among those wounded by American musketry.

When the ships eventually broke apart, *Guerriere* lost its other two masts and lay a defenceless hulk. Dacres struck to avoid further loss of life. The ship was too badly damaged to be saved and the Americans scuttled it the following morning.

Perry's victory
Commander Perry leaves his battered flagship *Lawrence* and crosses over to the *Niagara*, on board which he led the Americans to a remarkable and courageous victory.

THE BATTLE OF LAKE ERIE

In March 1813, 27-year-old Master Commandant Oliver Hazard Perry arrived on the southern coast of Lake Erie, charged with creating a squadron of warships to win control of the lake from the British. Building ships and procuring guns and crews was a difficult task in such a remote region, but by the end of July Perry had two 20-gun square-rigged brigs, *Lawrence* and *Niagara*, supported by smaller vessels. The British, based at Amherstburg, experienced the same difficulties in building, equipping, and manning a lake fleet. Royal Navy commander Robert Barclay, a one-armed veteran of Trafalgar, had two ships that could take on Perry's brigs, the 19-gun *Detroit* and the 15-gun *Queen Charlotte*.

AMERICAN VICTORY

On the morning of 10 September, the British came upon Perry's squadron in Put-in-Bay, in the lee of South Bass Island. Sailing out of the bay in line ahead, the Americans tacked for hours to gain the weather gage. Perry and Barclay both sought a conventional battle, in which each ship would place itself alongside an opponent of similar firepower and slug it out. However, for the Americans the approach went badly wrong. Perry placed his flagship *Lawrence* alongside Barclay's flagship *Detroit*, but Lieutenant Jesse Elliot on

the *Niagara* failed to engage *Queen Charlotte*. Thus Perry soon found himself occupied with both of the largest British ships. The carnage on board *Lawrence* after two hours' close fighting was horrendous, although the American carronades visited similar punishment upon the British. With most of his gun carriages shattered and more than half his crew casualties, Perry decided to shift his flag. He had himself rowed across to the still unengaged *Niagara*, standing upright in the boat through heavy fire, while *Lawrence* struck its colours.

The British cheered the American flagship's surrender, but their joy was shortlived. Perry re-entered the fight

Spyglass telescope
Retractable to a portable size, telescopes such as these were vital to the functioning of a warship. By 1813 they had impressive magnification.

with the fresh, undamaged *Niagara*. With most of his portside guns out of action, Barclay attempted to turn his ship to present the starboard broadside to the approaching American brig. For *Detroit* and *Queen Charlotte*, badly damaged and manned by mostly inexperienced crews now decimated by cannonfire, it was too complex a manoeuvre. The two ships ran into one another and became inextricably entangled. *Charlotte* had already lost her captain and first lieutenant; now Barclay was seriously wounded and his first lieutenant killed. Defenceless against *Niagara*'s broadsides, the two

ships struck. The smaller British vessels either followed suit or were pursued and captured attempting to slip away.

The battle gave the Americans undisputed control of Lake Erie, and made a hero of Commander Perry.

WAR OF 1812

BATTLE OF LAKE ERIE

Date	10 September 1813
Location	Lake Erie, Ohio
Result	American victory

⊂∾ COMBATANTS ∾⊃

UNITED STATES	BRITAIN

⊂∾ COMMANDERS ∾⊃

Oliver Hazard Perry	Robert Barclay

⊂∾ FORCES ∾⊃

Ships: 2 20-gun brigs, 7 other vessels	**Ships:** 2 ships, 2 brigs, 2 other vessels

⊂∾ LOSSES ∾⊃

Men: 27 dead, 96 wounded **Ships:** 1 brig damaged	**Men:** 41 killed, 306 captured, of which 93 wounded **Ships:** 6 captured

> ❝ THE DECK WAS IN A SHOCKING PREDICAMENT ... THE DEAD WERE STREWED IN EVERY DIRECTION ... IT WAS IMPOSSIBLE TO TAKE THE WOUNDED BELOW AS FAST AS THEY FELL. ❞
>
> **DAVID BUNNELL**, AMERICAN SAILOR, DESCRIBING THE SCENE ABOARD *LAWRENCE* IN HIS MEMOIRS

THE BATTLE OF LAKE CHAMPLAIN

In summer 1814 Sir George Prevost led a British army from Canada south into New York. He halted outside Plattsburgh, waiting to be joined by a naval force under Commodore George Downie. The British naval squadron appeared off Plattsburgh on the morning of 11 September, borne up the lake by a light northwesterly breeze. It was faced by a roughly comparable force of American vessels commanded by Master Commandant Thomas Macdonough.

Macdonough had his four main ships – his flagship *Saratoga*, the brig *Eagle*, the schooner *Ticonderoga,* and the sloop *Preble* – anchored in a line across Cumberland Bay. They lay between a shoal and a headland, with gunboats in support. Downie advanced to attack aboard the newly built 39-gun frigate *Confiance*, the most powerful ship in the battle. With him were the brig *Linnet* and two sloops, the *Chub* and the *Finch*, plus a dozen gunboats.

Saratoga and *Ticonderoga* were soon engaged in a ferocious exchange of broadsides in the centre of the line. Macdonough was temporarily disabled twice, once when a splintered boom struck him briefly unconscious, and a second time when the head of a decapitated sailor knocked him across the deck. Downie, less fortunate, was killed when struck by a long gun that had been blown off its carriage.

DESPERATE STRUGGLE

Meanwhile, at the south end of the line, *Finch* was crippled by broadsides from *Ticonderoga* and went aground on Crab Island, but on the American side *Preble* took a drubbing from British gunboats and drifted out of the battle. On the other flank fighting was no less fierce. The sloop *Chub* drifted dismasted into the American lines and was boarded, but in an encounter between the two brigs, *Eagle* and *Linnet*, the American *Eagle* came off worse. After two hours' fighting the fire began to slacken. Too many guns had been put out of action and too many men were dead or wounded. *Saratoga* was in poor shape, being raked by *Linnet* as well as facing what were left of *Confiance's* guns. But Macdonough would not accept defeat and summoned a last effort to gain the initiative. His starboard batteries, facing the British, were wrecked, but his port guns remained unused and largely intact. By hauling on cables his anchored frigate was turned about so its port broadside was brought to bear upon the *Confiance*. The British desperately strove to turn their own frigate but the exhausted remnants of the crew could not get the ship around. At the mercy of *Saratoga's* guns, *Confiance* struck, followed shortly by the battered *Linnet*.

The aftermath of the slaughter was handled with ceremonious dignity, the British officers handing their swords to Macdonough only to have them returned as a gesture of respect. As a result of the battle, Prevost abandoned his invasion of New York and the Americans were able to resist British claims to Lake Champlain and the Great Lakes in the peace negotiations.

WAR OF 1812

BATTLE OF LAKE CHAMPLAIN

Date	11 September 1814
Location	Cumberland Bay, Plattsburgh
Result	United States victory

COMBATANTS

UNITED STATES	BRITAIN

COMMANDERS

Thomas Macdonough	George Downie

FORCES

Ships: 1 frigate, 1 brig, 1 schooner, 1 sloop, 10 gunboats	**Ships:** 1 frigate, 1 brig, 2 sloops, 12 gunboats

LOSSES

Men: 52 killed, 58 wounded	**Men:** 84 killed, 110 wounded
Ships: none	**Ships:** 1 frigate, 1 brig, 2 sloops captured

Thomas Macdonough
This bronze medal, one of a series commemorating the War of 1812, features a bust of Thomas Macdonough, hero of the battle of Lake Champlain.

Battle of attrition
Commandant Macdonough's flagship *Saratoga* exchanges broadsides with HMS *Confiance* during fierce fighting on Lake Champlain. The battle was decided when *Saratoga* managed to bring her fresh portside guns against her exhausted opponent.

CONGREVE ROCKETS

The British discovered the effectiveness of rockets in war when the weapon was used against them by the army of Mysore in India in the late 18th century. Working at the Royal Arsenal at Woolwich, William Congreve developed the type that bears his name between 1801 and 1805. Propelled by black powder, Congreve rockets had a range of up to 3km (2 miles), although accuracy was poor and the warhead frequently exploded prematurely. The rockets could be fitted with a variety of warheads, including shrapnel and incendiary, ranging in size from 3 to 24 pounds. They were used by the Royal Navy in the Napoleonic Wars, notably at Copenhagen in 1807, and in the bombardment of Baltimore during the 1812 war with the United States – as immortalized in the line of the US national anthem, "And the rockets' red glare, the bombs bursting in air". Congreve's rockets were employed as anti-ship weapons during the First Opium War, fired by British gunboats to destroy Chinese junks.

Self-propelled missiles
The Congreve rocket was improved in 1815 with a guide stick fitted to the base of the rocket head, rather than along the side, reducing drag.

 WAR OF 1812

BOMBARDMENT OF BALTIMORE

Date 13–14 September 1814
Forces British: 19 ships; Americans: none
Losses British: none; Americans: none

Location Baltimore, Maryland

After capturing and burning Washington in August 1814, the British chose Baltimore as their next target. The city was a shipbuilding centre and the home port of privateers raiding British merchant shipping. The Americans had no naval force adequate to resist Vice Admiral Sir Alexander Cochrane's North American Station fleet, but the entrance to the harbour was covered by the guns of Fort McHenry and blocked by a line of sunken merchant ships.

The British put soldiers ashore to attack the city by land, but this force halted in the face of stiff resistance. At 6:30am on 13 September Cochrane began the naval attack. Anchored out of range of the fort's guns, four bomb vessels firing mortars kept up a sustained bombardment, while the rocket ship *Erebus* fired its Congreve rockets through a porthole from below deck. In the afternoon the ships shifted closer inshore and came under heavy fire from Fort McHenry. Cochrane eventually had *Erebus* towed back out of range. In foul weather the bombardment continued through the night, creating a spectacular pyrotechnic display, but to little practical effect.

At dawn Lieutenant Colonel George Armistead had a large stars-and-stripes flag raised over the fort, inspiring the lawyer and poet Francis Scott Key to write the verses that would become the American national anthem. The British gave up the attempt to take Baltimore.

LIEUTENANT COLONEL GEORGE ARMISTEAD
COMMANDER OF THE GARRISON AT FORT MCHENRY

BOMBARDMENT OF BALTIMORE

"One of the 24 pounders on the south-west bastion, under the immediate command of Capt. Nicholson, was dismounted by a shell, the **explosion from which … wounded several of his men**; the bustle produced in removing the wounded and remounting the gun, probably induced the enemy to suspect we were in a **state of confusion**, as he **brought in three bomb-ships** to what I believed to be good striking distance. I immediately **ordered a fire to be opened** … within half an hour those intruders again sheltered themselves by **withdrawing beyond our reach**. We gave three cheers and again ceased firing."

SECOND BARBARY WAR

ACTION OF 17 JUNE

Date 17 June 1815
Forces Americans: 3 frigates, 6 other ships; Algerians: 1 frigate
Losses Americans: none; Algerians: none

Location Western Mediterranean

In March 1815 the US Congress authorized the dispatch of a naval force to North Africa, where the Barbary pirates had resumed attacks on American shipping and the capture and ransom of American sailors. Commodore Stephan Decatur reached Gibraltar with a squadron of nine ships in mid-June. Hearing that Algerian raiders were at sea, he immediately set off and on 17 June had the good fortune to sight the *Meshuda*, the 46-gun flagship of the Algerian admiral Rais Hammidia. They gave chase as the Algerians raced for their home port, the 38-gun frigate USS *Constellation* leading the pursuit.

The *Constellation* succeeded in overhauling the *Meshuda* and her broadsides soon inflicted enough damage to convince Hammidia that Algiers was an impossibly distant refuge. The admiral turned his ship toward Spain, hoping to shelter in a neutral port. With the sloop *Ontario* joining the *Constitution*, however, Meshuda was soon closely engaged. Decatur then brought his flagship *Guerriere* alongside the Algerian ship and devastated it with point-blank broadsides. The Algerian admiral was killed but the crew fought on, inflicting casualties with musket fire from aloft. Finally the American sloop *Epervier* fired broadside after broadside into the Algerian ship, persuading the survivors to strike the colours.

Decatur sailed on to Algiers, whose bey soon accepted American terms, as did the rulers of Tripoli and Tunis. The following year, after the bombardment of Algiers by an Anglo-Dutch fleet, the privateering of the Barbary states was definitively brought to an end.

1550 – 1830

WARS OF INDEPENDENCE

AT THE START of the 19th century, South America was under the rule of Spain and Portugal. Between 1810 and 1826 a series of wars was fought that resulted in independence for these colonies, which then fought wars among themselves to define their new borders. Although the land campaigns of Simón Bolívar and José de San Martín played the leading part in the wars of independence against Spain, naval warfare also had a significant impact. The makeshift forces of the republican rebels performed remarkably well against the Spanish navy, but imported expertise was essential to their success. Maverick British admiral Thomas Cochrane became a hero of the independence struggle in Chile and Peru, while a previously undistinguished Irish sea captain, William Brown, earned legendary status in Argentina for his exploits both before and after independence. The battle of Lake Maracaibo was the final decisive victory in the struggle for the independence of Colombia, which briefly comprised also Venezuela and Ecuador. The Argentinian defeat at Monte Santiago was a key step toward the foundation of Uruguay as a separate country.

URUGUAYAN WAR OF INDEPENDENCE

MONTEVIDEO

Date 14–17 May 1814
Forces Argentinians: 10 ships; Spanish: 13 ships
Losses Argentinians: 1 ship sunk; Spanish: 2 ships sunk, 5 captured

Location Off Montevideo, Uruguay

In 1814 the Argentinians, engaged in an independence war against Spain, decided they needed a naval force to contest Spanish dominance at sea. William Brown, an Irish-born seaman who had recently settled in Argentina, was placed in command of the fledgling navy. He assembled a force of seven ships, taking as his flagship the frigate *Hercules*. The Argentine navy was blooded on 8 March in an attack upon Isla Martin Garcia, a Spanish stronghold in the mouth of the River Uruguay. Brown then established a blockade of Montevideo, his naval force augmented by three armed merchant ships. A Spanish squadron was in the harbour, protected by shore batteries. In mid-May, Brown pretended to lift the blockade, luring the Spanish ships into setting to sea, where he forced them to give battle. The fiercest engagement occurred on 16 May. Brown had his leg shattered by a cannonball, but his squadron got by far the better of the fight. As a result of this naval victory, Argentina was able to take control of Montevideo.

CHILEAN WAR OF INDEPENDENCE

VALDIVIA

Date 3–4 February 1820
Forces Chileans: 1 ship; Spanish: c.1600 men
Losses Chileans: 7 killed; Spanish: 100 killed

Location Corral Bay, Chile

In Chile's War of Independence against Spain, British admiral Sir Thomas Cochrane commanded the Chilean fleet in dashing style. He was convinced that the Spanish forces would crumble if subjected to unremitting aggression. Valdivia was the best defended Spanish stronghold in Chile – it had been compared to Gibraltar. Corral Bay, the approach to Valdivia from the sea, was protected by forts and other strongpoints mounting some 120 guns and manned by around 1,600 soldiers. Cochrane, with little over 300 men under his command and a leaky frigate *O'Higgins* as his sole effective warship, decided to take Valdivia by a nighttime amphibious assault. Achieving complete surprise, the Chileans landed in the darkness and attacked Fort Ingles, which was swiftly abandoned by its garrison. In the confusion Cochrane's men mingled with Spanish soldiers, compounding the problems of Spanish officers attempting to organize resistance. By the end of the night the four forts on the south side of the bay were in Cochrane's hands. Utterly demoralized, Valdivia itself surrendered shortly afterward.

Valdivian fort system
These extensive fortifications protected a port used by ships crossing the Straits of Magellan.

1775–1860

THOMAS COCHRANE

BRITISH COMMANDER OF THE CHILEAN FLEET IN THE CHILEAN WAR OF INDEPENDENCE

Serving in the Napoleonic Wars, Thomas Cochrane, Earl of Dundonald, made his name through bold exploits as a captain of sloops and frigates. His progress in his naval career was inhibited by his involvement in politics and criticism of corruption in high places. In 1814 he was disgraced for alleged involvement in stock market fraud. After a spell in prison, he sought employment abroad, serving in independence wars in Chile, Brazil, and Greece.

VENEZUELAN WAR OF INDEPENDENCE

LAKE MARACAIBO

Date 24 July 1823
Forces Colombians: 22 ships; Spanish: 32 ships
Losses Unknown

Location Lake Maracaibo, Venezuela

Despite the victories of Simón Bolívar, in 1823 the independence of Colombia was still contested by Spain. Spanish forces were holding the key town of Maracaibo, by the eponymous salt-water lake. Jose Prudencio Padilla, commander of a Colombian naval force comprising a corvette, three brigantines and a variety of small vessels, entered the lake from the Gulf of Venezuela to attack Maracaibo. Crossing the bar into the lake under the Spanish guns of Fort San Carlos, one of Padilla's ships was destroyed after running aground. The Spanish sent a squadron under Angel Laborde into the lake to pursue Padilla. On 24 July, in a fierce close-quarters mêlée fought more with machetes than with cannon, the Spanish were defeated despite superior numbers. Maracaibo was recaptured and Spanish forces in Colombia laid down their arms.

ARGENTINA-BRAZIL WAR

MONTE SANTIAGO

Date 7–8 April 1827
Forces Brazilians: c.14 ships; Argentinians: 4 ships
Losses Brazilians: none; Argentinians: 2 ships lost

Location Off coast of Argentina

In the war between Brazil and the United Provinces (Argentina and Uruguay) in 1825–28, the Argentinians had a naval squadron of small warships. Brazil had a far larger navy, but it was timidly led. Argentinian commander Admiral William Brown defeated a Brazilian river flotilla at Juncal in February 1827. The following April he took the brigs *Republic Argentina* and *Independencia*, plus a corvette and a schooner, out of his base at Los Pozos, evading a Brazilian blockade by hugging the coast (the Brazilian ships could not operate in the shallows). But Brown's two brigs ran aground. Captain James Norton, commanding the Brazilian blockade squadron, brought in four shallow-draught schooners and had a frigate towed into range to bombard the grounded ships. After a hard fight they were destroyed. Brown's other two ships escaped with heavy damage.

WEAPONS AND TECHNOLOGY

NAUTICAL INSTRUMENTS

BY THE 19TH CENTURY navigation at sea had reached a high level of accuracy. Previously, seamen had mostly kept within sight of shore, depending upon observation of the sun and stars for orientation. The introduction of the compass and of instruments such as the astrolabe by Chinese and Arab mariners in medieval times were major advances on which European navigators systematically built.

Early astrolabe Thirteenth-century navigators use an astrolabe in the Indian Ocean

TYPES OF INSTRUMENT

The compass was a difficult instrument to use at sea because of subtle and complex variations between readings of magnetic and true north. European mariners had made great progress in adjusting compass readings to true north by the end of the 16th century. The navigator's other prime instruments were devices such as the astrolabe, or the more advanced sextant for measuring the altitude of heavenly bodies such as the Pole Star or the Sun at noon. With the aid of astronomical almanacs this allowed him to calculate his latitude – how far his ship was north or south of the equator. It took until the mid-18th century for longitude to be calculated accurately.

The observer viewed the star through sights on the right-hand edge

A plumb bob hung from the centre of the arc

The plumb bob marked the angle of the star

Suspension ring

QUADRANT The quadrant was a primitive instrument for finding the altitude of stars, including the Sun. It was hard to use accurately on a rolling ship.

The index mirror is moved until the Sun appears on the horizon

Shade glasses

The telescope is pointed at the horizon

Horizon mirror

Shade glasses

The index bar moves the index mirror

Arc measures one-sixth of a circle

The *alidade* measures angle of the star

COMPASS The magnetic compass was in use in China from the 11th century. It needed skill and experience to use a compass accurately on oceanic voyages.

ASTROLABE The astrolabe was used by medieval astronomers to observe the stars. A simplified version was adopted by mariners.

SEXTANT Invented in the mid-18th century, the sextant was a great improvement over the astrolabe for measuring the altitude of the Sun.

1550 – 1830

MEASURING LONGITUDE

Until the 18th century calculations of longitude depended on dead-reckoning – the measurement of the ship's speed and direction of travel. This was often wildly inaccurate. A more precise calculation required the use of a clock that would keep accurate time at sea, but conventional timepieces could not cope with the movement of the ship. In response to a reward offered by the British government for solving this problem, clockmaker John Harrison produced a series of chronometers of increasing accuracy. His H4, tested on a voyage to the West Indies in 1761–62, allowed longitude to be calculated to within one nautical mile.

At a point in the mid-Atlantic the ship's navigator observes the height of the Sun to identify local noon. His chronometer tells him that at noon local time it is 2pm GMT. This means the ship must be 30° west, as for every hour, 15° longitude is travelled

Atlantic Ocean

Prime meridian

Greenwich

A ship leaves Lisbon and sails west into the Atlantic Ocean

Oscillating weights unaffected by rolling of ship

Marine chronometer This sea clock was built by John Harrison in 1730–35. It was designed to achieve accurate timekeeping at sea through a series of checks and balances.

Time in seconds
Time in hours
Time in minutes
Calendar dial

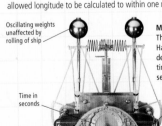

Sun passes through sky from east to west

90°

N

E

W

S

Ship's position

At local noon, Sun is highest in the sky and crosses imaginary north–south line

Lisbon

Calculating longitude To calculate their longitude, navigators carried a clock set to the time at a fixed location such as Greenwich. If the clock was accurate, the difference between the time shown by the clock and noon would correspond to the number of degrees they had sailed east or west of Greenwich.

LATER OTTOMAN BATTLES

THE OTTOMAN EMPIRE declined during the 18th and 19th centuries as it found itself unable to match the technological and organizational progress made by the European powers. Although still capable of defeating the similarly stagnant Venetians in the Mediterranean, the Turkish Navy had its weaknesses exposed during the wars with the expanding Russian Empire in 1768–74 and 1787–91. With the aid of foreign naval advisers, the Russians achieved a level of fighting efficiency and tactical flair far superior to that of the timidly led Ottoman fleet. Russian warships entered the Mediterranean for the first time to defeat the Turks at Chesma in 1770, and got the better of a series of engagements in the Black Sea, culminating in the victory at Tendra in 1790 – despite simultaneously fighting Sweden in the Baltic. The one-sided battle of Navarino in 1827, the last fleet engagement of the age of sail, completed the humiliation of the once proud Turkish navy. The Ottomans continued to spend heavily on warships – in 1875 they had the third largest navy in the world – but they never again fought a battle at sea.

⊡ RUSSO-TURKISH WAR

CHESMA

Date 5–7 July 1770
Forces Russians: 9 ships of the line; Ottomans: c.20 ships of the line
Losses Russians: 1 ship of the line; Ottomans: c.19 ships of the line

Location Near island of Chios, Aegean

After war broke out between Imperial Russia and Ottoman Turkey in 1768, two squadrons of Russian warships were sent from the Baltic Sea to the Mediterranean, under the command respectively of Admiral Grigory Spiridov and Rear Admiral John Elphinston, one of many British naval officers serving with the Russian navy. Count Alexsei Girgoryevich Orlov, an important figure at court, was given overall control of the naval force. His ultimate mission was to encourage a Greek revolt against Turkish rule.

On 5 July 1770 the two Russian squadrons found a Turkish fleet in Chesma Bay between the island of Chios and the Anatolian mainland. Lacking confidence in their seamanship, the Turks were anchored in two lines to form a floating battery, the ships in the second line positioned to fire through the gaps in the first. Although outnumbered, the Russian ships sailed in to attack. Spiridov's flagship *Yevstafy* closely engaged the Turkish flagship *Real Mustafa*, setting its mast on fire. Unfortunately for the Russians the blazing mast fell onto the *Yevstafy* and both ships were destroyed in the ensuing conflagration. Admiral Spiridov escaped, but more than 500 Russian sailors were killed.

After this engagement the Turkish fleet withdrew further into the bay, which was crowded with the ships of the line and a host of frigates, xebecs, galleys and other smaller craft. The Russian and British officers decided to attempt a night attack. A force of four ships of the line, two frigates, a bomb boat, and four fireships was put under the command of Scottish-born commodore Samuel Greig. The force advanced into the bay at around midnight while other ships targeted shore batteries and gave supporting fire.

Mortars of the bomb boat and the broadsides of the ships of the line soon took their toll and by the time the fireships were sent in,

Destruction of the Ottoman fleet
Turkish sailors abandon their burning ships during the Russian attack on the Ottoman fleet at Chesma.

several Turkish ships of the line were destroyed or on fire. Soon the bay was a mass of blazing ships, many set alight by explosions on board their neighbours. The entire Ottoman fleet at Chesma was destroyed except for one 60-gun ship and five galleys captured by the Russians. The battle left the Russian navy in command of the Aegean Sea.

GREEK WAR OF INDEPENDENCE

⊂∞ THE BATTLE OF NAVARINO ∞⊃

Date 20 October 1827
Location Off west coast of the Peloponnese
Result British, French, and Russian victory

⊂∞ COMBATANTS ∞⊃

BRITAIN, FRANCE, RUSSIA	**OTTOMAN EMPIRE, EGYPT**

⊂∞ COMMANDERS ∞⊃

Edward Codrington	**Ibrahim Pasha**

⊂∞ FORCES ∞⊃

Ships: 22 ships including 10 ships of the line	**Ships:** 78 ships including 3 ships of the line

⊂∞ LOSSES ∞⊃

Men: 181 **Ships:** none	**Men:** c.3,000 **Ships:** 70 ships

Victory for the Great Powers
British, French, and Russian ships attack the Ottoman-Egyptian fleet, anchored three-deep in a crescent formation at Navarino.

⊡ RUSSO-TURKISH WAR

TENDRA

Date 8–9 September 1790
Forces Russians: 10 ships of the line, 6 frigates; Ottomans: 14 ships of the line, 8 frigates
Losses Russians: none; Ottomans: 2 ships of the line

Location Off Tendra Island, Black Sea

During the Russo-Turkish War of 1787–91, Russia found an inspired naval commander in Rear Admiral Fyodor Fyodorovich Ushakov, who distinguished himself in victories at Fidonisi in 1788 and the Kerch Strait in July 1790. In September 1790 Ushakov surprised the Turkish fleet at anchor off Tendra Island in the Black Sea. He immediately attacked their rear, seizing the tactical initiative. The Ottomans had a clear numerical advantage, which Ushakov countered by including three frigates in his line of battle and positioning three other frigates alongside his ships in the van, to block any Turkish effort to double the line. The Russians had the better of the exchange of broadsides and the Turks, whose ships were copper-bottomed, used their superior speed to disengage. Ushakov pursued vigorously, inflicting significant damage on a number of the departing Turkish ships.

The following day Ushakov caught up with two ships of the line. One was easily captured but the other ship, the flagship of Admiral Said Bey, held out for hours despite being surrounded by Russian guns. The ship eventually caught fire and exploded before most of the 800 crew could be taken off. This victory, costing the Ottomans 1,400 casualties and 733 prisoners, gave the Russians command of the Black Sea which was confirmed by a victory at Kaliakria the following year.

THE BATTLE OF NAVARINO

In July 1827 Britain, France, and Russia signed the Treaty of London, agreeing joint action to end the war in Greece, where Greek nationalists were fighting for independence from the Ottomans. The British commander-in-chief in the Mediterranean, Sir Edward Codrington, was ordered to demand that both sides observe an immediate armistice.

In September an Egyptian fleet from Alexandria anchored in Navarino Bay, the principal Ottoman naval base in the Peloponnese. Nominally part of the Ottoman Empire, Egypt had achieved a notable degree of modernization under French influence and its navy was now superior to the Turkish fleet. Admiral Codrington blockaded the harbour and sought assurances that the Egyptian ships would not be used against the Greeks. Nonetheless the ships twice sortied out of the bay and had to be shepherded back into port by Codrington.

In October Codrington was joined by the French admiral Henri de Rigny and the Russian admiral Login Heyden, creating an allied force of 10 ships of the line plus a 60-gun frigate, de Rigny's flagship *Sirène*. Hoping to avoid a prolonged winter blockade, the admirals agreed on a bold plan of action: they would sail into the bay and anchor opposite the Ottoman-Egyptian fleet, whose commanders would be forced either to implement an armistice or have their fleet destroyed.

NO WAY BACK

At 2pm on 20 October Codrington's flagship *Asia* led two columns of British and French ships into the harbour, with the Russians following in the rear. It was on the face of it a desperately risky operation. The allied ships sailed between shore batteries to anchor in the middle of a horseshoe-shaped formation of Ottoman and Egyptian ships, with an onshore wind making any escape from the bay virtually impossible.

But the allied commanders' faith in the superiority of their guns and gunnery was well founded. *Asia* anchored with a band playing on deck, hoping the Ottomans and Egyptians would not put up resistance. In fact the fighting started almost immediately. Conducted at close range in a crowded harbour, the cannonade of the allied ships proved fearsomely effective. The

Smoothbore naval gun
Smoothbore naval guns remained in use until late in the 19th century. They were superseded by rifled breech-loaders.

Turks and Egyptians fought with courage and determination, but they lacked both adequate guns and training. Codrington's *Asia* took on the Ottoman flagship and an Egyptian 60-gun frigate simultaneously and shattered both. It was the same story elsewhere: three-quarters of the Ottoman and Egyptian ships were sunk by enemy gunfire or by their own crews, who set them on fire or blew them up to avoid

them falling into enemy hands. The news of the Ottoman defeat at Navarino was greeted with joy by the Greeks and with defiance by the Ottoman sultan, who declared a jihad against the infidel. This precipitated a war with Russia, which the Ottomans lost, and Greece eventually gained its independence. The battle is above all remembered as the last major naval encounter of the sailing ship era.

Navarino

At 2pm, 20 October, the allies entered Navarino Bay to help broker peace between the Greeks and the Turks. However, their approach was misunderstood as hostile activity by the anchored Ottoman-Egyptian fleet, which subsequently opened fire. By 6pm, the latter had all but been destroyed.

MOREA

Navarino Bay

The Ottoman-Eyptian fleet carries 2,000 guns, against the allies' 1,300

Sphacteria

Western flank guarded by allied frigates

Codrington's flagship *Asia*

Turkish flagship *Fahti Bahri*

Allies block enemy fireships and corvettes

Wind

Navarino

The allies enter the bay and anchor within the crescent of the Ottoman-Egyptian fleet

N

KEY
- 1 British ship of the line
- 1 French ship of the line
- 1 Russian ship of the line
- 1 allied frigate
- 1 Turkish ship of the line or frigate
- 1 Turkish corvette or smaller vessel
- 1 Turkish fireship

1550 – 1830

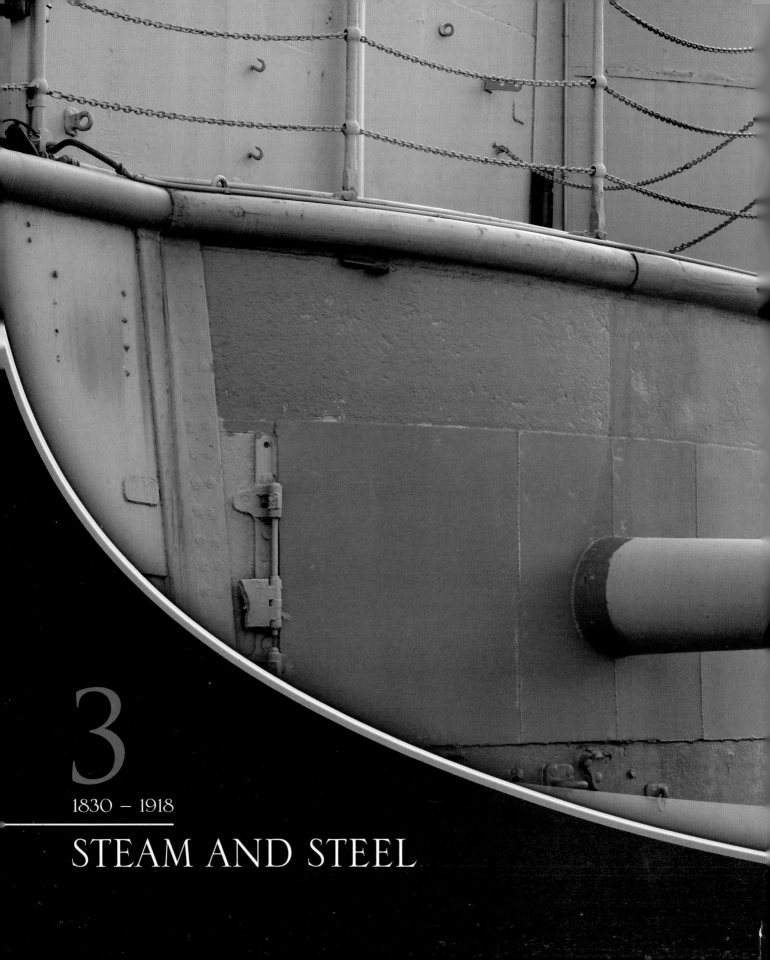

3

STEAM AND STEEL

I F ADMIRAL HORATIO NELSON had returned from the grave to view the navies of 1914, he would have been confronted by a startling technological metamorphosis. During a period of only occasional naval warfare, fragile wooden sailing ships with cannon firing broadsides of solid shot had been replaced by warships built of steel, powered by steam, and armed with huge turret-mounted rifled guns firing explosive shells. It was a transformation that had cost vast sums of money, reflecting the importance accorded to navies in a world of competing imperial powers – valued as much for prestige as for use in war. The outbreak of World War I in 1914 belatedly gave steam-and-steel warships a chance to show their paces in a global conflict.

Funnels and masts
Until the 1870s steam warships were built with masts and sails because of concerns about the unreliability of steam engines. These warships of the Argentinian navy are in action on the River Paraguay during the bloody War of the Triple Alliance (1864–70).

NEW SHIPS

The usefulness of a steam engine for making a vessel independent of the wind was obvious in the early 19th century, but the first steam boats were only suitable for rivers, lakes, and coastal waters. Steam gunboats were in use by the 1820s, but it was not until the 1860s that the new face of naval warfare began to emerge. The introduction of the first ocean-going steam warships – although fitted with sails as a supplementary form of propulsion – more or less coincided with the development of naval guns firing explosive shells and the use of iron cladding to protect wooden hulls from this augmented firepower. This revolution in warship design, which threw up many strange configurations and combinations, eventually settled down with the Royal Navy's *Devastation* of 1873, a screw-driven steamship with an iron hull, armour, no masts or sails, and guns mounted in turrets instead of broadside. *Devastation* set the style for

battleships, which replaced ships of the line as the fleet's capital ships. Frigates were supplanted by cruisers, designed for duties such as convoy escort and commerce raiding. The development of torpedoes led to the introduction of light torpedo boats and so of the torpedo-boat destroyer – soon shortened to "destroyer" – which defended larger ships against torpedo attack and served as a form of torpedo boat itself. When submarines emerged as submersible torpedo boats, the basic outline of a new kind of fleet was complete.

1850 British cannon
In the mid-19th century Royal Navy warships were still armed with muzzle-loading cannon firing solid shot and mounted on wooden carriages. Within 20 years such guns were obsolete.

SMARTENING UP

Crews changed as well as ships. The press-gang disappeared and was replaced either by the signing up of volunteers for long-term service, or short-term conscription as part of a wider system of universal military service. It became standard practice for navies to have uniforms for their men. The old idea of training officers and men through practical experience at sea from boyhood died out. The United States set up the Naval Academy at Annapolis in 1850; the Japanese established a cadet academy at Etajima; and even the tradition-bound British felt obliged to create a Royal Naval College at Dartmouth in the early 20th century. Special training ships came into use for ratings. Men were still taken on board at a young age and given a hard time, with lots of caning and flicking with ropes. In general, naval punishment remained harsh, although milder than in the 18th century. The German navy was atypical in still flogging its conscript ratings in 1914. But discipline in some ways became far more rigorous than before, with meticulous regard for details of personal appearance and the cleanliness and painting of ships. Harassment over such relatively minor matters, along with complaints over pay and conditions, caused occasional outbreaks of mutiny below decks. Officers in general tended to become more remote from the men than in Nelson's day. Victorian and Edwardian navies were acutely class-conscious and promotion from the ranks was virtually non-existent.

STEAMING TO WAR

Coal-fired engines meant a new breed of engineers and stokers appeared on board, keeping the machinery going in often difficult and unpleasant conditions deep inside the ship. Armour plating left even less chance for air or natural light below decks than previously, although the introduction of electricity was a boon. Fire was less of a hazard than on wooden ships and there were no falls from rigging. But there were disturbing losses of warships to explosions, a consequence of problems with coal stocks or boilers, or with the new propellants and high explosives that sometimes proved unstable. Taking on coal was back-breaking manual labour, and the need for it limited ships' tactical flexibility, requiring breaks from action to replenish fuel stocks from coaling ships or to put in at coaling stations. In war, engagements were fought at ever

Inspecting a torpedo
These British sailors are inspecting a self-propelled torpedo. Whether deployed on small torpedo boats or submarines, self-propelled torpedoes challenged the dominance of big-gun battleships.

increasing range but lost none of their savagery. New munitions produced new wounds, especially flash burns that proved a major source of casualties in World War I. Officers could no longer afford to stand exposed on an open deck swept by the blast of explosions and shards of steel. The old wooden ships had been hard to sink in battle, however much punishment they took, but a steel ship might go to the bottom in minutes, especially if a magazine was hit, taking most of the crew with her.

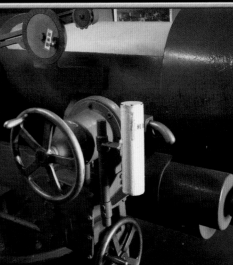

Civil war ironclads
The American Civil War was one of the first conflicts in which ironclad steamships went into battle. These Union gunboats and mortar boats are bombarding Confederate fortifications on the Mississippi.

Very pistol
Invented in 1877 by an American naval officer and ordnance expert, Edward Very, the Very pistol became the most common type of flare gun for signalling at sea.

GUNBOAT DIPLOMACY

Steam gunboats received their baptism of fire in a scattering of conflicts around the world from the 1820s to the 1860s – from the Opium War through the Crimean War to the American Civil War, which exhibited the strengths and limitations of their varieties. A complex relationship developed between the evolution of these steam warships and the rampant imperialism of the 19th century. These new technologies increased the ability of the European powers, later joined by the United States and Japan, to bully less developed nations into submission. "Sending in the gunboat" became the answer to most popular assertions of anti-imperialism. But steamships also necessitated imperial conquest, as the ships' frequent need for refuelling with coal required a global naval power to possess secure coaling stations around the world. Its later replacement with oil led Britain to put a high value upon controlling Iraqi oilfields during World War I.

RISING NAVAL POWERS

Growing rivalry between the imperialist powers gave the impetus to accelerating naval programmes from the late 19th century. Up to that point Britain enjoyed unparalleled maritime dominance, not only through the Royal Navy but also through the overwhelming size of its merchant fleet and the output of its shipyards. By the 1890s, however, Britain's naval pre-eminence was being increasingly contested, even though world t rade continued to be carried mostly in British ships. The influential writings of the American naval historian Alfred Mayer Mahan voiced a widespread view that a nation's global standing depended upon the strength of its navy. In an era of global competition, naval expansion became a popular cause promoted by jingoistic

1839
Start of First Opium War between Britain and China, an early instance of European "gunboat imperialism"

1843
Launch of *Great Britain*, first ocean-going screw-propelled ship

1855
French floating batteries bombard Kinburn; first ironclads used in battle

Case shot
This case or canister shot from the American Civil War, complete with small iron balls, was similar to grape shot.

1871
Launch of first mastless turret ship, HMS *Devastation*

1830 **1840** **1850** **1860** **1870**

Powder horn
This early 19th-century American powder horn was carried by marines and sailors for loading muskets and pistols.

1853
Start of Crimean War. First naval use of exploding shells at Sinope; race between shell and armour begins

1854
First strategic use of naval mines by Russians at Kronstadt

1859
France launches first seagoing ironclad warship *La Gloire*

1866
Battle of Lissa between Austria and Italy is first sea battle between armoured ships

nationalists, even in countries with no tradition of maintaining large fleets, such as the United States and Germany. Thus a global naval arms race gathered momentum. America and Japan in particular embarked on major naval construction programmes, followed by Germany. By 1914 the French had become the world's fifth-ranking naval power. The United States flexed the muscles of its new navy in a one-sided war with Spain in 1898, and then proudly sent the "Great White Fleet" around the world in 1907–09 in a pageant of American seapower. But it was the Russo-Japanese war of 1904–05 that provided the first thorough test of the new steam-and-steel navies. At the battle of Tsushima the Japanese were triumphant in a fleet encounter consciously inspired by Trafalgar, yet contested by ships capable of a speed of 16 knots with guns engaging effectively at a range of over 3 miles (5km).

BIG SHIPS AND SNEAKY DEVICES

Early 20th-century navies were involved in an arms race that led to every ship launched being bigger and more heavily armed than the last. The intense rivalry between Britain and Germany, in particular, triggered an astounding burst of naval construction, which proved one of the main causes for Britain entering World War I on the side of France.

The race started in 1906 when the Royal Navy's HMS *Dreadnought* set a new standard for battleships. However, the *Dreadnought* was soon surpassed by the oil-fired super-dreadnoughts, such as *Conqueror*, while cruisers put on weight to become battlecruisers, faster ships with more powerful guns. These mighty ships attracted huge public and press interest possibly in part because of the great expense involved in their

production. The main threats to these great ships – that naval commanders were well aware of – were mines and torpedoes. These were relatively cheap weapon systems against which ships had little protection.

When the long-awaited Great War came in 1914, the mighty fleets disappointed naval enthusiasts, avid for a repeat of the Battle of Trafalgar. Just as in the land war on the Western front, the new maritime technology favoured defensive tactics. The threatening presence of submarines and mines militated against the bold, aggressive use of large warships. Even when sailing with a defensive screen of destroyers, battleships and battlecruisers proved vulnerable to these devices. The Royal Navy's Grand Fleet spent much of the war out of U-boat range, only occasionally risking a foray

Super-dreadnought
The Royal Navy's *Queen Elizabeth* was an oil-fired battleship launched in 1913. With 15in guns and a top speed of 23 knots, she far surpassed the battleship *Dreadnought*, launched only seven years earlier.

into the North Sea. While the one full-scale encounter between the British and German fleets at Jutland in 1916 was indecisive, commerce raiding, in the form of U-boat attacks on merchant shipping, almost crippled Britain's war effort. By the end of World War I, with experiments in flying aircraft off ships becoming more successful and techniques of submarine and anti-submarine warfare becoming ever more sophisticated, a new profile of naval war was emerging that was no longer dependent on ships engaging with another at close quarters.

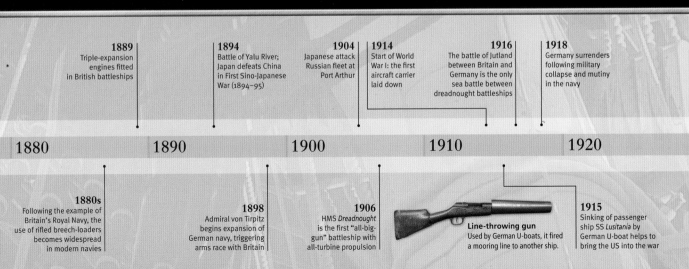

1889
Triple-expansion engines fitted in British battleships

1894
Battle of Yalu River; Japan defeats China in First Sino-Japanese War (1894–95)

1904
Japanese attack Russian fleet at Port Arthur

1914
Start of World War I: the first aircraft carrier laid down

1916
The battle of Jutland between Britain and Germany is the only sea battle between dreadnought battleships

1918
Germany surrenders following military collapse and mutiny in the navy

1880   1890   1900   1910   1920

1880s
Following the example of Britain's Royal Navy, the use of rifled breech-loaders becomes widespread in modern navies

1898
Admiral von Tirpitz begins expansion of German navy, triggering arms race with Britain

1906
HMS *Dreadnought* is the first "all-big-gun" battleship with all-turbine propulsion

Line-throwing gun
Used by German U-boats, it fired a mooring line to another ship.

1915
Sinking of passenger ship SS *Lusitania* by German U-boat helps to bring the US into the war

NEW NAVIES OF EUROPE

NAVIES PLAYED A MARGINAL ROLE in European warfare for most of the 19th century, and sea battles were few. In the Crimean War of 1854–56 sea power was essential in enabling Britain and France to install armies in the Black Sea, but the Russian navy refused to come out and fight. The battle of Lissa in 1866 was fascinating as a ramming combat between ironclads, but irrelevant to the outcome of the war between Austria and Italy. In the Franco-Prussian War of 1870–71 French naval superiority was impotent to offset the dominance of the Prussian army. Yet navies were central to European states' view of themselves as great powers and competition between nations provided the impetus for rapid innovation in warship design and naval armament. When new countries wanted to assert their status – Italy, unified in the 1860s, and Imperial Germany after 1871 – they inevitably built fleets.

Siege of Sevastopol
The largest naval operation in the early years of steam power was the Anglo-French expedition to the Black Sea in the Crimean War. Some 89 warships and 300 transports were sent to besiege the Russian naval base at Sevastopol.

The power of naval guns
With their powerful long-range guns, warships were often used to bombard targets on shore. Here, the British paddle sloop *Bulldog* joins in the attack on the Russian fort at Bomarsund in the Baltic during the Crimean War.

STEAM AND STEEL

BRITISH PREDOMINANCE

Britain's Royal Navy enjoyed an overwhelming dominance at sea, but the British nonetheless had to respond to rapid developments in naval technology if they were to stay ahead. In the mid-19th century the transition from wood and sail to steam and steel brought a new period of experimentation as designers and strategists juggled with the new technological possibilities. Emperor Napoleon III's France at first led the way with the construction of the battleship *Gloire* in 1859, the first ocean-going ironclad warship, sparking a brief naval race with the

British – a race Britain's industrial superiority ensured she would easily win. The success of the *Monitor* in the American Civil War put European navies in a flurry in the 1860s and led to a brief fashion for ramming as a style of combat. Gunports and broadsides were gradually supplanted by turret guns, and sails were somewhat reluctantly abandoned – the Royal Navy battleship *Devastation* launched in 1871 was the first all-steam capital ship.

By the 1880s warship design was settling down, but an arms race between the major European powers was beginning. Fear of the

Screw propulsion
As the design of blades improved through the 19th century with greater understanding of the physics involved, the propeller totally superseded the paddle wheel.

combined naval strength of France and Russia led Britain to formally adopt the "two-power standard". The Naval Defence Act of 1889 decreed that the Royal Navy should always be strong enough to defeat any other two navies, and pledged vast sums of public money to the construction of new battleships and cruisers. But Germany was to provide the real challenge to British naval superiority from the 1890s, when it placed its expanding industrial power behind a massive shipbuilding programme under Admiral Alfred von Tirpitz.

IMPERIAL ASSERTION

Sea travel became far more secure in the second half of the 19th century after the great powers formally renounced privateering and most piracy was quelled. As the arm of the world's dominant shipbuilding and commercial power, the Royal Navy took the lead in charting the seas – a major project that led to safer navigation for all – and the suppression of the slave trade. But European dominance of the oceans was most often experienced by the rest of the world as straightforward bullying. This was seen at its worst in the mistreatment of China by Britain and France from the 1840s to the 1880s. As long as European powers did not go to war with one another, however, there was little chance for these expensive steam fleets to show their worth in battle.

EARLY NAVAL STEAM ENGINES

The standard propulsion system for early steamships was a paddle wheel driven by a double-acting steam engine (see below). Steam would enter the cylinder alternately on the left and right, pushing the piston forward and back. The first ever ironclad battleships – the French *Gloire* of 1859 and British *Warrior* of 1861 – combined double-acting engines with screw propellers. In the 1880s the introduction of triple-expansion engines, with three cylinders instead of one, led to a major improvement in efficiency. Whereas *Warrior*'s engine needed 2.2kg (5lb) of coal to generate one horsepower for an hour, the triple-expansion engine of the British pre-dreadnought *Canopus* in 1899 needed only 0.75kg (1.7lb). In the early 20th century Charles Parsons's steam turbine would take steam propulsion to its peak of efficiency.

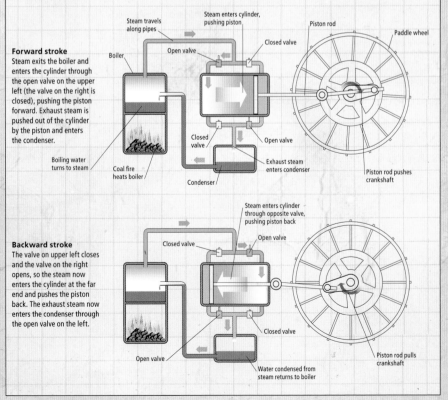

Forward stroke
Steam exits the boiler and enters the cylinder through the open valve on the upper left (the valve on the right is closed), pushing the piston forward. Exhaust steam is pushed out of the cylinder by the piston and enters the condenser.

Steam travels along pipes
Steam enters cylinder, pushing piston
Piston rod
Paddle wheel
Open valve
Closed valve
Boiler
Boiling water turns to steam
Coal fire heats boiler
Closed valve
Open valve
Condenser
Exhaust steam enters condenser
Piston rod pushes crankshaft

Backward stroke
The valve on upper left closes and the valve on the right opens, so the steam now enters the cylinder at the far end and pushes the piston back. The exhaust steam now enters the condenser through the open valve on the left.

Steam enters cylinder through opposite valve, pushing piston back
Closed valve
Open valve
Closed valve
Open valve
Water condensed from steam returns to boiler
Piston rod pulls crankshaft

EUROPEAN WARS: FROM SAIL TO STEAM

DURING THE PERIOD from 1850 to 1870, navies struggled to adapt their tactics as the switch was made to steam power, ironclad ships, and rifled guns firing explosive shells. There were few chances for the European powers to experiment with new technology in action. In 1854 Britain and France went to war against Russia in support of Ottoman Turkey. Although known as the Crimean War, this conflict was fought in the Baltic as well as the Black Sea. Confronted by the world's two leading naval powers, Russia refused to commit its fleet to battle. Anglo-French

command of the sea was essential to their land operations, but the Allies had less success than hoped with the naval bombardment of land fortifications. In the 1860s Prussian ambitions to rule Germany and Italian aspirations to nationhood provoked a series of wars in which sea power was marginal. Nonetheless there were a couple of intriguing naval battles. The encounter at Heligoland was the last significant conflict between wooden ships, and the battle between Austrian and Italian fleets at Lissa was a remarkable instance of the brief fashion for ramming as the prime means of attack.

STEAM AND STEEL

CRIMEAN WAR
SINOPE

Date 30 November 1853
Forces Russians: 11 ships; Ottoman Turkish: 12 ships
Losses Russians: none; Ottoman Turkish: 11 ships sunk

Location Sinope, northern Turkey

A month after the Russian Empire had gone to war with the Ottomans, a powerful Russian naval squadron under Admiral Pavel Nakhimov attacked an Ottoman force of seven frigates and five smaller ships in harbour at Sinope. Nakhimov's squadron included six battleships and

Exploding shells
Nakhimov's warships open fire on the Turkish fleet in an action that, with its use of exploding shells, saw an end to the era of unarmoured ships.

mounted a total of 720 guns, some of which were the revolutionary new Paixhans guns that fired explosive shells. This overwhelming weight of firepower devastated the Turkish ships in an hour, in a battle fought at anchor. Only one Ottoman vessel escaped destruction, a steam-powered auxiliary under an English captain. British and French public opinion responded to the attack (a legitimate act of war) with outrage. The battle was denounced in the press as the "massacre at Sinope" and provided the pretext for Britain and France to enter the war against Russia.

CRIMEAN WAR
SEVASTOPOL FORTS

Date 17 October 1854
Forces British and French: 27 ships
Losses British and French: 340 casualties; Russians: 1,100 casualties

Location Sevastopol, Crimea

The long siege of the Russian naval base of Sevastopol was the gruesome centrepiece of the Crimean War. The British and French fleets landed some 50,000 troops in September 1854 to besiege the city on land. The sea approach to Sevastopol harbour ran up a narrow creek, the mouth of which was guarded by forts Constantine and Alexander and blocked by five ships of the line and two frigates sunk there by the Russians. On 17 October a combined land and sea attack on Sevastopol was attempted. The task of the British and French fleets, under Vice Admiral James Dundas and Vice

Sevastopol besieged
A map of the siege of Sevastopol as it was on 18 June 1855. The Allied fleet enters the harbour to the north, while Russians flee from ruined fortifications.

Russian naval sword
Though originally designed as a boarding weapon, by 1860 the naval sword was only used when going ashore or on ceremonial occasions.

Admiral Ferdinand Hamelin, was to destroy the forts at the harbour mouth. They deployed a mix of steam and sailing ships of the line, the latter moved into position by small steamers used as tugs. In a long-range exchange of fire with the shore batteries, the unarmoured wooden ships proved excessively vulnerable to the Russians' shells and red-hot shot, several being forced to leave the line. Fort Constantine suffered severe damage when a magazine exploded, but the shore batteries were still firing when the Allied fleet withdrew to lick its wounds. The long siege lasted until September 1855, when Sevastopol was finally taken by Allied land forces after heavy loss of life.

SECOND SCHLESWIG WAR
HELIGOLAND

Date 9 May 1864
Forces Danish: 2 frigates, 1 corvette; Prussians and Austrians: 2 frigates, 3 gunboats
Losses Danish: none; Prussians and Austrians: 1 frigate badly damaged

Location Off Heligoland, North Sea

In 1864 Denmark fought Prussia and Austria over control of the duchies of Schleswig and Holstein. The Danes, who were superior to the Prussians at sea, blockaded ports in northern Germany with a squadron under Commodore Edouard Suenson. Captain Wilhelm von Tegetthoff took a small Austrian squadron to the North Sea to break the blockade. It encountered Suenson's smaller force on 9 May off the island of Heligoland, then a British possession.

Each side had two wooden-hulled steam-powered screw frigates: the Danish *Niels Juel* and *Jylland*, and the Austrian *Schwarzenberg* and *Radetzky*. The Danish steam corvette *Heimdall* also took part in the fighting. The hostile squadrons first steamed past one another on opposite tacks shelling furiously, then manoeuvered to follow a parallel course, Suenson's *Niels Juel* taking on Tegetthoff's *Schwarzenberg* while *Jylland* and *Heimdall* engaged *Radetzky*. After more than two hours' fighting, *Schwarzenberg* burst into flames. Unable to continue fighting, Tegetthoff fled for neutral British territorial waters around Heligoland. The Danes had also suffered damage, especially to *Jylland*, and withdrew for repairs. Both sides claimed a victory, the Danes having inflicted heavier casualties but the Austrians having succeeded in lifting the blockade.

Brief revival of ramming
The Austrian armoured frigate *Erzherzog Ferdinand Max* rams the Italian ship *Re d'Italia*, which sinks within minutes. It was one of the last times a ram was used in combat.

THE BATTLE OF LISSA

In 1866 Italy went to war with Austria in alliance with Prussia. From an Italian point of view the main aim of the war was to free Venice from Austrian rule. On 20 July an Italian fleet under Count Carlo di Persano was preparing to land troops on the island of Lissa, then part of the Austrian Empire. An Austrian fleet under Wilhelm von Tegetthoff was sent to prevent the landings.

Occurring at a transitional time in naval technology, the battle was fought by a mix of ironclads and wooden ships, all with both steam propulsion and sails, and most with guns in broadside.

Tegetthoff had the weaker force, but he hoped to compensate by breaking the battle into a mêlée in which his ships might win individual duels. He arranged his fleet in a V formation, advancing toward the Italians with the ironclads in the van. Due to a confusion of orders, the Italians ended up in a ragged line with ironclads and wooden ships interspersed and a large gap between the van and the centre. Toward this gap Tegetthoff gratefully plunged, braving the Italian broadsides that decapitated one of his captains but otherwise caused limited damage to his ships.

Once at close quarters the Austrians fought with outstanding skill. Tegetthof's ship *Erzherzog Ferdinand Max* rammed two ironclads, *Re d'Italia* (twice) and *Palestro*, as well as battering them with close-range gunfire. *Re d'Italia* was gouged open below the waterline by Tegetthoff's second ramming attack and sank in two minutes. *Palestro* eventually exploded, killing most of its crew who had gallantly refused a chance to abandon ship. Meanwhile, the large Austrian wooden battleship *Kaiser*, under Captain Anton von Petz, engaged no less than four ironclads in the Italian rear. Von Petz lost his stem and bowsprit ramming the *Re di Portogallo* and had his smokestack and mainmast shot off, but successfully withdrew his crippled ship from the battle. For his victory, Tegetthoff justly became an Austrian national hero.

AUSTRO-ITALIAN WAR

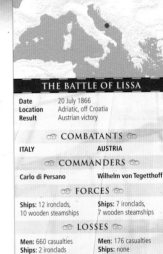

THE BATTLE OF LISSA

Date	20 July 1866
Location	Adriatic, off Croatia
Result	Austrian victory

∞ COMBATANTS ∞

ITALY	AUSTRIA

∞ COMMANDERS ∞

Carlo di Persano	Wilhelm von Tegetthoff

∞ FORCES ∞

Ships: 12 ironclads, 10 wooden steamships	Ships: 7 ironclads, 7 wooden steamships

∞ LOSSES ∞

Men: 660 casualties	Men: 176 casualties
Ships: 2 ironclads	Ships: none

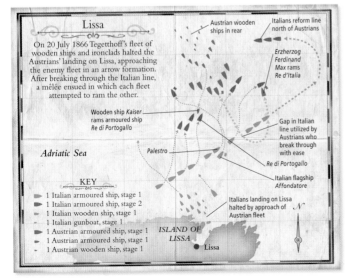

Lissa

On 20 July 1866 Tegetthoff's fleet of wooden ships and ironclads halted the Austrians' landing on Lissa, approaching the enemy fleet in an arrow formation. After breaking through the Italian line, a mêlée ensued in which each fleet attempted to ram the other.

Adriatic Sea

Austrian wooden ships in rear

Italians reform line north of Austrians

Erzherzog Ferdinand Max rams *Re d'Italia*

Wooden ship *Kaiser* rams armoured ship *Re di Portogallo*

Gap in Italian line utilized by Austrians who break through with ease

Palestro

Re di Portogallo

Italian flagship *Affondatore*

Italians landing on Lissa halted by approach of Austrian fleet

KEY

- 1 Italian armoured ship, stage 1
- 1 Italian armoured ship, stage 2
- 1 Italian wooden ship, stage 1
- 1 Italian gunboat, stage 1
- 1 Austrian armoured ship, stage 1
- 1 Austrian armoured ship, stage 1
- 1 Austrian wooden ship, stage 1

ISLAND OF LISSA

• Lissa

N

1827–1871

WILHELM VON TEGETTHOFF

COMMANDER-IN-CHIEF OF THE AUSTRIAN NAVY

Commissioned as an officer in the Austrian navy in 1849, Tegetthoff had no chance to show his talents as a naval commander in combat until the war with Denmark in 1864. His spirited engagement of a Danish squadron at Heligoland was hailed in Austria as an outstanding naval feat and he was raised from captain to rear admiral. As commander-in-chief of the Austrian navy in 1866, his bold attack upon the Italian fleet at Lissa contrasted vividly with the poor performance of Austrian land forces, which were crushed by Prussians.

SHOT TO SHELL

UNTIL THE 19TH CENTURY naval cannon fired varieties of solid shot. Explosive shells – hot shot filled with gunpowder – were employed in land warfare, but they were thought too unsafe for use at sea. From the 1830s, navies adopted shells as part of their munitions. The introduction of iron armour on warships around 1850 made solid shot obselete – it simply bounced off the cladding. By the 1880s rifled breech-loading guns firing high-exposive shells had become standard.

Swivel guns
Heavy mortar

OFFSHORE BOMBARDMENT

Bombarding targets on shore has always been a major application of ships' guns. In land warfare, mortars and howitzers were developed for the bombardment of besieged towns and fortresses. These were guns firing in a high arc, using "bombs" or explosive shells as their munitions. The French navy was the first to develop vessels designed to mount mortars in the 1680s, and was soon imitated by other navies. These bomb galiots or bomb ketches were built with reinforced structures to cope with the forces released by the guns. To avoid the danger of keeping stores of explosive shells on a vessel that had guns firing, the shells were usually carried by tenders that accompanied the bomb vessels.

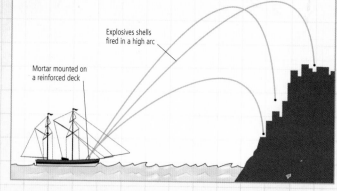

Explosives shells fired in a high arc

Mortar mounted on a reinforced deck

SHIP VERSUS SHIP GUN DUELS

In the age of sail, guns on warships had a limited range. While an 18th century cannon could fire traditional solid shot up to 1.6km (1 mile), its flat trajectory (the most accurate part of its flight) was about 200m (656ft). Just to be sure of the shot, however, vessels would frequently close to half that distance before opening up with huge broadsides. Different navies employed different tactics in gun engagements. The Royal Navy, for example, preferred to shoot into the enemy's hull to kill men or sink the craft, while the French Navy frequently concentrated on masts, sails and rigging in an attempt to hinder a ship's manoeuvrability.

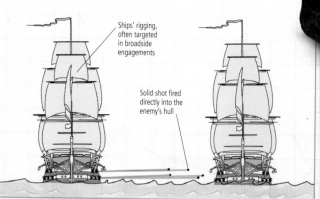

Ships' rigging, often targeted in broadside engagements

Solid shot fired directly into the enemy's hull

BOMB-KETCH
These were developed to carry heavy naval mortar. Here the mortar projects through a hatch in the deck to deliver its bombardment.

EXPLOSIVE SHELL
A bore hole was used to fill the shell with a small charge of gunpowder, which would then be detonated via a time-delay fuse.

Bore hole used to prime shell

Thick shell walls designed for explosion on impact

SHELL CUTAWAY
Firing the shell ignited a slow-burning fuse set into the bore hole, which then ignited the gunpowder. A wooden plug, or sabot, kept the fuse centred in the barrel during shell loading.

Sabot

Solid shot, usually an iron ball

SOLID SHOT
Before shells, shot was mainly used for penetrating heavy structures, in set-piece engagements. It had a formidable effect on personnel, guns, and equipment.

Metal canister, designed to rupture on firing

Small shot

Canister lid

CANISTER
The metal canister here would rupture as it left the muzzle of the cannon, allowing the small shot inside to continue in a wide formation against enemy personnel.

GUN FOUNDING

As the power requirements of cannon increased over the centuries, guns required corresponding strengthening to cope with the greater pressures on the breech. The search for the best cannon-founding method produced two main variants during the 18th and 19th centuries – bore drilling and Rodman casting (here seen applied to a Dahlgren Gun).

BORE DRILLING

The bore-drilling method was pioneered during the mid-18th century, and was a major improvement over the earlier hollow-casting method (casting the gun around a solid core, which was then removed). In bore drilling, the barrel was cast in one solid piece. Then the bore of the gun was drilled out of the metal. The problem with bore drilling was that the gun cooled from the outside in, creating weaknesses in the gun's structure through an outer tension in the metal. This would then place limitations on the power and range of the gun.

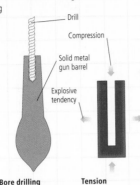

Drill

Compression

Solid metal gun barrel

Explosive tendency

Bore drilling
The bore of the gun is drilled from one piece of solid metal.

Tension
Cooling from outside, compression causes an explosive force.

RODMAN CASTING

Rodman casting was designed by Thomas Jackson Rodman, an American artilleryman. Rodman overcame the problems of bore-drilled guns by casting the cannon over an inner cooling core. This consisted of a cast iron tube, closed at one end but with inflow/outflow valves at the other, a design that allowed the operator to pump a constant flow of cooling water through the tube. The result was that the gun cooled from the inside out, meaning that each successive layer of metal that cooled contracted onto the one beneath it. The subsequent barrel was held together by compression rather than tension, making the gun much stronger and capable of taking heavier charges.

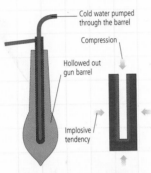

Cold water pumped through the barrel

Compression

Hollowed out gun barrel

Implosive tendency

Rodman core
The water-filled core cools the gun from inside out.

Compression
Cooling from inside, compression causes an an implosive force.

DAHLGREN BATTERY
Designed by American naval officer John A Dahlgren, the bulbous breech of the Dahlgren gun allowed shells to be fired at a higher velocity and, consequently, much further.

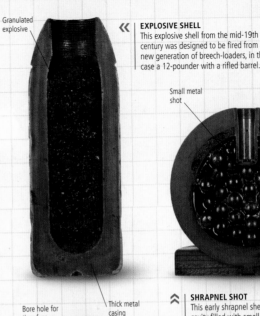

Granulated explosive

EXPLOSIVE SHELL
This explosive shell from the mid-19th century was designed to be fired from a new generation of breech-loaders, in this case a 12-pounder with a rifled barrel.

Small metal shot

Metal membrane between powder and shot prevents early explosion

Bore hole for time fuse

Thick metal casing

SHRAPNEL SHOT
This early shrapnel shell featured a hollow cavity filled with small metal balls. The shell would explode in the air and throw out a lethal cloud of anti-personnel shot.

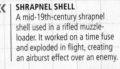

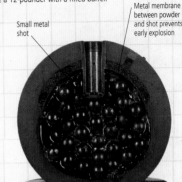

SHRAPNEL SHELL
A mid-19th-century shrapnel shell used in a rifled muzzle-loader. It worked on a time fuse and exploded in flight, creating an airburst effect over an enemy.

Shrapnel

HIGH-EXPLOSIVE SHELL
A modern naval shell with a high-explosive filling made from a mixture of TNT and beeswax. The shell's red cone contains dye to help identify which ship had fired the shell.

Shell cap holds red dye

Shell contains TNT and beeswax (TNT/BWX)

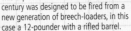

GUNBOAT IMPERIALISM

THE TRADITION OF "sending in a gunboat" to intimidate a non-European state was established by Britain in its first Opium War with China from 1839 to 1842. The flat-hulled steam-powered iron boats became a symbol of European imperialism because of their unique effectiveness in penetrating Asian or African rivers and coastal waters that otherwise might have offered some shelter from European naval power. Yet it was the overall strength of their fleets, rather than any specific type of vessel, that allowed Britain and France in particular to project power on a global scale in the 19th century. By using their navies, these imperialist European states could often achieve their objectives by limited punitive actions, without the need for costly campaigns of conquest. Non-European countries sometimes courageously resisted intimidation – the reverse suffered by the British at the hands of the Chinese at the Dagu forts in 1859 was a reminder that the outcome of battle was never inevitable. But most encounters were one-sided, European fleets crushing technologically inferior opposition with arrogant and ruthless efficiency.

STEAM AND STEEL

The Nemesis
The experimental gunboat *Nemesis* (far right) destroys a Chinese war junk with a Congreve rocket in Anson's Bay, 1841. Also armed with 32lb and 6lb guns, she played an outstanding part in the reduction of China's defences during the First Opium War.

 FIRST OPIUM WAR

FIRST OPIUM WAR

Date 1839–1842
Forces British: 16 sailing ships, 4 steam ships, 1 iron gunboat; Chinese: unknown.
Losses Unknown

Location
Southern China

In November 1839, tensions arose between the British East India Company and Chinese officials, who were attempting to stop the import of opium through Canton (Guangzhou). This led to open hostilities when Chinese war junks exchanged fire with the frigate *Volage* and sloop *Hyacinth*. The British government sent a force of warships and troop transports to blockade Canton and other Chinese ports. There were further clashes with junks, but the most decisive operations involved the experimental gunboat *Nemesis*. A flat iron-hulled steam-driven paddleboat, commanded by William Hall, *Nemesis* could negotiate the shallow waters of Chinese rivers, landing troops and bombarding strongpoints. Defeat in the war forced the Chinese to cede Hong Kong to Britain and open its ports to British traders.

HMS Nimrod
The 18-gun sixth-rate sloop *Nimrod*, launched in 1828, was commanded by Joseph Pearse during the First Opium War.

SECOND OPIUM WAR

ATTACK ON THE DAGU FORTS

Date 25 June, 1859
Forces British: 2 gun vessels, 9 gunboats; Chinese: shore batteries
Losses British: 4 ships; Chinese: unknown

Location Peiho River, northern China

On 8 October 1856 the Chinese authorities stopped and searched a merchant vessel, *Arrow*, that was later alleged to have been flying the British flag. On this flimsy pretext Britain launched a punitive action against China, soon abetted by France. On 20 May 1858 a dozen British and French gunboats bombarded the Dagu forts at the entrance to Peiho River, placing Tientsin and Beijing at their mercy. The Chinese were forced to sign another humiliating peace treaty.

But the Qing government did not implement the treaty in full. The next year, the British sent another naval force to Peiho River, under Rear Admiral James Hope. This time the Chinese were better prepared. They had blocked the river in front of the forts with three lines of obstacles, including iron stakes in the riverbed

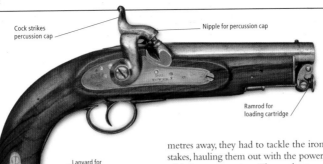

Cock strikes percussion cap
Nipple for percussion cap
Ramrod for loading cartridge
Lanyard for attaching gun to belt

and a chain stretched across the narrow channel. The forts' guns were protected by thick earth ramparts.

The night before the assault on the forts, Hope sent a party to blow up the river obstacles, but it had little success. In the morning, the nine gunboats and two larger gun vessels headed into the river mouth on the flood tide. Under the guns of the forts only a few hundred

Bombardment of Canton
In December 1857, during the Second Opium War, British and French warships bombarded, and then occupied, the port of Canton.

metres away, they had to tackle the iron stakes, hauling them out with the power of their steam engines. The gunboat *Plover*, where Hope had raised his flag, became trapped between the first and second line of obstacles and was battered by fire from the shore guns. Hope was among the wounded as the

Percussion pistol
Percussion pistols shared the same design as flintlocks, but had a different firing mechanism. The hammer struck a cap containing an explosive that lit the charge in the barrel.

boat became a slaughterhouse, only nine of her 40 crew still functioning. The gun vessel *Cormorant* and gunboats *Kestrel* and *Lee* were also sunk, and an attempt by marines to storm the forts was a costly failure. The surviving boats withdrew from the battle in the evening. This unusual reverse for the Royal Navy was eventually avenged the following year when an Anglo-French force sacked Beijing.

> # OCCUPATION WOULD GO FURTHER TO PROCLAIM OUR POWER AND ACCOMPLISH OUR ENDS.
>
> **LORD PALMERSTON**, AUTHORIZING THE OCCUPATION OF BEIJING

ANGLO-EGYPTIAN WAR

BOMBARDMENT OF ALEXANDRIA

Date 11–13 July, 1882
Forces Britain: 15 ships; Egyptians: shore batteries
Losses None

Location Alexandria, Egypt

In 1882 a government took power in Egypt opposed to Anglo–French dominance of the country. In June there were riots in Alexandria and many foreign residents took refuge on British and French warships offshore. The Egyptians set about reinforcing the forts defending the port. British admiral Sir Frederick Seymour interpreted this as a hostile act and issued an ultimatum. The French dissociated themselves, leaving the Royal Navy to fight alone. The British had a varied force of ironclads, including the giant turret ship *Inflexible*, the most powerful warship afloat, whose captain

was the future admiral of the fleet John Fisher. Seymour chose the centre-battery ironclad *Invincible* as his flagship.

The British opened fire on the Egyptian forts at 7am on 11 July. The shore guns returned fire and the action continued for the next ten and a half hours. *Invincible* and the corvette *Penelope*, which advanced into the harbour, both took hits, as did *Inflexible*, but the ships' armour provided good protection and casualties were light. The Egyptians, by contrast, suffered grievously under the fire of the big naval guns, losing about a quarter of their defending force. The shore guns were silenced the following morning.

WEAPONS AND TECHNOLOGY

GATLING GUN

Patented by American inventor Richard Jordan Gatling in 1862, the Gatling gun was an early machine-gun that found favour with the British Royal Navy. It had multiple barrels rotated by a hand-operated crank. As each barrel came round a cartridge automatically dropped into place and the gun fired. By this method the gun could achieve an effective rate of fire of 400 rounds a minute. The Royal Navy adopted the Gatling gun as an ideal weapon to repel boarders. It was never employed in this role, but Gatling guns were fired against Egyptian forts during the bombardment of Alexandria in 1882, and Naval Brigades used them on land in various colonial wars. They were superceded by Gardner guns in the late 1880s.

Magazine containing 240 rounds
Ten rotating barrels
Hand crank operates firing mechanism
Barrels fire in lower right-hand position
Elevation wheel
Wheel for turning gun
0.65in Gatling gun
This ten-barrel version of the Gatling gun was adopted by the British Royal Navy in 1875.
Naval gun mounting

THE BATTLE OF FOOCHOW

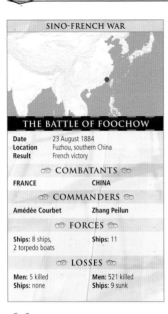

SINO-FRENCH WAR

THE BATTLE OF FOOCHOW

Date	23 August 1884
Location	Fuzhou, southern China
Result	French victory

☞ COMBATANTS ☜

FRANCE	CHINA

☞ COMMANDERS ☜

Amédée Courbet	Zhang Peilun

☞ FORCES ☜

Ships: 8 ships, 2 torpedo boats	**Ships:** 11

☞ LOSSES ☜

Men: 5 killed	**Men:** 521 killed
Ships: none	**Ships:** 9 sunk

In search of an Asian empire, France was extending its influence over Vietnam, traditionally regarded by the Chinese as under their suzerainty. In 1883 the French took control of Tonkin, the area of Vietnam closest to the Chinese border, after a French naval squadron commanded by Rear Admiral Amédée Courbet blockaded the Vietnamese capital Hue. Although France and China officially remained at peace, Chinese troops were sent to fight the French in Vietnam.

In August 1884 Courbet, promoted to vice admiral, took his squadron of warships north to the Chinese port of Foochow (Fuzhou). Lying on the Min River, this was the base of the Fukien Fleet, one of China's four regional navies. After a series of humiliating defeats by European forces, the Chinese government had embarked on a policy of "self-strengthening", which aimed to modernize its army and navy with the help of European experts. The condition of the Fukien Fleet revealed how limited the progress had been. Most of its few steamships had unarmoured wooden hulls. Its only large-calibre guns were carried by two Rendel gunboats, "flatiron" coastal defence vessels providing a platform for one 10in gun apiece. Antiquated sailing junks still made up a large part of the fleet.

IMPERIAL POWER

Because France and China were at peace, the French were permitted to anchor their warships in the Min River among the ships of the Chinese fleet and various other European vessels. Courbet kept two of his three armoured cruisers (the most powerful ships in his squadron) at the mouth of the Min River, where they played no part in the subsequent battle. One armoured cruiser, *Triomphante*, and three unprotected cruisers – *D'Estaing*, *Villars*, and *Duguay-Trouin* – anchored opposite the gunboat *Chen Wei* and two Chinese wooden warships. The smaller French ships moored further up river, where the rest of the Chinese fleet, including the flagship *Yang Wu* and the flatiron gunboats, were clustered.

At 1:56pm on 23 August the French opened fire without warning. Together *Triomphante* and the three unprotected cruisers mounted more than 40 guns, most of larger calibre than the Chinese guns. They made short work of *Chen Wei* and the two wooden ships. On the face of it, the French ships up river

> ❝
> HE WAS VERY CAREFUL NOT TO SHED FRENCH BLOOD. HIS BATTLES WERE HIGHLY ORGANIZED, WORKED OUT IN ADVANCE ... WITH RARE PRECISION ...
>
> **PIERRE LOTI**, FRENCH SAILOR AND WRITER, DESCRIBING ADMIRAL COURBET

faced a more difficult task. But the Chinese flagship was lost within minutes of the start of the action. The French had equipped two small steam launches with spar torpedoes (mines hung on long poles projecting from their bows). One of these exploded against *Yang Wu*'s hull, sinking the vessel. The flatiron gunboats were also sunk by the fire of French guns. Some Chinese ships ran aground attempting to flee up river. The sailing junks proved perfectly useless. In an hour every Chinese ship in Foochow had been sunk or disabled and the arsenal and docks were ablaze.

News of this display of imperial naval power was greeted with joy by a jingoistic French public. Vietnam was secured for France after some harder fighting on land. Courbet died the following year, ensuring his elevation to the status of a French national hero. France's first dreadnought, lanched in 1913, would bear his name.

Unequal contest
French armoured cruisers rain destruction down upon the wooden Chinese vessels at Foochow. All of the Chinese ships were destroyed, while the French lost none.

COMPOUND ENGINE

Early steam engines had a single cylinder. A simple compound steam engine is fitted with two cylinders, the first using the high-pressure steam from the boiler and the second exploiting the lower pressure steam emitted from the first cylinder as exhaust. Invention of the first truly practical two-cylinder compound steam engine is attributed to Scottish engineer William McNaught in 1845, but compound engines did not begin to be used at sea until the 1860s. "Compounding" greatly improved the efficiency of maritime engines. By increasing the distance ships could travel without refuelling, compound engines made steam vessels effective for oceanic travel. By 1880 they were almost universal in new-built ships. Over the following decade triple-expansion engines (with three cylinders) began to come into use. During the 19th century innovations in steam-engine design were usually pioneered by merchant vessels, naval development following in their wake.

Engine with two cylinders
The second cylinder of a compound engine uses steam that escapes from the first. Each cylinder drives a piston.

IRRAWADDY RIVER

Date 16–28 November 1885
Forces British: c.50 river boats
Losses British: none; Burmese: unknown

Location Irrawaddy River, Burma

Britain fought three wars against the kingdom of Burma in the 19th century, the first in 1823–26, the second in 1852, and the third in 1885. The first two wars ended in compromise, but the third was followed by the annexation of Burma. The 1885 war was rooted in colonial rivalry between Britain and France. The British government suspected that Burmese King Thibaw

Min was allowing his country to slip under French influence. To forestall the French they launched a military expedition to take over the country.

Major General Harry Prendergast was sent from Madras to the Burmese border with an army and naval force numbering some 9,000 men. They could not advance on land through the Burmese jungle, but the Irrawaddy River offered a clear highway from the Bay of Bengal to the royal capital of Mandalay. The British-owned Irrawaddy Flotilla Company provided river steam boats and pilots for the expeditionary force. Prendergast had brought with him 24 Maxim guns, the first ever appearance of these belt-fed machine-guns in military service. They were mounted on steamers to provide formidable firepower.

King Thibaw was slow to organize his defences. In principle the river was defended by shore batteries and forts. At Minhla, boats were to be sunk in the navigable channel as blockships, forcing the British to halt under the guns of a fort on the river bank. In practice there was little resistance. The blockships were never sunk and the shore positions were overrun by British-Indian troops and naval brigades with the support of devastating fire from the armed steamers. Wherever the guns of the steamships were trained upon the shore, the Burmese swiftly surrendered, their defeat completed by the fall of Mandalay on 28 November.

Snider-Enfield rifle, 1860
This breech-loading precussion-cap rifle was adopted by the British forces in 1866 and was used during the Third Anglo-Burmese War.

ZANZIBAR

Date 27 August 1896
Forces British: 5 ships; Zanzibar rebels: 1 armed yacht
Losses British: none; Zanzibar rebels: 1 yacht sunk

Location Zanzibar, off east coast of Africa

The Anglo-Zanzibar conflict of 1896 was the shortest war in recorded history and the ultimate exercise of "gunboat diplomacy". The island of Zanzibar was a British protectorate, its sultan Hamad bin Thuwaini accepting the advice of a British resident. There was, however, tension over Zanzibar's persistence with slave trading, which

the British wished to suppress. The political crisis that led to war came on 25 August 1896, when the sultan died. The succession to the sultanate of Britain's preferred candidate, Hamad bin Muhammed, was preempted by Hamid bin Thuwaini's nephew Khalid bin Bargash, who established himself in the royal palace with several thousand armed followers in what amounted to a coup d'état. The Royal Navy had two ships at Zanzibar, the third-class cruiser *Philomel* and the gunboat *Thrush*. These were joined by the sloop *Sparrow* and a body of Royal Marines was put ashore. Rear Admiral Harry Rawson then arrived on board the Cape Station flagship *St George*, a thoroughly modern first-class cruiser with 9.2in main armament, accompanied by the

torpedo cruiser *Racoon*. The Zanzibar navy consisted of a single British-built armed yacht, *Glasgow*, which was anchored in front of the palace.

Rawson presented an ultimatum: if Bargash did not surrender by 9am on 27 August, the Royal Navy would open fire. At 9.02am the bombardment began. *Glasgow* was soon sunk and the royal palace and harem were pulverized. After some 40 minutes of destruction by the naval guns, Bargash fled to seek refuge at the German consulate and his followers raised the white flag. Around 500 people lay dead amid the ruins of the royal buildings. Hamud bin Muhammed duly became sultan and, out of gratitude to the British, abolished the slave trade. Zanzibar was also obliged to pay the cost of the war.

THE AMERICAS AT WAR

An easy victory
On 25 April 1898 the American Asiatic squadron under Admiral Dewey totally destroyed the Spanish squadron in Manila Bay, without losing a single man during the battle. Here Dewey delivers the order "You may fire when ready, Gridley", from the bridge of his flagship *Olympia*.

Fighting far from home
The successful Confederate raider *Alabama* met her end on 19 June 1864 off Cherbourg, France, when she was tracked down by the USS *Kearsarge*. French and English spectators watched the uneven contest between the Confederate wooden cruiser and her armoured foe.

FROM A BROAD PERSPECTIVE of world naval history, the 19th century in the Americas is important as the period when the United States began its emergence as a major naval power. This development was slow to occur, however. Until the final decade of the century, naval operations in the Americas were on a relatively modest scale, whether involving the United States or not. Naval power played a significant role in the American Civil War of 1861 to 1865, and that conflict provided the perfect test-bed for new technologies such as iron armour and turret guns. Yet naval encounters never involved more than a handful of ships. Some intriguing naval battles were also fought in the seas and rivers of Southern America. But it was the creation of the "New Navy" of the United States from the 1880s that was to give the continent its first world-class fleet.

LIMITED FORCE

For much of the 19th century Americans simply saw no need for substantial naval forces. The United States was not seriously threatened by any external enemies and Britain's dominant Royal Navy saw to it that the seas were safe for merchant shipping. The United States did make a gesture toward the imperialist use of naval power with the dispatch of a squadron under Commodore Matthew Perry to intimidate Japan in 1854, but Perry's four paddle steamers would not have impressed even one of the lesser European powers. At the outbreak of the Civil War in 1861 the US Navy comprised around 90 vessels, mostly of indifferent quality and condition. The conflict was the occasion for improvisation on both sides, the South showing particular ingenuity and boldness in taking on a naval struggle for which it could hardly have been worse prepared. The Union government converted a host of steam merchantmen to naval use and instituted a blockade of Southern ports.

Percussion caps
Loading a round into a handgun in the Civil War era still required a separate cartridge, ball, and percussion cap.

Armoured ironclads, monitors, and river paddle steamers fought one another in coastal waters and along the Mississippi. The South bought cruisers from British shipyards to be used as commerce raiders and employed them to great effect. It deployed tethered mines, "torpedo boats" with explosive devices on long spars, and proto-submarines such as the *Hunley*, which sank the steam sloop *Housatonic* in Charleston harbour in February 1864. But the naval dominance of the North was never seriously challenged.

GLOBAL NAVY

Once the Civil War ended, the monitors, ironclads, converted merchantmen, and cruisers were sold off, mothballed, or scrapped. American naval power was allowed to run down as the country concentrated on opening up the West through railroad building and the defeat of Native American tribes.

In 1879, when the United States considered intervening in the War of the Pacific between Chile and Peru, it was unable to do so because it had no warships to match Chile's British-supplied battleships. Yet the rapid growth of

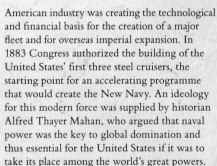

Colt Navy revolver
The Model 1961 Navy, a streamlined version of a successful model that had appeared a decade earlier, was used throughout the Civil War.

American industry was creating the technological and financial basis for the creation of a major fleet and for overseas imperial expansion. In 1883 Congress authorized the building of the United States' first three steel cruisers, the starting point for an accelerating programme that would create the New Navy. An ideology for this modern force was supplied by historian Alfred Thayer Mahan, who argued that naval power was the key to global domination and thus essential for the United States if it was to take its place among the world's great powers.

When the United States went to war with Spain in 1898, a conflict that was triggered by an accidental explosion on board US battleship *Maine* in Havana harbour, it gave the New Navy a chance to flex its muscles against distinctly inferior European opposition. After crushing victories at Manila Bay and off Cuba, the United States came out of the war with a permanent involvement in the Philippines and a string of island bases for its Pacific fleet, as well as assured dominance in the Caribbean. When President Teddy Roosevelt sent the "Great White Fleet" to show the Star and Stripes on a world tour in 1907, it included 16 battleships. The United States had arrived as a serious naval power.

THE AMERICAN CIVIL WAR

THE WAR FOUGHT IN 1861–65 between the 11 Confederate secessionist states of the South and the Union forces of the United States government (the North) was fuelled by their opposing views on slavery. Although largely decided on land, naval warfare also played a part. The Union, by far the stronger in naval terms, established a blockade of the Southern coast. The South used fast ships to run the blockade and commerce raiders to attack Northern shipping at sea. Small flotillas of paddle-wheel steamers fought for control of the major rivers. Occurring at a transitional point in naval technology, the war spawned a variety of experimental craft, from proto-submarines – used by the South to challenge the blockade – to ironclad "monitors". Overall, the Union had the better of the conflict at sea, as on land, because of superior resources of every kind.

THE AMERICAN CIVIL WAR 1861-1865

The naval war began with the Confederates' bombardment of Fort Sumter in April 1861. From then on, the war centred on the Union blockade of the ports and its attempts to take the forts along the Mississippi. When the latter fell, the Confederate States were effectively cut in half.

KEY

- ▬ Union states 1861
- ▬ Confederate states 1861
- — State border
- ⌄⌄⌄ Union front line December 1861
- ⌄⌄⌄ Union front line December 1863
- Ħ Union fort
- Ħ Confederate fort
- ⦿ Union blockade
- ⟹ Union attack/ landing
- ⚓ Union victory
- ⚓ Confederate victory
- ⚓ Inconclusive battle

THE FORCING OF THE MISSISSIPPI FORTS

A major strategic objective of the Union in the early stages of the war was to wrest control of the lower Mississippi River from the Confederates. In February 1862 Flag Officer David Farragut was entrusted with the capture of New Orleans. He was to take a task force, the West Gulf Blockading Squadron, across the sandbars at the mouth of the Mississippi and up the river past the Confederate strongholds of Fort Jackson and Fort St Philip. The Confederates had blocked the river at the line of the forts with sunken hulks linked by a chain. In principle Farragut's unarmoured sloops would be stopped by this obstacle and pulverized by the forts' heavy guns.

RUNNING THE GAUNTLET

Farragut had 19 barges mounting mortars capable of firing shells of up to 200lb. He also had transports carrying 15,000 troops to attack the forts on land if needed. The mortars began their bombardment on the morning of 18 April. More than a thousand shells a day raining down on the forts caused a deal of damage, but showed no signs of silencing their guns. Farragut decided to force a passage regardless.

In the early hours of 24 April, in total darkness, his 17 sloops and gunboats weighed anchor and steamed up river toward the barrier. Two gunboats had earlier succeeded in raiding the obstacle and opening a small navigable passage. Through this gap the Union ships began to pass in single file. At 3:40am the moon rose and more than a hundred guns opened up from the forts upon the sloops and gunboats revealed below. The Union mortars provided counter-fire upon the batteries; a rag-tag assemblage of Confederate gunboats behind the barrier hastened to join in the firing; and rafts heaped with pine and burning pitch were released to float down on the Yankees' wooden ships.

The ships in the centre and rear of Farragut's file took a heavy battering from the forts' guns, but only one was disabled and two others forced to turn back. CSS *Governor Moore* and CSS *Jackson*, cottonclads (gunboats with bales of cotton as armour) succeeded in ramming USS *Varuna*, which sank with guns blazing. The oddest vessel in the battle, CSS *Manassas*, a cigar-shaped propeller-driven ironclad ram, carried out a series of unsuccessful ramming attacks before she ran aground and was destroyed by broadsides from the sidewheel steamer USS *Mississippi*.

Brushing aside further resistance, on 25 April the Union squadron steamed into New Orleans. The fall of the city was a major blow to the Confederacy.

AMERICAN CIVIL WAR

THE MISSISSIPPI FORTS

Date	18–24 April 1862
Location	Mississippi River, near New Orleans
Result	Union victory

⚭ COMBATANTS ⚭

CONFEDERACY	UNION

⚭ COMMANDERS ⚭

John K Mitchell	David G Farragut

⚭ FORCES ⚭

Ships: 12 vessels including 2 ironclad rams	**Ships:** 8 steam sloops, 9 gunboats, 19 mortar schooners

⚭ LOSSES ⚭

Men: 782 dead and wounded **Ships:** 13	**Men:** 37 killed, 149 wounded **Ships:** 1

Pennant
This pennant belonged to the Confederate navy vessel CSS *McRae*, which fought Farragut's fleet at the Mississippi forts. Each star represents a Confederate state.

 AMERICAN CIVIL WAR

PLUM RUN BEND

Date 10 May 1862
Forces Union: 7 ironclad gunboats, 1 wooden gunboat, 16 mortar boats; Confederacy: 8 cottonclad gunboats
Losses Union: 2 gunboats; Confederacy: none

Location Near Memphis, Tennessee

In May 1862 Union forces advancing down the Mississippi were threatening Memphis. In their path lay Fort Pillow. Union mortar boats, defended by ironclad gunboats, bombarded the fort. Captain James E Montgomery of the Confederate River Defense Fleet commanded a small flotilla of paddle steamers that had been converted into fighting rams by the addition of one or two guns and an iron prow. They lacked iron cladding but had cotton bales functioning as light armour.

Steaming up river, Montgomery's cottonclads encountered the Union ironclad *Cincinatti*, one of the paddle-wheel gunboats known as "Pook's Turtles" after their designer Samuel Pook. Steaming through *Cincinatti*'s broadsides, three of the cottonclads rammed the gunboat, which sank in shallow water. Another ironclad, *Mound City*, was also sunk by ramming, settling half-submerged on a sandbar. As more Union gunboats rushed to the scene, the Confederates withdrew.

The skirmish at Plum Run Bend gave a welcome boost to Confederate morale but failed to affect the course of the river war. Fort Pillow was abandoned within a month.

Battle at Fort Pillow
Plum Run Bend demonstrated how steam propulsion had restored the effectiveness of the old galley tactic of ramming.

Battle of the ironclads
Union ironclad gunboats fire salvos into the Confederate fleet, bringing a swift end to the battle of Memphis

 AMERICAN CIVIL WAR

MEMPHIS

Date 6 June 1862
Forces Union: 5 ironclad gunboats, 4 rams; Confederacy: 8 cottonclads
Losses Union: none; Confederacy: 7 ships

Location Memphis, Tennessee

After their losses at Plum Run Bend in May 1862, the Union was convinced of the need for rams in river warfare. Charles Ellet, a civil engineer, had been tasked with building a ram fleet. He strengthened nine river tug boats for ramming, crewed them with riverboat men, and put them under the command of himself and his relatives. Four of Ellet's rams, together with five ironclad "Pook's Turtles", steamed down the Mississippi toward Memphis, Tennessee, on 6 June. There Captain James

Montgomery's cottonclads, victors of Plum Run Bend, steamed out to meet them, watched by a crowd of Memphis residents ready to cheer a Confederate triumph. But it was not to be.

Union rams, captained by Charles Ellet and his brother Alfred, collided with the van of the Confederate force at 15 knots. Two cottonclads were holed and crippled. The Union ironclad gunboats followed, firing salvos that sank one Confederate vessel and disabled three others. After two hours' fighting, the Confederate fleet had ceased to exist, losing 180 men and only one ship escaping down river. Charles Ellet was the only casualty on the Union side. Memphis was occupied and stars and stripes raised over the Confederate city.

> ## THE PASSING OF FORTS JACKSON AND ST PHILIP WAS ONE OF THE MOST AWFUL SIGHTS I EVER SAW ...
>
> **DAVID FARRAGUT**, UNION FLAG OFFICER, WRITING IN HIS MEMOIR

Moonlit battle
Farragut's flagship *Hartford* runs the gauntlet of Confederate incendiaries, forcing a passage up the Mississippi.

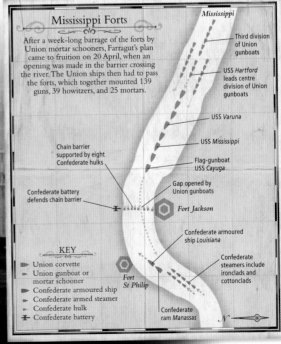

Mississippi Forts

After a week-long barrage of the forts by Union mortar schooners, Farragut's plan came to fruition on 20 April, when an opening was made in the barrier crossing the river. The Union ships then had to pass the forts, which together mounted 139 guns, 39 howitzers, and 25 mortars.

Mississippi

Third division of Union gunboats

USS *Hartford* leads centre division of Union gunboats

USS *Varuna*

USS *Mississippi*

Flag-gunboat USS *Cayuga*

Chain barrier supported by eight Confederate hulks

Gap opened by Union gunboats

Fort Jackson

Confederate battery defends chain barrier

Confederate armoured ship *Louisiana*

Confederate steamers include ironclads and cottonclads

KEY
- Union corvette
- Union gunboat or mortar schooner
- Confederate armoured ship
- Confederate armed steamer
- Confederate hulk
- Confederate battery

Fort St Philip

Confederate ram *Manassas*

US CIVIL WAR

CHARLESTON HARBOUR

Date 7 April 1863
Forces Union: 7 monitors, 2 ironclads
Losses Union: 1 ironclad sunk

Location Charleston, South Carolina

In preparation for an attack upon the Confederate port of Charleston, Rear Admiral Samuel Francis du Pont's South Atlantic Blockading Squadron attempted to overcome the defences of Charleston harbour by naval bombardment. Seven monitors and the ironclads *New Ironsides* and *Keokok* crossed the harbour bar on 6 April 1863, but poor visibility delayed the attack until the following morning. The Confederate defences were excellently prepared. The channel into the harbour was blocked with obstacles and "torpedoes" (mines), while the gunners in Fort Sumter and Fort Multrie had taken measures to ensure that their fire was accurate and deadly. The monitor *Weehawken* was first to open fire on the forts with her Dahlgren guns, but she was soon taking hits on her armour, as well as having a torpedo explode beneath her. The unfortunate *Keokuk* found herself swept into the van on the flood tide. Her experimental armour (she was dubbed a "tinclad") was quickly holed. In all, the shore batteries fired 2,200 shots, achieving 440 hits, while the ships only managed to fire 154 shots before retiring for the day. *Keokuk* sank the following morning and the assault on the forts was abandoned.

US CIVIL WAR

ALABAMA VS KEARSARGE

Date 19 June 1864
Forces Confederacy: 1 steam sloop; Union: 1 steam sloop
Losses Confederacy: 1 ship sunk; Union: none

Location Off Cherbourg, France

The Confederate steam sloop *Alabama* was a highly successful commerce raider. Commanded by Captain Raphael Semmes, she sank more than 60 merchant ships. On 14 June 1864 she was trapped in the French port of Cherbourg by the Union sloop *Kearsarge* under Captain John Winslow. Five days later Semmes boldly came out to fight. The engagement lasted 70 minutes. The two ships steamed in opposite directions in narrowing circles, pounding one another with shot and shell. *Kearsarge* was armoured with iron chains; *Alabama* was not. Holed and taking water, *Alabama* struck shortly before sinking. Semmes was among the 38 men saved by a private yacht.

THE BATTLE OF MOBILE BAY

US CIVIL WAR

THE BATTLE OF MOBILE BAY

Date 5 August 1864
Location Mobile Bay, Gulf of Mexico
Result Union victory

☞ COMBATANTS ☜

UNION	CONFEDERACY

☞ COMMANDERS ☜

David Farragut	Franklin Buchanan

☞ FORCES ☜

Ships: 4 monitors, 14 wooden steamships	**Ships:** 1 ironclad, 3 gunboats

☞ LOSSES ☜

Men: 315 **Ships:** 1 ironclad	**Men:** 35 casualties, 123 captured **Ships:** 1 ironclad and 2 gunboats captured

By the fourth year of the Civil War, Mobile, Alabama, was one of only two Confederate ports still successfully challenging the Union naval blockade (the other being Savannah, Georgia). In August 1864 Union forces under Admiral David Farragut sought to close this avenue for blockade-runners by taking control of Mobile Bay.

As the fog lifted around 6am on 5 August, Farragut's squadron crossed the bar at the entrance to the bay on the flood tide. His four armoured monitors led the way, steaming to starboard of his wooden ships to protect them from the fire of Fort Morgan's heavy batteries. Meanwhile, Confederate admiral Franklin Buchanan brought *Tennessee* (an unwieldy ironclad ram) and three unarmoured gunboats up to block the channel into the bay. The Union ironclads began a vigorous exchange of fire with Fort Morgan, creating such smoke that Farragut had to climb the mainmast of his flagship, the screw-sloop *Hartford*, to see what was happening.

The leading Union monitor was Commander Tunis Craven's *Tecumseh*. As Buchanan's ships opened fire from ahead, Craven manoeuvered to engage *Tennessee*. Veering to port, *Tecumseh* struck a mine (or "torpedo"), triggering a massive explosion. The monitor capsized and sank, taking Craven and more than 90 of the crew to the bottom. For a moment the Union squadron came to a halt under the fire of the fort's guns, as captains hesitated to press forward for fear of mines. Farragut's resolve saved the day. With the famous cry "Damn the torpedoes! Full speed ahead!", the Union admiral ordered his flagship forward through the mined channel, followed without further loss by the rest of the squadron.

Although facing overwhelming odds, Buchanan gallantly refused to accept defeat. *Tennessee's* guns did a great deal of damage to Union ships and

Battle of the ironclads
Commander David G Farragut (far right) stands in the rigging of his sloop-of-war *Hartford*. In the foreground, a gun crew readies a Dahlgren gun to fire point-blank at a Confederate ironclad.

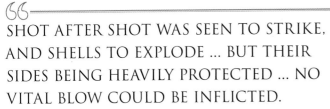

> SHOT AFTER SHOT WAS SEEN TO STRIKE, AND SHELLS TO EXPLODE ... BUT THEIR SIDES BEING HEAVILY PROTECTED ... NO VITAL BLOW COULD BE INFLICTED.

GENERAL RICHARD L PAGE, COMMANDER OF FORT MORGAN

proved a tough opponent to overcome. Three of the Union screw-sloops, including Farragut's *Hartford*, rammed the Confederate leviathan, but suffered more damage than they caused. The monitors *Chickasaw* and *Manhattan* moved in to fire their heavy guns at point-blank range, finally succeeding in blowing a hole in *Tennessee*'s armour.

Buchanan, himself wounded, at last ordered a white flag flown from the battered, disabled ironclad, bringing the battle of Mobile Bay to a close.

Over the following weeks, Union army and naval forces captured the forts at the mouth of the bay, completing the blockade of Mobile, which itself stayed in Confederate hands.

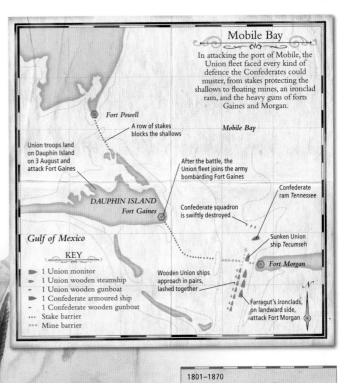

Mobile Bay

In attacking the port of Mobile, the Union fleet faced every kind of defence the Confederates could muster, from stakes protecting the shallows to floating mines, an ironclad ram, and the heavy guns of forts Gaines and Morgan.

Fort Powell

A row of stakes blocks the shallows

Mobile Bay

Union troops land on Dauphin Island on 3 August and attack Fort Gaines

After the battle, the Union fleet joins the army bombarding Fort Gaines

DAUPHIN ISLAND
Fort Gaines

Confederate ram *Tennessee*

Confederate squadron is swiftly destroyed

Gulf of Mexico

Sunken Union ship *Tecumseh*

KEY

Wooden Union ships approach in pairs, lashed together

Fort Morgan

▶ 1 Union monitor
▷ 1 Union wooden steamship
▷ 1 Union wooden gunboat
▶ 1 Confederate armoured ship
▷ 1 Confederate wooden gunboat
••• Stake barrier
••• Mine barrier

Farragut's ironclads, on landward side, attack Fort Morgan

N

1801–1870
DAVID G FARRAGUT

THE FIRST ADMIRAL OF THE US NAVY

Tennessee-born David Farragut was a midshipman in the US Navy aged nine, and, during the 1812 War with Britain, commanded a prize vessel at the age of 12. He saw further action in the Mexican War of 1846–48. Although born and bred a southerner, in the Civil War he opted for the Union and distinguished himself in the running of the forts to new Orleans in 1862. The assault on Mobile Bay, in 1864, was his finest hour. He was rewarded with the title of admiral in 1866, the first man to hold that rank in the US Navy.

FORCING OF THE MISSISSIPPI FORTS

On 24 April 1862, Commodore Farragut of the United States Navy sent his West Gulf Blockading Squadron of nine gunboats, eight steamboats, and several mortar vessels up the Mississippi to wrest New Orleans from Confederate control. The city fell peacefully, but Farragut's squadron had to endure a vicious bombardment from Confederate strongholds, forts Jackson (left) and St Philip.

FARRAGUT APRIL 24ᵗʰ 1862

Point-blank range
Monitor (right) opens fire with one of its Dahlgren guns at point-blank range. The *Virginia*'s barbette is riddled with damage, and its smokestack is shattered. It also takes fire from Union frigates.

Crew of USS Monitor
The *Monitor* had a crew of 59 officers and men, some of whom are gathered here on its deck. A gunner stands on the turret, which houses two 11in Dahlgren smoothbores.

THE BATTLE OF HAMPTON ROADS

Faced with overwhelming Union naval superiority and a blockade of its coasts, the Confederacy sought salvation in new technology: ironclad warships. Building upon the half-burned hull of the steam frigate USS *Merrimack*, captured at Gosport in the first days of the Civil War, the Confederates created a ship completely covered down to the waterline in 102mm (4in) thick iron plates. On 8 March 1862 this sinister, ungainly fighting machine, renamed CSS *Virginia*, steamed out from Norfolk Navy Yard to challenge the Union frigates blockading the Hampton Roads.

HISTORIC ENCOUNTER

Although it carried 12 assorted guns (four rifles, two howitzers, and six Dahlgren smoothbores), *Virginia*'s chief weapon was an iron ram, created in response to rumours that the Union, too, had an ironclad – one that might resist *Virginia*'s guns. *Virginia*'s captain, 61-year-old Franklin Buchanan, had orders to effect "prompt and successful action". Without hesitation he set his course directly for the wooden frigate USS *Cumberland*. Steaming inexorably forward, immune to *Cumberland*'s broadsides, *Virginia* smashed its ram into the frigate's hull. As *Cumberland* sank, the ironclad was almost dragged to the bottom, disengaging at the expense of snapping the ram. *Virginia*'s next victim was USS *Congress*. Deliberately run aground to escape ramming, the frigate provided target practice for *Virginia*'s gunners. *Congress* eventually struck its colours but *Virginia*'s acceptance of the surrender was interrupted by fire from Union soldiers on shore. Buchanan himself was shot in the leg – the limb was later amputated. Before handing over command, he angrily ordered his gunners to fire on *Congress* with heated iron shot, setting it aflame.

By the end of the day yet another Union frigate, *Minnesota*, was aground and at *Virginia*'s mercy. The ironclad, now under Lieutenant Catesby ap Roger Jones, retired to rest its crew, intending to finish the job the following day. This it would undoubtedly have done but for the timely arrival (for the Union) of an even stranger vessel. Aware of the Confederates' progress with *Virginia*, the Union had indeed rushed to complete its own revolutionary ironclad. USS *Monitor*, with no time for sea trials and with an inexperienced crew, reached the Hampton Roads on the night of 8–9 March.

US CIVIL WAR

BATTLE OF HAMPTON ROADS

Date	8–9 March 1862
Location	Off Sewell's Point, Virginia
Result	Inconclusive

∾ COMBATANTS ∾

UNION	CONFEDERACY

∾ COMMANDERS ∾

| John L Worden | Franklin Buchanan, |
| Samuel D Green | Catesby ap R Jones |

∾ FORCES ∾

Ships: 1 ironclad, 5 wooden frigates	**Ships:** 1 ironclad, 2 wooden warships, 1 gunboat

∾ LOSSES ∾

| **Men:** 261 killed, 108 wounded | **Men:** 7 killed, 17 wounded |
| **Ships:** 2 frigates | **Ships:** none |

> ❝ DURING THE ACTION THEY CHEERED AND CHEERED AGAIN. THEIR COOLNESS AND SKILL WERE THE MORE REMARKABLE FROM THE FACT THAT THE GREAT MAJORITY OF THEM WERE UNDER FIRE FOR THE FIRST TIME. ❞
>
> **LIEUTENANT CATESBY AP ROGER JONES**, WRITING OF HIS CREW ABOARD *VIRGINIA*

STEAM AND STEEL

1821–1877
CATESBY AP JONES
CONFEDERATE NAVY LIEUTENANT

Born in Fairfield, Virginia, Catesby ap Roger Jones ("ap" meaning "son of" in Welsh) was appointed midshipman in 1836 and served extensively at sea, becoming a lieutenant in 1849. In the 1850s he was involved in the development of naval weapons, and served as an ordnance officer aboard *Merrimack* when she began service in 1856. He became a Confederate Navy Lieutenant in 1861, and converted *Merrimack* into the ironclad *Virginia*, taking temporary command of her at the battle of Hampton Roads. He was killed in 1877 in a feud between his and another man's children.

USS *Monitor* was a semi-submerged armoured raft designed by Swedish engineer John Ericsson, driven by Ericsson's novel marine screw, and topped by a revolving iron gun turret containing two 11in smoothbore Dahlgren guns. The latter had reinforcing muzzle swells that permitted large amounts of explosives to be used without fear of the guns exploding (and gave them a soda-bottle shape), the pair aboard *Monitor* being of a higher calibre than the two aboard *Virginia*. Unlike her opponent, who was simply a wooden ship dressed in iron, *Monitor* was the first truly semi-submersible warship, having all of her features underwater save for the turret and a tiny pilothouse up front.

Flattened shot
One of the solid shots fired at *Virginia* by *Monitor* that flattened on impact with the former's thick, armoured barbette – *Merrimac* being the Union name for *Virginia*.

The duel that followed the next day, when *Virginia* steamed out and found *Monitor* defending *Minnesota*, may rank as the oddest in naval history. For four hours the two ships blasted at one another at close range, producing little more than dents in their iron armour. Visibility was poor for commanders and gunners on both ships. *Monitor* suffered problems with its turret, which had to be kept permanently rotating, firing as it turned. *Virginia* had the disadvantage of a V-shaped hull (*Monitor* was flat-bottomed) and at one point ran aground, refloating with a supreme effort of her overstretched engines. Ramming proved as ineffectual as gunfire. A shell exploded on the eye-slit of *Monitor*'s cramped pilothouse, and its captain, John L Worden, was burnt in the face and blinded. But his first officer, Samuel D Green, continued the stalemated fight, and in the afternoon *Virginia* withdrew to port.

Over the following two months *Virginia* made occasional sorties into Hampton Roads, but the epic duel was not repeated. Both sides claimed victory, but with the blockade still intact, the strategic balance remained in the Union's favour. When he heard of the engagement, *Monitor*'s designer John Ericsson criticized the crew for firing only solid shot at *Virginia*'s upper works, claiming that firing explosive shells beneath the waterline would have sunk the Confederate ship. Nevertheless, neither ironclad survived the year. *Virginia* was scuttled by her commander in May 1861 when the course of the land battle forced the Confederates to abandon Portsmouth. *Monitor*, which was never truly seaworthy, sank on 31 December while under tow in an Atlantic gale.

Duel in Hampton Roads
Virginia (right) fires its 7in stern and casement guns, while *Monitor* fires its 11in turret equivalents. *Virginia*'s use of molten shot enhanced the need for ships to be made of iron.

KEY
CONFEDERATE FLEET
1 Confederate ironclad ship: CSS *Virginia*
1 Confederate steam gunboat
UNION FLEET
1 Union ironclad ship: USS *Monitor*
1 Union frigate or other wooden warship

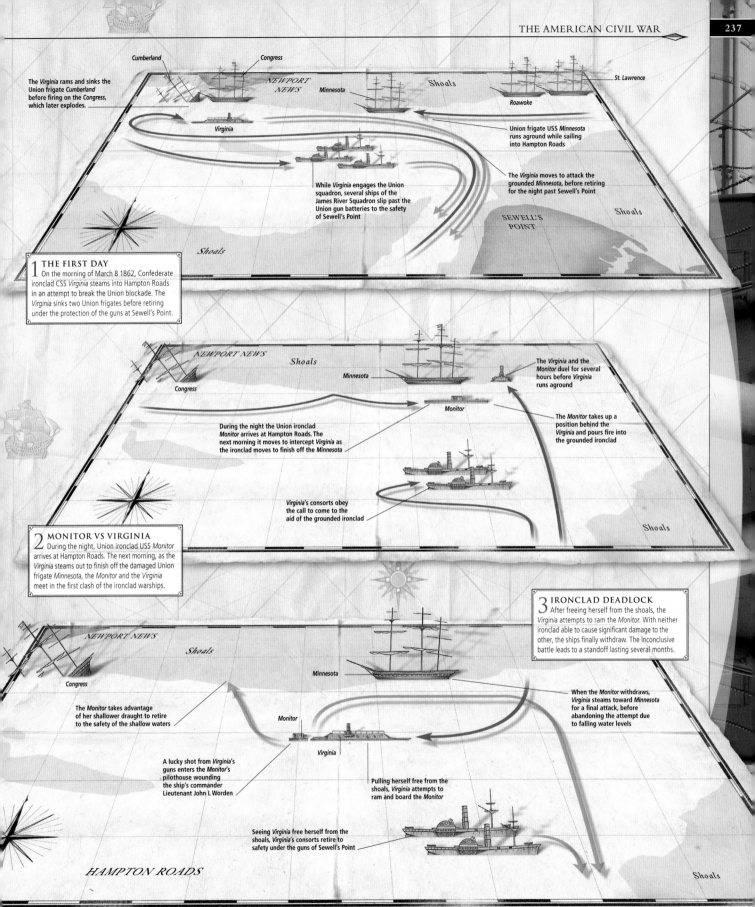

The *Virginia* rams and sinks the Union frigate *Cumberland* before firing on the *Congress*, which later explodes.

Cumberland

Congress

NEWPORT NEWS

Shoals

Minnesota

St. Lawrence

Roawoke

Virginia

Union frigate USS *Minnesota* runs aground while sailing into Hampton Roads

While *Virginia* engages the Union squadron, several ships of the James River Squadron slip past the Union gun batteries to the safety of Sewell's Point

The *Virginia* moves to attack the grounded *Minnesota*, before retiring for the night past Sewell's Point

SEWELL'S POINT

Shoals

Shoals

1 THE FIRST DAY
On the morning of March 8 1862, Confederate ironclad CSS *Virginia* steams into Hampton Roads in an attempt to break the Union blockade. The *Virginia* sinks two Union frigates before retiring under the protection of the guns at Sewell's Point.

NEWPORT NEWS

Shoals

Minnesota

Congress

The *Virginia* and the *Monitor* duel for several hours before *Virginia* runs aground

Monitor

During the night the Union ironclad *Monitor* arrives at Hampton Roads. The next morning it moves to intercept *Virginia* as the ironclad moves to finish off the *Minnesota*

The *Monitor* takes up a position behind the *Virginia* and pours fire into the grounded ironclad

Virginia's consorts obey the call to come to the aid of the grounded ironclad

2 MONITOR VS VIRGINIA
During the night, Union ironclad USS *Monitor* arrives at Hampton Roads. The next morning, as the *Virginia* steams out to finish off the damaged Union frigate *Minnesota*, the *Monitor* and the *Virginia* meet in the first clash of the ironclad warships.

3 IRONCLAD DEADLOCK
After freeing herself from the shoals, the *Virginia* attempts to ram the *Monitor*. With neither ironclad able to cause significant damage to the other, the ships finally withdraw. The inconclusive battle leads to a standoff lasting several months.

NEWPORT NEWS

Shoals

Congress

Minnesota

The *Monitor* takes advantage of her shallower draught to retire to the safety of the shallow waters

Monitor

When the *Monitor* withdraws, *Virginia* steams toward *Minnesota* for a final attack, before abandoning the attempt due to falling water levels

Virginia

A lucky shot from *Virginia*'s guns enters the *Monitor*'s pilothouse wounding the ship's commander Lieutenant John L Worden

Pulling herself free from the shoals, *Virginia* attempts to ram and board the *Monitor*

Seeing *Virginia* free herself from the shoals, *Virginia*'s consorts retire to safety under the guns of Sewell's Point

HAMPTON ROADS

Shoals

SPANISH AND LATIN-AMERICAN CONFLICTS

FROM THE 1840s to the 1890s the countries of Central and South America fought a number of wars that involved naval action. None of the naval conflicts was contested on a large scale, but some were of technical interest, providing a testing ground for the latest naval technology – as when the first sinking of a warship by a torpedo took place during the Chilean Civil War of 1891. The war that broke out between Spain and the United States in 1898, however, marked a major historical transition. The war was precipitated by the explosion of the battleship *Maine* in Havana harbour – an event that was almost certainly an accident, but which was blamed by the Americans on the Spanish authorities, thus providing the former with a pretext for war. Two one-sided naval battles, at Santiago de Cuba and Manila Bay, to a large degree determined the war's outcome. As a result of the conflict the United States effectively replaced Spain as the imperial power in Cuba and the Philippines. At the same time, the naval battles confirmed the terminal decline of the Spanish navy and the emergence of the United States as a potentially major naval power.

STEAM AND STEEL

Texan sailing ships
Sailing ships of the Texan navy head for the Yucatán Peninsula, where they engage and defeat the steam ships of Mexico at Campeche.

TEXAS-MEXICAN WARS

CAMPECHE

Date 30 April and 16 May 1843
Forces Texans, Yucatáns: 4 sailing ships; Mexicans: 2 ironclads, 4 sailing ships
Losses None

Location Bay of Campeche, Mexico

In 1843 the region of Texas was a self-declared republic whose independence was not recognized by Mexico. The Texan navy was in poor shape, its crews unpaid and mutinous. Its commander, Commodore Edwin Ward Moore, sought to fund the navy by selling its services to Yucatán, also fighting for independence from Mexico. In April 1843 Moore sailed from New Orleans for the Yucatán port of Campeche, under blockade by the Mexican navy.

Mexico had recently bought the British-built, iron-hulled, paddle-wheel frigate *Guadalupe*, the largest iron ship in the world. *Guadalupe* was supported by the ironclad steamer *Moctezuma*. Commanded by Commodore Thomas Marin, the Mexican ironclads were mostly manned by British officers and crews. The Texans had only wooden sailing ships, including Moore's flagship, the sloop-of-war *Austin*, and the brig *Wharton*. Joined by two schooners of the Yucatán navy, Moore met the Mexican steamships off Campeche on 30 April. The two-hour running battle was indecisive, but the Texans broke through the blockade and entered Campeche for rest and repairs.

Over the following fortnight the Texan sailing ships had long-range guns added to their armament, for they had had difficulty closing with the steam-driven ships. On 16 May Moore led his ships out of Campeche to renew battle. This time the fighting lasted three hours. *Austin* was badly damaged, but the Texan broadsides caused far heavier casualties. The Texans had the better of the two encounters, justifying the description of Campeche as the only battle in which sail defeated steam.

CHINCHA ISLANDS WAR

CALLAO

Date 2 May 1866
Forces Spanish: 14 warships; Peruvians: 5 warships, c.60 shore guns
Losses Spanish: none; Peruvians: unknown

Location Callao, Peru

In the 1860s relations between Spain and its former colonies Peru and Chile deteriorated into open warfare after the Spanish seized Peru's guano-rich Chincha Islands. Admiral Casto Mendez Nuñez steamed from Spain on board the newly built ironclad *Numancia* to take command of a Spanish squadron off the coast of Chile. He bombarded the port of Valparaiso in February 1866, then moved north to Peru, choosing the fortified naval base at Callao as his target. The Spanish fleet had 245 guns on board, arranged in broadside. The Peruvian armament totalled around 90 guns, including some very heavy shore guns in armoured emplacements. On the morning of 2 May, the Spanish ships advanced within range and a ferocious gun duel began; it lasted six hours. The Spanish vessels received many hits, especially *Numancia*, deliberately positioned by Mendez Nuñez in the place of greatest danger. More than 40 Spanish officers and men were killed and a further 160 were wounded, including the admiral. But the Spanish had the better of the duel, silencing almost all the shore guns with their more skilful shooting. There were some 600 Peruvian casualties, including the minister of war Juan Galvez, killed in the destruction of an armoured strongpoint. The Spanish squadron subsequently left for the Philippines, leaving the bombardment without consequence. Returning home to Spain, *Numancia* became the first ironclad to circumnavigate the globe.

WAR OF THE PACIFIC

IQUIQUE

Date 21 May 1879
Forces Chilians: 1 corvette, 1 schooner; Peruvians: 1 armoured frigate, 1 monitor
Losses Chilians: 1 corvette; Peruvians: 1 armoured frigate

Location Iquique, Peru

During the war between Chile and Peru in 1879, the Chilean navy left two obsolescent wooden steamships, the corvette *Esmeralda* and the schooner *Covadonga*, blockading the Peruvian port of Iquique. There they were surprised by two Peruvian ironclads, the armoured frigate *Independencia* and the monitor *Huascar*. *Esmeralda* became trapped between the Peruvian shore batteries and *Huascar*, and although most of her crew were killed or wounded, her captain, Arturo Prat, refused to surrender. When *Huascar* rammed the corvette, Prat led his surviving crew in an attempt to board the monitor. He was killed on its deck with a blow from an axe. Meanwhile, *Covadonga* fought a skilful running battle with *Independencia*, exploiting its shallow draught to lure the Peruvian ship into going aground. *Covadonga* was then able to batter *Independencia* with her guns. The Peruvians scuttled the ship while *Covadonga* escaped southward. On balance, the battle was a victory for Chile.

Battle hero
This medal commemorates the death of Chilean captain Arturo Prat, who died boarding the Peruvian monitor *Huascar*.

THE BATTLE OF SANTIAGO DE CUBA

When war broke out between the United States and Spain in April 1898, Spanish admiral Pascual Cervera was ordered to protect his country's West Indian colonies from American attack. This was a poor decision, for the forces at Cervera's disposal were inadequate to confront the battleships of the US "New Navy" – deficiencies ranging from faulty boilers to missing guns and dud ammunition. Nevertheless, Cervera anchored his squadron of armoured cruisers and destroyers at Santiago de Cuba, where it was swiftly blockaded by the Americans.

The commander of the American Atlantic Squadron, Admiral William T Sampson, had no intention of attacking the Spanish in harbour, where they were defended by shore batteries and mines, leaving Cervera with the slim hope that bad weather might interrupt the blockade. By July, however, American land forces were also threatening Santiago, so the Spanish admiral made the decision to attempt a breakout.

Cervera chose the morning of 3 July for the attempt. He had the good fortune of selecting the morning when Admiral Sampson, aboard the armoured cruiser *New York*, was heading off to meet with US Army commanders. *New York* was far from its blockade station when, at around 9:30am, the Spanish were spotted steaming out of harbour, with Cervera's flagship, the cruiser *Infanta Maria Teresa*, leading the line.

Cervera's only hope lay in speed. In principle, the Spanish ships had a fair chance of outrunning the blockade force once they were clear. In Sampson's absence, command of the American squadron devolved to Commodore Winfield Scott Schley aboard the armoured cruiser *Brooklyn*. As the Spanish steamed southward close to the shore, Schley manoeuvered so radically that he nearly collided with

American medal
Commemorating the destruction of the Spanish fleet at Santiago de Cuba, this medal shows a broadside view of USS *Brooklyn* under steam.

the battleship *Texas*. But *Brooklyn* was soon engaging *Maria Teresa*, which sought to hold off the enemy as the other ships slipped away.

The battle quickly degenerated into a debacle for the Spanish. Cervera's flagship was battered by *Brooklyn*'s guns and ran aground. Another armoured cruiser, *Vizcaya*, valiantly duelled with *Brooklyn* and the battleship *Texas* for over an hour, until it too was grounded. *Oquendo* was disabled and scuttled. The Spanish destroyers succumbed to the battleships *Iowa* and *Indiana*, and of *New York* hurrying to join the action. Only the cruiser *Cristóbal Colón* broke the blockade, but was overhauled by *Oregon* after an 80km (50-mile) chase.

SPANISH-AMERICAN WAR

BATTLE OF SANTIAGO DE CUBA

Date	3 July 1898
Location	Off Santiago de Cuba
Result	American victory

COMBATANTS

UNITED STATES	SPAIN

COMMANDERS

| William T Sampson | Pascual Cervera y |
| Winfield Scott Schley | Topete |

FORCES

Ships: 4 battleships, 2 armoured cruisers, 2 torpedo boats	Ships: 4 armoured cruisers, 2 destroyers

LOSSES

| Men: 1 dead, 1 wounded | Men: 474 casualties, 1,800 taken prisoner |
| Ships: none | Ships: 6 |

> ## NOTHING CAN BE EXPECTED OF THIS EXPEDITION EXCEPT THE TOTAL DESTRUCTION OF THE FLEET OR ITS HASTY AND DEMORALIZED RETURN.
>
> **SPANISH ADMIRAL PASCUAL CERVERA**, BEFORE THE BATTLE OF SANTIAGO DE CUBA

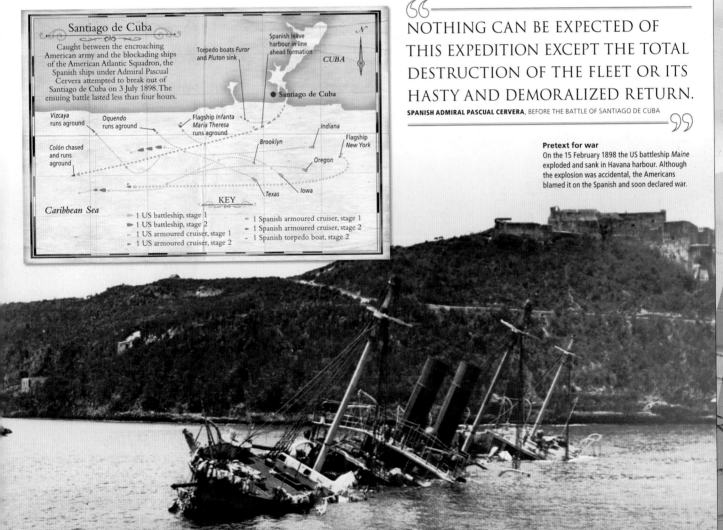

Santiago de Cuba

Caught between the encroaching American army and the blockading ships of the American Atlantic Squadron, the Spanish ships under Admiral Pascual Cervera attempted to break out of Santiago de Cuba on 3 July 1898. The ensuing battle lasted less than four hours.

Spanish leave harbour in line ahead formation

Torpedo boats *Furor* and *Pluton* sink

CUBA

Santiago de Cuba

Vizcaya runs aground

Oquendo runs aground

Flagship *Infanta Maria Theresa* runs aground

Colón chased and runs aground

Indiana

Flagship *New York*

Brooklyn

Oregon

Texas   *Iowa*

Caribbean Sea

KEY

- 1 US battleship, stage 1
- 1 US battleship, stage 2
- 1 US armoured cruiser, stage 1
- 1 US armoured cruiser, stage 2
- 1 Spanish armoured cruiser, stage 1
- 1 Spanish armoured cruiser, stage 2
- 1 Spanish torpedo boat, stage 2

Pretext for war
On the 15 February 1898 the US battleship *Maine* exploded and sank in Havana harbour. Although the explosion was accidental, the Americans blamed it on the Spanish and soon declared war.

1830 – 1918

WEAPONS AND TECHNOLOGY

BREECH-LOADING GUNS

In the mid-19th century the breech-loading rifled cannon began to replace the muzzle-loader, which took longer to load, was difficult to clean, and could mistakenly be double-loaded, as happened aboard HMS *Thunderer* in 1879, causing terrible loss of life. But breech-loaders had dangers of their own, and only became reliable with the invention of the interrupted screw and the French-designed De Bange obturation system. The former allowed the breech to be opened and closed quickly, while the latter created an airtight seal, preventing dangerous propellent gasses escaping through the breech when firing.

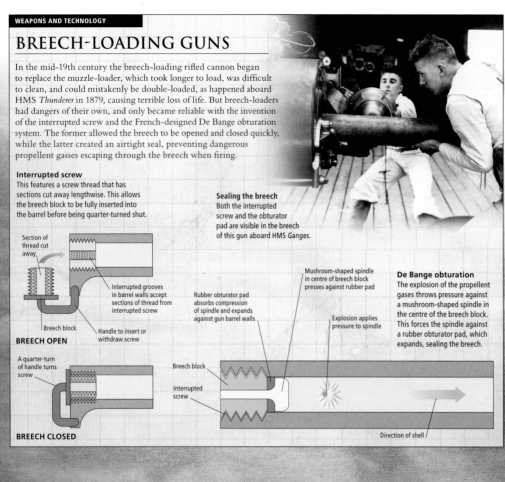

Interrupted screw
This features a screw thread that has sections cut away lengthwise. This allows the breech block to be fully inserted into the barrel before being quarter-turned shut.

Section of thread cut away

Interrupted grooves in barrel walls accept sections of thread from interrupted screw

Breech block

Handle to insert or withdraw screw

BREECH OPEN

A quarter-turn of handle turns screw

BREECH CLOSED

Sealing the breech
Both the interrupted screw and the obturator pad are visible in the breech of this gun aboard HMS *Ganges*.

Rubber obturator pad absorbs compression of spindle and expands against gun barrel walls

Breech block

Interrupted screw

Mushroom-shaped spindle in centre of breech block presses against rubber pad

Explosion applies pressure to spindle

De Bange obturation
The explosion of the propellent gases throws pressure against a mushroom-shaped spindle in the centre of the breech block. This forces the spindle against a rubber obturator pad, which expands, sealing the breech.

Direction of shell

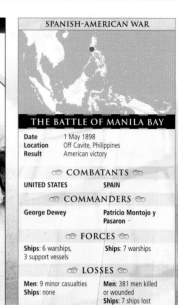

SPANISH-AMERICAN WAR

THE BATTLE OF MANILA BAY

Date	1 May 1898
Location	Off Cavite, Philippines
Result	American victory

∞ COMBATANTS ∞

UNITED STATES	SPAIN

∞ COMMANDERS ∞

George Dewey	Patricio Montojo y Pasaron

∞ FORCES ∞

Ships: 6 warships, 3 support vessels	**Ships:** 7 warships

∞ LOSSES ∞

Men: 9 minor casualties **Ships**: none	**Men**: 381 men killed or wounded **Ships**: 7 ships lost

THE BATTLE OF MANILA BAY

On 27 April 1898 Commodore George Dewey, commanding the US Asiatic Squadron anchored in Mirs Bay, China, received a cable from Navy Secretary John D Long: "War has commenced between the United States and Spain. Proceed at once to Philippine islands." Dewey had been expecting this order, but his preparations had been hampered by logistical problems. The nearest US base was in California, and his cruisers had only 60 per cent of their optimum ammunition supply – even less than the standard peacetime allotment.

Dewey's mission was to attack Spain's fleet in the Philippines, which, it was correctly assumed, would stay inshore, depending on land batteries for defence against the better-armoured, heavier-gunned American ships. The Spanish admiral Patricio Montojo originally planned to anchor in Subic Bay, north of Manila, but as shore batteries had negligently not been mounted there, he instead awaited the Americans in Manila Bay. Humane and defeatist, Montojo chose not to fight in front of Manila, where a battle

would have caused numerous civilian casualties. Instead, he anchored off Cavite Naval Yard, in shallow water so that his sailors would have a better chance of survival when their ships sank. Defeating the Americans was not an objective; for Montojo the fight was for the honour of the Spanish Empire.

On the night of 30 April, on board the protected cruiser *Olympia*, Dewey led his squadron into Boca Grande channel, steaming in column with all but stern lights extinguished. Tension was high, for there had been reports

that the channel had been mined and was defended by shore batteries. Their presence was revealed when a support vessel's smokestack flared with fire, but this brought only a brief exchange with guns on El Fraile island. By 1am Dewey's squadron had safely made its way inside Manila Bay.

The engagement between the two ill-matched naval squadrons began soon after dawn. After finding only merchant ships at Manila, Dewey led his cruisers toward Cavite in line ahead, a leadsman calling the depth at *Olympia*'s bow.

> 66
> ## THE STORM OF SHOT AND SHELL LAUNCHED AGAINST THE SPANIARD WAS DESTRUCTIVE BEYOND ALL DESCRIPTION.
> **JL STICKNEY,** LIEUTENANT ABOARD *OLYMPIA,* IN A NEWSPAPER ARTICLE, 1898
> 99

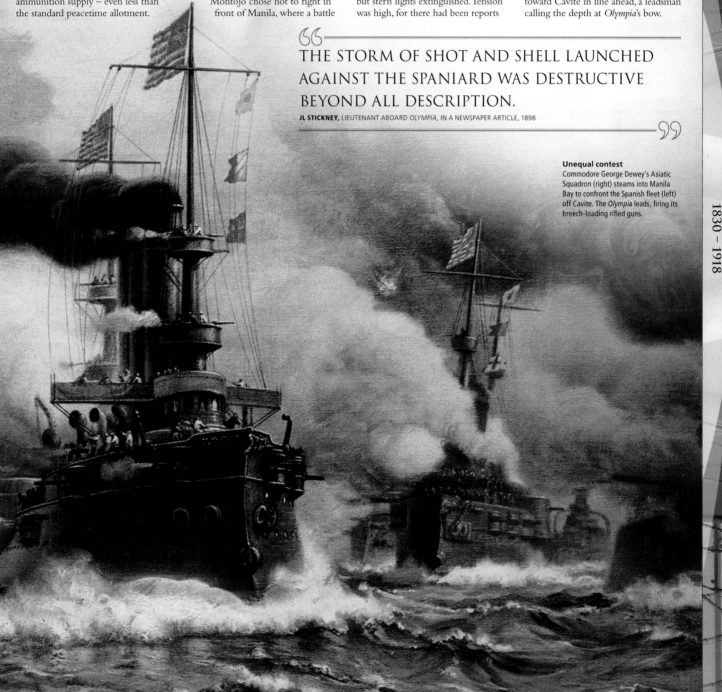

Unequal contest
Commodore George Dewey's Asiatic Squadron (right) steams into Manila Bay to confront the Spanish fleet (left) off Cavite. The *Olympia* leads, firing its breech-loading rifled guns.

STEAM AND STEEL

The Spanish battery on Sangley Point and Montojo's ships opened fire while still well out of range. Aware of his shortage of shells, Dewey waited half an hour before giving the laconic order to *Olympia*'s captain "You may fire when ready, Gridley". The American cruisers steamed back and forth on a course parallel to the static Spanish line, battering the enemy ships successively with port and starboard guns. By the fifth pass, just after 7am, the Americans, peering through dense smoke, could see little sign that their guns were having any great effect. And indeed their fire was woefully inaccurate, 99 out of 100 shots missing their target, the increased range of contemporary guns having outstripped techniques for aiming. Nonetheless, Montojo's ships had taken appalling punishment.

America in the ascendant
The second American assault on the Spanish fleet, made after the "breakfast break", saw the end of Spanish imperial power in the Pacific. The battle also marked the birth of America as a global power.

At 7:35am Dewey received the startling news that his 5in guns were running short of ammunition. He signalled for a withdrawal to the centre of the bay. His surprised crew were told this was a halt for breakfast, and took the chance to rest and eat.

FINAL PHASE

During the break, the smoke cleared, and the dire condition of the Spanish ships was revealed; most had been fatally mauled. And to make matters worse, the Americans' ammunition turned out to be plentiful; only 15 rounds per 5in gun

Anniversary medal
This commemmorative medal shows a port-bow view of Dewey's flagship *Olympia*. Battle-ready, she has flags flying from her mainmast.

had been fired, while the report had suggested only 15 rounds per 5in gun remained. American casualties were also minimal; nine men had been injured, and one, Chief Engineer Randall, had died of heart failure when the fleet had entered the bay.

At 11:15am, led by the cruiser *Baltimore*, Dewey's squadron returned to finish the job. With little resistance they pummelled the ships and shore batteries into surrender. In the afternoon, the Americans anchored off Manila and entertained Spanish sightseers gathered on the waterfront with the music of their bands.

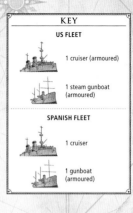

KEY
US FLEET
1 cruiser (armoured)
1 steam gunboat (armoured)
SPANISH FLEET
1 cruiser
1 gunboat (armoured)

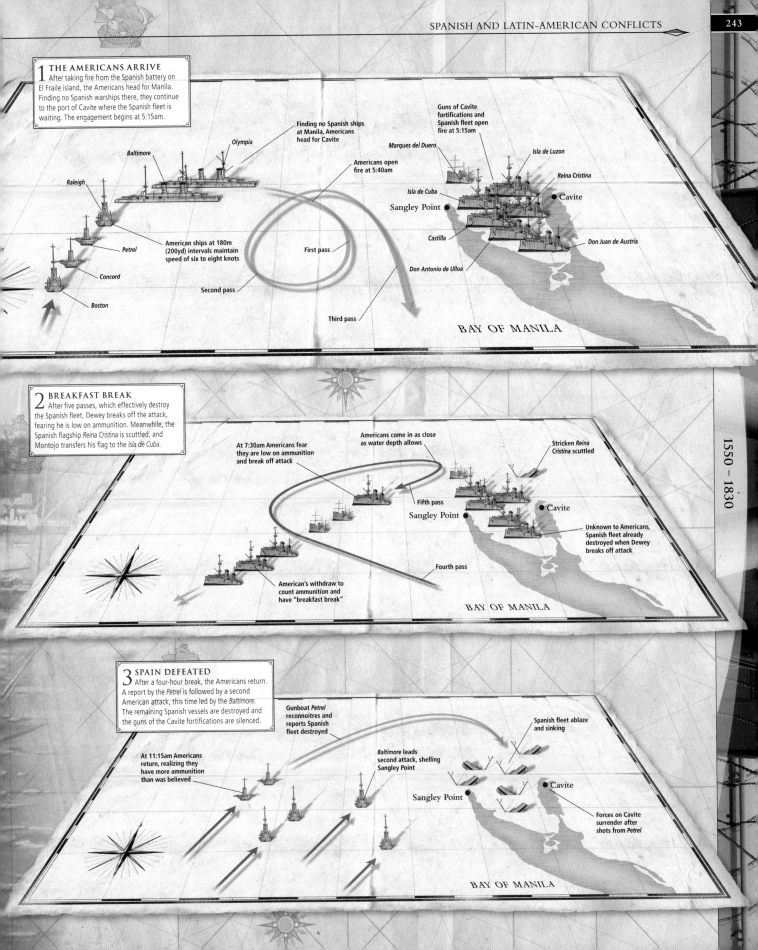

1 THE AMERICANS ARRIVE
After taking fire from the Spanish battery on El Fraile island, the Americans head for Manila. Finding no Spanish warships there, they continue to the port of Cavite where the Spanish fleet is waiting. The engagement begins at 5:15am.

Finding no Spanish ships at Manila, Americans head for Cavite

Olympia

Baltimore

Raleigh

Petrel

Concord

Boston

American ships at 180m (200yd) intervals maintain speed of six to eight knots

First pass

Second pass

Third pass

Americans open fire at 5:40am

Guns of Cavite fortifications and Spanish fleet open fire at 5:15am

Marques del Duero

Isla de Luzon

Reina Cristina

Isla de Cuba

Sangley Point

Cavite

Castilla

Don Juan de Austria

Don Antonio de Ulloa

BAY OF MANILA

2 BREAKFAST BREAK
After five passes, which effectively destroy the Spanish fleet, Dewey breaks off the attack, fearing he is low on ammunition. Meanwhile, the Spanish flagship *Reina Cristina* is scuttled, and Montojo transfers his flag to the *Isla de Cuba*.

At 7:30am Americans fear they are low on ammunition and break off attack

Americans come in as close as water depth allows

Stricken *Reina Cristina* scuttled

Fifth pass

Sangley Point

Cavite

Unknown to Americans, Spanish fleet already destroyed when Dewey breaks off attack

American's withdraw to count ammunition and have "breakfast break"

Fourth pass

BAY OF MANILA

3 SPAIN DEFEATED
After a four-hour break, the Americans return. A report by the *Petrel* is followed by a second American attack, this time led by the *Baltimore*. The remaining Spanish vessels are destroyed and the guns of the Cavite fortifications are silenced.

Gunboat *Petrel* reconnoitres and reports Spanish fleet destroyed

Spanish fleet ablaze and sinking

At 11:15am Americans return, realizing they have more ammunition than was believed

Baltimore leads second attack, shelling Sangley Point

Sangley Point

Cavite

Forces on Cavite surrender after shots from *Petrel*

BAY OF MANILA

RISE OF THE IMPERIAL JAPANESE NAVY

JAPAN'S IMPERIAL NAVY had an extraordinarily brief lifespan. Created during the late 1860s and first blooded in battle against China in 1894, it grew to be the world's third greatest naval force before abruptly ceasing to exist after the total defeat of Japan in 1945. The Imperial Navy was conceived as part of a wider project to modernize Japan and challenge the supremacy of the European powers and the United States. Its great victory over the Russian navy at Tsushima in 1905 was a stunning rebuff to the prevailing assumptions of white racial superiority. The Imperial Navy embodied both Japan's impressive ability to adopt Western technology and its own warrior tradition, which gave Japanese forces their particular spirit of disciplined, sometimes fatalistic self-sacrifice.

An archetypal hero in a modern setting
Japanese artists were quick to commemorate the navy's exploits in the Sino-Japanese War. Here, Lieutenant Commander Sakamoto of the *Akagi*, a gunboat that fought at Yalu River, gestures defiantly at the Chinese.

BORN OF HUMILIATION

When Commodore Matthew Perry anchored four American steam warships off Edo – now modern-day Tokyo – in July 1853, Japan had no national navy with which to repel this foreign intrusion. Its defencelessness was soon exploited, as the United States was joined later by Britain, France, and the Netherlands in bullying a small country for whose traditions they had no respect. In 1863 the British Royal Navy bombarded the Japanese city of Kagoshima, and the following year an international force shelled rebels opposed to foreign influence at Shimonoseki. These humiliations set in train a process of upheaval in Japan that resulted in the restoration of a strong central government under Emperor Meiji and the crushing of the samurai clans who opposed this. Japan then embarked on a breakneck rush to modernization in order to take on the West on its own terms.

During the civil strife surrounding the Meiji Restoration, an ad-hoc Imperial Navy was created from assorted ships of samurai clans

Triumph of the new navy
The first serious test for the Imperial Japanese Navy came when it took on a Chinese fleet at the battle of Yalu River in 1894. The Japanese cruisers sank five enemy ships, without suffering the loss of a single vessel.

Officer's dirk
This ceremonial dagger combines aspects of Western and Japanese weapons. Dirks of this kind were worn by officers from the time of the Russo–Japanese War.

supporting the emperor. The foundations for a modern navy were laid after the establishment of a Navy Department in 1872, which set about creating Western-style naval dockyards, a naval academy, and an arsenal. At first Japan was totally dependent upon a transfer of technology and skills from the West. Britain's Royal Navy provided cadet training and British shipyards supplied most of Japan's early warships. The Japanese proved supremely good learners in naval as in other matters and the scope of their ambitions was soon apparent. In 1885 Japan took delivery of two steel cruisers that were the largest and most advanced vessels of their type in the world. By the 1890s Japanese shipyards had begun delivering home-built armoured warships.

NAVAL POWER

The ethos of the new Japanese Imperial Navy was formed through a mix of British influence – Japan's greatest admiral Togo Heihachiro consciously modelled himself upon Nelson – and of the samurai tradition of loyalty to the death. Japan was historically inclined to value its army far above its navy; only the Satsuma samurai clan had a naval tradition. However, the defeat of China at sea in the Sino-Japanese war of 1894-95 raised the reputation of the Imperial Navy both at home and abroad. Naval strength became the key to the acceptance of Japan as

a major power on the world stage, in defiance of Western racial prejudice. The British, worried by the Royal Navy's inability to match combined French and Russian sea power in the Pacific, concluded a defensive alliance with Japan in January 1902. From the point of view of Britain this was a practical solution to the problem of finding a naval ally in the Pacific. To the Japanese it was above all about achieving the right to respect as equals of the West.

Bolstered by the alliance with Britain, in 1904-05 Japan took on and beat the Russian Empire both on land and at sea – beginning the conflict with a surprise attack on Port Arthur without a declaration of war, an ominous prefiguration of Pearl Harbor in 1941. The Russo-Japanese War was a triumph for Japan and a proving ground for cutting-edge naval technology, at least on the Japanese side. The war showed the importance of wireless communications, possessed by the Japanese but not by the Russians. It showed the frightful potential of mines, which sunk battleships on both sides, and the possible uses of torpedo-firing destroyers. Above all, it showed the devastating effect of the latest naval guns with advanced fire control, delivering concentrated fire at long range with explosive shells.

The period of peace in Japan after 1905 saw cutbacks in naval spending, but even so the first Japanese-built dreadnought was launched in 1910 and bigger and better warships followed. The startling reversal of Japan's naval weakness of only half a century before was clearly illustrated in World War I, when Japan was able to help out its overstretched ally Britain by sending destroyers to carry out anti-submarine duties in the Mediterranean. By then, however, potential conflicts of interest with Britain and the United States in the Pacific were already brewing.

CROSSING THE T

CONCENTRATING FIRE

The naval battles of the 1904-05 Russo-Japanese War demonstrated the new naval tactics of fleet encounters between steam-powered warships with their guns mounted in rotating turrets. As in the age of sail, ships entered battle in line astern and they might steam parallel to each other exchanging salvoes. However, the fleet with the faster warships could then potentially manoeuvre to cross in front of the enemy line, bringing to bear enfilading fire (directed along the enemy line) from all the guns of its line simultaneously, while the enemy could only reply with its forward guns. The range of effective fire at this period was over 5km (3 miles). This tactic, known in English as "crossing the T" and in Japanese as *tei sempo*, was a textbook ideal aspired to by naval commanders the world over, but it was rarely put into practice with complete success.

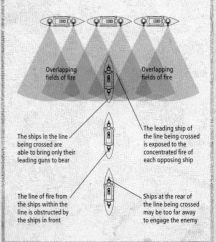

Overlapping fields of fire

Overlapping fields of fire

The ships in the line being crossed are able to bring only their leading guns to bear

The leading ship of the line being crossed is exposed to the concentrated fire of each opposing ship

The line of fire from the ships within the line is obstructed by the ships in front

Ships at the rear of the line being crossed may be too far away to engage the enemy

JAPANESE NAVAL MIGHT

THE JAPANESE IMPERIAL NAVY started its life as an ad-hoc force of mostly wooden steam warships assembled to fight the civil conflict known as the Boshin War, in which Emperor Meiji triumphed over Tokugawa loyalists in 1868-69. Over the next two decades Japan founded a modern navy complete with organizational structures copied from the British and the latest styles of warship from European shipyards. The Chinese had also been modernizing their navy and, although European observers were sceptical about the ability of either force, they were inclined to see China as the stronger naval power. In July 1894 a small-scale naval clash at Asan brought China and Japan to open war – as well as causing a diplomatic row with Britain over the Japanese sinking of a British-crewed ship carrying Chinese troops. The subsequent Japanese naval victories at the Yalu River and Weihaiwei revealed the gulf between an Asian power that was successfully modernizing and one that was not. At the end of the war Russia refused to allow Japan to take the Liaodung Peninsula and Port Arthur, which China had agreed to cede, sowing the seeds for the Russo-Japanese War of 1904-05.

BOSHIN WAR

HAKODATE BAY

Date 4–10 May 1869
Forces Meiji: 8 ships; Tokugawa: 5 ships
Losses Meiji: 1 ship; Tokugawa: 2 ships destroyed, 3 captured

Location Hakodate Bay, Hokkaido, Japan.

In 1868–69 forces loyal to the Tokugawa shogunate fought to resist the transfer of power to supporters of the Emperor Meiji. An Imperial Japanese Navy was hastily assembled, centred on the French-built American-supplied ironclad *Kotetsu*. When Imperial forces attacked the last Tokugawa stronghold at Hakodate, the Tokugawa warships failed to prevent the landing of troops and were worsted in a series of actions. The Tokugawa schooner *Banryu* succeded in sinking the Imperial ship *Choyo*, but later herself sank. Their paddle steamer *Kaiten* was also disabled. The Tokugawa rebellion collapsed after this naval defeat.

FIRST SINO-JAPANESE WAR

YALU RIVER

Date 17 September 1894
Forces Japanese: 10 protected cruisers, 2 other ships; Chinese: 2 battleships, 10 cruisers, 2 other ships
Losses Japanese: none; Chinese: 5 ships

Location Off mouth of Yalu River, Yellow Sea

The first major battle fought by the Imperial Japanese Navy occurred when Admiral Sukeyuki Ito led a fleet on a sweep through Korea Bay, hoping to interrupt Chinese troop landings at the Yalu River, which marks the border between Korea and China. The troop landings were being covered by the Chinese Beiyang Fleet under Admiral Ting Ju ch'ang. The two fleets sighted each other at 11:40am on the morning of 17 September 1894. They were of roughly equal strength. The Chinese had the most powerful vessels present, two German-built armoured turret ships *Ting Yuen* and *Chen Yuen*, which carried 12in Krupp guns. But the

Portable telescope
A lacquered Japanese telescope dating from the time of the First Sino-Japanese War.

Japanese naval firepower
Exotically attired Chinese sailors come under fire from Japanese warships in this fanciful French print showing the Japanese victory at Yalu River.

FIRST SINO-JAPANESE WAR

ASAN

Date 25 July 1894
Forces Japanese: 3 cruisers; Chinese: 1 cruiser, 2 gunboats
Losses Japanese: none; Chinese: 1 gunboat and 1 transport sunk, 1 gunboat captured

Location Off Asan, Korea

In July 1894 Japan and China both had troops in Korea. The Japanese protected cruisers *Yoshino*, *Akitsushima*, and *Naniwa* were blockading Chinese forces at Asan, south of Seoul. At 7am on 25 July the Chinese cruiser *Kwang-yi* and the gunboat *Tsi-yuen* steamed out of Asan Bay toward the Japanese ships. The Japanese opened fire: *Kwang-yi* was badly damaged and forced back into the bay; the gunboat ran onto rocks and exploded. *Kowshing*, a Chinese troop transport flying the British flag, then arrived, accompanied by a gunboat. The gunboat promptly surrendered, but the Chinese soldiers refused to allow *Kowshing*'s British captain to follow suit. The protected cruiser *Naniwa* sank the troop transport with heavy loss of life.

Japanese cruisers were on average larger and faster than their Chinese opposite numbers. The two fleets steamed toward one another through the morning, the Japanese in line-ahead formation and the Chinese in two lines abreast.

JAPANESE TRIUMPH

The battle that followed was confused and brutal. The Japanese steamed down both sides of the Chinese formation, pumping shells into the enemy ships. The Chinese armoured cruiser *Ting Yuen* rolled over and sank; several other Chinese ships were ravaged by fire, apparently rendered vulnerable by decorative woodwork and layers of flammable paint. Chinese gunnery proved inferior, as did the quality of their munitions, although they had their successes – for example, Admiral Ito's flagship *Matsushima* was damaged by an explosion when a shell ignited ammunition on board. In five hours' fighting, some ships were hit several hundred times. With five ships sunk, by nightfall the Chinese lay at the mercy of their enemies. But, exhausted and running out of ammunition, Admiral Ito withdrew his fleet short of total victory. The Chinese suffered some 850 men killed and had 500 wounded; Japanese losses numbered 90 killed, about 200 wounded, and not a single Japanese ship was destroyed.

WEAPONS AND TECHNOLOGY

TORPEDOES

The torpedo began life as a static mine. In the second half of the 19th century navies were seeking methods of moving a mine to strike a ship's hull. This led to the spar torpedo, a mine on a long pole projecting from the front of an attack craft, and the Brennan torpedo, a mine controlled by wires from shore. The first effective self-propelled torpedo was invented in the 1860s by Robert Whitehead, a British engineer working on a commission for the Austrian navy. The Whitehead torpedo had a propeller driven by compressed air and used a pressure gauge attached to horizontal rudders to keep a constant depth. Self-propelled torpedoes were unreliable for many decades – most of those fired in the Russo-Japanese war of 1904–05, for example, failed for one reason or another – but their potential was quickly recognized, leading to the development of purpose-built torpedo boats and of torpedo-boat destroyers to counter them.

Whitehead torpedo
The first effective self-propelled torpedo, the Whitehead torpedo had a range of over 300m (980ft).

247

Fierce sea battle at Weihaiwei
A heroic sword-wielding officer of the Imperial Japanese Navy spurs forward his men as they fire on a Chinese warship at Weihaiwei.

1830 – 1918

FIRST SINO-JAPANESE WAR

WEIHAIWEI

Date 30 January–12 February 1895
Forces Japanese: 41 vessels including 16 torpedo boats; Chinese: 2 battleships, 5 cruisers, 13 torpedo boats
Losses Japanese: none; Chinese: 1 battleship, 2 cruisers, 6 torpedo boats sunk, all others captured
Location Shantung Peninsula, China

After the punishing battle at the Yalu River, Chinese admiral Ting Ju ch'ang withdrew his fleet to the fortified harbour at Weihaiwei. Here his turret ships, cruisers, and torpedo boats were protected by shore guns and a barrier of tethered mines and steel hawsers across the harbour mouth. The Japanese fleet arrived at the end of January 1895 to blockade the harbour while troops attacked Weihaiwei by land. The weather was appalling with prolonged blizzards and on several occasions sailors froze to death at their posts. The Japanese ships engaged in gun duels with the Chinese shore batteries and warships day and night, with no decisive results.

Seeing that they would have to enter the harbour, the Japanese carried out risky minesweeping operations and cut one of the steel hawsers. They then sent torpedo boats into the harbour several times at night, sinking the armoured turret ship *Ting Yuen* and the cruisers *Ching Yuen* and *Lai Yuen*. In a desperate gesture, Admiral Ting sent all his torpedo boats out of the harbour in a daylight sortie that resulted in all of the boats being sunk or captured. By 12 February the Chinese had had enough of the extreme cold, continual bombardment, and terrifying night raids. Admiral Ting sent a surrender note to the Japanese admiral. Before the Japanese could take possession of the enemy fleet, the Chinese admiral committed suicide. Shortly after, China sought peace negotiations with Japan.

CREW PROFILE

JAPANESE IMPERIAL WARSHIP

1870s TO EARLY 1900s

WHEN THE JAPANESE SET OUT to create the Imperial Navy almost from scratch in the 1870s, they received most of their training and ships from Britain. The result was a service in most ways similar to Western navies of the time. All ranks were uniformed and formal discipline such as saluting of officers was strictly enforced. The navy was in the forefront of the headlong modernization of Japan, well ahead of most of civil society, so it was on board ship that many Japanese recruits first got to grips with technologies such as steam engines and electricity. Discipline was often enforced with slaps or punches, but this was apparently acceptable to the average Japanese sailor, brought up in an ordered and disciplined society.

OFFICER CLASS

Commissioned officers were more numerous in the steam era than in the age of sail, and more diverse. Many were given responsibility for specialist areas, such as gunnery, engines, or torpedoes. The first wave of Japanese officers was mostly recruited from the Satsuma samurai clan, and the founding ethos of the Imperial Navy mingled the samurai tradition with attitudes and practices learned from Britain's Royal Navy. The Etajima Naval Academy soon became the route into the Japanese naval officer corps. Entrants were picked by rigorous nationwide examinations, with many more applicants than places available. Those who passed were then subjected to four years intensive training, with an emphasis on physical fitness as well as academic education. Graduates from Etajima entered the navy as a self-conscious elite.

DISCIPLINE AND AUSTERITY

Despite holding a high sense of status and personal honour, Japanese officers tended to be frugal and spartan, sleeping on rush mats on the deck. When the men had to clean decks barefoot in freezing weather, Admiral Togo would reportedly come on deck barefoot himself. Obedience and loyalty were highly valued qualities in Japanese society and transferred well to the formal, hierarchical world of a warship.

Imperial Japanese officer
Smartly uniformed Japanese officers look on as well-drilled sailors of the Imperial Japanese Navy fire on the Chinese fleet at the Yalu River.

THE RUSSO-JAPANESE WAR

THE RUSSIAN AND JAPANESE Empires went to war in 1904 over their rival ambitions in northern China and Korea. In the naval war, the Japanese were from the outset more aggressively led and better trained and motivated than their opponents. The Russians also suffered from the dispersal of their naval forces – the squadrons in Port Arthur and Vladivostok never succeeded in joining up, and when the Baltic fleet was sent on an epic voyage around the world to the Pacific in 1905, it was crushingly defeated at Tsushima. The victory for an Asiatic over a European power upset assumptions of white racial superiority. Japan gained control of Port Arthur and soon took over Korea. The Japanese were confirmed as valuable allies for Britain in the Pacific, while defeat plunged Russia into the 1905 revolution that the tsarist regime barely survived.

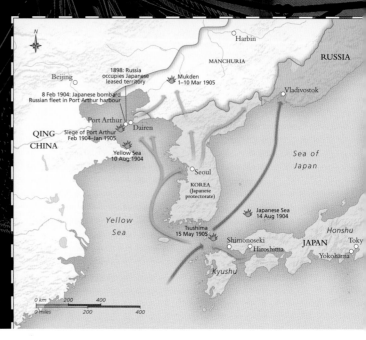

THE RUSSO-JAPANESE WAR 1904-1905

The main areas of operations during the Russo-Japanese War were the Korean and Liaodong peninsulas, southern Manchuria, and the seas around Japan and Korea. The Russians were particularly keen to control the warm-water Pacific port of Port Arthur – the other main Russian port on the Pacific, Vladivostok, was inaccessible during winter months.

KEY

▨	Japan
▨	Russia
▨	To Russia 1897, to Japan 1905
▨	Area leased to Japan 1895
⇒	Japanese advance/ landing
⇒	Route of Russian Baltic fleet 1905
⚓	Japanese victory

THE BATTLE OF PORT ARTHUR

The Russian First Pacific Squadron in harbour at Port Arthur was a potential threat that Japan decided to eliminate at the outset of hostilities. Admiral Togo planned a night attack that would enjoy total surprise since it would precede a declaration of war.

An attack squadron of 10 Japanese destroyers armed with Whitehead torpedoes reached Port Arthur shortly after midnight on 8 February. Most of the Russian fleet was lit up, as was the town behind it. Confusion and terror followed as torpedoes exploded against the hulls of the American-built pre-dreadnought *Retvizan* and the protected cruiser *Pallada*. The battleship *Tsesarevich* was also hit. But the operation was less effective than Togo had hoped. Many torpedoes were caught in Russian torpedo nets and failed to explode. Once Russian searchlights and guns were manned the destroyers found it hard to press home further attacks. The action was broken off at around 2am. No Russian ships had been sunk.

THE DAYLIGHT ACTION

The following morning, believing the Russian ships were more damaged than they were, Togo led his fleet toward Port Arthur to complete the destruction of the Russian fleet. He was to be disappointed. The Russians remained in harbour, drawing the Japanese within range of shore guns. A brisk exchange of long-range fire brought further damage to a number of Russian ships, but Togo's flagship *Mikasa* was also hit. After an hour the Japanese turned away.

The inconclusive result to the fighting forced the Japanese to mount a prolonged siege of Port Arthur by both sea and land. However, the arrival of the vigorous Russian admiral Stepan Makarov to take over command in Port Arthur put fresh heart into the Russian fleet. Maintaining a blockade over succeeding months the Japanese lost a number of ships to mines. Stepan Makarov was also a victim of a mine, going down on board his flagship *Petropavlovsk* during a rare sortie outside Port Arthur on 13 April.

Assault on Port Arthur
A line of Japanese battleships steams toward Port Arthur, the bombardment from the Russian shore defences sending up plumes of water around them.

1848-1934
TOGO HEIHACHIRO
FLEET-ADMIRAL OF THE IMPERIAL JAPANESE NAVY

Born into the Satsuma samurai clan, as a boy Togo Heihachiro witnessed the bullying of Japan by foreign naval forces, a humiliation he never forgot. Enrolled in the fledgling Imperial Navy, he went to Britain for training in 1871 and brought back an enduring respect for the traditions of the Royal Navy. Togo first attracted attention as captain of the cruiser *Naniwa* in the action at Asan that opened the war with China in 1894. A calm and confident commander during the Russo-Japanese War, victories at the Yellow Sea and Tsushima made him one of the world's most respected admirals.

YELLOW SEA

Date 10 August 1904
Forces Japanese: 4 battleships, 2 armoured cruisers, 8 other cruisers, 18 destroyers, 30 torpedo boats; Russians: 6 battleships, 4 cruisers, 8 destroyers
Location Off Shantung Peninsula, China
Losses Japanese: none; Russians: 1 battleship, 2 cruisers, 4 destroyers interned in neutral ports

After being blockaded in harbour for six months, on 10 August 1904 the Russian First Pacific Squadron steamed out into the Yellow Sea. Its commander, Rear Admiral Vilgelm Karlovich Vitgeft, was obeying a personal order from Tsar Nicholas II to join the rest of the Russian Pacific fleet in Vladivostok. Vitgeft personally considered the breakout attempt doomed to failure.

Admiral Togo, commanding the Japanese blockade from the battleship *Mikasa*, prepared to engage the Russians as they came out, but surprisingly missed them. Executing manoeuvres designed primarily to keep his own flagship in the van, he found himself

pursuing the Russians from a good distance behind. Fortunately for Togo the Russian ships were slow and by 5pm his four battleships and two armoured cruisers were in position to engage the six Russian battleships. Steaming in line ahead on a parallel course, the ships bombarded one another ferociously. Eyewitnesses described the gigantic columns of water thrown up by the shells, the noise of explosions, clouds of foul smoke, and decks streaming with blood. *Mikasa* was hit repeatedly but it was Vitgeft's flagship *Tsesarevich* that suffered worst. The key moment in the battle occurred when two shells struck *Tsesarevich's* bridge. Vitgeft and all his senior officers were killed. Out of control, the battleship was stuck in a turn to port that many other Russian ships blindly followed, looping pointlessly.

As night fell most of the Russian fleet headed back to Port Arthur. *Tsesarevich* and some other ships sought refuge in neutral ports, where they were interned. The First Pacific Squadron would play no further part in the war.

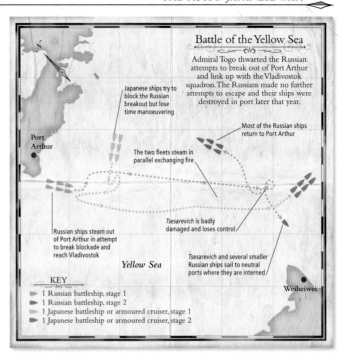

Battle of the Yellow Sea

Admiral Togo thwarted the Russian attempts to break out of Port Arthur and link up with the Vladivostok squadron. The Russians made no further attempts to escape and their ships were destroyed in port later that year.

KEY
- 1 Russian battleship, stage 1
- 1 Russian battleship, stage 2
- 1 Japanese battleship or armoured cruiser, stage 1
- 1 Japanese battleship or armoured cruiser, stage 2

> # THE ATTACK MUST BE DELIVERED WITH THE GREATEST ENERGY POSSIBLE BECAUSE, GENTLEMEN ... ONLY HE WHO ACTS FEARLESSLY CAN HOPE FOR SUCCESS.
>
> **TOGO HEIHACHIRO,** ADDRESS BEFORE PORT ARTHUR, 1904

THE BATTLE OF PORT ARTHUR

Date	8–9 February 1904
Location	Liaodong peninsula
Result	Inconclusive

COMBATANTS

JAPAN	RUSSIA

COMMANDERS

Heihachiro Togo	Oscar Stark

FORCES

Ships: Japan: 6 battleships, 5 cruisers, 35 destroyers and torpedo boats	**Ships:** Russia: 7 battleships, 5 cruisers, various smaller vessels

LOSSES

Men: 132 casualties **Ships:** none	**Men:** 150 casualties **Ships:** none

THE JAPANESE SEA

Date 14 August 1904
Forces Japanese: 4 armoured cruisers; 2 protected cruisers Russians: 3 armoured cruisers
Losses Japanese: none; Russians: 1 cruiser
Location Off Ulsan, Korea

Russian rear admiral Karl Jessen was sent out of Vladivostok with armoured cruisers *Rossia*, *Gromoboi*, and *Rurik* to meet the First Pacific Squadron coming from Port Arthur. Jessen was unaware of the defeat at the Yellow Sea, but turned for home when the squadron failed to appear. Unfortunately he ran into a stronger force of Japanese cruisers under Vice Admiral Kamimura. *Rurik*, the rearmost Russian ship, came under heavy bombardment. Disabled and with most of her officers dead, the cruiser gallantly maintained defensive fire until scuttled by the few survivors. *Rossia* and *Gromoboi*, at Kamimura's mercy, were inexplicably allowed to escape.

WITNESS TO WAR
LIEUTENANT ANDREI PETROVICH STEER
SINKING OF THE RUSSIAN FLAGSHIP PETROPAVLOVSK OUTSIDE PORT ARTHUR

> *In quick succession, **a series of perfectly deafening explosions**, and the big ship literally broken into several parts, **began to go down fast, head foremost**. We saw by degrees the propellers, still revolving, appear out of the water, then her bottom, painted bright green, **while positive sheets of flame ran along the upper deck** ... she finally disappeared in a veritable geyser of steam and columns of water.*

THE BATTLE OF TSUSHIMA

In October 1904 five divisions of the Russian Baltic Fleet, renamed Second Pacific Squadron, set off on a journey of 18,000 nautical miles (30,000km) to join the defence of Port Arthur against the Japanese. Commanded by Admiral Zinovi Rozhdestvenski, the squadron soon showed its inexperience by firing on British trawlers in the North Sea, taking them for Japanese torpedo boats. Slow and gruelling, the long and difficult voyage took a heavy toll on the labouring ships' engines and on crew morale. Rozhdestvenski was joined by Admiral Nikolai Nebogatov with more Baltic warships, designated Third Pacific Squadron, to create a fleet of impressive size, but dubious quality.

Port Arthur had fallen by the time this Russian armada reached East Asia, so Vladivostok became its substitute goal. Short of coal, Rozhdestvenski chose the shortest route past Japan, through the Tsushima Strait. Admiral Heihachiro Togo, commanding the Japanese Combined Fleet, had anticipated this choice. But on the night of 26–27 May, in fog and mist, the Russians might have slipped past had not the Japanese auxiliary cruiser *Shinano Maru* spotted a Russian hospital ship with its navigation lights lit. On board his flagship *Mikasa* in Chinae Bay, Admiral Togo was immediately informed by wireless – then a novel technology. Togo in turn informed his government: "The Russian fleet has been sighted. I will attack it and annihilate it." The admiral's confidence, shared by his officers and men, contrasted markedly with the state of mind of the Russians after their arduous journey. Togo's only fear was that the enemy fleet might escape in the mist and gloom. Once visual contact was made in the early afternoon, the Russians were doomed.

RELENTLESS PURSUIT

Togo was a great admirer of Nelson and, recognizing this as his Trafalgar, announced the start of the battle by hoisting the "Z" flag, conveying the signal: "The Empire's fate depends on the outcome of this battle, let every man do his utmost duty." Where the Russians had difficulty holding a line of battle in a chaos of confused orders and poor seamanship, the Japanese manoeuvred with precision and daring, exploiting to the full their speed advantage over the Russian ships. In the gunnery duel between battleships the Japanese proved far superior, due to better training and range-finding technology. Their high-explosive shells devastated the superstructure of Russian ships, scattering deadly steel splinters, starting fires, and ripping open armour. A Russian officer described how "iron ladders were crumpled into rings and guns hurled from their mountings."

By nightfall four Russian battleships had been sunk, with appalling loss of life. Rozhdestvenski was wounded by a shell fragment in the skull, leaving the inexperienced Nebogatov in command. Through the night attacks by Japanese destroyers and torpedo boats took a further toll, and morning found scattered remnants of the Russian fleet struggling for survival. At 10:30am Nebogatov abjectly surrendered the ships under his immediate command. Other Russian warships were hunted down through the day. Only three made it through to Vladivostok.

The battle forced Russia to accept defeat in the war with Japan and led to the 1905 revolutionary uprising against the tsarist regime.

RUSSO-JAPANESE WAR	
BATTLE OF TSUSHIMA	
Date	27–28 May 1905
Location	Tsushima Strait, between Japan and Korea
Result	Japanese victory

COMBATANTS	
JAPAN	**RUSSIA**

COMMANDERS	
Heihachiro Togo	**Zinovi Rozhdestvenski**
	Nikolai Nebogatov

FORCES	
Ships: 4 battleships, 24 cruisers, 20 destroyers, 16 torpedo boats	**Ships:** 8 battleships, 8 cruisers, 3 coastal monitors, 9 destroyers

LOSSES	
Men: 117	**Men:** 4,380 killed, 5,917 captured
Ships: 3 torpedo boats sunk	**Ships:** 17 ships sunk, 5 captured

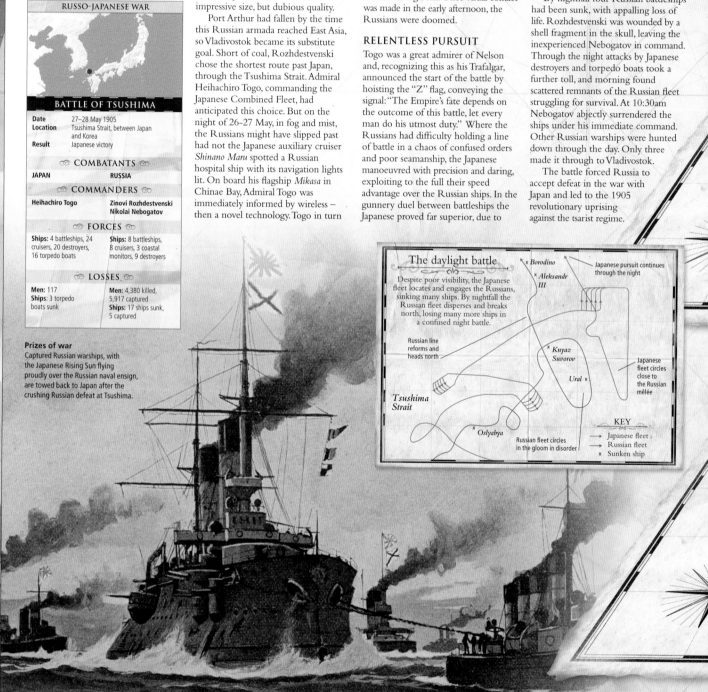

Prizes of war
Captured Russian warships, with the Japanese Rising Sun flying proudly over the Russian naval ensign, are towed back to Japan after the crushing Russian defeat at Tsushima.

The daylight battle

Despite poor visibility, the Japanese fleet locates and engages the Russians, sinking many ships. By nightfall the Russian fleet disperses and breaks north, losing many more ships in a confused night battle.

Japanese pursuit continues through the night

x *Borodino*

x *Aleksandr III*

Russian line reforms and heads north

x *Knyaz Suvorov*

Ural x

Japanese fleet circles close to the Russian mêlée

Tsushima Strait

x *Oslyabya*

Russian fleet circles in the gloom in disorder

KEY
→ Japanese fleet
→ Russian fleet
x Sunken ship

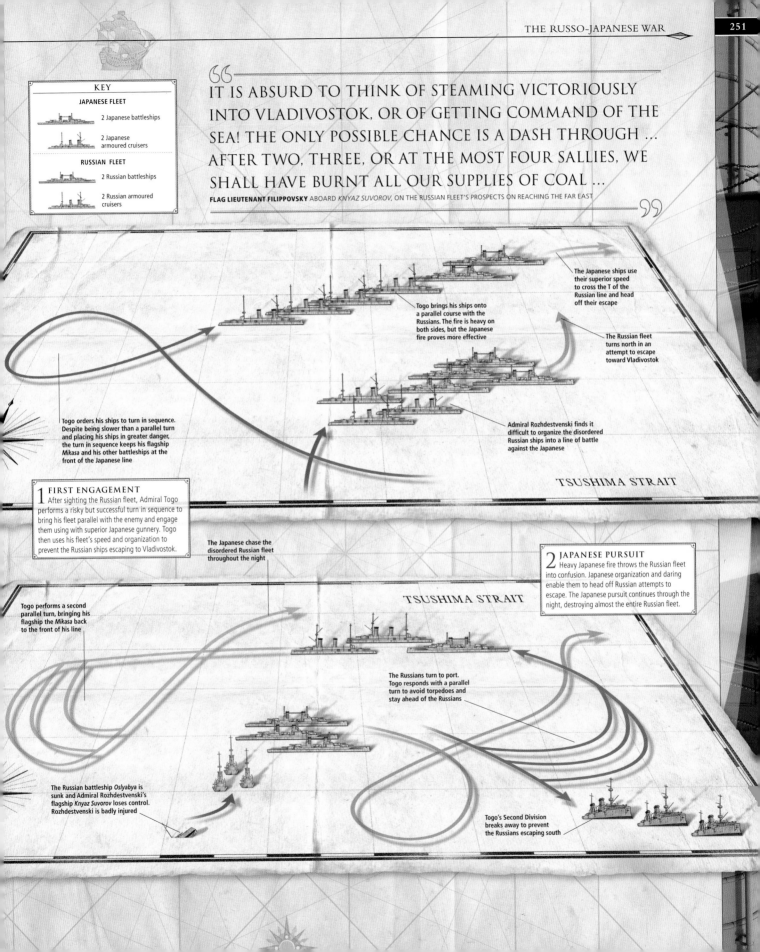

KEY

JAPANESE FLEET

2 Japanese battleships

2 Japanese armoured cruisers

RUSSIAN FLEET

2 Russian battleships

2 Russian armoured cruisers

> IT IS ABSURD TO THINK OF STEAMING VICTORIOUSLY INTO VLADIVOSTOK, OR OF GETTING COMMAND OF THE SEA! THE ONLY POSSIBLE CHANCE IS A DASH THROUGH … AFTER TWO, THREE, OR AT THE MOST FOUR SALLIES, WE SHALL HAVE BURNT ALL OUR SUPPLIES OF COAL …

FLAG LIEUTENANT FILIPPOVSKY ABOARD *KNYAZ SUVOROV*, ON THE RUSSIAN FLEET'S PROSPECTS ON REACHING THE FAR EAST

The Japanese ships use their superior speed to cross the T of the Russian line and head off their escape

Togo brings his ships onto a parallel course with the Russians. The fire is heavy on both sides, but the Japanese fire proves more effective

The Russian fleet turns north in an attempt to escape toward Vladivostok

Togo orders his ships to turn in sequence. Despite being slower than a parallel turn and placing his ships in greater danger, the turn in sequence keeps his flagship *Mikasa* and his other battleships at the front of the Japanese line

Admiral Rozhdestvenski finds it difficult to organize the disordered Russian ships into a line of battle against the Japanese

TSUSHIMA STRAIT

1 FIRST ENGAGEMENT

After sighting the Russian fleet, Admiral Togo performs a risky but successful turn in sequence to bring his fleet parallel with the enemy and engage them using with superior Japanese gunnery. Togo then uses his fleet's speed and organization to prevent the Russian ships escaping to Vladivostok.

The Japanese chase the disordered Russian fleet throughout the night

2 JAPANESE PURSUIT

Heavy Japanese fire throws the Russian fleet into confusion. Japanese organization and daring enable them to head off Russian attempts to escape. The Japanese pursuit continues through the night, destroying almost the entire Russian fleet.

Togo performs a second parallel turn, bringing his flagship the *Mikasa* back to the front of his line

TSUSHIMA STRAIT

The Russians turn to port. Togo responds with a parallel turn to avoid torpedoes and stay ahead of the Russians

The Russian battleship *Oslyabya* is sunk and Admiral Rozhdestvenski's flagship *Knyaz Suvorov* loses control. Rozhdestvenski is badly injured

Togo's Second Division breaks away to prevent the Russians escaping south

HIJMS MIKASA

THE JAPANESE BATTLESHIP MIKASA was Admiral Togo's flagship at the decisive battle of Tsushima in 1905. She has survived to be preserved as a museum ship at Yokosuka in Japan, the only pre-dreadnought battleship still in existence. When delivered by English shipbuilders Vickers in 1902, *Mikasa* was the most advanced warship in the world.

STEAM AND STEEL

MIKASA'S MAIN ARMAMENT consisted of four impressive 12in guns mounted in pairs in centreline turrets. There were also 14 smaller 6in guns arranged in broadside and 20 Quick Firing (QF) 3in guns distributed around the ship, intended for defence against torpedo boats. The battleship also had four submerged torpedo tubes. She was heavily armoured with Krupp steel plates, especially in a belt around the hull above the waterline and around the gun turrets. *Mikasa* proved capable of taking a lot of punishment. Some 30 hits from Russian guns at Tsushima failed to put her out of action. Ironically she was sunk in harbour shortly after the war with Russia ended, through an accidental explosion in a magazine. Although refloated, *Mikasa* was soon rendered obsolete as a new generation of dreadnought battleships took centre stage. She was decommissioned in 1923.

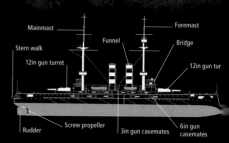

Victor of Tsushima
Admiral Togo's flagship *Mikasa* pictured around 1905, the year of the Japanese victory against the Russian fleet at Tsushima. The smoke from her powerful coal-powered engines billows through the ship's funnels.

Pre-dreadnought leviathan
Constructed for the Imperial Japanese Navy at Vickers shipyard in Britain and displacing more than 15,000 tons, *Mikasa* comfortably matched the size and firepower of the Royal Navy's own leading battleships.

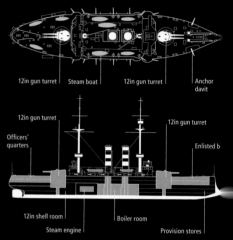

Mainmast · Foremast · Funnel · Bridge · Stern walk · 12in gun turret · 12in gun tur... · Rudder · Screw propeller · 3in gun casemates · 6in gun casemates

12in gun turret · Steam boat · 12in gun turret · Anchor davit

12in gun turret · 12in gun turret · Officers' quarters · Enlisted b... · 12in shell room · Boiler room · Steam engine · Provision stores

⌃ Fore anchor
The anchor rests on an indented area of the foredeck with a davit above to lift and drop it overboard. A chain runs through a hole in the bows to a capstan on the deck.

⌄ Imperial crest
The gold chrysanthemum on the *Mikasa*'s bow, the emblem used on all Imperial battleships, was the seal of the emperor of Japan.

《 12in gun turret
Mikasa's four main 12in guns are grouped in pairs in two armoured turrets, fore and aft, and could fire around three shells every two minutes. The power and range of *Mikasa*'s modern guns were a crucial factor at the battle of Tsushima.

⌃ Porthole
Small portholes run along the *Mikasa*'s hull, allowing a little natural light through the thick steel of the Krupp armour plating into the

> ❝
> JAPAN BLOSSOMED FORTH LIKE HER OWN CHRYSANTHEMUM ... HER BATTLESHIPS ARE PERHAPS THE FINEST IN THE WORLD.
> **NAVY AND ARMY ILLUSTRATED,** BRITISH MAGAZINE, 1902

Mainmast
Mikasa's fore- and aft- masts were used primarily as a mounting point for signals, lookouts, and wireless apparatus. Fortified "fighting tops" on the masts were armed with light guns for raking fire.

Broadside guns
Mikasa's armoured sides bristle with two rows of 3in and 6in broadside guns for use against smaller ships or to target the lightly armoured superstructure of larger warships.

Funnels and ventilators
The smoke produced by *Mikasa*'s 25 coal-fired Belleville boilers exited the ship through two large funnels in the centre of the deck. Several smaller ventilation shafts brought fresh air below deck.

Stern walkway
The admiral's cabin enjoyed direct access onto a narrow walkway around the stern end of the ship. The Japanese characters on the metal plate spell out the name of the battleship *Mikasa*.

Rangefinder
A Barr & Stroud FA3 rangefinder is mounted on the deck of the topgallant forecastle, behind the compass. A number of Russian ships at Tsushima were fitted with similar models, but better training meant the Japanese rangefinding proved far superior during battle.

Electric searchlight
A pair of long "wings" of decking extend on either side of the forecastle, down which the two large 90cm (35in) searchlights can be rolled. Powerful searchlights were essential at night and in fog to locate and target enemy ships and to prevent collisions.

Togo's command post
Admiral Togo commanded the fleet at Tsushima standing on the deck of the topgallant forecastle in front of this compass. Speaking tubes allowed him to send orders to the bridge below.

Forecastle
Underneath the foremast, looking toward the prow of the ship, are the main navigation and command areas: the pilothouse and bridge, the topgallant forecastle on the deck above, and two long "wings" on either side.

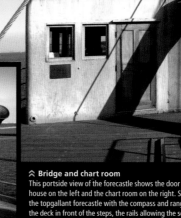

Bridge and chart room
This portside view of the forecastle shows the door to the pilot-house on the left and the chart room on the right. Steps lead up the topgallant forecastle with the compass and rangefinder. On the deck in front of the steps, the rails allowing the searchlights to be moved up and down the "wings" are just visible.

BELOW DECKS

THE ACCOMMODATION FOR *Mikasa*'s 840 officers and men was quite austere. Even the admiral's living space was simple, if comfortable. The other ranks slept in hammocks among the guns, as in Nelson's day. The ship could carry 2,000 tons of coal to fuel the triple expansion steam engines, which gave a maximum speed of 18 knots. Working conditions in the depths of the ship, amid the heat and noise of the engine rooms, were harsh. In battle men were acutely aware that a ship of this kind could be an iron coffin, sinking in minutes if badly holed. The upper deck where Admiral Togo stood in battle was protected only by sandbags from enemy fire. The ship was equipped with the newly invented wireless telegraph giving the Japanese fleet an advantage over the Russians in communications.

» Life ring
Mikasa carried several cork life rings in case of man overboard, as well as 14 lifeboats and launches of various sizes.

⩔ Ship's wheel
The polished wood and brass wheel from *Mikasa*'s pilothouse. A second wheel was located in an armoured conning tower for the helmsman to use during battle.

» 3in gun casemate
Eight 3in Quick Firing (QF) guns are mounted along the sides of the ship in armoured casemates. Too light to penetrate the armour of opposing battleships, the guns provided a defence against fast torpedo boats and destroyers.

⩔ Pilothouse
The ship was steered from the pilothouse using the wheel and engine order telegraphs. A compass is mounted inside a large brass binnacle case.

« ⩘ Entrance to 3in casemate
After the battle of Tsushima, the Russian Rear Admiral Nikolai Nebogatov entered the *Mikasa* through this door in the armoured casemate to present his sword and the surrender of his five remaining ships to Admiral Togo.

⩔ Morse key
Messages were tapped in using this Morse key and transmitted using *Mikasa*'s new wireless telegraphy equipment – a novel technology at the time *Mikasa* was launched in 1900.

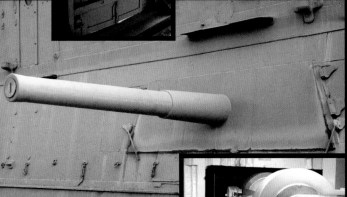

⩘ 6in broadside gun
Underneath each of the 3in gun casemates, fixed in place behind 15cm (6in) of steel plating, was a line of three 6in Quick Firing (QF) guns. Several more were fitted on the corners of the gun decks, bringing the total number to 14.

» 6in Quick Firing gun breech
The Quick Firing (QF) guns on *Mikasa* used a breech-loading mechanism and single-piece ammunition containing both the shell and propellant to enable more rapid loading.

Pantry

The petty officers' pantry was where the officers' food was prepared. Enlisted crewmen ate their meals in berthing areas in the bows of the ship.

Admiral's desk

The portrait of Admiral Togo on the desk in his cabin is inscribed with the only known example of his signature in English.

Admiral's bathroom

The washing facilities for the admiral and officers were simple but adequate – and a great deal more comfortable than those for the regular sailors.

Admiral's cabin

Admiral Togo's personal quarters are located on the second deck toward the stern of the ship. The admiral's cabin is austerely furnished with a desk and a high bed and drawers below for storage.

Togo's pocketbook

Admiral Togo's handwritten notebooks provide an intriguing window into the mind of the man who oversaw Japan's greatest naval victory.

Officer's wardroom

The large wardroom was used for meetings and as a dining area and recreation room for officers.

Admiral's saloon

The saloon is simply but comfortably furnished with carpets, cabinets, and a fireplace. Two Hotchkiss 3-pounder gun mounts on either side of the cabin provide the only reminder that the saloon is part of a ship of war.

Skylight over officers' quarters

Deck skylights connect directly to the admiral's cabin and captain's saloon below, allowing in light and fresh air. The skylights could be fixed shut during battle or in stormy weather.

Hotchkiss gun in admiral's saloon

Four Hotchkiss QF 3-pounder guns protrude from the rooms at the fore and stern of *Mikasa* – the admiral's saloon and the enlisted berthing – turning living areas into makeshift gun emplacements.

TRIUMPH OF THE JAPANESE NAVY
The French-built protected cruiser *Matsushima*, the flagship of the Imperial Japanese Navy at the time of the first Sino-Japanese War, fires a devastating broadside against a Chinese warship. Naval scenes such as this were a popular subject for Japanese artists of the period who revelled in the big ships and the imposing new technology of the rapidly modernizing Japanese Navy.

WORLD WAR I

PUBLIC INTEREST IN NAVAL AFFAIRS has never been greater than in the lead-up to World War I. German naval expansion, perceived as a threat to British security, triggered an expensive arms race in which the two countries competed to build bigger and better battleships. This growing hostility led to an agreement between Britain and France to split responsibility for naval defence in case of war, Britain taking on the English Channel and North Sea while France looked after the Mediterranean. Given this build-up, World War I undoubtedly proved a disappointment to naval enthusiasts. Although major engagements between surface warships did occur, a decisive Trafalgar-style battle simply did not come off. Instead the British and German battle fleets sparred and shadow-boxed indecisively while struggling to come to terms with the deadly threat posed by unglamorous submarines and mines.

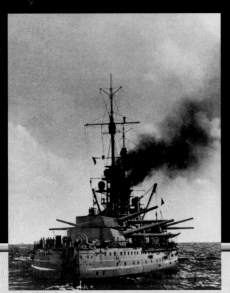

German battleship
Prinzregent Luitpold was a German Kaiser-class battle-ship, launched in 1912 as part of Germany's rapid naval expansion during the run-up to World War I. She fought at Jutland in 1916 – the only occasion when opposing battleships duelled in the war – and was scuttled with the rest of the High Seas Fleet at Scapa Flow in 1919.

DISTANT BLOCKADE

Britain entered World War I with clear naval superiority over Germany. The Royal Navy had 52 dreadnoughts, pre-dreadnoughts, and battlecruisers, as against 34 comparable German warships. Inevitably the German High Seas Fleet was unwilling to steam out and engage in a full-scale battle in the face of such uneven odds. Yet the Royal Navy could not bottle up the German navy with a close blockade of enemy ports as it had during the Napoleonic Wars, because of the extreme vulnerability of its large surface warships to submarines, mines, and torpedo boats. British naval dominance of the entrances to the English Channel and the North Sea was enough to close Germany off from world trade, but this blockade was actually so distant that squadrons of German warships were still able to sortie from harbour and shell the east coast of England.

German strategy was to weaken the Royal Navy by piecemeal sinkings until numbers were even enough for a showdown. The caution of Admiral Sir John Jellicoe, commander of the Grand Fleet, ensured that this never happened. His determination to keep the British fleet intact was matched only by Kaiser Wilhelm's concern to preserve his prized warships. The German High Seas Fleet was more aggressively led for a time after Admiral Reinhard Scheer took command of it in January 1916, and the British succeeded in luring Scheer into a fleet battle at Jutland the following May. The battle revealed clear defects in the Royal Navy – for instance, much of its gunnery was inferior to that of the Germans – and was claimed as a German victory in terms of ships lost and damaged. Yet it was fought as a defensive battle by a German fleet running for home and German surface warships hardly left port again for the rest of the war.

U-BOAT MENACE

The ease with which capital ships could be sunk by mines and submarines had been predicted before the war, yet navies were slow to develop countermeasures. They had continued to create ever bigger, faster, and more heavily gunned battleships, which over time would

DREADNOUGHTS AND SUPER-DREADNOUGHTS

The launch of the British battleship *Dreadnought* in December 1906 ignited an international naval arms race. With ten 12in guns and steam turbine engines giving a maximum speed of 21 knots, *Dreadnought* outclassed every other warship afloat. Its name became the general term for the new generation of battleships that started to appear around the world, including the South Carolina class in the United States, Germany's Nassau class, and France's Courbet class. The Royal Navy was determined to remain ahead of the competition and introduced even more powerful battleships dubbed "super-dreadnoughts". The first of these ships, *Orion*, launched in 1910, had 13.5in guns, but the much admired Queen Elizabeth class, built between 1912 and 1915, mounted astonishing 15in guns. Combined with heavy armour and oil-fired engines generating a maximum speed of 24 knots, this made for a truly formidable fighting machine.

Top of her class
Dreadnought may have represented the new kind of battleship that every navy hoped to acquire, but she had her faults. The arrangement of the main guns with three turrets in line and two at the sides was not a success, and with the mainmast just behind the front funnel, life was not easy for men in the spotting top.

Super-dreadnought
Conqueror was an Orion class battleship launched in 1911, the next generation after *Dreadnought*.

Anchor

Main 13.5in armament

Bridge

Spotting top

Gunnery control position

Searchlights

Booms for anti-submarine net

Secondary armament of 4in guns

Secondary bridge

Twin rudder

Propeller (one of four)

The world's two most powerful and expensive navies spent most of World War I facing each other across the North Sea, too cautious to go out and do battle. Both sides went out on patrol and laid mines as close as they could to the enemy's coast, but neither was prepared to risk its fleet. Two cruiser squadrons clashed briefly at Dogger Bank in 1915, but it was not until May the following year that the two sides finally met at Jutland for the only large-scale fleet action of the war. What became clear at the battle was that the British fleet was still much more powerful than the German one. Realizing this, the Germans tried to win the war by means of a U-boat campaign against Allied and neutral shipping, aimed at starving Britain into submission, a plan in which they very nearly succeeded. After Jutland the German High Seas Fleet never again ventured out into the North Sea.

KEY

- Allied Powers
- Central Powers
- Neutral states
- --- Western Front 1916
- British naval base
- German naval base
- British port bombarded by Germans 1914–16
- British raid on German base 1918
- British mine barrage 1914–15
- British minefield
- German minefield
- British naval blockade
- British victory
- Inconclusive action

Map labels: ATLANTIC OCEAN · Shetland Islands · Scapa Flow · Orkney Islands · Bergen · NORWAY · Rosyth · Kristiania · Stavanger · Cromarty · North Sea · Skagerrak · Belfast · Dublin · Irish Sea · Hartlepool · Whitby · Dogger Bank Jan 1915 · Scarborough · Jutland May–Jun 1916 · DENMARK · Queenstown · Hull · Heligoland Bight Aug 1914 · Copenhagen · Sinking of Lusitania 7 May 1915 · UNITED KINGDOM · Great Yarmouth · Kiel · Lowestoft · Borkum · Cuxhaven · Emden · Hamburg · London · Harwich · Bremerhaven · Chatham · Sheerness · Amsterdam · Wilhelmshaven · Plymouth · NETHERLANDS · Berlin · Portsmouth · Dover · Zeebrugge · English Channel · Calais · Ostend Bruges · GERMANY · Cherbourg · BELGIUM · Brest · FRANCE · LUX. · Paris · 0 km 200 · 0 miles 200

become irrelevant. Allied losses of warships to mines were grievous, for example at the Dardanelles in 1915, and German U-boats continued to be a threat even after the adoption of destroyer screens to protect battleships and cruisers.

It was when U-boats began to be deployed as commerce raiders, first in 1915 and then on a larger scale in 1917, that they threatened to change the course of the war. At the start of the war U-boat attacks against merchant shipping were conducted for the most part according to prize regulations, the traditional rules used by cruisers attacking unarmed civilian shipping. In February 1915, however, Germany declared the waters around Britain a war zone and authorized U-boat captains to launch attacks on merchant vessels, including neutrals, without

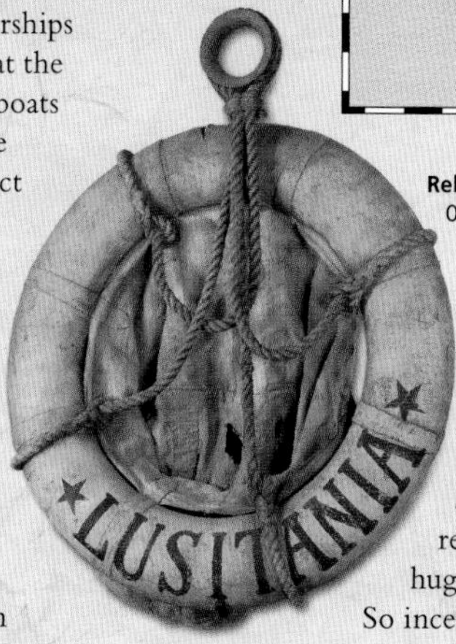

Relic of the Lusitania
Of the 1,201 passengers drowned when the *Lusitania* was sunk by a torpedo, 128 were US citizens.

warning. The sinking of the liner *Lusitania* in May 1915 and the cross-Channel ferry *Sussex* in March 1916 resulted in the deaths of huge numbers of US citizens. So incensed were the Americans that the Germans were forced to call off the campaign. But, when the idea of a full-scale surface battle was abandoned after Jutland, Germany resumed unrestricted submarine

warfare on 1 February 1917. The reluctance of the British to adopt a convoy system led to unsustainable losses of merchant ships to U-boat attack right up to May 1917, when the phasing in of convoys reversed the trend. But indiscriminate sinkings by U-boats brought America into the war against Germany, so ensuring the eventual victory of the Allies.

Morale in the German High Seas Fleet suffered from years of inactivity in port. When German commanders planned a sortie to engage the Grand Fleet in a death-or-glory final battle in October 1918, the sailors mutinied. Interned at Scapa Flow, the German fleet was scuttled by its crews in protest against the Versailles peace treaty in June 1919.

U-boat in port
Launched in 1911, U-8 had only a short career. She was trapped in nets off Folkestone in the English Channel in March 1915 and sunk by the British destroyers *Gurkha* and *Maori*. All her crew were rescued.

WARSHIP BATTLES 1914–18

MUCH OF THE NAVAL ACTION early in World War I concerned the Royal Navy's efforts to track down German surface raiders, which posed a serious threat to Allied shipping. After the British victory over Admiral Graf von Spee's squadron at the Falklands in December 1914, German commerce raiding was restricted to submarines, the U-boats proving a fearful menace for merchant shipping and warships alike (see pp268–269). An attempt to use Allied naval power to decisive effect against Germany's ally Turkey in the Dardanelles was a painful failure. Meanwhile, for almost two years the Royal Navy's Grand Fleet and the German High Seas Fleet, stationed at opposite ends of the North Sea, did not meet. After an early reverse at the Heligoland Bight, the Kaiser forbade his fleet to venture into the North Sea, although this prohibition was not absolutely respected. Probing raids by German squadrons met with some success, despite a serious setback at the Dogger Bank, before the British at last trapped their opponents into a full-scale fleet engagement at Jutland in May 1916 – without, however, achieving the victory which Britain craved.

STEAM AND STEEL

> ## POOR DEVILS! THEY FOUGHT THEIR SHIPS LIKE MEN AND WENT DOWN WITH COLOURS FLYING LIKE SEAMEN AGAINST OVERWHELMING ODDS ...
>
> **VICE ADMIRAL DAVID BEATTY** DESCRIBING THE GERMAN SAILORS AT HELIGOLAND BIGHT IN A LETTER TO HIS WIFE, 1914

WORLD WAR I

HELIGOLAND BIGHT

Date 28 August 1914
Forces British: 5 battlecruisers, 8 light cruisers, 31 destroyers, 3 submarines; Germans: 6 light cruisers, 19 torpedo boats
Losses British: none; Germans: 3 light cruisers, 1 torpedo boat

Location Heligoland Bight, northern Germany

Commodore Roger Keyes, in command of British submarines based at Harwich, conceived a plan for an impudent raid on German ships on patrol near their naval base at Heligoland. The raid was to be carried out by the light cruisers and destroyers of Commodore Reginald Tyrwhitt's Harwich Force, along with Keyes' submarines. It was decided at the last minute to provide back-up for the raid from Vice Admiral David Beatty's First Battlecruiser Squadron and the First Light Cruiser Squadron of Commodore William Goodenough.

As Keyes had planned, early on the morning of 28 August the presence of British submarines off Heligoland was detected by the Germans, who promptly sent out a flotilla of torpedo boats.

These were then engaged by Tyrwhitt's destroyers and two light cruisers, *Arethusa* and *Fearless*. Fought in mist, the ensuing battle was characterized by confusion on both sides. The German light cruisers *Stettin* and *Frauenlob* arrived on the scene and duelled with *Fearless* and *Arethusa* respectively. *Arethusa*, with Tyrwhitt on board, suffered heavy damage and withdrew to attempt repairs. Four more German light cruisers turned up, attacking in an uncoordinated fashion as Tyrwhitt's destroyers screened *Arethusa*.

Fortunately for the British, the arrival of Goodenough's light cruisers, followed by Beatty's battlecruisers, swung the balance of forces decisively in their favour. Rear Admiral Leberecht Maass's *Mainz* was sunk after being

Battlecruisers in line ahead
A column of Royal Navy warships is led by *Queen Mary* and *Princess Royal* of the First Battlecruiser Squadron, victorious at Heligoland Bight.

caught between the Harwich Force destroyers and Goodenough's cruisers. The light cruisers *Köln* and *Ariadne* were destroyed by the heavy guns of Beatty's *Lion*, looming unexpectedly upon them out of the mist. The British withdrew across the North Sea, *Arethusa* reaching home under tow.

Despite "friendly fire" incidents resulting from poor communication and worrying malfunctions of guns and fire-control systems, the British had scored an unquestionable victory, achieved with great boldness in German home waters.

QF 3-pounder Hotchkiss
Pedestal-mounted Quick Firing (QF) 3-pounders were common anti-torpedo boat guns on British cruisers at the start of the war, but were soon found to be too light to be very effective.

1863–1928
REINHARD SCHEER
GERMAN ADMIRAL

Born in Obernkirchen, Hanover, Scheer joined the Imperial German Navy in 1879. By 1907 he had risen to be chief of staff of the High Seas Fleet. On the outbreak of World War I he advocated the use of surface ships to lure British warships into the path of submarines lying in ambush. On being promoted to Admiral of the Fleet in 1916, he used a similar tactic at Jutland. The skill of his manoeuvres in the battle enabled the German fleet to escape and even to claim victory.

WORLD WAR I
SINKING OF SMS EMDEN

Date 9 November 1914
Forces Australians: 1 light
cruiser; Germans: 1 light cruiser
Losses Australians: none;
Germans: 1 light cruiser

Location Cocos
Islands, Indian Ocean

The light cruiser *Emden*, commanded by
Karl von Müller, was one of Germany's
most successful commerce raiders,
paralyzing trade in the Indian Ocean
and destroying oil tanks at Madras.
Müller earned a reputation for the
chivalrous treatment of the passengers
and crews of ships he sank. *Emden*
evaded or defeated all her pursuers for
three months until she encountered
the Australian light cruiser *Sydney*,
whose 6in guns had a greater range than
Emden's. Captain John Glossop was
able to bombard the ship almost with
impunity. Müller beached the battered
Emden on an island to avoid sinking
and reluctantly ran up the white flag.

WORLD WAR I
CORONEL

Date 1 November 1914
Forces Germans: 2 armoured
cruisers, 3 light cruisers; British:
2 armoured cruisers, 1 light
cruiser, 1 armed liner
Losses Germans: none;
British: 2 armoured cruisers

Location Off Coronel,
Chile

From the start of the war Vice Admiral
Graf Maximilian von Spee was at large
in the Pacific with a powerful squadron
that included two impressive armoured
cruisers, *Scharnhorst* and *Gneisenau*.
Rear Admiral Sir Christopher Cradock,
based in the Falkland Islands, was tasked
with seeking out and destroying Spee's
squadron, despite having far inferior
ships and crews. His armoured cruisers
Good Hope and *Monmouth* were slower
than their German equivalents, had
obsolescent guns, and were crewed by
recalled reservists and half-trained boys.
His light cruiser *Glasgow* was at least a
fully modern ship, but his armed liner
Otranto was effectively useless.

The German and British squadrons
met in heavy seas off the coast of Chile
in the late afternoon of 1 November.
Steaming to the east of the British, Spee
exploited the superior speed of his ships
to stay out of range until the sun had
set. With Cradock's ships silhouetted
against the afterglow, the German ships
opened an accurate fire to which the
British were barely able to reply. *Good
Hope* and *Monmouth*, battered by salvo
after salvo in the gathering darkness,
sank with all hands, including Cradock.
Otranto had been sent away at the start
of the battle and the badly damaged
Glasgow escaped into the night. It
was a humiliating defeat that the
Royal Navy was determined to avenge.

WEAPONS AND TECHNOLOGY
SEA MINES

Contact mines were chained to the seabed and
exploded when a ship's hull struck one of
the protruding spikes. They were used
to great effect by Germany, sinking a
greater tonnage of British warships than
any other weapon. The Royal Navy
entered the war without minelayers or
purpose-built minesweepers and did
not use mines effectively until 1917.

Contact mine
The length of chain was adjusted
so that the mine floated at the
desired depth below the surface.

Aboard the Glasgow
At the Falkland Islands *Glasgow* was
the first British ship to catch up and
exchange fire with the German light
cruiser *Leipzig*. Three months later she
helped track down *Dresden*, the only
German ship to escape the battle.

WORLD WAR I
FALKLAND ISLANDS

Date 8 December 1914
Forces British: 2 battlecruisers,
3 armoured cruisers, 2 light
cruisers, 1 pre-dreadnought
battleship; Germans: 2 armoured
cruisers, 3 light cruisers
Losses British: none;
Germans: 2 armoured cruisers,
2 light cruisers

Location Falkland
Islands, South Atlantic

After the defeat at Coronel, Vice Admiral
Frederick Sturdee was sent from Britain
with two battlecruisers, *Invincible* and
Inflexible, to destroy Spee's victorious
armoured cruisers *Scharnhorst* and
Gneisenau. Sturdee joined up with the
five cruisers of Rear-Admiral Archibald
Stoddart's South Atlantic Squadron and
steamed to the Falkland Islands, arriving
at Port Stanley on 7 December. The
next day, unaware of the British ships,
Spee's squadron appeared, having
rounded Cape Horn from the Pacific.

As *Gneisenau* and the light cruiser
Nürnberg approached Port Stanley they
were fired on by the antiquated pre-
dreadnought *Canopus*, which had been
grounded at the harbour mouth as a
shore battery. The
British warships,
caught in harbour
and some in the
middle of coaling,
were vulnerable
to attack, but the
Germans fled at
the sight of the

HMS Canopus
The opening shots at
the Falkland Islands
were fired by the pre-
dreadnought *Canopus*.

unexpected battlecruisers. The British
had time to get up steam and set to
sea in pursuit. Spee realized he had no
chance of outrunning the battlecruisers.
He decided to engage them with
Scharnhorst and *Gneisenau*, hoping
to buy time for the light cruisers at
least to escape.

THE SQUADRON DESTROYED
The German admiral fought a cunning
delaying action against an enemy with
superior guns and armour, but the end
was inevitable. On fire and listing
heavily, Spee's flagship *Scharnhorst* sank
with her admiral and all hands just after
4pm. *Gneisenau* lasted longer. She went
down at around 6pm after taking more
than 50 hits. Some 200 of her crew
were rescued from the icy waters. The
light cruisers *Nürnberg* and *Leipzig*
were pursued, engaged, and sunk
by the armoured cruisers *Kent* and
Cornwall and the light cruiser *Glasgow*.
The only German ship to escape was
the light cruiser *Dresden*, but she too
was eventually hunted down. It was a
crushing British victory, achieved by
the application of overwhelming force.

STEAM AND STEEL

WORLD WAR I

BOMBARDMENT OF THE ENGLISH COAST

Date 16 December 1914
Forces Germans: 3 battlecruisers, 1 armoured cruiser, 4 light cruisers, 18 torpedo boats; British: 6 battleships, 4 battlecruisers, 8 cruisers, 8 destroyers
Losses Germans: none; British: none

Location Coast of northeast England

Vice Admiral Franz von Hipper, commanding the German 1st Scouting Group, planned a raid across the North Sea against English coastal towns. If the Royal Navy responded by coming out in force, Hipper hoped to draw them onto mines laid in the area, or toward the guns of the High Seas Fleet advancing behind him. The British were forewarned of the raid by codebreakers in the Admiralty's Room 40, but unaware the High Seas Fleet was involved. For over an hour on the morning of 16 December Hipper's battlecruisers and light cruisers bombarded Hartlepool, West Hartlepool, Scarborough, and

Whitby, causing considerable damage and killing more than 100 civilians. Shore batteries at Hartlepool scored hits on three of the ships.

A much larger naval engagement was narrowly avoided. British forces sent to intercept Hipper blundered into sight of the High Seas Fleet, but Admiral Frederich von Ingenohl, fearing this was the Royal Navy's Grand Fleet, fled for home. This left Hipper exposed, surrounded by British battleships and battlecruisers, yet he was allowed to slip past and escape to safety. Outrage in Britain was directed equally at the Germans for shelling civilian targets and at the Royal Navy for failing in its duty to protect the country from attack.

German pistol
A Roth-Steyr M1907 taken from a German naval officer at the surrender of the High Seas Fleet at Scapa Flow in 1918.

WORLD WAR I

CUXHAVEN RAID

Date 25 December 1914
Forces British: 7 seaplanes, 3 seaplane tenders, 2 light cruisers, 2 destroyers, 10 submarines
Losses British: 4 seaplanes

Location Cuxhaven, northern Germany

On Christmas Day 1914 the Royal Naval Air Service executed the first air raid launched from the sea. Three converted cross-Channel steamers carried nine Short seaplanes to within flying range of Cuxhaven, escorted by Commodore Reginald Tyrwhitt's Harwich Force. The seaplanes were lowered onto the sea by cranes. Seven succeeded in taking off. Their objective was to bomb Zeppelin airship sheds, but they missed their target in low cloud. They caused some panic in Wilhelmshaven, where a battlecruiser and a cruiser collided taking evasive action. Three of the seaplanes found their way back to their tenders, while the pilots of the others were all rescued, three by British submarines and one by a Dutch trawler.

WORLD WAR I

BATTLE OF THE DARDANELLES

Date	18 March 1915
Location	Dardanelles, Turkey
Result	Ottoman Turkish victory

∞ COMBATANTS ∞

BRITAIN AND FRANCE	OTTOMAN TURKEY

∞ COMMANDERS ∞

Sir Sackville Carden	Mustafa Kemal
John de Robeck	
Emile Guépratte	

∞ FORCES ∞

Ships: 15 battleships (mostly pre-dreadnought), 1 battlecruiser, various cruisers, destroyers, and minesweepers	**Ships:** Shore guns and mines

∞ LOSSES ∞

Men: 700	**Men:** 40
Ships: 3 battleships	

Naval bombardment
The pre-dreadnought British battleship HMS *Cornwallis* uses her 12in guns to bombard Turkish gun positions on the Gallipoli Peninsula. *Cornwallis* fired the first shell of the first naval bombardment of the Turkish forts on 19 February 1915.

Sinking of the Blücher
German sailors scramble onto the hull of the stricken German cruiser *Blücher* as she rolls over following heavy British fire at Dogger Bank.

WORLD WAR I

DOGGER BANK

Date 24 January 1915
Forces British: 5 battlecruisers, 9 light cruisers, 31 destroyers; Germans: 3 battlecruisers, 1 armoured cruiser, 4 light cruisers, 18 torpedo boats
Losses British: none; Germans: 1 armoured cruiser

Location Dogger Bank, North Sea

On 23 January 1915 Admiral Franz von Hipper took the German 1st and 2nd Scouting Groups into the North Sea to attack British trawlers and patrol boats on the Dogger Bank. Radio intercepts by Royal Navy signals intelligence revealed the plans and Admiral David Beatty was sent out with the 1st and 2nd Battlecruiser Squadrons to surprise Hipper, joined by the light cruisers and destroyers of the Harwich Force.

Contact was made shortly after 7am on 24 January. Once Hipper realized that heavy British ships were present, he turned for home. Beatty's flagship

Lion led the chase and opened fire at extreme range around 9am. Hipper was leading the German line on the battlecruiser *Seydlitz*, with the armoured cruiser *Blücher* struggling to keep up. *Lion* drew first blood, blowing up *Seydlitz's* aft turrets with an armour-penetrating shell. A devastating explosion was averted through the heroism of German sailor Wilhelm Heidkamp who flooded *Seydlitz's* magazines despite suffering severe burns. *Blücher* also took a battering and fell further behind the rest of the German force.

However, as the range shortened, *Lion* came under accurate fire from all three battlecruisers. By 10:45am *Lion* was so badly damaged she slowed to a halt.

From this point the British effort lost all tactical coherence. Four British battlecruisers poured shells into the crippled *Blücher* until she capsized and sank, while Hipper led his battlecruisers home to safety. *Lion* was towed back to the Forth, to a hero's welcome. But an opportunity to inflict a crushing defeat on the German navy had slipped through Beatty's fingers.

> ❝
> IT WAS ONE CONTINUOUS EXPLOSION ... THE WOUNDED BLÜCHER SETTLED DOWN, TURNED WEARILY OVER AND DISAPPEARED IN A SWIRL OF WATER.
> **GERMAN SURVIVOR** FROM SMS *BLÜCHER*, 1915
> ❞

THE BATTLE OF THE DARDANELLES

In January 1915 the Royal Navy drew up plans for an ambitious operation designed to drive Ottoman Turkey out of the war. British and French warships would force a passage through the Dardanelles into the Sea of Marmara. There they would menace the Ottoman capital Constantinople with their guns, obliging the Turks to surrender.

The passage through the Dardanelles was blocked by minefields covered by the batteries of a series of forts and mobile howitzers. Admiral Sackville Carden began the naval attack on these defences on 19 February. He had a large force of British and French battleships at his disposal, although most of these were ageing pre-dreadnoughts whose heavy guns proved far less effective against shore batteries than had been anticipated. However, the greatest weakness of the Allied forces was a lack of efficient minesweepers.

On 25 February the Turks abandoned the forts at the entrance to the strait, but Carden made no further progress. Through the first two weeks of March the inner forts were shelled almost daily, but the minefields remained uncleared and the navy began taking casualties.

FORCING THE STRAIT

With Carden in poor health, it was Admiral John de Robeck who assumed command for the decisive bid to force the straits on 18 March. Almost the entire force of heavy warships advanced in three lines, one of them consisting of four French pre-dreadnoughts under Rear Admiral Emile Guépratte.

Opening around 11am the exchange of fire between sea and shore was intense. Ordered forward to engage the forts at close range, the French ships took heavy punishment, especially *Gaulois,* which ran aground to avoid sinking. At 2pm de Robeck ordered the French to withdraw so he could bring other ships forward to cover the

mineclearing. As the French wheeled right, *Bouvet* struck a mine and sank in minutes. Only 35 of the 674 crew were saved.

One disaster followed another. The battlecruiser *Inflexible* was next to hit a mine, withdrawing with a heavy list. Then it was the turn of *Irresistible* and *Ocean*; both were immobilized by explosions

Amphora from HMS Implacable
The *Implacable* supported the troop landings at Gallipoli – part of the failed attempt to open the straits to British and French warships.

and abandoned. With night approaching, de Robeck signalled for all the ships to retire. There was no further attempt to force a passage through the straits. Instead it was decided to land troops at Gallipoli – an operation that was to prove an even more costly failure.

Dardanelles
British and French forces attempted to force a passage through the straits using heavy warships to reduce the forts and provide protection for minesweepers.

GALLIPOLI PENINSULA

Dardanelles

The narrowest part of the straits strongly defended by Turkish forts and artillery

A series of 10 minefields blocks the passage through the narrows

KEY
- ◾ 1 British/French battleship
- ✕ 1 sunk battleship
- ▪▪▶ Allied landings, April 1915
- ◄ Major Turkish gun battery
- ⋯ Turkish minefields

Aegean Sea

The first British line opens fire while the French line passes through to advance on the forts

The battleships advance in three lines, two British and one French

TURKEY

As the French line turns starboard to withdraw, *Bouvet* strikes a mine. More ships hit mines as they withdraw

Outer defences cleared by naval bombardment

The night before the battle the Turks lay a minefield along the inside edge of the straits

N

WEAPONS AND TECHNOLOGY

WWI TURRET GUNS

The large calibre naval guns on World War I capital ships were mounted in turrets protected by armoured barbettes and supported on a bed of rollers to allow the guns to rotate. A gunhouse above deck was linked by a tube, known as the main trunk, to the magazine and shell room deep inside the ship. The shells were too heavy to lift by hand, so to load the gun the shells and propellant charges were placed on a hoist that carried them up the trunk to a working chamber. From there they were raised to the top of the turret and rammed into the breech of the gun for firing. A series of doors and scuttles was installed to prevent flash travelling from the gunhouse down to the magazine if the gunhouse was hit by a shell – although Royal Navy procedures at Jutland proved defective in this regard.

Battleship Texas
The battleship's ten 14in guns, mounted in five turrets along her centreline, could fire 680kg (1,500lb) shells a distance of 21km (13 miles).

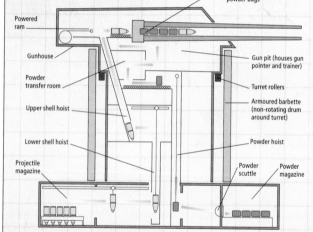

US battleship turret gun
The turret guns on most American battleships of the period were divided into two sections with separate hoists for the shells and the propellant. Royal Navy turret guns typically had just one hoist.

Powered ram

Gunhouse

Powder transfer room

Upper shell hoist

Lower shell hoist

Projectile magazine

Gun breech containing one shell and four powder bags

Gun pit (houses gun pointer and trainer)

Turret rollers

Armoured barbette (non-rotating drum around turret)

Powder hoist

Powder scuttle

Powder magazine

1859–1935

SIR JOHN JELLICOE

ADMIRAL OF THE BRITISH FLEET

Jellicoe joined the Royal Navy as a cadet in 1872 and saw action in the colonial wars of the late 19th century. As a senior administrator he participated in the reform of the Royal Navy before World War I, specializing in gunnery. Appointed commander-in-chief of the Grand Fleet at the outset of the war, he pursued a cautious strategy, ever-conscious of being in Winston Churchill's words, "the only man on either side who could lose the war in an afternoon". No politician, he was outmanoeuvred by his critics, who were numerous after the battle of Jutland. In November 1916 he was appointed First Sea Lord, only to be precipitately dismissed 13 months later, a scapegoat for Admiralty failings.

The Jellicoe Touch
Admiral John Jellicoe's image is borrowed to add a patriotic touch to this collection of "Naval Fantasia" sheet music.

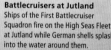

Battlecruisers at Jutland
Ships of the First Battlecruiser Squadron fire on the High Seas Fleet at Jutland while German shells splash into the water around them.

WITNESS TO WAR

COMMANDER HUMPHREY WALWYN

EXECUTIVE OFFICER ON HMS WARSPITE

BATTLE OF JUTLAND

*Very soon after the turn, could see leading ships of High Seas Fleet, hardly discernible but I counted six or eight. **Long lines of orange flame seemed to ripple along continuously, and I realised they were firing at us**. Felt heavy shakes but didn't think much of it … Crossed Cook's lobby to port side and was just going forward to the fo'c'sle deck, when a 12-inch shell came in through the starboard side and burst with a **terrific sheet of flame, impenetrable dust, smoke, stink**, and everything seemed to fall from everywhere at once. Called for number two fire brigade and several rushed out and we got the fire out fairly easily, but **place was full of smoke and several men were sick – awful stench**."*

THE BATTLE OF JUTLAND

At 2am on 31 May 1916 a scouting force of five modern battlecruisers under Admiral Franz von Hipper headed out into the North Sea. An hour and a half behind him, Admiral Reinhard Scheer followed Hipper with 16 dreadnought battleships of the German High Seas Fleet. With light cruisers and torpedo boats in support, almost a hundred German ships were at sea. Scheer's plan was for Hipper's scouting group to draw out part of the British Grand Fleet, which would then be surprised and destroyed by the German battleships.

Unbeknownst to the Germans, the Grand Fleet was already at sea. Royal Navy signals intelligence had detected that the High Seas Fleet was preparing to come out. With Admiral John Jellicoe in command, the Main Battle Fleet had set out from Scapa Flow after dark on 30 May. Jellicoe intended to rendezvous with Sir David Beatty's Battlecruiser Force and destroy the High Seas Fleet. Instead of surprising an inferior Royal Navy force, Scheer would himself be surprised by an overwhelmingly superior British force of 151 warships, including 28 modern battleships.

Into the early afternoon of 31 May, Jellicoe and Beatty's ships proceeded in quite leisurely fashion toward their rendezvous off Jutland, misled by a message from the Admiralty indicating that the High Seas Fleet had not yet left port. German commanders were equally ignorant of the movement of the Grand Fleet. U-boats in the North Sea had missed the British ships entirely while bad weather prevented the use of zeppelins for aerial reconnaissance. It was a surprise to both sides when, at around 2:20pm, two of Beatty's light cruisers sighted and engaged two of Hipper's torpedo boats.

BATTLECRUISER ACTION

As the first shots were fired, Beatty was steaming the wrong way, having just turned north to meet up with Jellicoe. He hastily turned south, a manoeuvre his 5th Battle Squadron was slow to follow. This was unfortunate, for the squadron's four Queen Elizabeth–class battleships would have given Beatty a clear superiority over Hipper. The five German and six British battlecruisers steamed on converging courses and sighted one another about an hour later. Hipper turned southeast to draw Beatty toward the High Seas Fleet. But since Scheer had inexplicably brought with him six slow-moving Deutschland-class pre-dreadnoughts his progress was not fast and there was time for Beatty to take on the German battlecruisers.

WORLD WAR I

THE BATTLE OF JUTLAND

Date	31 May–1 June 1916
Location	North Sea off the coast of Denmark
Result	Inconclusive

COMBATANTS

BRITAIN	GERMANY

COMMANDERS

John Jellicoe	Reinhard Scheer

FORCES

Ships: 28 battleships, 9 battlecruisers, 8 armoured cruisers, 106 other ships	Ships: 16 battleships, 5 battlecruisers, 6 pre-dreadnoughts, 72 other ships

LOSSES

Men: 6,094 Ships: 3 battlecruisers, 3 armoured cruisers, 8 destroyers	Men: 2,551 Ships: 1 battlecruiser, 1 pre-dreadnought, 4 light cruisers, 5 destroyers

Webley Mark VI revolver
The Mark VI was a standard sidearm issued to British officers and boarding parties during WWI. The owner of this example served at Jutland on the *Temeraire*.

> "
> SUDDENLY MY PERISCOPE REVEALED SOME BIG SHIPS, BLACK MONSTERS; SIX TALL, BROAD-BEAMED GIANTS STEAMING IN TWO COLUMNS.
> **COMMANDER GEORG VON HASE**, GUNNERY OFFICER OF BATTLECRUISER *DERFFLINGER*, 1916
> "

The battlecruisers were soon engaged in bitter earnest. Beatty closed with the German force at speed, neglecting to exploit the superior range of his guns. Hipper's ships opened fire first, with a clear view of their targets silhouetted against the westering sun. With good range-finding equipment and armour-piercing shells, the Germans recorded hit after hit on the Royal Navy ships. First *Indefatigable* and then *Queen Mary* exploded and sank, each taking almost her entire crew to the bottom. Beatty's flagship *Lion* and the other battlecruisers all took hits. It was some relief when the battleships of 5th Battle Squadron tardily arrived, but before they could have any decisive impact the High Seas Fleet loomed into view.

Still unaware of Jellicoe's Grand Fleet drawing ever closer, Scheer believed a major victory was in his grasp. Beatty's battlecruisers turned northward, both to flee Scheer's battleships and lead him to Jellicoe, but the balance

Jutland medal
The Victoria Cross – Britain's highest award for valour – bestowed posthumously on Jack Cornwell after Jutland.

First Battlecruiser Squadron
Beatty's flagship *Lion* and battlecruisers *Princess Royal* and *Queen Mary* steam through the waters off Jutland shortly before the sinking of the *Queen Mary*.

of losses continued to tip heavily against the Royal Navy. As elements of the Grand Fleet caught up with the battle, the battlecruiser *Invincible* and the armoured cruiser *Defence* were sunk charging heroically into the thick of the action. Meanwhile Jellicoe, still unsure of the location of the German ships in worsening visibility, deployed the Grand Fleet in line of battle behind the battleship *King George V*.

THE MAIN FLEETS ENGAGE

Scheer emerged from the murk to be confronted by the capital ships of the Grand Fleet spread out across his bow in a line 10km (6 miles) long. From the moment the guns of the British battleships opened up on his leading ships, the German admiral had only one objective: to escape back to harbour. The High Seas Fleet turned a full 180 degrees behind a thick smokescreen to disengage. As Jellicoe manoeuvred to cut off their retreat to the south, the German battleships ran into the Grand Fleet again, and then dodged to the west, deploying a screen of torpedo boats and cruisers to deter pursuit. Controversially, Jellicoe turned away to avoid the torpedoes, letting Scheer's fleet disappear in fog and smoke. As

night fell, Jellicoe was confident that he could force a decisive battle the following morning. But in the darkness Scheer drove his fleet full tilt through the rear of the Grand Fleet's line. The night was sporadically lit by searchlights, star shells, gunfire, and burning ships as confused clashes occurred here and there. There were more losses on both sides. However, Jellicoe failed to grasp that Scheer was escaping and remained on the wrong course until the following

morning, when he received the disappointing news that the German fleet was all but home.

In the immediate aftermath of the battle, the Germans were jubilant, and the British bitterly disappointed. The performance of the Grand Fleet drew howls of rage from the jingoistic British press. While the Germans had materially the better of the encounter, however, the Royal Navy remained in command of the North Sea.

> ## THERE'S SOMETHING WRONG WITH OUR BLOODY SHIPS TODAY.
> **SIR DAVID BEATTY,** COMMANDER OF THE BRITISH BATTECRUISER SQUADRON

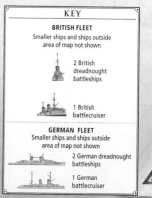

KEY

BRITISH FLEET
Smaller ships and ships outside area of map not shown
2 British dreadnought battleships
1 British battlecruiser

GERMAN FLEET
Smaller ships and ships outside area of map not shown
2 German dreadnought battleships
1 German battlecruiser

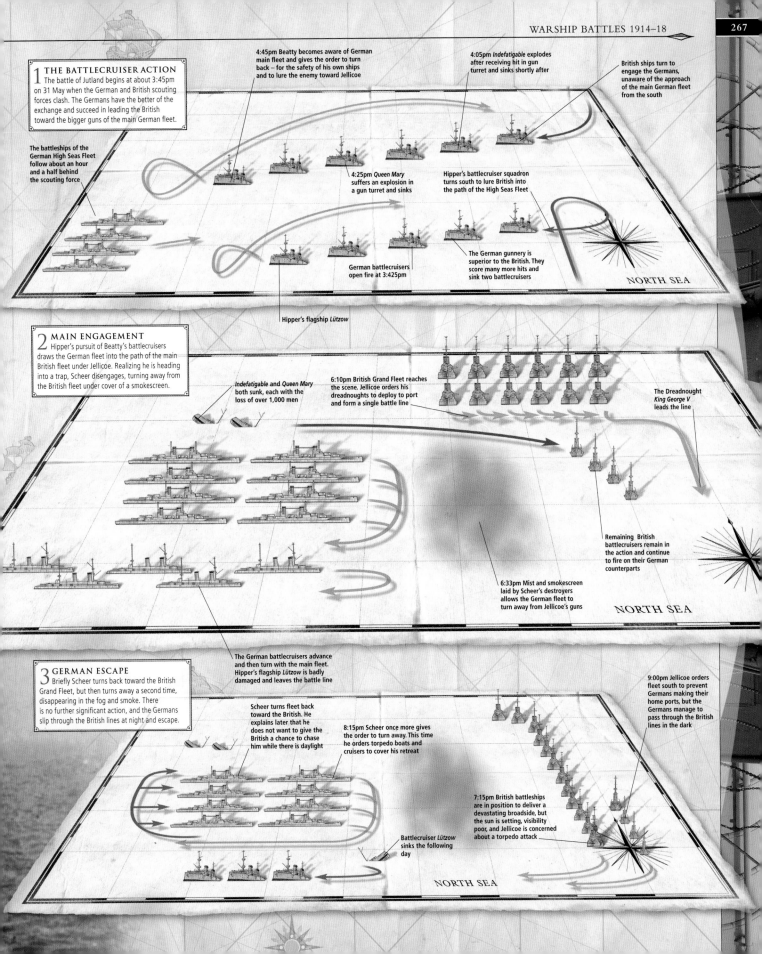

1 THE BATTLECRUISER ACTION

The battle of Jutland begins at about 3:45pm on 31 May when the German and British scouting forces clash. The Germans have the better of the exchange and succeed in leading the British toward the bigger guns of the main German fleet.

The battleships of the German High Seas Fleet follow about an hour and a half behind the scouting force

4:45pm Beatty becomes aware of German main fleet and gives the order to turn back – for the safety of his own ships and to lure the enemy toward Jellicoe

4:25pm *Queen Mary* suffers an explosion in a gun turret and sinks

German battlecruisers open fire at 3:425pm

Hipper's flagship *Lützow*

4:05pm *Indefatigable* explodes after receiving hit in gun turret and sinks shortly after

Hipper's battlecruiser squadron turns south to lure British into the path of the High Seas Fleet

British ships turn to engage the Germans, unaware of the approach of the main German fleet from the south

The German gunnery is superior to the British. They score many more hits and sink two battlecruisers

NORTH SEA

2 MAIN ENGAGEMENT

Hipper's pursuit of Beatty's battlecruisers draws the German fleet into the path of the main British fleet under Jellicoe. Realizing he is heading into a trap, Scheer disengages, turning away from the British fleet under cover of a smokescreen.

Indefatigable and *Queen Mary* both sunk, each with the loss of over 1,000 men

6:10pm British Grand Fleet reaches the scene. Jellicoe orders his dreadnoughts to deploy to port and form a single battle line

The Dreadnought *King George V* leads the line

Remaining British battlecruisers remain in the action and continue to fire on their German counterparts

6:33pm Mist and smokescreen laid by Scheer's destroyers allows the German fleet to turn away from Jellicoe's guns

NORTH SEA

3 GERMAN ESCAPE

Briefly Scheer turns back toward the British Grand Fleet, but then turns away a second time, disappearing in the fog and smoke. There is no further significant action, and the Germans slip through the British lines at night and escape.

The German battlecruisers advance and then turn with the main fleet. Hipper's flagship *Lützow* is badly damaged and leaves the battle line

Scheer turns fleet back toward the British. He explains later that he does not want to give the British a chance to chase him while there is daylight

8:15pm Scheer once more gives the order to turn away. This time he orders torpedo boats and cruisers to cover his retreat

Battlecruiser *Lützow* sinks the following day

9:00pm Jellicoe orders fleet south to prevent Germans making their home ports, but the Germans manage to pass through the British lines in the dark

7:15pm British battleships are in position to deliver a devastating broadside, but the sun is setting, visibility poor, and Jellicoe is concerned about a torpedo attack

NORTH SEA

THE U-BOAT WAR 1914–18

BRITAIN'S ROYAL NAVY was made inescapably aware of the threat posed by German U-boats on 5 September 1914, when U-21 sank the cruiser *Pathfinder* off eastern Scotland – the first warship ever sunk by a submarine-fired torpedo. Allied naval commanders were slow to face up to the full implications of this event, sometimes disastrously failing to provide large warships with protective destroyer screens. Laxness was eventually replaced by paranoia, with fear of submarines severely inhibiting the operation of surface fleets. The most effective role for U-boats, however, was as commerce raiders. In February 1915 Germany began sinking, without warning, merchant ships in the waters around the British Isles, a practice halted in the face of American protests, but resumed with a vengeance in 1917. U-boats based at Austrian ports in the Adriatic played havoc with Allied merchant shipping in the Mediterranean. The Allies tried various responses from creating anti-submarine barriers across the entrance to the Channel and the exit from the Adriatic to raids on U-boat bases in Belgium. They were inexplicably slow to adopt the best solution: a system of merchant convoys.

WORLD WAR I

SINKING OF ABOUKIR, CRESSY, AND HOGUE

Date 22 September 1914
Forces British: 3 armoured cruisers; Germans: 1 submarine
Losses British: 3 armoured cruisers; Germans: none

Location Southern North Sea

In September 1914, in the area known as the Broad Fourteens, between the Netherlands and Dogger Bank, a force of British submarines, destroyers, and armoured cruisers was on permanent patrol. Their role was to block any attempt by German surface warships to interfere with communications between Britain and continental Europe across the Narrow Seas. The cruisers were obsolescent ships that were manned mostly by reservists and cadets fresh out of naval college. Their position in the southern North Sea was so obviously exposed that the force had been sardonically dubbed the "Live Bait Squadron". By the third week of September heavy seas had led to the withdrawal of their destroyer screen, while the need of one of the cruisers for coaling left only three on patrol: *Aboukir, Cressy,* and *Hogue.*

THREE BEFORE BREAKFAST

At around 6am on 22 September Lieutenant Commander Otto Weddigen, in command of the submarine U-9, sighted the cruisers steaming straight in line ahead. He dived

Weddigen medallion
This commemorative German medallion shows a sinking British cruiser, with a portrait of Otto Weddigen on the obverse.

Engine room bell from U-9
Following her surrender in 1918, the bell from the submarine U-9 was engraved with the names of the sunken British cruisers *Aboukir, Cressy,* and *Hogue.*

to close for attack and fired a single torpedo at *Aboukir*. This struck home to such effect that the ship sank within 20 minutes. The captains of the other cruisers, assuming that *Aboukir* had run into a mine, stopped and sent out boats to pick up survivors. At about 6:45am the submarine unleashed more torpedoes against *Hogue*, which was now a sitting target. The cruiser was struck amidships twice in quick succession, the impact almost breaking her in half. The captain of *Cressy* made a belated attempt to flee, steaming away from the scene of the disaster where his ship's boats were still collecting survivors. It was too late, however, for the U-boat immobilized *Cressy* with one torpedo, then sent her to the bottom with a second. There were men rescued from *Aboukir* by *Hogue*, then from *Hogue* by *Cressy*, who were sunk three times.

Weddigen was awarded the Iron Cross for his exploit. He was killed in March 1915 when his submarine U-29 was rammed by the battleship *Dreadnought* in Pentland Firth.

Ready for patrol
Otto Weddigen and his crew pictured on board the submarine U-9. A month after sinking the *Aboukir, Cressy,* and *Hogue,* U-9 also sank the British cruiser *Hawke.*

> ❝
> ## SUBMARINES ARE UNDERHAND. UNFAIR. AND DAMNED UN-ENGLISH. THE CREWS OF ALL SUBMARINES CAPTURED SHOULD BE TREATED AS PIRATES AND HANGED.
> **SIR ARTHUR WILSON**, CONTROLLER OF THE ROYAL NAVY, 1901
> ❞

WORLD WAR I

ATTACK ON THE JEAN BART

Date 21 December 1914
Forces French: 1 dreadnought; Austrians: 1 submarine
Losses French: none; Austrians: none

Location Otranto Strait, off southern Italy

Admiral de Lapeyrère, commanding the French Mediterranean fleet at the outset of World War I, was noted for his scorn of submarine warfare and conviction that battleships would be the key to victory. In December 1914 Lapeyrère's flagship, the dreadnought *Jean Bart,* was leading a sweep of the southern Adriatic when an Austrian submarine, U-12, hit the battleship with a single torpedo. The explosion missed the forward magazine and the ship's compartmentalized hull served to keep her afloat. Lapeyrère reached Malta safely, but the damage to one of its most modern warships was a severe shock to the French Navy.

WORLD WAR I

SINKING OF THE LUSITANIA

Date 7 May 1915
Forces British: 1 passenger liner; Germans: 1 submarine
Losses British: 1 passenger liner; Germans: none

Location Off Old Head of Kinsale, Ireland

The luxury passenger ship *Lusitania* left New York for Liverpool on 1 May. She had more than 1,900 passengers and crew on board and a very small quantity of ammunition in her cargo hold. On the afternoon of 7 May *Lusitania* was sighted off southern Ireland by Walther Schwieger, commander of the submarine U-20. A single torpedo struck the liner amidships. The ship sank in 18 minutes, killing 1,198 people including 128 Americans and almost 100 children. The sinking was a propaganda disaster for Germany, contributing greatly to the eventual entry of the United States into the war on the Allied side.

WEAPONS AND TECHNOLOGY

Q-SHIPS

Special Service Vessels, code-named Q-ships by the British Admiralty, were created in response to U-boat attacks on merchant shipping. The Royal Navy took old tramp steamers and other vessels and fitted them with concealed guns. A U-boat coming upon such a vessel would not waste a torpedo on it, but instead closed with it on the surface. Once the U-boat approached, the Q-ship would unveil its guns and open fire. Manned by volunteers, the Q-ships achieved their first success in July 1915. In the course of the war they sank 14 U-boats. One of their unintended effects, however, was to encourage U-boats to sink any merchant vessel without warning.

U-boat trap
Volunteers man a hidden gun on board a Special Service Vessel or Q-ship.

 WORLD WAR I

OTRANTO STRAIT

Date 15 May 1917
Forces Austrians: 3 light cruisers, 2 destroyers, 3 U-boats; Allies: 2 light cruisers, 8 destroyers
Losses Austrians: none; Allies: 2 destroyers, 14 trawlers, 1 supply ship

Location Otranto Strait, off southern Italy

The Allies attempted to block U-boats in the Adriatic by establishing a barrier from Otranto in Italy across to the Dalmatian coast. Consisting of minefields and of trawlers with steel "indicator nets" to detect and entangle submarines, the Otranto Barrage was not especially successful, but the anti-submarine trawlers did present a tempting target for raids by Austrian destroyers. In May 1917 Austrian Captain Miklos Horthy planned a heavier raid using three light cruisers, *Novara*, *Helgoland*, and *Saida*.

Leaving the port of Cattaro at nightfall on 14 May, the cruisers reached the barrage around 3:30am and steamed along blowing hapless Allied trawlers out of the water. Two accompanying destroyers sank an Italian munitions ship and its destroyer escort. Heading for home, the Austrians were pursued by an Allied force including the cruisers *Dartmouth* and *Bristol*. *Dartmouth* and two destroyers succeeded in pounding *Novara* to a standstill and Horthy was badly injured. But reports of the approach of a stronger Austrian force led the Allies to break off the action. On the way back to Brindisi, *Dartmouth* was badly damaged by the lurking submarine U-25 and one destroyer was sunk by a mine. *Saida* towed the crippled *Novara* back to Cattaro. The Allies subsequently abandoned night patrols by trawlers on the barrage. Horthy survived to become an admiral and, eventually, dictator of Hungary.

 WORLD WAR I

RAIDS ON ZEEBRUGGE AND OSTENDE

Date 23 April 1918
Forces British: 75 ships; Germans: unknown
Losses British: 5 cruisers, 1 submarine; Germans: unknown

Location Ostende and Zeebrugge, northern Belgium

A bold but over-optimistic operation was planned by Commodore Sir Roger Keyes to block the exits from German submarine pens in occupied Belgium.

The main effort was to be directed at Zeebrugge. The plan was to scuttle three blockships loaded with concrete in the mouth of the Bruges Canal, which linked the U-boat pens to the sea. The approach to the canal was protected by batteries on the Zeebrugge mole, a stone breakwater. These were to be disabled by a party of seamen and Marines landed on the mole by the cruiser *Vindictive* and two modified ferries. The raid was executed on the night of 22–23 April. The attack went badly from the start. *Vindictive* was battered by gunfire as she approached and ran against the mole in the wrong place. The landing party could not take the batteries, making it hard for the blockships – the aged cruisers *Iphigenia*, *Intrepid*, and *Thetis* – to reach the canal entrance. With heroic effort two of the them were scuttled as planned, but one sank short of its target. The raid on Ostende was less successful, the blockships failing to reach the harbour entrance. The raids were immensely popular in Britain. Keyes was knighted and 11 Victoria crosses were awarded. But it cost 214 lives and failed significantly to inhibit U-boat operations.

German Imperial naval ensign
Taken from the submarine U-155 when she surrendered at Harwich in 1918 after a career in which she sank 42 ships.

Zeebrugge blockships
Although the Zeebrugge raid did briefly block the route of the U-boats down the Bruges Canal, the Germans simply created a channel to move the U-boats around the sunken blockships at high tide.

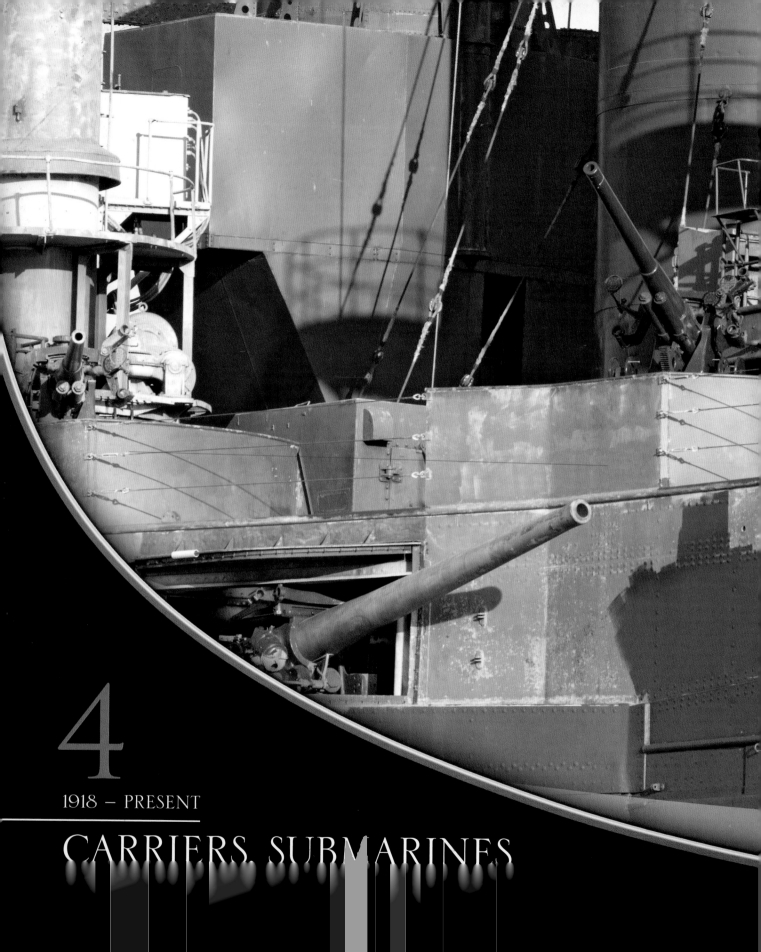

4

CARRIERS, SUBMARINES

DURING THE 20th century the long-established tradition of naval warfare fought between ships armed with guns was rendered increasingly obsolete by a series of technological innovations. Fleets found a new focus in the form of the aircraft carrier, which replaced the battleship as the capital ship. The introduction of missiles made guns largely redundant and missile-armed submarines became a crucial element in the awesomely destructive nuclear forces of the major powers. The successive transformations of naval warfare in the course of the century brought sea battles to an unprecedented climax in World War II – viewed as a whole, by far the greatest naval conflict in history – then appeared more or less to have abolished them, at least as large-scale engagements between opposing naval forces.

LIMITATION AND EXPANSION

After World War I, defeated Germany was temporarily banned from possessing a navy by the terms of the Versailles Treaty. In an attempt to avoid an expensive arms race between the remaining naval powers, an international agreement on fleet sizes was negotiated at the Washington Conference in 1922. Britain and the United States were accorded parity, with a fleet tonnage of 535,000 tons each, Japan was allowed 315,000 tons, and France and Italy 175,000 tons each. The British Royal Navy's acceptance of equality with America was a stark acknowledgement of Britain's waning power.

Nothing of this worthy attempt at arms limitation survived the rise of aggressive nationalist regimes in Japan, Germany, and Italy in the 1930s. The Japanese became increasingly restive at their restriction to third place in the pecking order and, after trying in vain to overturn this at the London Conference of 1930,

Amphibious landing
US troops disembark from a landing ship onto the Normandy beaches in June 1944. Amphibious operations, often conducted on a vast scale, made a crucial contribution to the Allied victory in WWII.

HIT 'EM WHERE IT HURTS!

33% OF JAPAN'S TONNAGE HAS BEEN SUNK. Of this
77% WAS SUNK BY SUBMARINES!

JOIN THE

Submarine Service

Hit 'em where it hurts
Naval commanders at the start of World War II were
generally complacent about the threat from
submarines. By the time this US Submarine Service
poster was designed in 1943, however, submarines
had more than proved their worth.

abandoned adherence to the Washington Treaty.
The rise to power of Adolf Hitler in Germany
in 1933 was inevitably followed by German
naval rearmament, which Britain tried to control
by agreeing to accept construction of a German
fleet a third of the size of its own.

DESCENT INTO WAR

Facing the possibility of having to
take on Germany, Japan, and Italy
simultaneously, with only France as
an ally, Britain was acutely aware
that the Royal Navy was no longer
adequate to the challenge it might
confront. Fortunately for the British,
Nazi Germany was only in the early
stages of naval expansion when war
broke out in 1939. The United States,

which had become accustomed to view Japan as
its major potential rival at sea, committed itself
in 1940 to the creation of a "Two Ocean Navy"
– capable of fighting simultaneously against the
Japanese in the Pacific and Nazi Germany in the
Atlantic. But the expansion of the US Navy was
barely under way when the Japanese attack on
Pearl Harbor brought America fully into the war
at the end of 1941, its destroyers having already
begun contributing to Atlantic convoy defence.

TRANSITIONAL TECHNOLOGY

World War II started at an uncertain transitional
moment in the evolution of naval technology
and tactics. Submarines had proved their
effectiveness in World War I, yet they remained
in practice only "submersibles" – craft that
could dive but had to spend most of their time
on the surface. Even in Germany, there was a
reluctance to accord the U-boats top priority,
and naval commanders used to focusing on
surface warships were often complacent about
their ability to cope with the underwater threat.

Aircraft meanwhile, although appreciated, were
underrated. The United States and Japan had
experimented in exercises with the aggressive
use of aircraft carriers as a prime strike force
capable of crippling an enemy fleet at long
range. But there was still a tendency even in
those air-conscious fleets to revert to regarding
carriers as ancillary to the battleships and
cruisers, simply providing reconnaissance or air
defence for the big-gun battlewagons. Japanese
naval aviation was the most advanced in the
world, yet at the end of the 1930s Japan devoted
vast resources to building the largest battleships
ever seen, the ill-fated Yamato class. A vision of
decisive battles between surface fleets with their
great guns continued to dominate naval thinking.

In the event, World War II did involve a
good number of battles in which exchange
of gunfire between large surface warships
was crucial, or even the sole action, and in most
engagements it played at least a part. But the
overwhelming importance of naval air power
was clear from start to finish of the conflict.

Sweetheart of the Marianas
Naval air power proved decisive during World War II
– the F-4U Corsair fighter-bomber was nicknamed the
"sweetheart of the Marianas" by US ground forces for its role
in the conquest of the Pacific Islands.

DECLINE OF THE GUNS

It was the Japanese strike on Pearl Harbor that first fully realized the potential of the aircraft carrier. Soon Japan and the United States were fighting naval battles conducted by shipborne aircraft at ranges of several hundred kilometres. In the Carrier Task Force, surface ships became escort screens for carriers, providing anti-aircraft and anti-submarine defence. Meanwhile submarines, as well as sinking a lot of warships, proved again their effectiveness as commerce raiders, especially for Germany in the Atlantic and the United States in the Pacific – although even submarines proved vulnerable to air power.

Whether under, on, or over the ocean surface, there was no doubting the importance of sea power in World War II. The Allies established dominance over the Atlantic, Mediterranean, and Pacific only after epic struggles. Amphibious operations, both landings and evacuations, were carried out on an unprecedented scale – the big guns of the battleships and cruisers proved above all important for shore bombardment in support of landings. The Allies won the race for technological development, with crucial progress in the use of radar, plus increasingly sophisticated systems of command and control, and superior naval intelligence. But the key to Allied

success, in the end, was the astonishing productive power of American shipyards. By the end of the war the US Navy had not only crushed its enemies, but established an overwhelming superiority over its Allies.

COLD WAR AND AFTER

The context for the development of navies in the 40 years after World War II was the Cold War confrontation between the United States and the Soviet Union. The US Navy had to prepare for a possible nuclear war with the Soviets and to counter what America regarded as communist expansionism around the globe. The navy enjoyed the resources made available by American economic dominance, always the ultimate basis for naval power. But the USSR was prepared to devote a large percentage of its

lesser national wealth to military development and thus over time created the world's second largest navy, a massive force especially strong in nuclear submarines. However, as a war between the two superpowers was ruled out by nuclear weapons, which made an all-out armed struggle between them in practice unwinnable, the Soviet Navy never fired a shot in anger. The US Navy by contrast saw plenty of action during the Cold War, notably in support of land operations in "limited" wars in Korea and Vietnam. Britain became America's subordinate ally, the Royal Navy still the third-largest naval force in the

Hunter-killer submarine
The Los Angeles-class nuclear-powered submarine *Salt Lake City* on exercises in 2005. The class was introduced during the Cold War as hunter-killers to track, and if necessary destroy, Soviet ballistic missile submarines.

Soviet submariner's uniform
The focus of the Soviet Navy during the Cold War was on matching the nuclear submarine and missile capacity of the United States.

Night vision goggles
A pair of World War II night vision goggles for use on board submarines during secret missions.

1922
Washington Naval Treaty places strict limits on tonnages of warships for major naval powers after World War I

1934
Japan announces intention to withdraw from the Naval Treaties

1935
Anglo-German naval agreement allows Germany to strengthen its fleet

1939
Britain and France declare war on Germany. Within hours, German U-boat sinks British cruise ship, marking the start of U-boat warfare in the Atlantic

1941
Attack by Japanese carrier aircraft on US fleet at Pearl Harbor brings US into WWII

1942
Coral Sea is the first battle between carrier fleets in which neither side's ships exchange direct fire or have visual contact with the opposing fleet

1944
First kamikaze suicide attacks by Japanese aviators against Allied shipping

1950
The largest amphibious landing since WWII takes place at Inchon in Korea, supported by a United Nations backed force of 230 ships

1954
First nuclear powered submarine launched, USS *Nautilus*

1955
Soviet Union fires first submarine-launched ballistic missile

1960
Nuclear-powered submarine USS *Triton* completes first submerged circumnavigation of the globe

1964
US Congress approves war in Vietnam

1920   **1930**   **1940**   **1950**   **1960**

Vietnam patch
America's war in Vietnam saw
an increasing focus on coastal
and riverine warfare – and
the formation of naval units
dedicated to fighting in these
"littoral" environments.

world but only just capable of independent
action – as it showed in the Falklands War in
1981. The end of the Cold War in the late 1980s
left the US Navy with an absolute predominance
over any potential enemies, though with plenty
of work for its aircraft and missiles to perform
in support of global interventions, especially
in the troubled Middle East.

CHANGING NAVIES

Battleships for many years continued to function
in a shore bombardment role, but the capital
ships of the postwar era were unquestionably
carriers and submarines. Carriers grew in size
to accommodate jet aircraft – although jump
jets and helicopters enabled all kinds of smaller
warships to mount their own aircraft – and
were equipped with nuclear engines that gave
them almost unlimited operational range.

Genuine submarines, in the sense of a vessel
capable of sustained operations underwater,
were brought into service by Germany at the
end of World War II, but it was nuclear power
that really made submarines come into their
own. Nuclear submarines, much bigger than
their predecessors, could travel under the sea
almost indefinitely. They diverged into two
types: those armed with ballistic missiles that
formed part of the "nuclear deterrent" and
hunter-killer submarines, chiefly to be used
to hunt an enemy's submarine forces.

The demise of the big guns did not mean
that the only valid surface warships were
carriers. Frigates, reintroduced during World
War II, and destroyers continued to fulfil a vital
role as platforms for anti-submarine, anti-ship,
and anti-aircraft missiles, as well as mounting
nuclear and non-nuclear land attack missiles.
The predominance of missiles was such that by
the 1970s some warships were being built with
no guns at all – but this proved a momentary
aberration. The use of missiles, with their
guidance systems and the countermeasures they
required, was necessarily linked to massively

sophisticated systems
of communications and
control. Combat was
in the hands of men or
women sitting in front
of computer screens in
control rooms who would
never see the enemy
they fought. By the 1991 Gulf War, shore
bombardment was being conducted at ranges
of hundreds of kilometres not only by naval
aircraft but also by Tomahawk cruise missiles.

THE 21ST-CENTURY NAVY

By the 21st century it was fair to say that, in
terms of world power, the US Navy was the
only force that really counted. The navy that
took part in attacks on Afghanistan and Iraq
was a refined instrument of global power-
projection. Its crews, ratings as well as officers,
consisted mostly of educated people – women
as well as men from 1993 – exercising some
special skill. Many were operating electronic
gadgetry related to sensors and guidance systems,
control and communications. Manual labour
formed only a relatively small part of life on
board any warship. Even on submarines, crew
experienced conditions – in terms of food,
comfort, and medical care – far more civilized
than any of their historical predecessors. What
role this superbly trained and equipped navy
would find to play in the context of the "War
on Terror" remained open to question.

Missile keys
The set of keys used
to arm the Polaris
nuclear missile on
board the ballistic
missile submarine
HMS *Repulse*.

1988
US Navy attacks Iranian
oil platforms in the
Gulf in retaliation for
Iranian minelaying

1990
Iraqi invasion of Kuwait
sparks the First Gulf War

2001
Muslim extremists
destroy World Trade
Center in New York

2003
US invasion of Iraq
opens the Second
Gulf War

2006
USS *Freedom* launched, the first
ship in US Navy's next generation
of Littoral Combat Ships

1970   **1980**   **1990**   **2000**   **2010**

1973
US troops
complete
withdrawl from
Vietnam

1973
Israeli missile boats sink
several Syrian ships near
Latakia in first engagement
between boats using surface-
to-surface missiles and
electronic countermeasures

1982
Falklands War between
Argentina and UK: sinking
of a British destroyer by
Exocet missile illustrates
the vulnerability of surface
craft to anti-ship missiles

1991
Collapse of Soviet
Union leaves USA
as the world's only
naval superpower

2001
US invasion of
Afghanistan begins,
supported by carrier
groups in the Gulf

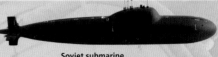

Soviet submarine
An Akula-class nuclear-powered attack
submarine, deployed by the Soviet Navy in 1986.

EUROPE BETWEEN THE WARS

AFTER THE END of hostilities with Germany in 1918, the British and French toyed with intervention in Russia against the Bolshevik regime, then engaged in conflicts on its western borders. The commitment of naval forces in the Baltic and the Black Sea brought little positive result besides a demonstration of British fighting spirit in a raid on Kronstadt. A mutiny aboard the French battleships *Jean Bart* and *France* in the Black Sea in April 1919 hastened disillusionment with interventionism and pressure to demobilize. No further naval conflict occurred in Europe until 1936, when right-wing Nationalist officers in Spain rebelled against the left-wing government of the Republic. Nazi Germany and Fascist Italy gave the Nationalists military support while the Soviet Union backed the Republic, and Britain and France operated a "non-intervention" policy. The Spanish navy split like the rest of the country and elements of it fought one another. Aided by Germany and Italy, which deployed submarines to attack Republican convoys, the Nationalists had the better of the naval war, although this was marginal to their eventual victory in 1939.

RUSSIAN CIVIL WAR

RAID ON KRONSTADT

Date 18 August 1919
Forces British: 1 carrier, 8 coastal motor boats; Russians: 1 dreadnought, 1 pre-dreadnought, and many other vessels
Losses British: 3 coastal motor boats; Russians: 1 dreadnought, 1 pre-dreadnought, 1 depot ship

Location Kronstadt, Baltic

The British navy developed Coastal Motor Boats (CMBs) during World War I, small torpedo craft designed to attack warships in harbour. After the war Lieutenant Augustus Agar was sent to the Baltic with two CMBs to help the British secret service destabilize the revolutionary Bolshevik government in Russia. Agar made a night raid on the Russian naval base at Kronstadt on 17 June 1919, sinking the cruiser *Oleg*.

Rear Admiral Sir Walter Cowan was commanding a Royal Navy force in the Baltic blockading the Russian navy in Kronstadt. Inspired by Agar's example, he had a flotilla of CMBs brought from Britain. Led by Commander Claude Dobson, they attacked Kronstadt on the night of 18–19 August, supported by aircraft from the carrier *Vindictive*. Dobson led the first wave of four boats into the harbour. His CMB 31 torpedoed the pre-dreadnought *Andrei Pervozvanny*. CMB 88 had her captain killed but Sub-Lieutenant Gordon Steele, taking control under heavy fire, torpedoed the dreadnought battleship *Petropavlovsk*. A second wave of CMBs faced intensifying Russian resistance. Two boats collided in the dark and another was cut in two by a shell. Both Steele and Dobson were awarded Victoria Crosses for their part in the raid.

Depot ship sunk
The British motor boats attacking Kronstadt sank the submarine depot ship *Pamyat Azova* as well as dreadnought and pre-dreadnought battleships.

SPANISH CIVIL WAR

CAPE ESPARTEL

Date 29 September 1936
Forces Republicans: 3 destroyers; Nationalists: 2 cruisers
Losses Republicans: 1 destroyer; Nationalists: none

Location Straits of Gibraltar

At the start of the Spanish Civil War Republican sailors took control of many naval vessels and blocked the movement of Nationalist troops by sea from Spanish Morocco to southern Spain. At the Atlantic port of El Ferrol Nationalists won control of warships including the light cruiser *Almirante Cervera* and heavy cruiser *Canarias*. Under Captain Francisco Moreno, the two ships sailed to the Strait of Gibraltar, where they attacked a Republican flotilla. *Almirante Ferrandiz* was sunk and another destroyer, *Gravina*, severely damaged. The rest fled for safety, leaving the sea route between North Africa and Spain open for Nationalist forces.

SPANISH CIVIL WAR

CAPE CHERCHELL

Date 7 September 1937
Forces Republicans: 2 light cruisers, 4 destroyers; Nationalists: 1 heavy cruiser
Losses Republicans: none; Nationalists: none

Location Off Cape Cherchell, Algeria

The Nationalist heavy cruiser *Baleares* intercepted a Republican convoy of four supply ships escorted by the light cruisers *Libertad* and *Mendez Nuñez* and four destroyers. Despite being outnumbered, *Baleares* engaged the Republican cruisers. *Libertad* scored a hit that damaged *Baleares*'s electronics, temporarily disabling her guns. The Republican cruisers then took the opportunity to steam after the convoy, but they were later caught again by *Baleares*, pursuing with her electronics repaired. Suffering further damage, the Nationalist cruiser broke off the engagement and, joined by the cruiser *Canarias*, sailed back to port at Malaga.

SPANISH CIVIL WAR

CAPE PALOS

Date 5–6 March 1938
Forces Republicans: 2 light cruisers, 5 destroyers; Nationalists: 2 heavy cruisers, 1 light cruiser
Losses Republicans: none; Nationalists: 2 heavy cruisers, 1 light cruiser

Location Off Cartagena, Spain

On the night of 5–6 March 1938, the cruisers *Baleares*, *Canarias*, and *Almirante Cervera*, under the command of Rear Admiral Manuel de Vierna, were escorting two Italian freighters to Nationalist Spain. At the same time a Republican force of cruisers and destroyers under Vice Admiral Luis de Ubieta left the port of Cartagena, intending to raid the Nationalist harbour at Palma on Mallorca.

Just after midnight the two forces chanced to run into one another. The Republicans fruitlessly fired a number of torpedoes before the Nationalist cruisers disappeared into the darkness. Around 2:15am the two forces met again. Neither side was capable of effective gun-aiming at night but the Nationalist cruiser *Baleares* made the mistake of opening fire and the gun flashes provided a target for the Republican destroyers to aim for. Three destroyers fired a total of 12 torpedoes, two of which struck *Baleares*, blowing up both the forward magazine and the bridge. Admiral Manuel de Vierna was among those killed.

Blazing from stem to stern, *Baleares* was almost run into by her fellow cruiser *Canarias*, following directly behind. *Canarias* and *Almirante Cervera* quit the scene, leaving *Baleares* to her fate. Fortunately there were two British destroyers in the area that rescued more than half of the sinking cruiser's 765 crew. The Republican ships meanwhile returned to port at Cartagena, allowing *Canarias*

Attack on Cartagena
Spanish Nationalists bomb the Republican naval base at Cartagena near Cape Palos. The battle of Cape Palos in 1938 was the last Republican victory in a war that the Republic was losing.

and *Almirante Cervera* to return at dawn to collect the survivors, transferring them to the Nationalist cruisers under Republican air attack. The battle of Cape Palos was a Republican success but had no strategic consequences.

EARLY NAVAL AVIATION

AMERICAN FLIER EUGENE ELY demonstrated in 1910–11 that it was possible to take off from and land on the deck of a ship. Navies were quick to see the usefulness of aircraft, especially for reconnaissance, and adopted both airships and heavier-than-air machines. In 1911 the French navy introduced the first ship to carry float planes and in 1914 Britain's Royal Naval Air Service was founded.

EARLY NAVAL AIRCRAFT

Float planes were used from the start of World War I. Lowered over the side of a seaplane tender to take off from the water, they were lifted back on board after their mission. Unfortunately, the float planes could only operate in optimum weather conditions. A heavy swell made landing and take-off impossible. The lightweight wood-and-canvas aircraft of the period were relatively easy to launch from an improvised platform on a ship, but safe landing was only just being mastered as the war ended. Thus even ship-launched machines had to be retrieved from the sea after a mission.

Wing flaps give lift at low speeds

British RAF biplane
Aircraft could be flown off improvised platforms on battleships or cruisers, such as one here laid on top of the warship's main guns.

Upper wing supported by struts and wires

Undercarriage support for the wheels

Wing braces to strengthen the wings

Lower of the fabric-covered wooden wings

SOPWITH CAMEL
The Sopwith 2F.1 could be split in two just behind the cockpit so it could be more easily moved and stored on the carriers of the period.

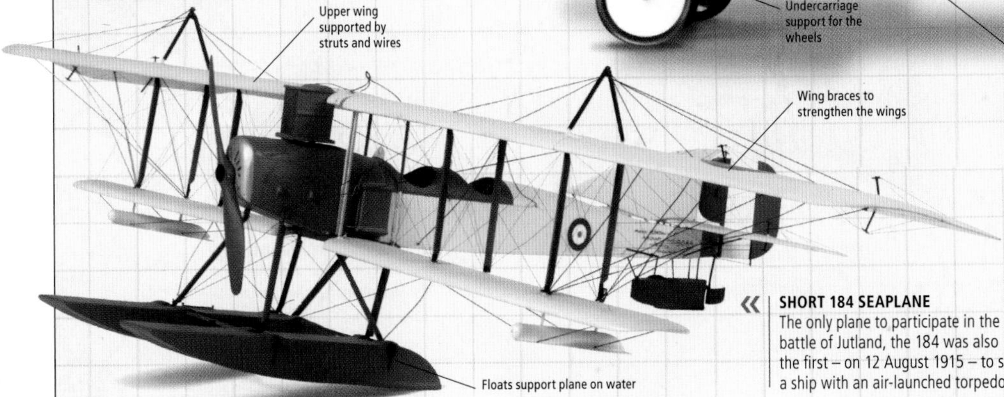

Floats support plane on water

SHORT 184 SEAPLANE
The only plane to participate in the battle of Jutland, the 184 was also the first — on 12 August 1915 — to sink a ship with an air-launched torpedo.

CARRIER CONVERSIONS

The first carriers evolved from experiments by the Royal Navy Air Service in 1916. The decks of the battlecruiser *Furious* were cleared to make a platform for take-off and landing, but it was found that the funnel and central superstructure created insuperable problems for pilots. In 1918 the British converted an Italian liner into the carrier *Argus*, with a funnel tucked away at the end of a long unobstructed deck. The US Navy followed this example with the converted collier *Langley* — dubbed the "covered wagon" — in 1922. A superstructure offset to starboard was generally adopted in the 1920s, but most carriers continued to be conversions — the US Navy's *Lexington* and *Saratoga*, for example, started life as battlecruisers.

HMS Hermes
The world's first purpose-built aircraft carrier, the Royal Navy's *Hermes*, was commissioned in 1923. She was sunk in 1942.

HMS Argus
Built in 1916, the British aircraft carrier *Argus* was the first carrrier to have a flush deck that let wheeled planes take off and land safely.

1918 – PRESENT

WORLD WAR II: THE WEST

THE OUTBREAK OF World War II in 1939 came too early for the German navy, which was looking forward to completing a large-scale expansion programme by the mid-1940s. Yet Britain's Royal Navy found itself fighting a defensive war on increasingly difficult terms. Germany's military successes in 1940 gave it control of the Norwegian side of the North Sea, France's Atlantic ports, and the southern Channel coast, and deprived the Royal Navy of the support of the French fleet. With Italy also entering the war, British naval forces were desperately stretched. German U-boats came very close to severing Britain's lifeline across the Atlantic through the savaging of merchant convoys. Yet whereas in World War I the Royal Navy had performed generally disappointingly, despite its superiority, in World War II it showed endurance and aggression under the most demanding circumstances.

Coming up for air
German U-boats were used mainly for economic warfare against Allied merchant shipping. With most U-boat war patrols lasting between three weeks and six months, any opportunities to get outside for fresh air were welcomed.

British binnacle compass
Nicknamed "Faithful Freddie", this submarine compass has a binnacle cover and two iron correcting spheres to protect it from magnetic distortion caused by the submarine's iron hull.

WEAKNESSES AT SEA

The British Royal Navy entered the war with some serious drawbacks. Failing to learn from the experience of World War I, the British had inadequate numbers of smaller ships for convoy escort duties to combat U-boats. Too much faith had been placed in new sonar underwater detection equipment and depth charges as a miracle cure for submarine attack. Corvettes and then frigates were rushed into service to fill this gap, while Canada made an invaluable contribution to convoy defence, followed by the United States from 1941. British inter-war neglect of carrier aircraft – a result of putting them under RAF rather than navy control up to 1937 – resulted in the Fleet Air Arm entering the war with some excellent aircraft carriers but

obsolescent naval aircraft. On the other side, Germany was slow to put sufficient resources into U-boats, and the Italian navy suffered from technical deficiencies including absence of radar and inadequate intelligence as well as poor command at the highest levels.

COURAGE AND AGGRESSION

Germany's surface fleet was never powerful enough to challenge the Royal Navy in the way its World War I predecessor had at Jutland. After heavy losses of destroyers in the 1940 Norwegian campaign the German navy was in no position to engage in fleet actions or cover a seaborne invasion of Britain. Its fast modern warships, used as surface raiders, were a serious threat to vital shipping lanes early

in the war but they were gradually hunted down and destroyed, albeit at considerable cost. The Royal Navy also inflicted heavy losses on Italian warships in a number of bold actions off Taranto and Cape Matapan. But the use of submarines and air power denied the British command of the sea. Although the Germans had no carriers, land-based Luftwaffe aircraft proved their deadly effectiveness against the Royal Navy in the Norwegian campaign, at Dunkirk, and in the Mediterranean, especially during the Allied evacuation of Crete in 1941 in which 24 British warships were sunk or badly damaged by air attack. Sea mines were rendered less effective than in World War I through the adoption of effective countermeasures by 1940, but Axis submarines took their toll of warships as well as

merchant shipping – Royal Navy ships lost to attack by U-boats included the battleships *Royal Oak* and *Barham* and the carriers *Courageous* and *Ark Royal*. Convoys had to be escorted through the Mediterranean, across the Atlantic, and into the Arctic under both submarine and air attack, gruelling and costly operations to keep supply lifelines open. It was not until 1943, more than a year after the entry of the United States into the war, that the Allies established effective command over the Atlantic and Mediterranean. Even then much was owed to air power – the battle of the Atlantic was not won until escort carriers and long range aircraft

British moored contact mine
Contact mines such as this were triggered by passing vessels brushing against the protruding horns. Other types of mine were set off by the magnetic field of a ship's hull.

brought the whole ocean under cover of air patrol. The Allied landings at Normandy in June 1944 were a staggering demonstration of naval power, but the operation depended on command of the air. The impressive productivity of Allied shipyards, especially those of the United States, meant that the odds mounted overwhelmingly against Germany as time passed. The U-boats never ceased to operate, with a superior new design even giving them a fresh lease of life in 1945, but it was far too little and too late.

Atlantic convoy
Allied survival during the war relied on a steady flow of supplies across the Atlantic. To defend merchant vessels from U-boat attack they were organized into convoys under the protection of warship escorts.

THE GERMAN NAVY was not capable of a fleet battle with the British Royal Navy in World War II. Germany possessed only a handful of large warships, no carriers, and an inadequate number of destroyers. But the best German ships were modern, fast, and heavily armed for their size. Despite the loss of *Graf Spee* at the River Plate in December 1939, commerce raiding by German warships such as *Scharnhorst* and *Gneisenau* was frighteningly effective in the first 18 months of the war. The hunting down and sinking of the battleship *Bismarck* in May 1941 was a turning point. Although substantial Royal Navy forces were tied down by the need to neutralize the threat posed by the presence of warships such as *Scharnhorst* and *Tirpitz* in the Norwegian fjords, Hitler lost all faith in his surface ships. Admiral Erich Raeder, who had masterminded the creation of the German fleet, was replaced as commander-in-chief by U-boat advocate Admiral Karl Dönitz in January 1943. From then onward the German warships were the hunted rather than the hunters. The mighty *Tirpitz* was eventually sunk without ever having fired its guns against an enemy ship.

THE BATTLE OF THE RIVER PLATE

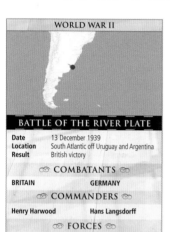

WORLD WAR II

BATTLE OF THE RIVER PLATE

Date	13 December 1939
Location	South Atlantic off Uruguay and Argentina
Result	British victory

⚓ COMBATANTS ⚓

BRITAIN	GERMANY

⚓ COMMANDERS ⚓

Henry Harwood	Hans Langsdorff

⚓ FORCES ⚓

Ships: 1 heavy cruiser, 2 light cruisers	**Ships:** 1 pocket battleship

⚓ LOSSES ⚓

Men: 100 casualties	**Men:** 96 casualties **Ships:** 1 pocket battleship later scuttled

In the early months of World War II, the Deutschland-class pocket battleship *Admiral Graf Spee* conducted a successful commerce raiding campaign in the Indian Ocean and the South Atlantic. Under the command of Captain Hans Langsdorff, the German warship sank nine merchant ships, while chivalrously ensuring that there was no loss of life.

At around 6:15am on the morning of 13 December 1939, a lookout on *Graf Spee* sighted a cruiser and, it was initially believed, two destroyers. The ships were in fact the Royal Navy's Force G, consisting of the heavy cruiser *Exeter* and the light cruisers *Ajax* and *Achilles*, the latter belonging to the New Zealand Division. Led by Commodore Henry Harwood on board *Ajax*, the cruiser squadron had been hunting for the German commerce raider and correctly guessed it might be lurking off the estuary of the River Plate between Argentina and Uruguay. The Royal Navy ships were outgunned by *Graf Spee*:

the pocket battleship had 11in main guns, compared with *Exeter*'s 8in and the 6in armament of the two light cruisers. In the true tradition of the Royal Navy, however, Harwood unhesitatingly attacked. He split his force, with *Exeter* steaming to the south of *Graf Spee* and the cruisers *Ajax* and *Achilles* manoeuvring to the north.

Fire opened within minutes as the range closed, *Graf Spee* initially focusing upon *Exeter* as the greater threat. The heavy cruiser was soon in trouble. Its bridge was swept by shrapnel, leaving the ship's captain, F S Bell, as one of the few survivors. Guns were put out of action, communications destroyed,

Glory of the Navy
The sinking of the *Graf Spee* was a huge boost for British morale. This commemorative magazine celebrates "How we beat the *Graf Spee*".

and fires started. *Ajax* and *Achilles* forced Langsdorff to divide his fire, depending on their speed to survive as salvoes fell around them. By around 7:40am *Exeter* could no longer fight and limped away from the battle. But without knowing it, *Exeter*'s gunners had succeeded in scoring a crucial hit on *Graf Spee*, destroying her fuel processing system. Langsdorff knew he could not long remain at sea without repairs and headed west for the River Plate. Damaged and short of ammunition, *Achilles* and *Ajax* settled for shadowing

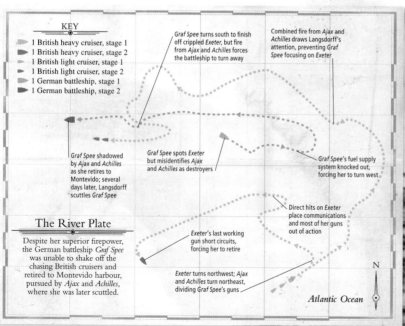

KEY

- 1 British heavy cruiser, stage 1
- 1 British heavy cruiser, stage 2
- 1 British light cruiser, stage 1
- 1 British light cruiser, stage 2
- 1 German battleship, stage 1
- 1 German battleship, stage 2

Graf Spee turns south to finish off crippled *Exeter*, but fire from *Ajax* and *Achilles* forces the battleship to turn away

Combined fire from *Ajax* and *Achilles* draws Langsdorff's attention, preventing *Graf Spee* focusing on *Exeter*

Graf Spee shadowed by *Ajax* and *Achilles* as she retires to Montevideo; several days later, Langsdorff scuttles *Graf Spee*

Graf Spee spots *Exeter* but misidentifies *Ajax* and *Achilles* as destroyers

Graf Spee's fuel supply system knocked out, forcing her to turn west

Direct hits on *Exeter* place communications and most of her guns out of action

The River Plate

Despite her superior firepower, the German battleship *Graf Spee* was unable to shake off the chasing British cruisers and retired to Montevideo harbour, pursued by *Ajax* and *Achilles*, where she was later scuttled.

Exeter's last working gun short circuits, forcing her to retire

Exeter turns northwest; *Ajax* and *Achilles* turn northeast, dividing *Graf Spee*'s guns

Atlantic Ocean

N

CHANNEL DASH 1942

Date 11–13 February 1942
Forces Germans: 2 battlecruisers, 1 heavy cruiser, 6 destroyers, 40 other vessels; British: 9 destroyers, 32 motor torpedo boats
Losses Germans: 17 aircraft; British: 42 aircraft

Location The English Channel

The German battlecruisers *Scharnhorst* and *Gneisenau* and the heavy cruiser *Prinz Eugen* were ordered to return to Germany from Brest through the Channel. Under Vice Admiral Otto Ciliax, they left port late on the night of 11-12 February and sailed 480km (300 miles) down the Channel before they were detected, even though the British had been expecting their move. They dodged fire from shore guns at Dover and brushed off destroyers and torpedo boats. A gallant attack by six Fairey Swordfish biplanes led by Lieutenant Commander Eugene Esmond also failed and all the aircraft were shot down. Despite hitting a number of mines, the ships successfully reached home, to the great embarrassment of the Royal Navy.

Graf Spee through the day, largely succeeding in keeping out of range of the battleship's guns.

That night, *Graf Spee* entered the port of Montevideo, the capital of neutral Uruguay. According to the accepted rules of war, the Uruguayans had either to order the German warship to leave after completing repairs or to intern both the ship and its crew. British misinformation convinced Langsdorff that a powerful Royal Navy force awaited him – whereas in fact only the heavy cruiser *Cumberland* had joined *Ajax* and *Achilles*. Langsdorff rejected the options of internment or a death-or-glory showdown. On 17 December *Graf Spee* steamed out into the River Plate estuary, the crew were taken off, and the ship was scuttled. Two days later, Langsdorff shot himself.

Ajax and Achilles
The light cruiser *Achilles* seen from underneath the guns of her sister ship *Ajax* after battle with *Graf Spee*. The guns are loaded and trained in the direction of the River Plate estuary to prevent *Graf Spee's* escape.

ATTACKS ON TIRPITZ

Date 22 September 1943; 3 April 1944
Forces Germans: 1 pocket battleship; British: 6 submarines, 6 midget submarines, 6 fleet and escort carriers, 2 battleships, 2 cruisers, 16 destroyers
Losses Germans: none; British: 5 midget submarines, 3 aircraft

Location Kafjord and Altenfjord, Norway

From early 1942 the German pocket battleship *Tirpitz* was stationed in the north of Norway, posing a threat to British Arctic convoys. The Royal Navy tried to sink *Tirpitz* in the fjords, twice inflicting serious damage. In September 1943 six X-craft – midget submarines with a three-man crew – were towed across the North Sea by conventional submarines. Two X-craft were lost en route but the rest made their run into Kafjord, steering a hazardous course through a minefield and past listening posts. One of the X-craft was sunk by gunfire and another failed to locate a target, but X-6 and X-7, commanded by Lieutenant Donald Cameron and Lieutenant Basil Place, succeeded in laying their explosive charges beneath *Tirpitz's* hull. These exploded, causing substantial damage that put the ship out of action for six

Hidden menace
The huge Bismarck-class battleship *Tirpitz* spent much of the war in the fjords of German-occupied Norway, where her mere presence was a threat to the Allied Arctic convoys.

months. The crews of the X-craft survived but were captured. Cameron and Place received the Victoria Cross.

OPERATION TUNGSTEN
Another attack on *Tirpitz* was carried out by the Fleet Air Arm in April 1944. The fleet carriers *Victorious* and *Furious*, supported by a powerful force including two battleships, launched 40 Fairey Barracuda dive-bombers with fighter escorts in two waves. The fighters strafed *Tirpitz* and the Barracudas dropped both general-purpose and armour-piercing bombs, the latter disappointingly failing to penetrate the battleship's deck. *Tirpitz* suffered more than 400 casualties and was put out of action for a further month. She was finally sunk by the Royal Air Force on 12 November 1944.

NORTH CAPE 1943

Date 26 December 1943
Forces Germans: 1 battlecruiser; British: 1 battleship, 4 cruisers, 9 destroyers
Losses Germans: 1 battlecruiser; British: none

Location Off northern Norway

The German battlecruiser *Scharnhorst*, under Rear Admiral Erich Bey, sortied from its harbour in Norway, intending to attack British Arctic convoy JW-55B. The British were aware of *Scharnhorst's* movements through signals intercepts and prepared to counterattack. Bey had dispersed his destroyer escorts to search for the convoy and the battlecruiser was alone when surprised by the cruisers *Sheffield*, *Belfast*, and *Norfolk* on the morning of 26 December. The weather was bleak, with a heavy snowstorm in progress. The British cruisers scored two hits on *Scharnhorst*, disabling her forward radar and radar-assisted fire control. They then tracked the German warship while calling in support from a larger force commanded by Admiral Sir Bruce Fraser on board the battleship *Duke of York*, with the cruiser *Jamaica* and a bevy of destroyers.

A desperate pursuit developed, *Scharnhorst* running for Norway and exchanging salvoes with *Duke of York* at long range. The crucial moment came when a shell from the Royal Navy battleship destroyed one of *Scharnhorst's* engine rooms, sharply reducing her speed. British (and one Norwegian) destroyers were then able to close for torpedo attacks. Despite taking some damage, the destroyers scored four hits. As star shells lit up the Arctic night, the crippled *Scharnhorst* was battered by the guns of *Duke of York* and the cruisers *Jamaica* and *Belfast*, then suffered multiple torpedo strikes as destroyers closed for the kill. She capsized and sank. Of her crew of 2,004 men, only 36 were rescued from the ice-cold sea.

THE HUNT FOR THE BISMARCK

On 18 May 1941 the German battleship *Bismarck*, accompanied by the cruiser *Prinz Eugen* sailed from the Baltic port of Gdynia. Admiral Lütjens' mission was to break out into the Atlantic and raid merchant convoys. The Royal Navy tracked the ships as far as the Norwegian coast, after which they disappeared. On the evening of 23 May, however, the pair were detected by the radar-equipped cruisers *Norfolk* and *Suffolk* patrolling the Denmark Strait.

SINKING OF THE HOOD

The new battleship *Prince of Wales* and the large but ageing battlecruiser *Hood* arrived in visual range at 5:35am the next morning. On paper the two sides looked well matched, but *Prince of Wales* had been rushed into action without proper preparation, while *Hood* lacked adequate armour. *Bismarck,* while not without flaw, was the largest warship commissioned at the time. The firing began at range, with the Royal Navy ships closing rapidly. At 6am a shell penetrated one of *Hood*'s magazines and the battlecruiser was split in two by a huge explosion. It sank in three minutes. Only three men from a crew of over 1,400 survived. The *Prince of Wales* prudently broke off the fight. The sinking of *Hood* was a severe shock to the Royal Navy, but *Bismarck* had not emerged unscathed. A shell had damaged its fuel tanks, forcing Lütjens to alter his plans. *Prinz Eugen* was despatched to fulfil the commerce raiding mission, while *Bismarck* made a dash for Brittany.

The Royal Navy devoted every available resource to hunting down the German battleship, but Admiral John Tovey, leading the pursuit on board *King George V,* found the enemy elusive. A torpedo attack by Swordfish aircraft from the carrier *Victorious* on the night of 24 May was ineffectual and the following day Lütjens gave his pursuers the slip. Tovey mistakenly suspected he was heading back to the Denmark Strait and sailed too far north.

THE END OF THE BISMARCK

On the morning of 26 May *Bismarck*'s luck changed, when she was spotted by a Catalina flying boat of RAF Coastal Command. Tovey was too far off to catch *Bismarck* before she came within the protective shelter of land-based Luftwaffe aircraft. But Force H, including the carrier *Ark Royal*, sailing north from Gibraltar, was well placed to intercept. The Force's commander, Admiral James Sommerville, sent the cruiser *Sheffield* to shadow *Bismarck* and Swordfish from *Ark Royal* to attack with torpedoes. The first Swordfish sortie was a fiasco – they attacked *Sheffield* by mistake. But a second sortie late in the day proved decisive. Flying unscathed through a barrage of anti-aircraft fire in the murky dusk, the flimsy biplanes managed two hits on *Bismarck*, one of which jammed the rudders. The ship was stuck in a circle to port. Knowing he was doomed, Lütjens sent a last message to headquarters: "We will fight to the last shell. Long live the Führer!"

British destroyers kept up the pressure on *Bismarck* through the night with torpedo attacks. The following morning the battleships *King George V* and *Rodney* arrived to batter Lütjens' crippled ship. *Bismarck* was a burning hulk by the time the cruiser *Dorsetshire* closed to finish her off with torpedoes. Only 110 of the crew were saved.

WORLD WAR II

HUNT FOR THE BISMARCK

Date	18–27 May 1941
Location	North Atlantic
Result	British victory

⟨∞⟩ COMBATANTS ⟨∞⟩

BRITAIN	GERMANY

⟨∞⟩ COMMANDERS ⟨∞⟩

John Tovey	Günther Lütjens

⟨∞⟩ FORCES ⟨∞⟩

Ships: 2 carriers, 7 battleships, more than 50 other ships	**Ships:** 1 battleship, 1 cruiser

⟨∞⟩ LOSSES ⟨∞⟩

Men: 1,500	**Men:** 2,100
Ships: 1 battlecruiser	**Ships:** 1 battleship

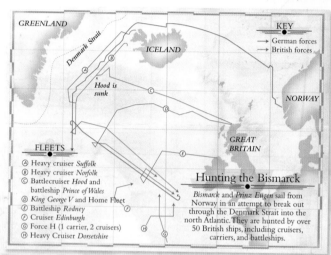

KEY
⟶ German forces
⟶ British forces

FLEETS
Ⓐ Heavy cruiser *Suffolk*
Ⓑ Heavy cruiser *Norfolk*
Ⓒ Battlecruiser *Hood* and battleship *Prince of Wales*
Ⓓ *King George V* and Home Fleet
Ⓔ Battleship *Rodney*
Ⓕ Cruiser *Edinburgh*
Ⓖ Force H (1 carrier, 2 cruisers)
Ⓗ Heavy Cruiser *Dorsetshire*

Hunting the Bismarck

Bismarck and *Prinz Eugen* sail from Norway in an attempt to break out through the Denmark Strait into the north Atlantic. They are hunted by over 50 British ships, including cruisers, carriers, and battleships.

Hood is sunk

GREENLAND
Denmark Strait
ICELAND
NORWAY
GREAT BRITAIN

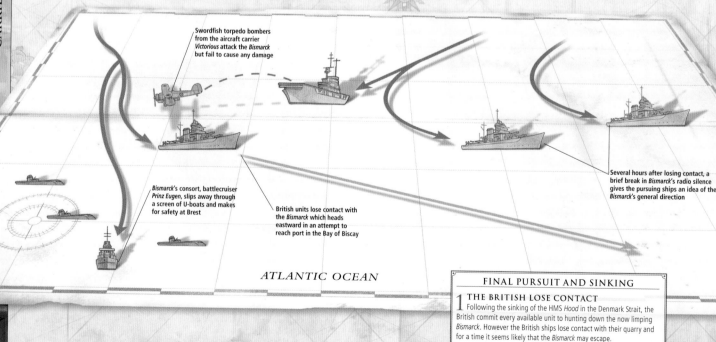

Swordfish torpedo bombers from the aircraft carrier *Victorious* attack the *Bismarck* but fail to cause any damage

Bismarck's consort, battlecruiser *Prinz Eugen*, slips away through a screen of U-boats and makes for safety at Brest

British units lose contact with the *Bismarck* which heads eastward in an attempt to reach port in the Bay of Biscay

Several hours after losing contact, a brief break in *Bismarck*'s radio silence gives the pursuing ships an idea of the *Bismarck*'s general direction

ATLANTIC OCEAN

FINAL PURSUIT AND SINKING

1 THE BRITISH LOSE CONTACT
Following the sinking of the HMS *Hood* in the Denmark Strait, the British commit every available unit to hunting down the now limping *Bismarck*. However the British ships lose contact with their quarry and for a time it seems likely that the *Bismarck* may escape.

Bismarck's last battle
Raked by gunfire from the British battleships, the crippled *Bismarck* puts up a desperate last fight.

KEY

GERMAN FORCES

1 German battleship: SMS *Bismarck*

1 German battlecruiser

German U-boat screen

BRITISH FORCES DURING FINAL PURSUIT
Destroyers and other small ships not shown.

1 British aircraft carrier

1 British battleship

1 British cruiser or battlecruiser

1 wave of British torpedo bombers

1 British reconnaissance plane

A reconnaissance plane from Northern Ireland spots the *Bismarck*, letting the British units renew their pursuit

A second bombing raid by *Ark Royal*'s Swordfish torpedo bombers damages the *Bismarck*'s steering

Admiral Tovey leads the pursuit of the *Bismarck* on board the battleship *King George V*. He is joined by the battleship *Rodney* and heavy cruiser *Norfolk*

Force H, including aircraft carrier *Ark Royal*, heads north from Gibraltar to block the *Bismarck*'s escape

Cruiser *Sheffield*, shadowing the *Bismarck*, is mistakenly attacked by *Ark Royal*'s aircraft, but escapes damage

ATLANTIC OCEAN

2 THE BISMARCK IS SPOTTED
After a break of over 30 hours, a Catalina flying boat from Loch Erne in Northern Ireland spots the *Bismarck*. Carrier *Ark Royal*, approaching from the south, launches Swordfish torpedo bombers against the battleship, damaging her steering.

3 THE END OF THE BISMARCK
Her rudders jammed, the *Bismarck* steams in large circles into the path of the approaching British battleships. Mortally damaged by torpedo attacks from the cruisers and destroyers and heavy fire from the battleships, the *Bismarck* finally succumbs.

Her steering irretrievably damaged, *Bismarck* steams in circles. Pounded by guns and torpedoes, the *Bismarck* sinks at last with heavy loss of life

Heavy cruiser *Dorsetshire* arrives from the south to join the attack. With *Bismarck*'s crew already scuttling the battleship, *Dorsetshire*'s torpedoes finally finish her off

Rodney and *King George* V close in on the incapacitated *Bismarck*. Despite heavy fire causing great damage, *Bismarck* does not surrender. Running low on fuel, the battleships head home

ATLANTIC OCEAN

USS TEXAS

THE NEW YORK-CLASS battleship *Texas*, commissioned in March 1914, was a "super-dreadnought", a product of the naval arms race that preceded World War I. She was especially prominent in World War II in a shore bombardment role, her big guns providing fire support for landings in North Africa, Normandy, Iwo Jima, and Okinawa.

THE USS *Texas* was built at Newport News, Virginia, for a cost of around $6 million. Her main armament of ten 14in guns made her the most powerful warship in the world in 1914, but in some respects she was behind the times, especially in depending upon coal-fired reciprocating engines instead of oil-fired steam turbines. An extensive modernization in 1927 replaced coal-fired boilers with oil-firing, improved the ship's armour, and upgraded her fire-control systems. Subsequent modifications included the addition of anti-aircraft guns and the installation of radar on board in 1939.

By the outbreak of World War II *Texas* was too slow to hold her own as a warship in battle with more modern capital ships, but her guns still packed a powerful punch and the battleship earned five battlestars during the war. The only combat fatality ever suffered by *Texas* occurred in a duel between the ship and German shore batteries at Cherbourg in June 1944, when a shell struck her armoured conning tower. *Texas* was decommissioned in 1946. Now a museum ship at San Jacinto, Texas, she is the last surviving dreadnought-era battleship.

American patriot
The USS *Texas* is adorned with flags for Navy Day in October 1940. During the early part of World War II, before America's entry into the war, *Texas* escorted merchant convoys crossing the Atlantic.

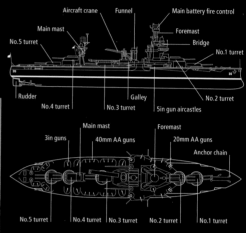

Aircraft crane — Funnel — Main battery fire control
Main mast — Foremast
No.5 turret — Bridge
No.1 turret
Rudder — Galley — No.2 turret
No.4 turret — No.3 turret — 5in gun aircastles

Main mast — Foremast
3in guns — 40mm AA guns — 20mm AA guns
Anchor chain
No.5 turret — No.4 turret — No.3 turret — No.2 turret — No.1 turret

USS Texas
The basis of *Texas*'s influence in both world wars lay with her ten huge 14in guns, which could fire a 680kg (1,500lb) shell a distance of over 20km (13 miles). The battleship had an active career of over 30 years.

> ❝
> SHE WAS A SHIP – THE SMARTEST MAN O' WAR AFLOAT, AND THE BEST. A HARD, TOUGH, SALTY, SHOOTIN' STEAMIN' FOOL. A TROPHY GRABBER, A FIGHTER, AND A HE-MAN BATTLE WAGON.
> **LIEUTENANT PAUL SCHUBERT,** CREWMAN ON USS TEXAS, 1919–1923
> ❞

≫ Paravane
Texas carried two torpedo-shaped paravanes which could be towed from the bow to snag the lines of floating naval mines. A sharp blade on the side would cut the mine loose so that it would float to the surface where it could be sunk or destroyed by gunfire.

≫ Ship superstructure
On the top of the foremast at the highest point of the ship sits the battery control and the radio and radar antennae. Below this are other areas of the ship that need a high, clear line of sight such as the pilot house and lookout platforms.

≪ Ship's bell
A large brass bell, located in the centre of the main deck was used to mark the time of day for the crew and regulate the duty watches. The bell is engraved with the name of the battleship.

« Tampion gun cap
When not in use, the ship's huge 14in guns were covered by metal caps designed to prevent water entering the barrels.

« Anti-aircraft barbettes
Most of the 20mm, 40mm, and 3in anti-aircraft guns down side of the battleship are protected by circular, armoured barbettes. The boxes on top of this 40mm mount are covers for the ammunition loading slots.

⌃ Inside view of 14in turret
Shells would be brought from the magazine up into the gunhouse through the upper shell hoist and rolled onto the loading tray. The shell and charge bags were then rammed into the open breech and the breech door shut. A trained gun crew could load and fire a round every 45 seconds.

⌃ Anchor capstan
Underneath the large guns at the bows of the ship, two large electric anchor capstans could rotate to raise or lower the ship's anchors. Capstans at the stern were used for towing.

⌄ Oven door
Texas was the first US battleship to use electric ovens, though these were later replaced with oil-fired ovens to reduce electricity consumption.

⌄ Crew galley
Located on the main deck with three sides that could be opened up for ventilation while cooking, the ship's galley handled three meals a day for a crew of almost 1,800 men. A dumbwaiter carried food down to a second serving area below deck.

« 20mm cannon
44 Oerlikon automatic cannon were fitted as a secondary anti-aircraft defence. The gunner was strapped against the shoulder rests and aimed using the sight.

⌃ Bofors anti-aircraft guns
The ship was fitted with ten sets of four Bofors 40mm guns to provide defence against enemy aircraft. Each of the four quad mounts was powered and controlled remotely using a Mk51 gun director located close to the mount.

» Bakery
The bakery was located near to the galley on the port side of the main deck where the ovens could be cooled by fresh air.

SUPERSTRUCTURE AND BELOW DECK

WITH A COMPLEMENT of around 1800 officers and men by 1945, the battleship *Texas* was in some ways like a small town, with its own post office, barber's shop, and dentist – although no liquor store, alcohol consumption being officially banned on all US Navy ships, in sharp contrast to the practice of Britain's Royal Navy. This was certainly a large ship, 175m (573ft) long and 32m (106ft) across the beam, yet there was little room for privacy and precious few frills. Toilet and bathing facilities in particular were quite primitive and most men ate where they slept. It was, however, a well-organized world in which each individual knew his place and his function, and in which the basic needs of health and nutrition were properly addressed.

» Chart House
Located close to the pilot house and the Captain's sea cabin, this room was used for chart navigation. The devices attached to the wall above the chart table are depth and speed indicators. The bulkheads surrounding the room are made of brass to avoid magnetic interference with compass readings.

⌄ Navigation dials
The equipment in the auxilliary CIC includes this speed indicator dial and chronometer – a precise timekeeper used to assist in navigation.

» Speaker system
Internal phones and speakers fitted around the *Texas* enabled effective communications between different areas on board the ship.

⌃ Combat information centre
The CIC provided the electronic eyes and ears of the ship, collecting and evaluating information from a variety of sources such as the ship's radar, and coordinating the fire control systems.

⌄ Pilot house
The ship was steered from the helmsman's station where the ship's wheel, tiller, rudder angle indicator, compass, and engine order telegraph were all located.

« Executive Officer's Office
The Executive Officer was the second-in-command of the ship. The staff in his office handled much of the ship's day-to-day administration, approved work assignments, and created the daily routine sheet – the orders and schedule for the ship's daily activities.

⌄ Adding machine
The Burrough's machine was an early calculator used to help the officers with their book-keeping.

« Auxilliary Combat Information Centre (CIC)
Located in the heart of the ship to provide back-up in case the main CIC was damaged, the auxilliary CIC contained a range of crucial information-gathering equipment such as the surface SG radar unit seen against the wall on the right. The large circular device in the foreground is an illuminated plotting table.

Barber's shop
Regulations specified that a sailor's hair should be no longer than 38mm (1.5in) on top and clipped short on the sides. This barber's looked after the enlisted men – officers had their own barber's shop further forward.

Ship's laundry
The large laundry was equipped with a washer, wringers, and clothes pressing machines. Laundry workers received additional pay because of the unpleasantly hot and humid working conditions.

Post office
Letters and news from loved ones back home reached the sailors through the ship's post office, providing an important boost to crew morale.

Cafeteria
Food came down from the galley on the deck above in a dumbwaiter and was put into heated containers for serving. Most enlisted men took their food back to their berthing areas to eat off stowaway wooden tables.

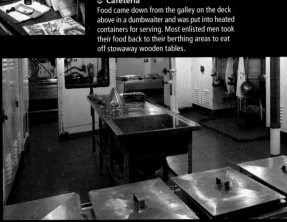

Surgical theatre
The ship's medical facilities included a surgery to deal with injuries sustained in battle and other emergencies. Instruments were sterilized using a pressurized device known as an autoclave, in the next room.

Tailor's shop
Alongside the ship's post office in the general service area was a busy tailor's shop where crew members could pay to have their uniforms mended or adjusted, and pressed.

Sick bay
Texas had a large sick bay and extensive medical facilities, and the battleship often provided medical services to smaller ships in the fleet. The ship also contained an isolation ward next to the main sick bay to prevent the spread of infectious diseases.

Prophylactic room
Condoms were made readily available to US sailors during World War II to prevent sexually transmitted diseases – one government educational film urged the sailors to "put it on before you put it in".

Dispensary drawers
The ship's doctor treated minor injuries and ailments in the dispensary, next door to the surgery and sick bay.

Dentist's room
Texas had her own dentist on board, as well as a well-equipped dental surgery. The dentist was also able to perform other types of surgery when required, something which could prove essential if the ship had to deal with large numbers of wounded.

BELOW DECK

⌃ Marine berths
The ship's complement of like the enlisted sailors, s bunks hung three or four high. Berthing areas were around the ship where th space, mostly on the seco

⌃ Crew heads
Crew toilets consisted of more than boards over a with seawater pumped d carry waste matter into

‹‹ Lieutenant's cabin
Only relatively senior offic have enjoyed the luxury of room. This cabin belonged Lieutenant Fred Winter, the command of Turret No.2's

⌃ Junior officer's racks
Accommodation for junior officers was in shared staterooms often only slightly less cramped than the areas for the enlisted men. Bunks in the passageway of the officers' quarters provided an overflow berthing space.

‹‹ Officer's washroom
Junior officers shared their own washing facilities and toilets in a small area on the second deck in the bows of the ship.

⌃ Ventilation holes
Small vents in the partition walls helped air between the berthing areas. Nonetheless t

Battle lantern

Although *Texas* was fitted with a regular electric lighting system, there were also a number of portable relay-operated lamps known as battle lanterns located around the ship for use in an emergency.

Bureau Express oil-fired boiler

The propellors and electrical generators were powered by steam engines driven by six oil-fired boilers. This boiler's triangular firebox has nine burners mounted on the front (three are removed to show the openings) and two large cylinders for water on either side. The steam drum above the firebox which fed the engine is out of shot.

Nozzle detail

The nine burners forced oil through atomizers to create a spray mist that was burned to heat the water. The red T-bar handles held the adjustable atomizer rods in place to control the volume and fineness of the spray.

Steering room

The rudder was normally turned using an electric motor, but if the battleship's steam and electric power systems were knocked out, it was possible to steer the ship manually using four large wheels along the main rudder shaft. It took 16 men to turn the rudder very slowly.

Powder scuttles

Propellent powder was stored in the powder magazines, well away from the shells. The powder bags were passed from the powder magazine to the turret handling room through flash-proof scuttles to prevent explosive flash travelling down from the gun and igniting the powder.

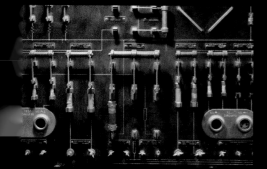

Power shop test unit

The workshop used for the repair of electrical items and the maintenance of the ship's electrical power systems was known as the power shop. This test unit allowed the engineers to check different parts of the ship's electrics.

14in shell magazine and hoist

Several decks below each of the five main gun turrets lay magazines for storing the 14in shells. The shells were lifted using a block and tackle and carried on ceiling mounted pulleys to the lower handing room, where they were hoisted to the gun turret for loading.

20mm ammo box

A wooden box from one of the ammo magazines containing two 60-round clips of ammunition for the 20mm anti-aircraft guns.

THE U-BOAT WAR 1939–45

FROM SUMMER 1940 TO SPRING 1943 German U-boats, led by Admiral Karl Dönitz, attempted to blockade Britain into submission by sinking convoys of merchant ships carrying much needed supplies across the Atlantic. Operating from bases in occupied Brittany, the U-boats attacked escorted convoys in groups known as "wolf packs". The period up to February 1941 became known as the "Happy Time" for U-boat crews, as British convoy escorts were inadequate in numbers, equipment, and training, and the U-boats sank many ships. Successful U-boat captains became celebrated in Germany as "aces". A second surge of U-boat success followed the entry of the United States into the war in December 1941, which allowed them to prey on ships on convoy routes up and down the US east coast. The climax of the U-boat war came in spring 1943. Just as Dönitz looked like winning the war, a combination of superior industrial production, improved technology and tactics, air cover, and intelligence allowed the Allies to turn the tide decisively against the U-boats. Overall, the U-boat war was exceptionally tough for Allied merchant and naval seamen, whether crossing the Atlantic or on the harsh Arctic route to Russia. However, it was U-boat crews that suffered the heaviest losses, with 60 per cent of all crew dying during the war.

THE U-BOAT WAR 1940–1943

The main areas of engagement between German and Allied forces during the U-boat war were in the North Atlantic along the major convoy routes connecting the US east coast with the UK, and along the convoys routes running around the US east coast. German U-boat wolf packs also targeted Allied merchant shipping on the routes running through the Arctic between the UK and northern Russia, and on convoys running between West Africa and the UK and from the Americas through the Straits of Gibraltar into the Mediterranean.

KEY

- ▢ Allied territory 1942
- ▢ Axis territory 1942
- — Major convoy route 1943
- ▢ Maximum extent of air cover 1940
- ▢ Maximum extent of air cover 1943
- ● U-boat base
- ① Main areas of U-boat success Jun 1940–Mar 1941
- ② Main areas of U-boat success Jan 1942–Feb 1943
- ③ Main areas of U-boat success Mar–Sep 1943

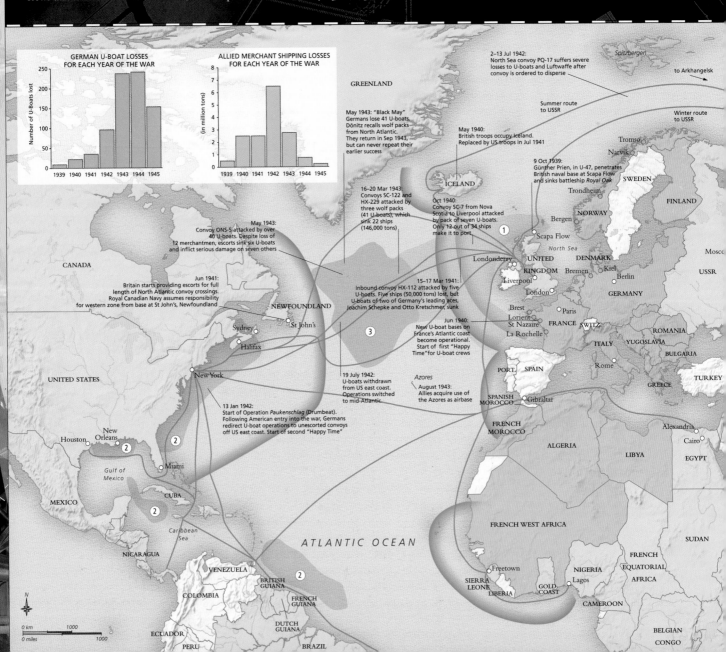

GERMAN U-BOAT LOSSES FOR EACH YEAR OF THE WAR

Number of U-Boats lost (vertical axis: 0, 50, 100, 150, 200, 250) — years 1939, 1940, 1941, 1942, 1943, 1944, 1945

ALLIED MERCHANT SHIPPING LOSSES FOR EACH YEAR OF THE WAR

(in million tons) (vertical axis: 0, 1, 2, 3, 4, 5, 6, 7, 8) — years 1939, 1940, 1941, 1942, 1943, 1944, 1945

2–13 Jul 1942: North Sea convoy PQ-17 suffers severe losses to U-boats and Luftwaffe after convoy is ordered to disperse

May 1943: "Black May" Germans lose 41 U-boats. Dönitz recalls wolf packs from North Atlantic. They return in Sep 1943, but can never repeat their earlier success

May 1940: British troops occupy Iceland. Replaced by US troops in Jul 1941

9 Oct 1939: Günther Prien, in U-47, penetrates British naval base at Scapa Flow and sinks battleship *Royal Oak*

16–20 Mar 1943: Convoys SC-122 and HX-229 attacked by three wolf packs (41 U-boats), which sink 22 ships (146,000 tons)

Oct 1940: Convoy SC-7 from Nova Scotia to Liverpool attacked by pack of seven U-boats. Only 12 out of 34 ships make it to port

May 1943: Convoy ONS-5 attacked by over 40 U-boats. Despite loss of 12 merchantmen, escorts sink six U-boats and inflict serious damage on seven others

Jun 1941: Britain starts providing escorts for full length of North Atlantic convoy crossings. Royal Canadian Navy assumes responsibility for western zone from base at St John's, Newfoundland

15–17 Mar 1941: Inbound convoy HX-112 attacked by five U-boats. Five ships (50,000 tons) lost, but U-boats of two of Germany's leading aces, Joachim Schepke and Otto Kretschmer, sunk

Jun 1940: New U-boat bases on France's Atlantic coast become operational. Start of first "Happy Time" for U-boat crews

19 July 1942: U-boats withdrawn from US east coast. Operations switched to mid-Atlantic

August 1943: Allies acquire use of the Azores as airbase

13 Jan 1942: Start of Operation *Paukenschlag* (Drumbeat). Following American entry into the war, Germans redirect U-boat operations to unescorted convoys off US east coast. Start of second "Happy Time"

Map labels: Spitzbergen; to Arkhangelsk; Summer route to USSR; Winter route to USSR; Tromsø; Narvik; SWEDEN; Trondheim; FINLAND; NORWAY; Bergen; Scapa Flow; North Sea; Londonderry; UNITED KINGDOM; DENMARK; Moscow; Liverpool; Bremen; Kiel; Berlin; USSR; London; GERMANY; Brest; Lorient; St Nazaire; Paris; FRANCE; SWITZ; La Rochelle; ROMANIA; ITALY; YUGOSLAVIA; BULGARIA; Rome; GREECE; TURKEY; PORT; SPAIN; SPANISH MOROCCO; Gibraltar; FRENCH MOROCCO; ALGERIA; LIBYA; EGYPT; Alexandria; Cairo; GREENLAND; ICELAND; CANADA; NEWFOUNDLAND; Sydney; St John's; Halifax; New York; UNITED STATES; Houston; New Orleans; Miami; Gulf of Mexico; MEXICO; CUBA; Caribbean Sea; NICARAGUA; VENEZUELA; BRITISH GUIANA; FRENCH GUIANA; COLOMBIA; DUTCH GUIANA; ECUADOR; PERU; BRAZIL; Azores; ATLANTIC OCEAN; FRENCH WEST AFRICA; Freetown; SIERRA LEONE; LIBERIA; GOLD COAST; NIGERIA; Lagos; FRENCH EQUATORIAL AFRICA; CAMEROON; SUDAN; BELGIAN CONGO

N — 0 km 1000 / 0 miles 1000

SINKING OF ROYAL OAK

Date 14 October 1939
Forces British: 1 battleship;
Germans: 1 submarine
Losses British: 1 battleship;
Germans: none

Location Scapa Flow,
Orkney Islands

At the start of World War II German U-boat chief Admiral Dönitz was looking for a prestige operation that would win Hitler's support for the submarine arm. He decided to attempt to penetrate the

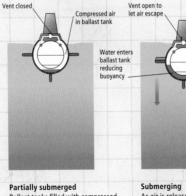

The Royal Oak
The breaching of Scapa Flow's defences, and subsequent sinking of Royal Oak so early in the war, came as a severe blow to the Royal Navy.

British deep-water anchorage at Scapa Flow. Although Scapa was well defended against submarine attack, German reconnaissance had shown narrow channels between the sunken blockships at the eastern end and Dönitz believed these were navigable by a U-boat on the surface. Lieutenant Günther Prien sailed U-47 out of Kiel on 8 October and proceeded across the North Sea, travelling on the surface by night and submerging during the daylight hours. After dark on 13 October, U-47

squeezed between the blockships, carried forward by a strong current. Prien emerged into the harbour after midnight to find it largely deserted. Most of the British fleet had left for fear of air attack and ageing battleship *Royal Oak* had been left behind, moored next to a seaplane carrier.

With his first volley of torpedoes Prien hit *Royal Oak* near the bows. The Royal Navy believed Scapa Flow impregnable to U-boats, so it was assumed the explosion had occurred in a storeroom. Most of the crew were still sleeping below decks when three more torpedoes ripped into the ship, causing a further huge explosion. *Royal Oak* swiftly sank. Of a crew of 1,200, 833 sailors were killed. Prien slipped away before dawn, to receive a hero's welcome on his return to Germany.

1908–1941
GÜNTHER PRIEN

COMMANDER OF GERMAN SUBMARINE U-47

U-boat commander Günther Prien originally trained as a merchant seaman. He joined the Reichsmarine and the Nazi Party in the early 1930s, transferring to U-boats in 1935. He was awarded the coveted Knight's Cross for the sinking of *Royal Oak* and was feted as the first U-boat ace. Prien carried out 12 patrols in 18 months and is credited with sinking 30 ships. After refusing a shore posting, he went down with U-47 in the Atlantic in March 1941.

CONVOY SC-7

Date 16–19 October 1940
Forces British: 5 escort ships, 35 merchant ships; Germans: 7 U-boats
Losses British: 20 merchant ships; Germans: none

Location Western Approaches, Atlantic

SC-7 was a convoy of slow merchant ships that set out from Nova Scotia for Britain on 5 October 1940 with a single sloop as escort. Although another two British sloops and two

corvettes met the convoy as it entered the Western Approaches, none of them had any idea how to cope with multiple attacks by submarines operating on the surface at night. The convoy itself was undisciplined, with too many ships out of formation. Four merchant ships, including two stragglers, were sunk by U-boats on 16 and 17 October, before the main attack on the night of 18–19 October. This involved five U-boats, including Otto Kretschmer's U-99, Engelbert Endrass's U-46, and Joachim Schepke's U-100. The U-boats sank 16 ships in six hours, while the escorts were reduced to picking up survivors.

CONVOY HX-79

Date 19–20 October 1940
Forces British: 11 escort ships, 49 merchant ships; Germans: 5 U-boats
Losses British: 12 merchant ships; Germans: none

Location Western Approaches, Atlantic

Shocked by the savaging of Convoy SC-7 on 19 October 1940, the British Admiralty rushed out 11 warships to escort another convoy, HX-79, which was then approaching Britain. The

escorts included two destroyers and four corvettes. Meanwhile, HX-79 was being shadowed by Gunther Prien's U-47. Four U-boats that had participated in the attack on SC-7, including Joachim Schepke's U-100 and Engelbert Endrass's U-46, joined Prien. That night the U-boats slipped through the escort screen on the surface and attacked the merchant vessels. Ten ships sank in the darkness, four of them claimed by Prien. Two more ships sank the next day, bringing total British losses over five days in the Atlantic to 32 ships totalling 150,000 tons. No U-boats were damaged.

HOW SUBMARINES WORK

Depending on its density, an object will either float or sink in water. When a submarine is about to dive vents at the top of the hull are opened, air escapes, and the reduced pressure allows water in through vents in the bottom. The density of the submarine increases and it sinks. With the aid of angled hydroplanes, the engine powers the submarine forward and down until the ballast tanks are completely full and a state of neutral buoyancy has been achieved. At this point the upper vents are closed. To reverse the process, compressed air is forced into the submarine's ballast tanks, forcing water out of the lower vents and increasing buoyancy, while the engine propels the submarine back to the surface.

Vent closed
Compressed air in ballast tank

Vent open to let air escape
Water enters ballast tank reducing buoyancy

Hydroplanes tilt forward to move submarine down

Ballast tanks full of water

Hydroplanes flat to keep submarine steady
Compressed air released into ballast tanks

Hydroplanes tilt back to assist movement to the surface
Compressed air forces water out of ballast tank, increasing buoyancy

Partially submerged
Ballast tanks filled with compressed air allow the submarine to float just below the surface of the water.

Submerging
As air is released the ballast tanks fill with water and the submarine starts to submerge.

Fully submerged
The submarine continues to sink until the ballast tanks are completely filled with water.

Surfacing
Compressed air released into the ballast tanks forces water out and the submarine surfaces.

ARCTIC CONVOY PQ-17

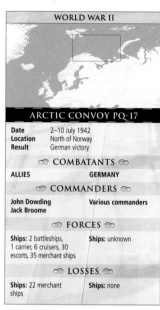

ARCTIC CONVOY PQ-17

Date	2–10 July 1942
Location	North of Norway
Result	German victory

∞ COMBATANTS ∞

ALLIES	GERMANY

∞ COMMANDERS ∞

John Dowding	Various commanders
Jack Broome	

∞ FORCES ∞

Ships: 2 battleships, 1 carrier, 6 cruisers, 30 escorts, 35 merchant ships	Ships: unknown

∞ LOSSES ∞

Ships: 22 merchant ships	Ships: none

Following the entry of the Soviet Union into the war in summer 1941, Britain and the United States began supplying Soviet forces with military equipment to fight the Germans. Some of these supplies were carried by convoys to the northern Russian ports of Arkhangelsk and Murmansk. Even without enemy action, Arctic convoys were a gruelling struggle against freezing cold, gales, fog, and ice. The convoys were exposed to attack by land-based Luftwaffe aircraft in occupied Norway as well as from U-boats, and they were constantly threatened by the presence of German warships in the Norwegian fjords.

PQ-17 SETS SAIL

In June 1942 the largest Arctic convoy yet to sail, consisting of 35 merchant ships, assembled at Iceland. It was given three levels of naval defence: a close

U-boat gunnery traverse table
German U-boats often surfaced to attack unescorted merchant ships with their guns, saving torpedoes for better defended targets.

escort force of destroyers, corvettes, minesweepers, armed trawlers, and anti-aircraft auxiliaries. In support was a covering squadron of heavy cruisers and destroyers. Yet further off lurked a powerful force centred around the carrier *Victorious* and two battleships, *Duke of York* and *Washington*, hoping that the German big-gun ships *Tirpitz*, *Admiral Hipper*, and *Admiral Scheer* might come out. The Germans had in fact decided to launch a major operation against the convoy, which therefore became the unfortunate

focus of a trial of strength between the two sides. Leaving Iceland on 27 June, the convoy started to run into air attacks from 2 July. The swarms of Luftwaffe aircraft met fierce resistance from the ships of the close escort and from guns on the merchant ships. Although two American merchantmen were lost on 4 July, the situation seemed broadly under control. At this point, however, the British Admiralty made

Arctic hunter
A German U-boat cruises on the surface of the ocean. Arctic convoys were at constant risk from both U-boats and Luftwaffe aircraft.

an assessment – not supported by any intelligence – that *Tirpitz*, *Hipper*, and *Scheer* were moving to intercept the convoy. The First Sea Lord Sir Dudley Pound ordered the convoy to scatter, concentrating all the escort and covering warships to meet the German sortie. It was an appalling error. The German warships never appeared, having returned to harbour after the briefest of forays. Meanwhile, the scattered convoy, escorted only by a handful of corvettes, minesweepers, and armed trawlers, was defenceless against the remorseless attacks of the Luftwaffe and the U-boats.

SITTING TARGETS

On 5 July 12 merchant ships were sunk, seven of them American. Six of the sinkings were claimed by U-boats and six by the Luftwaffe. Over the next two days five more ships went to the bottom, three of them victims of a single U-boat, Captain Reinhardt Reche's U-255. A final two sinkings occurred on 10 July, after which the remnants of the convoy crawled into Arkhangelsk or Murmansk. Out of the original 35 vessels, 22 had been sunk, among the worst losses of any convoy in the war. Along with 430 tanks, 200 aircraft, and almost 100,000 tons of cargo, the lives of 153 seamen had been lost. Many survivors endured days in open lifeboats in Arctic conditions before being rescued.

Freezing conditions
The icebound deck of a British cruiser sailing the convoy route between Britain and Russia in 1943 gives an idea of the risks and hardships facing sailors on the Arctic convoys.

WORLD WAR II

CONVOY HX-229 AND CONVOY SC-122

Date 16–19 March 1943
Forces Germans: 38 U-boats; Allies: 17 escort ships, 100 merchant vessels
Losses Germans: 1 U-boat; Allies: 22 merchant ships

Location North Atlantic Ocean

In early March 1943 two convoys left New York bound for Liverpool: HX-229 with 40 merchant ships and the 60 slower vessels of SC-122. Admiral Karl Dönitz knew of these convoys because his B-Dienst intelligence department had deciphered Britain's naval codes. Three U-boat wolf packs, codenamed Raubgraf, Stürmer, and Dränger, were positioned in the mid-Atlantic across the convoys' route. Raubgraf made contact with HX-229 on 16 March. The merchant ships had a weak escort of three destroyers and two corvettes, insufficient to prevent the eight-boat wolf pack from harrying the convoy mercilessly. Meanwhile, on their way to join the attack on HX-229, the other wolf packs stumbled upon SC-122. This had a stronger escort, but the wolf packs totalled 30 U-boats and simply swamped its defences. By 19 March, when the arrival of more escorts halted the attacks, HX-229 had lost 13 ships and SC-122 had lost nine. Some 300 merchant seamen were killed. The Germans lost a single U-boat to an air patrol. A Royal Navy report later stated that "there seemed real danger the enemy would achieve his aim of cutting the route which united Great Britain with the North American continent".

U-boat computer
This German HR2 slide computer helped U-boats to navigate using the stars.

CREW PROFILE

U-BOAT CREW

WORLD WAR II

A TYPE VII, THE STANDARD U-BOAT OF WORLD WAR II, typically had a crew of four officers – the captain, his two lieutenants or "watch officers", and an engineering officer – and some 40 petty officers and seamen. The petty officers were responsible for various specialist areas such as crew discipline, the torpedoes, the diesel and electric engines, the radio, navigation, and steering. At least in the early period of the war, U-boat crews were a self-conscious elite, with five years' intensive training before going operational. They needed to be exceptionally fit and well balanced to endure the rigours of a submariner's life. Most of the men were in their early 20s, and their captains were usually not much older.

U-BOAT SEAMAN

The seamen were housed in the bows of the boat, a space they shared with the forward torpedoes. There was usually one bunk for every two men, occupied on a shift system as one was on duty while the other rested. There was no privacy and little opportunity to wash or get a change of clothes while on patrol. The seamen performed the whole range of tasks required on board, from preparing food to manning the guns and loading the torpedoes in their tubes. The most onerous task was keeping watch. When the U-boat was on the surface there had to be four seamen on watch 24 hours a day, searching the horizon for a convoy to attack or a hostile warship or aircraft.

UNITY IN ADVERSITY

Each sailor stood at each corner of the conning tower and was responsible for observing a 90-degree sector of the sea. A four-hour watch, often in freezing cold with waves sweeping over the bridge, could be a feat of endurance. To avoid being swept overboard in rough weather seamen on watch wore safety belts that tied them to the column in the middle of the conning tower, as well as special waterproof suits. In the claustrophobic, cramped conditions on a U-boat, most crews became like a family for the seamen – one U-boat man wrote that "you felt engulfed by comradeship".

Torpedo ratings
Crew members load a torpedo into one of the tubes on board a German U-boat. Seamen usually had to share their sleeping quarters with spare torpedoes.

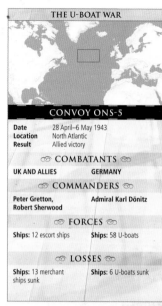

THE U-BOAT WAR

CONVOY ONS-5

CONVOY ONS-5	
Date	28 April–6 May 1943
Location	North Atlantic
Result	Allied victory

☞ COMBATANTS ☜

UK AND ALLIES	GERMANY

☞ COMMANDERS ☜

Peter Gretton, Robert Sherwood	Admiral Karl Dönitz

☞ FORCES ☜

Ships: 12 escort ships	Ships: 58 U-boats

☞ LOSSES ☜

Ships: 13 merchant ships sunk	Ships: 6 U-boats sunk

CONVOY ONS-5

In spring 1943 a convoy of 43 merchant ships left Liverpool bound for Halifax, Nova Scotia. It was escorted by escort group B-7, consisting of two destroyers, four corvettes, and a frigate under the command of Commander Peter Gretton. Convoy ONS-5 was always a sitting target for Admiral Dönitz's U-boat "wolf packs" swarming in the North Atlantic, the more so because the Allied codebreakers were temporarily unable to decipher German messages.

On 28 April, ONS-5 was spotted by U-650, one of 16 boats strung out in a line between Greenland and Iceland. Tracking the convoy, U-650 called in the other U-boats for a group attack. Aware of the U-boats' presence through "huff-duff" (HF/DF) radio detection equipment, Gretton organized his defence well – the convoy suffered small

losses, while two U-boats were severely damaged. Bad weather then led to an intermission. Reinforcements arrived for the convoy escort, but Gretton's destroyer *Duncan* was forced to leave, unable to refuel in the heavy seas.

THE SECOND ENGAGEMENT

Command passed to Lieutenant Commander Robert Sherwood on the frigate *Tay*. By the time the storm abated on 4 May, the main convoy had been reduced to 30 merchant ships with the rest detached stragglers.

The U-boats reformed a line of 29 vessels into which the convoy now blundered. Behind this lay a further line of 24 U-boats. Taken together it was the largest concentration of force Dönitz had ever achieved. He told his U-boat commanders to "fight with

everything you've got". On the night of 4–5 May the onslaught on ONS-5 began. It lasted more than 30 hours. U-boats preyed upon the stragglers and worked their way into the middle of the main convoy, sending a number of ships to the bottom with torpedoes. But the Allied escorts fought back tirelessly with well-rehearsed sweep patterns, using radar and ASDIC (sonar) to locate targets and depth-charges or ramming to attack them. On the night of 5–6 May fog set in. The escorts could see the U-boats on their radar screens, while the U-boat commanders could see neither their targets nor their pursuers.

By daybreak on 6 May, ONS-5 had lost 13 merchant ships, but the cost to the U-boats had been high – six boats sunk and at least four severely damaged.

U-BOAT TACTICS
WOLF PACKS

WORKING TOGETHER TO LOCATE AND ATTACK CONVOYS

The "wolf pack" was a group of U-boats hunting together to locate and attack convoys. Typically the U-boats formed a line spread out across an Atlantic convoy route. When one of them spotted a convoy it tracked it, radioing the location to headquarters, which directed other U-boats to join in the hunt. When the pack had assembled around a convoy, the U-boats would wait for nightfall and then surface to attack. The boldest of them would penetrate the escort screen into the heart of the convoy, picking targets to torpedo at will.

The rest fired their torpedoes from outside the convoy. Escort ships were frequently overwhelmed by the number of attackers and, at first, had little chance of spotting low-lying U-boats on the water's surface at night. However, wolf-pack tactics required much use of radio, which allowed the U-boats to be located by escort ships' "huff-duff" (HF/DF) radio direction finders. The subsequent introduction of shipborne radar transformed the ability of escort ships to cope with night surface attacks.

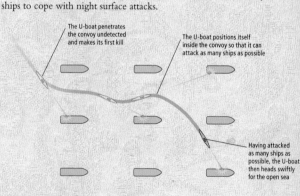

U-boat

Escort ship

U-boat

Unarmed merchant convoy

Escort ship

Several U-boats approach the front of the convoy to draw off the escort ships

With the convoy undefended, more U-boats move in to attack the unarmed merchant ships

The escort ships pursue the U-boats leaving the convoy undefended

U-boat

Escort ship

Drawing off the escorts
Once the U-boats located a convoy, they would be directed to assemble around it. The first wave of U-boats was often able to draw off the escort ships, leaving the convoy undefended against attack by other U-boats.

The U-boat penetrates the convoy undetected and makes its first kill

The U-boat positions itself inside the convoy so that it can attack as many ships as possible

Having attacked as many ships as possible, the U-boat then heads swiftly for the open sea

Surfacing inside the convoy
Once a convoy was exposed, the most effective strategy involved the U-boat surfacing inside the convoy before torpedoing individual ships. Accompanying U-boats might fire a spread of torpedoes from outside the convoy.

> 66 WE WERE ALMOST RAMMED BY A DESTROYER THAT SUDDENLY
> APPEARED BEHIND US, LIGHTING UP THE STERN OF OUR
> U-BOAT WITH A BIG SEARCHLIGHT ... I DIVED IMMEDIATELY.
> **CAPTAIN-LIEUTENANT HARTWIG LOOKS,** COMMANDER OF U-264 99

Atlantic convoy
A merchant convoy travelled at the speed of its
slowest ship, so was an easy target for U-boat or
air attack and difficult for escort ships to defend.

ANTI-SUBMARINE WARFARE

DURING THE BATTLE of the Atlantic from 1939 to 1945, German U-boats sent around 2,000 Allied merchant vessels to the bottom of the ocean. The U-boat war was the critical threat against Britain once the immediate danger of a German invasion had passed in 1940 – Winston Churchill once commented that "the only thing that ever really frightened me during the war was the U-boat peril". Yet over the course of six years, the Allies steadily gained the tactical and technological advantage, and by war's end nearly 80 per cent of operational U-boats were destroyed, giving the U-boat crews the highest percentage of fatalities of any German armed service.

AVOIDING U-BOATS

The primary measure adopted to avoid U-boats was the convoy system. Sending supplies in large convoys rather than single, independent vessels worked on probability. If a U-boat failed to detect a single ship, or failed in an attack, then probability assured that another target would be along soon. However, if the U-boat failed to detect or attack a convoy, then it would lose a mass of opportunities in one instance. Convoying certainly reduced casualties, but the convoys themselves took further evasive measures to throw off the U-boats. They adopted zigzag movements across the Atlantic, with slow convoys making shifts at angles of 20–40 degrees every few minutes. Convoy evasion did not always work, but on many occasions convoys of almost 200 vessels crossed the Atlantic perfectly safely without being spotted by U-boats.

AIR ATTACK U-boats were acutely vulnerable to surprise air attack when they surfaced. Here a U-boat is strafed by an Allied aircraft, receiving multiple hits to the conning tower.

ZIGZAG CLOCK Each convoy ship would have a clock synchronized to sound a bell at irregular intervals, instructing the ships when to change course with the rest of the convoy, helping to evade pursuing U-boats.

HUFF-DUFF

High-Frequency Direction-Finding (HF/DF), abbreviated to "huff-duff", became one of the crucial technological resources in the battle against the U-boats. It consisted of either shore-based or ship-mounted antennae that picked up German U-boat radio transmissions, from which it was possible to triangulate the enemy's rough position, and then make evasion or attack.

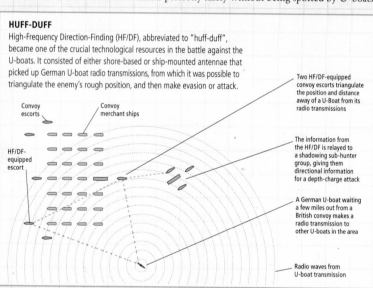

Convoy escorts

Convoy merchant ships

HF/DF-equipped escort

Two HF/DF-equipped convoy escorts triangulate the position and distance away of a U-Boat from its radio transmissions

The information from the HF/DF is relayed to a shadowing sub-hunter group, giving them directional information for a depth-charge attack

A German U-boat waiting a few miles out from a British convoy makes a radio transmission to other U-boats in the area

Radio waves from U-boat transmission

LOCATING U-BOATS

Even more than "huff-duff" (see above), radar systems were the critical U-boat locating tool. The first ship-mounted sets were crude and often ineffective, but by 1942 the British Type 271 centimetric radar was in operation, with enough sensitivity to detect a surfaced submarine at a distance of several kilometres. Once similar radar was fitted to long-range patrol aircraft, U-boats found it more difficult to hide. When the submarine was submerged, ASDIC (sonar) came into play. ASDIC used a sonar pulse that, if it hit and rebounded off a submarine's hull, would give depth and direction data. The Allies also used hydrophone sets, powerful underwater microphones that "listened" for propeller or other noises. The Americans had the Magnetic Anomaly Device (MAD) fitted to patrol aircraft, which searched for magnetic disturbances in the water.

12in mortar barrel

DESTROYING U-BOATS

Once a convoy escort group had located a U-boat they had several means of engaging it. If the U-boat was on the surface, it was attacked with gunfire or torpedoes, or sometimes even rammed (maritime patrol aircraft would make strafing or depth-charge runs). In most cases, however, the U-boat would submerge. In this case, the primary weapon was the depth charge, a cylinder of explosive with a hydrostatic fuze that was set to detonate the weapon at a particular depth. Escort vessels would circle the known or predicted U-boat position and "bracket" the area with depth charges. Typically, an escort would drop three depth charges from the stern and fire one from each side in every attack, varying the depth settings of each depth charge to maximize the possibilities of a kill. Several ships working in tandem would be able to blanket a wide area with explosive. In response, the U-boat commander would make constant evasive manoeuvres and depth changes in order to throw the enemy ships off his scent.

DEPTH-CHARGE LAUNCH PATTERNS

As the war progressed, two forward-firing main variations on the depth charge emerged. The Squid three-barrelled mortar fired three fast-sinking depth charges that produced triangular explosive patterns beneath the water, increasing the chances of a successful kill. The Hedgehog, by contrast, fired 24 small contact-detonated bomblets over a wide circular area.

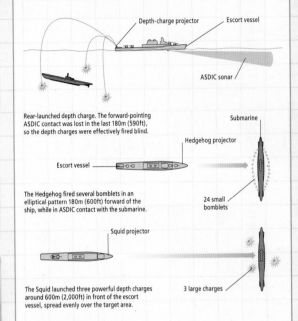

Depth-charge projector

Escort vessel

ASDIC sonar

Rear-launched depth charge. The forward-pointing ASDIC contact was lost in the last 180m (590ft), so the depth charges were effectively fired blind.

Submarine

Hedgehog projector

Escort vessel

The Hedgehog fired several bomblets in an elliptical pattern 180m (600ft) forward of the ship, while in ASDIC contact with the submarine.

24 small bomblets

Squid projector

The Squid launched three powerful depth charges around 600m (2,000ft) in front of the escort vessel, spread evenly over the target area.

3 large charges

READY FOR LAUNCH A British naval crew prepare a depth charge for launch from a thrower. Depth charges may have been the crudest anti-submarine weapon in the Allied arsenal, but they were also extremely effective, accounting for 43 per cent of all U-boats sunk.

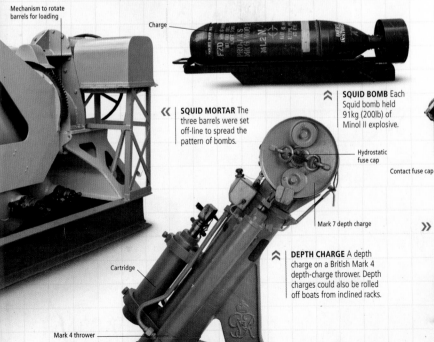

Mechanism to rotate barrels for loading

Charge

SQUID MORTAR The three barrels were set off-line to spread the pattern of bombs.

SQUID BOMB Each Squid bomb held 91kg (200lb) of Minol II explosive.

Hydrostatic fuse cap

Contact fuse cap

Mark 7 depth charge

Cartridge

Mark 4 thrower

DEPTH CHARGE A depth charge on a British Mark 4 depth-charge thrower. Depth charges could also be rolled off boats from inclined racks.

ANTI-SUBMARINE DEPTH CHARGES AND MORTARS

The limitations of British sonar (ASDIC) were critical in the development of new anti-submarine weaponry during World War II. ASDIC was forward pointing, and therefore lost contact with a U-boat if it was within 180m (600ft) of the front of the ship. New types of anti-submarine weapon such as the Hedgehog and Squid mortars, introduced in 1942–43, fired forward and far enough ahead to engage the U-boat while still within ASDIC contact. The shape of their bombs also meant that they sank faster than depth charges, so escort vessels could put their explosives on target more quickly if a contact was made.

Charge

Stabilizing fins

HEDGEHOG BOMBLET Four rows of six spigots launched a salvo of 24 spigot-mortar bomblets.

Spigot (solid rod)

FORMIDABLE FIREPOWER

Huge shockwaves spread across the water as the
battleship USS *Iowa* fires a full broadside from
her nine 16in guns. One of the most heavily armed
warships ever built, the *Iowa* entered US service in
1943 and participated in many of the key Pacific
battles of World War II. Iowa-class battleships
have since served in every major US conflict
of the second half of the 20th century.

EVACUATIONS AND LANDINGS

OPERATIONS IN SUPPORT of land forces constituted a major part of the naval war in the European theatre. In April 1940 the Germans landed troops in Norway, primarily by sea, precipitating an intensive air-sea battle as Britain and France attempted first to interrupt the landings and then to put their own soldiers ashore. Both sides suffered naval losses in the Norway campaign, which ended in victory for Germany in June 1940. By then the Germans had invaded France and the Low Countries, forcing a mass evacuation of Allied troops from Dunkirk, carried off by Royal Navy warships with the assistance of a flotilla of small craft under intensive air attack. From 1942, however, with the United States having entered the war and the tide of victory flowing in the opposite direction, Allied naval forces developed expertise in troop landings rather than evacuations. After British and American warships had successfully escorted troops to North Africa in late 1942, they went on to cover the landings in Southern Italy and Sicily in the following year, and finally played a crucial role in achieving the vast-scale invasion of Normandy in June 1944.

NARVIK

Date 10–13 April 1940
Forces British: 1 carrier, 1 battleship, 14 destroyers; Germans: 10 destroyers
Losses British: 2 destroyers, 2 aircraft; Germans: 10 destroyers, 1 U-boat

Location Narvik, Ofotfjord, Norway

Early in the Norway campaign, Captain Bernard Warburton-Lee, in command of a destroyer flotilla, decided to attack a German naval force in port at Narvik in northern Norway, which was outside the range of Luftwaffe air cover. He took his five H-class destroyers – *Hardy*, *Hotspur*, *Havock*, *Hunter*, and *Hostile* – stealthily up the Ofotfjord in a heavy snowstorm, approaching Narvik around dawn. The Germans had taken a picket ship off station and they were caught by surprise. Two German destroyers were sunk and three others were damaged. Having sunk some cargo ships and exchanged fire with German forces on shore, Warburton-Lee then set to leave, but on the way out he was surprised by five more German destroyers that had been concealed around the fjord. *Hardy* and *Hunter* were lost and *Hotspur* severely damaged. Killed on board *Hardy*, Warburton-Lee was awarded a posthumous Victoria Cross.

Three days later the Royal Navy sent the battleship *Warspite*, escorted by destroyers and supported by the carrier *Furious*, to Narvik. The eight German destroyers still in the fjord, several damaged and all short of fuel and ammunition, were annihilated by this overwhelming force. Troops were then landed at Narvik, but had to be evacuated two months later as Norway became indefensible.

DUNKIRK

Date 26 May–4 June 1940
Forces Allies: 222 naval vessels, 665 civilian craft
Losses British: 6 destroyers, 24 other naval vessels, c.200 small craft; French: 3 destroyers

Location Dunkirk, northern France

The evacuation of Allied troops trapped by German forces at Dunkirk was codenamed Operation Dynamo. Vice-Admiral Sir Bertram Ramsay was initially ordered to take off 45,000 men over two days, but once it became apparent more time was available, the operation was greatly expanded. The troops were mostly carried across the Channel on destroyers and minesweepers, but Ramsay also called for the aid of hundreds of civilian vessels including paddle steamers, trawlers, tug boats, and lifeboats. This was not a pure improvisation – most of the boats already belonged to the Royal Navy's "small vessels pool". The function of the little boats was to ferry soldiers from the Dunkirk beaches through the shallows to naval ships waiting off shore, since the port at Dunkirk had become unusable. The evacuation was carried out under repeated attack from the Luftwaffe, especially from Stuka dive-bombers. Ships were also lost to U-boats and German Fast Attack Boats (E-boats) as they crossed to England.

The evacuation peaked on 31 May when 68,000 men were rescued. The following day four destroyers were lost to enemy attack, after which the operation was restricted to night-time. In all 338,226 troops were brought safely across the Channel, the majority British but some 120,000 of them French.

Dunkirk little ship
At only 4.5m (15ft) long, *Tamzine* was the smallest vessel to take part in the evacuation of Dunkirk.

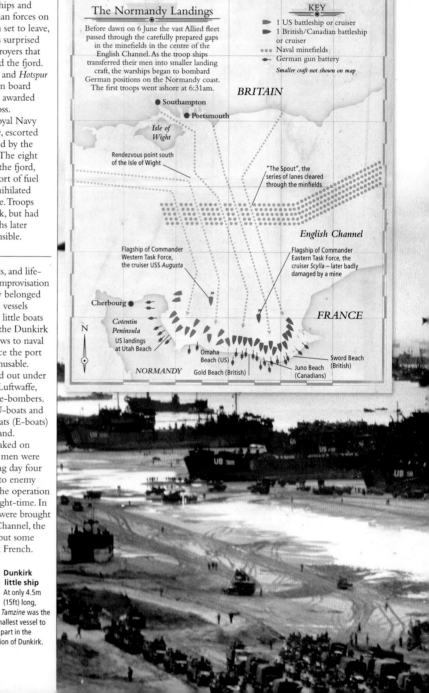

The Normandy Landings

Before dawn on 6 June the vast Allied fleet passed through the carefully prepared gaps in the minefields in the centre of the English Channel. As the troop ships transferred their men into smaller landing craft, the warships began to bombard German positions on the Normandy coast. The first troops went ashore at 6:31am.

KEY

➤ 1 US battleship or cruiser
➤ 1 British/Canadian battleship or cruiser
••• Naval minefields
➤ German gun battery
Smaller craft not shown on map

BRITAIN

● Southampton
● Portsmouth

Isle of Wight

Rendezvous point south of the Isle of Wight

"The Spout", the series of lanes cleared through the minefields

English Channel

Flagship of Commander Western Task Force, the cruiser USS *Augusta*

Flagship of Commander Eastern Task Force, the cruiser *Scylla* – later badly damaged by a mine

● Cherbourg

Cotentin Peninsula

US landings at Utah Beach

FRANCE

N

Omaha Beach (US)

Gold Beach (British)

Juno Beach (Canadians)

Sword Beach (British)

NORMANDY

THE NORMANDY LANDINGS

The invasion of Normandy by Allied forces on 6 June 1944 was the largest amphibious operation in military history. The naval aspect of the landings was known as Operation Neptune. The naval forces had three major functions: to transport troops and equipment across the English Channel; to protect the invasion force against attack by German surface warships or submarines; and to bombard the German land defences. That the operation succeeded should not hide the fact that it involved considerable risks.

From a naval point of view, bad weather was probably the most serious hazard, for heavy seas would have prevented the landings entirely. Weather did in fact force a postponement from the original planned D-day of 5 June, and conditions on 6 June were far from perfect. This resulted in most troops arriving at the beaches seasick, but put the German defenders off their guard,

Midget submarine helmet
The first craft off the shore of Normandy on D-Day were midget submarines that guided the invasion force toward the beaches with navigation beacons.

since they considered an invasion in such weather unlikely.

Intervention by German naval forces also had to be taken seriously. During a full-scale rehearsal for D-day at Slapton Sands in southern England in April 1944, several German Fast Attack Boats (E-boats) struck a convoy of landing craft and killed more than 600 American servicemen. If E-boats, U-boats, or even large surface warships had got among the landing craft during the actual landings the death toll could have been serious. In the event, the threat of the German navy was nullified. Air patrols kept U-boats out of the English Channel, while minefields and screening destroyers limited the possibility of German surface attacks.

The massive invasion fleet put to sea on the night of 5-6 June, the American Western Task Force under Rear Admiral Alan G Kirk and the British-Canadian Eastern Task Force under Rear Admiral Sir Philip Vian. The convoys formed up south of the Isle of Wight and crossed

Normandy beachhead
Fleets of US transport and landing craft disgorge their cargoes onto the beaches at Normandy. Barrage balloons overhead protect against German strafing aircraft.

over the English Channel through "the Spout", a series of lanes swept clear of mines. Several midget submarines laid navigation beacons approaching the Normandy coast to guide in the landing forces. The naval bombardment of the coastal defences behind the five landing beaches was formidable. Kirk's force consisted of three battleships – *Nevada, Texas,* and *Arkansas* – nine cruisers, and 20 destroyers. Vian had the battleships *Warspite* and *Ramillies,* accompanied by 12 cruisers and 37 destroyers.

The operation did not end with the landings. Naval forces had to maintain the supply lifeline across the English Channel, using the famous Mulberry artificial harbours towed across to Normandy. The naval guns continued to bombard German land forces as the fighting moved inland. There were losses to mines and air attacks, duels with coastal artillery, and occasional fights with German destroyers. But taken as a whole the Normandy invasion was a remarkable demonstration of the command of the sea and the importance of logistics.

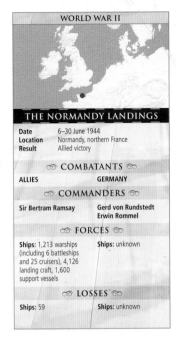

WORLD WAR II

THE NORMANDY LANDINGS

Date	6–30 June 1944
Location	Normandy, northern France
Result	Allied victory

COMBATANTS
ALLIES	GERMANY

COMMANDERS
| Sir Bertram Ramsay | Gerd von Rundstedt |
| | Erwin Rommel |

FORCES
Ships: 1,213 warships (including 6 battleships and 25 cruisers), 4,126 landing craft, 1,600 support vessels	**Ships:** unknown

LOSSES
| **Ships:** 59 | **Ships:** unknown |

D-Day landing craft
A British Landing Craft Assault (LCA) ferries US troops to shore during the rehearsals for the Normandy landings.

WAR IN THE MEDITERRANEAN

ITALY'S ENTRY INTO THE WAR in June 1940 initiated a three-year naval struggle for control of the Mediterranean. The Italian navy, the Regia Marina, fought bravely, although its effectiveness was limited by lack of radar. When the Italians were joined by the land-based aircraft of the German Luftwaffe, Britain's Royal Navy came under severe pressure. Running convoys from Alexandria and Gibraltar to Malta, a key British base less than 100km (62 miles) from Sicily, was always difficult and sometimes impossible. Although British victories at Taranto and Cape Matapan weakened the Italian fleet, the Royal Navy's losses were grievous, mostly to air attack but also to German and Italian submarines. By the start of 1942 the Axis was winning control of the Mediterranean. The progress of Allied ground forces in North Africa, facilitated by naval attacks on Axis supply ships, eventually relieved the pressure on sea communications. Italy was defeated in September 1943.

THE MEDITERRANEAN THEATRE 1940–1943

By 1942 the Mediterranean was in danger of becoming an Axis lake. The Germans had invaded Greece in 1941, and by October 1942 British land forces had been driven back almost to Alexandria. Yet the Royal Navy continued to operate, escorting convoys to isolated Malta. The situation changed in November 1942 with the Allied victory in Egypt and US landings in Algeria.

KEY
- ▭ Under Allied control Jul 1940
- ▭ Under Axis control Jul 1940
- ▭ Vichy French possessions
- ✦ Axis airbase
- ➤ Main British convoy routes
- ➤ Main Axis convoy routes
- ⚓ Allied victory
- ⚓ Axis victory
- ⚓ Inconclusive action

CARRIERS, SUBMARINES, AND MISSILES

WORLD WAR II

MERS-EL-KEBIR

Date 3 July 1940
Forces British: 1 carrier, 2 battleships, 1 battlecruiser, 2 light cruisers, 11 destroyers; French: 4 battleships, 6 destroyers, 5 submarines
Losses British: none; French: 3 battleships sunk or disabled
Location West of Oran, French Algeria

As German forces overran France in June 1940, the French Navy made vigorous efforts to keep its warships out of Nazi hands. Ships dispersed to British ports and the French overseas empire, including Mers-el-Kebir in French Algeria. The armistice terms agreed on 24 June specified that the French Navy would not be handed over to the Germans. The British, however, did not trust Germany or France to stick to the terms of the agreement. The addition of the French fleet to the Axis naval forces would have dangerously altered the balance of power at sea. Britain decided to ensure this could never happen. A force consisting of the battlecruiser *Hood*, the battleships *Valiant* and *Resolution*, and the carrier *Ark Royal* was sent to Mers-el-Kebir. Its commander, Admiral Sir James Somerville, had orders to

demand that the French either join the British war effort, surrender their ships into British hands, or sail to internment in the Americas. If they refused these options they had to scuttle their ships or be fired upon. Admiral Marcel Gensoul, the French naval commander in Mers-el-Kebir, preferred to fight. He cleared his four battleships – *Dunkerque*, *Strasbourg*, *Bretagne*, and *Provence* – for action and attempted to get under way. The British gunnery was accurate and destruction swift. *Bretagne* was hit by 15in salvoes, exploded and capsized,

Dunkerque was immobilized, and *Provence* set on fire and forced to beach. Only *Strasbourg* escaped to Toulon, but she was scuttled with the rest of the Vichy fleet in 1942 to prevent her falling into German hands. Almost 1,300 French sailors died at Mers-el-Kebir, an action regretted by the Royal Navy and bitterly resented in France.

French fleet at Mers-el-Kebir
A French soldier stands guard next to the battleships *Dunkerque* and *Strasbourg*. The sister ships were of an unusual design with all their main guns mounted forward.

WORLD WAR II

CALABRIA

Date 9 July 1940
Forces British: 1 carrier, 3 battleships, 5 cruisers, 16 destroyers; Italians: 2 battleships, 14 cruisers, 16 destroyers
Losses none
Location East of Punta Stilo, Calabria

One month after Italy had entered the war, a British naval force under Admiral Sir Andrew Cunningham escorting convoys from Alexandria to Malta was intercepted by Italian warships under Admiral Inigo Campioni. The British had suffered damage in attacks by Italian land-based aircraft, leading the Italians to believe they were in worse shape than was actually the case. After a clash between opposing cruisers, Cunningham's flagship *Warspite* duelled at maximum range with the Italian battleships *Giulio Cesare* and *Conte di Cavour*. *Warspite* hit *Giulio Cesare* with a 15in shell from a distance of 24km (15 miles), causing considerable damage. As the other British battleships, *Malaya* and *Royal Sovereign*, came up the Italians turned for home. The Italian air force concluded the engagement by bombing both fleets indiscriminately.

THE BATTLE OF TARANTO

Admiral Sir Andrew Cunningham approved a bold plan for a night attack by the Fleet Air Arm upon the Italian naval base at Taranto. For the first time in history a naval attack would use only planes, launching the aircraft from offshore aircraft carriers. The raid was originally scheduled for Trafalgar Day, 21 October, and was to involve the carriers *Eagle* and *Illustrious*. However, fire damage to one ship and structural damage to the other delayed the action. Eventually it was decided to go ahead with *Illustrious* only, bolstered by the transfer of five aircraft from *Eagle*.

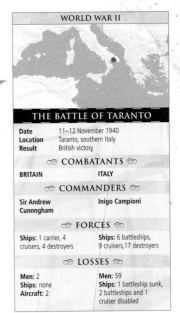

Fairey Swordfish
British Fairey Swordfish torpedo-bombers used modified torpedoes dropped from a low height to attack the Italian fleet at Taranto.

THE AIRCRAFT

It was a peculiarity of the Fleet Air Arm that its carriers were superb but its aircraft were obsolescent. The raid was carried out by slow-moving Fairey Swordfish, two-seater biplanes that had first entered service in 1936 and were affectionately known as "Stringbags". Escorted by cruisers and destroyers, *Illustrious* approached within striking range of Taranto on the evening of 11 November, flying off two waves of 12 and nine Swordfish an hour apart. Half the aircraft were armed with torpedoes and the rest with bombs. The torpedoes were used against the six battleships and three cruisers moored in Taranto's outer harbour, while the bombs were dropped on the smaller ships in the inner harbour.

THE OUTCOME

The Italians were well prepared for an aerial attack. The Swordfish flew into an inferno of anti-aircraft fire, some keeping so low their wheels touched the sea. Their torpedoes had been skilfully adapted to run in the shallow harbour waters and explode beneath the torpedo nets protecting the capital ships. Five struck home, hitting the battleships *Vittorio Veneto*, *Caio Duilio*, and *Conte di Cavour*. A cruiser in the inner harbour was badly damaged by bombs. Remarkably only two of the Swordfish were shot down during the conflict. For this trivial cost, the Fleet Air Arm succeeded in halving the Italian battleship strength in a single night. *Vittorio Veneto* and *Caio Duilio* were recommissioned the following year, but *Cavour* was never salvaged.

The victory tilted the balance of power in the Mediterranean in favour of the Allies. Any Italian ships that survived the attack were moved further north to Naples and La Spezia.

WORLD WAR II	
THE BATTLE OF TARANTO	
Date	11–12 November 1940
Location	Taranto, southern Italy
Result	British victory
❧ COMBATANTS ❧	
BRITAIN	ITALY
❧ COMMANDERS ❧	
Sir Andrew Cunnngham	Inigo Campioni
❧ FORCES ❧	
Ships: 1 carrier, 4 cruisers, 4 destroyers	**Ships:** 6 battleships, 9 cruisers, 17 destroyers
❧ LOSSES ❧	
Men: 2 **Ships:** none **Aircraft:** 2	**Men:** 59 **Ships:** 1 battleship sunk, 2 battleships and 1 cruiser disabled

Italian firepower
Italian battleship *Vittorio Veneto* fires a salvo from her nine 15in guns. The *Vittorio Veneto* was the most powerful warship to survive the attack on Taranto.

1883–1963
ANDREW B CUNNINGHAM
BRITISH ADMIRAL OF THE FLEET

Admiral Andrew B Cunningham, known as "ABC", was the commander-in-chief of the Royal Navy's Mediterranean Fleet from the outbreak of World War II to the Italian surrender in September 1943. A forthright man of action, Admiral Cunningham best showed his nerve and aggression in the night-time pursuit and destruction of the Italian fleet at Cape Matapan. His iron will helped keep his fleet going through the savage losses of the Malta convoy battles and the Crete campaign. In October 1943 he was appointed First Sea Lord and was responsible for British naval strategy through the rest of the war.

CARRIERS, SUBMARINES, AND MISSILES

WORLD WAR II

OPERATION EXCESS

Date 10–11 January 1941
Forces British: 1 carrier, 2 battleships, 3 cruisers, 7 destroyers; Axis: 2 destroyers, land-based aircraft
Losses British: 1 cruiser and 1 destroyer; Italians: 1 destroyer

Location Off southern Sicily

The Luftwaffe's Fliegerkorps X moved to bases in Sicily in January 1941. The British mounted a complex convoy operation, Operation Excess, in which merchant ships from Gibraltar were escorted to the south of Sicily by a force, including the carrier *Illustrious*, and passed to cruiser escorts from Alexandria to continue eastward. *Illustrious* was attacked by Stuka dive-bombers on 10 January. Hit by eight bombs and partially disabled, she limped to Malta, where air attacks continued. The next day the cruiser *Southampton*, heading for Alexandria, was so badly damaged by dive-bombing that she had to be scuttled.

THE BATTLE OF CAPE MATAPAN

On 27 March 1941 a substantial force of Italian warships assembled off southern Italy, commanded by Admiral Angelo Iachino on the Littorio-class battleship *Vittorio Veneto*. Iachino had been misled by intelligence reports suggesting the Royal Navy had only one battleship and no aircraft carriers in the waters around Crete. In reality, Admiral Sir Andrew Cunningham had the battleships *Warspite*, *Barham*, and *Valiant*, and the carrier *Formidable*. Once the Italian fleet was at sea, Cunningham set out from Alexandria to intercept, calling on Vice Admiral Henry Pridham-Wippell to join him with a destroyer flotilla and light cruiser squadron from Piraeus.

On 28 March, an Italian aircraft spotted Pridham-Wippell's light cruisers and destroyers and Iachino headed to intercept. Shortly after 8am Pridham-Wippell came under fire from Italian heavy cruisers. Iachino skilfully executed a pincer movement that threatened to trap Pridham-Wippell's force between the heavy cruisers and *Vittorio Veneto*, but at around 11am torpedo bombers from Andrew Cunningham's carrier *Formidable* arrived on the scene. While the Italian warships were preoccupied with evading air attack, Pridham-Wippell slipped away.

THE ITALIAN RETREAT

Without air cover, Iachino wisely decided to withdraw. Meanwhile Cunningham ordered further air attacks during which *Formidable*'s airmen succeeded in scoring hits on *Vittorio Veneto* and the heavy cruiser *Pola*, slowing down the former and immobilizing the latter. Still unaware that heavier Royal Navy forces were in the vicinity, Iachino ordered Admiral Carlo Cattaneo's heavy cruisers *Fiume* and *Zara* plus three destroyers, to stay behind to rescue *Pola*.

Cape Matapan medallion
Two warships on a parallel course with aircraft overhead adorn this unofficial Italian medal commemorating the defeat at Cape Matapan.

By this time night had fallen. The Italians had no radar and no training in night fighting. Totally undetected by the Italians in the pitch darkness, Cunningham's battleships, which had radar, advanced to around 3,500m (3,800 yards) of the ships clustered around *Pola* before opening fire. Struck repeatedly by heavy armour-piercing shells from *Valiant* and *Barham*'s 15in guns, *Fiume* and *Zara* were disabled in minutes, on fire, and listing heavily. British destroyers sank two Italian destroyers; only the destroyer *Gioberti* escaped. *Fiume* sank around 11pm. *Zara* and *Pola* were finished off by torpedoes in the early hours of the following morning.

The battle ended Italian hopes to control the Mediterranean. Mussolini's once proud fleet would not emerge in force again until it surrendered in 1943.

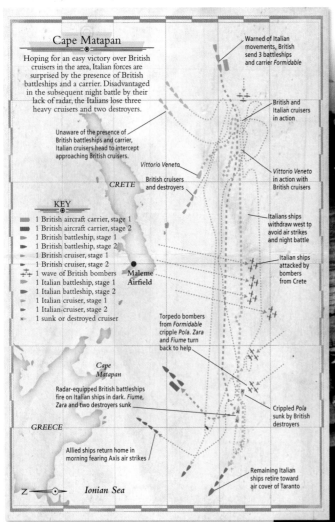

Cape Matapan

Hoping for an easy victory over British cruisers in the area, Italian forces are surprised by the presence of British battleships and a carrier. Disadvantaged in the subsequent night battle by their lack of radar, the Italians lose three heavy cruisers and two destroyers.

Unaware of the presence of British battleships and carrier, Italian cruisers head to intercept approaching British cruisers.

Vittorio Veneto

British cruisers and destroyers

CRETE

KEY

- ◼ 1 British aircraft carrier, stage 1
- ◼ 1 British aircraft carrier, stage 2
- ▶ 1 British battleship, stage 1
- ▶ 1 British battleship, stage 2
- ▶ 1 British cruiser, stage 1
- ▶ 1 British cruiser, stage 2
- ✚ 1 wave of British bombers
- ▶ 1 Italian battleship, stage 1
- ▶ 1 Italian battleship, stage 2
- ▶ 1 Italian cruiser, stage 1
- ▶ 1 Italian cruiser, stage 2
- ✕ 1 sunk or destroyed cruiser

Maleme Airfield

Torpedo bombers from *Formidable* cripple *Pola*. *Zara* and *Fiume* turn back to help.

Cape Matapan

Radar-equipped British battleships fire on Italian ships in dark. *Fiume*, *Zara* and two destroyers sunk

GREECE

Allied ships return home in morning fearing Axis air strikes

N

Ionian Sea

Warned of Italian movements, British send 3 battleships and carrier *Formidable*

British and Italian cruisers in action

Vittorio Veneto in action with British cruisers

Italians ships withdraw west to avoid air strikes and night battle

Italian ships attacked by bombers from Crete

Crippled *Pola* sunk by British destroyers

Remaining Italian ships retire toward air cover of Taranto

WORLD WAR II

THE BATTLE OF CAPE MATAPAN

Date	28–29 March 1941
Location	Off coast of Greece
Result	Allied victory

∞ COMBATANTS ∞

BRITAIN	ITALY

∞ COMMANDERS ∞

Sir Andrew Cunningham	Angelo Iachino

∞ FORCES ∞

Ships: 1 carrier, 3 battleships, 24 other ships	**Ships:** 1 battleship, 6 heavy cruisers, 19 other ships

∞ LOSSES ∞

Men: 3	**Men:** c.2,300
Ships: none	**Ships:** 3 heavy cruisers, 2 destroyers

Ambush at Cape Matapan
HMS *Valiant*, together with her fellow Queen Elizabeth-class battleships *Barham* and *Warspite*, fires her 15in guns. The three British battleships destroyed two Italian cruisers and two destroyers at Cape Matapan.

WORLD WAR II

CRETE

Date 21 May–1 June 1941
Forces British: 1 carrier, 4 battleships, 12 cruisers, 32 destroyers; Axis: unknown
Losses British: 3 cruisers and 6 destroyers sunk; Axis: unknown

Location Crete, eastern Mediterranean

On 20 May 1941 German paratroopers launched an assault upon Crete, held by British Commonwealth troops. British naval commander Admiral Cunningham was determined to prevent German troop reinforcements arriving by sea from Greece. His principle throughout was that "the Navy must not let the Army down". Since his ships were operating without air cover within range of German land-based aircraft, losses were inevitably heavy. On 21 May a first flotilla of German troop transports was forced to turn back. The next day a larger invasion force was attacked and scattered, but this time Luftwaffe air attacks took their toll – the cruiser *Gloucester* sunk and 723 lives were lost.

From 28 May, with the land battle on Crete lost, the Royal Navy's task was to evacuate as many troops as possible to Egypt. This was a perilous task. The destroyers *Hereward* and *Imperial* were sunk evacuating troops from Heraklion on 29 May. Most troops were taken off from Sphakia in southern Crete. In all some 16,000 soldiers were evacuated. The last Royal Navy ship sunk was the cruiser *Calcutta*, sent from Alexandria to cover the withdrawal, on 1 June. The British had lost nine ships, all to aerial attack, and had 15 others damaged. Some 2,000 sailors lost their lives.

WORLD WAR II

RAID ON ALEXANDRIA

Date 17–18 December 1941
Forces British: unknown; Italians: 1 submarine, 3 midget submarines
Losses Italians: 3 midget submarines; British: 2 battleships, 1 destroyer severely damaged, 1 tanker sunk

Location Alexandria, Egypt

The Italian Regia Marina developed midget submarines known as *Maiali*, for underwater raids on British harbours. On the night of 17–18 December 1941 three Italian *Maiali* were carried to the entrance of Alexandria harbour, home of the British Mediterranean Fleet, by the submarine *Scire*. Released under water, the midget submarines penetrated the harbour's defences undetected by following behind a British cruiser, the entry of which required the harbour's anti-submarine barrier to be opened. Two of the crews attached their charges to the hulls of the battleships *Valiant* and *Queen Elizabeth* – Admiral Andrew Cunningham's flagship. The third was destined for the absent aircraft carrier *Eagle*, so a large tanker, *Sagona* was targeted instead. The time-delayed charges exploded the next morning. The two battleships were severely damaged, *Queen Elizabeth* settling on the bottom of the shallow harbour. The explosion under the tanker also damaged the destroyer *Jervis*. All of the Italian commandos were taken prisoner. Both of the battleships were eventually returned to action, but the short-term loss to British naval strength in the Mediterranean was serious.

Italian manned torpedo
Nicknamed *maiali* (pigs) by their crews because of their poor handling, the manned torpedo carried a detachable warhead of up to 300kg (660lb).

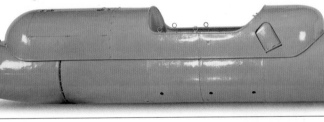

WORLD WAR II

SECOND SIRTE

Date 22 March 1942
Forces British: 5 cruisers, 18 destroyers, 1 submarine; Italians: 1 battleship, 3 cruisers, 8 destroyers, 1 submarine
Losses British: none; Italians: none

Location Gulf of Sirte, Mediterranean

The First Battle of Sirte, on 17 December 1941, was an inconclusive fight between Italian and British convoy escort forces under Admiral Angelo Iachino and Rear-Admiral Philip Vian. The same commanders clashed at the same location three months later. Vian was escorting four supply ships from Alexandria to Malta, with four light cruisers, an anti-aircraft cruiser, and a bevy of destroyers. The Italian Regia Marina intercepted with a squadron that included the heavy cruisers *Gorizia* and *Trento*, and the battleship *Littorio*. The weather was stormy, with heavy seas. Vian sighted the heavy cruisers and, leaving five destroyers to escort the supply ships, turned the rest of his escort force to confront the enemy. The Italians manoeuvered to draw the British toward their battleship, which loomed into sight around 4pm. Heavily outgunned, the British laid down a thick smoke screen, from behind which they dodged out intermittently to engage the Italians with their guns and torpedoes. The destroyer *Kingston* was almost torn apart by a hit from *Littorio*'s 15in armament and *Havock* was so badly damaged she was for a time dead in the water. Most of the British cruisers also took hits. Toward nightfall Admiral Iachino withdrew, and all the British ships were able to escape. The aftermath of the battle was painful for both sides. Two Italian destroyers foundered in a storm returning home; all the British supply ships were sunk by air attack on arrival at Malta.

WEAPONS AND TECHNOLOGY

ENIGMA INTERCEPTS

The Enigma machines used by the German Navy for encoding communications used three (later four) rotors to scramble the messages. They were considered utterly secure because the receiver needed to know the exact settings of the rotors, which changed daily. British codebreakers, however, intermittently managed to decipher these messages, providing advance warning of the movements of Axis warships, supply convoys, and submarines. The Enigma intelligence is credited, among other things, with contributing to the victory at Cape Matapan and the defeat of German U-boats in the Atlantic.

Enigma machine
By rotating the cylinders at the rear of the machine, code settings could be changed daily. Viewing windows on the lid showed the encoded letters.

FOOD AND DRINK

AN AGE-OLD PROBLEM of naval warfare is how to keep ships supplied with food and drink at sea. In the ancient world galleys carried only enough supplies for a few days of sailing. Hugging the coastlines, they beached to buy food and usually ate on shore, although when the galley was in a hurry the oarsmen might snack while they rowed. As sailing ships ventured far from land, however, they had to carry their own supplies with them for long periods of time. This led to health problems because of the lack of fresh food available and inadequate methods of food preservation.

A SAILOR'S DIET

Sailors basically consumed the food and drink typical of their society. In the 16th century Spanish sailors ate squid, tuna, sardines, oil, rice, and wine, while the English ships carried beef, butter, and beer. The distinguishing feature of shipboard food was that it needed to last. So freshly baked bread was replaced by biscuit, provided for Venetian galley crews as "biscotti" and the Royal Navy as "hard tack". Although liable to infestation by weevils and other pests, it provided a good basic foodstuff. Salted meat and fish ("stockfish") were also near universal staples, along with cheese and peas or lentils. That these lacked essential vitamins found in fresh food was recognized long before any scientific explanation was available. Navies in the 18th century tried to provide fresh fruit and vegetables when possible and carried live animals for slaughter. Sailors were on the whole not badly fed by the standards of their day. Scurvy, a disease formed by a deficiency of vitamin C, was found on land as well as at sea.

STORAGE Provisions in the hold of a reconstructed Spanish royal galley from 1570. Typical daily fare issued to the oarsmen would have included a 720g (26oz) biscuit, made by baking bread and legumes without oil. Pork and wine was added to the volunteers' rations.

> *The crew made haste that they [did not stop for meals but] pulled and ate at the same time, barley bread mixed with wine and olive oil.*
>
> **THUCYDIDES** (c. 400 BCE), on the exceptional circumstances when a trireme crew did not go ashore to take their meal.

COOKING AND MESSING

Arrangements for messing (eating) and cooking on a packed wooden sailing ship were always unsatisfactory. Men messed on the gun deck where they slept, letting down tables that hung from the deckhead. There were typically eight men to a mess. One man from each mess prepared the rations and brought them to the ship's cook – a petty officer, often a disabled man unfit for other service. For safety reasons the cooking fire was small and in the safest place that could be found. All food was typically cooked in a single large pot. Until the mid-19th century men provided their own table utensils. Naturally, life for officers was very different and quite luxurious by comparison. They could pay for their own more refined food and drink, and were waited on by servants, sometimes eating from silver plates.

FRESH FOOD
Live animals were brought on board when space permitted in order to overcome the problem of meat spoiling in storage. This meant that men and livestock shared the confines of the lower gun deck, lending additional odour and noise to already overcrowded conditions.

HARD TACK "Ship's biscuits" were so hard that sailors would dunk them in liquid to soften them up.

BEER TANKARD Beer was standard in Nelson's navy since water soon went stagnant in the storage barrels.

CLOSE QUARTERS The crew on a 19th-century warship would have eaten elbow to elbow amidst guns and hammocks. Eight adults and one boy would have sat around this table.

WATER AND ALCOHOL

Keeping water fresh at sea was beyond the technological capacity of the age of sail. It corrupted in the barrels, a problem only solved by the use of iron storage tanks in the 19th century. Instead, sailors mostly drank beer or wine. A sailor in the Royal Navy of Nelson's time was allowed a gallon (4.5 litres) of beer a day. There was also a daily rum ration of half a pint (280ml) per man, drunk mixed with water as "grog". However, punishments for men drunk on duty were severe. Concern about alcohol led to the reduction of the Royal Navy rum ration to an eighth of a pint (70ml) by the 1850s. The US Navy stopped spirit rations in 1862 and banned all alcohol on board warships in 1914.

» **ISSUING THE GROG**
Men gather aboard the *Royal Sovereign* in 1895. Teetotallers could claim the money value of the rum, or its equivalent in cocoa and sugar.

» **RUM BARRELS** The red line on the top of the barrel indicated its contents of rum. Rum gradually replaced brandy as the Royal Navy's official daily ration after the British capture of Jamaica in 1655.

» **COMPACT KITCHEN**
With room for only two to three people, this is one of several cooking areas on board the Greek armoured cruiser *Georgios Averof*, active from 1910 to 1952.

≪ **CRAMPED CONFINES** The unchanging problem of limited space calls for multi-purpose areas. Here 1950s sailors bunk and mess in the same room.

> *The stench of 51 sweating seamen, diesel oil, rotting food, and mouldy bread mingled with the noisome odours that emanated from the galley and the two tiny washrooms.*
>
> **HERBERT A WERNER**, *Iron Coffins*, describing the unappetising conditions in a U-Boat in World War II

⌃ **MASS PRODUCTION** The bakery on board the US aircraft carrier *George Washington* provides bread for 6,000 crew members. A far remove from early days of unvarying fare, there are specially catered meals and even an ice-cream booth available on board.

MODERN INNOVATIONS

The introduction of canned foods, followed later by refrigeration, improved nutrition on board through the 19th century. Also the increase in the speed of steamships shortened times at sea, making use of fresh ingredients more feasible. In Britain's Royal Navy in 1914, potatoes, powdered soup, smoked salmon, and milky tea were on the menu, although men still ate in messes eight to a bench with a table that probably doubled as a bed. During World War II self-service canteens became common on larger ships, though this brought no end to seamen's grumbling about food.

WORLD WAR II: THE PACIFIC

LAUNCHING A WAR in the Pacific was a desperate gamble by the Japanese. The temporary weakness of Britain, France, and the Netherlands – the colonial powers in southeast Asia – created an irresistible opportunity for Japan to seize control of the oil and other natural resources of British-ruled Malaya and the Dutch East Indies. But Japanese military leaders knew they would also have to fight the United States, with its vastly superior long-term warmaking potential. Admiral Isoroku Yamamoto, commander-in-chief of the Imperial Navy, proposed a surprise attack on the US naval base at Pearl Harbor, Hawaii. By crippling the US Pacific fleet, the Japanese would buy enough time to establish a defensive perimeter across the Pacific, ready to resist an eventual US counterattack. The raid on Pearl Harbor on 7 December 1941 initiated the most intensive large-scale naval conflict ever seen.

Kamikaze suicide attack
Smoke billows from US carrier *Belleau Wood* after an attack by a kamikaze pilot in October 1944. The battle of Leyte Gulf saw the first organized attacks by Japanese suicide planes – a tactic that became increasingly widespread in the closing stages of the Pacific War.

EARLY SUCCESSES

At the start of the Pacific War the Japanese and US fleets were quite evenly balanced, except in terms of carriers. Japan had more, and its carrier aircraft were the best in the world. For the first six months of the war Japanese forces ran amok. The Pearl Harbor raid subdued the US Navy briefly, and Britain's Royal Navy, committed to the war against Hitler's Germany, could offer little resistance. In early 1942 the formidable British base at Singapore fell to an attack from the land. Part of the Japanese fleet entered the Indian Ocean and there was nothing to stop it sailing up the Red Sea to the Suez Canal or attacking Iraq, a vital source of British oil supplies. But the Japanese never went further west than Sri Lanka. By May 1942 they were thoroughly occupied in the South Pacific, as the Americans

fought back sooner than expected. US carrier aircraft checked Japanese carriers at the Coral Sea and then dealt them a severe blow at Midway – one from which the Imperial Japanese Navy never fully recovered.

Neither the Americans nor the Japanese shied away from a fight. Particularly fierce sea battles were fought around the island of Guadalcanal in the Solomon Islands, with heavy losses on both sides. The Americans benefited from superior naval intelligence – having broken the Japanese naval codes – but the Japanese proved

Desperate fighting
USS *Bunker Hill* burns after being hit by two kamikaze planes in the space of 30 seconds near Okinawa in 1945. Around 1,500 kamikaze planes were crashed into US ships or shot down during the Japanese defence of the island.

Next! Japan
A poster advertising bonds to help the US government finance the war in the Pacific and the drive on the Japanese home islands.

THE JAPANESE ADVANCE

The Pacific War began with Japan's invasion of China and Manchuria in 1937–39 before moving into a second more intensive phase after Japan's attack on Pearl Harbour in December 1941. This was followed by the invasion of the Philippines, Burma, Malaya, and the Dutch East Indies (Indonesia) and the seizure of their economic resources.

KEY

- Under Japanese control Dec 1941
- Under Japanese control Jun 1942
- Japanese invasion/landing
- Route of Pearl Harbor carrier fleet
- Doolittle Raid on Tokyo 18 Apr 1942
- Japanese victory
- US/Allied victory
- Inconclusive battle
- Japanese bombing raid
- US/Allied bombing raid

Submarine binoculars
A pair of Japanese conning tower binoculars. Despite the vulnerable Allied supply line in the Pacific, Japanese submarines generally focused on sinking warships rather than merchant vessels.

better at night-fighting and had more effective torpedoes. At the end of 1942, the Imperial Japanese Navy was still holding its own, but against the huge industrial potential of the United States Japan's long-term prospects looked more grim.

INDUSTRIAL MIGHT

The United States embarked on the largest shipbuilding programme in history. From 1943 onward the US Navy expanded its resources in the Pacific until it had achieved an overwhelming superiority over the Japanese. New heavy carriers, light carriers, and escort "jeep" carriers were organized into Carrier Task Forces, each with a protective screen of escort vessels. They soon surpassed their target of 27,500 naval aircraft to equip the new carriers. Landing craft were produced on a massive scale for assaults on the Pacific islands, for which the big guns of their ships, plus carrier aircraft, provided fire support. Meanwhile US submarines overcame problems with non-functioning torpedoes to take a mounting toll on Japanese merchant shipping and warships. The US Navy handled its rapid expansion remarkably well, achieving a high level of training for fresh pilots and sailors and the provision of an efficient supply line to keep the massive new fleets at sea. New tactics were

developed, turning amphibious landings into precisely coordinated operations, and evolving robust systems of fleet defence against air attack such as the use of destroyer "pickets" to identify incoming enemy aircraft and the coordination of ship anti-aircraft fire with air combat patrols.

Acutely aware of their growing material inferiority, the Japanese fell back upon their fighting spirit. Naval commanders remained committed to seeking a decisive fleet encounter in which they would destroy the enemy against all the odds. The result in 1944 was a series of epic battles as the Japanese Imperial Navy attacked US ships supporting landings on the Marianas and the Philippines. The absolute superiority of US naval aviation, with improved aircraft and better-trained pilots, achieved the destruction of Japanese carrier-borne air power at the battle of the Philippine Sea. At Leyte Gulf the Japanese fleet made its last serious bid for a decisive victory and lost.

DESPERATE OFFENSIVES

Japan's adoption of kamikaze suicide tactics in the final phase of the war was in part a practical response to the problem of how to inflict damage on the now well-defended US fleet. What the Japanese really needed was guided missiles, but a suicide pilot could perform a similar function. For the final battles, as the war approached Japan itself, the Japanese had no useable warships and no time or fuel to train naval pilots operating from land bases. A vast fleet of US, British, and Australian ships was the object of mass suicide attacks by pilots who could barely fly.

The kamikazes inflicted much damage, but by this stage the Allied shipyards could replace ships faster than they were lost. By the end of the war Japan was under almost total naval blockade. In September 1945 Japan's formal surrender took place on board USS *Missouri* in Tokyo Bay.

1884–1943
ISORUKU YAMAMOTO

COMMANDER-IN-CHIEF OF JAPANESE COMBINED FLEET

Born Isoroku Takana, the future admiral entered the Etajima Naval Academy aged 16 and fought as an ensign at the battle of Tsushima in 1904, losing two fingers on his left hand. Isoruku became part of the Yamamoto samurai family by adoption in 1914. As an admiral in the 1930s he was an advocate of naval air power, deploring Japan's obsession with outsize battleships. He was deeply pessimistic about Japanese chances of success in a war against the US, and he opposed Japan's alignment with Nazi Germany. On being appointed commander-in-chief of the Japanese Combined Fleet in 1939, he pushed through the plan for a pre-emptive attack on Pearl Harbor. On 18 April 1943, pinpointed by American intelligence, the aircraft in which he was travelling was shot down over Bougainville.

CARRIERS, SUBMARINES, AND MISSILES

THE JAPANESE OFFENSIVE

THE SURPRISE ATTACK by Japanese naval aircraft on the American naval base at Pearl Harbor on 7 December 1941 was the first of a series of bold aggressive moves that within six months gave Japan control of all of southeast Asia and much of the Pacific. The navies of Britain and the Netherlands were able to put up little more than token resistance to an enemy overwhelmingly superior both in heavy-gun warships and in land- and carrier-based aviation. It fell to the US Navy to contest the dominance of the Japanese at sea. The Americans faced an opponent not only superior in numbers but also highly motivated, well trained, and in some departments, better equipped. Yet at the decisive battle of Midway in June 1942 the Japanese carrier force that had humiliated the United States at Pearl Harbor was itself crushingly defeated. The fierce battles fought around the island of Guadalcanal during the second half of 1942 showed that the Japanese Imperial Navy was still confident and aggressive, but Japan had ultimately failed to achieve a decisive naval victory while the balance of power at sea was most in its favour.

PEARL HARBOR

WORLD WAR II

PEARL HARBOR

Date	7 December 1941
Location	Pearl Harbor, Oahu, Hawaii
Result	Japanese victory

☞ COMBATANTS ☜

JAPAN	UNITED STATES

☞ COMMANDERS ☜

Isoroku Yamamoto	Husband E Kimmel
Chuichi Nagumo	

☞ FORCES ☜

Ships: 2 battleships, 6 carriers, 28 submarines, 23 other ships, 432 aircraft (353 on raid)	**Ships:** 90 ships including 8 battleships, 300 aircraft

☞ LOSSES ☜

Men: 55	**Men:** 2,403
Ships: 1 submarine, 5 midget submarines	**Ships:** 18 ships sunk or seriously damaged

On 26 November 1941 a Japanese naval task force under the command of Vice Admiral Chuichi Nagumo slipped out of Hitokapu Bay in the Kurile Islands bound for Hawaii. The force included six aircraft carriers: *Akagi, Kaga, Zuikaku, Shaokaku, Hiryu,* and *Soryu.* Its goal was to attack and destroy the US Pacific Fleet in its base at Pearl Harbor. The key figure behind the Pearl Harbor raid was Admiral Isoroku Yamamoto: Japan had decided to seize Malaya and the Dutch East Indies and, convinced this must mean war with the United States, Yamamoto planned a preemptive strike against the US fleet, to coincide with, rather than follow, a declaration of war.

The operation depended on total surprise. Observing strict radio silence, Nagumo's force would cross thousands of kilometres of ocean undetected, refuelling from tankers en route. A separate force of Japanese submarines also proceeded to Pearl Harbor, full-size boats carrying midget submarines to penetrate the American defences. At dawn on 7 December, 400km (250 miles) north of Hawaii, the first wave of 183 Japanese aircraft took off from their carriers – Nakajima "Kate" torpedo-bombers, Mitsubishi "Zero" fighters, and Aichi "Val" dive-bombers.

Although Japan and the US were not at war, diplomatic relations had reached a breaking point and American forces should have been on full alert. But Pearl Harbor was enjoying a sleepy peacetime Sunday morning. The incoming aircraft were picked up on radar and one midget submarine was spotted, but none of this disturbed the Americans. The ship's band was playing on the deck of the battleship *Nevada* as the bombs began to fall. The aircraft that should have defended the base were destroyed as they sat on the ground.

Japan's naval pilots were a highly trained elite flying the world's best carrier aircraft. It is reckoned that 90 per cent of the torpedoes at Pearl Harbor found their target, as did around 60 per cent of the bombs dropped by dive-bombers. Within 20 minutes of the start of the attack the battleship *Oklahoma* had capsized after hits by five torpedoes, while *Arizona* had suffered

Binoculars from USS *Arizona*
The first ship to be sunk at Pearl Harbor, the battleship *Arizona* was ripped apart by an explosion in its forward magazine.

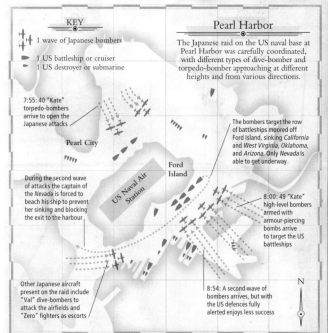

KEY

✈ 1 wave of Japanese bombers

➤ 1 US battleship or cruiser

▸ 1 US destroyer or submarine

7:55: 40 "Kate" torpedo-bombers arrive to open the Japanese attacks

Pearl City

During the second wave of attacks the captain of the *Nevada* is forced to beach his ship to prevent her sinking and blocking the exit to the harbour

Other Japanese aircraft present on the raid include "Val" dive-bombers to attack the airfields and "Zero" fighters as escorts

US Naval Air Station

Ford Island

Pearl Harbor

The Japanese raid on the US naval base at Pearl Harbor was carefully coordinated, with different types of dive-bomber and torpedo-bomber approaching at different heights and from various directions.

The bombers target the row of battleships moored off Ford Island, sinking *California* and *West Virginia, Oklahoma,* and *Arizona.* Only *Nevada* is able to get underway

8:00: 49 "Kate" high-level bombers armed with armour-piercing bombs arrive to target the US battleships

8:54: A second wave of bombers arrives, but with the US defences fully alerted enjoys less success

N

> ❝ YESTERDAY, DECEMBER 7, 1941 – A DATE WHICH WILL LIVE IN INFAMY – THE UNITED STATES OF AMERICA WAS SUDDENLY AND DELIBERATELY ATTACKED. ❞
>
> **PRESIDENT FRANKLIN D ROOSEVELT**, SPEECH TO CONGRESS ON 8 DECEMBER 1941

1919–1943
DORIS "DORIE" MILLER
COOK THIRD CLASS, USS WEST VIRGINIA

Like most black sailors in the US Navy in 1941, Doris Miller was a mess attendant. When the Japanese struck Pearl Harbor he was on board the battleship *West Virginia*. Amid the inferno of the burning ship, Miller first attempted to save his wounded captain and then manned an anti-aircraft gun. He is credited with shooting down at least one Japanese aircraft, despite having no training. Miller was awarded the Navy Cross for "distinguished devotion to duty, extraordinary courage, and disregard for his own personal safety". He died in 1943 when the ship on which he was serving was sunk by a Japanese submarine.

an even worse fate: an armour-piercing bomb penetrated its forward magazine, setting off an explosion that ripped the battleship in two, killing more than a thousand of its crew.

A second wave of 170 aircraft arrived later in the morning to add to the mayhem. By the time it was all over, 18 American ships were sunk or disabled, including all the battleships.

There were a few glimmers of light in an otherwise grim scene. The attempted attack by Japanese midget submarines was a total failure. The Japanese also failed to destroy the oil tanks at the base. And most important of all, the US Navy's four aircraft carriers were absent when the raid took place. But for the time being, the Japanese navy had established dominance in the Pacific.

USS Nevada on fire
Despite being damaged in the first wave of attacks, *Nevada* was the only battleship to get underway during the raid. The battleship was struck again and beached during the second wave of attacks.

 WORLD WAR II
SINKING OF PRINCE OF WALES AND REPULSE

Date 10 December 1941
Forces British: 1 battleship, 1 battlecruiser, 4 destroyers; Japanese: 84 aircraft
Losses British: 1 battleship, 1 battlecruiser; Japanese: 6 aircraft

Location South China Sea

On 2 December 1941 the battleship *Prince of Wales* and the battlecruiser *Repulse* arrived at the British base at Singapore, along with four destroyers. They had been sent in the vain hope of deterring the Japanese from going to war. The ships should have been accompanied by a carrier, but a mishap en route left this under repair in the US.

On the same day as Pearl Harbor, the Japanese began landing troops in Malaya. Admiral Sir Tom Phillips sailed north from Singapore to intercept the landings. His ships, designated Force Z, were spotted by Japanese submarines and cruiser-carried reconnaissance aircraft. Aware that he had lost the advantage of surprise, Phillips turned back on the night of 9–10 December.

Japanese naval aircraft of the 22nd Air Flotilla, based at airfields around Saigon in Japanese-occupied Indochina, failed to find Force Z that night, but the following morning they located the ships off Kuantan. Force Z was not unprepared for air defence – *Prince of Wales* alone mounted 175 anti-aircraft guns – but waves of attacks by conventional bombers and, in particular, torpedo-bombers were devastatingly effective. The air attacks began shortly after 11am; *Repulse* sank at 12:30pm and *Prince of Wales* at 1:20pm. Some 2,000 men were rescued by the destroyers, although Admiral Phillips was among those lost. This naval disaster left the Japanese navy in command of the seas and Malaya and Singapore exposed to Japanese conquest.

Air raid on Tokyo
A US Army Air Force B-25 takes off from the deck of the USS *Hornet* on its way to take part in the first US air raid on Japan – an important propaganda coup for the United States military.

 WORLD WAR II
DOOLITTLE RAID

Date 18 April 1942
Forces Americans: 2 carriers, 4 cruisers, 8 destroyers, 16 aircraft
Losses Americans: 16 aircraft; Japanese c.50 civilians

Location Pacific Ocean and Tokyo, Japan

With Americans in desperate need of a morale boost, a plan was devised for a carrier raid on the Japanese homeland. The US Navy reckoned it could advance a carrier task force to within 650km (400 miles) of Tokyo. As no naval airplane had sufficient range, the US Army Air Force agreed to supply B-25 Mitchell bombers, although no B-25 had ever taken off from a flight deck. Lieutenant Colonel James Doolittle led the air side of the mission.

The carrier *Hornet* set to sea on 2 April 1942 with 16 B-25s tethered on the flight deck – they were too large to be stowed below. North of Hawaii *Hornet* rendezvoused with the carrier *Enterprise* and its escort of cruisers and destroyers. Maintaining strict radio silence, they had advanced to within 1,000km (650 miles) of Tokyo when, on the morning of 18 April, they were spotted by a Japanese patrol boat. The decision was taken to launch the planes immediately, although the extra distance meant they would be unlikely to reach the airfield in a friendly area of China where they planned to land.

Doolittle had exhaustively practised short take-offs with his volunteer crews, but no one actually knew if the aircraft, laden with fuel and bombs, would launch from a pitching deck in a heavy sea. Remarkably, they took off without mishap and, four hours later, bombed Tokyo and other cities. All the aircraft were subsequently lost but most of the crews found their way back to the US. The raid was a severe embarrassment to Japanese military leaders and partly motivated their fateful decision to attack Midway the following June.

Heavy cruiser Nachi
The Japanese cruiser *Nachi* and her sister ship *Haguro* outclassed their opponents at the Battle of the Java Sea. *Nachi*'s "longlance" torpedoes, more reliable than the Allied torpedoes, sunk the Dutch light cruiser *Java*.

WORLD WAR II

JAVA SEA

Date 27 February–1 March 1942
Forces Allies: 5 cruisers, 9 destroyers; Japanese: 4 cruisers; 14 destroyers
Losses Allies: 5 cruisers; 5 destroyers; Japanese: 4 troop transports

Location
Java Sea

An American-British-Dutch-Australian (ABDA) force under Dutch admiral Karel Doorman was created to prevent the Japanese landing troops on Java. On 27 February 1942 an invasion force was spotted and Doorman sailed from Surabaya to intercept it. His force consisted of two heavy cruisers – the Royal Navy's *Exeter* and the US Navy's *Houston* – one Australian and two Dutch light cruisers, and nine destroyers, four of them American. They found the Japanese troop transports defended by Admiral Shoji Nishimura with the heavy cruisers *Nachi* and *Haguro* supported by light cruisers and destroyers.

Although on paper the two forces were comparable, the Japanese were superior in guns, torpedoes, organization, and morale. After two hours' gunfire *Exeter* was forced to withdraw by a hit on her boiler room and two ABDA destroyers were sunk. At around 6pm the US destroyers

Dutch medallion
Admiral Doorman's flagship *De Ruyter* appears below his reputed last words at the battle of the Java Sea: "I'm attacking, follow me".

WORLD WAR II

CORAL SEA

Date 4–8 May 1942
Forces US and Australians: 2 carriers, 8 cruisers, 13 destroyers; Japanese: 2 carriers, 1 light carrier, 6 cruisers, 6 destroyers
Losses US and Australians: 1 carrier, 1 destroyer, 74 aircraft; Japanese: 1 light carrier, 1 destroyer, 70 aircraft

Location
Coral Sea

In April 1942 the Japanese, pushing south toward Australia, sent a force to occupy Tulagi in the Solomon Islands and Port Moresby in New Guinea, supported by the carriers *Shokaku* and *Zuikaku*. The US Navy was well informed of Japanese plans through radio intercepts and Rear Admiral Frank Fletcher was ordered to seek out and attack the Japanese forces. He assembled the carriers *Lexington* and *Yorktown* and a number of cruisers and destroyers in the Coral Sea, including a contingent from the Royal Australian Navy under Rear Admiral John Crace.

The Americans struck the first blow on 4 May when aircraft from *Yorktown* attacked the Japanese at Tulagi, sinking a destroyer and several merchant vessels. For the next two days the rival carrier forces, concealed by cloud cover, failed to find one another. Fletcher was, however, informed of the course of the invasion force bound for Port Moresby, which was located by the US Army Air Force. On 7 May carrier aircraft attacked the Japanese troop convoy escorts. US fliers piled in to sink the light carrier *Shohu* with a plethora of torpedoes and bombs. But the overkill on a single ship meant other available targets were neglected. Meanwhile, Japanese carrier aircraft attacked and sank an American destroyer and oil tanker that had been mistakenly identified as a carrier and a cruiser. As night fell six Japanese planes tried to land on *Yorktown*, believing it was one of their own ships.

The following morning both sides flew off their aircraft to attack. Many of the American pilots had trouble finding the Japanese carriers, which were sailing through a tropical rainstorm. *Zuikaku* escaped in the poor visibility but *Shokaku* was left ablaze and incapable of operating aircraft. Meanwhile, Japanese bombers, enjoying better conditions, attacked with excellent coordination. *Yorktown* was hit by a bomb that exploded below decks, killing or seriously injuring 66.

covered a tactical withdrawal by laying a smokescreen, Doorman intending to maonoeuvre around the Japanese escorts and get among the troop ships at night. However, the destroyers then left for Surabaya and by the time Doorman encountered the Japanese again he had only his four remaining cruisers. In the darkness, a devastating Japanese torpedo attack sank two light cruisers including Doorman's flagship. The admiral was not among the few survivors.

Two days later the damaged *Exeter*, with two destroyers as escorts, unluckily encountered *Nachi* and *Haguro* as she headed for Sri Lanka. All three ships were sunk. Also on 1 March, *Houston* and the Australian light cruiser *Perth* were sunk in night action in the Sunda Strait. This completed a comprehensive naval disaster for the Allies, who had lost more than 2,000 men and 10 warships.

Lexington took the worst of the damage, struck by at least two torpedoes and two bombs, and had to be scuttled.

Overall the US Navy came off the worse in the world's first battle fought exclusively between carriers. But the Japanese were forced to abandon their intended invasion of Port Moresby, an important strategic setback.

Preparing for launch
SBS Dauntless dive-bombers stand on the flght deck of the US carrier *Yorktown*. Coral Sea was the first battle fought as a duel between between carrier aircraft, without opposing ships sighting one another.

CREW PROFILE

US AIRCRAFT CARRIER

WORLD WAR II

WITH A CREW NUMBERING OVER 2,000 men, a World War II American fleet aircraft carrier was a complex social world, in which divisions of function were often as important as differences of rank. Some officers and men executed tasks required on all warships, while others did jobs specific to the business of operating warplanes from carriers. These included the aviation machinists and electricians who serviced the aircraft in the hangars, the aviation ordnance teams responsible for arming the planes, the aviation boatswain's mates whose tasks included supervising the catapults and arresting gear on the flight deck, and the landing signal officer – usually a trained aviator – who stood prominently on deck using coloured paddles to guide pilots attempting to land. Until 1943 the navy accepted no draftees, so all crew members were volunteers, many going to sea to avoid conscription into the army.

NAVAL PILOT

American naval pilots were a gung-ho body of men, keen on a fight and justly proud of their skills. Between 1942 and 1944 more than 50,000 were trained, most passing through Naval Air Station Pensacola in Florida. Officers became Naval Aviators while the enlisted men were designated Naval Aviation Pilots (NAPs). On flying operations rank was disregarded, the most experienced fliers taking command even if this meant non-commissioned men giving orders to officers. As in all aerial warfare, a few pilots proved exceptionally gifted and these men led from the front. In fighter squadrons pilots flew in divisions of four aircraft. The leader of the division was the man expected to shoot

Navy cadet
A US Navy pilot climbs into the cockpit of a gleaming T-6 Texan trainer aircraft during flight training at Naval Air Station Corpus Christi in Texas in 1942.

down enemy aircraft, the other three were there primarily to cover his back. A carrier pilot's task was exceptionally demanding because of the need to launch from and land on a small pitching flight deck crowded with aircraft. Taking off even with the aid of a catapult was only possible if the carrier was making speed into the wind. Landing posed even more complex problems. Once the pilot got "into the groove" to land, he was in the hands of the landing officer who would give him "the cut" to authorize landing or the "wave off" if all was not well. Pilots tended to be competitive individualists by nature, but they acknowledged that they needed the help and support of many other crew members to stay operational.

Pilot briefing
The commanding officer of Fighting Squadron 16 briefs his pilots in front of an F6F-3 Hellcat fighter on board the USS *Lexington* in 1943.

THE BATTLE OF MIDWAY

In June 1942 Japan embarked upon an invasion of the American-held Midway atoll. One of the objectives was to draw the US Pacific Fleet into a decisive battle that Japanese commanders were confident they would win. Admiral Yamamoto dispersed his forces in a complex plan to distract and envelop his adversaries. Since the Americans had broken Japanese naval codes they were aware of Yamamoto's intentions and, ignoring a diversionary attack on the Aleutians, concentrated their efforts against Vice-Admiral Nagumo's force of four carriers. US Admiral Chester Nimitz sent two carrier task forces to defend Midway. Rear Admiral Fletcher

commanded Task Force 16 with the carriers *Enterprise* and *Hornet*, while Rear Admiral Raymond Spruance led Task Force 17 with *Yorktown*, repaired at Pearl Harbor in a mere three days after its battering at the Coral Sea.

DECISIVE AIR STRIKES

Battle was joined on 4 June. Unaware of the proximity of the US carriers, Nagumo launched an early morning air strike on Midway. He was planning a follow-up when a reconnaissance aircraft reported sighting enemy ships, tardily identified as including carriers. By then the Americans had already flown off their aircraft. Launched in haste and some confusion, the Wildcat fighters, Dauntless dive-bombers, and Devastator torpedo-bombers from *Hornet* and *Enterprise* searched for the enemy in uncoordinated groups. Unfortunately the slow-moving torpedo-bombers were first to locate Nagumo's carriers. Without fighter cover, they were pounced upon by Zero fighters. Not one of *Hornet's* 15 Devastators survived.

Aircraft from *Yorktown*, launched later than those from the other two carriers, arrived together at around 10:20am. By chance, two squadrons of dive-bombers from *Enterprise* found Nagumo's force at the same moment. While *Yorktown's* Wildcats took on the Zeros, dive-bombers from *Yorktown* and *Enterprise* were left free to attack the carriers. Bomb after bomb struck the decks of Japanese carriers packed with

Purple encoding machine
The Americans never captured the Japanese "Purple" encoding machine, but Japanese naval code was understood well enough to warn the US Navy of the attack on Midway.

aircraft, munitions, and fuel lines. In five minutes *Akagi*, *Kaga,* and *Soryu* were all burning wrecks.

The Japanese still had one carrier intact. *Hiryu* flew waves of bombers to deliver a counter-strike against *Yorktown*. Showing great determination in the face of American fighters and anti-aircraft fire, the Japanese pilots inflicted crippling damage upon the carrier. It was small compensation for a day of disaster for the Imperial Japanese Navy, capped late on when *Hiryu* was destroyed by dive-bombers from *Enterprise*.

Over the following days American aircraft and submarines harassed the withdrawing Japanese fleet, sinking the cruiser *Mikuma*. Meanwhile, efforts

were made to salvage *Yorktown*, until a Japanese submarine hit the heavily listing carrier with two torpedoes, also sinking a destroyer alongside. But nothing could detract from the scale of the American victory. That the invasion of Midway had been defeated was a minor point compared with the blow inflicted upon Japan's naval aviation. The loss of four carriers and so many naval pilots was a setback from which the Imperial Navy never recovered.

WORLD WAR II

BATTLE OF MIDWAY

Date	4–7 June 1942
Location	Pacific Ocean near Midway Island
Result	American victory

COMBATANTS
UNITED STATES	JAPAN

COMMANDERS
Chester Nimitz, Frank Fletcher, Raymond Spruance	Isoroku Yamamoto, Chuichi Nagumo

FORCES
Ships: 3 carriers, 8 cruisers, 15 destroyers **Aircraft**: 233 carrier-based, 127 land-based	**Ships**: 4 carriers, 9 battleships, 6 cruisers, 25 destroyers **Aircraft**: 248

LOSSES
Men: 307 **Ships**: 1 carrier, 1 destroyer **Aircraft**: 98	**Men**: 3,057 **Ships**: 4 carriers, 1 cruiser **Aircraft**: 228

KEY

US FLEET
Cruisers, destroyers, and smaller ships in US carrier task forces not shown.

1 US aircraft carrier

Wave of US bomber aircraft

JAPANESE FLEET
Cruisers, destroyers, and smaller ships in Nagumo's carrier strike force not shown. Main Japanese invasion force is off area of map.

1 Japanese aircraft carrier

Wave of Japanese bomber aircraft

1 Japanese cruiser

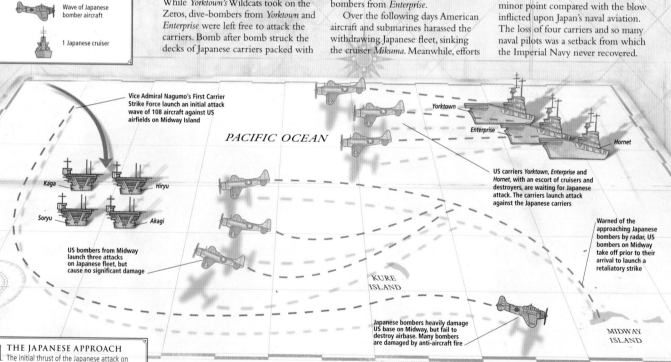

Vice Admiral Nagumo's First Carrier Strike Force launch an initial attack wave of 108 aircraft against US airfields on Midway Island

PACIFIC OCEAN

Yorktown

Enterprise

Hornet

US carriers *Yorktown*, *Enterprise* and *Hornet*, with an escort of cruisers and destroyers, are waiting for Japanese attack. The carriers launch attack against the Japanese carriers

Kaga

Hiryu

Soryu

Akagi

US bombers from Midway launch three attacks on Japanese fleet, but cause no significant damage

Warned of the approaching Japanese bombers by radar, US bombers on Midway take off prior to their arrival to launch a retaliatory strike

KURE ISLAND

Japanese bombers heavily damage US base on Midway, but fail to destroy airbase. Many bombers are damaged by anti-aircraft fire

MIDWAY ISLAND

1 THE JAPANESE APPROACH
The initial thrust of the Japanese attack on Midway comes from Vice Admiral Nagumo's carrier strike force. Warned of the Japanese approach, two US carrier task forces are laying in wait and launch retaliatory air strikes against the Japanese carriers.

Crippled carrier at Midway
USS *Yorktown* lists heavily after being attacked by bombers from the Japanese carrier *Hiryu*. *Yorktown* was sunk the following day by a Japanese submarine.

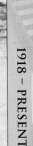

> **I SAW THIS GLINT IN THE SUN AND IT LOOKED JUST LIKE A BEAUTIFUL, SILVER WATERFALL, THESE DIVE-BOMBERS COMING DOWN. I'D NEVER SEEN SUCH SUPERB DIVE-BOMBING.**
>
> **US PILOT JIMMY THATCH**, RECALLING THE BATTLE OF MIDWAY, 1942

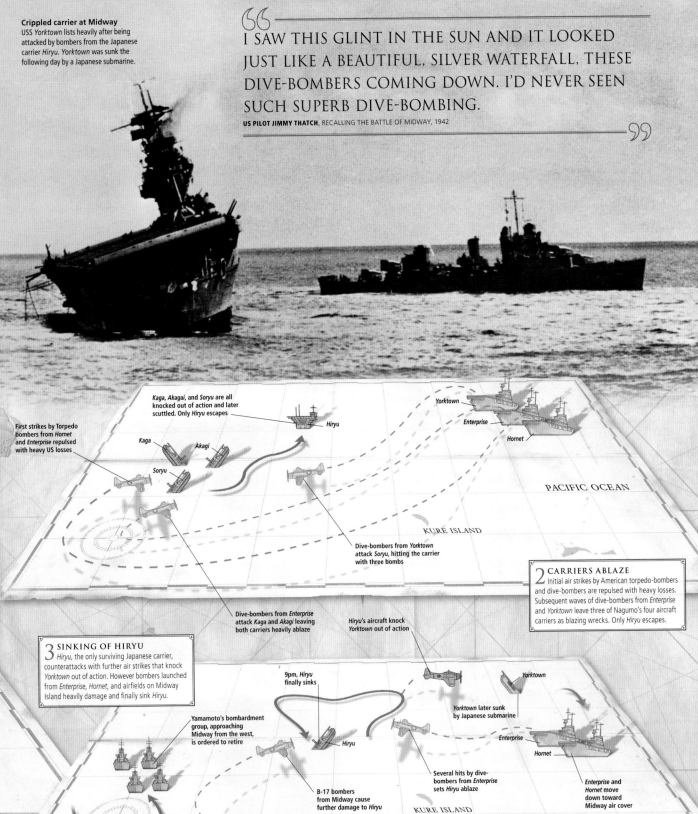

Kaga, *Akagai*, and *Soryu* are all knocked out of action and later scuttled. Only *Hiryu* escapes

Hiryu

Kaga

Akagi

Soryu

First strikes by Torpedo bombers from *Hornet* and *Enterprise* repulsed with heavy US losses

Dive-bombers from *Yorktown* attack *Soryu*, hitting the carrier with three bombs

Dive-bombers from *Enterprise* attack *Kaga* and *Akagi* leaving both carriers heavily ablaze

Yorktown

Enterprise

Hornet

PACIFIC OCEAN

KURE ISLAND

2 CARRIERS ABLAZE
Initial air strikes by American torpedo-bombers and dive-bombers are repulsed with heavy losses. Subsequent waves of dive-bombers from *Enterprise* and *Yorktown* leave three of Nagumo's four aircraft carriers as blazing wrecks. Only *Hiryu* escapes.

3 SINKING OF HIRYU
Hiryu, the only surviving Japanese carrier, counterattacks with further air strikes that knock *Yorktown* out of action. However bombers launched from *Enterprise*, *Hornet*, and airfields on Midway Island heavily damage and finally sink *Hiryu*.

Hiryu's aircraft knock *Yorktown* out of action

9pm, *Hiryu* finally sinks

Yamamoto's bombardment group, approaching Midway from the west, is ordered to retire

Hiryu

B-17 bombers from Midway cause further damage to *Hiryu*

Several hits by dive-bombers from *Enterprise* sets *Hiryu* ablaze

Yorktown

Yorktown later sunk by Japanese submarine

Enterprise

Hornet

Enterprise and *Hornet* move down toward Midway air cover

KURE ISLAND

MIDWAY ISLAND

PACIFIC OCEAN

THE BATTLE FOR GUADALCANAL

AMERICAN FORCES LANDED on Guadalcanal and other islands in the Eastern Solomons on 7 August 1942. As the Japanese were determined to retake Guadalcanal and the Americans equally determined to hold it, the island became the focus for intense naval warfare. The Japanese Navy was at first supremely confident, viewing the fighting as a chance to draw American forces into battle and destroy them. After a stunning initial victory at Savo Island, however, the Japanese failed to crush the Americans in fleet encounters at the Eastern Solomons and the Santa Cruz Islands. The US Navy equally failed to prevent the Japanese running supply convoys – the "Tokyo Express" – down New Georgia Sound at night to land reinforcements on Guadalcanal and shell the airbase at Henderson Field. The climax of the campaign came in two major night encounters in mid-November, known as the naval battle of Guadalcanal, during which the Japanese lost two battleships. Their attempt to retake the island was eventually abandoned. The Japanese Navy successfully evacuated troops from Guadalcanal in February 1943, but it had been unable to achieve decisive naval superiority.

CARRIERS, SUBMARINES, AND MISSILES

THE BATTLE OF SAVO ISLAND

Japanese vice admiral Gunichi Mikawa, based at Rabaul, organized a rapid naval response to the initial American landings on Guadalcanal. With no air cover, Mikawa planned to attack under cover of darkness, as his cruisers were well trained in night-fighting. On the evening of 8 August, the Allied naval forces covering the landings were far from alert. Admiral Frank Fletcher had withdrawn his carriers and British admiral Victor Crutchley, commanding the warships screening the landings, had departed from his station with his flagship *Australia* to discuss this move with the overall commander, Admiral Turner.

On the ships of the screening force it was hot and crews were tired. Captain Howard Bode, left in command on Crutchley's departure, slept soundly on board his cruiser *Chicago*. The approach of Mikawa's force was undetected until far too late. The destroyer *Patterson* raised the alarm at almost the same moment that Japanese floatplanes dropped flares to illuminate *Chicago* and the Australian cruiser *Canberra*. Hit by gunfire and torpedoes from four Japanese cruisers, *Canberra* was wrecked in minutes. Bode, rudely torn from his sleep, succeeded in extracting *Chicago* from the action with relatively little damage, but his flight left the rest of the ships exposed. Other Allied warships fatally hesitated to open fire on Japanese searchlights, unsure whether they would be hitting friendly vessels. The cruisers *Astoria*, *Quincy,* and *Vincennes* were all sunk after multiple hits from shells and torpedoes.

Mikawa could have gone on to destroy the Allied transport ships, but he was unaware that the US carrier aircraft were no longer there and wanted to get away before daylight. The Japanese cruiser *Kako* was sunk by a submarine on its way back from the action, a small consolation for the battered Allies.

Torpedo damage
Crewmen on the heavy cruiser USS *Chicago* cut away torpedo-damaged plating on the day after the battle of Savo Island.

Mikawa withdraws before daylight in case US carriers are present

Savo Island

The Japanese raid caught US forces largely by surprise. However, Mikawa missed the opportunity to destroy the transports supporting the US troops on Guadalcanal.

Vincennes

Savo Island

US transports

Florida Island

Astoria

Quincy

Pacific Ocean

Canberra

San Juan and Hobart guard eastern entrance to passage and take no part in battle

Chicago and Canberra, guarding Southern approach, are surprised by Japanese. Chicago flees battle leaving the transports exposed

US transports

Admiral Crutchley is in conference on Australia and takes no part in battle

KEY

▶	1 Japanese cruiser, stage 1
▶	1 Japanese cruiser, stage 2
▶	1 US cruiser, stage 1
▶	1 US cruiser, stage 2
▶	1 sunk US cruiser

Guadalcanal Island

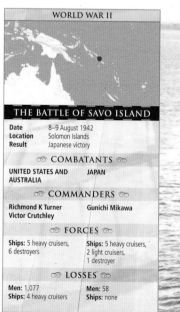

WORLD WAR II

THE BATTLE OF SAVO ISLAND

Date	8–9 August 1942
Location	Solomon Islands
Result	Japanese victory

◌ COMBATANTS ◌

UNITED STATES AND AUSTRALIA	JAPAN

◌ COMMANDERS ◌

Richmond K Turner Victor Crutchley	Gunichi Mikawa

◌ FORCES ◌

Ships: 5 heavy cruisers, 6 destroyers	**Ships:** 5 heavy cruisers, 2 light cruisers, 1 destroyer

◌ LOSSES ◌

Men: 1,077 **Ships:** 4 heavy cruisers	**Men:** 58 **Ships:** none

1918 – PRESENT

WORLD WAR II

EASTERN SOLOMONS

Date 24 August 1942
Forces Americans: 2 carriers, 1 battleship, 4 cruisers, 11 destroyers; Japanese: 2 carriers, 1 light carrier, 2 battleships, 16 cruisers, 25 destroyers
Losses Americans: 25 aircraft; Japanese: 1 escort carrier, 75 aircraft

Location Off Solomon Islands

Encouraged by their victory at Savo Island, the Japanese devised Operation Ka, a counter-offensive whose twin objectives were to retake Guadalcanal from the US Marines and to establish naval dominance in the South Pacific by the destruction of American fleet carriers. On 20 August 1942 3,000 soldiers embarked on transport ships at the Japanese base of Rabaul and headed for Guadalcanal to reinforce a first wave of troops already ashore. Admiral Yamamoto, commander-in-chief of the Japanese Combined Fleet, hoped this troop convoy would lure the American carriers into a trap. His fleet carriers *Shokaku* and *Zuikako*, under Admiral Chuichi Nagumo, would surprise and destroy them, allowing a powerful force of battleships and cruisers to mop up the remaining American ships and support the retaking of Guadalcanal.

In the event, the American carriers *Enterprise*, *Saratoga*, and *Wasp*, under Admiral Frank Fletcher, were already heading toward Guadalcanal in response

to the original Japanese landings. Because of confused intelligence reports, Fletcher was unsure whether the Japanese Combined Fleet was in the area. On 23 August an American reconnaissance aircraft spotted the troop transports, but in the absence of any sighting of carriers Admiral Fletcher sent *Wasp* away to refuel. The following morning there were more sightings of Japanese ships, including the light carrier *Ryujo*.

BOMBER ATTACKS

In the early afternoon, still unaware of the approaching Japanese fleet carriers, Fletcher ordered a strike by aircraft from *Saratoga* against *Ryujo*, which was duly sunk. Meanwhile, Admiral Nagumo, having located the American carriers, launched waves of torpedo-bombers and dive-bombers to attack

Japanese navy sextant
Sextants were used to calculate latitude so Japanese officers could navigate around the Pacific Ocean.

them. The incoming Japanese aircraft were picked up on US radar and carrier-based F4F Wildcat fighters flown off to engage them, but despite their best efforts and those of anti-aircraft gunners on the ships, some of the Japanese bombers got through. *Enterprise* received the brunt of the aerial onslaught. Hit by three bombs in rapid succession, the carrier was on fire, listing, and for a time without steering control, yet she survived.

After this the battle petered out, the Japanese battleships and cruisers giving up efforts to locate the US carriers soon after nightfall. The attempt to land einforcements was abandoned the following day.

BEFORE GUADALCANAL THE ENEMY ADVANCED AT HIS PLEASURE – AFTER GUADALCANAL HE RETREATED AT OURS.

ADMIRAL WILLIAM HALSEY, DESCRIBING THE SIGNIFICANCE OF THE CAMPAIGN FOR GUADALCANAL

WORLD WAR II

CAPE ESPERANCE

Date 11–12 October 1942
Forces Americans: 4 cruisers, 5 destroyers; Japanese: 3 cruisers, 2 destroyers
Losses Americans: 1 destroyer; Japanese: 1 cruiser, 1 destroyer

Location Off Cape Esperance, Guadalcanal

Both sides reinforced their troops on Guadalcanal as the ground fighting intensified. On the night of 11-12 October a group of Japanese destroyers was ferrying in soldiers and equipment while another force under Rear Admiral Goto was sent to bombard the airbase at Henderson Field. A US Navy task force of cruisers and destroyers, commanded by Rear Admiral Norman Scott aboard *San Francisco*, had orders to stop Japanese ships entering Ironbottom Sound. Goto's force of three cruisers and a destroyer, detected by radar, was surprised off Savo Island around midnight. Goto's flagship *Aoba* was immediately hit and the admiral fatally wounded. Two other Japanese ships were sunk by gunfire and torpedoes, but the Americans also suffered losses. The light cruiser *Boise*'s magazine exploded killing almost 100 men, and the destroyer *Duncan* was sunk, shelled by both sides in the confusion. Although on balance an American victory, the battle failed to stop the Japanese continuing to land troops.

ANTI-AIRCRAFT DEFENCE

American naval defence against air attack improved steadily in the course of the Pacific War. Carrier task forces adopted a circular formation, with carriers in the centre surrounded first by a circle of battleships and cruisers and then by an outer ring of destroyers. These ships between them threw up an impressive weight of anti-aircraft fire. The carriers also provided aerial defence, their fighter aircraft guided onto incoming aircraft by radar controllers on the ships. Naval anti-aircraft guns ranged from 5in guns for long-range fire

to 40mm Bofors for medium-range and 0.50in machine guns or 20mm Oerlikons for close-range fire. Improving fire-control systems increased the chances of hitting a rapidly moving target, but probably the most important development in the war was the adoption of radar proximity fuses. These made shells explode when close to an enemy aircraft, rather than at a pre-set time after firing. The sheer number of guns on ships vastly increased as well as their quality. By 1945 the American battleship *South Dakota*, for example, mounted 16 5in, 68 40mm and 76 20mm guns.

Oerlikon 20mm cannon
The Swiss-designed Oerlikon was one of the most widely used anti-aircraft guns of World War II.

Anti-aircraft gun crew
Sailors man a Oerlikon 20mm anti-aircraft gun during training on board the USS *Iowa* in 1943.

WORLD WAR II

SANTA CRUZ

Date 26 October 1942
Forces Americans: 2 carriers, 1 battleship, 6 cruisers, 14 destroyers; Japanese: 4 carriers, 2 battleships, 10 cruisers, 22 destroyers

Location Off Santa Cruz Islands, Solomon Islands

Losses Americans: 1 carrier, 1 destroyer, c.80 aircraft; Japanese: c.200 aircraft

In October 1942 the United States had only two carriers, *Hornet* and *Enterprise*, operational in the Pacific. Rear Admiral Thomas Kinkaid, on board *Enterprise*, led them on a sweep north of the Santa Cruz Islands, searching for a Japanese naval force bound for Guadalcanal. The Japanese, under Vice Admiral Kondo, had the carriers *Shokaku*, *Zuikaku*, *Zuiho*, and *Junyo*, as well as a powerful force of battleships and cruisers.

On the morning of 26 October the opposing carriers located one another and launched air strikes. The first American and Japanese attack waves crossed in flight. The American attack put the carriers *Zuiho* and *Shokaku* out of action, along with the cruiser *Chikuma*. But the Japanese strike was more deadly. Combat air patrols failed to stop the Japanese dive-bombers and torpedo-bombers and the US carriers took a pounding. *Hornet* was hit first and worst. The Japanese struck her with bombs and torpedoes, and with two aircraft that, deliberately or not, crashed into the ship. *Hornet* was left dead in the water and on fire. *Enterprise*, initially hidden by a rain-shower, soon came in for her own share of attention and suffered serious bomb damage. Many US aircraft were forced to ditch in the sea for lack of a deck to land on. Japanese losses of aircraft were, however, far heavier, for they pursued their attacks with relentless courage through a storm of anti-aircraft fire.

An attempt to take *Hornet* under tow failed as further waves of Japanese aircraft attacked. The carrier was eventually abandoned and finally sunk by a torpedo. For a short period after the battle, until *Enterprise* had been repaired, the United States had no aircraft carriers in the Pacific. Yet the Japanese had suffered such heavy losses of experienced pilots – 148 aircrew killed – that they were in no position to exploit this temporary advantage.

Dive-bomber attack
A Japanese "Val" bomber dives on the USS *Hornet* during the battle of Santa Cruz. Seconds later the plane crashed into the *Hornet*'s signal bridge.

THE NAVAL BATTLE OF GUADALCANAL

In November 1942 the Japanese planned to turn the battle for Guadalcanal decisively in their favour by mounting a naval bombardment on the American airstrip at Henderson's Field and landing thousands of reinforcements on the island. The operation would take place by night to avoid attack by aircraft from the airfield and the carrier *Enterprise*.

On the night of 12–13 November Vice Admiral Hiroaki Abe led a force of two Japanese battleships and 12 smaller warships into "Ironbottom Sound" off northern Guadalcanal – so named for the number of ships sunk there. As usual, the Americans had forewarning of the Japanese movements and sent a force of five cruisers and eight destroyers to meet them. The Japanese and American ships blundered into one another in the dark and a brutal, disorganized fight broke out at close quarters – memorably described by one US officer as like "a bar-room brawl after the lights had been shot out". In the confused mêlée both Admiral Callaghan and his second-in-command were killed – the latter probably by "friendly fire". The Japanese battleship *Hiei* took significant damage, but the Americans suffered worse. By the time the Japanese disengaged only two US ships were still in a condition to fight. The next day the limping *Hiei* was attacked by American land-based and carrier aircraft and eventually scuttled.

ROUND TWO

Nothing could be done to stop the Japanese bombarding Henderson's Field the following night, but by 14–15 November the Americans had brought a new force into play, consisting of the battleships *Washington* and *South Dakota* and four screening destroyers. This force encountered the advancing Japanese

Japanese Naval Landing Forces helmet
Japanese attempts to land troop reinforcements on Guadalcanal were repulsed after two nights of savage naval fighting.

battleship *Kirishima* and 13 other ships shortly before midnight. The destroyers screening the American battleships performed their role courageously, but two were quickly sunk, a third so badly damaged it sank the following day, and the fourth disabled. Meanwhile the battleship *South Dakota* suffered a series of electrical failures that left her exposed to a pounding from the Japanese guns.

Washington, however, succeeded in stealing up on the Japanese ships unnoticed and hit *Kirishima* with a sudden devastating salvo that set the battleship ablaze. The night's action ended with the Japanese scuttling *Kirishima*.

The battle of Guadalcanal doomed Japanese plans to reinforce the island. By 15 November seven Japanese transport ships had been sunk by air attack. The remaining four transports beached that morning and were quickly destroyed by American bombardment from air, land, and sea. The ultimate outcome of the battle was that the Americans could strengthen and supply their forces on Guadalcanal while the Japanese could not.

WORLD WAR II

GUADALCANAL

Date 12–15 November 1942
Location Off Guadalcanal, Solomon Islands
Result American strategic victory

COMBATANTS

UNITED STATES	JAPAN

COMMANDERS

Daniel J Callaghan	Hiroaki Abe
Willis A Lee	Nobutake Kondo

FORCES

Ships: 1 carrier, 2 battleships, 5 cruisers, 12 destroyers	**Ships:** 2 battleships, 8 cruisers, 16 destroyers

LOSSES

Men: 1,732	**Men:** 1,900
Ships: 2 cruisers, 7 destroyers	**Ships:** 2 battleships, 1 cruiser, 3 destroyers

WITNESS TO WAR

COMMANDER CHIHAYA MASATAKA

OFFICER ON BOARD JAPANESE BATTLESHIP HIEI, NIGHT OF 12–13 NOVEMBER 1942

BATTLE OF GUADALCANAL

*"I think it was **about a minute** before I was due to give the order to **start bombarding** [Henderson's Field] when, all of a sudden, the look-out on the bridge shouted out: "**Enemy ships starboard ahead!**" – I can still remember it. There was no time to get permission from my commanding officer. I shouted: "**Change target! New target!** Enemy ships starboard ahead! Start bombardment with searchlights on!"… **The ships fought at close quarters**, almost falling aboard each other. We missed our antiquated rams very badly."*

1886–1969
RAYMOND A SPRUANCE

US ADMIRAL AND COMMANDER OF US FORCES AT MIDWAY AND THE PHILIPPINE SEA

A career naval officer, Raymond Spruance commanded a cruiser division in the early stages of the Pacific War. Despite having no previous experience of carriers, he was given command of Task Force 16 in time to play a vital part in the crucial battle of Midway in June 1942. As commander of the US 5th Fleet from 1943 he spearheaded the drive through the central Pacific, presiding over the destruction of Japanese naval aviation at the battle of the Philippine Sea. Sometimes criticized as over-cautious, Spruance enjoyed an exceptional record of success in major naval engagements.

WEAPONS AND TECHNOLOGY

FIRE CONTROL SYSTEMS

The increasing range of naval guns and speed of warships from the late 19th century onward led to the introduction of fire control systems to replace gunners sighting by eye. Personnel aloft in the director tower were equipped with optical instruments to gauge the bearing and range of a target to a fine degree of accuracy. They also "spotted" the splash of shells to provide feedback to correct the aim. Information from aloft was transmitted to an armoured plotting room below the decks, where the data was combined with other input – the movement of the ship, wind speed and direction, and so on – to produce a "firing solution". Analogue computers were developed to permit fast and accurate update of the calculation in a rapidly changing situation. The firing solution was then transmitted electronically to the gun turrets, usually appearing as a visual pointer indicating the correct elevation and bearing. The gunner matched the pointer on his gun to the desired position and the guns were ready to fire. The use of radar and increasingly complex computers allowed large strides to be made in speed and accuracy of fire during World War II.

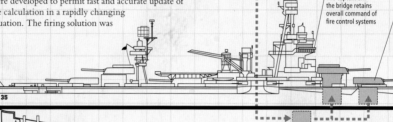

The adoption of radar during World War II increased the speed and accuracy of readings

Observers in gun director tower take readings for range, speed, and bearing and send the information to the plotting room

The captain on the bridge retains overall command of fire control systems

The pointer and trainer in the gun turret aims the guns by matching needles in the director indicator. The guns fire when the ship rolls to a level position.

Data is processed in the plotting room at the fire control table (a kind of simple analog computer) and the gun elevation and train angles are transmitted to the turret

Director firing
Most of the guns on a large warship were directed – the person firing the gun relied on a series of readings and calculations taken elsewhere on the ship.

Wrecked Japanese transport
Japanese cargo ship *Kinugawa Maru* lies beached and gutted on the Guadalcanal coast, destroyed by US aircraft after the naval battle of Guadalcanal.

WORLD WAR II

TASSAFARONGA

Date 30 November 1942
Forces Americans: 5 cruisers, 4 destroyers; Japanese 8 destroyers
Losses Americans: 5 cruisers, 4 destroyers; Japanese: 8 destroyers

Location Off Guadalcanal, Solomon Islands

In response to a shortage of supplies, Japanese destroyers under Rear Admiral Raizo were delivering drums of food by night to troops based on Guadalcanal when they were intercepted by Task Force 67 commanded by Rear Admiral Wright. The five cruisers in Wright's force had an overwhelming superiority in firepower and possessed radar, which the Japanese did not. On detecting the Japanese ships there was a brief delay before permission to start firing was granted. Once the word was given the Americans concentrated their fire on a single ship, *Takanami*. She was quickly incapacitated, but in the interim the other Japanese destroyers had converged. None of the torpedoes that were fired by the American force found their mark. Guided onto target by the flashes of the American guns, however, the Japanese destroyers delivered a series of devastating torpedo attacks that left *Minneapolis*, *New Orleans*, and *Pensacola* holed and on fire. *Northampton* was the last cruiser hit; struck by two torpedoes, she sank in the course of the night. All of the Japanese destroyers except *Takanami* escaped unscathed, but did not succeed in delivering the supplies.

DRIVE TO VICTORY

THE AMERICAN WAR EFFORT in the Pacific began inexorably to gather momentum after 1943. At first naval action was confined to relatively small-scale engagements around the Solomons and in the North Pacific, but from November 1943 the United States began a drive through the Central Pacific to the Marshall and Mariana Islands, and from New Guinea to the Philippines. Attempting to resist this advance, the Japanese navy committed its forces to major battles at the Philippine Sea and Leyte Gulf. These epic engagements revealed the overwhelming naval superiority the Americans had achieved by this stage in the war. After Leyte Gulf the Japanese navy could only put up meaningful resistance by operating naval aircraft from land bases. Using kamikaze tactics they inflicted heavy losses on the Allied fleet at Okinawa in 1945, but by then Japan had already lost the naval war.

THE WAR IN THE PACIFIC 1943–1945

By late 1943 the tide of the Pacific War had turned and the US Navy began its long, inexorable advance through the Pacific toward Japan, one island to the next. The destruction of the Japanese Navy and naval aviation at Leyte Gulf and the Philippine Sea opened the way to the Japanese home islands.

KEY
- – – Area under Japanese control Jan 1943
- ⇨ US/Allied landing/advance
- ⚔ US/Allied victory
- ⚔ Inconclusive battle

WORLD WAR II
BISMARCK SEA

Date 2–3 March 1943
Forces Americans: 168 aircraft; Japanese: 8 destroyers, 8 transports
Losses Americans: 5 aircraft; Japanese: 4 destroyers, 8 transports
Location Off Papua New Guinea, Bismarck Sea

In 1943 the Allies installed elements of the US 5th Army Air Force and the Royal Australian Air Force at bases on New Guinea to intercept Japanese convoys ferrying troops from their base at Rabaul across the Bismarck Sea. On 1 March 1943 a convoy of eight Japanese troop transports with destroyer escorts, under Rear Admiral Masatomi Kimura, was spotted heading for Lae in New Guinea. One of the transports was sunk by B-17 bombers on 2 March, but the main air strike was delivered on the following morning. American B-25 Mitchell bombers and Australian Bristol Beaufighters attacked at low altitude with torpedoes, "skip" bombs – released onto the water to bounce into their target – and strafing guns.

The Japanese destroyers *Shirayuki*, *Arashio*, *Tokitsukaze*, and *Asashio* were sunk, along with all the troop transports. On the day after the bombings Allied aircraft and torpedo boats systematically machine-gunned all the survivors they found in the water. Almost 2,900 Japanese soldiers and sailors were killed in what General Douglas MacArthur described as "one of the most complete and annihilating combats of all time".

WORLD WAR II
KOMANDORSKI ISLANDS

Date 27 March 1943
Forces Americans: 2 cruisers, 4 destroyers; Japanese: 4 cruisers, 4 destroyers
Losses Americans: none; Japanese: none
Location South of Komandorski Islands, North Pacific

The heavy cruiser *Salt Lake City*, the light cruiser *Richmond*, and four American destroyers, all commanded by Rear Admiral Charles McMorris, were sent into the North Pacific to block the path of a Japanese convoy bound for the Aleutian Islands. McMorris encountered the convoy on 27 March, only to find it escorted by a stronger force of warships than his own. Vice Admiral Boshiro Hosogaya had the heavy cruisers *Nachi* and *Maya*, plus light cruisers and destroyers.

The Americans first steamed toward the convoy, but soon judged it wiser to stage a fighting withdrawal. *Nachi* was the first ship hit, but *Salt Lake City* ran into serious difficulties as the shelling intensified, losing steering and power. As she sat dead in the water, the US destroyers laid a protective smokescreen in front of her and launched torpedo attacks against the Japanese cruisers while under heavy fire. *Salt Lake City* fortunately got her engines restarted and the Japanese turned away, short of ammunition and fuel. This inconclusive encounter was one of the last in naval history in which large ships battled almost exclusively with gunnery.

WORLD WAR II
KULA GULF

Date 6 July 1943
Forces Americans: 3 cruisers, 4 destroyers; Japanese: 10 destroyers
Losses Americans: 1 cruiser; Japanese: 2 destroyers
Location Solomon Islands, South Pacific

In summer 1943 the Americans were fighting for control of the Solomons. On the night of 5-6 July 10 Japanese destroyers commanded by Rear Admiral Teruo Akiyama on board *Niizuki*, were carrying reinforcements to Kolombangara Island. This "Tokyo Express" was intercepted by Rear Admiral Walden Ainsworth's force of light cruisers and destroyers. The Japanese, newly equipped with search radar, spotted the Americans first and three destroyers turned for a torpedo run. *Niizuki* was hit by radar-directed fire from the US cruisers and sank, with Admiral Akiyama among those killed. But the two other destroyers fired longlance torpedoes before turning away. The cruiser *Helena* was struck by several torpedoes and sank. Another Japanese destroyer ran aground and was demolished by American aircraft after daylight, leaving honours roughly even.

WORLD WAR II
EMPRESS AUGUSTA BAY

Date 2 November 1943
Forces Americans: 4 cruisers, 8 destroyers; Japanese: 4 cruisers, 6 destroyers
Losses Americans: none; Japanese: 1 cruiser, 1 destroyer
Location Off Bougainville Island, South Pacific

On 1 November 1943 14,000 US Marines were landed on Bougainville in the Solomon Islands. In response the Japanese sent a hastily assembled naval force from Rabaul under Admiral Sentaro Omori. American light cruisers and destroyers commanded by Rear Admiral Aaron "Tip" Merrill took up position to defend the landings. In principle the Japanese force was much the stronger, as it included the heavy cruisers *Myoko* and *Haguro*. Both sides engaged in complex manoeuvres in the dark, creating considerable confusion.

The US destroyer *Foote* lost touch with its formation and was hit by a stray torpedo that blew off the back of the ship, although she was eventually towed to safety. Various Japanese ships careered just past or into one another, *Myoko* slicing through the destroyer *Hatsukaze* – she carried the destroyer's bow back to port with her. The light cruiser *Sendai* was disabled by multiple hits from American guns, but in general both sides expended shells to little effect. *Omori* broke off the engagement before daybreak, convinced he had inflicted far more damage than was actually the case. *Sendai* and *Hatsukaze* were left behind to be finished off by the Americans. Several hundred Japanese were killed in the engagement; 19 American lives were lost.

THE BATTLE OF THE PHILIPPINE SEA

By the summer of 1944 the Americans held the strategic initiative in the Pacific War. Without any source of intelligence on US planning, the Japanese were reduced to guessing where the next blow might fall. The target chosen by the Americans in June 1944 was the Mariana Islands, which would provide bases for bomber aircraft within range of Japan. Admiral Raymond Spruance sent Task Force 58 under Vice Admiral Marc Mitscher to support landings on Saipan with bombardment by carrier aircraft and naval guns. Japanese Vice Admiral Osawa Jisaburo, with a force of carriers and battleships, was 3,000km (2,000 miles) to the south when the Japanese realized the Marianas would be the next battleground. He steamed north at speed, hoping to catch the Americans between his carriers and airbases on the islands.

The battle began on the morning of 19 June. For the Japanese it was an unmitigated disaster. The waves of aircraft sent to attack the American fleet met a sophisticated defence system. Incoming aircraft were detected by radar, allowing the carrier Combat Information Centres to scramble fighters and vector them onto the intruders. The Japanese pilots were less experienced than the Americans and had no aircraft to match the Grumman Hellcats. The few who survived being pounced on by the fighters were shot down by anti-aircraft fire. In total the Japanese lost over 300 aircraft in what became known as the "Marianas Turkey Shoot". Meanwhile, American submarines preyed on the Japanese carrier force with first *Taiho* and then *Shokaku* struck by torpedoes.

The following day Mitscher sought to complete the victory with an air strike on the Japanese fleet. The Americans did not locate the enemy naval force until late in the afternoon. Mitscher decided to launch his aircraft although they would be operating at extreme range and would have to return after nightfall. The attack was largely successful, sinking the carrier *Hiyo* for the loss of just a handful of aircraft, but the return journey proved to be a nightmare for the naval aircrews. Some 80 aircraft ran out of fuel before reaching the US carriers and were forced to ditch in the ocean, although the majority of the aircrews were rescued.

The battle of the Philippine Sea destroyed the Japanese carriers as a fighting force. The losses of aircraft and pilots were even more crippling than the losses of ships. Another step had been taken toward the total dominance of the US Navy in the Pacific.

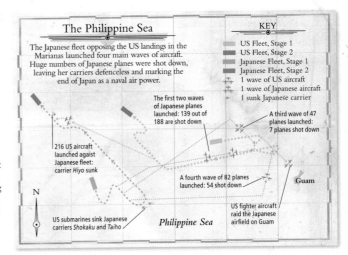

The Philippine Sea

The Japanese fleet opposing the US landings in the Marianas launched four main waves of aircraft. Huge numbers of Japanese planes were shot down, leaving her carriers defenceless and marking the end of Japan as a naval air power.

KEY

- US Fleet, Stage 1
- US Fleet, Stage 2
- Japanese Fleet, Stage 1
- Japanese Fleet, Stage 2
- 1 wave of US aircraft
- 1 wave of Japanese aircraft
- 1 sunk Japanese carrier

The first two waves of Japanese planes launched: 139 out of 188 are shot down

A third wave of 47 planes launched: 7 planes shot down

216 US aircraft launched agaist Japanese fleet: carrier Hiyo sunk

A fourth wave of 82 planes launched: 54 shot down

Guam

US fighter aircraft raid the Japanese airfield on Guam

US submarines sink Japanese carriers Shokaku and Taiho

Philippine Sea

N

WORLD WAR II

THE PHILIPPINE SEA

Date	19–20 June 1944
Location	Philippine Sea, Western Pacific
Result	United States Victory

∞ COMBATANTS ∞

UNITED STATES	**JAPAN**

∞ COMMANDERS ∞

Raymond Spruance	**Osawa Jisaburo**
Marc Mitscher	

∞ FORCES ∞

Ships: 15 carriers, 7 battleships, 21 cruisers, 69 destroyers	**Ships:** 9 carriers, 5 battleships, 13 cruisers, 28 destroyers

∞ LOSSES ∞

Ships: none	**Ships:** 3 carriers
Aircraft: 123	**Aircraft:** 600

Battleship Iowa
USS *Iowa*'s huge 16in guns were used to bombard Japanese positions on Saipan and Tinian during the Marianas campaign, and helped to protect the US carriers at the battle of the Philippine Sea.

Turkey Shoot
Part of the propeller from a Japanese plane that crashed into the carrier *Essex* during the one-sided air battle American aviators and sailors nicknamed the "Marianas Turkey Shoot".

THE BATTLE OF LEYTE GULF

On 20 October 1944 US forces began landing on Leyte island as the first stage in the invasion of the Philippines. Admiral Thomas Kinkaid's 7th Fleet was responsible for the amphibious operation, while Admiral William Halsey's 3rd Fleet was on hand to help resist any effort by the Japanese navy to disrupt the invasion. Japan had in fact drawn up plans to meet this contingency and these were swiftly implemented. Virtually all available Japanese naval forces were to be thrown into a death-or-glory battle on an awesome scale.

By this stage in the war, after the disaster of the battle of the Philippine Sea, Japan had few carriers and barely any carrier aircraft, but still possessed a formidable tonnage of large battleships and cruisers. These would have to rely on land-based aircraft from the Philippines for air cover. The Japanese plan, Operation Sho-Go, envisaged

simultaneous thrusts by Admiral Takeo Kurita's Centre Force through the Sibuyan Sea and by Admiral Shoji Nishimura's Southern Force through the Sula Sea, emerging to the east of the Philippines to catch Kinkaid's ships in a pincer from north and south. Admiral Ozawa's force of four impotent aircraft-less carriers was to provide a suicidal decoy for the Americans, drawing some of their fleet away to the north. The plan was ambitious, complex, and very unlikely to succeed.

THE BATTLES BEGIN

Admiral Kurita's Centre Force, with five battleships including the giants *Yamato* and *Musashi*, set out for the Philippines on 22 October. It suffered its first losses within 24 hours when two cruisers, including Kurita's flagship *Atago,* were sunk by American submarines. Picked up out of the sea, the admiral shifted

his flag to *Yamoto* and pressed on, entering the Sibuyan Sea on 24 October. There his ships were spotted by Halsey's carrier aircraft and an air-sea battle commenced. Japanese aircraft based on Luzon succeeded in destroying the light carrier *Princeton* at great cost to themselves in aircraft and pilots lost, but they could not prevent waves of American carrier aircraft striking the Japanese fleet, putting 19 bombs and 17 torpedoes into *Musashi* before the leviathan finally sunk.

At this point the Americans made an error that could have cost them dearly. Believing that Kurita had turned back to escape air attack, Halsey departed northward, accepting the bait offered by

> ## WOULD IT NOT BE A SHAME TO HAVE THE FLEET REMAIN INTACT WHILE OUR NATION PERISHES? ... YOU MUST ALL OF YOU REMEMBER THAT THERE ARE SUCH THINGS AS MIRACLES.
>
> **ADMIRAL TAKEO KURITA** BRIEFING HIS OFFICERS BEFORE THE BATTLE OF LEYTE GULF

1885–1966
CHESTER NIMITZ
COMMANDER-IN-CHIEF OF PACIFIC NAVAL FORCES

Born in Texas into a family of German origin, Chester Nimitz graduated from the US Naval Academy in 1905. After earning a reprimand as a young ensign for running a destroyer aground, he transferred to submarines and during World War I acted as chief of staff of the US Atlantic Submarine Force. Promoted to rear admiral in 1938, he was chief of the Bureau of Navigation when the Japanese attacked Pearl Harbor. Ten days later he was appointed commander-in-chief of the Pacific Fleet. During a period of Japanese naval superiority, Nimitz followed an aggressive strategy based on calculated risk. This bore fruit in the crucial victory at Midway in 1942. He masterminded the subsequent "island-hopping" drive through the Central Pacific toward Japan. Nimitz was appointed a fleet admiral in 1944 and was a signatory at the Japanese surrender ceremony in Tokyo Bay in October 1945.

Ozawa's carrier force. Communication between the two American commanders was poor and Kinkaid mistakenly thought Halsey had left part of his fleet covering the northern flank of the invasion force. He had not. Meanwhile, Kinkaid sent most of his warships south to meet Admiral Shoji Nishimura's two battleships, cruiser, and four destroyers coming through the Surigao Strait.

Emerging from the strait in line ahead in the dark early hours of 25 October, the Japanese ships were ambushed by US destroyers firing a total of 27 torpedoes and sinking the battleship *Fuso* and three destroyers.

Landings at Leyte Gulf
Two US Coast Guard-manned LSTs (Landing Ships Tank) open their jaws onto Leyte Beach. While the initial landings were not strongly opposed, the Japanese Navy subsequently threw all the forces they had left against the invading forces.

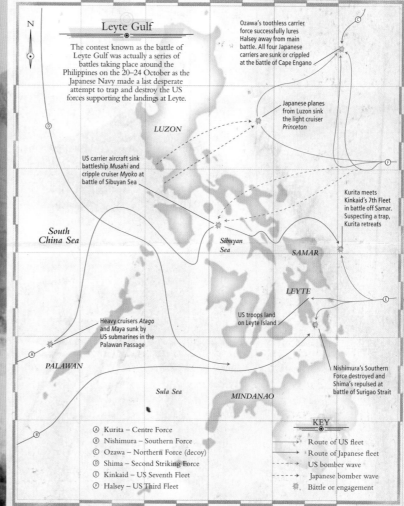

Leyte Gulf

The contest known as the battle of Leyte Gulf was actually a series of battles taking place around the Philippines on the 20–24 October as the Japanese Navy made a last desperate attempt to trap and destroy the US forces supporting the landings at Leyte.

Ozawa's toothless carrier force successfully lures Halsey away from main battle. All four Japanese carriers are sunk or crippled at the battle of Cape Engano

Japanese planes from Luzon sink the light cruiser *Princeton*

US carrier aircraft sink battleship *Musashi* and cripple cruiser *Myoko* at battle of Sibuyan Sea

Kurita meets Kinkaid's 7th Fleet in battle off Samar. Suspecting a trap, Kurita retreats

Heavy cruisers *Atago* and *Maya* sunk by US submarines in the Palawan Passage

US troops land on Leyte Island

Nishimura's Southern Force destroyed and Shima's repulsed at battle of Surigao Strait

LUZON

South China Sea

Sibuyan Sea

SAMAR

LEYTE

PALAWAN

Sula Sea

MINDANAO

KEY
Ⓐ Kurita – Centre Force
Ⓑ Nishimura – Southern Force
Ⓒ Ozawa – Northern Force (decoy)
Ⓓ Shima – Second Striking Force
Ⓔ Kinkaid – US Seventh Fleet
Ⓕ Halsey – US Third Fleet

→ Route of US fleet
⇢ Route of Japanese fleet
----→ US bomber wave
------ Japanese bomber wave
✺ Battle or engagement

CARRIERS, SUBMARINES, AND MISSILES

Exhausted survivors
A US patrol torpedo boat hoists Japanese survivors out of the water after the destruction of the Japanese forces at Leyte Gulf.

Nishimura's flagship *Yamashiro* was hit but pressed on. At 3:52am the darkness ahead suddenly erupted as a semicircle of waiting American warships opened fire. The most modern of them had radar fire control that left the Japanese no chance. Nishimura was already dead by the time *Yamashiro* sank.

Approaching this scene of carnage, some way behind Nishimura, a second group of warships under Admiral Shima added an element of farce to the tragedy by colliding with the crippled cruiser

No chance of escape
A Japanese heavy cruiser desperately manoeuvres while US bombers send up plumes of water around it. The raid on Manila Bay was part of the American campaign to reconquer the Philippines after Leyte Gulf.

Mogami and then torpedoing an island misidentified as an enemy ship, before fleeing back down the strait.

To the north, meanwhile, Kurita led his ships undetected through the San Bernadino Strait and on the morning of 25 October sailed south down the coast of Samar island toward Leyte. First light revealed a force of 16 American escort carriers and seven destroyers and destroyer escorts lying in his path. As the Japanese ships opened fire, Rear Admiral Sprague radioed desperately for help, believing his carriers would be destroyed in minutes. With outstanding bravery the destroyers attacked the Japanese capital ships, winning the carriers a breathing space. All but one were eventually sunk by Japanese guns and many of the carriers

took hits. But the destroyers and carrier aircraft between them sank three of Kurita's heavy cruisers and badly damaged three more. Although Sprague's carriers were still theoretically at his mercy, Kurita had had enough and turned back, safely withdrawing the remainder of his ships from the battle.

DESPERATE LAST GAMBLE
Admiral Ozawa's carriers and cruisers had performed their function bravely by drawing Halsey's 3rd Fleet away from Leyte, though all to no avail. Their destruction, which took place off Cape Engano, at the northern tip of Luzon, was inevitable – indeed, formed part of the Japanese plan. The only use that remained for the once proud Japanese carrier force was as sacrificial victims.

It was as a response to his pilots' inability to damage enemy ships with conventional tactics that Admiral Ohnishi, commander of the 1st Air Fleet on the Philippines, called for volunteers to carry out suicide attacks. On 21 October, off Leyte, a pilot flew his aircraft into the cruiser *Australia*. Four days later Ohnishi's Special Attack Unit, formally dedicated to kamikaze tactics, began systematic suicide attacks.

On 25–26 October they crashed onto 47 US ships, including seven carriers. The first to be sunk by a kamikaze attack was the escort carrier *St Lô*.

The suicide attacks were a disturbing conclusion to an important American victory. By any measure it had been one of the largest sea battles in history, and the Japanese had lost. Their surface warships would take no further active part in the war, beyond a suicidal gesture at the very end.

KEY	
US FORCES AT SURIGAO STRAIT	
	1 US Battleship
	1 US cruiser
	1 US destroyer squadron
	Several US torpedo boat squadrons
JAPANESE FORCES AT SURIGAO STRAIT	
	1 Japanese battleship
	1 Japanese cruiser
	1–3 Japanese destroyers

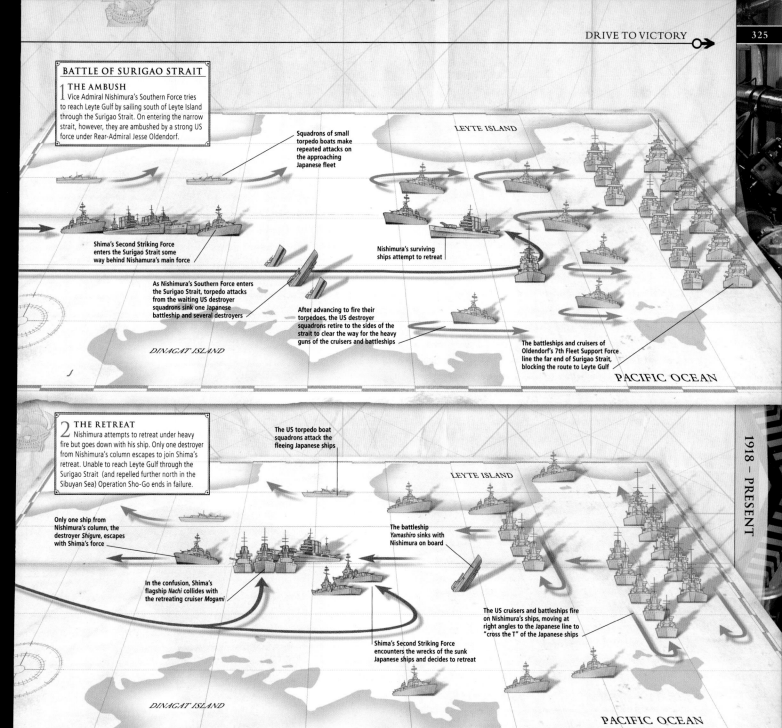

BATTLE OF SURIGAO STRAIT

1 THE AMBUSH

Vice Admiral Nishimura's Southern Force tries to reach Leyte Gulf by sailing south of Leyte Island through the Surigao Strait. On entering the narrow strait, however, they are ambushed by a strong US force under Rear-Admiral Jesse Oldendorf.

Squadrons of small torpedo boats make repeated attacks on the approaching Japanese fleet

LEYTE ISLAND

Shima's Second Striking Force enters the Surigao Strait some way behind Nishimura's main force

Nishimura's surviving ships attempt to retreat

As Nishimura's Southern Force enters the Surigao Strait, torpedo attacks from the waiting US destroyer squadrons sink one Japanese battleship and several destroyers

After advancing to fire their torpedoes, the US destroyer squadrons retire to the sides of the strait to clear the way for the heavy guns of the cruisers and battleships

DINAGAT ISLAND

The battleships and cruisers of Oldendorf's 7th Fleet Support Force line the far end of Surigao Strait, blocking the route to Leyte Gulf

PACIFIC OCEAN

2 THE RETREAT

Nishimura attempts to retreat under heavy fire but goes down with his ship. Only one destroyer from Nishimura's column escapes to join Shima's retreat. Unable to reach Leyte Gulf through the Surigao Strait (and repelled further north in the Sibuyan Sea) Operation Sho-Go ends in failure.

The US torpedo boat squadrons attack the fleeing Japanese ships

LEYTE ISLAND

Only one ship from Nishimura's column, the destroyer *Shigure*, escapes with Shima's force

The battleship *Yamashiro* sinks with Nishimura on board

In the confusion, Shima's flagship *Nachi* collides with the retreating cruiser *Mogami*

Shima's Second Striking Force encounters the wrecks of the sunk Japanese ships and decides to retreat

The US cruisers and battleships fire on Nishimura's ships, moving at right angles to the Japanese line to "cross the T" of the Japanese ships

DINAGAT ISLAND

PACIFIC OCEAN

> ❝
> I HEARD ONE OF THE SIGNALMEN YELL: "GODDAMIT, BOYS, THEY'RE GETTING AWAY!" I COULD NOT BELIEVE MY EYES, BUT IT LOOKED AS IF THE WHOLE JAPANESE FLEET WAS INDEED RETIRING … AT BEST I HAD EXPECTED TO BE SWIMMING BY THIS TIME.
>
> **VICE ADMIRAL CLIFTON SPRAGUE** DESCRIBING THE BATTLE OFF SAMAR
> ❞

WORLD WAR II

IWO JIMA

Date 19 February–26 March 1945
Forces Americans: Over 800 ships, 74,000 Marines; Japanese: 23,000 soldiers
Losses Americans: 1 escort carrier, 1 tank landing craft, 1 infantry landing craft

Location Iwo Jima, Ogasawara Islands

Lying halfway between the Marianas and the Japanese mainland, the small volcanic island of Iwo Jima was of limited military value. But the Americans decided to take the island as a stepping stone across the Pacific, and the Japanese defended it to the death.

The Iwo Jima landings were an amphibious operation on an awesome scale. Almost 500 ships were dedicated to transporting and landing more than 70,000 men of the 3rd, 4th, and 5th Marine Divisions. Hundreds of other ships were deployed in support, including battleships, cruisers, and escort carriers. The US Navy was not expecting interference from the Imperial Japanese Navy, which was no longer a viable

fighting force, and Iwo Jima was far distant from Japanese air bases. The function of the US armada was to bombard the island and land Marines.

The naval bombardment of Iwo Jima began three days before the landings – a much shorter softening-up than the Marines would have liked. Six battleships and an array of cruisers fired a total of 22,000 shells into the island. The actual damage caused by this onslaught and the accompanying aerial bombardment was slight. Under Lieutenant General Tadamichi Kuribayashi, the 22,000 soldiers on the island had created a network of strongpoints and bunkers linked by tunnels deep inside the cave-riddled volcanic rock. When the first wave of Marines came ashore at 8:59am on the morning of 19 February, the Japanese were ready to receive them.

MARINE ASSAULT

The initial landing was not contested. The Japanese only opened fire when a log-jam of Marines and equipment had built up on the beaches, trapped by the volcanic terrain. Sailors bringing landing craft into shore had to contend

WITNESS TO WAR

US SEAMAN WILLIAM P CAMPBELL
CREWMAN ON AMPHIBIOUS VEHICLE DURING LANDINGS AT IWO JIMA

BATTLE OF IWO JIMA

*"We made it in all right carrying in troops off the ship. **My trouble started when I went back** and picked up a load of medical supplies a little after dark. **I went onto the beach and couldn't get off**. They'd shoot flares and it would **light the whole island up, just like it was daylight** … I was at the back of the boat when a shell or mortar hit the front of the boat. **It blew the bow door off it**. We got off that thing and dug a foxhole …"*

not only with enemy fire but also with waves that dashed boats onto the beach. Close support for the Marines from naval guns and carrier aircraft was inhibited by worsening weather. On 21 February the attack carrier *Saratoga* and escort carrier *Bismarck Sea* were hit by attacks from Japanese kamikaze aircraft. *Saratoga* limped away for repairs after fires and explosions caused over 300 casualties on board; *Bismarck Sea* was blown apart and sank with the loss of 318 men.

The outcome of the battle was never in doubt, however the human cost was appalling. By the time the island was finally secured the Marines had suffered over 23,000 casualties and the US Navy around 2,000. Almost all the Japanese soldiers on the island died.

The beaches of Iwo Jima
US Marines make their way up the volcanic beaches on Iwo Jima. The Japanese waited until the beaches were full of men and equipment before opening fire.

WEAPONS AND TECHNOLOGY

AMPHIBIOUS WARFARE

The Americans deployed an impressive range of landing craft and amphibious vehicles during the Pacific War. The most basic was the LCVP (Landing Craft Vehicle Personnel) or Higgins Boat. Men climbed down netting from transports into these shallow-draught wooden boats to be ferried ashore. More than 23,000 LCVPs were built in World War II, along with 11,000 LCMs (Landing Craft Mechanized) designed to carry tanks and other vehicles. The larger LCI (Landing Craft Infantry) was an ocean-going vessel capable of carrying 200 soldiers. Alongside these landing craft a number of inventive types of amphibious vehicle were used. These included the DUKW, an amphibious wheeled truck, and various forms of LVT (Landing Vehicle Tracked). LVTs were basically designed to carry men ashore, but they developed in the course of the war into armoured vehicles, some equipped with turret guns so that they could function as amphibious tanks.

DUKW amphibious truck
This US Navy six-wheel drive truck carried 25 soldiers and could maintain a speed of 5 knots in the water.

Shore bombardment
USS *Idaho*'s big 14in guns Okinawa shortly before the first amphibious assault on 1 April 1945.

THE BATTLE OF OKINAWA

The assault on Okinawa was the largest amphibious operation of the Pacific war. More than half a million Allied personnel were involved in the battle for control of an island regarded by the Japanese as part of their homeland. In many ways the operation resembled the struggle for Iwo Jima, only on a much larger scale. The preliminary naval bombardment to soften up the defences, begun on 21 March, was so intensive that Okinawans called it the "Typhoon of Steel". As at Iwo Jima, the initial landings on 1 April were unopposed. The Japanese soldiers on Okinawa,

numbering over 100,000, were hidden in well-prepared defensive positions from which they could only be removed by months of hard infantry fighting.

OPERATION TEN-GO
The Allied naval forces at Okinawa consisted of the American Fifth Fleet – which included an astonishing 40 carriers and 18 battleships – and Vice Admiral Sir Bernard Rawlings's Royal Navy Task Force, under American operational control. The fleet was in an exposed position, within range of Japanese air bases on Kyushu island in

southern Japan. It was also close enough to tempt the remnants of the Japanese navy into a final sortie, Operation Ten-go. On 6 April Admiral Seiichi Ito sailed out of the Inland Sea on board *Yamato*, the largest

Kamikaze attack
A Japanese suicide pilot can be seen about to crash his plane into the side of the battleship *Missouri* during the battle for Okinawa.

battleship in the world, accompanied by the cruiser *Yahagi* and a handful of destroyers – at that point the entire naval force that Japan could muster. His mission was to attack the Allied fleet off Okinawa. None of the ships was expected to return; they had only been supplied with fuel for a one-way trip.

On 7 April the 11 carriers of Marc Mitscher's Task Force 58 launched three waves of aircraft. Swarming around *Yamato*, they struck time and again with bombs and torpedoes until the battleship turned turtle and exploded, sending up a plume of smoke that could be seen 200km (125 miles) away. The cruiser and four destroyers were also sunk and the operation abandoned.

FINAL SACRIFICE
The Allied fleet did not find it so easy to cope with air attack, however. On 6 April Japanese naval and army aircraft under Vice Admiral Ugaki launched the first mass kamikaze attack with over 300 aircraft. By crashing their aircraft onto warships, young half-trained pilots caused fearsome damage, even though only a small percentage of them penetrated the combat air patrols and

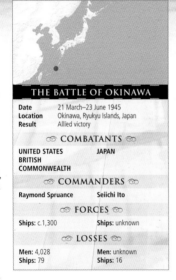

WORLD WAR II

THE BATTLE OF OKINAWA

Date	21 March–23 June 1945
Location	Okinawa, Ryukyu Islands, Japan
Result	Allied victory

COMBATANTS
UNITED STATES	JAPAN
BRITISH COMMONWEALTH	

COMMANDERS
Raymond Spruance	Seiichi Ito

FORCES
Ships: c.1,300	Ships: unknown

LOSSES
Men: 4,028	Men: unknown
Ships: 79	Ships: 16

anti-aircraft fire of the Allied fleet. In raids that continued through to the third week of June, the kamikazes sank more than 40 ships and damaged some 200 others, killing over 5,000 sailors. The fall of Okinawa was a huge relief to the battered and exhausted naval personnel.

> ❝ WE WATCHED EACH PLUNGING KAMIKAZE WITH THE DETACHED HORROR OF ONE WITNESSING A TERRIBLE SPECTACLE RATHER THAN AS THE INTENDED VICTIM. ❞
>
> **VICE ADMIRAL C R BROWN,** DESCRIBING JAPANESE KAMIKAZE ATTACKS

POSTWAR CONFLICTS

IN THE SECOND HALF of the 20th century, the developments in naval tactics and technology evident during World War II continued apace. Big-gun naval vessels were reduced to a shore bombardment role, before virtually disappearing as ever larger aircraft carriers and submarines took centre stage. By the 1960s carriers were operating missile-armed jet aircraft from their decks and nuclear-powered, nuclear-armed submarines had become a central part of the Cold War "nuclear deterrent". Surface warships gained a new lease of life through the introduction of shipborne missiles, which not only equipped escort ships for fleet defence but also provided powerful offensive weapons. The days of pitched battles between fleets seemed over, but the relevance of maritime strength to military power projection remained essential, in particular to the global role of the United States, from the Korean War through to modern Middle East conflicts.

Global reach
Fast Combat Support Ship USS *Bridge* leads a flotilla of vessels in support of Operation Enduring Freedom in 2001. Auxiliary vessels such as the *Bridge* enable the US Navy to refuel, rearm, and restock warships wherever they are in the world, extending US naval power across the globe.

NO BIG BATTLES

Since the end of World War II there have been no major battles at sea. The end of the war found the United States in possession of what was in practice an unchallenged worldwide naval supremacy. Defeated Germany and Japan were denied any significant naval forces. Britain and France still maintained navies of significant size, but were not potential opponents of the United States. The Soviet Union emerged as a global superpower rival for the United States in the Cold War, but the Soviet navy was not a major force in the first decades after the war. When the Soviet Union did develop a major fleet, by the 1970s, both sides planned for a sea conflict that never happened. Indeed, the Soviets and Americans observed rules to prevent hostile encounters between their navies. Thus the Soviet Union did not intervene with its navy during the Korean War in the 1950s, although the United States and its Allies operated large fleets close to the Soviet Pacific coast, and during the Vietnam War the Americans mostly did not interfere with Soviet seaborne supplies of war material to North Vietnam. With the demise of the Soviet Union in 1991, the United States was left with no credible enemy for a

---

WEAPONS AND TECHNOLOGY

NUCLEAR POWER

Nuclear propulsion has now been in existence for over half a century – the first nuclear-powered vessel, the submarine USS *Nautilus,* was launched in 1955. Nuclear power has some impressive advantages over conventional propulsion systems since nuclear reactors produce a high power output and rarely need refuelling. For these reasons, and the fact that nuclear reactors do not require air to operate, nuclear propulsion is ideal for submarines, which spend long periods of time submerged and away from refuelling ships or ports.

Nuclear power has also been used in some surface vessels. A basic steam-turbine nuclear reactor works by generating heat through the fission of nuclear material. The heat converts water to steam, and the steam is used to drive a turbine that powers the vessel's propshaft and generators. Nuclear propulsion is not without disadvantage: heavy and expensive structures need to be put in place to contain the radiation, and the reactor core will continue to be radioactive for hundreds of years after the ship is decommissioned.

Nuclear-powered propulsion
A nuclear engine uses heat exchangers to transfer energy between three systems: a primary system of water pumped through the reactor core; a secondary system that drives the turbines; and a cooling circuit.

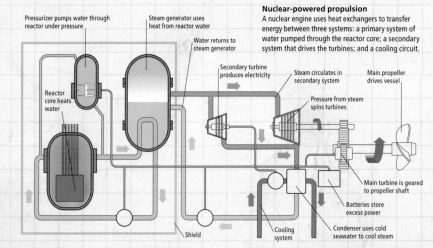

Pressurizer pumps water through reactor under pressure

Steam generator uses heat from reactor water

Water returns to steam generator

Secondary turbine produces electricity

Steam circulates in secondary system

Main propeller drives vessel

Reactor core heats water

Pressure from steam spins turbines

Main turbine is geared to propeller shaft

Batteries store excess power

Shield

Cooling system

Condenser uses cold seawater to cool steam

major war. But the Middle East offered plenty of scope for US power-projection in which naval forces could play a central role.

SUPPORTING LAND FORCES

The largest naval operations since 1945 have been conducted in support of land forces, with firepower deployed for the bombardment of targets on land. During the Korean War and the Vietnam War, big naval guns and carrier aircraft were used by the Americans and their allies on a massive scale to provide fire support and to devastate targets in enemy territory. This pattern was repeated in Iraq and Afghanistan in the 1990s and more recently – although with ship-launched missiles replacing the big warships' heavy guns.

These large-scale operations were largely uncontested at sea, but during the same period several of the world's smaller navies engaged in

some sharp, if mostly limited, naval combat that provided the opportunity for real-life use of developing new technologies and tactics. The Middle East and the Indian subcontinent were the scenes of interesting encounters, including the successful use of a ship-to-ship missile in the sinking of the Israeli destroyer *Eilat* by Egyptian missile boats in 1967. The Falklands War of 1982 was an unequal contest between the Royal Navy and Argentina's small and ageing fleet, but a more balanced contest between the British ships and shore-based Argentinian aircraft armed with advanced missiles as well as bombs.

AWESOME POWER

By the early 21st century the firepower of navies was far beyond anything that had previously existed, even if nuclear warheads were left out of account. The aircraft and missiles of the fleets

assembled by the United States and its allies for operations in Afghanistan and Iraq constituted an awesome concentration of force and sophisticated technology. Nuclear submarines were among the technological wonders of the modern world. Whether such supremely impressive naval forces were a weapon that would continue to suit 21st-century strategic needs in the age of the "War on Terror" remained to be demonstrated.

WEAPONS AND TECHNOLOGY

BALLISTIC MISSILES

Unlike cruise missiles, which take a guided flight path to their targets, ballistic missiles are guided only during the relatively brief powered multi-stage lift-off and initial flight, which takes the missile to sub-orbital altitudes. Thereafter the missile flies on using its own ballistic, free-flight energy, eventually deploying nuclear or conventional warheads at supersonic speeds to the target area. The ranges of these ballistic missiles vary from a few hundred kilometres to more than 5,500km (3,418 miles) in inter-continental versions. Naval ballistic missiles are primarily submarine-launched weapons. The first operational naval model was the Polaris, which entered service with the US Navy in 1961 after a five-year development programme. The latest Trident ballistic missiles have a range of 11,300km (7,000 miles), can reach speeds of 29,0500kph (18,000mph) in sub-orbit, and use star-sighting and inertial guidance systems.

Polaris nuclear missile
The Polaris missile was a submarine-launched, solid-fuel, nuclear-armed, ballistic missile (SLBM), which was carried by British submarines from 1968. It was later replaced by Trident I.

Quiet sentinels
Modern nuclear-powered submarines such as HMS *Astute*, launched by the Royal Navy in 2007, are able to remain submerged for months at a time.

COLD WAR CONFLICTS

AFTER THE END OF World War II the United States and it allies became involved in global resistance to the spread of Communism. Communist triumph in the Chinese Civil War in 1950 was followed by a major war in Korea, where Communist North Korean and Chinese forces fought South Korean and US-led United Nations forces. The navies of the United States and its allies were deployed on a large scale through the three years of the war, operating unchallenged around the whole Korean peninsula. As well as the amphibious operations such as that at Inchon in September 1950, they provided close air support for UN ground forces with carrier aircraft, and flattened North Korean coastal towns with naval gunfire. The fact that both the Communist Soviet Union and the United States possessed nuclear weapons deterred them from fighting one another directly, but a dangerous confrontation developed after Fidel Castro came to power in Cuba in 1959 and allied his country with the Soviets. The possibility that the Soviets might defy a naval blockade imposed on Cuba by the United States during the missile crisis of 1962 brought the world close to nuclear disaster.

CARRIERS, SUBMARINES, AND MISSILES

THE COLD WAR

YANGTZE INCIDENT

Date 20 April–31 March 1949
Forces British: 4 frigates; Chinese: shore batteries
Losses British: none; Chinese: none

Location Yangtze River, near Jiangyin, China

On 20 April 1949, the British frigate HMS *Amethyst* sailed up the politically fraught waters of the Yangtze River in China. At this time, China was split between Chiang Kai-Shek's beleaguered Nationalists and the Communists of Mao Tse-tung's ascendant People's Liberation Army (PLA). The Yangtze River formed one of the frontlines in the conflict. The *Amethyst* was tasked with shipping supplies to the British community at Nanking, and with the relief of the guardship HMS *Consort* stationed there, a journey that would take it through the heart of a war zone. From the outset the *Amethyst* was shelled at close range by several PLA shore batteries, resulting in over 50 hits that killed 17 crewmen and wounded another 30. The commanding officer of the ship, Lieutenant Commander Bernard M Skinner, was among those who were killed during the shelling.

RESCUE MISSION

With the *Amethyst* run aground off Rose Island near Jiangyin, HMS *Consort* launched a spectacular high-speed rescue effort, knocking out several Chinese shore batteries before being forced to retreat. Other rescue attempts by the vessels HMS *Black Swan* and HMS *London* were similarly roughly handled, resulting in many dead and wounded. Thereafter, *Amethyst* remained trapped for 14 weeks during negotiations – during this time the ship's company (under Lieutenant Commander John Kerans) managed to complete major temporary repairs. On the night of 30–31 July *Amethyst* fired up her engines and made a break for the sea in a storm of gunfire. The ship punched through the boom at the mouth of the Yangtze River and made open water and safety. The incident was feted in Britain, and the crew were hailed as heroes.

THE INCHON LANDINGS

In August 1950 United Nations and South Korean forces were pinned in the Pusan area of southern Korea. UN Supreme Commander General Douglas MacArthur planned a bold amphibious operation to land troops behind North Korean lines at Inchon. The conditions for landings were difficult. Inchon had one of the most extreme tidal ranges in the world – around 11m (36ft) maximum variation between low and high tide – and was surrounded by treacherous mudflats. The two sea approaches, the Flying Fish Channel and the Eastern Channel, were narrow and difficult to negotiate. The approaches were dominated by the fortified island of Wolmi-do, which would have to be captured first. On the other hand, the UN forces had total command of the sea and air. The operation, codenamed Chromite, was set for 15 September, when the tide would be high enough to allow large tank landing craft to reach the shore.

AMPHIBIOUS OPERATION

A force of 261 ships, including British and Canadian vessels as well as American, assembled under Vice Admiral Arthur D Struble, although preparations for the landings were disrupted by a typhoon in early September. Diversionary attacks were mounted to disperse the North Korean defences, but Inchon itself was thoroughly softened up with strikes by carrier aircraft. Seven destroyers made a risky foray into the Flying Fish Channel

THE KOREAN WAR

THE INCHON LANDINGS

Date	15 September 1950
Location	South Korea
Result	UN victory

COMBATANTS

UNITED STATES	NORTH KOREA

COMMANDERS

Douglas MacArthur Arthur D Struble	Choi Yong-kun

FORCES

Ships: 261 ships, 40,000 troops	**Ships:** 1,000 troops

LOSSES

Men: 196 **Ships:** none	**Men:** unknown **Ships:** none

US troops land at Inchon
In the course of operations around the port of Inchon, UN forces landed some 50,000 US troops. The Inchon landings led to the recapture of Seoul and turned around UN fortunes in the Korean War.

THE COLD WAR

BAY OF PIGS

Date 17 April 1961
Forces Americans/Cuban exiles:
1 aircraft carrier, 6 destroyers,
4 freighters, 2 landing craft;
Cubans: 15,000 men
Losses Americans/Cuban exiles:
1 freighter sunk; Cubans:
unknown

Location Off coast of
southwest Cuba

In the early 1960s, with Communist dictator Fidel Castro firmly in power in Cuba, relations between the United States and it's Caribbean neighbour were deteriorating fast. In 1961 the US government decided to pursue a military solution. The Central Intelligence Agency (CIA) trained a group of 1,500 Cuban exiles for an invasion of Cuba, with the aim of removing Castro from power. The exiles were to land at the Bay of Pigs in four freighters, alongside two CIA landing craft, with heavy air and fire support from the US carrier *Essex* and six US Navy destroyers.

The landing went in on 17 April 1961. Air strikes destroyed initial Cuban resistance and the landing was successful. However, the landed invasion force was subsequently destroyed over three days of fighting, much to the embarrassment of the US government. Four US pilots also died during engagements over Cuba and Cuban strike jets managed to sink one enemy freighter.

US blockade of Cuba
Soviet tanker *Polzunov* is inspected by the US Navy picket ship *Vesole* as it carries a cargo of ballistic missiles away from Cuba on 9 November, during the Soviet withdrawal of missiles from the island.

---

to test North Korean defences. When shore guns opened up, revealing their location, these were destroyed by air attack and salvoes from cruisers.

On the night of 14–15 September US Marines travelled toward Wolmi-do on board three high-speed destroyers *Bass*, *Diachanko*, and *Wantuck*, preceded by a destroyer escort, followed by large landing craft with heavy equipment, and covered by a force of cruisers. The Marines transferred to landing craft and went ashore at first light, exploiting the morning flood tide. An intense naval bombardment ensured that resistance was slight. The follow-up landings, to the north and south of Wolmi-do, had to

wait for the late afternoon tide. The North Koreans proved unable to mount a swift counterattack, however, and by around 5:30pm Marines were swarming up ladders over sea walls in Inchon itself. Marine casualties on the day amounted to 22 killed and 174 wounded.

The success of the landings led to the recapture of the South Korean capital Seoul and obliged North Korean forces to retreat northward in an effort to avoid encirclement. It also unfortunately tempted MacArthur to take the war into North Korea, leading to the involvement of Chinese troops and a bloody stalemate lasting into 1953. UN naval dominance around Korea was never contested.

THE COLD WAR

CUBAN MISSILE CRISIS

Date 1962
Forces Americans/Allies: 183 warships; Soviets: unknown
Losses Americans/ Allies: none; Soviets: none

Location Atlantic, northeast of Cuba

During the summer of 1962, Soviet engineers and scientists began work on the Communist-controlled island of Cuba, establishing a series of medium-range ballistic missile launch facilities. By using Cuba as a nuclear missile launch-pad, the USSR could target almost the whole of the southern United States. When the facilities were revealed by U-2 reconnaissance flights over the island in October 1962, the missile deployments terrified the US authorities.

The government of John F Kennedy opted to take a tough stance against the Soviets, issuing a demand that the missiles and their facilities be withdrawn from Cuban soil immediately, and threatening a nuclear response against the Soviet Union should it attempt any aggression. The stakes were raised when the United States, with maritime support from Venezuela, Argentina, and Dominica, imposed a naval blockade off Cuba with warships, aircraft carriers, and nuclear-

armed submarines. On 24 October the blockade faced its first challenge with the approach of 19 cargo ships, mostly containing missile equipment, shadowed by Soviet submarines. A dramatic stand-off ensued, which finally resolved itself when most of the Soviet ships turned around in the face of US intransigence.

Only one Soviet ship, the tanker *Bucharest*, managed to make it through to Havana. Tensions escalated and for a time the world teetered on the brink of nuclear war. Ultimately, however, the US naval blockade convinced the Soviet government under Nikita Khrushchev that Cuba was not a viable investment for missile defence. Khrushchev agreed to remove the missile sites from Cuba under UN inspection. In return, the US agreed to respect Cuban borders. The blockade was lifted on 20 November.

Submarine Geiger counter
The US deployed nuclear submarines during the Cuban blockade. Geiger counters such as this one were used to check levels of radiation in the vessels and monitor how much radiation had been absorbed by crews.

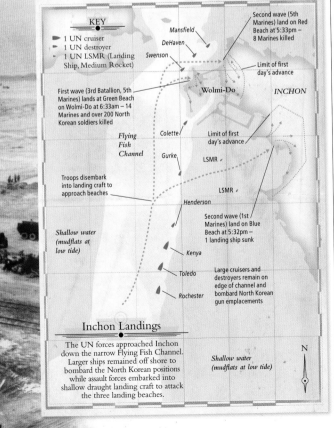

KEY

- ▶ 1 UN cruiser
- ▶ 1 UN destroyer
- ▶ 1 UN LSMR (Landing Ship, Medium Rocket)

First wave (3rd Batallion, 5th Marines) lands at Green Beach on Wolmi-do at 6:33am – 14 Marines and over 200 North Korean soldiers killed

Flying Fish Channel

Troops disembark into landing craft to approach beaches

Shallow water (mudflats at low tide)

Mansfield
DeHaven
Swenson

Colette
Gurke

Henderson

Kenya

Toledo

Rochester

Second wave (5th Marines) land on Red Beach at 5:33pm – 8 Marines killed

Wolmi-Do   *INCHON*

Limit of first day's advance

Limit of first day's advance

LSMR

LSMR

Second wave (1st Marines) land on Blue Beach at 5:32pm – 1 landing ship sunk

Large cruisers and destroyers remain on edge of channel and bombard North Korean gun emplacements

Inchon Landings

The UN forces approached Inchon down the narrow Flying Fish Channel. Larger ships remained off shore to bombard the North Korean positions while assault forces embarked into shallow draught landing craft to attack the three landing beaches.

Shallow water (mudflats at low tide)

N

❝

THE SOVIET GOVERNMENT CANNOT INSTRUCT THE CAPTAINS OF SOVIET VESSELS BOUND FOR CUBA TO OBSERVE THE ORDERS OF THE AMERICAN NAVAL FORCES BLOCKADING THAT ISLAND.

NIKITA KRUSHCHEV, SOVIET PREMIER, LETTER TO US PRESIDENT JOHN F. KENNEDY

❞

COLD WAR WARRIOR

The crew of the USS *Nautilus*, the world's first ever nuclear-powered submarine, take to her deck as she enters New York harbour in 1957. The following year *Nautilus* made the first submerged transit of the North Pole. Nuclear submarines, able to stay submerged for weeks or even months at a time and carrying a payload of ballistic missiles, soon became a key part of the Cold War stalemate.

THE VIETNAM WAR

THE POPULAR IMAGE of the Vietnam War is of foot-slogging search-and-destroy operations. The impression does little justice to the key US and South Vietnamese naval operations during the decade-long conflict. US involvement in the Vietnam War began in earnest at sea with the Gulf of Tonkin engagement in 1964, and ended with major evacuations from the South Vietnamese coastline in 1975. In between were a huge range of maritime operations. Aircraft carrier groups sat at two locations off the Vietnamese coast ("Yankee Station" and "Dixie Station") to launch naval air strikes against North Vietnam and Viet Cong targets in South Vietnam. Navy and Coast Guard units cut Communist supply lines during Operation Market Time, while a composite US Navy and US Army "Brown Water Navy" fought the Communists along the waterways of the Mekong Delta. Vietnam also saw more traditional forms of naval warfare, with the battleship *New Jersey* deployed to provide fire support to ground troops with her huge 16in guns. Although the Vietnam War ultimately ended in defeat for the West, the efforts of the US maritime forces were arguably the most successful component of the war.

RIVERINE OPERATIONS

The Mekong River Delta in South Vietnam was home to over 50 per cent of the country's population during the Vietnam war and contained the most fertile rice-producing land. It was also laced with 4,800km (3,000 miles) of tangled, jungle-shrouded waterways that provided superb covert transportation lanes for Communist insurgents, the Viet Cong, to traffic people, supplies and weapons. Taking the war to the Viet Cong along the Mekong was the task of the "Brown Water Navy" a collection of US Army, Navy, and South Vietnamese riverine patrol units.

The first unit tasked with patrolling the Mekong was the River Patrol Force (RPF), established in 1965. In terms of vessels, US forces made use of almost anything that could float and be armed, including World War II-era landing craft and French colonial monitor gunboats. Yet the arsenal also included purpose-designed vessels such as the Patrol Boat, River (PBR) whose shallow draft, high-speed of 25 knots, and armament of machine-guns and grenade launchers made it an ideal river assault craft.

The US launched Operation Game Warden in 1966, aimed at stopping and searching vessels on the Mekong waterways. The patrols could be violent affairs – in 1967 alone Game Warden operations destroyed 2,000 enemy vessels, boarded 400,000, and killed around 1,300 Viet Cong. Yet US forces were soon looking for more aggressive solutions.

The result was the formation of a joint army-navy unit, the Mobile Riverine Force, dedicated to search-and-destroy operations. Soldiers (principally the 9th Infantry Division) were carried into battle in Armored Troop Carriers (ATCs) with fire support provided by gun-bristling monitor gunboats. Forward headquarters were created from floating base ships – often converted LSTs (Landing Ships, Tank) left over from World War II. Pontoons provided platforms for floating artillery firebases.

The Mobile Riverine Force was critical in curtailing Viet Cong influence in the Mekong, particularly during the Communist Tet offensive of 1968, when the riverine craft were used to deploy troops around South Vietnam to douse the fires of Viet Cong uprisings. In 1969 the MRF was reorganized under the SEALORDS programme (the Southeast Asia Lake, Ocean, River, and Delta Strategy). The 9th Infantry were detached for other land warfare duties, but the boat force grew in scale and included the now 258-boat strong RPF.

Slow but sure
The turtle emblem on this uniform patch is an affectionate nod to the armoured monitor gunboats used by riverine units in Vietnam.

1943–PRESENT
JOHN KERRY
SWIFT BOAT COMMANDER AND ANTI-WAR ACTIVIST

Future US Senator and presidential candidate John Kerry served in Vietnam from 1968–1970, his first tour of duty being aboard the frigate USS *Gridley*. Kerry voluntarily transferred to be the commander of a Patrol Craft, Fast (PCF) Swift boat, performing coastal and river interdiction. In this role he saw much action, receiving three Purple Hearts for wounds sustained in action. After leaving Vietnam, Kerry became an anti-war activist and was the first Vietnam veteran to testify about the war before Congress.

CARRIERS, SUBMARINES, AND MISSILES

THE VIETNAM WAR

THE GULF OF TONKIN INCIDENT

Date 2–4 August 1964
Forces Americans: 2 destroyers; North Vietnamese: 5–8 torpedo boats
Losses Americans: none; North Vietnamese: c.3 boats destroyed

Location Gulf of Tonkin, North Vietnam

The Gulf of Tonkin incident provided a pretext for escalating US involvement in the Vietnam War. On 2 August 1964 the destroyer USS *Maddox* was engaged in intelligence gathering off the Gulf of Tonkin when she was approached by three North Vietnamese torpedo boats. Warning shots failed to deter the attackers, and US gunfire subsequently destroyed one boat and damaged another. Two days later *Maddox* was on patrol with another destroyer, *Turner Joy*. Radio operators on board suddenly reported five enemy torpedo boats approaching, resulting in a blaze of US gunfire and reports that two enemy craft had been sunk. Later analysis contended that the reports were false and no enemy craft were present. Nonetheless, the incidents led to retaliatory air attacks on North Vietnam and persuaded US Congress to effectively commit to war.

Jet warfare
Deck crew on board the carrier *Bon Homme Richard* prepare F-8 Crusader fighter jets for action against North Vietnamese aircraft in 1965.

The SEALORDS programme ran until 1970, when the Brown Water efforts began to wind down, having killed thousands of Viet Cong personnel and stemmed the Communist flow of supplies to and from Cambodia. The Riverine War was a dirty, violent campaign, but it had played a vital role in the efforts to destroy the Viet Cong.

Monitor on patrol
An American Swift patrol boat converted into an armoured monitor gunboat churns slowly past defoliated vegetation during counter-insurgency operations on the Saigon River.

THE VIETNAM WAR

RIVERINE OPERATIONS

Date	1965–1970
Location	Principally the Mekong River Delta
Result	US superiority

COMBATANTS

UNITED STATES | VIET CONG

COMMANDERS

William Westmoreland | Local commanders

FORCES

Ships: In 1969: 258 patrol and minesweeping boats, 184 monitors and transports, 25 helicopter gunships, 15 aircraft | **Ships:** unknown

LOSSES

Men: 5,182 | **Men:** unknown
Ships: unknown | **Ships:** unknown

THE VIETNAM WAR

OPERATION ROLLING THUNDER

Date 2 March1965–1 November 1968
Forces Americans: 600 ships; North Vietnamese: extensive Soviet-supplied air defences
Losses Americans: 922 aircraft; North Vietnamese: unknown

Location Gulf of Tonkin and North Vietnam

Rolling Thunder was the name of the aerial bombing campaign over North Vietnam, initiated in March 1965 with the intention of pounding the North Vietnamese government into submission. Sustained bombing over several years inflicted huge damage – air force, navy, and Marine Corps aircraft dropped 783,807 tonnes (864,000 tons) of bombs – but it ultimately failed to break North Vietnamese resistance or convince the government not to aid the Communist insurgency in South Vietnam.

The US Navy and Marine Corps component of Rolling Thunder was primarily delivered by the carrier aircraft of "Yankee Station" based 140km (75 miles) off the Gulf of Tonkin. Yankee Station consisted of multiple US aircraft carriers during the Rolling Thunder operations, including *Coral Sea*, *Hancock*, *Constellation*, and *Midway*. By operating in a multi-carrier unit, Yankee Station could keep up the round-the-clock commitments of the air war. Its aviators ran terrible risks from Soviet-supplied SA-2 Guideline missiles and vast barrages of conventional anti-aircraft fire. There were also some horrific offshore accidents, the most famous of which resulted from the accidental firing of a Zuni rocket aboard USS *Forrestal* on 29 July 1967. The missile ignited fuel and ordnance, and subsequent fires and detonations killed 134 and destroyed or damaged 64 aircraft. In total, 454 naval aviators and many more air force pilots, died during Operation Rolling Thunder.

THE VIETNAM WAR

OPERATION MARKET TIME

Date 11 March 1965–December 1972
Forces Americans: unknown; North Vietnamese: unknown
Losses Americans: unknown; North Vietnamese: unknown

Location Coastal waters of South Vietnam

On 16 February 1965 a US helicopter flying down the coast of central South Vietnam spotted a North Vietnamese trawler unloading arms and ammunition at Vung Ro Bay – the first tangible evidence that North Vietnam was using open sea routes to supply Communist insurgents in South Vietnam. The US Navy responded to the incident by launching Market Time, a major coastal patrol and surveillance operation designed to cut the open water supply lines between North and South Vietnam.

Operation Market Time ran for seven years along a 2,000km (1,200 mile) stretch of the South Vietnamese coast. It was delivered by Task Force 115, the Coastal Patrol Force. By 1966 hundreds of US Navy, Coast Guard, and South Vietnamese Navy craft were involved. The screening operation was organized around nine patrol sectors stretching 65km (40 miles) out to sea. Close to the shore, US Navy Patrol Gunboats, armed junks, and Coast Guard Cutters performed stop-and-search operations. Further from the coast, larger navy minesweepers and destroyers intercepted deep-water traffic. US Navy surveillance aircraft patrolled the waters beyond.

The effect of Market Time on the Communist supply lines was profound. Out of 50 North Vietnamese trawlers that attempted the run south between 1965 and 1972, US forces captured or destroyed 49. Communist forces almost entirely abandoned the coastal route in favour of the inland Ho Chi Minh Trail.

USS LEXINGTON

THE FIRST AIRCRAFT CARRIER to bear the name *Lexington* was sunk at the Coral Sea in 1942. The name was transferred to a new fleet carrier commissioned in 1943, which played a prominent part in the battles of the Philippine Sea and Leyte Gulf. *Lexington* remained in service until 1991, making her the longest serving carrier in the US Navy.

KNOWN AS THE "BLUE GHOST" because of her dark blue paint scheme, *Lexington* operated some 80 aircraft during World War II. The ship had the standard layout for a World War II carrier, with an island superstructure offset to starboard and aircraft taking off and landing along a straight flight deck stretching from the stern to the bow. With the aid of a steam-operated catapult and an arrestor cable, aircraft could take off and land using half the length of the flight deck, leaving the rest free for shifting planes up from and down to the hangars on lifts. If a landing went wrong, only a crash barrier prevented an aircraft piling into planes being marshalled on the deck. After the war, carriers were designed with a landing deck angled to port, so that if anything went wrong the landing pilot could accelerate off and come round for a second try. *Lexington* was given an angled flight deck during extensive

modernization in the 1950s. By the time she was decommissioned in 1991, *Lexington* was the oldest working aircraft carrier in the US Navy. She is now a museum ship at Corpus Christi, Texas.

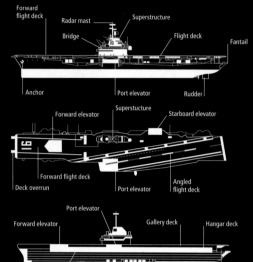

The Blue Ghost
At her permanent mooring in Corpus Christi, Texas, the floodlit shape of the *Lexington*, affectionately nicknamed the "Blue Ghost", can be seen from around the bay.

USS Lexington
The second Essex-class aircraft carrier to be commissioned, *Lexington* is 275m (910ft) long and displaces 33,000 tons. She can carry enough fuel in her tanks to sail nonstop for a distance of 50,000km (30,000 miles).

⌄ Superstructure
The island superstructure is the ship's command-and-control centre. The radar mast carries six different radar systems as well as radio antennae and other equipment. Below this, the island houses the bridge, pilot-house, radar room, flight control centre, and other key command areas.

⌃ Whaler MK11
Suspended from the starboard aft edge of the flight deck, the lightweight 8m (26ft) long Mk11 Whaler motorboat was used to ferry personnel to shore. It could carry up to 22 passengers.

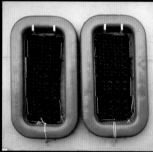

⌃ Life rafts
Two rigid, puncture-proof life rafts known as Carley floats are fixed to the starboard side of the island. In case of emergency, the lightweight rafts could be launched simply by casting them into the water.

> PILOTS ARE THE WEAPON OF THIS FORCE. PILOTS ARE THE THINGS YOU HAVE TO NURTURE. PILOTS ARE THE PEOPLE YOU HAVE TO TRAIN ... YOU HAVE TO TRAIN OTHER PEOPLE TO SUPPORT THE PILOTS.
>
> **ADMIRAL MARC MITSCHER,** COMMANDER OF FAST CARRIER TASK FORCE 58 ON *LEXINGTON*, 1941

CARRIERS, SUBMARINES, AND MISSILES

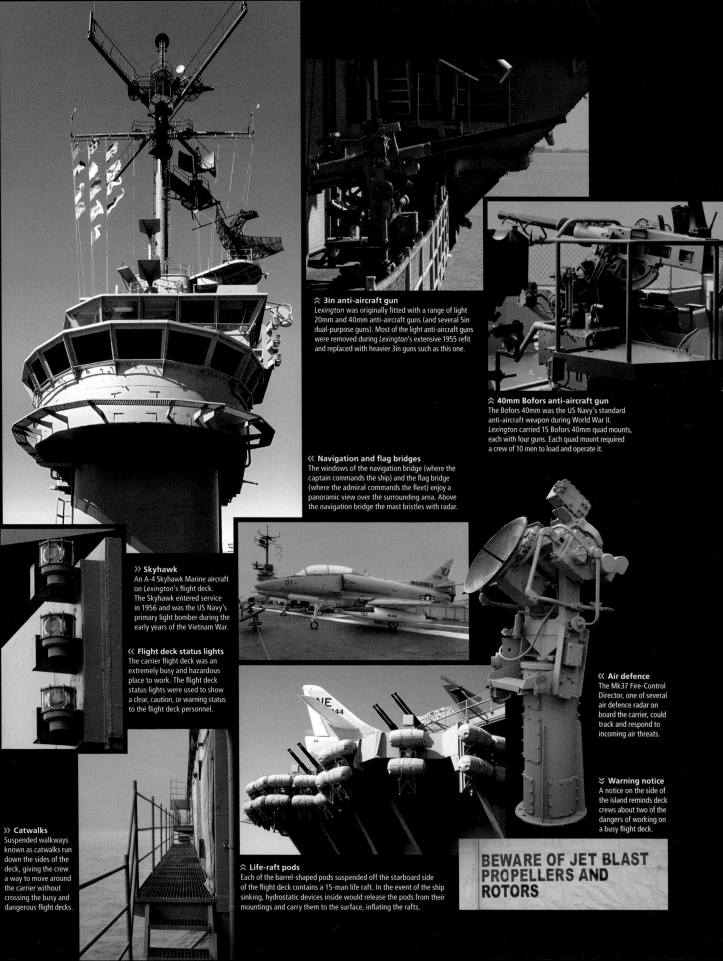

3in anti-aircraft gun
Lexington was originally fitted with a range of light 20mm and 40mm anti-aircraft guns (and several 5in dual-purpose guns). Most of the light anti-aircraft guns were removed during *Lexington*'s extensive 1955 refit and replaced with heavier 3in guns such as this one.

40mm Bofors anti-aircraft gun
The Bofors 40mm was the US Navy's standard anti-aircraft weapon during World War II. *Lexington* carried 15 Bofors 40mm quad mounts, each with four guns. Each quad mount required a crew of 10 men to load and operate it.

Navigation and flag bridges
The windows of the navigation bridge (where the captain commands the ship) and the flag bridge (where the admiral commands the fleet) enjoy a panoramic view over the surrounding area. Above the navigation bridge the mast bristles with radar.

Skyhawk
An A-4 Skyhawk Marine aircraft on *Lexington*'s flight deck. The Skyhawk entered service in 1956 and was the US Navy's primary light bomber during the early years of the Vietnam War.

Flight deck status lights
The carrier flight deck was an extremely busy and hazardous place to work. The flight deck status lights were used to show a clear, caution, or warning status to the flight deck personnel.

Air defence
The Mk37 Fire-Control Director, one of several air defence radar on board the carrier, could track and respond to incoming air threats.

Warning notice
A notice on the side of the island reminds deck crews about two of the dangers of working on a busy flight deck.

Catwalks
Suspended walkways known as catwalks run down the sides of the deck, giving the crew a way to move around the carrier without crossing the busy and dangerous flight decks.

Life-raft pods
Each of the barrel-shaped pods suspended off the starboard side of the flight deck contains a 15-man life raft. In the event of the ship sinking, hydrostatic devices inside would release the pods from their mountings and carry them to the surface, inflating the rafts.

BEWARE OF JET BLAST PROPELLERS AND ROTORS

BELOW DECKS

LEXINGTON HAD A complement of 2,600 officers and men, berthed in generally spartan conditions. *Lexington* represented a step forward from earlier carriers in some respects, however, notably the comfort of its pilot's briefing room. Much space below deck was devoted to the stowage of aircraft. The operation of aircraft in the confined space of a ship inevitably led to accidents, such as gruesome encounters between men and propellers.

» Navigation bridge
High in the island superstructure, with slanted windows to reduce the glare, the navigation bridge was the main command centre of the ship. The large device in the centre of the bridge is the navigational radar monitor.

⋙ Port engine control panel
Eight steam boilers powered the ship's four Westinghouse steam turbine engines. Control panels in each of the two engine rooms were used to control the turbine pressures and operate the engines.

« Bridge indicators
The bridge is fitted with a range of instruments, including this wind speed and direction indicator and the equipment for the bridge officers to talk to other areas of the ship.

» Pilothouse
Situated behind the bridge, the pilothouse is where the ship would have been steered and its speed controlled. In the centre of the room stand the engine order telegraph, helm wheel, and magnetic compass.

⋙ Pilot's ready room
The air-conditioned ready rooms were where pilots and air crew were briefed prior to their missions. Foldaway desks allowed the airmen to make notes during briefings.

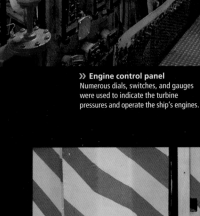

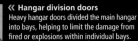

» Engine control panel
Numerous dials, switches, and gauges were used to indicate the turbine pressures and operate the ship's engines.

« Hangar division doors
Heavy hangar doors divided the main hangar into bays, helping to limit the damage from fires or explosions within individual bays. Each door section weighs over eight tons.

» Air Operations room
Planning and coordination for flight operations took place in the Air Ops room. The plot board listed all the day's flying schedules.

« Tow truck
With so many planes to move around the hangars, tow trucks were an indispensable piece of the ship's equipment.

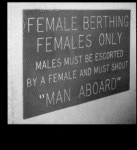

≪ ≫ Female berthing
Lexington was the first US Navy ship to have women serving on board. A sign at the entrance of the female berthing area indicates the protocol expected from male crewmen entering the women's living quarters.

≪ Surgery room
Lexington was equipped with extensive medical facilities. As well as this surgery, the ship also had a triage emergency room, a dental surgery, a diagnostics laboratory, an X-ray room, and a prosthetics lab.

≪ Captain's galley
There were separate galleys and messes for the enlisted men and officers. The captain had his own galley which was used to make meals for the captain and his guests.

≫ Bed pans
This set of bed pans and "piss pots" in the ship's sick bay was designed with utility in mind.

≫ Sick bay
The sick bay was located below the hangar deck, a common site for accidents. Beds could be raised to make room for stretchers.

≫ Admiral's quarters
The rooms reserved for the admiral, when he was on board, were comfortable but by no means lavish.

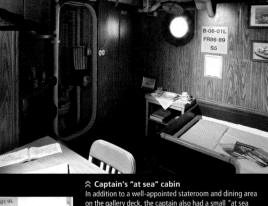

≫ Soup kettles
With more than 2,000 enlisted men on board, feeding the crew was a 24-hour operation. These gigantic soup kettles, like much of the kitchen equipment, were made out of stainless steel for ease of cleaning and maintenance.

≪ Galley ovens
The ship's ovens are much larger than normal, and there are lots of them. The size of the ship meant that feeding the crew was more like feeding a small city than a regular ship. The ovens, like the rest of the galley, were in constant use.

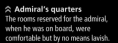

≫ Captain's "at sea" cabin
In addition to a well-appointed stateroom and dining area on the gallery deck, the captain also had a small "at sea" cabin nearer the bridge. The room is simply furnished with a small bathroom, a table and chair, and a bed with raised sides to prevent the captain rolling out during rough weather.

≪ Crew shelter and food service area
Small shelters around the ship provided areas for the gun crews to relax while remaining close to their guns in case of emergencies. Though sparsely furnished, the rooms provided a refuge from bad weather and a place to unwind and eat in comparative safety.

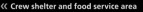

THE FALKLANDS WAR

ARGENTINA LAUNCHED A MILITARY campaign to invade and occupy South Georgia and the Falkland Islands, disputed British possessions in the South Atlantic, on 19 March 1982. The British government opted to retake the islands by military force, which it achieved by the middle of June. The British victory was made possible by the rapid deployment of a naval task force across 12,900km (8,000 miles) of Atlantic Ocean. The task force consisted of two small carriers, *Hermes* and *Invincible*, operating Harrier jump-jets, and ships carrying troops and equipment, screened by destroyers

and frigates. A separate force of submarines was sent to keep the Argentinian navy away from an "exclusion zone" around the islands. As the task force drew closer to the Falklands in early May, both sides suffered naval losses. The ageing Argentinian cruiser *General Belgrano* was sunk by a submarine while the Royal Navy lost a destroyer to air attack from land-based aircraft. On 21 May British troops landed at San Carlos, but air attacks intensified. Argentinian forces on the Falklands surrendered on 14 June, but it proved a close-run conflict. British losses were high, with 15 ships either sunk or badly damaged.

The sinking of HMS Antelope
On 24 May, while on air defence duty at the entrance to San Carlos Water, the British frigate HMS *Antelope* was attacked and sunk by two Argentine A-4 Skyhawk jets.

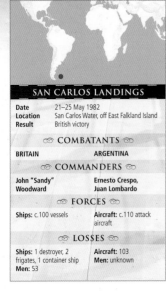

LANDINGS AT SAN CARLOS WATER

The landing of British troops on the Falklands began on 21 May, initiating the most intensive phase of the air-sea conflict. The Royal Navy positioned its destroyers and frigates in Falkland Sound to intercept air attacks with their missile defences, while the carriers *Hermes* and *Invincible*, operating far to the east for fear of Exocet missile attack, flew off Sea Harriers to provide a combat air patrol. The amphibious assault began at dawn with 4,000 men being landed by a variety of amphibious ships around San Carlos bay. Within 24 hours the beachhead had been secured and the land campaign had begun.

The naval forces, however, were still fighting for their lives. Argentinian air attacks began two hours after first light on 21 May, the principal attackers being Skyhawk and Mirage fighters flying low-level bombing and strafing runs from bases on the Argentine mainland. The British ships replied with machine-gun and cannon fire, as well as numerous Sea Slug, Sea Cat, and Sea Wolf missiles – although many of the missiles suffered technical failures. The County-Class destroyer *Antrim* was hit by a dud bomb that knocked out her surface-to-air missile systems; the Type 22 frigate *Brilliant*

was strafed; and the Leander Class frigate *Argonaut* was crippled in the water by multiple bomb strikes. Worse still, the Type 21 frigate *Ardent* was hit by two 454kg (1,000lb) bombs and sank. The only compensation was that the Argentine air force had lost 16 aircraft during the first day's fighting, an unsustainable daily loss.

It was the beginning of a difficult week for the British naval forces around San Carlos Water. The frigate *Antelope* was sunk on 24 May and on 25 May the destroyer *Coventry* and frigate *Broadsword* were attacked by waves of A-4 Skyhawks in Falkland

THE FALKLANDS WAR

SAN CARLOS LANDINGS

Date	21–25 May 1982
Location	San Carlos Water, off East Falkland Island
Result	British victory

∞ COMBATANTS ∞

BRITAIN	ARGENTINA

∞ COMMANDERS ∞

John "Sandy" Woodward	Ernesto Crespo, Juan Lombardo

∞ FORCES ∞

Ships: c.100 vessels	Aircraft: c.110 attack aircraft

∞ LOSSES ∞

Ships: 1 destroyer, 2 frigates, 1 container ship Men: 53	Aircraft: 103 Men: unknown

> 66
> **I WAS TWO DECKS DOWN AND COULD SEE NO WAY OUT. THE SMOKE WAS SUFFOCATING AND THE DOORS WERE BLOCKED BY FIRE. I WAS CALM AND PREPARED TO DIE.**
> **CAPTAIN DAVID HART DYKE**, DESCRIBING THE SINKING OF THE HMS *COVENTRY* ON 25 MAY 1982
> 99

CARRIERS, SUBMARINES, AND MISSILES

1932–PRESENT
JOHN "SANDY" WOODWARD

SENIOR COMMANDER OF THE SOUTH ATLANTIC TASK FORCE

After joining the Royal Navy at the age of just 13, John "Sandy" Woodward spent most of his early career on submarines, where he gained his first command, the submarine *Warspite*, in 1969. Promoted to rear admiral in 1981, the following year he was given command of the British Task Force sent to the Falklands. Woodward received a knighthood for his service during the war, finishing his career as a full admiral.

SINKING OF THE BELGRANO

Date 2 May 1982
Forces British: 1 submarine; Argentine: 1 cruiser
Losses British: none; Argentine: 1 cruiser

Location South of Falkland Islands, South Atlantic

The sinking of the Argentine cruiser *General Belgrano* remains one of the most controversial incidents of the Falklands War. By 30 April, when the *Belgrano*'s presence was first registered by British surveillance, the Royal Navy had established a circular exclusion zone around the Falkland Islands with a radius of 370km (230 miles). The *Belgrano*, accompanied by two Argentine destroyers, was actually 64km (40 miles) outside this exclusion zone and might therefore have been considered safe

Mark 8 torpedo
Despite carrying modern Mark 24 Tigerfish torpedoes, HMS *Conqueror* opted to use the much older but more reliable Mark 8 torpedo to attack the ARA *Belgrano*.

Silent hunter
HMS *Conqueror* is the only nuclear-powered submarine to have sunk an enemy ship using torpedoes, and one of only two to have sunk an enemy warship since World War II.

from attack. The British authorities, however, decided that the *Belgrano* did pose a serious threat to the British Task Force. It was directing aircraft attack missions and carried a powerful array of long-range and anti-aircraft guns. On 2 May the order came from London that the *Belgrano* was to be sunk. The tool for this job was the nuclear-powered submarine *Conqueror*, which had been shadowing the enemy cruiser since 30 April. When she received the order to attack, *Conqueror* closed to firing range at 3:57pm on 2 May, firing three Mark 8 mod 4 torpedoes. These were old, unguided weapons compared to the modern Tigerfish homing torpedoes that *Conquerer* also had on board at the time, but there were some concerns about the Tigerfish's reliability. Two of the torpedoes, each carrying

364kg (800lb) of Torpex explosive, hit the cruiser and detonated, ripping open her hull and killing around 275 men. Within 20 minutes the *Belgrano*'s crew were abandoning ship; many men would float in the South Atlantic for several days, some surviving, some not. In total 321 men out of the *Belgrano*'s crew of 1,000 died in the attack.

Sound. *Broadsword* was hit by a bomb that failed to explode; *Coventry* was not so lucky. The destroyer was hit by three bombs, two of which exploded. The operations room was devastated, killing or injuring most of the senior officers. Another victim was the transport ship *Atlantic Conveyor*, sunk by an Exocet missile that ironically had been diverted from its original warship target by the successful use of chaff decoys.

Nonetheless, 25 May proved to be something of a turning point for the British ships around the Falklands. With the Argentine air force unable to sustain its daily losses, British forces were able to establish a degree of air superiority over San Carlos Water. The Harrier jets performed outstandingly, shooting down 32 aircraft for the loss of five of their own – none in air-to-air combat. Thereafter the Argentine air force was able to make only brief assaults, though it would claim many more British lives during the attack on the landing ship *Sir Galahad* at Port Fitzroy on 8 June.

SINKING OF THE SHEFFIELD

Date 4–10 May 1982
Forces English: 1 destroyer; Argentine: 2 aircraft
Losses English: 1 destroyer; Argentine: none

Location Off Port Stanley, Falkland Islands

On 4 May 1982 the Type 42 guided-missile destroyer HMS *Sheffield* was on defensive station off the Falkland Islands when her ageing radar systems picked up what appeared to be two inbound missiles, although no launch aircraft were detected. Two Exocet anti-ship missiles had however been launched by Argentine Super Etendard aircraft, and only a few seconds after their detection, one of the missiles struck the HMS *Sheffield* amidships. The missile started a raging fire that could not be extinguished because of the destruction of many of the ship's fire-control systems in the initial impact. Eventually the captain gave the order for the ship to be abandoned – 21 men had been killed. The empty, stricken ship was towed out to sea and scuttled on 10 May. The sinking of the *Sheffield* was the first major loss for the British Task Force around the Falklands – and the first Royal Navy vessel to be sunk in battle for almost 40 years.

WEAPONS AND TECHNOLOGY

MODERN AIR DEFENCE SYSTEMS

Hostile aircraft armed with anti-ship missiles are one of the most potent threats to modern warships. As a response, navies tend to use three levels of onboard air defence technology. First are the electronic countermeasures (ECM) suites dedicated to jamming missile homing systems, or the radar systems of the attack aircraft themselves. ECM might include chaff and radar-jamming equipment, but these pose no real danger to the aircraft itself. The second level is more aggressive, and consists of automated missile or gun defence systems. These are linked to fire-control systems that can automatically acquire the targets and fire either a guided missile or, in the case of gun systems like the US Phalanx, deliver hails of radar-aimed cannon or machine-gun fire. The final, and most basic, level of air defence is usually provided by optically aimed and fired machine-guns and light cannon. Even the most modern vessels often have pintle mounts for machine-guns dotted around the ship's rails, and these can provide a last-ditch method of air defence.

Phalanx anti-missile system
The US Navy's Phalanx close-in weapon system (CIWS) uses an automated radar and fire-control system to track incoming anti-ship missiles and destroy them with its M61 Vulcan cannon.

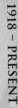

POSTWAR CONFLICTS

REGIONAL CONFLICTS

ALTHOUGH MOST POST-1945 conflicts have been largely restricted to land warfare, the "war in peace" has nonetheless featured some major regional naval engagements. Significant naval actions occured, for example, around the troubled Middle Eastern region during the Arab-Israeli wars of the 1960s and 70s, and in the waters around the Indian subcontinent during the later decade. The navies involved in these engagements have not been the world's largest by any means, but in many cases they were pioneers in testing out modern ship-versus-ship weapon

systems and electronic countermeasures in actual combat situations. In this capacity they often had a formative role in the development of naval weaponry by the major Western and Soviet bloc powers. The diversity of postwar regional naval engagements has also been impressive, and has ranged from gunboat missile actions through to well-organized suicide bombings and carrier aircraft attacks. Sheer cost has limited the capacity of many regional powers to maintain navies in recent years, but investment in modern weapons technology has enabled them to remain a potent threat to far larger forces.

ARAB-ISRAELI WARS

SINKING OF THE EILAT

Date 21 October 1967
Forces Israelis: 1 destroyer;
Egyptians: 2 missile boats
Losses Israelis: 1 destroyer;
Egyptians: none

Location Off Egyptian
coastline, near Port Said

Prior to her sale to Israel in 1955, the *Eilat* had seen service in World War II as the British Z-Class destroyer HMS *Zealous*. Renamed *Eilat*, she enjoyed a long operational record, including the sinking of two Egyptian vessels.

On 21 October 1967 the *Eilat* was on a routine patrol of the Sinai coastline, which took her some 25km (15 miles) from the Egyptian city of Port Said, when she suddenly came under attack from an Egyptian Komar-class missile boat. The boat fired a Russian-built SS-N-2 Styx anti-ship missile that struck the *Eilat* squarely, destroying her communications and powerplant. The *Eilat* was attacked again 90 minutes later, receiving another missile strike that caused her magazine to detonate. The crew abandoned ship, but many were wounded in the water when one of the ship's depth charges exploded. A total of 47 Israeli sailors were killed.

The *Eilat* was the first ship to be destroyed in battle by a ship-launched anti-ship missile. It was a huge blow to the Israeli navy and led to a major review of Israeli naval strategy. The resulting focus on fast, missile-armed boats and missile countermeasures would reap major benefits for the Israeli navy six years later at Latakia.

Styx anti-ship missile
A fast missile boat launches a Soviet SS-N-2 Styx missile of the type that sunk the Israeli destroyer INS *Eilat*.

THE BATTLE OF LATAKIA

The battle of Latakia was a milestone in postwar naval engagements – never before had anti-ship missiles and missile-jamming technology been pitted against one another in open combat. The context of the battle was the opening actions of the 1973 Yom Kippur War.

On 6 October Egyptian forces launched a surprise eastward thrust across the Suez Canal against Israeli forces in the Sinai. Syria made a simultaneous attack from the north across the Golan Heights. In an attempt to check the potential threat to Israeli ships from Syrian missile

boats, Israeli commanders decided to mount a preemptive naval strike, sending six Saar-class corvettes to draw the Syrian missile boats out of their harbour at Latakia and destroy them. The Syrian vessels posed a realistic threat to Israeli shipping. They were armed with the same SS-N-2 Styx anti-ship missiles that had sunk the Israeli destroyer *Eilat* in 1967. The Israeli warships were also armed with anti-

ship missiles, but since the Israeli Gabriel – which had yet to be used in battle – had only half the range of the Styx, the crews would have to rely on newly developed, and still unproven, electronic countermeasures (ECM). These consisted of two principal elements: chaff dispensers to fill the air with metallic strips, clouding the incoming missile's target picture; and jamming systems designed to confuse the missile's tracking system. At Latakia both systems would be tested for the first time against real threats.

MISSILE DUEL

Contact was made quickly as the six Israeli missile boats approached Latakia. An offshore Syrian P-4 torpedo boat was picked up on radar, and the Israeli corvette *Hanit* moved to engage her, sinking the boat with long-range gunfire.

Assuming that the Syrian torpedo boat had reported their presence off Latakia, the Israeli boats waited for new threats to emerge. The radar soon threw up another contact, a Syrian T-43 minesweeper to the northeast. This time *Reshef* peeled off to deal with her, hitting the ship with a Gabriel missile at a range of 18km (11 miles). *Reshef* rejoined the main group, now coming within Styx missile range of Latakia. At this point the Syrians responded in earnest. Three Syrian fast missile boats

Israeli missile boat
A group of Saar 4-class Israeli missile boats of the type used at Latakia. The side of one of the Gabriel missile launchers is just visible at the stern.

344

ANTI-SHIP MISSILES AND MISSILE DEFENCE

Although anti-ship missiles were trialled to some degree during World War II, it was only during the late 1950s and 1960s that they began to challenge gunnery as the primary weapon of combat vessels. Pioneering missiles such as the SS-N-2 Styx proved their worth in action, most notably sinking the Israeli destroyer *Eilat* in 1967, and inspired the US Navy to develop its own Harpoon missile during the 1970s. By the 1980s all major world navies had equipped themselves with ship-launched missile systems plus, in

many cases, electronic countermeasures (ECM) to combat enemy missile threats. Among the more effective of the anti-ship missiles developed in the 1980s, the Exocet gained particular notoriety in its air-launched form during the Falklands War. Most such missiles use active radar or infrared homing systems, and some of the longer-range examples are able to hit targets well over 100km (62 miles) away. Even terrorist units have used missiles against ships – in 2006 a Hezbollah unit hit and damaged an Israeli corvette with a Chinese-made C-802 missile.

Sea Sparrow
Fitted on board many US and NATO warships, the RIM-7 Sea Sparrow is a lightweight, radar-guided missile system used to provide point defence against air attack, incoming missiles, or small surface craft.

Excocet MM38 ship-launched missile
The French-built Exocet missile is designed to target large warships – the Type-42 destroyer HMS *Sheffield* was sunk by an Exocet during the Falklands War.

(two Komar-class and one Osa-class) left the harbour and fired their Styx missiles, well beyond the range of the Gabriels. As the missiles approached the Israelis deployed their jamming systems and chaff – both worked, and the missiles splashed harmlessly into the sea. The Israelis now closed to range, and a missile exchange ensued in which all three Syrian boats were destroyed.

ARAB-ISRAELI WARS

THE BATTLE OF LATAKIA	
Date	7 October 1973
Location	Off the port of Latakia, Syria
Result	Israeli victory
🔗 COMBATANTS 🔗	
ISRAEL	**SYRIA**
🔗 COMMANDERS 🔗	
Benjamin Telem	Fuad Abu Zikry
🔗 FORCES 🔗	
Ships: 6 missile boats	Ships: 3 missile boats, 1 torpedo boat, 1 minesweeper
🔗 LOSSES 🔗	
Men: none	**Men:** unknown
Ships: none	**Ships:** 3 missile boats, 1 torpedo boat, 1 minesweeper

INDO-PAKISTAN WAR

1971 INDO-PAKISTAN WAR

Date 3–16 December 1971
Forces Indians: c.100 ships; Pakistanis: c.40 ships
Losses Indians: 1 frigate; Pakistanis: 1 destroyer, 1 minesweeper, 1 submarine, 4 patrol boats

Location Off coast of East Pakistan and Karachi

The two week war between India and Pakistan over the separatist movement that led to the creation of Bangladesh, featured some of the largest naval engagements seen in Asia since World War II. The priority for the Indian navy was to stop the flow of supplies between East and West Pakistan. The Indian aircraft carrier *Vikrant* was dispatched to blockade the port of Chittagong in East Pakistan, its Sea Hawk aircraft seriously damaging the harbour facilities. The Pakistani submarine *Ghazi*, sent to oppose the *Vikrant*, was sunk, possibly by Indian depth charges. On 3 December, India launched a night-time attack on Karachi harbour in West Pakistan, sinking a destroyer and crippling several other vessels.

The short conflict confirmed the superiority of the Indian navy. India lost only one major vessel, the former British frigate *Khukri*, torpedoed by a Pakistani submarine, and largely achieved its goal of a naval blockade.

SRI LANKAN CIVIL WAR

SRI LANKA AND THE SEA TIGERS

Date 1984–present
Forces Sri Lankans: c.50 combat, support, and patrol vessels in 2008; Sea Tigers: unknown
Losses Sri Lankans: 30 gunboats, 1 freighter; Sea Tigers: unknown

Location Off coast of Sri Lanka

The Sea Tigers are the naval element of the Liberation Tigers of Tamil Elam, or Tamil Tigers, an insurgency force conducting a long-standing war aimed at creating a separatist Tamil state in northern Sri Lanka. The naval force was founded in the mid-1980s, and went on to specialize in speedboat suicide attacks, fast patrol boat assaults, and small-scale amphibious landings. In these tactics they have been notably successful – at the time of writing the Sea Tigers have sunk over 30 Sri Lankan gunboats and one freighter. They have also proved elusive opponents – following an operation, the small craft are generally brought ashore and hidden in the jungle on trailers. They have experienced setbacks, however. In one engagement on 20 October 2006,

the Sri Lankan navy destroyed nine rebel boats and reportedly killed over 170 Tamil Tiger insurgents.

The Sea Tigers have a particularly advanced structure and logistical network. Larger freighters are used to bring in supplies, which are transferred to shore in the fast patrol boats. They also have their own version of Special Forces – frogmen using rebreather apparatus have made stealth attacks on shipping, in one case sinking a freighter at the Kankesanturai naval base. With these capabilities, the Sea Tigers are likely to be a thorn in the side of the Sri Lankan navy for years to come.

Sea Tiger suicide vessel
Sea Tiger suicide soldiers – known as Black Tigers – ride a patrol boat through shallow waters near the rebel-controlled town of Mullathivu in 2005.

MIDDLE EAST AND TERRORISM

SINCE THE END of World War II the Middle East has been both a flashpoint for conventional conflicts and a breeding ground for terrorism. Much of the impulse for this has derived from the particular political and historical conditions in the region – questions of land, oil, nationhood, and religion. The other great catalyst for war has been the relations between Iraq and the wider world. The Iran-Iraq War led to around one million deaths in the 1980s, and generated many of the political conditions that led to the Gulf War of 1990–91. Following the terrorist attacks on New York in September 2001 and the subsequent US-led "War on Terror", tensions in the Middle East remained high. The invasion of Taliban-controlled Afghanistan and the ongoing conflict in Iraq mean that foreign troops continue to be deployed throughout the region. In all these conflicts, the waters of the Gulf have been a critical battle zone. Controlling the shipping lanes through this vital oil-producing region remains essential, hence the United States Navy still maintains a forceful presence in the region, guarding against terrorist and conventional foe alike.

OPERATION PRAYING MANTIS

PRAYING MANTIS

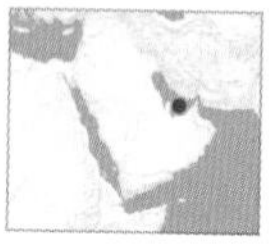

Date 18 April 1988
Forces Americans: 10 ships; Iranians: 13 ships
Losses Americans: 1 helicopter; Iranians: 3 speedboats, 1 frigate, 2 oil platforms damaged

Location
Persian Gulf

On 14 April 1988, the US Perry class frigate *Samuel B. Roberts* was patrolling the Gulf waters off Qatar when it spotted three naval mines in the water. In its attempt to evade the devices the ship hit a fourth mine that detonated, injuring 10 and blowing open the side of the hull. The mines were identified from their serial numbers as Iranian. With America committed to keeping the Gulf navigable for Kuwaiti tankers, a strong US reaction was inevitable.

US RETALIATION

The American response was codenamed Operation Praying Mantis. Commanded by Rear-Admiral Anthony Less, Praying Mantis had as its main objective the destruction of Iranian oil platforms in the Gulf by amphibiously deployed US Marine and Navy SEAL units. As a by-product, it was hoped that this would draw Iranian warships into the Gulf waters, where they could be destroyed by the US surface vessels plus carrier aircraft flying from the *Enterprise*.

The attack was launched on 18 April when two units of frigates, destroyers, and amphibious ships assaulted the Sassan and Sirri oil platforms. Resistance was first crushed by naval gunfire, then Marines were dropped by helicopter onto the platforms, where they placed demolition charges and left.

The Iranian navy responded in force. It sent out a group of armed Boghammar speedboats, though three of these were quickly sunk by bombing runs from US A-6E Intruder aircraft. A Kaman-class fast attack craft was similarly despatched by Harpoon missiles and naval gunfire. Two Iranian F-4 fighters made a run at the guided-missile cruiser *Wainwright*, but were scared off when *Wainwright* replied with Standard surface-to-air missiles. The Iranians now committed their most significant naval vessels – the frigates *Sahand* and *Sabalan*. *Sahand* went first, but was intercepted by aircraft and destroyed by three Harpoon missiles and four laser-guided bombs. The *Sabalan* was crippled by a single bomb dropped down its funnel; the US aircraft and ships then left it dead in the water.

Operation Praying Mantis, the largest US military engagement since the end of World War II, dealt a major blow to the Iranian navy and to Iranian pride. US losses amounted to two men killed in a helicopter crash, an unusually light toll for such a high-risk mission.

Sassan oil platform
US Marines inspect an anti-aircraft gun on one of the two Iranian oil platforms destroyed during Operation Praying Mantis.

WITNESS TO WAR

COMMANDER BUD LANGSTON

A-6 INTRUDER PILOT DURING THE ATTACK ON IRANIAN FRIGATE SABALAN

OPERATION PRAYING MANTIS

"My bombardier-navigator was looking at this [Iranian ship] on our ***forward looking infrared*** *and it certainly matched the silhouette that we're looking for. So we made a* ***high speed dive right down*** *to on top of the water a couple miles behind the ship and as we approached* ***the ship opened fire on us and that gave a pretty good idea it wasn't a friendly*** *… she clearly had the number of the Sabalan and tracers were going over the canopy from its* ***anti-aircraft guns and shoulder fired weapons*** *and rounds were going off all around the canopy."*

WEAPONS AND TECHNOLOGY

MARK 45 GUN

Although naval cannon have been largely superceded by guided missiles as the primary anti-ship and anti-aircraft defence on modern warships, the fully-automated Mark 45 proves that there is still a role for a fast and accurate lightweight naval gun. First developed in the 1960s by BAE Systems, the 5in Mark 45 has gone on to become the principal lightweight naval gun of the US Navy and several other navies worldwide. Aboard US ships the Mark 45 is controlled by the Mark 86 Gun Fire Control System or the Mark 160 Gun Computing System, both of which give rapid automated target acquisition and fire control. The gun is fed by an automatic loading system that can fuel automatic rates of fire of up to 20 rounds per minute, and the gun can engage naval, land, or even (with air burst shells) aerial targets. Although most Mark 45s have a range of about 24km (15 miles), the latest Mod 4 version has a greater velocity and, with advanced rocket-assisted, satellite-guided ammunition, a range of up to 115km (71 miles). The qualities of the Mark 45 will doubtless keep the gun in service for many more years to come.

Lightweight naval artillery
The guided-missile destroyer USS *Forrest Sherman* fires a rocket-assisted 5in shell from her Mk45 Mod4 gun during exercises in the Atlantic.

Shore bombardment
The battleship USS *Wisconsin* fires one of her nine 16in guns at an Iraqi shore target during Operation Desert Storm.

THE FIRST GULF WAR

The Gulf War of 1990–91 was a massive naval operation as well as a major air and land campaign. At the time of Saddam Hussein's invasion of Kuwait on 2 August 1990, the US Navy, Royal Navy, Saudi Arabia, and others already had significant naval assets on station. Once Operation Desert Shield – the Coalition operation for the protection of Saudi Arabia – was implemented, the naval presence expanded enormously.

The US had to provide naval logistics for a swelling land army – during the first six months of Desert Shield sealift accounted for over 2 million tons of supplies shipped ashore. Two carrier battlegroups (centred on *Eisenhower* and *Independence*) were on station by 8 August, providing huge offshore air capability. Four more carrier battlegroups and several surface warfare battlegroups would soon join them, including two battleships (*Wisconsin* and *Missouri*). The Coalition also enforced a naval embargo, resulting in hundreds of stop-and-search operations in Gulf waters: by January 1991 the US Navy had conducted 6,221 challenges and 749 boardings.

> ## YOU'D FLY ALONG THE ROAD, LOOKING FOR SOMETHING. IT WAS UNBELIEVABLE, THE NUMBER OF TARGETS AVAILABLE.
>
> **CAPTAIN ANDREW HALL**, MARINE AV-8B HARRIER PILOT DURING FIRST GULF WAR

On 17 January 1991 Desert Shield turned into Operation Desert Storm, and the shooting war began with a heavy, prolonged air attack on Iraq's forces and infrastructure. Desert Storm opened with naval vessels launching Tomahawk cruise missiles at key targets throughout Iraq, destroying much of Saddam's command-and-control structure. The carrier groups in the Gulf and Red Sea then contributed naval and Marine air assets to the Coalition air campaign, destroying vast amounts of Iraqi military material and killing many thousands of Iraqi troops. Navy E6-AB Prowler ECM aircraft also played a critical role in jamming Iraqi air defences to open a door for strike aircraft attacks. In total, US Navy and Marine Corps pilots flew some 30,000 sorties from the US carriers during the war.

DENOUEMENT

Out at sea there were skirmishes with Iraqi craft. Lynx helicopters from Royal Navy vessels destroyed 15 Iraqi vessels, including minesweepers and patrol boats, using anti-ship missiles. US vessels wrecked Iraqi positions atop several oil platforms, while naval aircraft took out Iraqi minelayers. When the land offensive opened, not only did Coalition marine forces take leading roles, but US naval units conducted simulated amphibious landings off the Kuwaiti coast to hold the attention of Iraqi coastal troops, who were actually being outflanked from behind. US battleships delivered massive offshore bombardments. By 27 February, the offensive operations had effectively ceased and Kuwait was back in Kuwaiti hands.

THE FIRST GULF WAR

THE FIRST GULF WAR	
Date	2 August 1990–11 April 1991
Location	The Gulf, Red Sea, Kuwait, and Iraq
Result	Coalition victory

☞ COMBATANTS ☜

US-LED COALITION	IRAQ

☞ COMMANDERS ☜

Stanley R Arthur	Saddam Hussein
Norman Schwartzkopf	

☞ FORCES ☜

Ships: c.150 combat and logistical ships, including 6 US carrier battlegroups	**Ships:** c.80 military vessels, mostly gunboats and missile boats

☞ LOSSES ☜

Men: 64 US Marines and US Navy personnel	**Men:** unknown
Ships: none	**Ships:** unknown

Sea Skua anti-ship missile
The British Sea Skua radar-guided anti-ship missile was first used in the Falklands War. A total of 26 missiles were fired during the First Gulf War, sinking 11 Iraqi vessels.

ATTACK ON USS COLE

ATTACK ON THE USS COLE

Date 12 October 2000
Forces Americans: 1 destroyer; terrorists: 1 suicide boat
Losses Americans: 1 destroyer damaged; terrorists: 1 suicide boat sunk

Location Port of Aden, Yemen

On 12 October 2000 the Arleigh Burke-class guided-missile destroyer USS *Cole* made a routine refuelling stop in Aden harbour, Yemen. The *Cole* was a new addition to the US Navy arsenal. She had been launched in 1996 and was equipped with the latest Aegis integrated guided-weapons system. The Middle East

was a potentially dangerous part of the world for the ship and its crew, but Aden was classed as a relatively safe harbour. The ship had been refuelling for some 50 minutes when, at 11:18am, a speedboat made an approach to the port side of the destroyer, piloted by two men. The vessel seemed to present no threat; indeed, many of the US sailors thought that it was the local garbage collection boat. Yet on board the speedboat was a large quantity of explosives, which the suicide bombers then detonated right against the side of the ship. The explosion ripped open the port side

Waterline blast
A gaping 10.6m (35ft) hole mars the side of USS *Cole*. The ship was carried back to the US for repairs aboard a heavy transport ship.

of the *Cole*; its force was directed into the galley area, where many men where lining up to eat, killing 17 and injuring another 39.

AFTERMATH

Although the keel of the vessel was not significantly damaged, water poured into the ship through the open hull, and it took the whole day to bring the flooding under control. The first naval assistance to the *Cole* came in from the Royal Navy Type-23 frigate HMS *Marlborough*, which was sailing through the Gulf and diverted

to provide medical and engineering aid. A force of US Marines arrived shortly afterward to provide additional security.

The bombing was planned by the Al-Qaeda terrorist group and carried out by operatives most likely acting with the support of Sudanese officials. The US Navy subsequently changed its rules of engagement – which had prevented the ship's guards firing on the approaching boat – to protect US vessels from similar attacks. Nonetheless, the bombing was a grim reminder of the vulnerability of modern warships, however well defended against conventional attack, to small vessels posing as non-combatants.

USS Cole limps home
The damaged destroyer is towed out of Aden by a Military Sealift Command tug before returning to the United States for repairs lasting 14 months.

"WAR ON TERROR"

INVASION OF AFGHANISTAN

Date 2001–
Forces Coalition forces: unknown; Afghans: none
Losses Coalition forces: none; Afghans: none

Location Persian Gulf and Afghanistan

The invasion of Afghanistan by US, UK, and Coalition forces in 2001 – named Operation Enduring Freedom – presented significant problems in terms of air support. Afghanistan is a land-locked country with no substantial infrastructure, hence there was little in the way of Forward Operating Bases (FOBs) for Allied aircraft. For much of

the early part of the campaign, therefore, air support was almost exclusively provided by US Navy and Marine Corps aviation operating from carrier battle groups in the Gulf. The attack sorties ran in over Pakistan (Iran was, and remains, prohibited airspace) to bomb enemy bunkers and positions, the great distance to the inland target leaving scant time for loitering over the target.

Only once the US Air Force began deploying heavy bombers to Diego Garcia, a British overseas territory in the Indian Ocean, did responsibility for the attacks become shared. Today the US Marine Corps (USMC) deploys

9-11 Let's Roll
Crew members assemble on the deck of amphibious assault ship USS *Belleau Wood* to remember the September 2001 terrorist attacks on New York, the catalyst for the invasion of Afghanistan.

aviation combat elements to support its ground forces on operations, deploying from FOBs established since the invasion.

US Marine and Navy aircraft were also integral to the invasion itself. The Marine Corps force that established the first strategic base in Afghanistan, for

example, deployed in Marine helicopters from the amphibious assault ships *Peleliu* and *Boxer*. The US Navy and USMC continue to provide support operations to ground troops, particularly as the US Marine Corps has been so heavily in demand for the ground fighting.

INVASION OF IRAQ

Date 20 March–11 April 2003
Forces Americans: 115 ships;
British: 22 ships; Iraqis: unknown
Losses Coalition forces:
unknown; Iraqis: unknown

Location Persian Gulf,
Red Sea, and Iraq

In many ways the invasion of Iraq in 2003 was very different to the war conducted against Saddam Hussein's forces in 1991. Instead of repeating the first Gulf War's prolonged air campaign as preparation for the ground assault, the second war against Iraq saw a near simultaneous launch of air and ground assets, with land forces making a direct, fast strike toward the Iraqi capital Baghdad. Nonetheless, as with the 1991 conflict, it was the US Navy that fired the opening shots.

At 5:15am on 20 March 2003 the Ticonderoga-class destroyer USS *Bunker Hill* fired the first of many US Navy Tomahawk missiles targeted at command-and-control centres and political targets deep in Iraq. Shortly afterward, US and UK ground forces attacked Iraq from across the Kuwaiti border. The US forces, with a large Marine Corps spearhead, would strike up to Baghdad, while British troops took responsibility for securing Basra, Iraq's second city.

SHOCK AND AWE

The order of battle of the coalition's naval contingent was formidable. The US Navy element alone (by far the biggest portion) ran to 115 ships, including five carrier battle groups

centred around the carriers *Kitty Hawk, Constellation, Theodore Roosevelt, Abraham Lincoln,* and *Harry S Truman.* The aviation striking power of these carrier groups was truly enormous, and F-18 Hornets, F-14 Tomcats, and US Marine Corps AV-8B Harriers provided close-air support for the advancing troops. The *Constellation* carrier group alone flew more than 1,500 sorties during Operation Iraqi Freedom – as the US operations were codenamed – during which it dropped more than 450,000kg (1 million lb) of ordnance. Tomahawk-armed destroyers within the group (including *Bunker Hill*) fired a total of 408 cruise missiles.

SUPPORT MISSIONS

Allied warships also provided offshore gunnery platforms for missions on land. For example, HMAS *Anzac* and the Royal Navy warships HMS *Richmond, Marlborough,* and *Chatham* delivered bombardments in support of British Royal Marine and USMC assaults on the Al-Faw peninsula, a critical southern action that included the capture of Umm Qasr, the only deep-water port in Iraq.

Baghdad was finally secured in the first week of April 2003, after what appeared to be a vigorously successful operation. The post-invasion conflict, however, far exceeded the worst expectations in terms of fighting, and US Marine and Navy air assets remain on call to deliver strikes in support of counter-insurgency operations.

US Carrier Strike Group
Nuclear-powered supercarrier *George Washington* is accompanied by ships from her strike group during their deployment in the Gulf in support of Operation Iraqi Freedom in June 2004.

SHIP-LAUNCHED CRUISE MISSILES

The development of cruise missiles that track to a target in a sustained, guided flight pattern began during World War II on both sides of the Allied-Axis divide, but was refined to operational level during the postwar period. The Regulus was the first US ship-launched version. It had a range of 926km (575 miles) and could be launched from both submarines and surface vessels. Regulus was deployed between 1955 and 1964. In the 1970s and 80s the world caught up with US advances and a wide range of ship-launched cruise missiles emerged in other world navies, such as the SS-N-12 (USSR) and the HY-2 Haiyang (China). The most famous of all the cruise missiles, however, remains the Tomahawk, used to powerful effect during both the 1991 and 2003 Persian Gulf Wars. Based on this success, new generations of long-range cruise missiles have recently entered service with many navies, including Pakistan, India, France, and Russia.

Tomahawk cruise missile
A subsonic Tomahawk missile is fired from an armoured box launcher during Operation Desert Storm.

Regulus cruise missile
The turbojet-powered supersonic Regulus was the US Navy's main strategic nuclear deterrent during the early days of the Cold War.

USS DONALD COOK

THE ARLEIGH BURKE-CLASS guided-missile destroyer *Donald Cook*, named for a Marine hero of the Vietnam War, was launched in 1997. Deployed in Operation Iraqi Freedom in March 2003 as part of the Battle Group led by the carrier *Harry S Truman*, she was among the first ships to launch Tomahawk cruise missiles against targets in Iraq.

THE FIRST ARLEIGH BURKE-CLASS destroyer was commissioned in 1991. *Donald Cook* belongs to Flight II, incorporating significant advances in armament and electronics. The ship is packed with diverse weaponry, giving her what the US Navy calls "multi-mission offensive and defensive capabilities". The Mk41 vertical launch system fires anti-aircraft missiles, anti-submarine missiles, missiles for destroying other surface ships, and cruise missiles for strike operations against land targets. The destroyer does not have the covered helicopter hangar fitted to later ships in the class, but a launch-pad allows an attack helicopter to be embarked. Survivability is a key concept in the destroyer's design and equipment. The Arleigh Burke-class were among the first ships to incorporate elements of "stealth" technology, with buried funnels and rounded shapes to reduce the ship's radar profile, as well as features to suppress infrared emissions. They were also the first American all-steel warships. Replacing the aluminium superstructure with steel was meant to reduce damage in case of a missile hit. The destroyer has a crew of 30 officers and more than 300 enlisted personnel.

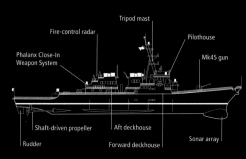

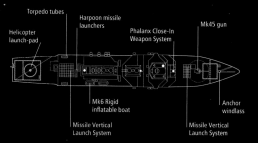

USS Donald Cook
Donald Cook is the 25th Arleigh Burke-class guided-missile destroyer to be built for the US Navy. Despite being classed as a destroyer, *Donald Cook* is over 150m (500ft) in length and displaces 8,400 tons when full, making her similar in size to many World War II cruisers.

Stealth warship
The USS *Donald Cook* and her fellow Arleigh Burke-class destroyers are among the most advanced surface combatants in service today.

> THESE DESTROYERS ... ARE A SPECIAL CLASS OF SHIPS, THE CLASS OF ARLEIGH BURKE. ADMIRAL BURKE WAS THE INSPIRATION FOR THESE SHIPS. THEY WERE MEANT TO BE FEARED AND FAST, THE VERY ATTRIBUTES THAT EARNED THEIR NAMESAKE THE NICKNAME "31-KNOT BURKE".
>
> **PRESIDENT BILL CLINTON**, SPEECH AT THE FUNERAL SERVICE OF ADMIRAL ARLEIGH BURKE, 1996

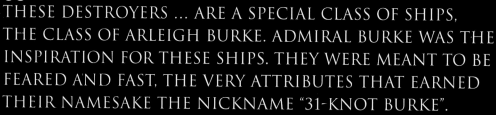

⌃ Landing indicator lights
A system of lights helps to guide the helicopter in to land. A green light indicates a good approach, amber caution, and red that the helicopter is too low. Two flashing red lights tell the pilot to abort.

» Helicopter landing-pad
Donald Cook can embark and refuel an SH-60 Seahawk helicopter, providing search and attack capabilities as well as an effective way to move cargo and personnel.

⌃ Torpedo tubes
Two sets of Mk32 triple torpedo tubes can be used to target submarines. The system fires the torpedoes using compressed air from a flask at the rear of tubes.

⌃ Ship's bridge
The helmsman steers the ship from the helm station in the centre of the bridge. The ship also has an automated digital steering system, allowing a course to be entered and automatically maintained

⌃⌄ 25mm chain gun
Two Mk38 chain guns provide close-range defence against small surface threats such as hostile patrol boats or floating mines. The guns are manually aimed and operated and can fire up to 200 rounds per minute

≪ Anchor chain
This lightweight 1,800kg (4,000lb) anchor and the *Donald Cook*'s heavier 4,000kg (9,000lb) main anchor are both carefully positioned to stop them striking the large sonar dome on the hull as they are lowered.

⌃ Mk45 gun and deckhouse
The 5in-gun on *Donald Cook*'s forward deck is the guided-missile destroyer's only large artillery weapon, designed for use against surface warships or aircraft, or for shore bombardment. The mast and deckhouse behind the gun bristle with radomes, antennae, jamming devices, and other types of navigational and electronic warfare equipment.

⌃ Chaff and decoy launcher
The Mk36 Super Rapid Bloom Offboard Chaff (SRBOC) system can fire a range of chaff and infrared decoys to confuse hostile missiles and fire-control systems.

≪ Phalanx weapon system
USS *Donald Cook* is fitted with two Phalanx Close-In Weapon Systems (CIWS) using automated radar-controlled 20mm rotary cannon that can identify, track, and destroy incoming threats such as missiles

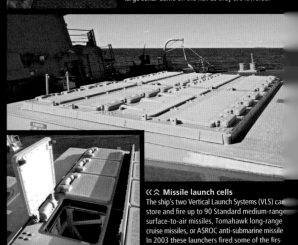

≪⌃ Missile launch cells
The ship's two Vertical Launch Systems (VLS) can store and fire up to 90 Standard medium-range surface-to-air missiles, Tomahawk long-range cruise missiles, or ASROC anti-submarine missiles. In 2003 these launchers fired some of the first Tomahawk strikes of Operation Iraqi Freedom.

BELOW DECKS

THE AEGIS COMBAT SYSTEM at the heart of the ship's operations detects incoming missile and aircraft threats and deploys countermeasures, missiles, and gunfire. The ship's AN/SPY 1-D phased array radar can track hundreds of targets simultaneously. There are steel bulkheads throughout the ship in case a hit is suffered, and especially vital equipment is given extra armour by Kevlar shields. An air filtration system forms part of the comprehensive protection against nuclear, biological, and chemical attack. The gas turbine engines are derived from the engines used on jet airliners such as the Boeing 747.

» Main passageway
Double-plated bulkheads and interior air-lock doors provide protection and allow vital areas – such as the Central Control Station at the end of this corridor – to be isolated.

« Tactical Coordinator
The CIC is manned by a team of highly trained specialists, each with a specific role to play. The Tactical Information Coordinator seen here, for example, handles tactical data coming in from allied ships.

⌃ Airtight hatch
To protect the ship and crew against contamination from chemical or biological agents, the Collective Protection System (CPS) divides the ship into zones, separated by airtight hatches, enabling the crew to maintain a pressurized, filtered environment.

«⌃ Combat Information Centre
The Combat Information Centre (CIC), the tactical heart of the ship, is dominated by the AEGIS combat system, an advanced computer-based control and information system that integrates the data coming in from the radar and satellite systems and controls the ship's weapons and electronic countermeasures.

» Ratings' mess
Enlisted men on *Donald Cook* eat most of their meals in an informal self-service canteen next to the ship's galley. Officers have a separate mess.

⌄ Ship's galley
The spacious and well-equipped kitchens on board *Donald Cook* allow the galley staff to prepare three hot meals a day, with a choice of dishes, for a crew of over 300 officers and enlisted men.

⌃ ≫ 5in gun magazine
Located underneath the Mk45 gun mounting, the 5in shell magazine on *Donald Cook* stores 680 rounds of ammunition. The yellow markings on the shells indicate high explosive. Propellent powder is stored nearby.

⌃ Ammunition loading systems
A small team inside the magazine operates a computerized loading system that ensures an uninterrupted supply of ammunition to the Mk45 gun on the deck above. It can select and load different types of ammunition, from high-explosive to illumination, at the touch of a button.

≪ ⌄ Gas turbine
The four LM2500 gas turbine engines are key to *Donald Cook*'s speed and manoeuvrability, powering her to over 56kph (30 knots).

⌃ Main engine room
The ship's two fuel oil transfer and purification systems, one in each of the two main engine rooms, remove water and solid contaminants from the engine fuel supply.

⌃ Halon room
The halon system forms a key part of the *Donald Cook*'s damage control systems. Fire-suppressant halon gas can be directed from canisters in the halon room throughout the ship to fight internal fires.

≫ Reducer gear
The two propulsion reducer gears (one in each engine room) are among the most expensive pieces of machinery on board. They convert the high-speed, low-torque output of the gas turbine engines into low-speed high-torque output suitable for driving the ship's propeller shafts.

≪ ⌃ Firefighting gear
As part of the ship's extensive fire-control systems, several fire stations containing protective overalls, fire hoses, and closed breathing apparatus are located around the decks.

CARRIER STRIKE FIGHTER JET
Deck crew direct an F/A-18 Hornet strike fighter and ground attack aircraft as it prepares to launch from the supercarrier *Kitty Hawk* during American operations in the Persian Gulf. Around 85 aircraft are deployed on the carrier, which ranks among the largest warships ever built, with a crew of over 5,000 men. The F/A-18 has been the mainstay of American naval aviation since the 1980s.

INDEX

ACKNOWLEDGEMENTS

The publisher would like to thank the following for their kind permission to reproduce their photographs:

Key:
(a-above; b-below/bottom; c-centre; f-far; l-left; r-right; t-top)
AA – The Art Archive;
AAA – Ancient Art & Architecture Collection;
BAL – Bridgeman Art Library;
IWM – Imperial War Museum;
MEPL – Mary Evans Picture Library;
NMM – National Maritime Museum;
UK Crown – © Crown Copyright 2008 reproduced with the permission of the Controller, HMSO, London

1 DK Images: Barcelona Maritime Museum. **2-3** Getty Images: Digital Vision. **4-5** Corbis: The Gallery Collection. **6** DK Images: Barcelona Maritime Museum (tc) (tr); Hellenic Maritime Museum (bl) (bc) (br). **7** DK Images: © UK Crown (tr); USS Donald Cook (bl); USS Lexington (br) (bc). **8** DK Images: Hellenic Maritime Museum (tl) (cr). Science & Society Picture Library: (b). **9** DK Images: Hellenic Maritime Museum (t) (c). MEPL: (b). **10** DK Images: Statens Historiska Museum, Stockholm (bc). Science & Society Picture Library: (t)

(cl) (cr). **11** BAL: Musee de la Marine, Paris, France, Lauros / Giraudon (br). DK Images: Hellenic Maritime Museum (t). Science & Society Picture Library: (c). **12** John Hamill: (cl). NMM: (tr). Science & Society Picture Library: (cr). **13** akg-images: Nederlands Scheepvaart Museum (bl). AA: Private Collection Italy / Alfredo Dagli Orti (cl). BAL: Private Collection, Photo © Bonhams, London, UK (cr). NMM: (br). **14** BAL: Private Collection, Photo / Bonhams (cr). DK Images: NMM (bl). NMM: (cl). **15** NMM: (tr) (br) (cl) (cr). **16** DK Images: Gettysburg National Military Park, PA (b). © Musée National de la Marine: (tr). NMM: The Royal Navy Submarine Museum: (tl). **17** DK Images: Getty Images: Imagno (br). NMM: (ca) (cb). **18** DK Images: IWM (b). NMM: (t) (c). **19** Cody Images: NMM: (ca) (cb) (t). **20** DK Images (cb); Explosion! Museum of Naval Firepower (b); NMM (t). NMM: (ca). **21** DK Images: Andy Crawford (cb); NMM: (ca). www. ww2incolor.com: (br). **22** DK Images: NMM (ca); Gary Ombler (t). NMM: (cb). **23** DK Images: Tim Ridley (t); © UK Crown (ca) (cb). Courtesy of US Navy: Todd P. Cichonowicz (b). **24-25** DK Images: Averof Museum. **26** AA: Gianni Dagli Orti (bl). British Library: (br). Corbis:

Araldo de Luca (c). DK Images: Averof Museum (bc). Photo Scala, Florence: National Archaeological Museum (tl). **27** Alamy Images: North Wind Picture Archives (tr). AA: Topkapi Museum Istanbul / Alfredo Dagli Orti (bc). BAL: Palazzo Pubblico, Siena, Italy (bl). DK Images: Barcelona Maritime Museum (br). **28** AA: AA379160 (tl). DK Images: Hellenic Maritime Museum (bl); Hoplite Society (br). **29** AA: Museo Correr Venice / Alfredo Dagli Orti (t). DK Images: NMM (b). **30** AAA: (c). AA: Dagli Orti / Museo Naval Madrid (b). Corbis: Bettmann (t). **31** Corbis: Bettmann (b). DK Images: Hellenic Maritime Museum (c). **32** Corbis: Werner Forman (br). DK Images: Averof Museum (bl). **33** Alamy Images: broombank (b). **34** MEPL: (b). Werner Forman Archive: British Museum (t). **36** Alamy Images: Visual Arts Library (London) (c). **37** Corbis: Bettmann (b). DK Images: Hoplite Society (t). **38** AAA: (b). AA: Dagli Orti / Museo Naval Madrid (t). **39** Corbis: Dagli Orti (b). **40** MEPL: Hans Bohrdt (c). **40-41** DK Images: Hellenic Maritime Museum. **42** Corbis: Araldo de Luca (t). Peter Newark's Military Pictures: (b). **43** Corbis: Araldo de Luca (t). Photo Scala, Florence: Ministero Beni e Att. Culturali (b). TopFoto.co.uk: Alinari (c). **44** akg-images: Peter Connolly (b);

Nimatallah (c). **45** MEPL: (b). **46** AAA: (t). **47** Photo Scala, Florence: (t). **48** AAA: (bl) (fbl). DK Images: Dave King (cr). **49** AA: Dagli Orti / Museo Prenestino Palestrina (t). BAL: Louvre, Paris (cl). **50** Corbis: Fine Art Photographic Library (t). NMM: (b). **52** British Library: (tl). China Tourism Photo Library: (bl). **53** British Library: (tr). China Tourism Photo Library: (bc). DK Images: The Wallace Collection, London (cr). **54-55** China Foto Press. **55** Corbis: Asian Art & Archaeology, Inc. (tc). **56** Corbis: Asian Art & Archaeology, Inc (cl). DK Images: University Museum of Archaeology and Anthropology, Cambridge (br). **57** British Library: (bl). Corbis: Asian Art & Archaeology, Inc. (t). **58** The Trustees of the British Museum: (tl). **59** V&A Images: (tc). **60-61** AA: Oriental Art Museum Genoa / Alfredo Dagli Orti. **62** BAL: Prado, Madrid, Spain (bl). Photo Scala, Florence: Doge's Palace (t). **63** AA: Naval Museum Genoa / Alfredo Dagli Orti (cl). Photo Scala, Florence: Doge's Palace (t). **64** DK Images: Hellenic Maritime Museum (b). **65** AAA: (c). **66** BAL: Louvre, Paris, France, Lauros / Giraudon (t). **67** DK Images: The Wallace Collection, London (tr). North Wind Picture Archives: (br). **68** AA: Museo Bottacin Padua / Gianni Dagli Orti (tc) (tr). **68-69** AA: Museo

Correr Venice / Alfredo Dagli Orti. **70** akg-images: British Library (cb). iStockphoto.com: (b). **71** AA: Bibliothèque Nationale Paris / Alfredo Dagli Orti (b). DK Images: Max Alexander (tr). **72** BAL: Museu Maritim Atarazanas, Barcelona, Catalunya, Spain, Index (b). NMM: (c). SuperStock: age fotostock (tr). **74** AA: Historiska Muséet Oslo / Alfredo Dagli Orti (tl). British Library: (cr). **75** AA: Marine Museum Lisbon / Gianni Dagli Orti (br). BAL: Musee de la Marine, Paris, France, Archives Charmet (t). **76** Corbis: The Gallery Collection (b). **77** TopFoto.co.uk: The British Library / HIP (c). The Viking Ship Museum, Roskilde, Denmark: (l). **78** DK Images: The British Museum (cl). Museu Maritim de Barcelona: (br). **79** BAL: Private Collection (t). DK Images: Hellenic Maritime Museum (cl); © UK Crown (bc). IWM: (br). **80** DK Images: Private Collection (cr). **80-81** BAL: Musee de la Tapisserie, Bayeux, France, With special authorisation of the city of Bayeux (b). **81** Alamy Images: Nick Miners. MEPL: (cr). **82** NMM: (tr). **82-83** AA: Bibliothèque Nationale Paris / Harper Collins Publishers. **84** The Mary Rose Trust: (cr). **84-85** Artists Harbour Ltd./www. artistsharbour.com. **85** DK Images:

360

ACKNOWLEDGMENTS

NMM (t). **86** AA: Museo Correr Venice / Alfredo Dagli Orti (cr); Topkapi Museum Istanbul / Alfredo Dagli Orti (tl). BAL: Topkapi Palace Museum, Istanbul, Turkey (bl). **87** AA: Museo Don Alvaro de Bazan Viso Del Marqués / Gianni Dagli Orti] (b). **88** BAL: British Museum, London, UK (cr). DK Images: Hellenic Maritime Museum (b). **89** Corbis: Arte & Immagini srl (c). Istanbul Naval Museum: Turkish General Staff, Ankara (tl) (b). **90-91** AA: University Library Geneva / Gianni Dagli Orti. **92** BAL: Bibliotheque Nationale, Paris, France, Lauros / Giraudon (b). Corbis: Araldo de Luca (tl). **93** akg-images: (bl). Photo Scala, Florence: Maps Gallery (t). **94** DK Images: Barcelona Maritime Museum (tl). NMM: (b). **96** BAL: Museu Maritim Atarazanas, Barcelona, Catalunya, Spain, Index (c). **96-97** DK Images: Barcelona Maritime Museum. **98-99** DK Images: Barcelona Maritime Museum. **99** DK Images: © UK Crown (cl). **100** DK Images: © UK Crown (bl). NMM: On loan from Lymington and Pennington Town Council (c). San Diego Historical Society : (tr). **100-101** MEPL: ILN Pictures (b). **101** DK Images: © UK Crown (crb). NMM: (tr). Wellcome Library, London: (cra). **104** Corbis: Bettmann (br); Macduff Everton (bc); Joel W. Rogers (c). DK Images: Hellenic Maritime Museum (bl). **105** AAA: (br). BAL: Private Collection, Photo © Rafael Valls Gallery, London, UK (t); Timothy Millett Collection (cl). DK Images: © UK Crown (bc). NMM: (bl). **106** DK Images: © UK Crown (br). NMM: (cl). **106-107** DK Images: © UK Crown. **107** DK Images: Courtesy of the Gettysburg National Military Park, PA (c). NMM: (tr). **108** AAA: Europhoto (tl). Korean War Academy: (b). **109** AAA: Europhoto (cl) (br). **110** AAA: Europhoto (bl). www.koreanhero.net: Chesungdang (Victory Hall) (tc). **110-111** AAA: Europhoto (c). **111** AAA: Europhoto (c) (br). **112** AAA: Europhoto (t). **113** AAA: Europhoto (t). **114** akg-images: Nederlands Scheepvaart Museum (tl). AA: Biblioteca Nazionale Marciana Venice / Gianni Dagli Orti (cr). BAL: The Crown Estate (bl). **115** akg-images: Nederlands Scheepvaart Museum (tr). Rijksmuseum Amsterdam: (b). **116** AAA: University Library Geneva / Gianni Dagli Orti (b). **117** AA: Museo Don Alvaro de Bazan Viso Del Marqués / Gianni Dagli Orti (cl); San Carlos Museum Mexico City / Gianni Dagli Orti (cr). **118** NMM: (cr). **118-119** AA: Society of Apothecaries / Eileen Tweedy (b). **119** NMM: (tr). **120** NMM: (tl) (b). **122-123** AAA. **124** AA: Marine Museum Lisbon / Gianni Dagli Orti (b). BAL: NMM, UK (c). **125** AA: University Library Geneva / Gianni Dagli Orti (br). MEPL: (t). **126** akg-images: Rijksmuseum (b). NMM: (cr). **127** Alamy Images: AAA Photostock (tc). MEPL: Rue Des Archives (bl). NMM: (c). **128** DK Images: Hellenic Maritime Museum (c). **128-129** NMM: (b). **129** NMM: (tc). **130** Alamy Images: MEPL (b). NMM: (tl). **131** DK Images: Kim Sayer (cl). Peter Newark's Military Pictures: (br). **132** MEPL: (b). NMM: (c). **133** DK Images: Royal Armouries (tr). NMM: (t). **134** MEPL: (cr). NMM: (c). **135** NMM: (tl) (b). **136-137** NMM. **138** BAL: Bonhams, London, UK (bl). NMM: (cr). **138-139** NMM: (b). **139** NMM: (tr). **140** DK Images: © UK Crown (bl); Dave King (tr); © UK Crown (c). IWM: (cl). MEPL: (br). **141** DK Images: USS Donald Cook (cr). NMM: (tc) (b). **142** Peter Newark's Military Pictures: (tl) (bl). **143** AA: Musée Saint Denis Reims / Gianni Dagli Orti (br). Peter Newark's Military Pictures: (tr). Rama: Musée national de la Marine, Paris, France (c). **144** DK Images: Explosion! Museum/Royal Armouries (b). NMM: (c). **145** NMM: (t). Réunion des Musées Nationaux Agence Photographique: Martine Beck-Coppola. **146** BAL: British Museum, London, UK (tr). NMM: (b). **148** Corbis: Stapleton Collection (tc). NMM: (cr) (b). **149** NMM: (t). **150** AA: Maritime Museum Stockholm Sweden / Alfredo Dagli Orti (tl). **150-151** AA: Naval Museum Genoa / Alfredo Dagli Orti (b). **151** akg-images: Residenzmuseum (br). AA: Maritime Museum Stockholm Sweden / Alfredo Dagli Orti (tr). NMM: (c). **152** DK Images: Royal Armouries (c). NMM: (b). **153** AA: Maritime Museum Stockholm Sweden / Alfredo Dagli Orti (c). NMM: (br). **154** BAL: Hermitage, St. Petersburg, Russia (b). **155** Det Nationalhistoriske Museum på Frederiksborg: (tr). State Hermitage, St Petersburg: (cr) (b). **156** State Hermitage, St Petersburg: (bc). **156-157** Wikipedia, The Free Encyclopedia: (b). **157** BAL: Radichtchev Museum, Saratov, Russia (tr). NMM: (cl). **158** BAL: Private Collection, © Royal Exchange Art Gallery at Cork Street, London (tl). DK Images: NMM (c). NMM: (bl). **158-159** NMM: Greenwich Hospital Collection (b). **159** NMM: (tr). **160** Corbis: Michael Freeman (br). NMM: (cl) (bl). **161** DK Images: Explosion! Museum of Naval Firepower (t). BAL: Yale Center for British Art, Paul Mellon Collection, USA (b). **162** NMM: (cr). **162-163** BAL: Musee des Beaux-Arts, Marseille, France, Giraudon (b). **163** NMM: (t). Peter Newark's Military Pictures: (br). **164-165** NMM: (b). **165** DK Images: Royal Armouries (cr). NMM: (br). **166** BAL: Collection of the New-York Historical Society, USA (t). DK Images: © UK Crown (br). **167** Corbis: Stapleton Collection (cr). NMM: (c); Greenwich Hospital Collection (b). **168** NMM: (bl) (cr). **168-169** BAL: NMM, UK (t). **169** BAL: Chateau de Versailles, France, Giraudon (c). **170** Réunion des Musées Nationaux Agence Photographique: Daniel Arnaudet / Gérard Blot (tl). **171** Corbis: (tc). NMM: (cl). **172** DK Images: © UK Crown (cl) (c); © UK Crown (tr) (bl). **172-173** MEPL: (b). **173** Corbis: Bettmann (tl). DK Images: USS Lexington (cr). **174** Alamy Images: Frumm John / Hemis.fr (bl). DK Images: Explosion! Museum/Royal Armouries (c). NMM: Greenwich Hospital Collection (tl). **174-175** NMM: (b). **176** DK Images: Judith Miller / Wallis and Wallis (c). NMM: (b). **177** NMM: (tr) (cl). **178** NMM: (b). **178-179** NMM: Greenwich Hospital Collection. **180** NMM: (tr) (b). **184** AA: Nelson Museum Monmouth / Eileen Tweedy (br). **184-185** DK Images: © UK Crown. **185** NMM: (bl). **186** NMM: (cl). **186-187** NMM: (b). **187** DK Images: Royal Armouries (t). **188-189** BAL: Private Collection (b). **189** AA: Eileen Tweedy (cr); Royal Naval Museum Portsmouth / Harper Collins Publishers (tr). **190** akg-images: NMM (b). NMM: (c). **192** Alamy Images: Rolf Richardson (cr). DK Images: Explosion! Museum/Royal Armouries (b); Royal Armouries (tl) (c). **193** DK Images: IWM (ca); © UK Crown (br). Peter Newark's Military Pictures: (tr). **194** BAL: Royal Naval Museum, Portsmouth, Hampshire, UK (c). **194-195** DK Images: © UK Crown. **196-197** DK Images: © UK Crown. **198** DK Images: © UK Crown (tr) (bl) (br). NMM: (bc). **199** Corbis: (br); Hulton-Deutsch Collection (tr). DK Images: Judith Miller / Branksome Antiques (tl). © UK Crown (br). **200** Corbis: Smithsonian Institution (c). DK Images: Wallace Collection (bl). **201** NMM: (tl) (b) (tr). **202** BAL: Atwater Kent Museum of Philadelphia/ Courtesy of Historical Society of Pennsylvania Collection (cl). NMM: (bc). United States Naval Institute: (cr). **203** Corbis: PoodlesRock (t). NMM: (c). **204** NMM: (c). **204-205** BAL: Courtesy of the Council, National Army Museum, London, UK/ BAL Nationality. **205** Science & Society Picture Library: Science Museum (tl). **206** AA: Private Collection Scotland (cr). **207** BAL: Bibliotheque Nationale, Paris (tr). NMM: (cr) (bl) (c) (cra). **208** akg-images: Coll. Archiv f.Kunst & Geschichte (c). **209** DK Images: Hellenic Maritime Museum (cl). **210-211** DK Images: Mikasa Preservation Association; Museo Nacional de Historia Lima / Gianni Dagli Orti (br). **212** AA: Museo Nacional de Bellas Artes Buenos Aires / Gianni Dagli Orti (bc); Nacional de Bellas Artes Buenos Aires / Gianni Dagli Orti (cl). DK Images: Explosion! Museum (cr). **213** akg-images: Coll. Archiv f.Kunst & Geschichte. (bc). BAL: Collection of the New-York Historical Society, USA (bl). DK Images: Mikasa Preservation Association (br). Science & Society Picture Library: (t). **214** BAL: Chicago History Museum, USA (tl). DK Images: Explosion! Museum of Naval Firepower (cl); Gettysburg National Military Park, PA (br); NMM (bl). **215** AA: IWM / Eileen Tweedy (tr). DK Images: Explosion! Museum of Naval Firepower (br). **216** BAL: Royal Hospital Chelsea, London, UK (tl). MEPL: (b). **217** BAL: Royal Hospital Chelsea, London, UK (tr). DK Images: Tim Ridley (cl). **218** BAL: Central Naval Museum, St. Petersburg, Russia (cl); Private Collection/ Archives Charmet (br). DK Images: Explosion! Museum of Naval Firepower (cr). **219** Getty Images: Imagno (t) (br). **220** DK Images: US Army Heritage and Education Center - Military History Institute (br). NMM: (tr). **220-221** DK Images: Explosion! Museum of Naval Firepower. **221** Stapleton Collection: (b). **222** AA: Eileen Tweedy (cr). NMM: (br). **223** AA: John Meek (cr). DK Images: Explosion! Museum of Naval Firepower (t) Explosion! Museum/NMM (br). **224-225** Getty Images: Roger Viollet. **225** DK Images: Explosion! Museum of Naval Firepower (b); NMM (tr). **226** Peter Newark's Military Pictures (tl) DK Images (c). **226-227** AA: Naval Museum Genoa / Alfredo Dagli Orti (b). **227** Peter Newark's Military Pictures (tr). **228** DK Images: Confederate Memorial Hall, New Orleans (bl). **228-229** BAL: Atwater Kent Museum of Philadelphia/ Courtesy of Historical Society of Pennsylvania Collection (b). **229** Corbis: (tr). Naval Historical Center: (cl). **230-231** Corbis: Burstein Collection (b). **231** AA: (br). **232-233** BAL: Chicago History Museum, USA. **234** Corbis: Bettmann (tr). **234-235** Corbis: Bettmann. **236** BAL: Private Collection/ Peter Newark Military Pictures (bl). Corbis: Medford Historical Society Collection (tl). DK Images: US Army Heritage and Education Center - Military History Institute (cl). **238** NMM: (br). San Jacinto Museum of History: (cl). **239** Corbis: (b). NMM: (tc). **240** Corbis: Hulton-Deutsch Collection (tr). **240-241** Naval History & Heritage Command: Courtesy of the Naval Historical Foundation, donation of Mrs F. Parotto. **242** Corbis: (b). NMM: (tc). **244** BAL: Bibliotheque Nationale, Paris, France/ Lauros / Giraudon (bl). Corbis: Philadelphia Museum of Art (tl). **245** Corbis: Philadelphia Museum of Art (tr). NMM: (cl). **246** Alamy Images: The Print Collector (bl). NMM: (c). The Royal Navy Submarine Museum: (br). **247** Corbis: Philadelphia Museum of Art (t) (br). **248** Corbis: (bl). **248-249** Corbis: Bettmann. **250** MEPL: (bl). **252** Getty Images: Hulton Archive (ca). **252-253** DK Images: Mikasa Preservation Society. **254-255** DK Images: Mikasa Preservation Society (b). **256-257** Corbis: Philadelphia Museum of Art. **258** Alamy Images: MEPL (c). Cody Images: (t). DK Images: NMM (b). **259** Cody Images: (b). DK Images: Gary Ombler (c). **260** DK Images: Explosion! Museum of Naval Firepower (bc). MEPL: Albrecht Meyer (br). **261** Cody Images: (bl) (br). DK Images: Explosion! Museum/Royal Naval Museum (tr). **262** AA: IWM (cb). DK Images: Explosion! Museum of Naval Firepower (ca). **263** NMM: (t). **263-264** Corbis: Bettmann (b). **264** DK Images: Texas Parks and Wildlife Department (tl). Getty Images: Popperfoto (tr). Peter Newark's Military Pictures: (c). **264-265** AA: Eileen Tweedy (b). **265** NMM: (r). **266** Alamy Images: Classic Image (r). AA: IWM (b). DK Images: IWM (cl). **268** Cody Images: (b); © UK Crown (ca). DK Images: © UK Crown (c). **269** Cody Images: (tl) (b). DK Images: © UK Crown (cr). **270-271** DK Images: Texas Parks and Wildlife Department. **272** DK Images: Texas Parks and Wildlife Department (bl) (bc); USS Donald Cook (br). TopFoto.co.uk: Ullsteinbild (c). **273** Cody Images: (t). DK Images: Old Flying Machine Company (c); Texas Parks and Wildlife Department (bc); USS Donald Cook (bl); USS Lexington (br); © UK Crown (bl). **274** DK Images: © UK Crown (cl). Courtesy of US Navy: Danielle M. Sosa (cr). **275** DK Images: © UK Crown (bl) (br). Mc Grogan's Patch Design LLC: Donald Mc Grogan BMCS (SW) USN Ret. DAV (cl). Courtesy of US Navy: Jeremie Yoder (t). **276** MEPL: (br). TopFoto.co.uk: (c). **277** Cody Images: (br). Corbis: Bettmann (tr). DK Images: IWM (cl). MEPL: (crb). US Air Force: (cr). **278** DK Images: © UK Crown (bl). Getty Images: Fox Photos (t). **279** Corbis: Bettmann (t). DK Images: Explosion! Museum/Royal Naval Museum (c). **280** Peter Newark's Military Pictures: (c). **280-281** TopFoto.co.uk: (b). **281** Naval Historical Center: (cr). **283** akg-images: Ullstein Bild (t). **284-285** DK Images: USS Texas. **286-287** DK Images: USS Texas. **288-289** DK Images: USS Texas. **291** Cody Images. Getty Images: Hulton Archive (r). **292** The Museum of World War II: (t). **292-293** MEPL: (cl). TopFoto.co.uk: (b). **293** The Museum of World War II: (t). TopFoto.co.uk: (b). **294-295** TopFoto.co.uk: Topham / AP (b). **296** Cody Images: (t). DK Images: © UK Crown (c). **296-297** DK Images: Explosion! Museum of Naval Firepower (b). **297** Cody Images: (t). **298-299** Corbis: Phan J. Alan Elliott. **300** DK Images: IWM (bl). **300-301** www.ww2incolor.com: (b). **301** DK Images: © UK Crown (t). www.ww2incolor.com: (cr). **302** Cody Images: (b). **303** DK Images: Gary Ombler (t). MEPL: (cr). TopFoto.co.uk: (b). **304** NMM: (t). **304-305** TopFoto.co.uk: (b). **305** DK Images: IWM (c) (br). **306** DK Images: Barcelona Maritime Museum (t); © UK Crown (b). **307** DK Images: Explosion! Museum / Museum of Naval Firepower (tc); Hellenic Maritime Museum (cr). Getty Images: Hulton Archive (br). MEPL: (tr). **308** Cody Images: (tr) (b). Courtesy of The Museum of World War II, Natick, Massachusetts: (cl). **309** Christie's Images Ltd.: (cl). Cody Images: (br). **310** Courtesy of The Museum of World War II, Natick, Massachusetts: (c). **310-311** Getty Images: MPI (b). **311** Corbis: (cr). Getty Images: Hulton Archive (tl). **312** Cody Images: (tl) (b). NMM: (tr). **313** Naval Historical Center: (br). **314** National Museum of The United States Air Force: (t). **315** Corbis: (t). **316** Naval Historical Center: (b). **317** DK Images: (t); Explosion! Museum of Naval Firepower (br); IWM (tc). Naval Historical Center: (bl). **318** www.historicalimagebank.com: (cr). Naval Historical Center: (bl). PA Photos: (t). **319** Getty Images: American Stock (cl). **321** Cody Images: (br). **322-323** TopFoto.co.uk: Jon Mitchell (b). **323** Corbis: Bettmann (tr). **324** Cody Images: (tl). Corbis: (b). **326** Bovington Tank Museum: Roland Groom (br). Naval Historical Center: (c). **327** Getty Images: US Navy/Time & Life Pictures (bl). Naval Historical Center: (t). **328** Corbis: Reuters (tl). **328-329** Getty Images: BAE Systems (b). **329** Corbis: Reuters (tr). DK Images: The Trustees of the IWM (br). **330** Getty Images: C. K. Rosk/US Army/National Archives/ Time Life Pictures (b). **331** DK Images: © UK Crown (br). Getty Images: Carl Mydans/Time & Life Pictures (tr). **332-333** Corbis: Hulton-Deutsch Collection. **334** Corbis: Tim Page (b). Getty Images: Kerry Campaign (bl). Mc Grogan's Patch Design LLC: Donald Mc Grogan BMCS (SW) USN Ret. DAV (ca). **335** Corbis: Bettmann (tr). **336** Alamy Images: Ian Leonard (bl). USS Lexington: (c). **336-337** DK Images: USS Lexington. **337** Alamy Images: Ian Leonard (bc). **338-339** DK Images: USS Lexington. **340** Rex Features: John W Jockel (c). **341** Cody Images: (tr). DK Images: © UK Crown (c). Rex Features: Nils Jorgensen (cl). Courtesy of US Navy: Kenny Swartout (b). **342** Cody Images: (cr) (bl). **343** DK Images: Explosion! Museum of Naval Firepower (c). Getty Images: R. Beesley/U.S. Navy (t). PA Photos: Gemunu Amarasinghe/AP (br). **344** Department of Defense, Media: (cl). Courtesy of US Navy: Joshua Adam Nuzzo (br). **345** Corbis: (t). DK Images: Explosion! Museum of Naval Firepower (b). **346** Corbis: Reuters (c). Department of Defense, Media: (b). Getty Images: US Navy (t). **347** Alamy Images: Bob Pardue (cr). Department of Defense, Media: (b). Rex Features: Roger-Viollet (tr). **348** Courtesy of US Navy: Michael W. Pendergrass (cl). **348-349** DK Images: USS Donald Cook. **350-351** DK Images: USS Donald Cook. **352-353** Corbis: Thomas Hartwell

All other images © Dorling Kindersley
For further information see:
www.dkimages.com

Dorling Kindersley would like to thank the following:

Mariana Evmolpidou, Anastasia Anagnostopoulou-Paloubi, Kleopatra Rigaki (Hellenic Maritime Museum); P. Sofikitis, Captain Dalianis, John Rigas, Dimitris Grigoropoulos (Averof Museum/Trireme Olympias); Alba Espargaró, Miriam Vallvé (Barcelona Maritime Museum); Marc Farrance, Nick Bremner, Derek Gurney, Phil Hazell (Explosion! Museum of Naval Firepower); Alexandra Geary (Royal Navy Submarine Museum); Sandi McNorton (USS *Lexington*); Andy Smith & staff (USS *Texas*); Chief Kreidel, staff & crew (USS *Donald Cook*)
Jacket design: Duncan Turner
Additional design and DTP assistance: Stephanie Allingham, Adam Brackenbury, Almudena Diaz, Peter Draper, Luca Frassinetti, John Goldsmid, Edward Kinsey, Tim Lane, Dean Morris, Phil Sergeant, Balwant Singh, Becky Tennant, Adam Walker

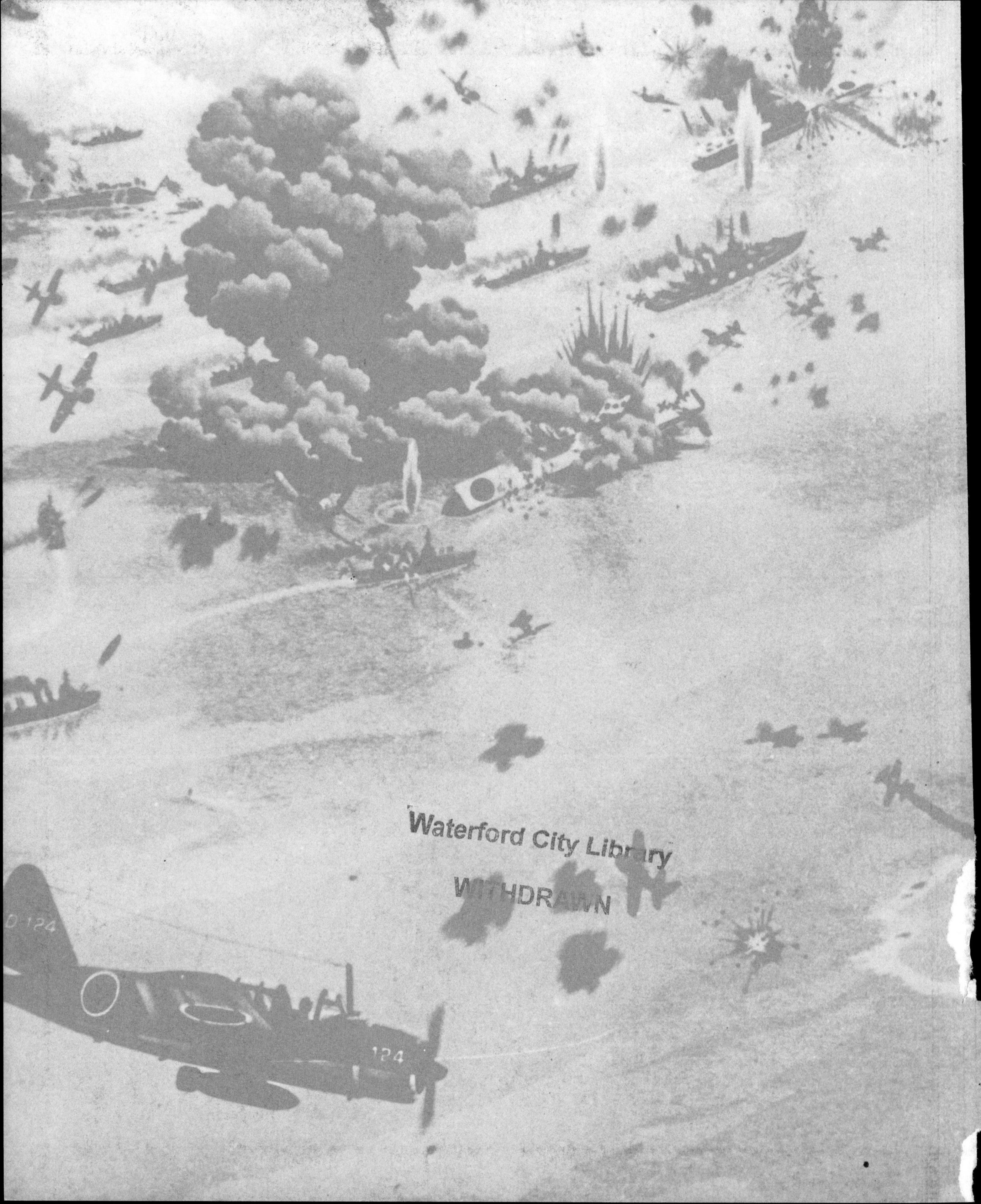
D-124
124